The Almanac of World Military Power

Third Edition

Colonel Trevor N. Dupuy, U.S. Army, Retired

Grace P. Hayes, Former Lieutenant, U.S. Navy

Colonel John A.C. Andrews, U.S. Air Force, Retired

1974

R.R. Bowker Company
New York and London

T.N. Dupuy Associates
Dunn Loring, Virginia

Third Edition

*Published by T.N. DUPUY ASSOCIATES,
Dunn Loring, Virginia, in association with
R.R. Bowker Co. (a Xerox company) New York, N.Y.*

Copyright © 1974 by Trevor N. Dupuy

*All rights reserved. No part of this publication may be
reproduced, stored in a retrieval system, or transmitted
in any form or by any means, electronic, mechanical,
photocopying, recording or otherwise, without the prior
permission of the copyright owner.*

Printed and bound in the United States of America

ISBN 0 8352 0730 7

Library of Congress Catalog Card No. 74-7578

CONTENTS

The Nature of Military Power vii
Preface xi

I. North America Regional Survey 1
    Canada 2
    Mexico 6
    United States 9

II. Central America and West Indies Regional Survey 21
    Barbados 23
    Bahamas 24
    British Dependent and Associated States 24
    Costa Rica 25
    Cuba 26
    Dominican Republic 28
    El Salvador 30
    French Guiana, Guadeloupe and Martinique 31
    Grenada 32
    Guatemala 32
    Haiti 33
    Honduras 33
    Jamaica 34
    Netherlands Possessions in the Western Hemisphere 35
    Nicaragua 36
    Panama 37
    Trinidad and Tobago 38

III. South America Regional Survey 41
    Argentina 42
    Bolivia 44
    Brazil 47
    Chile 50
    Colombia 53
    Ecuador 55
    Guyana 57
    Paraguay 58
    Peru 61
    Uruguay 61
    Venezuela 67

IV. Western Europe Regional Survey 71
    Austria 74
    Belgium 76
    Cyprus 78
    Denmark 80
    Finland 83

	France	85
	Germany (West)	90
	Greece	94
	Iceland	97
	Ireland	98
	Italy	100
	Luxembourg	103
	Malta	104
	Netherlands	104
	Norway	107
	Portugal	110
	Spain	112
	Sweden	117
	Switzerland	119
	Turkey	122
	United Kingdom	125
V.	Eastern Europe Regional Survey	133
	Albania	135
	Bulgaria	137
	Czechoslovakia	139
	Germany (East)	142
	Hungary	146
	Poland	148
	Romania	152
	Union of Soviet Socialist Republics	154
	Yugoslavia	164
VI.	Middle East Regional Survey	169
	Arab Gulf States	171
	Egypt	173
	Iran	176
	Iraq	179
	Israel	182
	Jordan	186
	Kuwait	189
	Lebanon	190
	Oman	191
	Saudi Arabia	193
	Syria	196
	Yemen (Aden)	199
	Yemen (San'a)	200
VII.	Africa Regional Survey	203
	Algeria	207
	Botswana	209
	Burundi	210
	Cameroon	211
	Central African Republic	212
	Chad	213
	Congo	214
	Dahomey	215

CONTENTS v

	Equatorial Guinea	215
	Ethiopia	216
	French Territory of Afars and Issas	220
	Gabon	221
	The Gambia	222
	Ghana	222
	Guinea	224
	Ivory Coast	225
	Kenya	226
	Lesotho	227
	Liberia	228
	Libya	229
	Malagasy Republic	232
	Malawi	233
	Mali	234
	Mauritania	235
	Morocco	236
	Niger	238
	Nigeria	240
	Portuguese Africa	242
	Rhodesia	247
	Rwanda	249
	Senegal	250
	Sierra Leone	251
	Somalia	252
	South Africa	254
	Sudan	259
	Swaziland	261
	Tanzania	262
	Togo	264
	Tunisia	265
	Uganda	267
	Upper Volta	268
	Zaire	269
	Zambia	271
VIII.	Central and East Asia Regional Survey	275
	Chinese People's Republic	276
	Republic of China (Taiwan)	283
	Japan	286
	Korea (North)	290
	Korea (South)	293
	Mongolia	295
IX.	South and Southeast Asia Regional Survey	299
	Afghanistan	300
	Bangladesh	302
	Bhutan	303
	Brunei	304
	Burma	304
	Cambodia	307
	India	309

vi ALMANAC OF WORLD MILITARY POWER

Laos	313
Malaysia	315
Nepal	317
Pakistan	318
Sikkim	321
Singapore	321
Sri Lanka	323
Thailand	324
Vietnam (North)	327
Vietnam (South)	331

X. South and Southwest Pacific Regional Survey 335
    Australia 335
    Indonesia 339
    New Zealand 341
    Philippines 344

Glossary 349
Sources 383
Index of Countries, Regions and International Organizations 385

THE NATURE OF MILITARY POWER

What is military power? We define it as the capability of a nation to employ armed forces effectively in support of national objectives by exerting influence on the performance of other nations.*

Some would assert that military power is the only effective power in the world today. There is, for instance, the perhaps apocryphal story of Stalin's contemptuous dismissal of the power of the Pope: "How many divisions does he have?" Stalin pretended, at least, to recognize no power but that of naked military force. And it was unquestionably the apparent willingness of the United States to use such force, if necessary, which caused him to withdraw from Persian Azerbaijan in 1946, and to call off the Berlin Blockade in 1949.

Stalin's successors, however, have revealed that they understand, and respect, other kinds of power, including that indefinable and unquantifiable influence which the Pope can still exert, even without divisions. They have also demonstrated considerable respect for the power of ideas. Sometimes this has been shown by modifying aspects of their autocratic and dictatorial rule of their own country and its satellite neighbors. Sometimes, also, they have shown that respect quite negatively, by armed aggression, as in Hungary in 1956, and Czechoslovakia in 1968.

Soviet leaders have also demonstrated an awareness of the importance of economic power. Khruschev's famous threat to America: "We will bury you," made in 1956, shortly after he came to power, was a declaration of economic war combined with a promise to greatly increase Soviet economic power to match that of the United States. It is noteworthy, however, that either because he was impatient, or because he recognized that the promise was not achievable during his lifetime (if ever), he resorted to the more traditional Soviet concepts of power in 1962 by threatening the United States with Cuban-based nuclear blackmail. However, like Stalin before him, he backed down when he recognized that the United States was ready, if necessary, to employ superior nuclear and conventional power against the Soviet Union.

These three examples of power confrontation between the US and USSR—Azerbaijan, Berlin, and Cuba—suggest that, no matter how persuasive and influential non-military forms of power may be, they cannot *in themselves*, and as a last resort of national policy, prevail against military power. Also, all three instances involved the use, or threatened use, of military forces actually in being.

There is, however, a very important difference between military power in being, and potential military power. Many relatively weak nations have been able to achieve their objectives, in peace and in war, despite the contrary objectives of more powerful neighbors, because the weaker nation could apply superior military strength readily available. Sparta earned a place in history by the careful cultivation of the maximum possible military strength from a small, sparsely populated area with scanty resources. Macedonia dominated the world briefly because the rulers of that otherwise undeveloped country created the most sophisticated military machine in the world for its time. A major factor in the rise of the Roman republic was the willingness of Rome's citizens to convert their resources into highly-organized military strength. The ability of Genghis Khan to implement a similar decision was the sole reason for the earthshaking conquests of the Mongols.

These historical examples must have been in the mind of a thoughtful American general, active a century ago, Winfield Scott Schofield, when he wrote: "Population and wealth do not constitute military strength. They are only the elements from which military strength may be developed in good time and by appropriate means. They are like the fat of the over-fed giant, which may be converted into muscle in due time by appropriate training. But it is too late for the giant to commence training after he has met his well-trained antagonist."*

In modern history, Japan in the first half of this century provides two classic case studies of the difference between actual and potential military power.

In 1904 Japan challenged Russia for dominance in northeast Asia. At that time the population of Russia was nearly 150 million, the population of Japan was 45 million; the total military strength of Japan was 280,000 troops (with 400,000 reserves); Russia had about 1,000,000 men in its active army (with perhaps double that number in reserves); the

---

*For a valuable theoretical discussion of military power, see Klaus Knorr, *Military Power and Potential*, Lexington, Mass., 1970.

*Annual Report, Secretary of War, 1887, GPO, Washington, D.C.

Japanese Navy had 59 warships (not counting 85 torpedo boats); Russia's navy was almost twice as large. A pygmy was defying a giant. Furthermore, the record of the war demonstrates that man-for-man, division-for-division, the Japanese on land had no discernible superiority in combat effectiveness. And, while their warships were slightly more modern, even there the man-for-man, ship-for-ship difference was not—in itself—enough to offset the tremendous Russian numerical superiority.

But most of this Russian military strength was not available to influence the outcome of a war fought in and near Manchuria. Even less relevant to such a war was the still greater disparity in manpower, economic, and industrial strength. Had Russia been willing, or able, to continue the fight, its potential power must inevitably have overwhelmed Japan. But Japanese military leaders were aware of the limitations of the 6,000 mile-long Trans-Siberian Railway, aware of the inability of Russia to unite its scattered fleets without overcoming a concentrated Japanese fleet stronger than any of them, and perhaps above all aware of internal social weaknesses in Russia. Thus they were confident that they could keep the war limited to their part of the world, that they could overwhelm in detail Russian piecemeal reinforcements, and that internal troubles would preclude determined Russian prosecution of the war. It was a close thing, but the Japanese calculations proved right.

A similar situation seemed to face Japan in 1941. The potential military strength of the United States was obviously far greater than anything Japan could possible mobilize. The similarities of the 1904 and 1941 situations were remarkable, particularly in the exposure of a sizable naval force to a surprise pre-war attack, and in the existence of major internal divisions among the people of the larger and potentially more powerful opponent. And, as in 1904, in 1941 the Japanese had a substantial military superiority on land and sea in the part of the world they had selected as the theater of combat.

There were two major differences in these situations, however, which Japanese planners in 1941 did not sufficiently appreciate. The major internal divisions in the United States at that time were political, not social and socio-economic as they had been in Russia in 1904. The Japanese offensives in Manchuria in 1904 increased the divisive social pressures in Russia; the 1941 attacks on Pearl Harbor and Southeast Asia united the divergent political forces in America. Japanese planners also failed to recognize that geography and distance affect a land power differently from a naval power. The land masses of the Eastern Hemisphere effectively hobbled both the Russian Army and the Russian Navy by creating long and extremely limited and inflexible lines of communication both on land and on sea. The vast reaches of the Pacific Ocean were a barrier to American land and naval power (and air power, of course!) only so long as Japan could maintain sufficient force to interfere with American use of the sea as a broad and flexible line of communications.

On the other hand, as Alfred Thayer Mahan pointed out, although the seas afford great strategic flexibility and versatility to a maritime power, the absolute limiting effects of geography on the employment of its power are greater than for a continental power. This was demonstrated in Britain's many wars against continental powers in Europe, and against this country in both the Revolution and the War of 1812. This was one of the limiting factors affecting the United States effort in Vietnam recently.

From these random examples from history it is possible to draw some conclusions about the interrelationship of actual and potential military power as components of national power. The following are generally accepted as the classic elements of national power:

1. Natural resources
2. Industrial capacity
3. Social-political structure
4. Military strength

Another formulation, presented in an official publication of the US Air University at Maxwell Air Force Base, Alabama, lists the factors of national power as follows:

Geographic (including location, configuration, topography, and size)
Demographic (including rate of growth, age, and productivity)
Economic (including mineral, agricultural, energy, and water resources, and the production policies for employing these resources)
Organizational (including social and governmental structure and management skills and methods)
Psychosocial (relating to attitudes, values, and motivation)
Military (with consideration to national policy, military policies, forces in being, research and development, and education and training)

These two formulations of national power are really different ways of slicing the same loaf of bread—at least if "natural resources" in the first is assumed to include "geographic situation." In either formulation, military strength, or power, comprises only one of several elements, or factors. Yet in terms of absolute national power, the others are significant in an ultimate test only to the extent that they contribute to potential *military* power and, more precisely, to the extent that they can be converted or mobilized to become *actual* military power.

Military power can be considered to have twelve characteristics:

1. Size of the armed forces;
2. Composition of the armed forces (in terms of balance or allocation of resources to the military services, and within services);

3. Quantity and performance of equipment or hardware;
4. Logistical reach, or range;
5. Availability of forces for effective employment;
6. Capability of performing sustained, active operations;
7. Mobilizable resources and productive capacity;
8. National willingness to employ force;
9. Leadership and doctrine;
10. Communications and control;
11. Military intelligence effectiveness;
12. Manpower quality in terms of skill, training, physical stamina, morale.

In his splendid study of *Military Power and Potential*, Dr. Klaus Knorr suggests that there are at least three different aspects of military power: (1) its exercise-in war as by threat or by readiness, (2) its availability, and (3) its effectiveness.

He suggests that effectiveness is essentially a reflection of quality, and stresses the danger of "accepting the power of sheer numbers," or even of "superior industrial capability," by itself. This aspect of quality as a determinant of effective military power can raise disturbing questions in the minds of those who can recall how twice in this century Germany, overwhelmingly outmatched by the potential military power of its enemies, came alarmingly close to military victory.

There is a fourth aspect of military power, which Knorr recognizes, but which has been most aptly described by Dr. Henry Kissinger as its "usability." The concept of "usable" military power is quite a different thing from "actual" or "available" military power. Power can in fact be actual, it can be available, and yet still not conceivably, or credibly, or rationally usable in relation to certain national objectives. This idea of "usable" military power is to some extent a reflection of changed political attitudes in a post-colonial era world, but it is to an even greater extent a consequence of the existence of nuclear weapons with cataclysmic destructive power, weapons which are terribly important components of the military power of the nations that possess them. But the use of nuclear weapons is credible only in support of the most fundamental national objectives. Thus, a tremendous proportion of American power, vital in any confrontration between the US and USSR, was simply not usable in Vietnam against either the Vietcong or North Vietnam.

A slightly different perspective of this concept of "usable" military power can be found in another recent historical example involving the United States. In January 1968, the North Korean Navy attacked and seized on the high seas the American electronic intelligence vessel USS *Pueblo*. In earlier times a major power would have responded to such an insult by sending a naval task force to inflict a certain amount of punishment upon such a brash, small power. In fact, in 1871, the US did respond in just such a fashion when earlier Koreans seized and destroyed an American vessel stranded off the Korean coast.

It should be noted that the United States was not reluctant to respond forcefully to much more blatant Korean lawlessness 97 years later because the United States was afraid of North Korea, or lacked the means to inflict the punishment. It is doubtful if we were inhibited seriously by the possibility of some censure in the United Nations. We simply were unwilling to incur the risk, small though it might be, of precipitating a war which could become nuclear war with one of North Korea's neighbors, over an issue, or an objective, not worth such a risk, not vital to American national security.

This one example shows three new concepts affecting the employment of military power which have emerged as a result of the development of nuclear weapons. There is a higher "threshold" of response, inhibiting actions by a nuclear power which would have been taken as a matter of course by an insulted or damaged major nation in the pre-nuclear era. The raised "threshold" is a result (despite mixing of metaphors) of the "umbrella" of mutual nuclear deterrence, which permits smaller powers considerably more leeway in their dealings with greater powers than would have been possible in those earlier eras.

Finally, and most significant, there are limits on "usable" military power (conventional as well as nuclear) because of the existence of the threshold and the umbrella.

T.N. Dupuy
Colonel, U.S. Army, Retired

PREFACE

This, the third edition of *The Almanac of World Military Power*, is built on the framework established by the authors and editors of the first and second editions, whose contributions have been described in the Prefaces to those editions. While the framework, like the geographical features of the world, remains unchanged, there have been many changes in political features, in strategic situations, in statistical data, and in types of military equipment since the first edition was produced in 1970. As many as possible of these changes have been reflected in this edition.

In the preparation of this edition comments and information were requested from defense ministries of many nations, and the editors appreciate greatly the considerable useful material received from these sources, either directly or through their attaches in Washington. Many points were cleared up in conversations with various US Government officials. But the bulk of the data has been taken from open, unclassified sources, including standard reference works, periodicals and daily newspapers. A list of the chief sources used is at the end of this volume.

For each nation three principal sets of data are presented: (1) statistics related to power potential, (2) general politico-military-strategic situations, and (3) inventories of armed forces strength, organization and equipment. The figures in all cases are the most recent ones available in mid 1974. The majority of them represent the end of year figures for 1973; some are earlier, some later, but an effort has been made to prepare as current a compilation as possible. When conflicting figures have been encountered official US Government figures have been used when available.

The Glossary for this edition has been considerably revised and expanded, to include all weapons in current arsenals as well as military terms for which a definition may be useful. Some items no longer in use have been dropped.

The editors have received valuable help from three other members of the staff of T.N. Dupuy Associates. Col. Angus M. Fraser, USMC, Ret., updated the sections on Central and East Asia, South and Southeast Asia, and South and Southwest Pacific; Gay M. Hammerman updated the sections on North America and Africa; and Paul Martell updated the sections on Eastern Europe and the Middle East. Updating of the other sections, revision of statistical information throughout, and editing have been a joint effort of the three co-editors who jointly assume full responsibility for the contents of this book.

John A.C. Andrews
T.N. Dupuy
Grace P. Hayes
Dunn Loring, Va.
August 1974

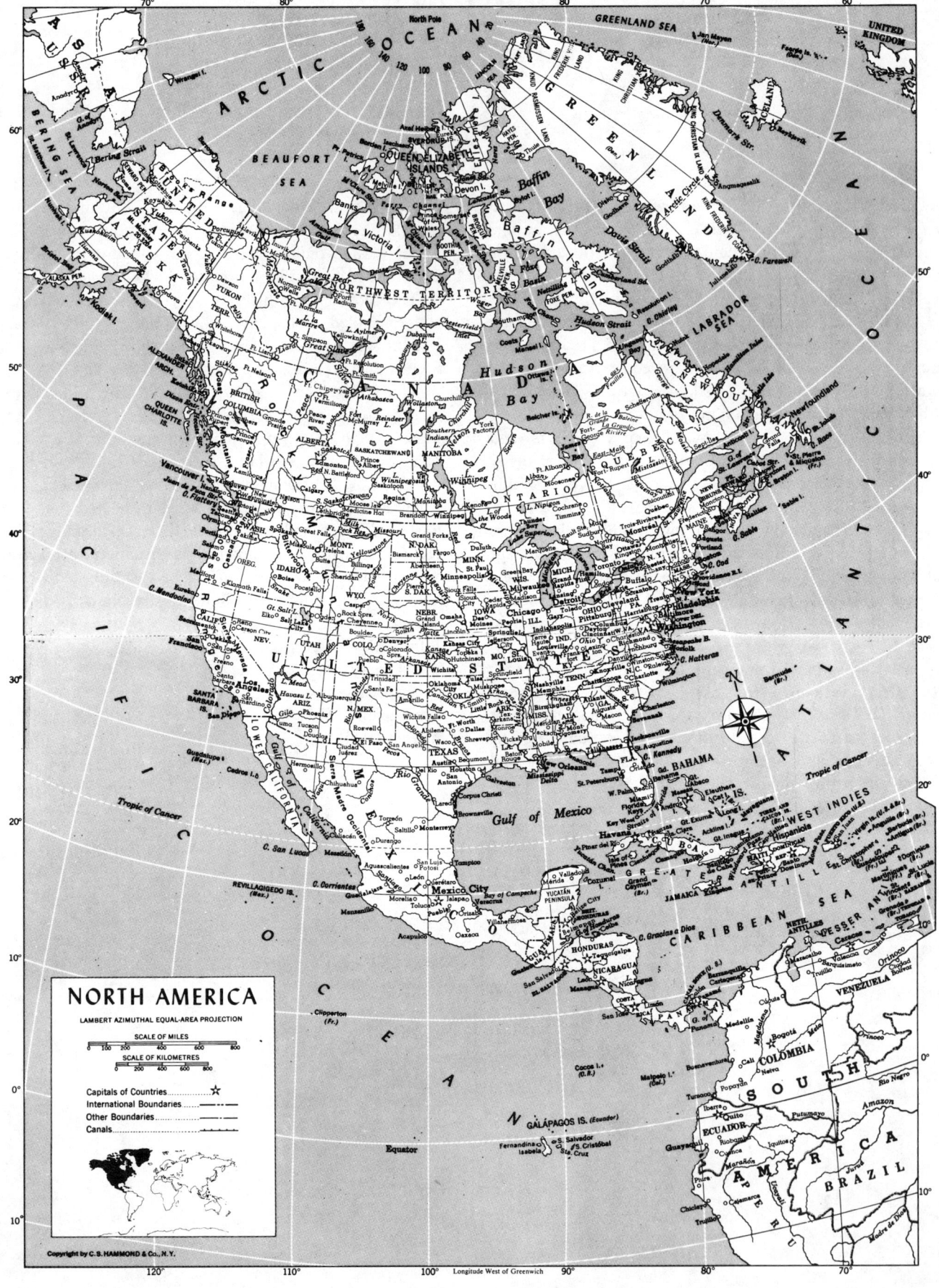

1
NORTH AMERICA

Regional Survey

MILITARY GEOGRAPHY

The North American continent, here understood to include the United States, Canada, Mexico, and the massive and largely unpopulated island of Greenland, has a total area of about nine million square miles.

Northern North America has generally sparse to moderate population density, moderate birth rates of 17.5 to 27.5 per 1,000, high literacy, and high per capita income, while Mexico shares with the other Latin American countries to the south an extremely high birth rate, relatively low literacy, and low (but growing) per capita income.

The political systems of all North American countries are stable. All are in reality democratic republics, although the Dominion of Canada nominally owes allegiance to the British Crown. The centrally placed United States is bound to each of its contiguous neighbors by a tradition of peaceful relations stretching back at least 50 years, and by mutual assistance defense treaties. The psychological ties with Canada are especially strong.

The continent is crossed by north-south mountain ranges, dividing it into an eastern coastal plain; an eastern mountain region comprising the Laurentian plateau and the Appalachian and Ozark Mountains; the great central plains; and the rugged Cordilleran highlands, which comprise the Rockies and the Pacific coastal ranges, and stretch from Alaska and northern Canada down through Mexico. Mexico falls almost entirely in this mountainous western region and has only very narrow coastal plains. The Great Lakes and St. Lawrence River form the most important inland waterway, stretching across most of the eastern half of the continent between Canada and the United States.

STRATEGIC SIGNIFICANCE

The area is dominated—although not controlled—politically, economically, and militarily by the United States. Eastern North America, including the eastern United States and southeastern Canada, is one of the four leading economic power regions of the world, along with Western Europe, Eastern Europe, and Japan. This power is derived from generally literate, technically skilled populations, wealth in a variety of natural resources, and highly developed methods of economic management. The area's great military strength, including the United States' nuclear-warhead ICBMs, is based on this economic power.

Military invasion from outside the continent has not occurred for more than 100 years.* The central fact of North American military geography for at least two centuries has been the isolation of this land mass, separated from other world powers by the world's two largest oceans. The new significant fact is the revolution in vulnerability that occurred with the development of thermonuclear weapons and ICBM delivery systems. With these weapons in the hands of the United States' chief political power adversary, the Soviet Union, with no tested defense available against them, and with air distance across the North Polar region the significant military distance under current technological circumstances, the United States and its North American allies are in constant danger of devastation by military might—as is their adversary beyond the Pole. The danger of amphibious invasion remains as negligible as ever.

REGIONAL ALLIANCES

The United States and Mexico are both members of the Organization of American States (see Central America and West Indies Regional Survey).

The United States and Canada are members of the North Atlantic Treaty Organization (see Western Europe Regional Survey).

The United States has no formal bilateral treaties with either Mexico or Canada, but bilateral planning agencies exist with both nations, permitting direct military planning for defense of the North American continent (see following articles on Canada and Mexico).

RECENT INTRA-AND EXTRA-REGIONAL CONFLICTS

There have been no international armed conflicts or incidents involving the use of force in North America since 1917, nor have there been any internal conflicts, except in Mexico, shortly after World War I. Both the United States and Canada, however, have been engaged in conflict or crisis operations outside the region. A list of the more important of these since World War II follows:

1948-1949   Berlin Blockade (US)
1950-1953   Korean War (US and Canada)

---

*The French involvement in Mexico in the 1860s was the last such event; prior to that had been British actions against the United States in 1814.

1954-1965	Assistance to South Vietnam (US)
1955-1965	Formosa Straits crises (US)
1958	Intervention in Lebanon (US)
1961	Bay of Pigs abortive invasion of Cuba (US)
1961-1962	Berlin Crisis (US and Canada)
1962	Cuban Missile Crisis (US)
1965-1973	Indochina War (US)
1965	Intervention in Dominican Republic (US)

CANADA

POWER POTENTIAL STATISTICS

Area: 3,851,809 square miles
Population: 22,095,000
Total Active Armed Forces: 83,000 (0.38% population)
Gross National Product: $110 billion ($4,979 per capita)
Annual Military Expenditure: $2.42 billion (2.2% GNP)
Iron and Steel Production: 54.3 million metric tons
Fuel Production: Coal: 14.4 million metric tons
   Crude Oil: 75.5 million metric tons
   Refined Products: 74.9 million metric tons
   Natural Gas: 77.5 billion cubic meters
Electric Power Output: 215.0 billion kwh
Merchant Fleet: 1,228 ships; 2,366,175 gross tons
Civil Air Fleet: 243 jet, 50 turboprop, and 124 piston transports, operated by scheduled carriers. Over 169 other companies operate fleets of all types of aircraft, performing such services as charters and non-scheduled passenger and cargo flights.

DEFENSE STRUCTURE

Canada is the only important nation in the world to have a completely unified defense structure, in which there are no separate or distinct services within the armed forces, but rather (in the words of the legislation by which this was accomplished) "One service called the Canadian Armed Forces." Civilian control over the Canadian Armed Forces is exercised by the Prime Minister and the Cabinet, with the Minister of Defence having direct responsibility. Under him the senior military man of the armed forces is the Chief of the Defence Staff, who in 1964 replaced the former four-man Chiefs of Staff Committee, and who is responsible for administering the armed forces through Canadian Forces Headquarters.

POLITICO-MILITARY POLICY

Canada has, for all practical purposes, linked its security requirements with those of the United States. Thus Canada has become a junior—but important and independent—partner in integrated defense arrangements for the defense of the North American continent. This does not imply that Canada feels obligated to follow the lead of the United States in foreign or military policy. But it does represent Canadian convictions that the principal objectives of the two nations are parallel, and many of their defense problems mutual.

Canada has been one of the leading proponents of the establishment of peacekeeping forces by the UN in instances where internal disorders, or danger of war, pose threats to international peace. Canadian forces have participated in all of the various UN forces and observer groups that have been established by the UN Security Council.

There were three principal reasons why the Canadian government made the policy decision first to integrate, then to unify, its armed forces. The first reason was budgetary; a study of the nation's force structure concluded that there was much unnecessary duplication of functions, personnel, and equipment among the three armed services. Second was the belief that future military requirements upon Canada, either for the defense of North America or for peacekeeping forces, would be in terms of relatively small mission forces including components of two, or of all three, of the conventional services. Third, and aside from the likelihood of requirements for mission forces, was a belief that in modern war all military functions for large forces, as well as small ones, involve joint operations of the conventional services.

In 1968 unification had become a fact, and there is now only one service of the Canadian Armed Forces. All personnel have a common uniform for duty (other than special purpose clothing) and off duty; a common grade structure has been established on a single promotion list.

Manpower for the Canadian Armed Forces is obtained by voluntary enlistment.

STRATEGIC PROBLEMS

Canada's principal strategic problems are geographical. First and most importantly, Canada lies athwart most of the likely paths of Soviet attack on the United States, either by manned aircraft or by ICBM. Second, most of Canada's relatively small population is concentrated in the far southern strip of the nation, close to the American border. Canada does not have the population or other resources to provide adequate defense against Soviet attacks, which would also threaten Canadian population and industrial centers. Thus, it is to Canadian interest to have the assistance of the United States in establishing passive and active defense means along the far-flung northern and northeastern periphery of the continent; it is to American interest to have Canadian cooperation in the Establishment of early warning and interceptor bases along this same periphery, most of which is on Canadian soil.

The great bulk of Canada (second largest nation in the world) in relation to the size of the population, and in relation

NORTH AMERICA 3

to its far-northern location, has other strategic implications. It is difficult for Canada to maintain naval forces sufficiently large to provide protection for one seacoast; without American help it is impossible to protect two seacoasts on the opposite shores of a great continent. Similarly, Canada would be indefensible against attack from the south (the experience of the War of 1812 is no longer valid) were it not that both Canada and the United States for more than a century (since the Treaty of Washington, 1871) have acted on the assumption that war between the two nations would be unthinkable, and both are proud that theirs is the longest unfortified frontier in the world.

MILITARY ASSISTANCE

Canada has no foreign assistance program as such, nor is it the recipient of any such programs. However, Canadian military personnel attend service schools and staff colleges in the United States and Great Britain, and students from America, Britain, and other members of NATO attend Canadian military schools.

ALLIANCES

Canada is a member of three overlapping alliances. First, as a member of the Commonwealth, Canada retains close and cordial military ties with the United Kingdom, and with a number of other Commonwealth countries, particularly Australia and New Zealand. The importance of Commonwealth ties has lessened in the years since World War II, however, as Canada has ever more firmly related its defense requirements and arrangements to those of the United States.

Canada was one of the original members of NATO. Until 1969, in addition to one brigade group and six tactical air squadrons stationed in Germany, committed to NATO's Allied Command Europe, approximately half of the remainder of Canada's combat forces was earmarked for NATO in the event of war or grave emergency. However, the land force contingent in Germany has been reduced, but in emergency will be reinforced by airlift from Canada.

Canada's relationship with the United States is perhaps the closest military alliance in the world between fully sovereign nations. This dates back to August 18, 1940, when at Ogdensburg, N.Y., President Franklin D. Roosevelt and Prime Minister William L. Mackenzie King announced the establishment of a Permanent Joint Board of Defense to consider in a broad sense the defense of the north half of the Western Hemisphere. This Ogdensburg Declaration was considered by Canada to be a treaty, although in the United States, for Constitutional reasons, it is classed as an Executive Agreement.

The Permanent Joint Board on Defense, with mixed civilian-military membership representation from both nations, is still the primary instrument for integrating the defense efforts of the two nations. It does not make decisions, but rather prepares recommendations to the two governments. Other bilateral consultative bodies have been established since World War II, including: the Military Cooperation Committee, established in 1946; the Senior Policy Committee on the Canada-United States Defense Production and Development Sharing Program, established in 1958; and the Canada-United States Ministerial Committee on Joint Defense, also established in 1958.

One of the most significant aspects of the alliance is the Defense Development Sharing Program. The origins of this also go back to the period just before American entry into World War II when, on April 20, 1941, President Roosevelt and Prime Minister Mackenzie King agreed at Hyde Park on cooperation in defense production. This close cooperation continued until 1958, when the governments of the two nations agreed upon the virtual integration of their weapons systems design, development, and production procedures, to assure the most complete possible coordination of their defense economies.

The most significant of the various operational military cooperative programs between the two nations is the North American Air Defense Command (NORAD) which was established in 1958 by a 10-year agreement which brought about the virtual integration of the Air Defense Commands of the two nations. In 1968 the agreement was renewed for an additional five years, and in 1973 for two years more.

Canada, while recognizing the necessity for close military, political, and economic ties with the United States, is careful to maintain and proclaim its complete sovereign independence from its giant neighbor. Prime Minister Pierre Elliott Trudeau visited Moscow and signed consultation agreements with the USSR a year before President Nixon's 1972 visit, and Canada also established cordial relations with the People's Republic of China well in advance of US moves.

Canada participated in the three-nation International Commission of Control and Supervision (ICCS) set up to supervise the Vietnam ceasefire in 1973 but withdrew July 31, citing the ICCS's inability to cope with constantly occurring truce violations.

CANADIAN FORCES ORGANIZATION

In subsequent sections, the land, sea and air components are treated separately, for comparative purposes, under the headings of Army, Navy, and Air Force. However, these components are no longer separate services but are unified as one service within the Canadian Armed Forces. These unified forces are organized within functional commands:

Mobile Command: Headquarters: North Bay, Ontario. Includes ground combat forces and tactical air forces including operational training units.

Air Defense Command: Headquarters: North Bay, Ontario. Includes air and ground installations required to detect and counter possible air or missile attack on Canada.

Maritime Command: Headquarters: Halifax, Nova Scotia. Includes bases and naval and air elements required for anti-submarine warfare (ASW) and other naval operations; also maritime transport for Mobile Command

Air Transport Command: Headquarters: Trenton, Ontario. Includes all air transport functions.

Training Command: Headquarters: Winnipeg, Manitoba. Provides for all common and basic training requirements and coordination of other training by the various commands.

Materiel Command: Rockcliffe, Ontario. Responsible for procurement and distribution of weapons and equipment for all commands.

Communications Command: Headquarters: Ottawa. Manages, operates and maintains strategic communications for the Canadian forces.

ARMY

Personnel: 33,000

Organization:
- 4 mechanized combat groups (one in West Germany with 2,800 men, and one—Air Mobile—prepared for quick transit to Europe) each group comprised of: 3 infantry battalions, 1 reconnaissance regiment, 1 reduced light artillery battalion (2 batteries)
- 1 airborne regiment
- 1 reduced battalion assigned to UNFICYP (Cyprus)
- 1 supply and logistics contingent in the UN Emergency Force Middle East

Major Equipment Inventory:
- 248 medium tanks (Centurion; to be replaced with Scorpion APC)
- 200 light tanks (M-24)
- 1,000 APCs (M-113)
- 72 M-109 155mm howitzers
- 260 105mm howitzers
- helicopters (CUH-IN and COH-58A)

Missiles: Blowpipe SAM

Reserves: A total of about 19,000 men are organized for short-notice mobilization.

NAVY

Personnel: 14,000

Organization:
- Maritime Command (Halifax, N.S.)
  - Maritime Forces Atlantic (Halifax)
  - Maritime Forces Pacific (Esquimalt, B.C.)
  - Maritime Reserve Forces
  - Maritime Air Forces

Major Units:
- 4 submarines (SS)
- 4 ASW helicopter destroyers with Sea Sparrow SAM, DDH 280 type (DDG)
- 9 ASW helicopter destroyers (DD)
- 11 ASW destroyer-escorts (DE)
- 3 operational support ships (AOR)
- 6 training vessels
- 4 oceanographic research vessels (AGS)
- 4 gate vessels (YNG)
- 1 diver depot ship
- 1 hydrofoil ASW, minesweepers, sub-chasers, etc., assigned to the reserve fleet

Major Naval Bases: Halifax, Esquimalt, Hamilton, Greenwood, Summerside, Shearwater, Comox, Patricia Bay

Reserves: There are approximately 2,615 naval reservists.

Maritime Air Forces:
- 4 maritime patrol squadrons (CL-28)
- 1 maritime patrol squadron (S-2)
- 1 ASW squadron (Sea King)
- 2 utility squadrons (T-33, C-47, UH-1N)
- 2 training squadrons (S-2, Sea King)

AIR FORCE

Personnel: 36,000

Organization:
- 3 tactical fighter squadrons (CF-104) Europe

2 tactical fighter squadrons (CF-5) Mobile Command
3 fighter-interceptor squadrons AW (CF-101) Air Defence Command
1 electronic warfare training squadron (CF-100, T-33)
1 fighter-interceptor training squadron (CF-101)
5 operational training squadrons, fighter (1 CF-101, 1 CF-104, 3 CF-5)
3 transport squadrons (1 Boeing 707, 2 C-130)
1 medium range transport squadron (Falcon, Cosmopolitan)
4 transport/rescue squadrons (Buffalo, Twin Otter, Labrador)
3 tactical helicopter squadrons (Iroquois, Kiowa)
28 long range radar squadrons
1 satellite tracking unit

Major Aircraft Types:
235 combat aircraft
   169 fighter-bombers (72 CF-104, 97 CF-5)
   66 CF-101 fighter-interceptors
585 other aircraft
   81 transports (5 Boeing 707, 23 C-130, 7 Falcon, 7 Cosmopolitan, 15 Buffalo, 24 Twin Otter)
   142 helicopters (18 Labradors, 50 Iroquois, 74 Kiowa)
   362 trainers and utility (7 C-47, 25 Musketeers, 84 Tutor, 80 T-33, 6 CF-100, 100 C-45, 25 T-34, 25 Otter, 10 HU-16)

Major Air Bases: Penhold, Sea Island, Moose Jaw, Edmonton Rivers, Cold Lake, Chatham, St. Jean, Lincoln Park, Fort Churchill, Uplands, Trenton, Clinton, Winnipeg, North Bay, St. Hubert, Dawson Creek, Rockcliffe, Halifax, Greenwood, Goose Bay, Gander, Resolute Bay, White Horse.

Reserves: Approximately 800, manning six squadrons with DHC-3 Otters (30 aircraft) for flight training.

PARAMILITARY

The Royal Canadian Mounted Police, approximately 8,000 strong, performs internal security as well as regional police functions, mostly in the lightly inhabited northern territories. The force is equipped with 13 aircraft, approximately 2,000 vehicles, and 24 vessels in the Marine Division of 245 men.

The provinces of Quebec and Ontario have provincial police forces, totaling about 5,000 men. Most of these perform routine regional police functions.

MEXICO

Estados Unidos Mexicanos
United Mexican States

POWER POTENTIAL STATISTICS

Area: 761,600 square miles
Population: 56,200,000
Total Active Armed Forces: 72,000 (not including constabulary: 0.13% population
Gross National Product: $38.3 billion ($681 per capita)
Annual Military Expenditure: $329 million (0.86% GNP)
Steel Production: 3.8 million metric tons
Fuel Production: Coal: 1.5 million metric tons
   Crude Oil: 26.0 million metric tons
   Refined Products: 26.6 million metric tons
   Natural Gas: 18.2 million cubic meters
Electric Power Output: 30.9 billion kwh
Merchant Fleet: 185 ships; 400,665 gross tons
Civil Air Fleet: 28 jet and 19 piston transports

DEFENSE STRUCTURE

The President is Commander in Chief of the armed forces. The Army and the Air Force are administered by the Ministry of National Defense, the Navy by the Ministry of the Navy.

The nation is divided into 33 military zones. Zone commanders are responsible for maintaining order, particularly during elections.

POLITICO-MILITARY POLICY

Beginning in 1920 after a decade of revolutionary turmoil, a strong executive initiated measures to break the political strength of the revolutionary generals and produce a loyal, professional army. At the same time social and economic reforms stabilized the government. Today the Mexican Army is among the least militaristic and most nonpolitical in Latin America. It has been modeled on that of the United States and is modern in organization, training, discipline, and proficiency. Military personnel surrender their political rights and may not even express political opinions in public without incurring penalties under the law.

The Army is composed of volunteers. Military training is compulsory for all 18-year-old male citizens for one year, but generally is accomplished by Sunday drill. There appears to be

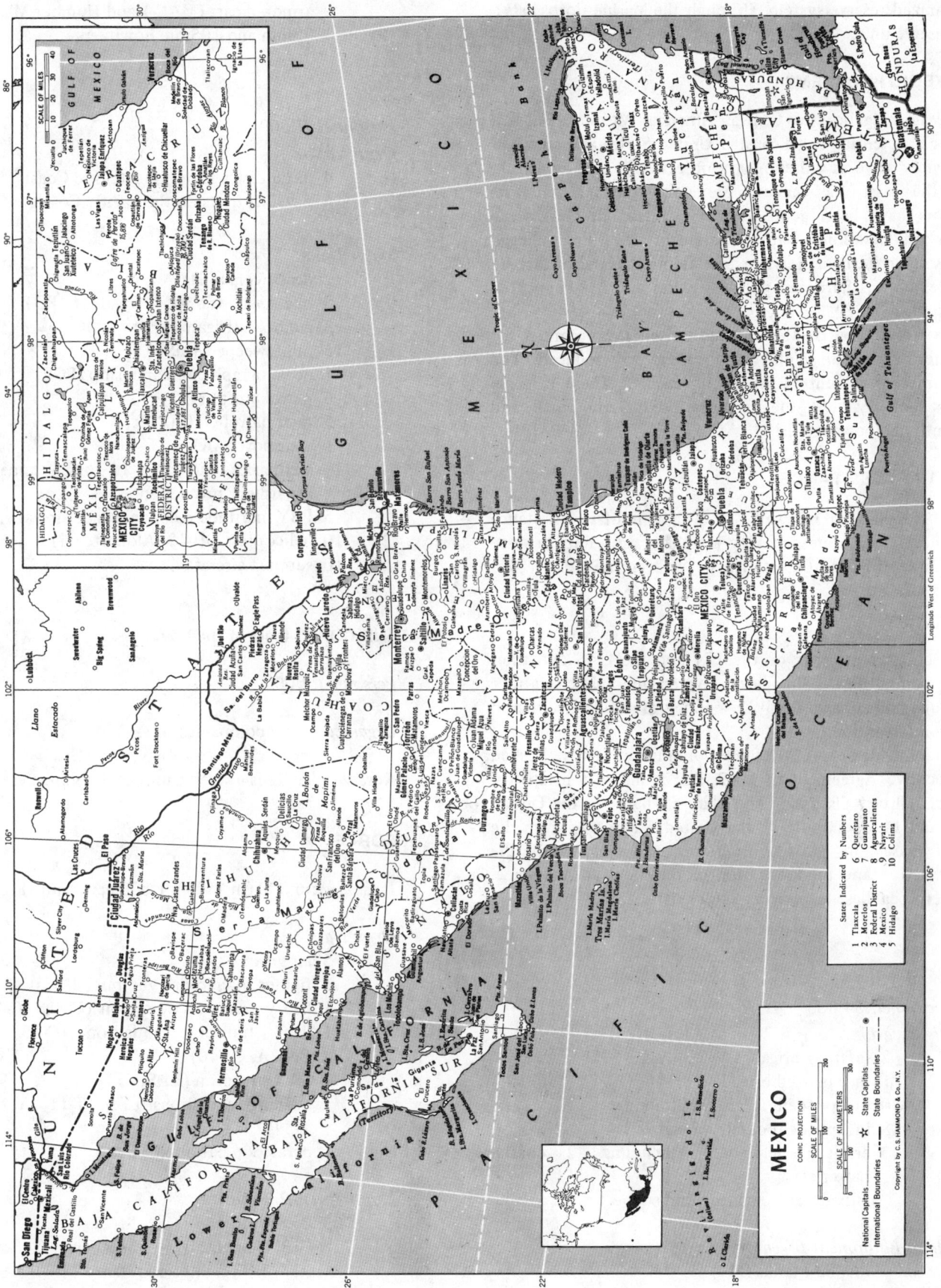

no organized reserve system, although the Marine Corps lists a small reserve unit.

STRATEGIC PROBLEMS

Like its neighbors in Central America, Mexico affords a base for a potential attack on the United States and so might conceivably serve as a preliminary objective in such an attack.

In the past half-century Mexico's relations with its neighbors have been good. However, there has been some tension in relations with Guatemala regarding alleged trespassing in territorial waters; Guatemala has also charged that Mexico has harbored political exiles and has supported subversion.

With the decline of Mexican militarism, the potential for revolution and coup d'etat has been greatly reduced. The Communist movement is small and divided. There is some terrorist activity, but the terrorist groups are small and apparently uncoordinated.

MILITARY ASSISTANCE

In 1972 Mexico received $99,000 in military assistance from the United States, making a total of $2.1 million since 1950. Under the MAP 659 students have been trained.

ALLIANCES

Mexico is a member of the UN and the OAS and their various committees. It has never severed diplomatic relations with Cuba and adheres firmly to a policy of self-determination and nonintervention.

The Joint Mexican-US Defense Commission was established by Executive Agreement in 1942, and is the only means for bilateral military discussion and planning between the United States and Mexico. In 1941 the United States was given the use of bases in Mexico in return for help with the reorganization and modernization of the Mexican Air Force. This reciprocal base use privilege still exists.

ARMY

Personnel: 54,000

Organization:
- 2 infantry brigades
- 1 mechanized brigade
- 40 independent infantry battalions
- 18 independent cavalry squadrons
- 3 artillery regiments (including 2 coastal batteries)
- antiaircraft, engineer, and support units

Major Equipment Inventory:
- medium tanks (M4)
- armored cars (MAC-1 and Humber Mk.IV)
- 75mm and 105mm howitzers

NAVY

Personnel: 7,600

Organization:
- 4 naval districts on the Atlantic Coast
- 4 naval districts on the Pacific Coast

Major Units:
- 2 destroyers (DD)
- 5 high speed transport/frigates (APD)
- 3 gunboats/frigates (PF)
- 15 minesweepers (MSF)
- 1 oceanographic research ship (PCE)
- 6 patrol craft (YP)
- 5 river patrol craft (PBR)
- 1 transport (AK)
- 19 auxiliaries, including 12 ex-US minesweepers for fishery protection
- 5 PBY maritime reconnaissance aircraft
- 10 helicopters OH-13, Alouette III)
- 10 support aircraft

MARINE CORPS (part of the Navy)

Personnel: 900

Organization: 7 companies

Reserves: There is a reserve unit of 3 companies

AIR FORCE

Personnel: 6,000 (including 1,800 paratroops)

Organization:
- 5 air groups
- 2 fighter squadrons (Vampire, T-33)
- 1 heavy transport squadron (C-118, C-47, C-54)
- 1 light transport squadron (C-45, IAI-201, BN-2A, C-140)
- 1 SAR squadron (LASA-60)
- 7 training squadrons (T-6, T-11, T-28, T-33, T-34)
- 1 paratroop battalion

Major Aircraft Types:
- 103 combat aircraft
  - 13 Vampire fighter-bombers
  - 15 T-33 fighter-bombers

30 T-28 armed trainers
45 T-6 armed trainers
107 other aircraft
37 transports (2 C-118, 4 C-54, 6 C-47, 19 C-45, 2 IAI-201, 3 BN-2, 1 C-140)
30 helicopters (13 OH-13, 1 OH-23, 6 Alouette III, 5 Bell 205, 5 Bell 206)
40 trainer/support aircraft (12 T-11, 10 T-34, 18 LASA-60)

PARAMILITARY

Police forces are about 60,000 strong, including the *Rurales*, a constabulary.

UNITED STATES

POWER POTENTIAL STATISTICS

Area: 3,615,210 square miles (50 states, including interior waterways and bodies of water)
Population: 211,600,000
Total Active Armed Forces: 2,201,539 (1.32% population)
Gross National Product: $1,304.5 billion ($6,165 per capita)
Annual Military Expenditure: $87.1 billion (6.68% GNP)
Iron and Steel Production: 84.3 million metric tons
Fuel Production: Coal: 495.1 metric tons
Crude Oil: 465.8 million metric tons
Refined Products: 557.2 million metric tons
Natural Gas: 636.9 billion cubic meters
Electric Power Output: 1,718 billion kwh
Merchant Fleet: 3,327 ships; 16.27 million gross tons
Civil Air Fleet: 2,192 jet, 431 turboprop, and 955 piston transports operated by scheduled carriers. Over 2,000 other companies perform such services as charters and non-scheduled passenger and cargo flights, operating fleets of all types of aircraft.

DEFENSE STRUCTURE

Under the US Constitution, responsibility and authority for national defense are divided between the Executive and Legislative branches of government. The President is Commander in Chief of the Armed Forces in peace and war; he is responsible for the formulation and execution of defense policy and for the administration of the defense establishment. His administrative defense responsibilities are carried out by the Department of Defense, whose top officials he appoints; these officials also assist him in policy making. The Congress has broad military powers that are largely limited to the making or withholding of appropriations. Since World War II, there has been a considerable and continuing increase in the practical powers of the Executive Branch over military policy and posture, with a corresponding decrease in Congressional power. Two factors have, in recent years, intensified the struggle over defense power between the President and Congress, with Congress attempting to regain its virtually abandoned prerogatives: (1) the long and frustrating Vietnam War, initiated and conducted by successive presidents and their Defense Department officials; (2) the fears of a strong and irresponsible Presidency engendered by the Watergate affair, and the opportunity it offered Congressmen to place pressure on the President. In June 1973 Congress forced a compromise with the President providing that bombing in Cambodia could continue until August 15, provided that it stopped permanently on that date. Later in 1973 a War Powers Act, passed over the President's veto, required that any future emergency war action taken by a President would have to cease after 30 days if it had not been approved by Congress.

Under the 1947 National Security Act, as amended, the Department of Defense (DOD) is a unified instrument for policy and action under the direction of the Secretary of Defense. The three autonomous military departments (Army, Navy, and Air Force, with the Marine Corps within the Navy Department), and their civilian secretaries, are subject to centralized authority of the Secretary of Defense. For instance, supply purchases for all services are made by one Defense Supply Agency; military intelligence reports and interpretation are handled in Washington by one Defense Intelligence Agency; The Readiness Command is a mission-centered headquarters to be made up of both Army and Air Force elements. Weapons development for all services is under the DOD Director of Research and Engineering.

POLITICO-MILITARY POLICY

At the conclusion of World War II, collective security and preparedness had replaced isolation and disarmament as the US national security principles for preventing war. Collaboration with allies during World War II developed into full and sponsoring participation in the United Nations and a number of regional mutual-assistance agreements. Lend-Lease Aid to allies, begun in 1940, developed after the war into both military and economic aid to friendly and neutral countries.

Nuclear explosives and the great military power of the hostile Soviet Union have been the determining factors in US military policy since World War II. The relative decline of British and French economic and military power left the United States in the position of world leader against continued Communist-Soviet encroachment in Europe and elsewhere. In recent years the rising power of the People's Republic of China, and its development of nuclear weapons, have been an additional significant factor.

US policy on control and disarmament of nuclear weapons has been that such measures must be predicated on reliable inspection procedures; Soviet policy has been that all weapons

should simply be destroyed, and that inspection would be an intolerable security threat to the Soviet Union. The little common ground between these positions yielded in 1963 the Treaty for a Partial Nuclear Test Ban and the Hot Line agreement providing a direct communications link between leaders of the two super-powers. The Nuclear Nonproliferation Treaty was ratified by the Senate in early 1969. Recent technological advances, including observation by man-made earth satellites, have eased the inspection controversy by making possible reasonable assurance that arms control agreements are being complied with, without necessity for on-site inspection. These advances, together with practical, and reasonably permanent, nuclear-weapon parity between the United States and the Soviet Union, seem to have opened the possibility of more fundamental strategic arms agreements. A new destabilizing force has appeared, however—MIRVs (multiple independently targeted warheads delivered by a single launcher).

"Massive retaliation," or instant response against aggression "by means and at places of our own choosing," was the strategic doctrine of the years from 1953 to about 1957. By the time Soviet testing of intercontinental ballistic missiles (ICBM) with thermonuclear warheads foreshadowed the end of the massive retaliation policy in 1957, the policy was already under thorough reevaluation.

Under the Kennedy administration, the policy of "flexible response," or "graduated response," became official US doctrine. All use of force was to be carefully controlled, with responses to aggression carefully selected to turn back the aggression at hand but not to trigger a nuclear reaction from the adversary power. Development of conventional forces, including special forces for counterinsurgency, was pushed. The country was to have the capability to fight limited war, so that it would not have to choose between survival and holocaust.

The Vietnam War demonstrated forcefully, however, that mere possession of a diversified array of weapons systems does not make it easy, or even necessarily feasible, to fight a limited war in the late 20th Century.

Production of long-range nuclear-warhead missiles, emphasized in the late Eisenhower administration to close the hypothetical missile gap with the Soviet Union, gave the United States a preponderance of nuclear offensive power. In the early 1960s efforts were concentrated on protecting (hardening) and dispersing the missile launching sites, thus resulting in relative invulnerability of missiles to enemy attack, without making them more provocative. The same purpose was served by the development of nuclear-powered submarines, with the ability to cruise under water at great speed, for long periods, and armed with long-range Polaris nuclear-warhead missiles.

During the early 1960s mutual nuclear deterrence of the United States and USSR became fairly stable, with each nation having enough striking power to survive a first nuclear strike by the other and still inflict unacceptable damage on its adversary. US policy then was that this condition was better than the instability, uncertainty, and consequent danger of nuclear war that might result from deployment of new weapons systems. More recently, technological improvements in ABMs (antiballistic missiles), some ABM deployment by the Soviet Union, and an approaching long-range nuclear capability of Communist China have brought reassessment. In September 1967 a limited ABM shield, stated to meet the kind of nuclear threat China could pose during the next 10 years, was proposed, but was never put into effect. In 1969 the Nixon administration proposed, and the Senate narrowly approved, the Safeguard ABM system, which was designed to protect a minimum nuclear deterrent force rather than attempting to protect any cities. Meanwhile, both the Johnson and Nixon administrations pushed for negotiations with the Soviet Union aimed at limiting the strategic arms race. The Strategic Arms Limitation Talks (SALT) began in 1969, and in May 1972 yielded two major agreements: (1) a treaty of unlimited duration limiting the installation of antiballistic missile sites in each country to two—one protecting the nation's capital and the other protecting a single ICBM site; (2) an interim executive agreement providing for a five-year moratorium on the deployment of strategic offensive rocket launchers. Its purpose was to freeze ICBM and SLBM (submarine-launched ballistic missile) deployment during the time necessary to work out a comprehensive agreement limiting strategic arms; its obvious weakness—perhaps unavoidable, for verification reasons—was the failure to limit the number of warheads per launcher, leaving the way open for deployment of MIRVs, the new destabilizing factor now threatening mutual deterrence.

A new development in 1974 was Secretary of Defense James R. Schlesinger's advocacy of a new, more flexible US targeting strategy for strategic missiles that would make it possible for the United States to strike at Soviet missile forces (that is, deliver counterforce strikes) as well as at Soviet cities. Critics of Schlesinger's approach consider it an attempt at building a US first-strike capability and thus a gravely destabilizing move. Schlesinger has asserted, however, that the Soviet Union's current missile projects have the "potential net throw weight for a major counterforce capability" and that the United States must not fall behind. The Schlesinger program passed a crucial test in summer 1974 when the Senate failed to delay funds for new projects to (1) increase the accuracy of the land-based intercontinental Minuteman missile, (2) double its nuclear yield, and (3) develop a terminally-guided warhead that would have almost perfect accuracy.

Evidence that the USSR has accelerated its efforts to strengthen its forces on land, in the air, and on the sea has caused further revision in US policy, to provide a more realistic deterrence. Involved are policies calling for improving strategic nuclear weapons, including submarine-launched missiles; the strengthening and modernization of the Navy; and increased research and development looking to the improvement of weapon systems for all services and the development of new ones. The observance of existing treaties is to be maintained, as is military assistance, but planning with our allies has the end of assuring that friendly countries increase their self defense efforts.

New factors in US politico-military policy include the detente with the Soviet Union and the end of hostile relations and establishment of diplomatic contact with the People's Republic of China, both accomplished in 1972. The end of US participation in the war in Indochina, in 1973, also removed a source of friction among the major powers.

Within the United States, despite the easing of anti-defense-establishment feelings brought by withdrawal from Vietnam, 1973 public opinion polls showed declining public support for defense spending. In 1973 it appeared that $5-6 billion would be cut from the President's FY 1975 defense budget of $79 billion, a figure he had stressed must not be cut at all. Congressional conservatives, usually strongly for defense, joined with liberals critical of the Pentagon to threaten the cuts. This attitude was a product of concern about inflation, anger at revelations that Defense officials had lied to Congress in official reports on bombing in Cambodia, and lessening of the President's political leverage as a result of the Watergate scandal, as well as of the drop in public support for defense spending. The October War in the Middle East, however, reversed the previous Congressional thinking, and the eventual cut was less than $3 billion.

Manpower for US armed forces is now obtained through voluntary service, with conscription legislation remaining in force should there not be enough volunteers to reach force level requirements. To implement the all-volunteer policy, determined efforts are being made to make military service attractive to young people.

STRATEGIC PROBLEMS

In the era of long-range nuclear bombing and nuclear-armed ICBMs, the nation's major strategic problem is security from possible attack by a hostile nuclear power. At present, only the USSR is a potential attacker, although China may soon achieve a limited ICBM capability. In addition to, and essential to, the policy of deterrence discussed above, is a realistic defense capability.

Air and aerospace defense of North America is the responsibility of the joint US-Canadian North American Air Defense Command (NORAD). The US component, more than 70 percent of NORAD's resources, is the US Air Force's Aerospace Defense Command (ADC). NORAD operational headquarters is under Cheyenne Mountain, near Colorado Springs, Colorado. When NORAD was established in 1958, the greatest danger was still from nuclear-armed bombers, and the NORAD force was composed largely of interceptor aircraft, plus some Bomarc and Nike missiles. A Distant Early Warning (DEW) line was established, stretching from the Aleutians to Greenland, with a radar, computer, and communications network that would immediately mobilize air defense to meet any threat from the north. It is recognized that the chief current threat is from missiles, and although the DEW line is maintained, NORAD's anti-bomber fighter and radar strengths are being reduced. A Ballistic Missile Early Warning System (BMEWS) was established in 1960, with stations in Alaska, the United Kingdom, and Greenland. NORAD's fighter-interceptor force of 530 aircraft (27 US and 3 Canadian squadrons) is to be cut to 336 aircraft by July 1975, and the 48 battery SAM force of US Army Nike-Hercules will be phased out. However, new missile warning systems and hardware are being integrated into NORAD, including Over-the-Horizon Forwardscatter early warning satellites and new phased array radar facing the southern approaches. Combined with BMEWS, DEW line and the network of SLBM warning radars there is a global air and space surveillance capability to prevent any kind of surprise attack on the United States.

The Panama Canal has had a crucial place in US strategy since its construction early in this century. With a two-ocean navy and the availability of massive air transport, the Canal has a less pivotal role in US national security. It is, however, still of great strategic and economic importance. A US garrison in the Canal Zone, the US base at Guantanamo, Cuba, and close surveillance of Caribbean regimes, are measures designed to protect the Canal and its approaches.

There is at present no serious threat to US national, state, or local government from internal subversion, although scattered outbreaks of civil disorder and isolated terroristic acts may be expected.

ALLIANCES

North Atlantic Treaty Organization (NATO). NATO members are pledged to consider an attack on one as an attack on all (see Western Europe, Regional Survey).

Organization of American States (OAS). The United States is signatory of the Inter-American Treaty of Reciprocal Assistance, approved for signature at Rio de Janeiro, September 2, 1947. Under the treaty the OAS Council can call a meeting of the Foreign Ministers of member nations to make decisions in crises (see Central America and West Indies Regional Survey).

The United States is a signatory of the Agreement for Mutual Defense Assistance in Indochina, signed at Saigon, December 23, 1950. Cambodia, France, Laos, the United States, and Vietnam are parties to the treaty.

ANZUS Pact. Security treaty signed at San Francisco, September 1, 1951. Australia, New Zealand, and the United

States are parties (see South and Southwest Pacific, Regional Survey).

Southeast Asia Collective Defense Treaty (SEATO). Signed at Manila, September 8, 1954. Australia, France, New Zealand, Pakistan, the Philippines, Thailand, and the United Kingdom are also parties (see South and Southeast Asia, Regional Survey).

The Pacific Charter. Signed at Manila, September 8, 1954. Australia, France, New Zealand, Pakistan, the Philippines, Thailand, and the United Kingdom are also parties.

The United States is not a member of the Central Treaty Organization of the Middle East (CENTO), formed in 1959 by Iran, Turkey, Pakistan, and the United Kingdom. The United States did, however, encourage the formation of CENTO, its representative sits as an observer at CENTO Council meetings, and the United States is a full member of CENTO committees. The US also has bilateral defense agreements with Turkey, Iran, and Pakistan, signed on March 5, 1959, in Ankara, pledging aid against aggression aimed at any of these countries.

The United States has bilateral alliances with the following nations: Japan, Republic of Korea (South Korea), Spain, and the Republic of China (Taiwan).

The United States has bilateral alliances or agreements, including military assistance agreements, with most of the other participants in the regional alliances listed above.

MILITARY ASSISTANCE

The table on p. 14 lists the nations which have received US military assistance since World War II under the Mutual Defense Act of 1949 and the Foreign Assistance Act of 1961.

ARMY

Personnel: 782,000

Organization:
- 2 commands in continental United States: Forces Command and Training and Doctrine Command (plus Materiel, Communications, etc.)
- 2 overseas armies: US Army Europe and US Army Pacific
- 3 armored divisions
- 2 airborne divisions
- 3 infantry divisions
- 4 mechanized infantry divisions
- 1 experimental division (air cavalry, airmobile, armored brigades)
- 3 independent infantry brigades
- 1 independent airborne brigade
- 1 independent armored cavalry brigade
- 30 SSM battalions
- 4 special forces groups
- 5 independent armored cavalry regiments
- independent artillery battalions (tube and missile)
- 200 independent aviation units
- independent SAM battalions

Deployment:
- Continental US: 1 airborne corps with 2 airborne divisions, 2 mechanized infantry divisions (less 1 brigade), 1 triple capacity division, 1 armored division, and 1 infantry division
- South Korea: 1 field army headquarters, 1 infantry division, and 1 missile command
- Hawaii: 1 infantry division
- Germany: 1 field army of 2 corps, 2 infantry divisions plus 1 brigade (mechanized), 2 armored divisions, 1 brigade (Berlin), 1 air defense command
- Italy: 1 task forces headquarters, 1 SSM (Sergeant) battalion

Major Equipment Inventory:
- M-60 medium tanks (M-60A1 with 105mm gun, M-60A1E2 with 152mm Shillelagh MGM-51A guided missile system)
- M-48 medium tanks (90mm gun)
- M-551 Sheridan assault vehicle (Shillelagh)
- M-41 light tanks (76mm gun)
- M-113 and M-114 armored personnel carriers
- MGM-31 Pershing SSM (about 250 in service)
- MGM-29A Sergeant SSM (about 500 in service)
- Lacrosse SSM
- MGR-1A/B Honest John SSM
- MGR-3A Little John SSM
- MGM-52A Lance SSM (replacing Honest John and Little John)
- MIM-23A Hawk SAM (2 battalions*)
- MIM-14A Nike-Hercules SAM (40 batteries* plus 36 National Guard batteries)
- Chaparral/Vulcan low-altitude air defense system
- Redeye man-portable SAM
- heavy artillery pieces (mostly M-107, M-109, and M-110 self-propelled guns and howitzers)

*Forming Army elements of the Air Defense Command.

VALUE OF MILITARY AID (Military Assistance Program) (Dollars in millions)*

Country	FY 1972	FY 1950-1972	Country	FY 1972	FY 1950-1972
East Asia			**Africa**		
Burma	0.3	80.7	Cameroon	-	0.3
Cambodia	129.2	310.2	Dahomey	-	0.1
China (Taiwan)	44.8	2,844.4	Ethiopia	11.7	171.7
Indochina	-	716.9	Ghana	0.02	0.2
Indonesia	8.5	98.4	Guinea	-	0.9
Japan	-	913.4	Ivory Coast	-	0.1
Korea	174.2	3,421.9	Liberia	0.4	8.0
Laos	-	347.6	Libya	-	16.2
Malaysia	0.1	1.3	Mali	0.04	2.9
Philippines	16.5	364.5	Morocco	1.4	42.7
Thailand	-	610.6	Niger	-	0.1
Vietnam	-	1,544.4	Nigeria	0.1	1.5
Regional Costs	0.1	248.2	Senegal	-	2.8
			Sudan	-	0.7
East Asia Total**	343.7	11,602.4	Tunisia	2.4	33.5
			Upper Volta	-	0.1
Near East and South Asia			Zaire	0.4	27.4
Afghanistan	0.2	4.4	Regional Costs	0.02	0.02
Greece	43.9	1,717.1			
India	0.2	101.3	Africa Total**	16.5	309.8
Iran	6.3	853.7			
Iraq	-	47.8	**Latin America**		
Jordan	23.4	96.2	Argentina	0.7	46.0
Lebanon	0.4	10.2	Bolivia	2.6	28.1
Nepal	0.02	1.9	Brazil	0.9	248.2
Pakistan	0.1	681.3	Chile	2.2	102.6
Saudi Arabia	0.4	36.7	Colombia	1.1	100.0
Sri Lanka	0.6	1.5	Costa Rica	-	1.9
Syria	-	0.1	Cuba	-	12.4
Turkey	117.3	3,173.6	Dominican Republic	0.9	27.2
Regional Costs	0.02	19.3	Ecuador	-	45.9
			El Salvador	0.3	7.2
NESA Total**	192.7	6,745.0	Guatemala	0.9	19.3
			Haiti	-	3.3
Europe			Honduras	0.8	9.5
Austria	0.01	100.2	Jamaica	-	1.1
Belgium	-	1,244.7	Mexico	0.1	2.0
Denmark	-	624.9	Nicaragua	0.8	14.4
Finland	0.01	0.1	Panama	0.4	4.7
France	-	4,249.7	Paraguay	1.9	12.3
Germany	-	901.0	Peru	1.2	95.4
Italy	-	2,361.8	Uruguay	1.6	47.5
Luxumbourg	-	8.3	Venezuela	0.6	10.9
Netherlands	-	1,231.7	Regional Costs	0.2	15.8
Norway	-	908.2			
Portugal	0.6	327.1	Latin America Total**	17.1	855.6
Spain	17.9	627.4			
United Kingdom	-	1,058.8	Non-Regional Costs	-	100.8
Yugoslavia	-	703.0	General Costs	22.8	2,785.7
Regional Costs	0.3	211.6			
Europe Total**	18.9	14,558.4	Grand Total**	641.7	36,957.8

*Department of Defense, Security Assistance Agency, *Military Assistance and Foreign Military Sales Facts*, May 1973.
**Rounding of items causes slight variations from these official regional totals.

medium artillery pieces
light artillery pieces
TOW antitank weapons
9,000 helicopters (including 1,100 UH-1)
3,900 fixed-wing aircraft

Reserves: The United States Army has two separate and independent reserve components. The Army National Guard has approximately 400,000 members, and the Army Reserve has about 260,000 members.

The Army National Guard is organized in eight combat divisions and 16 infantry, one airborne, one armored, one artillery, two engineer brigades, plus combat and combat service support units. The Army Reserve is organized in 19 Army Reserve Commands, 12 training divisions, and two maneuver area commands, 12 brigades (including 2 infantry and 1 mechanized infantry) plus combat and combat service support units. National Guard and Army Reserve units are to be ready for action five weeks after mobilization is ordered. Reserve units, in any number and combination, are mobilized by order of the President. Call up of individual reservists requires Presidential declaration of a national emergency or Congressional action. These provisions apply to all services.

NAVY

Personnel: 641,000 (not including Marine Corps)

Organization: The Chief of Naval Operations (CNO) commands the operating forces of the Navy. The Commandant of the Marine Corps (see below) is responsible to the Chief of Naval Operations for the readiness and performance of Marine Corps elements assigned to the operating forces of the Navy. Under the CNO are: The two major fleets (the Atlantic Fleet and the Pacific Fleet); the Naval Forces, Europe; the Military Sea Transportation Services; and, in time of war, the Coast Guard. There are four numbered fleets, Second, Third, Sixth, and Seventh. The two principal operational fleets are the Sixth Fleet in the Mediterranean, which is under the operational control of CINCNAVEUR, but which is administratively supported by CINCLANTFLT, and the Seventh Fleet, in the Western Pacific and South China Sea, under operational and administrative command of CINCPACFLT. MSTS provides sea transportation for military cargo and personnel of all services.

Major Units:
- 14 attack carriers (including the 76,000 ton nuclear-powered *Enterprise*; CVA/CVAN)
- 2 antisubmarine warfare (ASW) carriers (*Essex* class; CVS)
- 115 submarines (41 nuclear-powered ballistic missile submarines—10 with Poseidon missiles, 10 with Polaris undergoing conversion to Poseidon, and 21 with Polaris A-3, SSBN; 60 nuclear-powered attack submarines, SSN; 14 conventionally-powered attack submarines, SS, SSR, SSG)
- 6 guided missile cruisers (including 1 nuclear-powered; CG/CGN; CLG)
- 1 gun cruiser (CA)
- 28 guided missile frigates (including 4 nuclear-powered; DL, DLG/DLGN)
- 29 guided missile destroyers (DDG)
- 33 destroyers (DD, DDR)
- 63 escort ships (DEG, DER, DE, DH)
- 14 patrol craft (PG, PCER)
- 2 amphibious command ships (LCC)
- 14 transport dock ships (LPD)
- 65 amphibious assault ships (including 7 amphibious assault helicopter carriers)
- 20 tank landing ships (LST)
- 22 other amphibious ships
- 9 mine warfare ships (MSO, MSC, MM)
- 135 auxiliaries

There is a large Naval Reserve Training Command, with destroyers (DD), destroyer escorts (DE), ocean minesweepers (MSO), and coastal minesweepers (MSC), and a Training Fleet with submarines (AGSS), destroyers (DD), ocean minesweepers (MSO) and coastal minesweepers (MSC).

Naval Air Organization:
- 70 fighter/attack squadrons
- 10 reconnaissance squadrons
- 5 helicopter squadrons
- 24 patrol squadrons
- 16 ASW squadrons (fixed wing and helicopter)
- 33 other squadrons (training, etc.)

Naval Aircraft:
- 2,963 combat aircraft
- 38 F-14 Tomcat fighters

240 F-8 Crusader fighters
617 F-4 Phantom II fighter-bombers
521 A-7 Corsair II attack aircraft
401 A-4 Skyhawk attack aircraft
338 A-6 Intruder attack aircraft
226 other attack aircraft
582 shore- and carrier-based ASW, reconnaissance, ECM, and patrol aircraft (S-2, S-3, E-2, Tracker, P-3 Orion, SH-3 Sea King helicopters)
3,329 other aircraft
706 transport and support aircraft (C-130, KC-130)
1,179 other helicopters (AH-1, UH-1N)
1,444 trainer aircraft

Missiles:
656 SSM Polaris and Poseidon long-range ballis- missiles
ASROC anti-submarine
SUBROC submarine-launched anti-submarine
AAM Sparrow, Sidewinder
ASM Bullpup, Shrike, Standare ARM, Walleye
SAM Terrier, Tartar, Talos

Reserves: There are approximately 133,000 members of the Naval Reserve. In addition there are hundreds of reserve warships—mostly escort vessels, a few battleships and cruisers—in the so-called "mothball fleet." The major operational Naval Reserve units are naval aviation: 35 squadrons of fixed-wing aircraft and four squadrons of helicopters.

AIR FORCE

Personnel: 645,420

Organization:

Strategic Air Command (SAC: Commander in Chief, SAC, is responsible directly to the President, through the Secretary of Defense and the Joint Chiefs of Staff)
3 air forces (2 in United States, 1 in Guam), with 9 air divisions and 1 strategic areospace division, made up of:
23 bomb wings (B-52/KC-135)
2 bomb wings (FB-111/KC-135)
3 strategic missile wings (Titan II)
6 strategic missile wings (Minuteman)
1 strategic reconnaissance wing (SR-71)
1 strategic reconnaissance wing (RC/EC-135)
1 strategic reconnaissance wing (U-2, DC-130)
4 air refueling wings (KC-135)

Tactical Air Command (TAC: Commander TAC is also air commander of the joint US Readiness Command)
2 air forces, with 3 air divisions made up of:
13 tactical fighter wings (7 F-4, 3 F-111, 3 A-7)
2 tactical reconnaissance wings (RF-4, EB-66)
4 tactical airlift wings (C-130)
1 special operations wing (O-2, OV-10, UH-1, C-123, C-130, AC-130)
1 fighter weapons wing (F-4, F-111, F-105, A-7, T-38)

Aerospace Defense Command (ADC; the US element of North American Defense Command, NORAD, Joint US-Canadian defense command)
1 Aerospace Defense Force
6 air divisions
27 fighter-interceptor and squadrons, including 20 squadrons Air National Guards (6 F-101, 10 F-102, 4 F-106) and 7 squadrons Regular Air Force (F-106)

Pacific Air Forces (PACAF)
3 air forces (1 each in Thailand, Philippines, and Japan and Korea), with 4 air divisions, made up of:
6 tactical fighter wings (F-4, F-111, F-105, A-7)
1 tactical reconnaissance wing (RF-4)
1 special operations wing (CH-53, OV-10)
1 tactical airlift wing (C-130)

US Air Forces in Europe (USAFE)
3 air forces (1 each in England, Spain, and West Germany), with:
8 tactical fighter wings (7 F-4, 1 F-111)

2 tactical reconnaissance wings (RF-4)
2 tactical airlift wings (C-130)
US Air Forces, Southern Command (USAFSO)
Alaskan Air Command (AAC)
Military Airlift Command (MAC)
    2 air forces, with 13 C-141, 4 C-5, and 3 VC-137 and VC-140 squadrons
Air Training Command
Air Force Systems Command
Air Force Logistics Command
(supporting services and special centers)

Major Equipment Inventory:
Missiles:
    Surface-to-surface ICBMs (SAC)
        54 Titan II (6 squadrons)
        450 Minuteman II
        550 Minuteman III (with MIRV warhead)
    Surface-to-air
        480 Nike-Hercules in NORAD (to be phased out)
    Air-to-air
        AIR-2 Genie rocket (ADC, Air National Guard)
        AIM-4 Falcon (9 configurations, some nuclear, some conventional; TAC, ADC, PACAF, USAFE, Alaskan Air Command)
        AIM-7 Sparrow III (TAC, PACAF, USAFE)
        AIM-9 Sidewinder (TAC, ADC, PACAF, USAFE)
        AIM-20 Quail (carried by SAC B-52s)
    Air-to-surface
        AGM-12 Bullpup (nuclear and conventional; TAC, PACAF, USAFE)
        AGM-28 Hound Dog (SAC)
        AGM-62 Walleye (TAC, PACAF)
        AGM-45 Shrike (TAC, PACAF, USAFE)
        AGM-65 Maverick (TAC, PACAF, USAFE)
        AGM-69A SRAM (Short Range Attack Missile, on SAC B-52 and FB-111 aircraft)
        AGM-78A Standard ARM (TAC, PACAF)

3,662 combat aircraft
    350 B-52 long range heavy bombers
    70 FB-111 long range bombers
    75 F-105 fighter-bombers
    1,500 F-4 fighter bombers
    410 F-111 fighter-bombers
    320 A-7 fighter-bombers
    210 F-106 fighter-interceptors
    375 electronic warfare/tactical reconnaissance aircraft (25 EB-66, 350 RF-4)
    227 strategic/weather reconnaissance/ electronic warfare aircraft (SR-71, EC/RC-135, EC-121, DC/WC-130, U-2, WB-57)
    125 special operations aircraft (CH-53, UH-1, O-2, OV-10, C-123, C/AC-130)

4,518 other aircraft
    657 KC-135 tankers
    295 strategic and VIP airlift (72 C-5, 208 C-141, 4 VC-137, 11 VC-140)
    272 C-130 tactical airlift transports
    447 other transports (C-119, C-123, C-9)
    56 HC-130 search and rescue aircraft
    312 helicopters (UH-1, HH-3, HH-43, HH-1H, HH-53)
    2,365 trainers (T-29, T-33, T-37, T-38, T-39, T-41, T-43)
    114 utility/observation

Reserves: The Air National Guard has 92,000 paid personnel, organized in 92 squadrons, with 1,816 aircraft. They are committed as follows:

Tactical Air Command
    27 fighter-bomber squadrons (18 F-100, 4 F-105, 1 F-104, 1 F-4, 3 A-7)
    7 tactical reconnaissance squadrons (4 RF-101, 3 RF-4)
    2 light ground attack squadrons (A-37)
    9 tanker squadrons (KC-97)
    3 special operations squadrons (C-119/U-10)
    13 transport squadrons (C-123, C-130, C-7)
    5 ground-air coordination squadrons (O-2)
    1 early warning squadron (EC-121)

Aerospace Defense Command
- 20 interceptor squadrons (6 F-101, 10 F-102, 4 F-106)
- 2 electronic warfare squadrons (EB-57)

Military Airlift Command
- 3 airlift squadrons (C-124)

The Air Reserve has 56,000 paid and 101,000 unpaid personnel, organized in 37 squadrons with 427 aircraft. They are capable of immediate active service.
- 24 transport squadrons (2 C-7, 4 C-123, 18 C-130)
- 3 fighter-bomber squadrons (F-105)
- 4 light ground attack squadrons (A-37)
- 4 aerospace rescue squadrons (2 HC-130, 2 HH-1/3)
- 1 airborne early warning squadron (C-121)
- 1 special operations squadron (CH-3)

Personnel of an additional 18 squadrons fly with MAC in C-5, C-141, C-9 MAC squadrons.

MARINE CORPS

Personnel: 212,000

Organization:
- 3 Marine divisions (1st in California, 2d in North Carolina (elements in Mediterranean and Caribbean), 3d in Okinawa)
- 3 tank battalions (each associated with a division)
- 3 SAM battalions (24 missiles each; each associated with a division)
- 3 Marine Aircraft Wings (1st in Japan, 2d in North Carolina, 3d in California)
- 25 fighter-attack squadrons (F-4, A-4, A-6, AV-8)
- 3 composite reconnaissance squadrons (RF-4 and EA-6)
- 3 refueller/transport squadrons (KC-130)
- 3 observation squadrons (OV-10 and AH-1)
- 22 helicopter squadrons (CH-46, CH-53, UH-1)

Major Equipment Inventory:
- M-103 heavy tanks
- M-48 medium tanks
- LVTP-5 amphibious APCs
- M-113 APCs
- Hawk SAMs
- light artillery pieces
- medium artillery pieces
- heavy artillery pieces
- 550 combat aircraft
- 320 helicopters
- 100 other aircraft

Reserves: There are approximately 50,000 Marine Corps reservists, mostly in the 4th Marine Division and 4th Marine Aircraft Wing.

COAST GUARD

Personnel: 36,092

Organization: Under Department of Transportation. In time of war or by Presidential declaration, the Coast Guard is under the Navy Department.

Major Units:
- 44 high endurance cutters (WHEC)
- 19 medium endurance cutters (WMEC)
- 85 patrol craft (WPB)
- 4 training ships
- 8 icebreakers (WAGB)
- 98 buoy tenders
- 6 lightships
- 4 ferries
- 2 supply ships
- 18 tugs
- 2,054 non-commissioned boats
- 168 non-combat aircraft
- 110 helicopters
- 52 other aircraft

PARAMILITARY

There is no national police force or constabulary, nor is there any central law enforcement authority; this power is divided among the Federal, State, and local governments.

The Civil Air Patrol is an official auxiliary of the US Air Force. It numbers 85,000 volunteers, of which 25,000 are teen-age cadets, and operates 3,500 privately owned and 800 CAP-owned aircraft in more than 2,300 individual units, in eight regions. There is a wing in each state, the District of Columbia, and the Commonwealth of Puerto Rico. Missions include search and rescue, civil defense augmentation, disaster relief, and communications in support of emergency and civil defense activities and internal operations. More than 155,000 sorties have been flown, assisting over 16,000 people threatened by disaster and saving more than 1,250 lives.

The Office of Civil Defense under the Secretary of the Army directs the nation's civilian response to a nuclear attack. There are 10,000 civilian employees and about 20,000 part-time volunteers. The national organization is decentralized under State and local government. The program includes development of a nationwide fallout shelter system through dual-pupose use of available buildings, marking these shelters, stocking them with food, water, medical supplies, and radiological monitoring instruments. The program also includes some 3,000 protected Emergency Operating Centers (EOCs) for use by key State and local officials in directing emergency operations; the Emergency Broadcast System employing stations of the civilian boradcasting industry; a Broadcast Station Protection Program of fallout protection, emergency power, and radio links to the EOCs for over 600 radio stations; a warning system linking over 1,500 warning points to the North American Air Defense Command Center in Colorado; and a radiological monitoring system of more than 65,000 monitoring locations and communications, linking with US military communications, to tie all of these elements together.

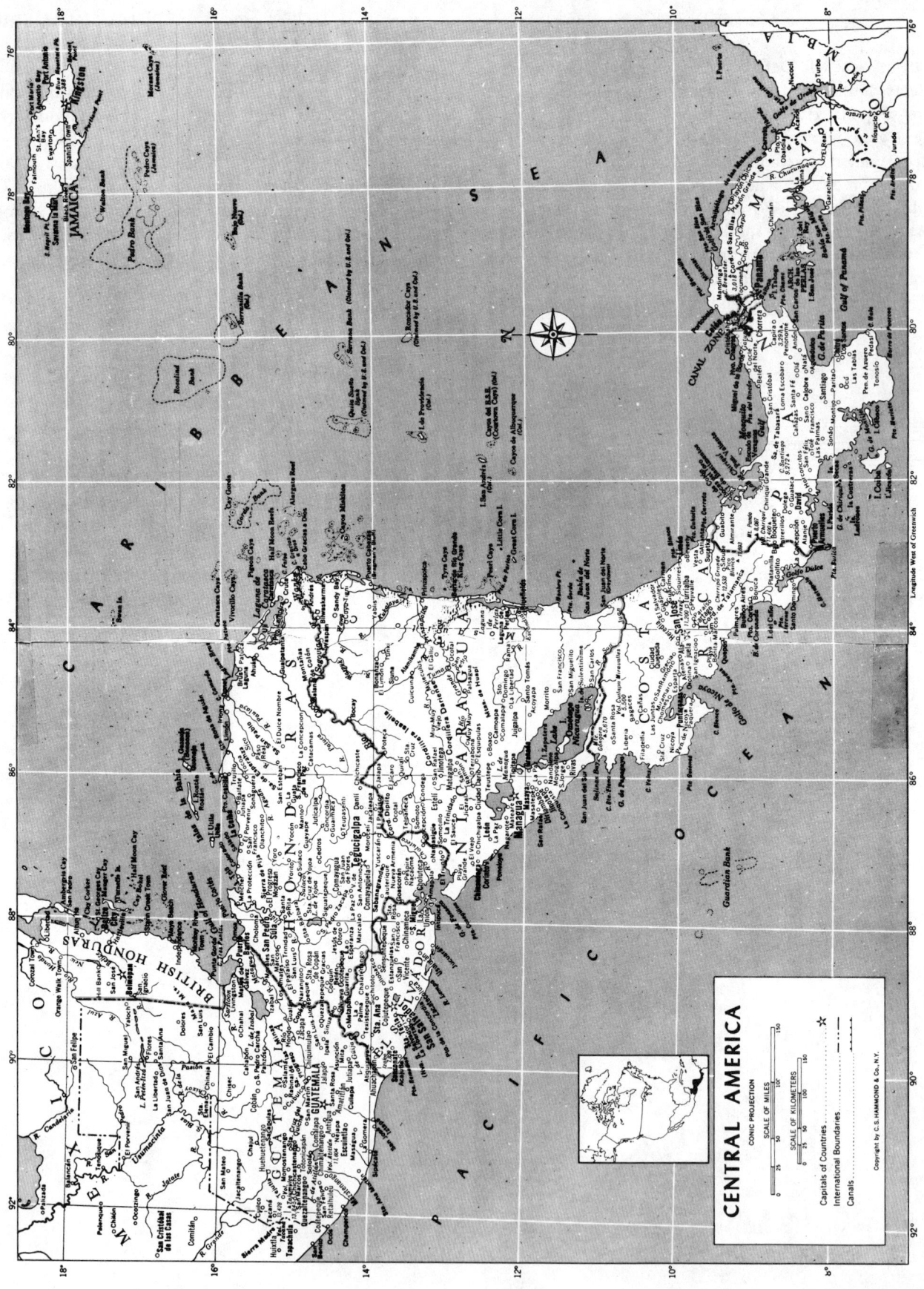

2
CENTRAL AMERICA AND ISLANDS OF THE WESTERN HEMISPHERE

Regional Survey

MILITARY GEOGRAPHY

This region includes two principal geographical groupings: the states of Central America and the Islands of the West Indies. The first is made up of Belize, Costa Rica, El Salvador, Guatemala, Honduras, Nicaragua, and Panama on a long isthmus connecting North and South America. The West Indies is a collection of islands in the Caribbean Sea and the Gulf of Mexico, east of Central America. The major political entities of the West Indies are Cuba, the Dominican Republic, Haiti, Jamaica, Trinidad and Tobago, Puerto Rico, the British Caribbean Islands, the Netherlands Antilles and the French possessions of Guadeloupe and Martinique. Also included in this selection are other islands of the Western Hemisphere.

STRATEGIC SIGNIFICANCE

The Central America-West Indies area has strategic importance for the United States and for the northern republics of South America as well. The island chain dominates the Atlantic Ocean approaches to the Panama Canal, to the Gulf coasts of the United States and Mexico, and to the Caribbean coasts of Venezuela and Colombia. Under friendly or neutral governments these islands comprise a protective screen; in unfriendly hands they could become dangerously hostile bases. The states of Central America, to a lesser degree, cover the Pacific Ocean approaches to the Panama Canal and to the most vulnerable areas of North and South America, and could also provide potential bases for attack against these areas.

The most important single feature of the region is the Panama Canal. In the half-century since it was opened it has stimulated regional and intercontinental commerce. It has been particularly valuable for the Pacific republics of South America. It has also made possible the rapid transfer of US naval forces between the two oceans. While this feature has been less significant since the advent of air-power and the growth of US naval strength during and since World War II, it is still important, particularly for the defense of the region itself.

Responsible for the security of the Canal area is the US Southern Command (SOUTHCOM), which also is responsible for administering all US forces and missions in Latin America. Headquarters of SOUTHCOM is in the Canal Zone.

In June 1972, after a conference on maritime problems held in Santo Domingo, the foreign ministers of 15 Caribbean nations announced support for a 12-mile limit for territorial waters and patrimonial limits (sovereignty over natural resources but not navigational rights) at 200 miles from their coastlines.

REGIONAL ALLIANCES

Because of the conventional grouping of Central and South America as Latin America, alliances involving both are discussed in this survey.

Organization of American States (OAS). Barbados, Costa Rica, Cuba, the Dominican Republic, El Salvador, Guatemala, Haiti, Honduras, Jamaica, Nicaragua, Panama, and Trinidad and Tobago are members, along with the United States, Mexico and all countries of South America except Guyana. (Cuba, although officially a member, has been excluded from active participation since the 1962 Punta del Este conference.) Eight countries (Belgium, Canada, France, West Germany, Guyana, Israel, The Netherlands, and Spain) have observer status. The origins of the OAS go back to the First International Conference of American States in 1889-1890, leading to the establishment of the Pan-American Union. Creation of the Inter-American Defense Board in 1942, and the signing of the Treaty of Rio (Inter-American Treaty of Reciprocal Assistance), finally led in 1948 to the formalization of the regional organization as the Organization of American States within Article 51 of the United Nations Charter. The OAS Charter, drawn up and signed at Bogota in April 1948, recognizes the sovereignty of each member, calls for non-intervention in the affairs of other states and contains certain provisions to maintain peace and security.

Inter-American Defense Board (IADB). This defense organization was established in 1942 in response to concern among Western Hemisphere states—and particularly the United States—regarding the need for coordination of defense against possible Axis attack. Now an organ of the OAS, the IADB prepares plans for hemispheric defense and operates the Inter—American Defense College to provide advanced study of hemispheric politico-military problems. Membership is identical with that of the OAS, except that Cuba was expelled at Punta del Este (1962). Unlike NATO, the IADB maintains no joint forces.

22 ALMANAC OF WORLD MILITARY POWER

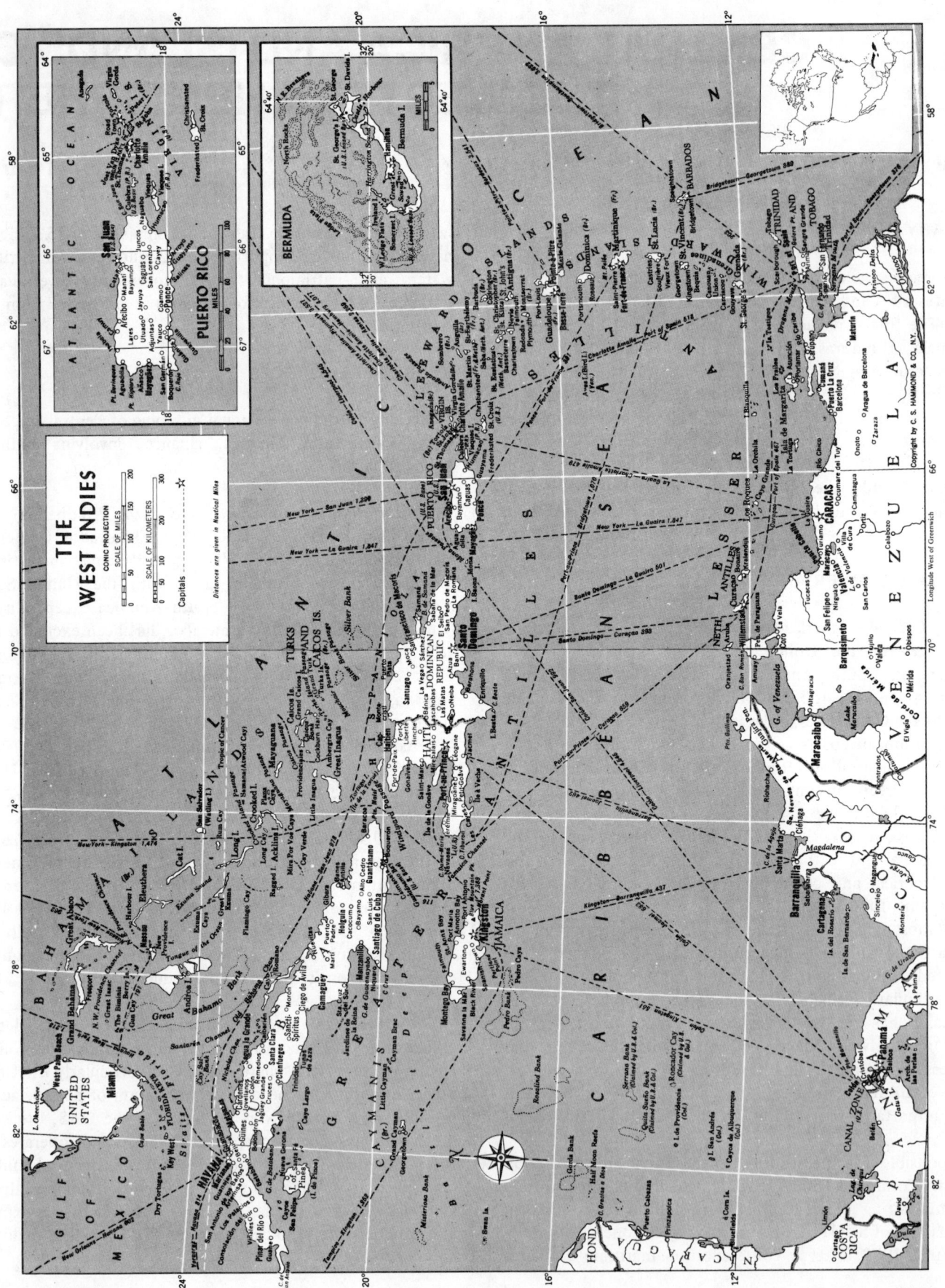

Organization of Central American States (ODECA) and Central American Defense Council (CONDECA). ODECA was established in 1962 by Costa Rica, Nicaragua, Honduras, El Salvador and Guatemala in an attempt to create a more localized OAS-type organization. CONDECA was created in the following year and concerns itself with matters of regional defense and collective security. Although CONDECA coordinates its planning with the IADB, and ODECA is informally involved with the OAS, neither organization is controlled by the OAS.

CONDECA has conducted a series of joint annual sea-surveillance exercises against the seaborne infiltration of guerrillas from Cuba. Similar counter-guerrilla land exercises have also been conducted. A permanent joint staff is headquartered in Guatemala.

Latin American Solidarity Organization (OLAS). Founded in Havana in 1966, this is a Cuban-based organization which seeks to unite various revolutionary groups throughout Latin America. Generally unsuccessful in raising overt revolution in Latin America, it has, however, promoted the formation of international brigades of agitators and students. One was sent to aid the Marxist President of Chile in creating a new Chilean society.

Unitas. To promote cooperation among the naval forces of the Western Hemisphere for its defense, each August or September since 1961 the US Navy has conducted joint naval exercises with the navies of various South American countries.

A Treaty for the Prohibition of Nuclear Weapons in Latin America, approved by the UN General Assembly in 1967, has been ratified by 18 nations and signed but not yet ratified by four others. It is overseen by the Agency for the Prohibition of Nuclear Weapons in Latin America.

Several regional organizations have been formed in an attempt to foster free trade and common markets. The Central American Common Market (CACM), created in 1960 with five members (Costa Rica, El Salvador, Guatemala, Honduras, Nicaragua) has had economic success although affected by controversy. The Caribbean Free Trade Association (CARIFTA) became operational in 1968, and presumably will be superseded by the Caribbean Community (CARICOM), based on a 1973 agreement providing for a Caribbean common market. Initially it consists of Barbados, Guyana, Jamaica and Trinidad and Tobago; other former and present British territories are being invited to join.

RECENT INTRA-AND EXTRA-REGIONAL CONFLICTS

1964	Anti-US and anti-Canal riots in Panama
1965	Dominican Republic civil war, US and OAS intervention
1967	El Salvador-Honduras border dispute
1968	Military coup in Panama
1969	British invasion of secessionist Anguilla
1969-1971	El Salvador-Honduras border conflict
1969	Surinam-Guyana border clash
1970	Disorder in Trinidad-Tobago
1972	Military coup in Honduras

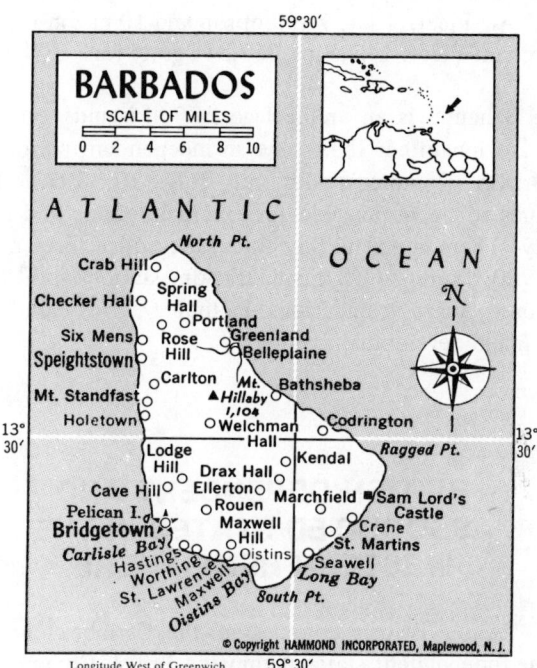

BARBADOS

POWER POTENTIAL STATISTICS

Area: 166 square miles
Population: 256,000
Gross National Product: $150 million ($570 per capita)
Electric Power Output: 63.0 million kwh
Civil Air Fleet: 2 jet transports

POLITICO-MILITARY POLICIES AND POSTURE

Barbados, the easternmost of the West Indies, is an independent, sovereign state within the British Commonwealth. Although relatively stable economically and socially, the island has one of the densest populations in the world and a high annual birth rate. The island is a member of the UN and the OAS.

Barbados has no regular military force, but maintains its own militia Territorial Force, the Barbados Regiment, consisting of one battalion equipped with light arms. Internal security is provided by a police force of 675 men.

BAHAMAS

Commonwealth of the Bahamas

Area: 5,382 square miles (land area)
Population: 185,000
Gross National Product: $390 million ($211 per capita)
Electric Power Output: 558 million kwh
Refined Oil Products: 11.7 million metric tons
Civil Air Fleet: 1 jet, 7 turboprop and 10 piston transports
Merchant Fleet: 145 ships, 357,845 gross tons

The Bahamas is an archipelago of 700 islands, only 40 of which are inhabited. It became an independent nation under the British Commonwealth on July 10, 1973. Britain continues to be responsible for external defense and internal security. There is no military force; the police force numbers about 900. There are US missile tracking stations and US Navy and Coast Guard installations, including a Navy underwater research and development center.

BRITISH DEPENDENT AND ASSOCIATED STATES IN THE WESTERN HEMISPHERE

Six former British colonies in the Caribbean area have become independent states within the British Commonwealth since 1962: The Bahamas, Barbados, Guyana, Jamaica, Trinidad and Tobago, and most recently (February 1974) Grenada. Of the 13 still dependent colonies, five are associated states, i.e., have control over their internal affairs, but not over foreign relations and defense. Each of the associated states and two of the dependencies (British Virgin Islands and Montserrat) has its own separate police force. Britain maintains only a small force in the area (two frigates and a battalion and a half of men).

ASSOCIATED STATES

Antigua
One of the Leeward Islands, Antigua (together with the nearby island of Barbuda) has an area of 170 square miles and a population of about 60,000.

Dominica
One of the Windward Islands, Dominica has an area of 205 square miles and a population of 75,000.

St. Christopher (St. Kitts)-Nevis
These two islands in the Windwards have a combined area of 118 square miles and a population of about 56,000. Anguilla, formerly associated with them, has been administered separately since 1971.

St. Lucia
One of the Windward Islands, St. Lucia has an area of 238 square miles and a population of 103,000.

St. Vincent
One of the Windward Islands, St. Vincent, including the northern Grenadines, has an area of 150 square miles and a population of 95,000.

DEPENDENCIES

Anguilla
One of the Leeward Islands, Anguilla was formerly associated with St. Christopher-Nevis. Since 1971 it has been administered separately. The people have requested (1973) a referendum to determine their future status.

Bermuda
Bermuda is a close cluster of seven main islands (the only ones permanently inhabited), all connnected by bridges, and perhaps 150 islets, with a total area of 21 square miles and a total population of 55,000. There is a local defense militia force of 360 and a police force of 350. The United States maintains a naval air base and a NASA tracking station.

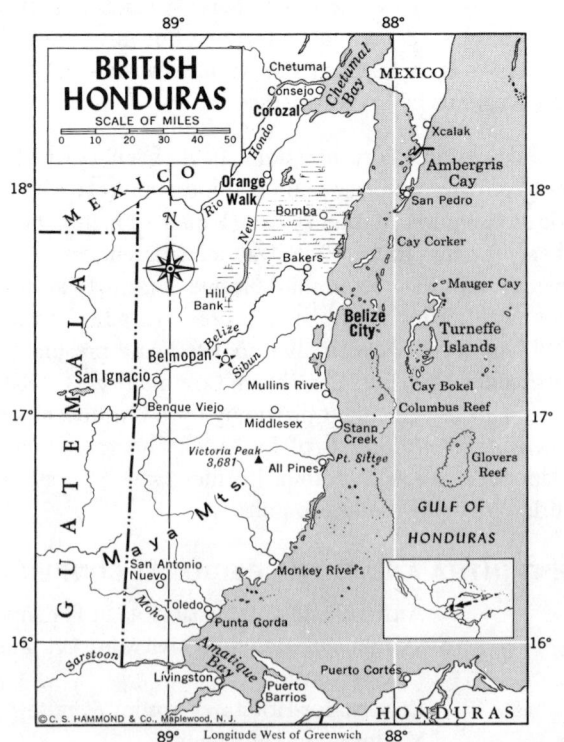

Belize
Area: 8,867 square miles
Population: 126,000
Per Capita Income: $550

Formerly British Honduras, Belize was renamed officially on June 1, 1973. It remains a British colony. Because of a claim by Guatemala to sovereignty of the territory, when rumors that it was about to become independent in 1972 spread to Guatemala the Guatemalan government sent troops to the border. The British responded by sending 1,000 troops to Belize and two ships and an aircraft carrier to the area, claiming that this was a previously annonced maneuver. Guatemala put its troops on alert. After OAS intercession the British troops were withdrawn, except for the small permanent garrison. Earlier attempts by the United States to mediate the dispute had failed.

British Virgin Islands

The British Virgin Islands, which lie to the east of the US Virgin Islands, have an area of 59 square miles and a population of 11,000. There are 36 islands, of which 16 are inhabited. The islands are economically interdependent with the US Virgin Islands.

Cayman Islands

Formerly administered by the Governor of Jamaica, the Caymans became dependencies when Jamaica became independent. The islands have an area of 100 square miles, with a population of 10,000. A local airline operates two light transport planes.

Falkland Islands

Located in the South Atlantic Ocean, about 480 miles northeast of Cape Horn, the islands and their dependencies, South Georgia and South Sandwich, have a total land area of 6,280 square miles and a total population of about 2,200.

Although Britain originally colonized West Falkland, Argentina colonized East Falkland, which Britain seized and occupied in 1833. Argentina has continued to protest British occupation of this territory and has submitted a claim to the United Nations. Guatemala in 1972 agreed to support Argentina's claim in return for Argentine support of Guatemala's claim to British Honduras (Belize). Britain in 1971 agreed to open up communications between the mainland and the islands but would allow no change in status without the consent of the islands' inhabitants.

Montserrat

One of the Leeward Islands, Montserrat has an area of 32 square miles and a population of about 14,000.

Turks and Caicos Islands

Geographically these islands are two southeastern groups of the Bahamas. There are over 30 small islands, with a total area of 166 square miles. Only six of the islands are inhabited, by about 6,000 people. On Grand Turk Island the United States maintains a missile tracking station and a naval base.

COSTA RICA

Republica de Costa Rica
Republic of Costa Rica

POWER POTENTIAL STATISTICS

Area: 19,650 square miles
Population: 1,727,000
Total Active Armed Forces: none (Civil Guard only)
Gross National Product: $970 million ($562 per capita)
Electric Power Output: 1,028 million kwh
Refined Oil Products: 442,000 metric tons
Merchant Fleet: 1 ship; 5,000 gross tons
Civil Air Fleet: 4 jet and 6 piston transports

POLITICO-MILITARY POLICIES AND POSTURE

The Costa Rican Army was abolished in 1948 and replaced by a Civil Guard of about 1,200, which has paramilitary capabilities. There are about 3,000 other police. There are also a number of private armies controlled by political parties and wealthy landowners. For revenue purposes the nation maintains one patrol gunboat (PGM) and an armed tug (YT) on the Atlantic and another PGM on the Pacific coast. Service in the Civil Guard is voluntary. Costa Rica claims exclusive fishing rights within 200 miles of its coasts.

The United States has furnished $1.8 million in military assistance and $38,000 of excess military stocks in the years 1950-1972 for use by the Civil Guard and various police units. Under the MAP 529 Costa Rican students have been trained.

Costa Rica is a member of the UN, ODECA, and OAS and is a vigorous supporter of an inter-American defense and economic system. A contingent of the Civil Guard participated in the Inter-American Peace Force in the Dominican Republic in 1965.

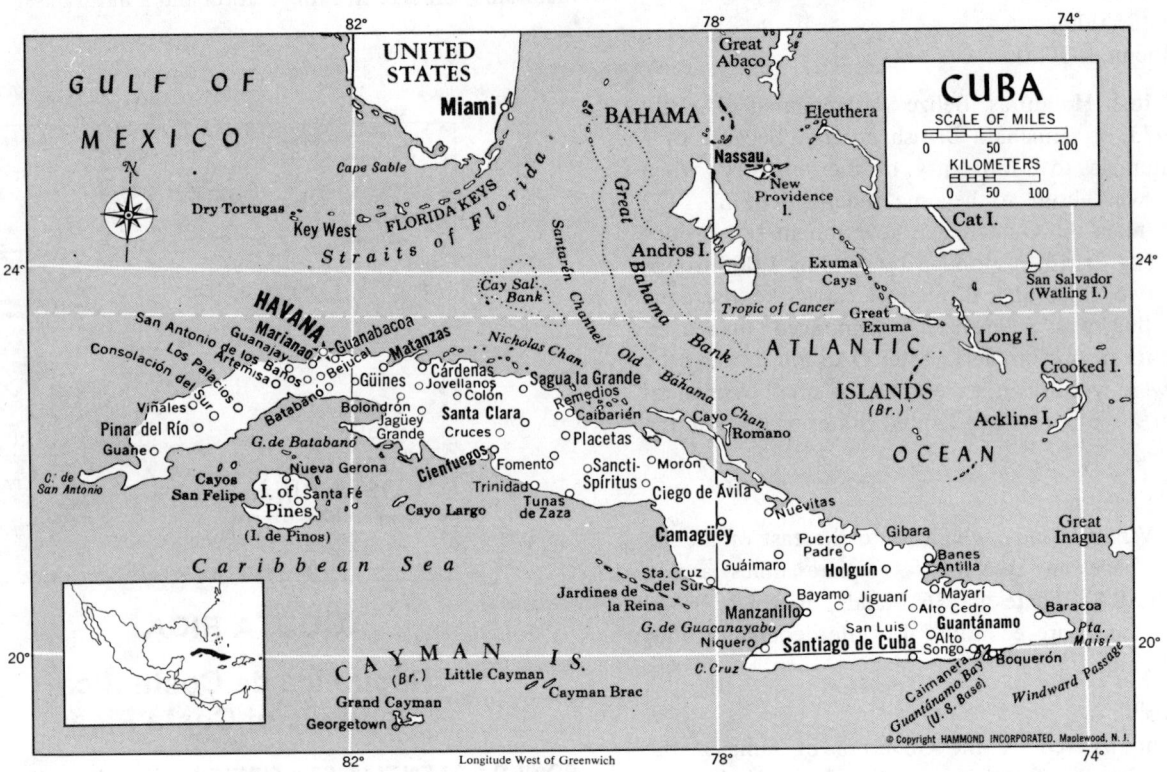

CUBA

Republica de Cuba
Republic of Cuba

POWER POTENTIAL STATISTICS

Area: 44,218 square miles
Population: 8,657,160
Total Active Armed Forces: 108,000 (1.24% population)
Gross National Product: $4.5 billion ($520 per capita)
Annual Military Expenditures: $290 million (6.44% GNP)
Fuel Production: Crude Oil: 116,506 metric tons
Electric Power Output: 4.7 billion kwh
Merchant Fleet: 264 ships; 384,885 gross tons
Civil Air Fleet: 9 turboprop, 14 piston transports

DEFENSE STRUCTURE

The Revolutionary Armed Forces includes the Army, the Air Force, the Navy, and the Militia. Fidel Castro is Prime Minister, First Secretary of the Cuban Communist Party, and Commander-in-Chief of the Revolutionary Armed Forces. His brother, Raul, is Vice-Premier, Minister of the Revolutionary Armed Forces, and Party Second Secretary.

POLITICO-MILITARY POLICY

The history of Cuba for more than a century has been one of instability, unrest and revolution. Early efforts to win independence from Spain failed, and it was not until 1898 that Cuba became formally independent. The first decade of independence was characterized by US administration, occupation, and intermittent interventions.

On January 1, 1959, after three years of insurgency against the dictatorship of Fulgencio Batista, Fidel Castro and his guerrilla forces took over the government in what they termed a nationalist revolution. In 1961, the Castro regime became avowedly communist.

Although Castro's revolution has led to a more even distribution of the internal wealth, it had disastrous initial effects on the general economy and has substantially reduced the wealth to be distributed. While industry has recently expanded and sugar exports once again bring in a sizeable income, the formerly lucrative tourist trade has ceased, as has much other trade. Improved prospects for international trade have led to plans for tripling Cuba's fleet of ocean-going vessels by 1980 and replacing its coastwise and harbor vessels. Ships for Cuba are currently under construction in Argentina, Japan and Spain. To man these new vessels training programs at the Mariel Naval Academy and the Heroic Viet Nam Training Ship have been greatly expanded.

Many Latin American and African insurgents have been

trained in Cuba in guerrilla warfare and revolutionary tactics. Members of the radical US youth who have gone to Cuba as sugarcane cutters are reported to have received the same training. Cuban military experts have been sent clandestinely to other nations, especially in Africa and Latin America, to encourage and direct revolutionary movements.

The volunteer guerrilla army with which Castro seized power proved inadequate as a permanent force. On November 13, 1963, conscription was introduced. Men between 17 and 45 years of age are required to serve for three years. Women between 17 and 36 may volunteer for two years of duty. Women are admitted to armed forces officers' schools, to be trained principally as anti-aircraft artillery and signal corps officers. Military personnel are assigned to agricultural duties during the cane-cutting season, probably with a detrimental effect on military efficiency.

STRATEGIC PROBLEMS

Cuba's location makes the island vulnerable to attack from several directions. Its proximity to the US (only 90 miles from Florida) makes Cuba an easy target for the overwhelming US military power. The presence of the US Navy base at Guantanamo Bay makes Cuba even more vulnerable. Proximity to Caribbean islands, Central America and northern South America increases Cuba's strategic security problems. Castro has repeatedly used this vulnerability as a propaganda theme to unify the nation behind his government.

Cuba's location on the other hand has the advantage of rendering it a useful base for an attack on any of these same places. Thus, the stationing there of Russian missiles in 1962 was immediately interpreted by the US Government as a clear threat to the US and its Latin American allies and led to the so-called Cuban Missile Crisis. In the fall of 1970, the US protested the evident USSR construction of a base capable of harboring and servicing missile-equipped nuclear submarines in Cienfuegos Bay. Cuba's location has also facilitated Castro's policy of exporting revolution in Latin America.

So stringent are the controls of the Castro government that internally generated insurgency is highly unlikely. But, millions of Cuban refugees stand ready to take advantage of any opportunity to return and overthrow the government.

MILITARY ASSISTANCE

Soviet military aid began arriving in Cuba in 1960 and by 1972 was estimated at about $150 million a year. All types of ground weapons from small arms to medium tanks, the latest jet fighters, surface-to-air missiles, land and sea tactical surface-to-surface missiles, and ASW craft have been included. Some 5,000 Soviet instructor-advisers still are in Cuba.

In 1962, in an attempt to overcome its deficiency in ICBMs targeted against the US, the Soviet Union introduced 42 IRBMs, MRBMs and 36 Il-28 nuclear-capable jet light bombers into Cuba. Their crews, plus protective ground units, and armored units to stiffen the Cuban army, numbered 25,000. As a result of the US-Soviet confrontation of October 1962 the missiles and bombers were immediately withdrawn. The troops, except for advisers, followed in subsequent months, but some are reported to have returned by 1972.

Many of the smaller Soviet weapons have been reexported with instructor-advisers to Cuban-supported insurgent movements in Latin America and Africa. A Cuban SAM battery is reported to be serving in North Vietnam.

ALLIANCES

Cuba is a member of the United Nations, but its membership in the OAS was suspended by the other members at Punta del Este in February 1962. A resolution introduced by Peru to the OAS in April 1972 that member nations should be free to consider individually their economic and diplomatic relationships with Cuba was defeated. Subsequently Peru, Mexico, Chile, Jamaica and Trinidad and Tobago have established full diplomatic relations. To further its attempts to export revolution, Cuba sponsored the Latin America Solidarity Organization (OLAS), a federation of left-wing groups, particularly of those sympathetic to violent revolutionary methods.

A treaty of friendship and mutual defense with the Soviet Union governs economic and military assistance and presumably defense arrangements. In July 1972 Cuba was admitted as the ninth member of COMECON (Council 1 for Mutual Economic Assistance), the Soviet-led economic alliance, which may be expected to result in less direct aid from the Soviet Union as the other member nations increase theirs.

ARMY

Personnel: 90,000
Organization:
    Three armies: East Army, Central Army, and West Army.
        9 infantry divisions (probably little more than brigade strength)
        2 armored brigades
Major Equipment Inventory:
    560 heavy and medium tanks (JS-2, T-34, T-54/55)
    light tanks (PT-76)
    100 assault guns (SU-100)
    200 APC (BTR-40, BTR-60, BTR-152)
     45 short-range SSMs (Frog and Salish)
    152mm, 122mm, 85mm, 76mm artillery pieces
    57mm AAA guns
    Snapper anti-tank missiles

Reserves: 85,000 trained reserves can be mobilized within 2 to 3 days to bring the divisions to full combat strength (see Paramilitary, below).

NAVY

Personnel: 6,000

Major Units:

    3 escort/frigates (PF)
    2 patrol escorts (PCE)
  18 submarine chasers (12 SO-1 and 6 Kronstadt class; SC)
  20 guided missile boats (18 Komar and 2 Osa class; PTFG)
  26 motor torpedo boats (P-4 and P-6 class; PT, PTF)
  13 Coast Guard Cutters (US and Cuban)
  12 patrol boats (YP)
     auxiliary and service craft
  18 Mi-4 Hound helicopters
     Styx SSM on Komar and Osa PTFGs
  50 Samlet SSMs for coastal defense

Naval Bases: Mariel, Havana, Varadero, Cienfuegos and 4 new bases

AIR FORCE

Personnel: 12,000

Organization:

  12 fighter-bomber/interceptor squadrons
  24 SAM battalions (SA-2/Guidelines, 144 launchers—6 per battalion)

Major Aircraft Types:

  220+ combat aircraft
    80 MiG-21 interceptors
    50 MiG-19 interceptors
      Su-7 fighter-bombers
    70 MiG-17 fighter-bomber/interceptors
    20 MiG-15 fighter-bombers
  241 other aircraft
    70 transport (An-2, An-24, Il-14)
    71 helicopters (Mi-1 Hare and Mi-4 Hound)
  100 trainer/support aircraft (MiG-15, Zlin 326)

Missiles:

  600 VK750 SAMs (SA-2/Guideline)
     Atoll AAMs (on MiG-21 interceptors)

PARAMILITARY

Cuba has a well-armed People's Militia of about 200,000. These can perform home guard functions, and also serve as a reserve for the Army. They are feared as block-wardens, having the duty of informing on citizens who may make statements or commit acts deemed disloyal to the regime. There is also a body of about 13,000 State Security troops and border guards. In addition, units known as Youth Technical Brigades, in uniform and armed, serve as technicians in industry and agriculture to make sure that the workers produce and that they are loyal to the regime.

DOMINICAN REPUBLIC
Republica Dominicana

POWER POTENTIAL STATISTICS

Area: 18,816 square miles
Population: 4,660,000
Total Active Armed Forces: 29,300 (including gendarmerie; 0.63% population)
Gross National Product: $1.89 billion ($406 per capita)
Annual Military Expenditures: $30.0 million (1.6% GNP)
Electric Power Output: 855 million kwh
Merchant Fleet: 17 ships; 8,881 gross tons
Civil Air Fleet: 2 jet and 6 piston transports

DEFENSE STRUCTURE

The President is Supreme Chief of the armed forces. He appoints the Secretary of State for the Armed Forces, whose job is primarily policy-making and supervision. Administration is exercised by the Chiefs of Staff of the several services.

POLITICO-MILITARY POLICIES

Since the Civil War in 1965, when the United States landed troops in the Dominican Republic to protect the lives of the resident Americans and to prevent the possibility of a Castro-like Communist takeover of the government, the Dominican Republic has weathered plots to overthrow the administration of President Joaquin Balaguer, numerous episodes of political violence, and clashes between police and politically-motivated guerrillas. A program of economic and social reform initiated in 1972 has provided a basis for somewhat increased internal stability.

Males between 18 and 54 are eligible for service in the armed forces; they are enlisted up to the number the budget will support. Since many enlisted men remain on active duty for years, often until retirement age, the number of applicants regularly exceeds the number of available billets. A law

CENTRAL AMERICA AND WEST INDIES 29

requires those not enlisted to do two months a year service in the reserves. This provision is apparently not universally applied.

The Army is involved in several civic action programs. It runs a civilian school for adults and children, cooperates with other governmental agencies on highway construction and maintenance, and participates in social assistance programs with medical and other supplies.

STRATEGIC PROBLEMS

The Dominican Republic occupies the eastern portion of the island of Hispaniola, having a common border of 193 miles with Haiti. Historically the two nations have been hostile, and have been close to war several times in the past decade. The security of the border, and particularly of the narrow valleys that give access from Haiti, is a prime objective of military planning.

The proximity of Cuba presents a threat of invasion by sea, or of infiltration by dissident elements or guerrillas. Consequently another major objective is defense of the coastline and elimination of the small number of dissidents who operate in the mountainous central region of the island.

MILITARY ASSISTANCE

The US Military Assistance and Advisory Group numbers about 50. Military assistance from the United States has totaled $26.1 million since 1950. Between 1950 and 1970, $1,100,000 in excess stocks was provided. Under the MAP, 3,056 students have been trained.

ALLIANCES

The Dominican Republic is a member of the UN and the OAS.

ARMY

Personnel: 12,000

Organization:
- 4 infantry brigades of 2 battalions each
- 1 artillery regiment
- 1 AAA regiment

Major Equipment Inventory:
- 20 light tanks (AMX-13)

30 ALMANAC OF WORLD MILITARY POWER

armored cars
3 Cessna 170 liaison aircraft

NAVY

Personnel: 3,800

Major Units:

- 3 patrol escorts (PF)
- 4 escorts (PCE)
- 2 fleet minesweepers (MSF)
- 3 subchasers (PC)
- 6 patrol gunboats and patrol boats (PGM and YP)
- 3 landing ships (1 LSM and 2 LCU)
- 15 auxiliaries

Naval Bases: Las Calderas, San Pedro de Macoris

AIR FORCE

Personnel: 3,500

Organization:

- 1 fighter squadron (Vampires)
- 1 fighter-bomber/light bomber squadron (F-51/B-26)
- 1 transport squadron (C-45, C-46, Beaver)

Major Aircraft Types:

- 43 combat aircraft
  - 15 Vampire fighters
  - 20 F-51 fighters
  - 6 B-26 light bombers
  - 2 PBY maritime patrol craft
- 54 other aircraft
  - 20 transports (C-45, C-46, Beaver)
  - 30 trainers and utility (T-6, T-11, BT-13, PT-17, Cessna 170)
  - 4 helicopters (Bell 47 and H-19)

Air Bases: San Isidoro, Santo Domingo, Puerta Plata, Santiago, La Romana, Saibo, Barahona, La Vega, Monte Cristi, Azua

PARAMILITARY

The Dominican Republic has a gendarmerie of about 10,000 men.

EL SALVADOR

Republica de El Salvador
Republic of El Salvador

POWER POTENTIAL STATISTICS

Area: 8,260 square miles
Population: 3,650,000
Total Active Armed Forces: 8,130 (including 2,500 National Guard; 0.22% population)
Gross National Product: $1,007 million ($276 per capita)
Annual Military Expenditures: $10.4 million (1.03% GNP)
Refined Oil Production: 471,000 metric tons
Electric Power Output: 736 million kwh
Civil Air Fleet: 2 jet, 2 turboprop, and 3 piston transports

POLITICO-MILITARY POLICIES AND POSTURE

The President is Commander in Chief of the armed forces with control exercised through the Minister of Defense, an Army officer. Men between 18 and 30 are all eligible for service but are called on a selective basis for one-year service. The National Assembly annually sets the strength of the Army, which must have at least 3,000 men. During peacetime El Salvador utilizes its armed forces in nationbuilding through military civic action.

The 19th and 20th Century history of El Salvador has been characterized by violence, chaos, and military intervention. Eight of the past ten governments have been led by military personnel. Relations with neighboring Honduras have been strained and erupted in warfare in mid-1960. Movement between the two countries was restricted until 1972.

El Salvador is small, with a heavy population pressure which grows more serious yearly (annual growth rate is 3.5%).

Serious economic problems of the 1960s have been ameliorated by improvements in the market for agricultural products and strict corrective measures taken by a politically stable government.

US financial military assistance for 1972 was $240,000, making a total of $6.9 million since 1950. Excess stocks were provided, 1950-1972, to a value of $312,000. In addition, 1,277 students have been trained under the MAP.

El Salvador is a member of the UN, the OAS, and ODECA. The headquarters of ODECA is in San Salvador.

The 4,500-man Army is organized in three infantry battalions, one cavalry squadron, two artillery battalions and one parachute company. These are expandable to regimental size upon mobilization of reserves, the Territorial Service, which has 30,000 men organized to produce 12 additional infantry units. The 130-man Navy has two patrol boats (YP). The Air Force, reorganized in 1954 with US assistance, has 1,000 men, one fighter-bomber squadron and one transport squadron. Equipment includes six F-4U5 and six F-51D piston fighter-bombers, four C-47 and one C-54 transports, one FH-1100 helicopter and about 30 trainers, mainly T-34 and T-11. The only air base is at Ilopango, but airstrips exist throughout the country.

The National Guard, a constabulary, has 2,500 men.

FRENCH GUIANA, GUADELOUPE AND MARTINIQUE

POWER POTENTIAL STATISTICS

Area:
   French Guiana: 34,740 square miles
   Guadeloupe: 687 square miles
   Martinique: 431 square miles
Population:
   French Guiana: 50,000
   Guadeloupe: 332,000
   Martinique: 341,800
Total Active Armed Forces: 2,500 (French; .34% population)
Per Capita Income:
   Guadeloupe: $450
   Martinique: $550
Civil Air Fleet: 12 piston transports (8 French Guiana, 4 Guadeloupe)

POLITICO-MILITARY POLICIES AND POSTURE

French Guiana, Guadeloupe and Martinique are all overseas departments of France and thus have representation in the

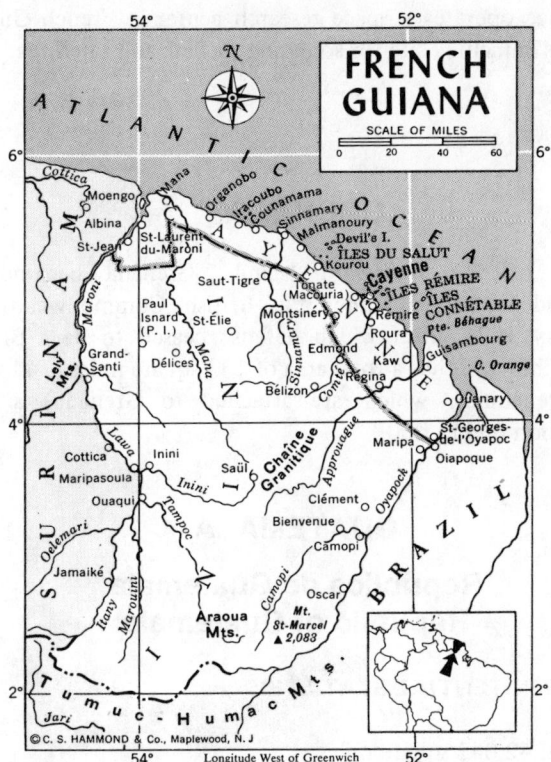

Senate and the National Assembly in Paris; their people have full rights as French citizens. While there has been some support for more self-rule in all three departments, there is no serious movement toward complete independence from France. During the 1940s and early 1950s Communist parties had considerable local influence; in Martinique they received 60 percent of the vote for local representation. The Communists still remain strong in Guadeloupe but have lost influence in Martinique.

Martinique and Guadeloupe both have essentially two-crop economies, based on sugar and bananas, with the only real industry being sugar refineries and rum distilleries. Because France buys its sugar about 20 percent above the world price, and because the government gives the islands more financial support per capita than to any of the other departments, the per capita GNP remains high.

Most of the inhabitants of French Guiana live along the coast; the interior is largely wilderness. Agriculture is primitive and the population is so small that Guianans are fully dependent on France.

Defense is the responsibility of the French government. The area comprises the French Antilles and Guiana Defense Zone, headquartered in Fort-de-France, the capital of Martinique. France maintains 2,500 troops in the zone, under a joint service command *(Commandement Superieur Interarmees du Groupe Antilles-Guyane)*. There is one marine battalion stationed on Guadeloupe. One naval squadron with a patrol escort ship and two minesweepers are stationed on Martinique, plus a small air detachment of transport and trainer aircraft.

France operates a space research center in French Guiana which is launching site for sounding rockets and satellites.

GRENADA

One of the Windward Islands, Grenada became an independent nation under the British Commonwealth in February 1974, after which defense ceased to be a British responsibility. It has a total area of 133 square miles (144 with the Grenadines, which are attached to Grenada) and a population of 115,000.

GUATEMALA

Republica de Guatemala
Republic of Guatemala

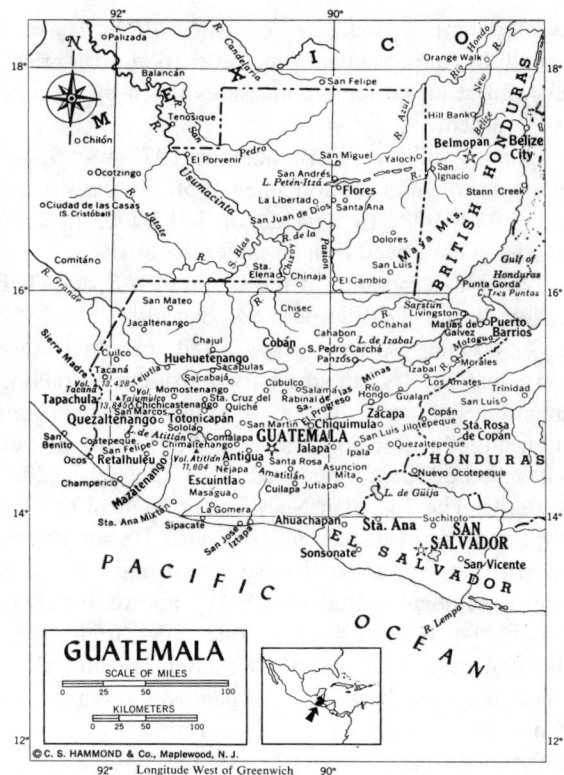

POWER POTENTIAL STATISTICS

Area: 42,042 square miles
Population: 5,603,840
Total Active Armed Forces: 17,000 (including security police; 0.30% population)
Gross National Product: $1.8 billion ($321 per capita)
Annual Military Expenditures: $15 million (0.83% GNP)
Electric Power Output: 589 million kwh
Refined Oil Products: 858,500 metric tons
Merchant Fleet: 2 ships; 3,629 gross tons
Civil Air Fleet: 1 jet and 9 piston transports

POLITICO-MILITARY POLICIES AND POSTURE

The President is Commander in Chief of the Armed Forces, exercising his control through the Minister of Defense in his Cabinet. The Minister of Defense appoints most of the officers of the armed forces.

Since the overthrow of the Arbenz government in 1954, the Communist Party has been outlawed, and there have been numerous guerrilla incidents in the countryside and, since a concerted effort by the army to break up guerrilla groups in the late 1960s, much terrorist activity in Guatemala City. Chiefly responsible are the Communist *Fuerzas Armadas Rebeldes*, but there are other terrorist groups as well, both leftist and rightist.

Guatemala has long claimed sovereignty over the bordering British colony of Belize (British Honduras) on the grounds that it inherited Spanish sovereignty. Britain asserts that an 1859 treaty voids that claim. In 1972, rumors that British Honduras was about to become independent caused the Guatemalan government to concentrate troops on the border.

The British sent three warships and an aircraft carrier to the area and airlifted 1,000 troops to Belize, claiming that these were previously-announced maneuvers. Guatemalan forces were put on alert. Under OAS pressure Britain removed its troops.

In 1972, the United States provided $637,000 in military assistance, making a total of $17.9 million since 1955. Excess stocks to a value of $1.5 million were provided between 1950 and 1970. Under the MAP program 2,576 students have been trained.

Guatemala is a member of the UN, the OAS, and ODECA.

Military service in Guatemala is compulsory for two years for men between ages 18 and 50. Until age 30, men are in a special reserve force. The armed forces have a program for education of illiterates and work on communications, agriculture and reforestation.

The Army numbers 8,000 and is organized in six infantry battalions, an artillery battery, an armored cavalry troop, an engineer battalion, a parachute battalion and a medical battalion. All weapons and vehicles are US: 105mm howitzers, M3A1 scout cars, M3A1 light tanks, M4 medium tanks, M8 armored cars and M113 armored personnel carriers.

The 200-man Navy has one 170-foot patrol boat, one 63-foot patrol boat and four 40-foot boats, all armed with machineguns of different calibers and some equipped with radar. There is a Marine rifle company of 120 men.

The 1,000-man Air Force has one fighter-bomber squadron

equipped with eight A-37 light ground attack jet aircraft, and T-33 armed jet trainers, one light bomber squadron of B-26 light bombers, one reconnaissance squadron of light aircraft, one transport squadron of C-47s, and one helicopter squadron of 10 UH-12, H-19 and UH-1 helicopters. Air bases are at La Aurora in Guatemala City, Puerto Barrios on the Atlantic coast and Puerto San Jose on the Pacific coast.

The younger generation of Army officers are all graduated from the Guatemalan Military Academy and most have taken specialized courses in foreign service schools, principally in the United States, but also in France, Italy, Spain, and West Germany. About 80 percent of all company grade officers are qualified parachutists.

The *Policia Nacional* has a strength of 3,000 men. In the event of a national emergency, they automatically come under control of the Army. There is also a secret or judicial police, strength unknown. These police as well as the *Policia Nacional* are used in counter-terrorist activities.

HAITI
Republique d'Haiti
Republic of Haiti

POWER POTENTIAL STATISTICS

Area: 10,714 square miles
Population: 5,500,000
Total Active Armed Forces: 16,000 (including security militia; 0.29% population)
Gross National Product: $514 million ($93 per capita)
Annual Military Expenditures: $8 million (1.55% GNP)
Electric Power Output: 88 million kwh
Merchant Fleet: 1 ship; 7,000 gross tons
Civil Air Fleet: 4 piston transports

POLITICO-MILITARY POLICIES AND POSTURE

Before his death in 1971, President Francois Duvalier, absolute dictator for 14 years, made his son, Jean-Claude, his successor and President-for-Life. He is nominal Commander in Chief of the armed forces.

Haiti shares the island of Hispaniola with the Dominican Republic. The boundary has been a cause of friction between the two nations, partly because of Haitians crossing into the more prosperous and productive Dominican Republic. Communist Cuba, to the west, has occasionally attempted the landing of exiles and Cuban guerrillas to overthrow the regime.

Haiti is a member of the UN and the OAS. The United States had provided considerable amounts of military assistance, both financial ($3,200,000) and in the form of military missions, before it halted in 1963 at the request of the Haitian government. In 1972 the United States licensed sales of military equipment to Haiti through a US company. The following year Haiti was again placed on the list of countries eligible for US military sales and credit. Recently Haitian Air Force officers have been trained in the United States.

Haiti's Army of some 5,000 men is organized as small combat teams for internal security and border and frontier patrol. There is a Presidential Guard of 265 men, and a new elite 567-man counter-insurgency battalion, the Leopards. Equipment includes nine obsolete light tanks and armored cars, and ten light artillery pieces. The Coast Guard of 290 men operates 2 patrol motor gunboats (PGM), 4 patrol boats (YP), 1 landing craft tank (LCT), and 3 miscellaneous craft (including a presidential yacht). The 250-man Air Force operates a composite squadron with the main function of maintaining internal air service. Aircraft are: 6 F-51 piston fighters, 15 trainers, 2 C-45 light transports, 3 C-47 medium transports and six helicopters.

HONDURAS
Republica de Honduras
Republic of Honduras

POWER POTENTIAL STATISTICS

Area: 43,277 square miles
Population: 2,900,000
Total Active Armed Forces: 7,235 (including internal security forces; .25% population)
Gross National Product: $714 million ($246 per capita)
Annual Military Expenditures: $7.0 million (0.98% GNP)
Electric Power Output: 310 million kwh
Refined Oil Products: 593,700 metric tons

34 ALMANAC OF WORLD MILITARY POWER

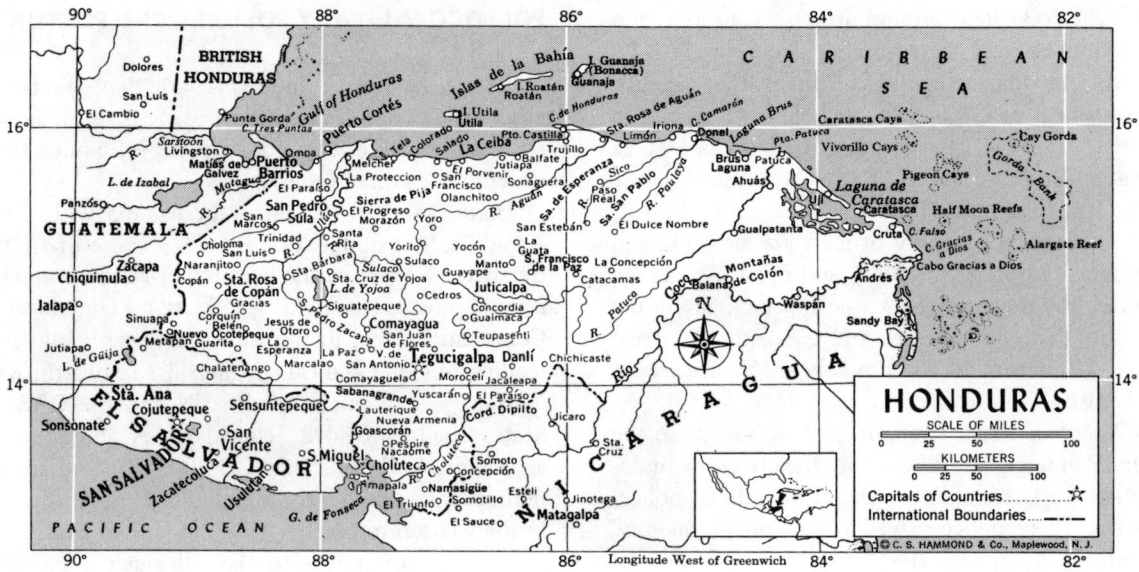

Merchant Fleet: 54 ships; 69,683 gross tons
Civil Air Fleet: 4 turboprop and 35 piston transports

POLITICO-MILITARY POLICIES AND POSTURE

The President is Commander in Chief of the armed forces, which are administered by the Department of the Armed Forces. The commander of the combined services is elected by the Honduran Congress for a six-year term. The military have repeatedly intervened in the government by coup d'etat, most recently in December 1972.

Honduras has been involved in boundary disputes with its neighbors, Guatemala, Nicaragua, and most recently El Salvador, which erupted into open warfare in mid-1969 until the OAS arranged mediation in June 1970. The border was closed until late 1972.

The Communist Party has been illegal since 1957, but two covert communist groups and a pro-Castro organization now exist. All are weak and divided. The military government is under great pressure for agrarian reform, with peasants illegally occupying private lands, and peasant groups, notably the National Union of Peasants, demanding action. At the same time land holders are exerting pressure against government action. Violence has occurred, and the situation threatens the stability of the government.

Honduras belongs to the UN, ODECA, and the OAS. Honduran troops participated in the Inter-American Peace Force sent to the Dominican Republic in 1965. In 1972 the United States provided $703,000 in military aid, making a total of $8.8 million since 1950. Excess stocks to a value of $.6 million were provided between 1950 and 1972. Under the MAP 2,012 students have been trained.

Every male citizen is liable for 8 months service between the ages of 18 and 55, but the Army is adequately filled with volunteers. Between 32 and 55, men may be in a reserve status. The Army of 3,500 men is organized as two infantry battalions and about 20 infantry companies with a supporting light artillery battery (8 pieces) and light tank company (17 tanks). The Coast Guard of 35 men operates three coastal patrol craft (YP). There are 1,200 men in the Air Force, which is organized as two fighter-bomber squadrons and one transport squadron. There are a few jet trainers (F-86), three armed jet trainers (RT-33), 12 piston fighters (F-4U), 2 C-47 and C-46 transports, 3 helicopters and 27 other aircraft, including T-41 trainers. Airfields are at Tegucigalpa and San Pedro Sula. There is a Civil Guard of 2,500.

JAMAICA

POWER POTENTIAL STATISTICS

Area: 4,411 square miles
Population: 2,000,000
Total Active Armed Forces: 4,160 (including Constabulary; .20% population)
Gross National Product: $1.27 billion ($635 per capita)
Annual Military Expenditures: $6 million (0.47% GNP; 2.7% total budget)
Electric Power Output: 1.55 billion kwh
Refined Oil Products: 1.7 million metric tons
Merchant Fleet: 6 ships; 12,899 gross tons
Civil Air Fleet: 5 jet, 2 turboprop and 6 piston transports

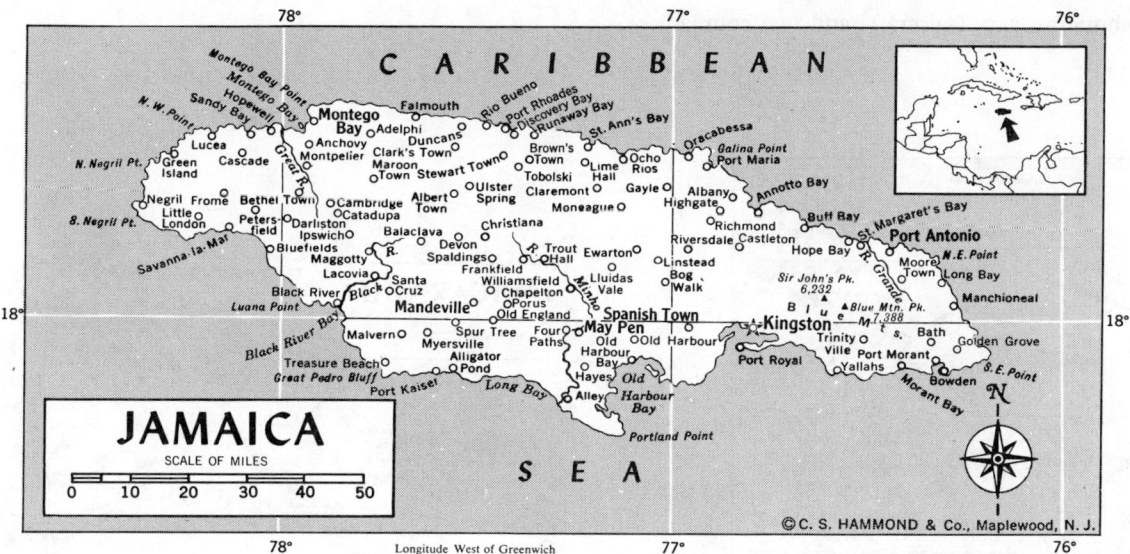

POLITICO-MILITARY POLICIES AND POSTURE

Jamaica is an independent nation (since 1962) within the British Commonwealth, with a Governor General representing the Sovereign. The Prime Minister also holds the portfolio of Minister of Defense; he commands the integrated Jamaica Defense Force (Army, Coast Guard, Air Wing) through its military commander.

Jamaica endorses all efforts to ensure the stability and security of the Western Hemisphere. In international affairs it follows an independent but anti-communist policy. Jamaica is a member of the UN and joined the OAS in August 1969.

Despite a flourishing industry, and production of 20 percent of the world's bauxite (12 million metric tons annually), Jamaica is plagued by socio-economic problems which have potential for internal dissent. These include a population growth rate of 2.5% annually, which robs the substantial economic growth rate of much of its importance, plus urban overcrowding, an overburdened education system, unemployment, underemployment and underproduction.

Jamaica has received US military aid valued at a total of $1.1 million since independence. The initial outfitting of the Army upon independence was British. A British training mission for the three services is retained.

The Defense Force Army numbers 1,000 and is organized as one infantry battalion and headquarters and supporting units. There is also one reserve infantry battalion. The Air Wing has about 250 men and operates two Bell 47, two Alouette II and one Bell 206 Jet Ranger helicopters and three light aircraft (Twin Otter, Cessna 185) for coastal patrol, reconnaissance, and liaison. It is headquartered at Up Park Camp, Kingston. There are international airports at Palisadoes (Kingston) and Montego Bay. The Coast Guard of 60 men operates three ex-USCG WPB patrol craft. It is based at Kingston. There is also a Coast Guard reserve of 8 officers and 27 men.

Jamaica has a Constabulary of 2,850.

NETHERLANDS POSSESSIONS IN THE WESTERN HEMISPHERE

NETHERLANDS ANTILLES

The Netherlands Antilles consist of two sets of islands: northern (St. Martin, Saba, St. Eustatius) and southern (Curacao, Aruba, Bonaire).

Area: 385 square miles
Population: 229,261
Electric Power Output: 1.26 billion kwh
Refined Oil Products: 39.7 million metric tons
Civil Air Fleet: 3 jet, 2 turboprop and 7 piston transports

The Netherlands Antilles are one of the three equal components of the Kingdom of the Netherlands (the other two being the Netherlands proper and Surinam). All are pledged to mutual support. The islands have full autonomy in internal affairs, the self-governing units being Curacao, Bonaire, Aruba, and the Leeward Islands.

Curacao is the principal island, with a per capita income of $1,090. The major economic activity of Curacao and Aruba is refining crude oil from Venezuela.

Netherlands naval units, based on Aruba and Curacao, consist of two escorts, one landing craft utility, one squadron of Tracker antisubmarine patrol aircraft, and two companies of Marines.

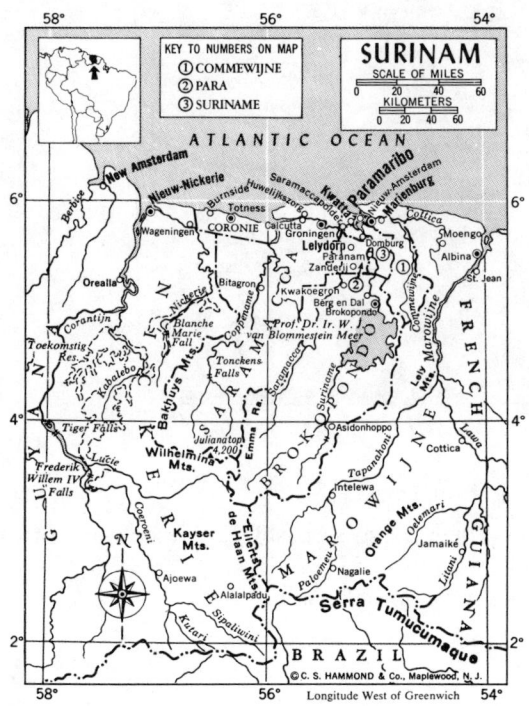

SURINAM

Area: 70,060 square miles
Population: 389,000
Electric Power Output: 1.24 billion kwh
Civil Air Fleet: 2 turboprop transports

Surinam, like the Netherlands Antilles, is a full member of the Kingdom of the Netherlands, with complete internal autonomy. Its most important economic activities are the mining of bauxite (6 million metric tons in 1970) and timber extraction.

One Netherlands infantry battalion with support units is stationed in Surinam. Service is voluntary.

A southern district along the Guyanan border is in dispute and in August 1969 Guyanan troops landed on a local airfield and drove off a Surinam police detachment. The dispute is not juridically settled, but troops of both sides were withdrawn in 1970.

NICARAGUA

Republica de Nicaragua
Republic of Nicaragua

POWER POTENTIAL STATISTICS

Area: 57,143 square miles
Population: 2,100,000
Total Active Armed Forces: 11,100 (including gendarmerie; 0.52% population)
Gross National Product: $893 million ($425 per capita)
Annual Military Expenditures: $12 million (1.34% GNP)
Electric Power Output: 551 million kwh
Refined Oil Products: 490,600 metric tons
Merchant Fleet: 6 ships; 10,877 gross tons
Civil Air Fleet: 2 jet and 7 piston transports

POLITICO-MILITARY POLICIES AND POSTURE

During the period of American military occupation of Nicaragua (1912-1933) the US Marines established and trained a professional Guardia Nacional designed to maintain internal order in Nicaragua and to promote democratic government. However, this elite body took advantage of its position and, under General Anastasio Somoza, soon took control of the country, which has been dominated by the Somoza family and the Guardia ever since. The Guardia serves as army and police force, and includes a coast guard and the air force.

On May 1, 1972, President Anastasio Somoza resigned in favor of a three-man junta, which was to govern until elections in 1974. Somoza retained command of the Guardia Nacional. Following a severe earthquake, which levelled Managua in December 1972, Somoza made himself president of the

National Emergency Committee and declared martial law, thereby becoming the country's chief executive.

Guerrillas, believed to be supported by Cuba, have been increasingly bothersome in the mountainous northern portion of the country.

There is a dispute with Venezuela over claims to the oil-bearing undersea platform north of Guajira Peninsula.

The United States provided Nicaragua $.6 million in military assistance in 1972, making a total of $13.7 million since 1950. In the period 1950-72, $600,000 in excess stocks was provided. Under the MAP 4,397 students have been trained.

Nicaragua is a member of the UN, the OAS, and ODECA.

The ground arm of the Guardia is about 5,400 strong, consisting of volunteers enlisted for three years. It is organized into infantry companies, a motorized detachment, engineers, and an antiaircraft battery. It is equipped with US materiel, including armored personnel carriers and two Cessna U-17A liaison aircraft. There is a Guardia reserve of 4,000. The Coast Guard numbers about 200 and operates six patrol craft (YP) divided between Pacific and Caribbean coasts. The Air Force has about 1,500 men. It has 6 T-33 armed jet-trainers, 6 B-26 light piston bombers, 6 T-28 light armed piston trainers and 14 transports (C-47, Cessna 180). There are also about 15 trainers (PT-13, PT-19, T-6). Air bases are at Managua and Puerto Cabeza with small strips throughout the country. There is a gendarmerie of 4,000 men.

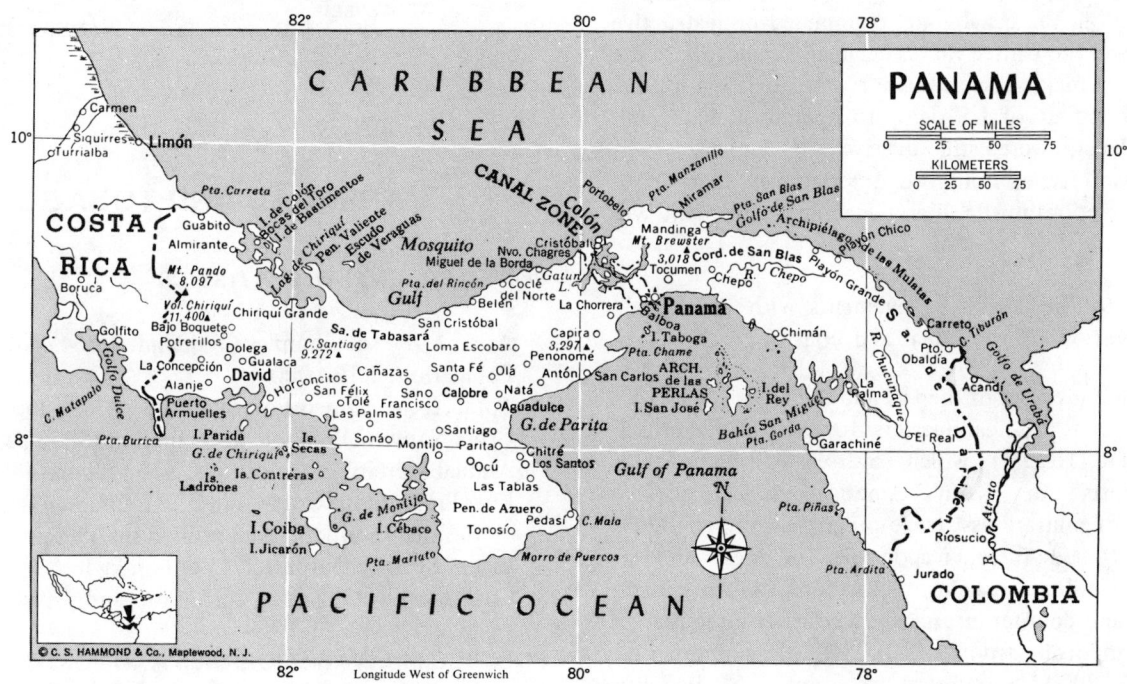

PANAMA

Republica de Panama
Republic of Panama

POWER POTENTIAL STATISTICS

Area: 29,208 square miles
Population: 1,600,000
Total Active Armed Forces: 4,800 (.30% population)
Gross National Product: $1.3 billion ($813 per capita)
Annual Military Expenditures: $2.0 million (.15% GNP)
Electric Power Output: 859 million kwh
Refined Oil Products: 3.9 million metric tons
Merchant Fleet: 1,031 ships; 6.26 million gross tons (most are foreign-owned, with convenience registries)
Civil Air Fleet: 4 jet and 24 piston transports

POLITICO-MILITARY POLICIES AND POSTURE

Constitutional government in Panama was overthrown in 1968 and the recently elected President replaced by a military junta. A new constitution was adopted in 1972, creating a constitutional dictatorship with a titular presidency and all executive, legislative and judicial power actually vested in the Commander-in-Chief of the National Guard, Brigadier General Omar Torrijos Herrera. Responsibility for external protection and for internal security in the Canal Zone, which bisects the country, belongs to the United States government.

Panama became independent by secession from Colombia in 1903, followed by immediate recognition and protection by the United States. This intervention had the primary purpose of permitting construction of the trans-isthmian canal, which had been blocked by what Americans considered Colombian intransigence. The Canal is considered essential to the defense of the United States and the United States holds special treaty rights. Through the years the United States has directly and indirectly exerted influence over internal Panamanian affairs when this has been deemed necessary for the defenses of the Zone. Resentment against the US presence is widespread; this has periodically flared into anti-American incidents, despite favorable modifications of the original treaty with the United States. Panama's long-standing discontent with the treaty of 1903, which gave the United States in perpetuity all the rights "as if sovereign" in the canal zone, culminated in destructive riots in 1964, and the United States decided to renegotiate the treaty. Although major issues, such as the duration of the treaty and the extent of US rights to operate, defend, and extend the Canal, were still divisive, in January 1974 agreement was reached on broad principles, and both governments were optimistic that a detailed agreement was now possible.

In addition to the treaty arrangements with the United States for operation of the Canal and control of the Canal Zone, Panama is a member of the UN and the OAS.

The Canal Zone is headquarters for the US Southern Command (SOUTHCOM) which oversees United States defense interests in Latin America, including the administration of military assistance programs. About 10,000 troops are stationed there, responsible for local and air defense, for four military training schools for Latin Americans, and for jungle and counter-insurgency warfare courses for US and Latin American troops. SOUTHCOM supports 43 missions, with 800 US military personnel, in all Latin American nations except Cuba.

In 1972 the United States provided military assistance valued at $340,000 making a total of $4.6 million since 1950. Excess stocks worth $81,000 were provided between 1950 and 1972. A total of 3,330 students have been trained under the MAP.

The National Guard of 4,800 is a lightly armed constabulary-type force for police and internal security duties. Arms and equipment come from the United States. There is a Coast Guard of about 25 men which operates one patrol craft (YP) on each coast. A small air unit of about 60 men is being trained for Canal inspection duties. It operates a few PBM-5 patrol planes, a Twin Otter transport, small training aircraft, and three Bell 47 helicopters. Air bases are Albrook AFB, France Field, and Tocumen (Panama City). Fields for light planes and landing strips are found in all provinces.

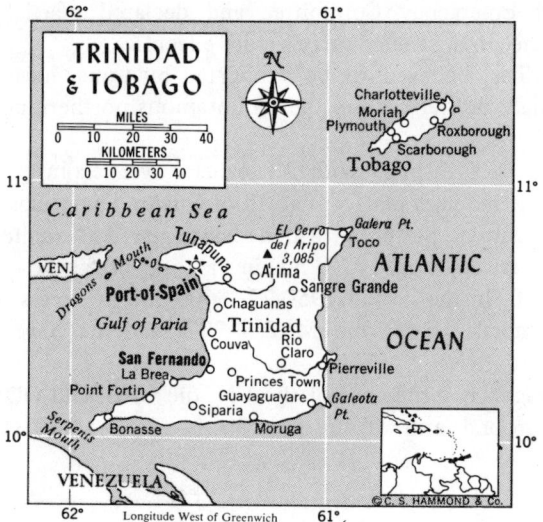

TRINIDAD AND TOBAGO

POWER POTENTIAL STATISTICS

Area: 1,980 square miles (Trinidad: 1,864, Tobago: 116)
Population: 1,100,000
Total Active Armed Forces: 1,125 (.11% population)
Gross National Product: $880 million ($800 per capita)
Annual Military Expenditures: $15 million (1.7% GNP)
Fuel Production: Crude oil: 10.2 million metric tons
    Refined Products: 20.3 million metric tons
Electric Power Output: 1.23 billion kwh
Civil Air Fleet: 6 jet, 1 turboprop and 3 piston transports

POLITICO-MILITARY POLICIES AND POSTURE

As an independent member of the British Commonwealth, Trinidad and Tobago maintains a link with Britain through a Governor General appointed by the Sovereign. The Prime Minister, appointed by the Governor General from a bicameral legislature, directly commands the Army, while the Coast Guard and Police come under the Minister of Home Affairs.

Trinidad and Tobago is a member of the UN and in 1967 became a member of the OAS. It takes an independent stand on many international issues but because of its small size relies on Britain, and on mutual security provided through membership in international organizations, to prevent foreign economic or military domination.

The favorable per capita GNP results from substantial petroleum production. However, declining production, high population density and growth rate, unemployment, and other economic problems have produced tensions threatening to internal stability. Severe riots fomented by Black Power agitators and affecting a part of the Army took place in April 1970. More disorders in 1971 resulted in declaration of a state of emergency and lasted into 1972.

In 1941 the United States and Britain signed a lend-lease agreement which included the granting of the former of base rights on Trinidad for 99 years. In response to a request by Trinidad and Tobago the United States relinquished the last of these, the naval base at Chaguaramas, in 1967.

Britain has provided arms and training for Trinidad and Tobago's armed forces. The Army has a strength of about 1,000 organized as one infantry battalion and supporting headquarters and services. There is a 1,000-man reserve which includes a second infantry battalion. A 200-man Coast Guard mans four 95-foot patrol craft (PGM), one 60-foot patrol craft (YP), one 45-foot patrol craft (YP) and four inshore patrol runabouts (YP). Naval base facilities exist at Chaguaramas and Port of Spain. Airfields include Piarco on Trinidad and Crown Point on Tobago, plus twelve small strips on Trinidad. There is no air force.

3
SOUTH AMERICA

Regional Survey

MILITARY GEOGRAPHY

South America comprises the nations of Argentina, Bolivia, Brazil, Chile, Colombia, Ecuador, Guyana, Paraguay, Peru, Uruguay and Venezuela, plus Dutch Surinam and French Guiana. Several major geographical features create natural defense barriers for parts of the frontiers of most nations of the continent: the Pacific Ocean, the Atlantic Ocean, the Andes mountain chains, and the jungle areas of the Amazon River basin. There are few natural divisions protecting the various nations from neighbors to the north or south, although some protection is provided by the lack of roads and of ground transportation in relatively unpopulated border regions. This lack of natural frontiers has resulted in numerous border disputes since the break-up of the Spanish domain in the early 19th Century. Many of these have yet to be settled to the satisfaction of all parties concerned.

Most South American countries share the common vulnerability of concentration of population, services, and industry in a single core region. Because of the difficulty of overland travel within the continent, however, this vulnerability is mainly susceptible to air attack or internal insurgency.

STRATEGIC SIGNIFICANCE

The strategic significance of this region for the United States is to a large degree related to US interests in the Panama Canal. The location of the northern republics, close to the Canal Zone, makes it important to the United States that they not fall into unfriendly hands. The two southern countries, Argentina and Chile, also have an importance to the United States indirectly related to the Canal: should the Canal be closed these countries dominate the alternate route through the Straits of Magellan or around Cape Horn. Argentina, to some extent, and Brazil, particularly, have further significance because of their proximity to South Atlantic sea lanes. An important development in 1969-70 was the announcement by Peru, Chile, Ecuador, Argentina, Brazil, Uruguay, Panama, Nicaragua and El Salvador that their claims to territorial waters extended 200 miles from their coasts. A similar declaration was made by the Caribbean nations in 1972. The Inter-American Juridical Committee of the OAS endorsed the claim on February 11, 1973.

Perhaps the greatest strategic significance of this continent is its wealth of natural resources, many relatively untapped: a variety of extensive mineral reserves, e.g., copper and nitrates in Chile; agricultural products such as Argentinian beef and wheat; and petroleum reserves in the northern part of the continent, especially Venezuela; and the vast, only partially explored, resources of Brazil. In addition, there is interdependence of the economies and transportation systems among the South American nations that in turn produces mutual concern with regard to strategic and political matters.

Almost without exception the nations of Latin America have been going through a period of serious social and political unrest resulting from severe economic problems and their exploitation by dissidents of various political factions. Inflation is rampant. Despite reform programs and increased industrialization, the gap between rich and poor remains, and a more equitable distribution of income and new solutions to old problems are imperative. Recent years have seen greater military influence in government, even in Uruguay, long a proud civilian democracy, and many of the nations are now headed by self-appointed military rulers.

Although each nation maintains armed forces, in the event of an attack in force from outside the Hemisphere the continent would be dependent upon the United States for effective defense.

Economically the South American nations are increasingly becoming less dependent upon the US market. Japan, Communist China and the Soviet Union in particular are participating in trade and industrial development in many areas.

REGIONAL ALLIANCES

For the Organization of American States (OAS), the Inter-American Defense Board (IADB), the Organization of Latin American Solidarity (OLAS) and UNITAS, see the Regional Survey for Central America.

The Latin American Free Trade Association (LAFTA), presently with eleven members (Mexico, Brazil, and the Spanish-speaking countries of South America) came into existence as a result of the Treaty of Montevideo signed in 1960. The Andean Group, a sub-group of LAFTA, with five members (Colombia, Ecuador, Peru, Bolivia, Chile) was established in 1969. Venezuela's entry was approved in 1973.

INTRA- AND EXTRA-REGIONAL CONFLICTS

1964	Military coup in Bolivia
1964	Military coup in Brazil
1966	Military coup in Argentina
1966	Anti-military coup in Ecuador
1967	Cuban-sponsored insurgency in Bolivia
1968	Military coup in Peru
1969	Uprising by Indians and planters in Guyana
1969	Military coup in Bolivia
1969	Frontier clashes between Guyana and Surinam
1970	Military coup in Argentina
1970	Military coup in Bolivia
1971	Military junta replaces President in Argentina
1971	Military coup in Bolivia
1972	Military coup in Ecuador
1973	Military coup in Chile

ARGENTINA

Republica Argentina

POWER POTENTIAL STATISTICS

Area: 1,073,700 square miles (excluding claimed Antarctic and South Atlantic Island areas of 481,177 square miles)
Population: 24,400,000
Total Active Armed Forces: 167,000 (including gendarmerie; 0.68% population)
Gross National Product: $28.3 billion ($1,160 per capita)
Annual Military Expenditures: $560 million (1.98% GNP)
Steel Production: 1.9 million metric tons
Fuel Production: Crude Oil: 22.1 million metric tons
   Refined Products: 23.6 million metric tons
   Coal: 631,000 metric tons
   Gas: 6.45 billion cubic meters
Electric Power Output: 18.7 billion kwh
Merchant Fleet: 335 ships; 1.3 million gross tons
Civil Air Fleet: 26 jet, 20 turboprop, 8 piston transports

DEFENSE STRUCTURE

The President of Argentina is commander in chief of the armed services. Administrative matters are handled through the Ministry of Defense.

POLITICO-MILITARY POLICY

Seven years of military rule came to an end in May 1973 when Hector J. Campora was inaugurated President of Argentina. Campora had been picked by Juan Peron, the dictator who was overthrown in 1955, to lead his supporters in the elections in March. Campora resigned in July, and Peron, who had returned to Argentina in June, was elected President on September 23.

Males between the ages of 20 and 45 are required to serve in the armed forces. Ten years of service are required, usually one year of it in continuous active service or training in the Army or Air Force, or two years in the Navy. Another ten years are served in the National Guard, which is called out only in the event of war. The final five years are in the Territorial Guard. Naturalized citizens are exempt from military training for a period of ten years after naturalization. Reservists can be called up periodically for training.

STRATEGIC PROBLEMS

Argentina claims about 474,897 square miles of Antarctica and the British colony of the Falkland Islands (Islas Malvinas) off the southeast coast. Talks with Britain in 1973 about the islands reached no solution. A long-standing dispute with Chile over possession of islands in the Beagle Channel, south of Tierra del Fuego, remains unsettled.

During the years of military rule Argentina was plagued by strikes, riots, and guerrilla and terrorist activity in protest against a variety of things, including the rapid increase in the cost of living (80% in 1972), foreign, and particularly US, ownership of industries, military government, and government treatment of Peron. The return of Peronistas to power saw little slackening in terrorist activity as the various factions of the party clashed with one another in a jockeying for power. Before his death on July 1, 1974, Peron had been unable to unify his supporters, and in the light of his disappearance from the scene the future course of government in Argentina is highly uncertain.

MILITARY ASSISTANCE

Deliveries of military equipment under the US Military Assistance Program from 1950 to 1972 were valued at $44.6 million. For 1972 the value was $.6 million. Much of this assistance consisted in credits for the purchase of material. Under the excess stocks program, $1.4 million in military equipment was provided between 1950 and 1972. Under the MAP 3,268 students have been trained.

ALLIANCES

Argentina belongs to the UN and the OAS and their related agencies. In 1962 the government signed an agreement on cooperation and exchange of information with the European Atomic Energy Community.

ARMY

Personnel: 85,000 (20,000 regulars; 65,000 national servicemen)

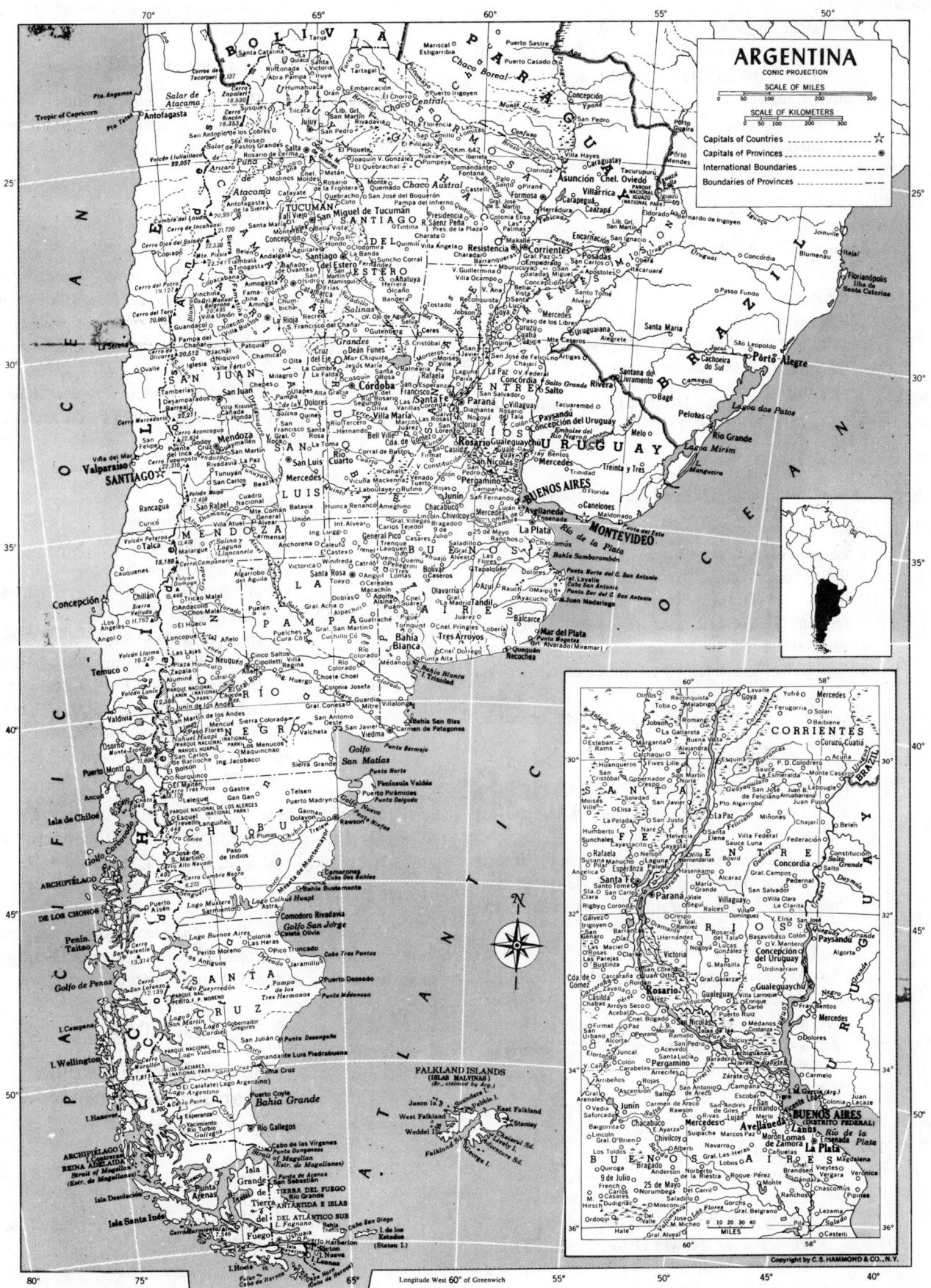

Organization:
- 2 armored brigades
- 3 infantry brigades (expandable to divisions upon reserve mobilization)
- 2 mountain brigades
- 1 airborne brigade
- 2 mechanized brigades
- 10 artillery regiments

Major Equipment Inventory:
- 120 light tanks (AMX-13 and M-24)
- 120 medium tanks (M-4)
- 200 APCs (M-113)
- armored cars
- light artillery
- 32 transport and liaison aircraft (Twin Otters, Bell 47 and FH 1100 helicopters)

Reserves: About 250,000 (trained) comprising the National Guard (200,000) and Territorial Guard (50,000)

NAVY

Personnel: 36,000 (including Naval Air and Marines)

Major Units:
- 1 carrier (CVL/CVS)
- 3 light cruisers (CL)
- 10 destroyers (DD) (2 under construction)
- 2 frigates (PF) (training ships)
- 4 submarines (SS)
- 4 fast patrol craft (PCF) (2 under construction)
- 6 landing ships (LST & LSD)
- 8 costal transports (APC) (1 under construction)
- 6 coastal minesweepers (MSC)
- 41 landing craft (LSM, LSIL, LCI & LCVP)
- 33 auxiliaries (including a floating dock and an icebreaker)
- 4 naval aviation squadrons (distributed among three main shore bases--Commandante Espora, Puerto Belgrano, Punta de Indio--and the carrier *25 de Mayo*)
- 77 combat aircraft
    - 14 A-4 attack aircraft (for service aboard *25 de Mayo*)
    - 8 MB-326GB, light attack
    - 45 T-28 armed trainers
    - 6 S-2 ASW aircraft
    - 4 P-2 patrol aircraft
- 49 other aircraft
    - 25 transports (14 C-45, 7 C-47, 1 C-54, 3 Electras)
    - 11 utility/trainers (5 Beech Queen Air, 4 PC-6 Porter, 1 Twin Otter, 1 HS-125)
    - 10 helicopters (S-31 Alouette, S-61 Sea King)
    - 3 HU-16 Albatross

Missiles: Seacat and Tigercat SAMs

Naval Bases: Puerto Belgrano, Zarate, Rio Grande, Ezeiza, Rio Santiago, Darsena Norte, Trelew, Madryn, Ushuaia

AIR FORCE

Personnel: 21,000

Organization:
- Air Operations Command directs all flying operations, bomber, fighter-bomber, and fighter, 4 brigades and 3 groups, each.
- Personnel Command directs administration and training.
- Materiel Command directs logistics and technical matters, 1 brigade transports and helicopters.
- Air Regions Command

Major Aircraft Types:
- 93 combat aircraft
    - 12 Canberra bombers
    - 20 F-86F fighters
    - 47 A-4 fighter-bombers
    - 14 Mirage III-E & -B fighter/fighter-bombers
- 244 other aircraft
    - 114 transports (C-130, Twin Otters, F-27, C-47, Aero Commander, IA-50, HU-16, Beaver, HS-748, F-28, Cessna 182)
    - 28 helicopters (Hughes-500, UH-1, H-13)
    - 102 trainers (Mentor, MS-760A, IA-35)
    - 50 IA-58 Pucara on order for delivery in 1974

Major Air Bases: Chamical, Rio Gallegos, Mar del Plata, El Palomar, Tandil, Parana, Comodoro Rivadavia, Reconquista, Moron, Reynold, Mendoza

PARAMILITARY

A gendarmerie of 17,000 men under Army command is used mainly for frontier guard duties. There are 8,000 additional men in the National Maritime Prefecture.

BOLIVIA

Republica de Bolivia
Republic of Bolivia

POWER POTENTIAL STATISTICS

Area: 424,162 square miles
Population: 5,038,000
Total Active Armed Forces: 26,800 (including National Police; 0.5% population)

SOUTH AMERICA 45

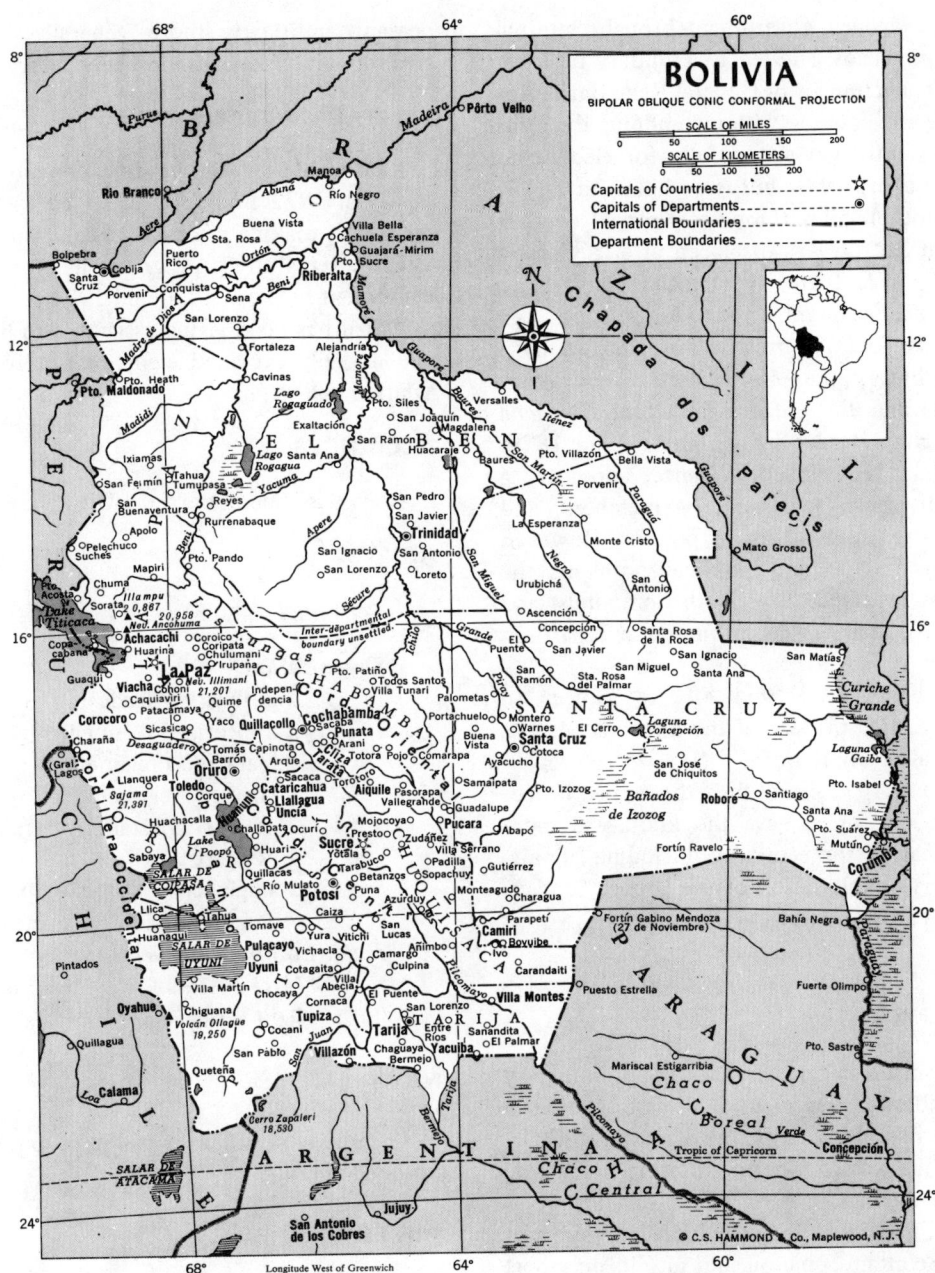

Gross National Product: $1.1 billion ($218 per capita)
Annual Military Expenditures: $25 million (2.27% GNP)
Tin Production: 28,000 metric tons
Fuel Production: Crude Oil: 1.97 million metric tons
　Refined Products: 640,000 metric tons
Electric Power Output: 731 million kwh
Civil Air Fleet: 1 jet, 3 turboprop and 7 piston transports

DEFENSE STRUCTURE

The President is ex-officio Captain-General of the Armed Forces, which consist of an Army, an Air Force, and a small semiautonomous River and Lake Force under a flag officer. He presides over a Supreme Council of National Defense and appoints the service commanders as well as the Commander in Chief of the Armed Forces. Administrative responsibility for the armed forces is in the hands of the Minister of National Defense.

POLITICO-MILITARY POLICIES

Bolivia's history has been one of political unrest and repeated changes of government, with the military frequently involved. An increasingly leftward trend in the revolutionarily-imposed civilian government brought internal dissension and economic chaos, and led to a military takeover in 1964, with the new government of General Rene Barrientos attempting to stabilize the country without undoing the gains of the revolution. Barrientos ran successfully for election as constitutional president in 1966, but was killed in an air accident in 1969. Another coup (bloodless) placed another general in control, but he too was displaced after a year by left-leaning General Juan J. Torres, who made overtures to Cuba and invited a Soviet economic and trade mission. Ten months later, in August 1971, Torres was overthrown by a coalition of the military, the *Movimiento Nacionalista Revolucionaria* (MNR) and the *Falange Socialista Boliviana* (FSB), under Colonel Hugo Banzer Suarez. This was the 187th coup in 146 years since independence. Banzer appointed a coalition cabinet with only two military members, and manifested a definite rightist trend in his policies. However, because of internal economic and political problems the government has sought assistance from both Communist and non-Communist nations. Banzer has promised a bipartisan government by October 1974.

All male citizens between 19 and 49 are subject to conscription, but in practice the size of the armed services is limited by Congressional appropriations.

Government decrees in 1972 established the Armed Forces Development Corporation, which gave the military a more active role in most areas of the economy, including mining, agriculture, and industry. Exploitation of the copper deposits in the Oruro region was a first concern.

STRATEGIC PROBLEMS

Bolivia has been involved in several unsuccessful boundary disputes with its neighbors. Resentment at these losses is still strong. In 1884 it lost its only seaport, Antofagasta, to Chile. Recent reports that Chile was considering offering Bolivia the port of Arica aroused feelings in Peru, which had lost it to Chile in 1884. In the Chaco War Bolivia lost not only most of the Chaco, reputed to contain some oil, but also its only port on the Paraguay River, an indirect outlet to the Atlantic. Earlier it had lost other areas to Peru and Brazil. Diplomatic relations with Chile were broken in 1962 over use of water of the Rio Lauca. In 1973 after Brazil took over a small strip of territory in Santa Cruz, there were reported threats of Brazilian expansion across the Abuna River, which forms Bolivia's northern boundary in the department of Pando.

Bolivia today has little need for concern about external aggression because of its high altitude and the natural defense barriers of the Andes Mountains. Internally, however, there remain substantial threats. The major center of opposition is in the tin mining region, where strikes and violence are frequent. The miners are organized in a now unofficial people's militia, often turbulent and subject to leftist manipulation. A similar peasant militia is more generally supportive of orderly government. Guerrillas have been active in rural areas.

MILITARY ASSISTANCE

United States military missions have been in Bolivia since 1942. In 1972 Bolivia received $2.1 million in US grant aid programs, making a total of $25.9 million between 1950 and 1972. Excess stock programs had provided $2.1 million in equipment between 1950 and 1972.

Brazil has been giving assistance to Bolivia in road-building, and in 1972 provided eight aircraft for the Bolivian military aviation college.

ALLIANCES

Bolivia is a member of the OAS and of the UN.

ARMY

Personnel: 20,000

Organization:
    2 infantry brigades
    2 motorized regiments
    1 paratroop regiment
    5 artillery regiments
    2 ranger battalions trained in antiguerrilla warfare
    5 engineer combat-construction battalions, largely used in civic action

Major Equipment Inventory:
    M-113 APCs
    light artillery and mortars

NAVY

Comprises a small patrol unit on Lake Titicaca on the border of Peru.

AIR FORCE

Personnel: 1,800

Organization:
    1 fighter-bomber squadron (F-51)
    1 counterinsurgency squadron (COIN T-28)
    1 transport squadron (C-47, C-54, Convair 440)

Major Aircraft Types:
    28 combat aircraft
        18 F-51 fighter-bombers
        10 T-28 armed trainers (COIN)
    86 other aircraft
        22 transports (15 C-47, 1 C-54, 6 Convair 440)

27 trainers (6 T-41, 13 T-33, 8 Fokker S-11)
12 helicopters (Hughes 500 M)
25 utility and liaison (U-17, U-3)

Major Air Bases: La Paz, El Trompillo, Charana, Colcapima, Santa Cruz, La Florida, El Tejar, Puerto Suarez

PARAMILITARY

The armed Corps of National Police and Carabineros numbers about 5,000.

BRAZIL
Republica Federativa do Brasil
Federative Republic of Brazil

POWER POTENTIAL STATISTICS

Area: 3,286,470 square miles
Population: 101,300,000
Total Active Armed Forces: 204,350 (0.20% population)
Gross National Product: $48.21 billion ($476 per capita)
Annual Military Expenditures: $1.66 billion (3.44% GNP)
Steel and Iron Production: 10.74 million metric tons
Fuel Production: Coal: 2.5 million metric tons
  Crude Oil: 8.35 million metric tons
  Refined Products: 32.68 million metric tons
Electric Power Output: 45.5 billion kwh
Merchant Fleet: 420 ships; 1.73 million gross tons
Civil Air Fleet: 45 jet, 45 turboprop and 30 piston transports

DEFENSE STRUCTURE

The President of Brazil is Supreme Commander of the armed forces, with the assistance of a National Security Council, an Armed Forces General Staff, Ministries of War, Navy, and Air Force, and a personal staff known as the Military Household. The National Security Council is responsible for strategic defense planning. The General Staff develops war plans and organization. The ministries supervise and control their respective forces. The Military Household is responsible for the President's security and serves as liaison for him with the service ministries.

POLITICO-MILITARY POLICY

Brazil has generally avoided foreign war, having been engaged in only five since becoming independent in 1822. In both World Wars Brazil attempted to remain neutral but finally declared war on Germany after some of its ships were sunk by submarines. In World War II Brazil granted use of bases to the United States, as well as collaborating in antisubmarine warfare and sending some 20,000 men to fight in Italy.

A 1964 military coup ousted the left-wing government of Joao Goulart. Elections were held in 1966, and a civilian-miliary government was established under Army Marshal Artur da Costa e Silva. In December 1968 da Costa e Silva, yielding to pressure by hard-line military leaders, assumed extraordinary powers, voided the constitution and prorogued Congress. After da Costa e Silva died in December 1969 Congress was convened by the junta of service ministers to confirm his successor, General Emilio Garrastazu Medici. On March 15, 1974, Medici's successor, General Ernesto Geisel, began his five-year term, after an election controlled by the military. Since 1969 the government has assumed the character of a military dictatorship, curbing civil liberties, notably freedom of the press, and taking extreme measures to root out opposition and control guerrillas. It is training officers to run the nation as well as the armed forces and proceeding to improve land, sea and air forces.

Military service is compulsory for all males at age 21, and service in the reserves continues to age 45. The first nine years are served in the "first line," one on active duty, the remainder in the organized reserve. The next seven years are in the "second line," and the final years in the unorganized reserve. In order to qualify for public office a man must prove that he is a reservist, that he has fulfilled his military obligations, or has been officially exempted.

The armed forces participate in a variety of civic action projects. In the frontier regions of the north and west, the military provide the only educational and medical services available to civilians. In addition to maintaining two paramilitary training schools, the military provides literacy training for conscripts.

STRATEGIC PROBLEMS

Traditionally supporting a military policy of defense rather than offense, Brazil has concentrated on protecting its frontiers. The northeastern portion of the country lies closer to the Eastern Hemisphere than any other Western Hemisphere country. Although this makes that area slightly vulnerable to trans-Atlantic attack, it also can assure a useful air link from the United States to the Middle East via Africa, as in World War II.

Because of jungles, mountains, and swamps, most of Brazil's frontiers — touching every South American nation except Ecuador and Chile — are physically inaccessible except by a few large rivers. The southern borders with Uruguay and Argentina, however, are less forbidding, and for many years Brazil has maintained half of its army in the southern third of the country.

48 ALMANAC OF WORLD MILITARY POWER

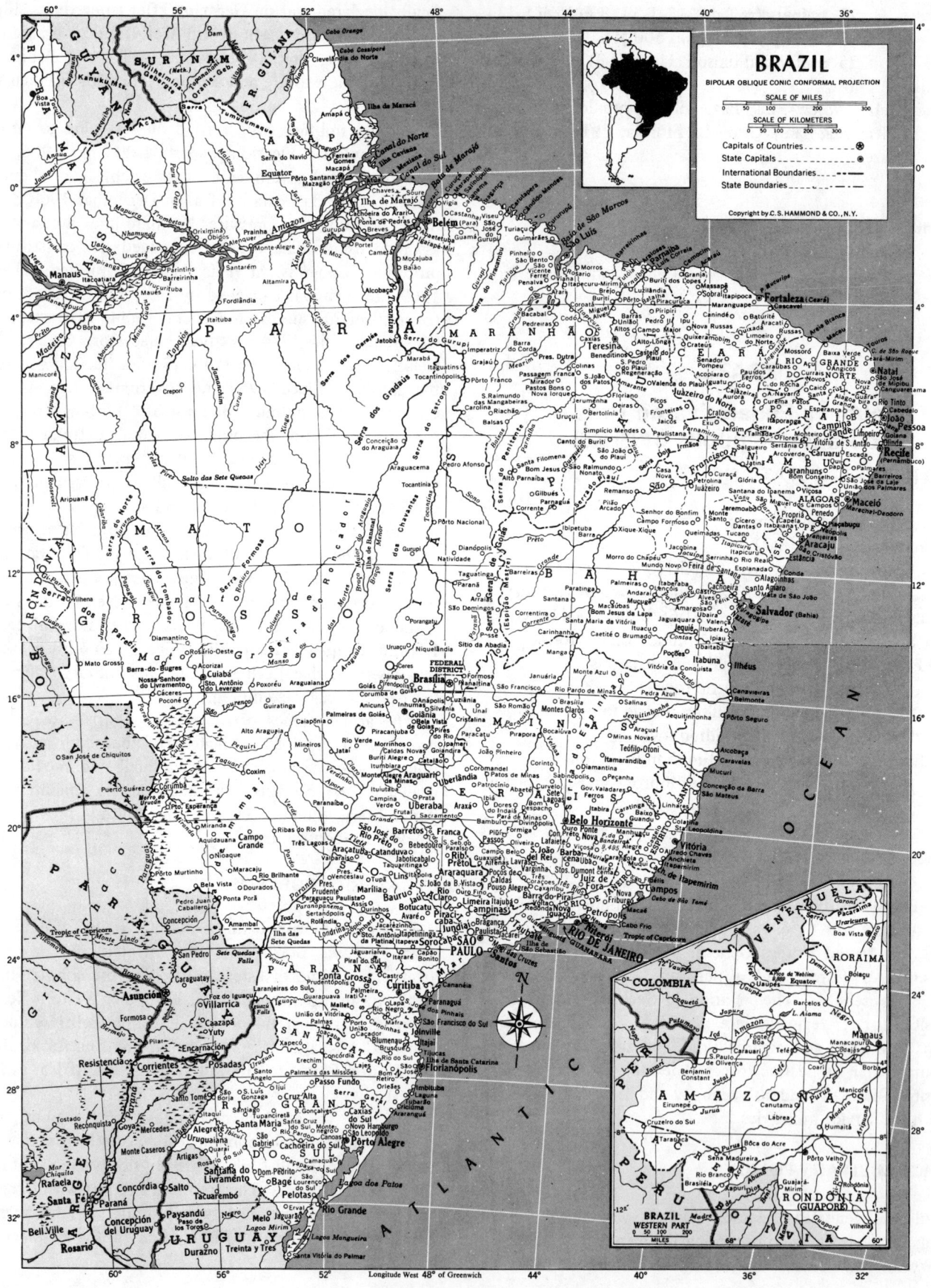

Offshore, Brazil has declared a 200-mile territorial limit, and protection of fishing restrictions within it is a concern of the Brazilian Navy, which is being built up with new ships designed for this purpose.

The Brazilian economy has been expanding rapidly as Brazilians and foreign investors have been developing some of Brazil's enormous natural resources. The construction of a hydroelectric plant on the Parana River has been a source of tension with both Paraguay and Argentina, who share the river as a border with Brazil. Brazil has provided assistance to other nations of Latin America, some of it military but most of it economic or industrial.

There is continuing internal unrest and violence in Brazil. Successful insurgency to the extent of overthrow of the government is, however, highly unlikely. Inflation, labor troubles, government controls on commercial credit, a high population gain and urban migration are all important problems. Unitl 1969 the poverty stricken northeast section of Brazil was considered the most vulnerable to insurgency, but leftist group efforts to organize the peasantry were unsuccessful. The focus of insurgency shifted to urban guerrilla activity: robbing banks for funds, attacks on government buildings, seizure of radio stations, and kidnapping of foreign diplomats. During 1969 and 1970, the ambassadors of the United States, West Germany, and Switzerland, and a consul-general of Japan were seized; they were released after Brazil had turned over a total of 130 jailed subversives to asylum in Mexico, Chile and Algeria. Government antiterrorist efforts were intensified, and allegations of mistreatment and torture of prisoners were decried. The government reported in January 1973 that the urban guerrilla movement, the Popular Revolutionary Vanguard, had been virtually "dismantled," but at the same time a Marxist-Leninist guerrilla group in the jungles of the Amazon claimed it was gaining popular support.

MILITARY ASSISTANCE

The United States sent a joint service mission to Brazil in 1948 to establish an advanced school for senior officers. Since 1953 a military mission has been maintained in Brazil. US grant aid to Brazil in 1970 was $4.3 million. During the period 1950-1970 it totalled $217.7 million. Excess stocks delivered between 1950 and 1970 were valued at $27.6 million. US AID police training was cancelled effective July 1971.

ALLIANCES

Brazil is a member of the OAS, the UN, and their related organizations. Brazilian units formed part of the UNEF in Suez, and Brazilian Air Force units participated in the United Nations transport operation in the Congo. In 1965, Brazil supported the United States in its action in the crisis in the Dominican Republic, and was among the first to send troops to the Inter-American Peace Force. By resolution of the OAS, overall command of the IAPF was given to a Brazilian.

ARMY

Personnel: 130,000

Organization:
    7 infantry divisions
    4 mechanized divisions
    1 armored division
    1 airborne division

Major Equipment Inventory:
  180 medium tanks (M-4, M-47)
  100 light tanks (M-41, M-3)
      APCs (M-113, M-59)
      light and medium artillery pieces
      Hawk surface-to-air missiles
   49 liaison aircraft
   15 helicopters (Bell 206A and UH-1D)

NAVY

Personnel: 44,350 (includes 1,000 Marines)

Organization: 6 naval commands and 1 fleet command

Major Units:
   1 ASW aircraft carrier (CVS)
   1 light cruiser (CL)
   8 diesel submarines (SS)
 14 destroyers (DD; 3 with Seacat SAMs)
   7 destroyer escorts (DE)
 10 patrol escorts (PCE)
   6 coastal gunboats (PGM)
   8 coastal minesweepers (MSC)
   4 transports (APA)
   2 landing ships (LST)
   2 river gunboats (PRB)
   1 river monitor (PRG)
 22 auxiliaries (including 6 survey ships, AGS, oilers, tugs)
 14 P-2E patrol aircraft (operated by Air Force)
 50 helicopters (S-55, Wasp, SH-3D)
 13 S-2A ASW aircraft (operated by Air Force)

Missiles: Seacat, Exocet and Ikara SAMs on CVS, CLs and 3DDs

Naval Bases: Rio de Janeiro, Belem, Natal, Recife, Salvador, Ladario (at Corumba on the Paraguay River), and Sao Pedro da Aldeia Naval Station

50 ALMANAC OF WORLD MILITARY POWER

Equipment on Order:
- 6 frigates
- 2 diesel submarines
- 4 minesweepers

AIR FORCE

Personnel: 30,000
Organization:
- 6 air zones (headquarters at Belem, Recife, Rio de Janeiro, Sao Paulo, Porto Alegre, Brasilia)
- 6 fighter-bomber COIN squadrons (AT-26, F-80/T-33, T-28, T-6)
- 1 fighter squadron (Mirage III E/B)
- 2 light bomber squadrons (B-26)
- 8 transport squadrons (C-54, DC-6/C-118, C-130, Buffalo, C-82/119, HS-748, Viscount, HS-125, C-95)
- 3 liaison-observation squadrons (C-42, L-42)
- 2 naval cooperation squadrons (P-2, S-2, HU-16)

Major Aircraft Types:
- 169 combat aircraft
    - 32 AT-26 Xavante fighter-bombers
    - 16 Mirage III fighters
    - 16 F-80/T-33 fighter-bombers
    - 18 B-26 light bombers
    - 48 armed trainers (T-28, T-6)
    - 27 ASW patrol aircraft (P-2, S-2)
    - 12 HU-16 maritime patrol aircraft
- 588 other aircraft
    - 168 transports (C-130, DC-6/C-118, C-54, Buffalo, C-82/119, HS-748, Viscount, HS-125, C-95 Bandeirante)
    - 48 liaison-observation (C-42, L-42)
    - 72 helicopters (H-13, UH-1, H-23)
    - 300 trainer/miscellaneous support aircraft (T-23, Fokker S-11, Magister, T-37)

Equipment on Order:
- 80 T-25 Universal trainers
- 80 AT-26 Xavante fighter-bombers
- 48 F-5 fighters
- 20 T-23 Uirapura primary trainers

Air Bases: Rio de Janeiro, Sao Paulo, Recife, Belem, Galeao, Cumbica, Santarem, Balterra, Cachijo, Jacareacanga, Salvador, Guarantinqueta, Campos do Alfonsos, Fortaleza, Porto Alegre, Natal, Manaus

PARAMILITARY

Public security forces of various kinds total about 120,000. They also serve as an auxiliary reserve force for the Army. In addition, militia organizations exist in some states. Sao Paulo's, the largest, comprises about 250,000 men.

As a result of prevalent insecurity some large landholders have developed their own security forces, and former policemen have formed death squads to eliminate those they adjudge to be criminals.

CHILE
Republica de Chile
Republic of Chile

POWER POTENTIAL STATISTICS

Area: 292,256 square miles
Population: 9,782,300
Total Active Forces: 90,500 (including constabulary; 0.92% population)
Gross National Product: $8.1 billion ($828 per capita)
Annual Military Expenditures: $175 million (2.16% GNP)
Steel and Iron Production: 1.11 million metric tons
Fuel Production: Coal: 1.38 million metric tons
  Crude Oil: 1.61 million metric tons
  Refined Products: 4.83 million metric tons
Electric Power Output: 7.55 billion kwh
Merchant Fleet: 135 ships; 387,810 gross tons
Civil Air Fleet: 8 jet, 9 turboprop and 19 piston transports

DEFENSE STRUCTURE

Since the military coup in September 1973, Chile has been ruled by a military junta composed of the commanders in chief of the Army, Navy, Air Force and National Police (Carabineros), with the Commander in Chief of the Army, General Augusto Pinochet Ugarte, as President of the junta. Operational and policy matters concerning all the services are the responsibility of the junta. Administration of the armed services is through the Ministry of Defense.

POLITICO-MILITARY POLICY

After a period of increasing unrest in the 1960s, in the 1970 elections Senator Salvador Allende, an avowed Marxist and a Socialist Party leader, formed a coalition of leftist parties—Socialist, Communist, Radical and splinter groups—which won the election as the Popular Unity Movement, although receiving only 37% of the popular vote. With both houses of the Chilean Congress controlled by the opposition parties, however, Allende had great difficulty in obtaining support from the Congress. He nationalized the copper industry and instituted land reforms, which failed because leftist guerrillas took over farm lands by force. The

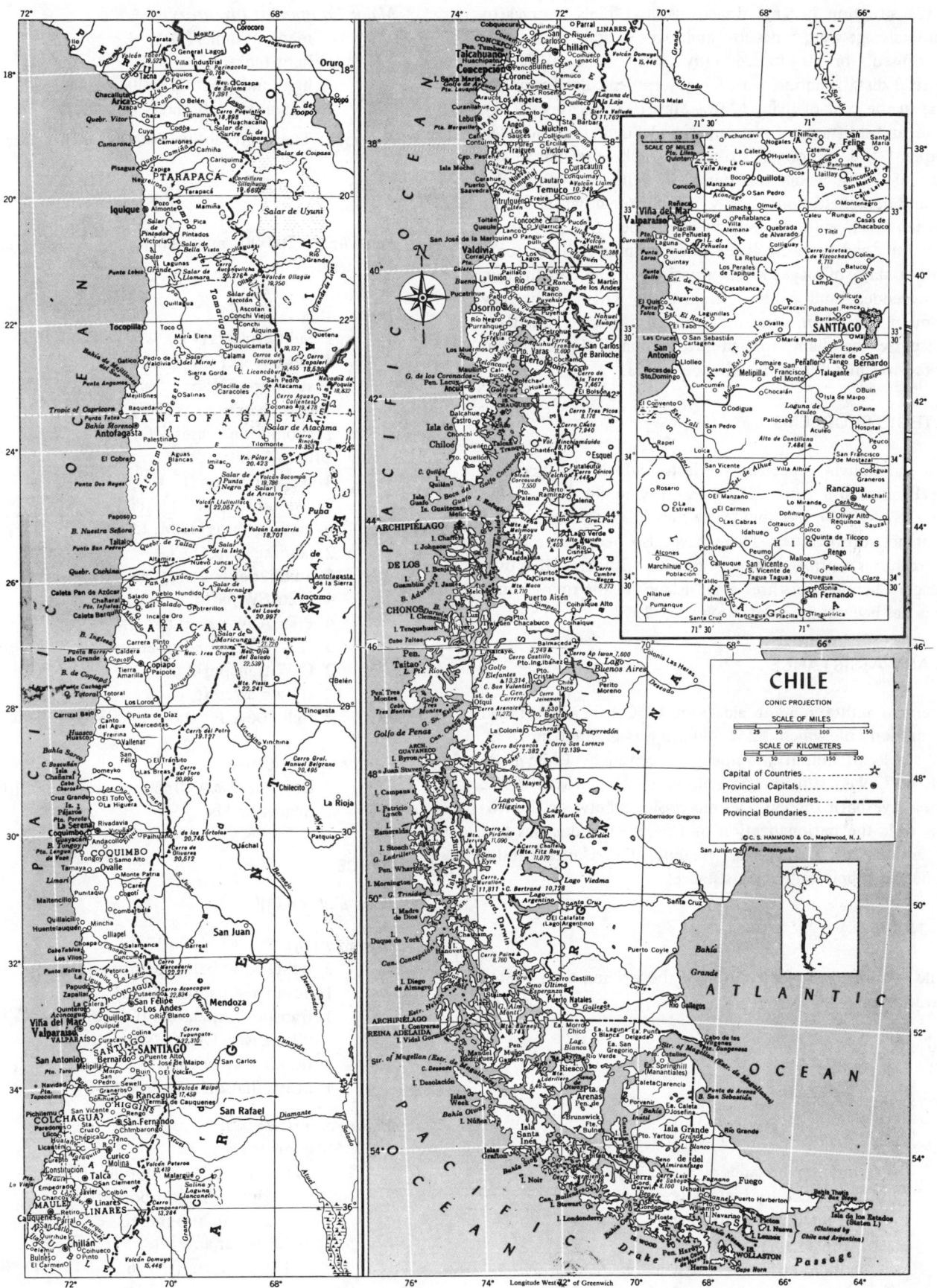

economic situation became disastrous, as Chile's reserves of foreign exchange were exhausted and loans of additional funds were refused, or negotiated only with great difficulty. Widespread dissatisfaction with the government, the enormous increase in the cost of living (238% May 1972 to May 1973), inflation, and shortages of consumer goods, including food, led to frequent and prolonged strikes. A truckers' strike in the summer of 1973, which was joined by numerous sympathy strikes and demonstrations, finally brought the downfall of the government in a military coup in September. (An attempted coup in June had been crushed.) The four-man military junta declared a state of siege. Most provisions of the constitution were suspended, and a new one is to be written. The new government has taken strict measures to eradicate dissidents and disperse the many foreign revolutionary elements that gravitated to Chile during the Allende period.

STRATEGIC PROBLEMS

Peru and Bolivia, especially the latter, which lost its outlet to the Pacific, still resent Chile's victory in the War of the Pacific (1879-1883), but their bitterness has not come to the point of active hostilities. There have also been some minor border disputes with Argentina. A dispute with Argentina over the Beagle Channel and three small islands at the tip of South America has been under arbitration since 1971.

MILITARY ASSISTANCE

American military grant aid from 1950 to 1972 totalled $94.6 million, of which $2.2 million was granted in 1972. Excess stocks of military equipment received by Chile from 1950 to 1972 were valued at $8 million. Under the MAP 4,932 students have been trained. Despite coolness between the two nations over the nationalization of US-owned industries and other actions of the Allende regime, the United States continued to supply military assistance.

ALLIANCES

Chile is a member of the OAS and the UN and their related organizations.

ARMY

Personnel: 38,000

Organization:
    6 infantry brigades
    4 horse cavalry regiments
    2 armored cavalry regiments
    8 artillery regiments
    antiaircraft artillery battalions

Major Equipment Inventory:
    medium tanks (M-4)
    light tanks
    light and medium artillery
    8 liaison aircraft and helicopters

Reserves: There are about 300,000 men in the reserves.

NAVY

Personnel: 20,000 men, including Marines and coast artillery

Major Units:
    2 light cruisers (CL)
    4 destroyers (DD; 2 with Seacat SAM)
    4 submarines (SS)
    4 destroyer escorts (DE)
    1 submarine chaser (PC)
    2 patrol craft (YP)
    4 torpedo boats (PT)
    3 coastal transports (APC)
    6 landing ships (LSM, LCU)
    2 landing craft (LCU)
    15 auxiliaries (oilers, tugs, survey ships)
    4 P-2 ASW patrol aircraft
    4 PBY ASW patrol aircraft
    3 HU-16 ASW patrol aircraft
    2 C-47 transports
    12 trainer aircraft
    4 Bell 206A Jet Ranger ASW/SAR helicopters

Equipment on Order:
    2 Leander-class frigates, to be fitted with Seacat SAMs

AIR FORCE

Personnel: 10,000

Organization:
    2 fighter-bomber squadrons (Hunter F-80/T-33)
    1 bomber squadron (B-26)
    1 transport squadron (C-118, C-54, C-47, Beech 99, Beaver, Otter, Twin Otter)
    1 training squadron (T-33, T-34, T-37, Vampire)
    1 utility/liaison squadron (T-6)

Major Aircraft Types:
    58 combat aircraft
        18 F-80/T-33 fighter-bombers
        25 Hunter fighter-bombers
        15 B-26 light bombers
    186+ other aircraft
        91 transports (C-118, C-54, C-47, Beech 99,

Beaver, Otter, Twin Otter)
20 liaison aircraft (T-6)
45 trainer aircraft (T-34, T-37, T-33, Vampire)
30+ helicopters (Bell 47 and UH-1, Sikorsky UH-19, Hiller UH-12)

Air Bases: Los Cerrillos, Puerto Moutt, Cerro Moreno, Antofagasta

PARAMILITARY

The national military police, *Carabineros*, number about 22,500. This force is elite, competent, and respected. Its equipment and training include the latest available for control of urban disorders. It has been heavily engaged in civic action such as medical services, social services, and literacy programs.

COLOMBIA
Republica de Colombia
Republic of Colombia

POWER POTENTIAL STATISTICS

Area: 439,734 square miles
Population: 23,600,000
Total Active Armed Forces: 98,200 (including National Police; 0.41% population)
Gross National Product: $7.6 billion ($322 per capita)
Annual Military Expenditures: $97 million (1.27% GNP)
Steel Production: 248,000 metric tons
Fuel Production: Coal: 3.0 million metric tons
  Oil: 10.16 million metric tons
  Refined Products: 8.41 million metric tons
  Gas: 1.47 billion cubic meters
Electric Power Output: 8.75 billion kwh
Merchant Fleet: 50 ships; 208,837 gross tons
Civil Air Fleet: 17 jet, 7 turboprop and 34 piston

DEFENSE STRUCTURE

The President is commander in chief of the armed forces. The Minister of War, who is the senior general officer of the Army, has supervision over the three services and the National Police. A Superior Council of National Defense — comprising the Ministers of Government, Foreign Relations, and Finance, and the Commanding General of the Armed Forces — acts in an advisory capacity. General Secretary of the Council is the Chief of Staff of the Armed Forces. A second advisory body is the high Military Council, whose membership includes all general officers normally stationed at or near Bogota, i.e., the Commanding General and Chief of Staff of the Armed Forces, the three service commanders, commander of the Military Institutes Brigade, and directors of the War College and the Military Institute divisions. Each service has full command responsibility in its own element, under its Commanding General. Civic action receives command and staff attention.

POLITICO-MILITARY POLICY

Internally, the history of Colombia has often been characterized by bloody strife. Exchanges of government since 1957 have been peaceful, but inflation and the prevalence of poverty have resulted in widespread discontent, manifested in riots, and in guerrilla activity. The three main guerrilla groups, National Liberation Army (ELN), which is pro-Cuba, Colombian Revolutionary Armed Forces, which is pro-Soviet, and People's Liberation Army (EPL), which is pro-China, singly and occasionally in coordinated efforts, have been so active that in January 1973 the government adopted security measures designed to control them.

Externally, boundary disputes with its neighbors, Panama, Peru, Ecuador, and Venezuela, have resulted in bad feeling but not in open warfare. Following the breaking away of Panama in 1903, and the prompt recognition of its sovereignty by the US Government (eager to proceed with construction of the Panama Canal), relations between Colombia and the United States were strained for many years. Increasing economic ties, since the ratification of a treaty between the two nations in 1921, have produced a generally amicable relationship.

The armed forces of Colombia are among the most modern in Latin America. All males are obligated for military service between the ages of 18 and 45. At least one year of active duty is served between 18 and 30. For the last 15 years men are in a reserve status.

Colombia is the only Latin American country that participated actively in the Korean War. A battalion of 1,000 men served in the United Nations forces, and two Colombian patrol escorts operated in the area.

STRATEGIC PROBLEMS

Colombia's position, straddling the isthmus of Panama, with coastlines on both the Pacific Ocean and the Caribbean Sea, is a strategic one with respect to the approaches to the vital Panama Canal. In September 1972 the United States agreed to abandon to Colombia claims to sovereignty over the islet of Quitasueno and the lighthouse it had maintained there and to the keys of Roncador and Serrana in the San Andres-Providencial archipelago, retaining fishing rights. Nicaragua promptly announced its claim to the territory. A dispute with Venezuela over the undersea platform extending north from Guajira Peninsula remains unsettled.

54 ALMANAC OF WORLD MILITARY POWER

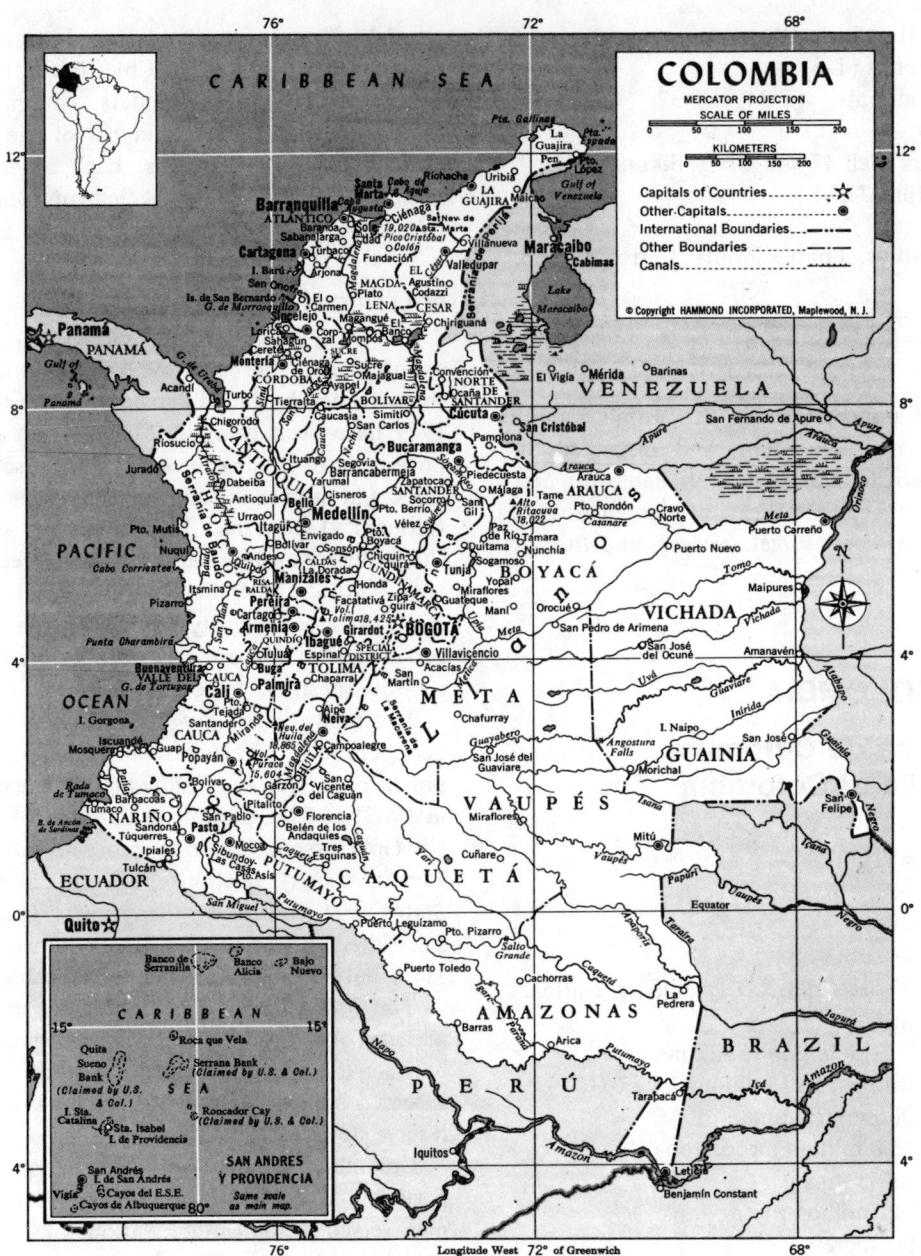

MILITARY ASSISTANCE

From the time of Colombia's independence, foreign advisers from a number of European countries have assisted in the organization and training of the armed forces. Since 1939 US missions have been active, and Colombian officers have received training at US service schools. A Mutual Assistance Treaty with the United States was signed in 1952.

In the period 1962-1972 Colombia received $99.97 million worth of military equipment from the United States. A total of 5,124 students were trained under the MAP.

ALLIANCES

In August 1958 Colombia, Venezuela, and Ecuador joined in a Declaration of Bogota, expressing the intention to maintain harmony in their external relations and aim to develop a common market. This was followed by Colombian participation in the Latin American Free Trade Area on September 29, 1961, and signature of the Charter of Bogota with Chile, Ecuador, Peru, and Venezuela on August 10, 1966, as a step toward advancing the trade agreement.

Colombia is a member of the OAS and the UN and their subsidiary organizations.

ARMY

Personnel: 50,000

Organization: 8 infantry brigades, with light armor, motorized artillery and engineer detachments

Major Equipment Inventory:
light tanks (M-3)
APCs (M-8)
light artillery pieces (105 mm)

Reserves: About 250,000 men but with no mobilization organization

NAVY

Personnel: 7,200 naval (including 1,000 Marines)

Major Units:
  2 submarines (SS)
  4 destroyers (DD)
  1 destroyer escort (DE)
  4 destroyer escort/high speed transports (DE/APD)
  8 patrol gunboats (PGM)
  5 river gunboats (PGR)
12 patrol boats (YP)
  5 river patrol boats (PBR)
  4 transports
26 auxiliaries (oilers, tugs, survey ships)

Naval Bases: Barranquilla, Balanquero, Cartagena, Santa Marta

AIR FORCE

Personnel: 6,000

Organization:
1 fighter-bomber squadron (Mirage 5)
1 bomber squadron (B-26)
1 reconnaissance and rescue squadron (PBY)
1 transport squadron (C-130, C-47, C-54, HS-748, F-28)

Major Aircraft Types:
  17 combat aircraft
      6 Mirage 5 fighter-bombers
      8 B-26 light bombers
      8 PBY maritime patrol aircraft
140 other aircraft
     50 transports (C-130, Fokker F-28, C-54, C-47, C-45, Beaver, Otter, HS-748)
     45 trainers (T-34, T-37, T-41, T-6, T-33)
     45 helicopters (Bell 47, UH-23, UH-1, HH-43, OH-6A)
      8 B-26 light bombers
      8 PBY-5A patrol aircraft

Air Bases: Barranquilla, Cali, Buenaventura, Bogota, Medellin, Cucuta, Cartagena, Leticia, Santa Marta, Bucaramanga, Paranquero

PARAMILITARY

The National Police Force of about 35,000 men is headed by a Commandant, who is responsible to the Commanding General of the Armed Forces. The Police Force is organized in divisions, one for each department of the country. It operates 36 helicopters.

ECUADOR

Republica del Ecuador
Republic of Ecuador

POWER POTENTIAL STATISTICS

Area: 109,438 square miles (including Galapagos Islands)
Population: 6,600,000
Total Active Armed Forces: 26,600 (including National Police; 0.4% population)
Gross National Product: $1.87 billion ($283 per capita)
Annual Military Expenditures: $38.95 million (2.08% GNP)
Fuel Production: Crude Oil: 3.77 million metric tons
   Refined Products: 1.33 million metric tons
Electric Power Output: 949 million kwh
Merchant Fleet: 18 ships, 45,441 gross tons
Civil Air Fleet: 4 turboprop, 24 piston transports

DEFENSE STRUCTURE

Since the coup in February 1972 the government of Ecuador has been a military dictatorship under General Guillermo Rodriguez Lara. As President he is commander in chief of the armed forces, responsible for internal order and external security. He is advised by the National Security Council and the General Staff of the Armed Forces. The Minister of National Defense is responsible for matters affecting external security, with the assistance of the Chief of the Armed Forces General Staff. The Minister of Government controls the police and is responsible for internal security.

The country is divided into four defense zones with headquarters in Quito, Guayaquil, Cuenca, and Pastaza.

56 ALMANAC OF WORLD MILITARY POWER

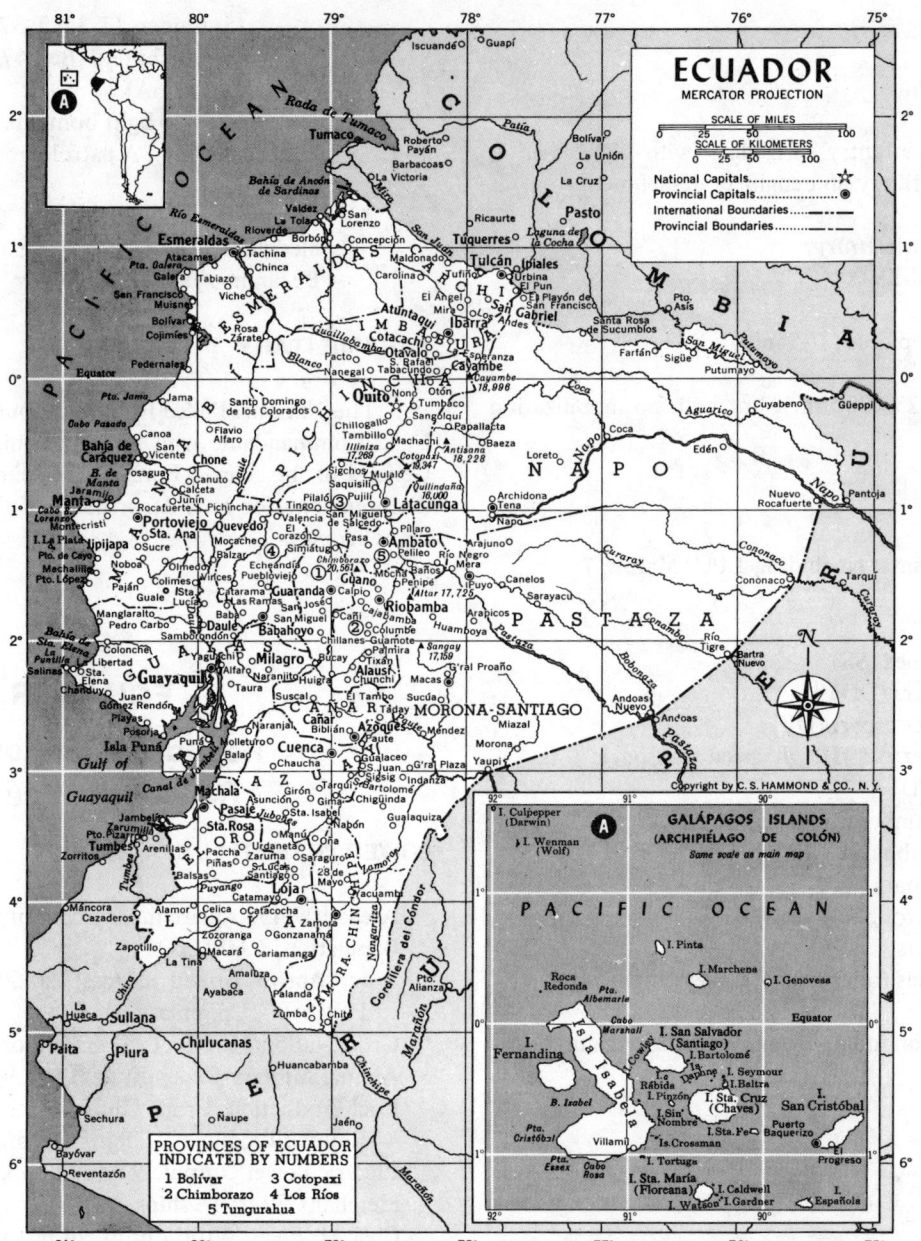

POLITICO-MILITARY POLICY

The Army has been involved in politics almost continuously throughout Ecuador's history. Traditionally the Army has considered itself the guardian of democratic institutions, although it has overthrown numerous elected heads of state.

A border dispute of many years' standing with Peru flared into open conflict in July 1941. Under pressure from the United States, Argentina, and Brazil, a ceasefire was imposed, and in January of 1942 an arbitration agreement (generally known as the Rio Protocol) gave Peru most of the disputed territory. Ecuadorians, however, have continued to hope for access to the Maranon River, which is a major tributary of the Amazon; they continue to regard Peru as an aggressor who stole half of their national territory.

Ecuador claims jurisdiction over the Pacific Ocean 200 miles from its coast, and defense of this area is a prime function of the military forces. Since 1968, naval patrol boats have seized many American fishing vessels within this 200-mile limit and imposed fines on them.

Military training for one year is compulsory for all men when they reach the age of 20. However, because of lack of vacancies, actual conscription is determined by lottery.

There are extensive military civic action programs. The military maintains a secondary school and has special literacy classes for conscripts. A military institute trains officers in the skills and disciplines of civilian administration.

STRATEGIC PROBLEMS

The Communist Party is weak and divided among pro-Moscow, pro-Peking, and pro-Cuban elements. All of these groups have influence in labor and student circles. The Indians, who make up over half of the population, have shown little susceptibility to subversion.

MILITARY ASSISTANCE

Since Ecuador signed the Treaty of Rio (Inter-American Treaty of Reciprocal Assistance) of 1947, its armed forces have been reorganized and reequipped with US aid, a total of $42.4 million since 1950. Excess stocks amounting to $3.5 million were provided by the United States in 1950-1971. A total of 4,400 students were trained under the MAP. In 1971, the US suspended military sales and assistance because of seizures of fishing vessels, and Ecuador expelled the US military aid staff. Israel gives assistance in the civic action program.

ALLIANCES

Ecuador is a member of the UN and the OAS.

ARMY

Personnel: 12,800

Organization:
- 11 infantry battalions
- 1 parachute battalion
- 3 artillery groups
- 3 mechanized reconnaissance squadrons
- 2 engineer battalions
- 2 antiaircraft battalions
- 3 signal companies
- independent infantry companies

Major Equipment Inventory:
- 80 M-3 light tanks
- 50 light artillery pieces
- light AAA pieces
- 8 T-41A light aircraft

NAVY

Personnel: 4,500

Major Units:
- 1 frigate (PF)
- 3 destroyer escorts (DE)
- 2 coastal escorts (PCE)
- 3 fast patrol torpedo boats (PT)
- 6 patrol boats (YP)
- 2 patrol gunboats (PGM)
- 1 cargo ship (AKL)
- 2 landing ships (LSM)
- 5 auxiliaries (oilers, survey ships, tugs)
- 2 patrol aircraft (PBY)

Naval Bases: Guayaquil, Salinas, San Lorenzo, Galapagos

AIR FORCE

Personnel: 3,500

Organization:
- 1 fighter/fighter-bomber squadron (F-80)
- 1 fighter-reconnaissance squadron (Meteor)
- 1 light bomber squadron (Canberra)
- 1 transport squadron (C-47, DC-6, HS-748)

Major Aircraft Types:
- 26 combat aircraft
  - 12 fighter/fighter-bomber (F-80)
  - 8 fighter-reconnaissance (Meteor)
  - 6 light bombers (Canberra)
- 68 other aircraft
  - 18 transports (C-47, DC-6, 3 HS-748, 1 Skyvan)
  - 45 trainers (T-28, T-33, T-34, T-41)
  - 3 helicopters (OH-13)
  - 2 liaison aircraft (Cessna 180)

On order: 8 BAC 167 Strikemaster light attack, 6 Alouette III helicopters

Air Bases: Quito, Loja, Latacunga, Manta, Riobamba, Salinas

PARAMILITARY

The National Civil Police, under the Minister of Government, number 5,800. In case of national emergency they can be transferred to the Minister of Defense.

GUYANA

POWER POTENTIAL STATISTICS

Area: 83,000 square miles
Population: 800,000
Total Active Armed Forces: 1,600 (0.20% population)
Gross National Product: $274 million ($342 per capita)
Annual Military Expenditures: $3 million (1.09% GNP)
Electric Power Output: 323 million kwh

58 ALMANAC OF WORLD MILITARY POWER

Bauxite Production: 4.31 million metric tons
Merchant Fleet: 39 ships; 13,647 gross tons
Civil Air Fleet: 6 piston transports, 2 turboprop

POLITICO-MILITARY POLICIES AND POSTURE

Guyana was granted independence by Great Britain in May 1966 as a member of the Commonwealth. The first general elections since independence took place in December 1968. The almost wholly black People's National Congress won a clear majority, and formed the government. The People's Progressive Party, largely East Indian and announced as Marxist-Leninist, and the small United Force made up the opposition. In 1969 the government announced the establishment of a cooperative Republic, remaining within the Commonwealth but having a president as head of state instead of the Queen. This was accomplished in February 1970, and the Prime Minister became also Defense Minister.

Despite improvements made with US aid (Guyana was the largest per capita recipient in the Western Hemisphere 1964-71), Guyana is still a poor country. The interior remains empty while 90 percent of the population lives on the coastal plain. Unemployment is high. This, and the claims of the People's Progressive Party that they will bring the government down by strikes and demonstrations, pose considerable threats to stability.

In January 1973 Guyana entered into a bilateral trade agreement with China, and in April a technical assistance agreement was signed.

Guyana's strategic significance, especially to the United States, is twofold. First, its position relative to the South Atlantic puts it on the best air route between the US and Africa. Second, there are large deposits of bauxite (4.7 million tons mined annually) and manganese (200,000 tons mined annually).

Guyana has been involved in border disputes with Surinam and Venezuela, the former claiming 6,000 square miles of uninhabited land, and the latter claiming three-fifths of Guyanese territory. The long-standing dispute with Venezuela has at least been put in abeyance by the 1970 Protocol of Trinidad whereby the two nations agreed not to press claims to each other's territory for 12 years. Still tension between the two nations remains. An armed clash of 1969 with Surinam was also stilled after a mixed commission agreed that both forces would quit the disputed area. A brief Amerindian revolt fomented by white ranchers was suppressed in 1969. Troops were sent to the Brazilian border in 1972 after guerrilla incidents there.

The Guyana Defence Force has a strength of over 2,000, with a women's corps of 60. It is organized in two infantry battalions and has two U-10 and two BN-2A STOL liaison aircraft and four 45-foot armed patrol launches armed with two 30 cal. machine guns.

PARAGUAY
Republica del Paraguay
Republic of Paraguay

POWER POTENTIAL STATISTICS

Area: 157,047 square miles
Population: 2,640,000
Total Active Armed Forces: 14,400 (0.54% population)
Gross National Product: $740 million ($280 per capita)
Annual Military Expenditures: $19 million (2.56% GNP)
Refined Oil Products: 0.22 million metric tons
Electric Power Output: 220 million kwh
Merchant Fleet: 26 ships, 21,884 gross tons
Civil Air Fleet: 3 turboprop and 2 piston transports

DEFENSE STRUCTURE

The President is commander in chief of the armed forces, with an Army general as Minister of National Defense.

POLITICO-MILITARY POLICY

After more than 20 years of foreign war, civil war, and political instability, in 1954 General Alfredo Stroessner took

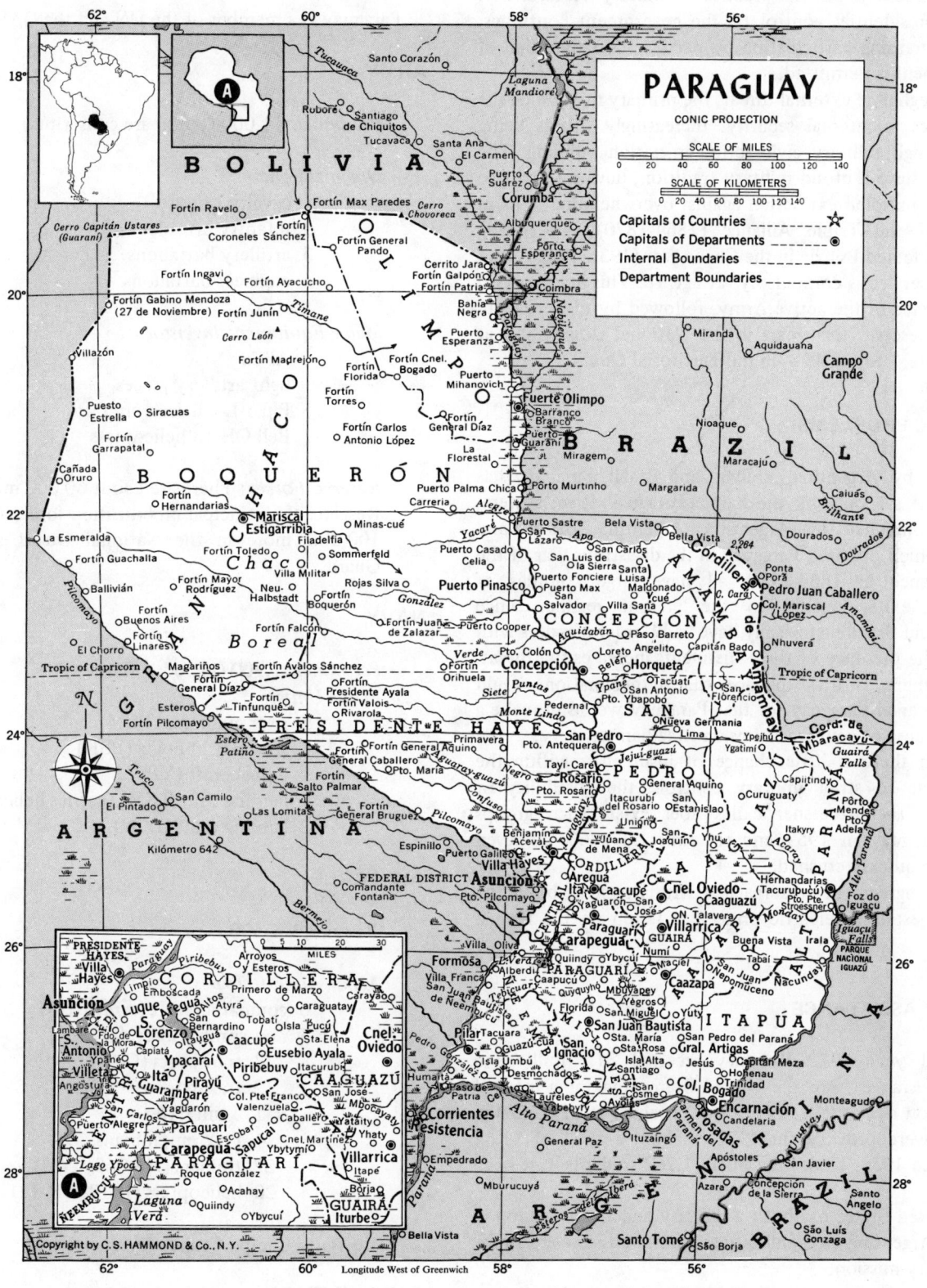

power in Paraguay and has since run the country as a nominal elective democracy but in practice a military dictatorship. Complete presidential control of the government continues, although increasing participation by parties other than that of the government is permitted.

With a negligible external threat, the primary mission of the armed forces is internal security. Increasingly this is being sought through military civic action in nation building. The Paraguayans have a proud military tradition, having fought to the verge of national extinction against overwhelming odds in the War of the Triple Alliance (1864-1870) and having decisively defeated Bolivia in the Chaco War (1932-1935).

Military service is compulsory, at age 18. This involves two years of service in the active Army, followed by nine years in the Army Reserve, ten years in the National Guard, and at least six years — to age 45 — in the Territorial Guard.

STRATEGIC PROBLEMS

Bounded by Argentina, Bolivia, and Brazil, Paraguay has access to the sea only by the Parana-Paraguay River system, which is controlled by Argentina. Argentina, Brazil, and Uruguay, which opposed Paraguay in the disastrous War of the Triple Alliance in 1864-1970, all have large colonies of Paraguayan exiles hostile to the present regime. Since Argentina and Brazil historically have had border disputes with Paraguay, the presence of these dissidents increases the threat. However, there is little chance that either nation would provoke a war in Paraguay, or that Paraguay would provoke a conflict because of counter-claims on Brazilian territory.

Although there is little chance of insurgency within the country, due to strict military controls, the possibility of invasion by anti-Stroessner exiles does exist. Such groups invaded Paraguay in 1959 and six times in 1960; all seven efforts were quickly crushed.

In 1973 agreement was reached with Brazil to build the world's largest hydroelectric project at Itaipu on the Parana River.

MILITARY ASSISTANCE

In fiscal year 1972 Paraguay received $1.1 million in military assistance from the United States, making a total of $10.7 million since 1950. Excess stocks valued at an estimated $810,000 were provided in 1972, making a total of $1.62 million since 1950. Under the MAP, 1,262 students have been trained.

The United States has both a military and an air mission in Paraguay. Argentina has a military and naval mission and Brazil has a military mission.

Paraguay sent a contingent of 200 troops to the Dominican Republic during the crisis of 1965, to serve with the OAS Inter-American Peace Force.

ALLIANCES

Paraguay is a member of the UN and the OAS.

ARMY

Personnel: 11,000 (8,000 are conscripts)

Organization:
    1 cavalry brigade
    3 infantry brigades
    3 artillery battalions
    6 engineer battalions

Major Equipment Inventory:
    APCs
    light artillery pieces
    6 Piper L-4 liaison aircraft
    2 Bell OH-13 helicopters

Reserve Forces: There are about 60,000 men in the Army Reserve, the principal mobilization force. There are about 100,000 more in the National Guard and Territorial Guard.

NAVY

Personnel: 1,900 (includes Marines)
Major Units:
    5 river gunboats (PGM)
    8 river patrol boats (PBR)
    2 patrol craft (YP)
    1 landing ship (LSM) (carries helicopters)
    2 landing craft (LCU)

AIR FORCE

Personnel: 1,500

Major Aircraft Types:
    6 combat aircraft (armed T-6)
    5 non-combat aircraft
        7 transports (C-47)
        2 transports (C-54)
        1 Twin Otter
        4 PBY amphibians
        22 trainers (MS-760, T-23)
        20 helicopters (H-13, UH-12)

Air Base: Campo Grande (Asuncion)

PARAMILITARY

Civil Police forces in Paraguay number 8,500 with a

responsibility for internal security as well as normal police functions.

PERU

Republica del Peru
Republic of Peru

POWER POTENTIAL STATISTICS

Area: 496,222 square miles
Population: 14,864,000
Total Active Armed Forces: 70,500 (including constabularies; 0.47% population)
Gross National Product: $7.3 billion ($491 per capita)
Annual Military Expenditures: $240 million (3.28% GNP)
Iron and Steel Production: 6.5 million metric tons
Fuel Production: Coal: 162,000 metric tons
  Crude Oil: 3.14 million metric tons
  Refined Products: 4.58 million metric tons
Electric Power Output: 5.32 billion kwh
Merchant Fleet: 582 ships; 356,783 gross tons
Civil Air Fleet: 2 jet and 17 piston transports

DEFENSE STRUCTURE

The President is the commander in chief of the armed forces, which are administered by independent Ministries of War, Air, and Navy. Control of the government is in the hands of a military junta, since the October 1968 coup d'etat.

POLITICO-MILITARY POLICY

The Revolutionary Government of the Armed Forces which seized power in 1968 has firm control of Peruvian society as well as the government, in which all cabinet posts are held by military men. In an attempt to gain support from the people and further its reform measures, the government has established the National System to Support Social Mobilization (SINAMOS), with a general as its head. A major economic measure, also designed to solidify public opinion behind the military, was the nationalization of the International Petroleum Company (IPC), a subsidiary of Standard Oil of New Jersey, in late 1968. Peru claims that the company owes more than $600 million in back taxes, and will not compensate the company for the expropriation. This has provoked a crisis with the United States government, which is bound by the Hickenlooper Amendment to take action against any government which does not provide necessary compensation for nationalized industries. IPC's appeal on the Peruvian seizure ruling was denied in September 1969, but the Hickenlooper Amendment was not applied, as Peru offered compensation of $71 million, though this was placed in escrow against the payment of the alleged debt.

As evidenced by a recent purchase of supersonic jets from France, Peru seems to be endeavoring to maintain the most modern air forces in Pacific South America. The armed forces are also contributing to the nation-building effort through a number of military civic action programs.

Two years' active military service is obligatory, although only a small number of men between 20 and 25 are actually drafted. Following active duty, five years are required in the Reserve, and 20 more in the National Guard.

STRATEGIC PROBLEMS

Peruvian history is replete with boundary disputes, losses, and gains. One long-standing dispute with Ecuador still persists, although the disputed region is firmly under Peruvian control. Peru remains unreconciled to the loss of territory to Chile following the war of the Pacific.

Peru's claim to sovereignty over waters 200 miles from the coastline has created friction with US tuna fishermen. Several incidents since 1969 in which Peru has seized 18 US tuna boats in these waters have exacerbated already strained relations with the United States, which suspended military sales to Peru briefly in 1969.

Socio-economic problems have created great discontent among Peruvian citizens, and were a major cause of the military take-over. Although the economic growth rate of the country continues to climb, so does the population. While development of petroleum and mineral resources has improved Peru's economy, a change in the pattern of ocean currents off the coast in 1972 resulted in the temporary disappearance of the anchovies that were one of the principal export resources of Peru. Loss of the fish meal in world markets had serious economic results in the nations which imported it, of which the United States, China, Cuba and West Germany were the largest buyers. The anchovies reappeared in 1974, again causing economic problems in areas which had developed substitute products.

Guerrilla activity in the eastern mountain-jungle areas of Peru has been troublesome but is currently under control. This is in part due to loss of leadership following the death of Che Guevara, with whom Peruvian Communists and guerrillas were cooperating.

MILITARY ASSISTANCE

In 1972 Peru received $1.2 million in US military aid, making a total of $88.6 million since 1950. Estimated deliveries of excess US stocks in 1971 were valued at $346,000, making a total of $6.8 million since 1950. Under the MAP 5,785 students have been trained. By expropriation

62 ALMANAC OF WORLD MILITARY POWER

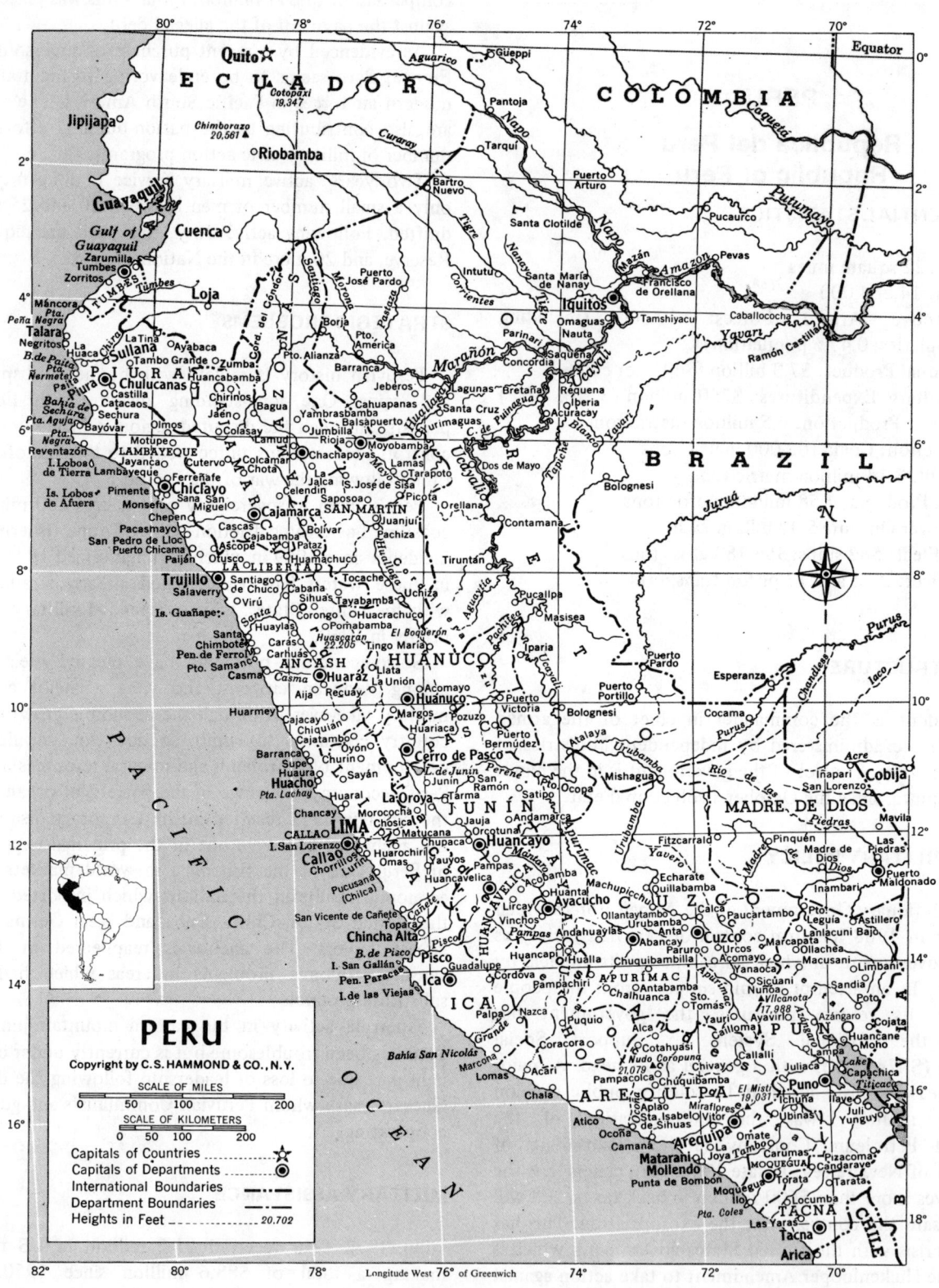

of American oil company assets, however, Peru is jeopardizing continuation of this assistance.

ALLIANCES

Peru is a member of the UN and the OAS.

ARMY

Personnel: 35,500

Organization:
- 4 infantry brigades
- 1 armored brigade
- 1 jungle unit (paratroops, commando, and mountain brigades)
- cavalry, artillery and engineer battalions

Major Equipment Inventory:
- 60 medium tanks (M-4 Sherman)
- 100 light tanks (AMX-13)
- 50 armored cars (M-3)
- 105mm and 155mm artillery pieces
- 4 U-10 STOL aircraft

NAVY

Personnel: 8,000

Major Units:
- 4 diesel submarines (SS)
- 2 light cruisers (CL)
- 4 destroyers (DD)
- 3 destroyer escorts (DE)
- 2 escort frigates (PCE)
- 2 coastal minesweepers (MSC)
- 4 landing ships (2 LST, 2 LSM)
- 2 motor gunboats (PGM)
- 6 fast patrol craft (PTF)
- 3 patrol launches (YP)
- 6 river gunboats
- 10 auxiliaries (oilers, transports, etc.)
- 8 Bell 47G/OH-13 helicopters
- 2 Beech Queen Air utility transports
- 24 PV-2 Harpoon patrol bombers (operated by Air Force)

Missiles:
- 30 short Seacat SAMs

Naval Bases: Callao, La Punta, Iquitos, San Lorenzo

AIR FORCE

Personnel: 9,000

Organization:
- Three groups made up of 2 to 3 squadrons each of fighter-bombers and light bombers (Mirage, Hunter, F-86, T-33, Canberra, B-26)
- 1 maritime reconnaissance squadron (PV-2)
- 1 transport squadron (C-130, Buffalo, F-28)
- 1 ASW squadron (HU-16, PBY)
- 1 helicopter squadron (Alouette II/III, UH-1)

Major Aircraft Types:
- 99 combat aircraft
  - 22 Canberra light bombers
  - 8 B-26 light bombers
  - 30 T-33 fighter-bombers
  - 16 Hunter fighter-bombers
  - 9 ASW patrol aircraft (HU-16, PBY)
- 196 other aircraft
  - 23 helicopters (Alouette II/III, UH-1, H-23)
  - 73 transport/utility (C-130, Buffalo, C-46, C-118, C-47, Beaver, Twin Otter, Queen Air)
  - 100 trainers (T-33, T-37, T-41, T-42, PC-6, Mirage)

On Order: 25 IA-28 Pucara attack (COIN)

Air Bases: Lima, Trujillo, Talara, Chiclayo, Pisco, Ancon, Arequipa, Cusco

PARAMILITARY

There are about 18,000 men in the Guardia Civil and the Guardia Republicana, which are under the direction of the Ministry of Interior and Police.

URUGUAY

Republica Oriental del Uruguay
Eastern Republic of Uruguay

POWER POTENTIAL STATISTICS

Area: 72,172 square miles
Population: 3,010,000
Total Active Armed Forces: 21,340 (including internal security police; 0.70% population)

64 ALMANAC OF WORLD MILITARY POWER

Gross National Product: $2.45 billion ($814 per capita)
Annual Military Expenditures: $61.0 million (2.49% GNP)
Refined Oil Products: 1.65 million metric tons
Electric Power Output: 2.13 billion kwh
Merchant Fleet: 42 ships; 162,774 gross tons
Civil Air Fleet: 1 jet, 4 turboprop and 4 piston transports

DEFENSE STRUCTURE

Following a week-long rebellion by the armed services in February 1973 agreement was reached with the elected President, Juan M. Bordaberry, which established military control of the government within the Constitution. The heads of the three services form the National Security Council, which advises the President, who remains nominally chief of state and commander of the armed forces. The Minister of Defense in the President's Cabinet is a civilian.

POLITICO-MILITARY POLICY

Uruguay strongly advocates nonintervention in the affairs of other nations, and in 1965 voted in the OAS against intervention in the Dominican Republic. However, the Secretary General of the OAS at the time was a Uruguayan who personally went to the Dominican Republic to mediate the internal dispute and the intervention.

Severe economic distress and runaway inflation have reduced the standard of living and created a general atmosphere of discontent. Strikes, rioting, and kidnappings plagued Uruguay and caused government crises from 1968 to 1972. A urban guerrilla group called the Tupamaros was responsible for most of the violence.

President Jorge Pacheco declared a state of siege in 1971 but was unable to control the Tupamaros or gain congressional support. As terrorism became more widespread the army was called in, and a state of internal war was declared by Bordaberry in April 1972, suspending some individual rights and giving the army powers of search and arrest. The campaign was successful in uncovering most of the Tupamaro organization and delivering about 3,000 members of the movement into custody.

Success in this area led the military to move against corruption in business and politics and finally resulted in early 1973 in the confrontation with Bordaberry, and creation of the National Security Council. In June the Congress was dissolved. An appointed Council of State of prominent leaders replaces it for some functions, but the real power lies in the military members of the National Security Council.

The communist-manipulated and politically active National Convention of Workers, the principal labor organization, was outlawed in 1973, temporarily eliminating an important instrument for communist penetration. A new labor law in August 1973 authorized other unions and federations, prohibited political activity by unions, and required union officers to be elected by secret ballot.

STRATEGIC PROBLEMS

With the suppression of the Tupamaros and subsequent outlawing of the Communist Party in Uruguay, threats to internal security from dissident groups under a military-controlled government seem minimal.

A dispute with Argentina over the limits of territorial claims in the broad waters of the River Plate which flared into near-confrontation in 1973 was settled with agreement on a treaty late in the year.

MILITARY ASSISTANCE

The United States keeps a small Military Assistance Advisory Group in Uruguay and provided $1.1 million worth of military assistance in 1972, making a total of $43.4 million since 1950. Further, an estimated $493,000 in excess US military stocks was provided in 1972, making a total of $4.1 million since 1950. Under the MAP 2,044 students have been trained.

ALLIANCES

Uruguay is a member of the UN and of the OAS.

ARMY

Personnel: 16,000

Organization:
- 4 infantry regiments
- 2 armored regiments
- 9 cavalry squadrons
- 4 artillery groups
- 6 engineer battalions

Major Equipment Inventory:
- light tanks (M-24 and M-3)
- light artillery pieces (105mm)
- 11 APCs (M-113)

Reserves: 100,000 are available to expand all army units to the next larger unit upon mobilization. These are men who have completed voluntary service, and citizens who have received part-time training.

NAVY

Personnel: 2,740

Major Units:
- 2 destroyer escorts (DE)
- 2 patrol escorts (PF) (one used as training ship)
- 2 submarine chasers (PC)
- 1 coastal minesweeper (MSC)
- 2 patrol gunboats (PGM)
- 4 auxiliaries (oilers, salvage vessels, etc.)
- 3 S-2 ASW aircraft
- 7 trainers
- 2 L-21A liaison aircraft
- 6 helicopters (Bell 47, OH-23)

Naval Base: Montevideo

Naval Air Bases; Carrasco, Laguna del Sauce, Laguna Negra

AIR FORCE

Personnel: 1,600

Organization:
- 1 fighter-bomber squadron (F-80, T-33)
- 2 transport squadrons (C-47, F-27, F-227, Beaver, U-8)

Major Aircraft Types:
- 16 combat aircraft
  - 10 F-80 fighter-bombers
  - 6 T-33 fighter-bomber/trainers
- 55 other aircraft
  - 26 transports (14 C-47, 5 C-46, 2 F-27, 2 F-227, 3 Beaver and U-8)
  - 25 trainers (T-6, T-33)
  - 4 helicopters (Bell 47, H-23)

Air Bases: Carrasco, Isla de la Libertad, Laguna del Sauce, Punta del Este, Melilla, Laguna Negra

PARAMILITARY

Police forces number 22,000 of whom about 1,000 are specially trained to cope with urban guerrilla warfare.

VENEZUELA
Republica de Venezuela
Republic of Venezuela

POWER POTENTIAL STATISTICS

Area: 352,143 square miles
Population: 11,560,000
Total Active Armed Forces: 32,500 (0.28% population)
Gross National Product: $11.6 billion ($1,003 per capita)
Annual Military Expenditures: $270 million (2.33% GNP)
Fuel Production: Crude Oil: 168.24 million metric tons
  Refined Products: 58.79 million metric tons
  Natural Gas: 9.4 billion cubic meters
Electric Power Output: 12.63 billion kwh
Merchant Fleet: 109 ships; 411,696 gross tons
Civil Air Fleet: 12 jet, 12 turboprop and 8 piston transports

DEFENSE STRUCTURE

The President of the Republic is commander in chief of the National Armed Forces, which consist of four independent services: Army, Navy, Air Force, and National Guard. The President administers the armed forces through the Minister of Defense (who is usually Chief of the Joint Staff). In his defense responsibilities the President is advised by a Supreme Council of National Defense, consisting of the Council of Ministers, the Chief of the Joint Staff, the commanders of the four services, and any other officials or experts whom the President wishes to include.

POLITICO-MILITARY POLICY

Since the overthrow of dictator Marcos Perez Jimenez through joint civilian and military efforts in 1958, the country has been controlled by civilian democratic forces. The presidential election of December 1973, in which the party of the incumbent administration was defeated by the major opposition party, was peaceful and legal. Extremist splinter parties gathered few votes.

Since 1917, when the exploitation of oil began, Venezuela's economy has progressed from an agrarian base to one that is highly industrialized. Venezuela is fifth among the world's oil producers. The large revenue from oil, and the resultant economic prosperity, have been major factors in relative governmental stability. Decreasing oil production and the world oil crisis of late 1973 stimulated the government to raise prices and move toward nationalization.

Recent governments, attempting to ensure stability in the face of guerrilla warfare threats, and to ensure their own power in a nation whose history is replete with military coups, have conscientiously shown their interest in the well-being of the military. Despite these attempts, conservative military elements continue to be suspicious of the liberal-democratic governments.

Under a long-standing border dispute, Venezuela claims 58,000 square miles of Guyanese territory, about three fifths of Guyana. An agreement between representatives of the two countries in 1970 not to press claims for the ensuing 12 years has not yet been approved by the Venezuelan Congress.

A latent dispute with Colombia over oil rights in the Gulf of Venezuela and one with The Netherlands on territorial boundaries between Venezuela and Aruba have not been resolved.

The bulk of the armed forces is made up of two-year conscripts, who are selected through a state lottery system from all able-bodied 18-year-olds. There are no organized reserves.

STRATEGIC PROBLEMS

Venezuela's major strategic problem arises from the avowed aim of Cuba's Castro to foment revolution in Venezuela. Violence and guerrilla activity were widespread in the early 1960s, the principal agency of unrest being the *Fuerzas Armadas de Liberacion Nacional* (Armed Forces of National Liberation). The most serious threats have been two uprisings by pro-Castro naval officers in 1962, and guerrilla efforts to influence the 1968 elections.

In 1963 the government, largely through the influence of the military, and led by the Interior Minister, Carlos Andres Perez (elected president ten years later), took strong action against terrorism and ordered mass arrests of all known Communists and sympathizers. Terrorism continued at a somewhat decreased rate until the pre-election guerrilla activity of mid-1968, when pro-Castro guerrillas were able briefly to take over some towns and villages. This continued after the elections, taking advantage of the confusion of a governmental change-over. Recent terrorism near Caracas reveals that the guerrillas are better trained and armed than ever before.

It is difficult to estimate the current potential of the terrorists. While there was initially some popular support for Castro, this has subsided considerably. The Venezuelan people place great faith in their young democracy. It appears, at least for the present, that despite sporadic violence, there is no great danger from the left.

MILITARY ASSISTANCE

From 1950 to 1972 Venezuela obtained $10.8 million in military assistance and $108,000 through the excess stock program. Under the MAP 4,648 students have been trained. Each US service has a resident mission in Venezuela. In July 1972 Venezuela purchased $60 million in arms from France.

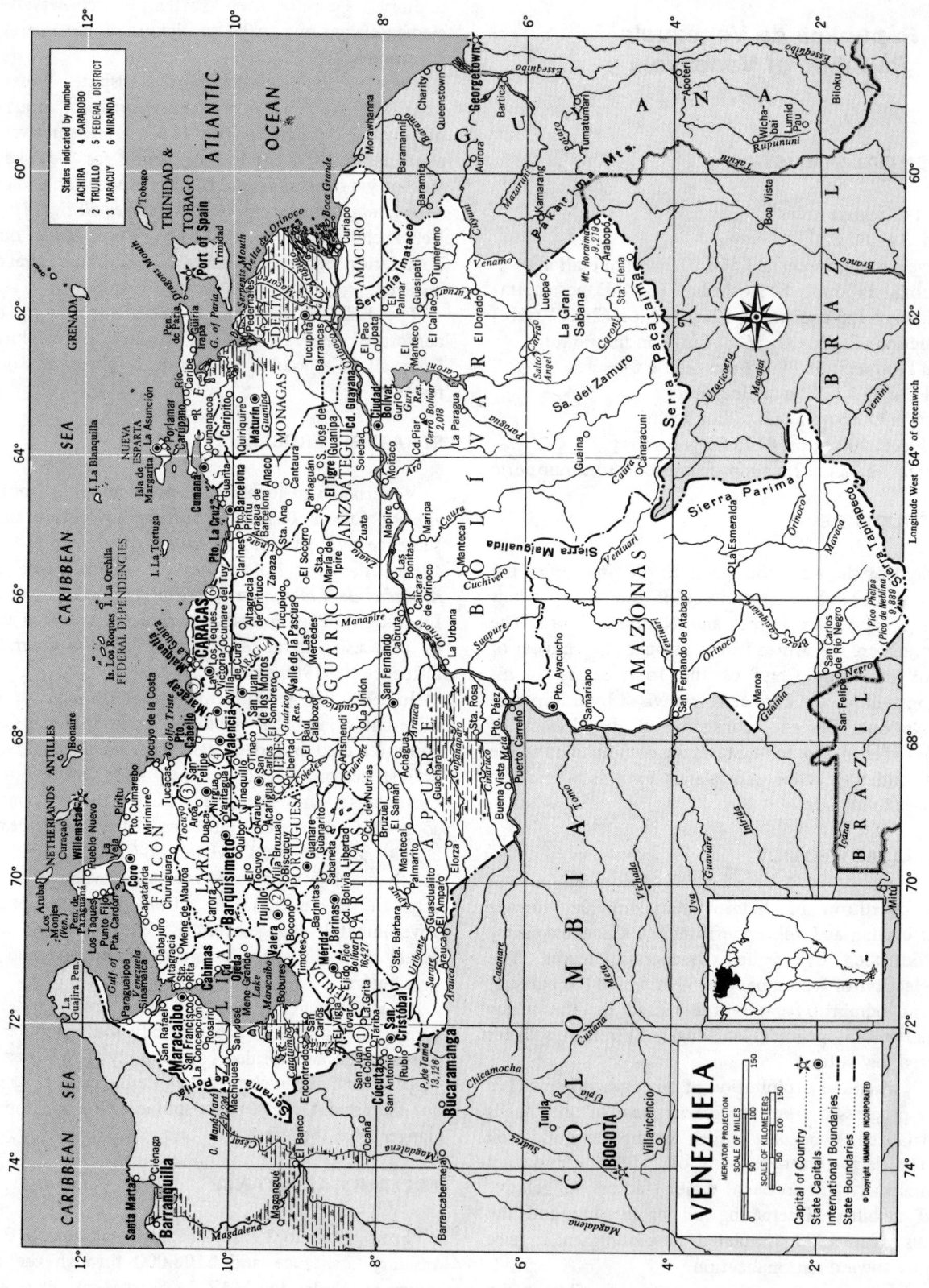

The United States has agreed to provide 100 air-to-air missiles, the first in Latin America.

ALLIANCES

Venezuela is a member of the UN and the OAS.

ARMY

Personnel: 18,000

Organization:
- 1 armored brigade
- 1 cavalry regiment
- 12 infantry battalions
- 2 tank squadrons
- 6 artillery groups
- 5 engineer and antiaircraft battalions supply groups

Major Equipment Inventory:
- 70 medium tanks (AMX-30)
- light tanks (AMX-13)
- tank destroyers (M-18)
- 10 SP artillery 155mm (AMX-155SP)
- light artillery pieces

On order: 72 AMX-30 tanks, 10 AMX-155 SP

NAVY

Personnel: 6,500 (including 2,500 Marines)

Major Units:
- 3 diesel submarines (SS)
- 4 destroyers (DD) (Seacat missiles on 1 destroyer)
- 6 destroyer escorts (DE)
- 10 submarine chasers (PC)
- 5 landing ships (4 LSM and 1 LST)
- 3 coastal transports (APC)
- 6 miscellaneous auxiliaries (netlayers, tugs, salvage vessels)
- 16 coast guard craft (YP)

On order: 6 fast patrol boats (PTF) (3 with SSM, 3 with guns)

AIR FORCE

Personnel: 8,000

Organization: 3 Commands: Combat Command (Combat-Transport), Instruction Command (Training), Logistics Command (Supply)
- 3 fighter/fighter-bomber squadrons (CF-5, F-86K(AW), F-86(FB), Mirage III & 5)*
- 2 bomber squadrons (Canberra, B-25, OV-10)*
- 1 training group (T-34, Queen Air, Jet Provost)
- 1 transport group (C-47, C-123, C-130)
- 1 liaison group (Alouette III, UH-1, UH-19, U-17, Queen Air)

Major Aircraft Types:
- 125 combat aircraft
    - 40 F-86 fighter/fighter-bombers
    - 20 CF-5 fighters
    - 15 Mirage III & 5 fighter/fighter-bombers
    - 25 Canberra bombers
    - 12 B-25 bombers
    - 16 OV-10 counter insurgency (COIN)
- 115 other aircraft
    - 50 trainers (T-2, T-34, Queen Air, Jet Provost)
    - 40 transport/liaison (C-47, C-123, C-130, Queen Air, U-17)
    - 25 helicopters (Alouette III, UH-1, UH-19)

Air Bases: Caracas, Maracay, Maiquetia, La Carlota, Maturin, Maracaibo, Barcelona, Barquisimeto, Palo Negro

PARAMILITARY

The *Fuerzas Armadas de Cooperacion,* popularly known as the National Guard, is composed of about 10,000 men, and is used for internal security, customs, and forestry. The National Guard operates its own military academy, officers' school of application, and staff college. The Guard operates the eleven coast guard vessels which nominally belong to the Navy.

*Mirages are replacing F-86; OV-10 are replacing B-25.

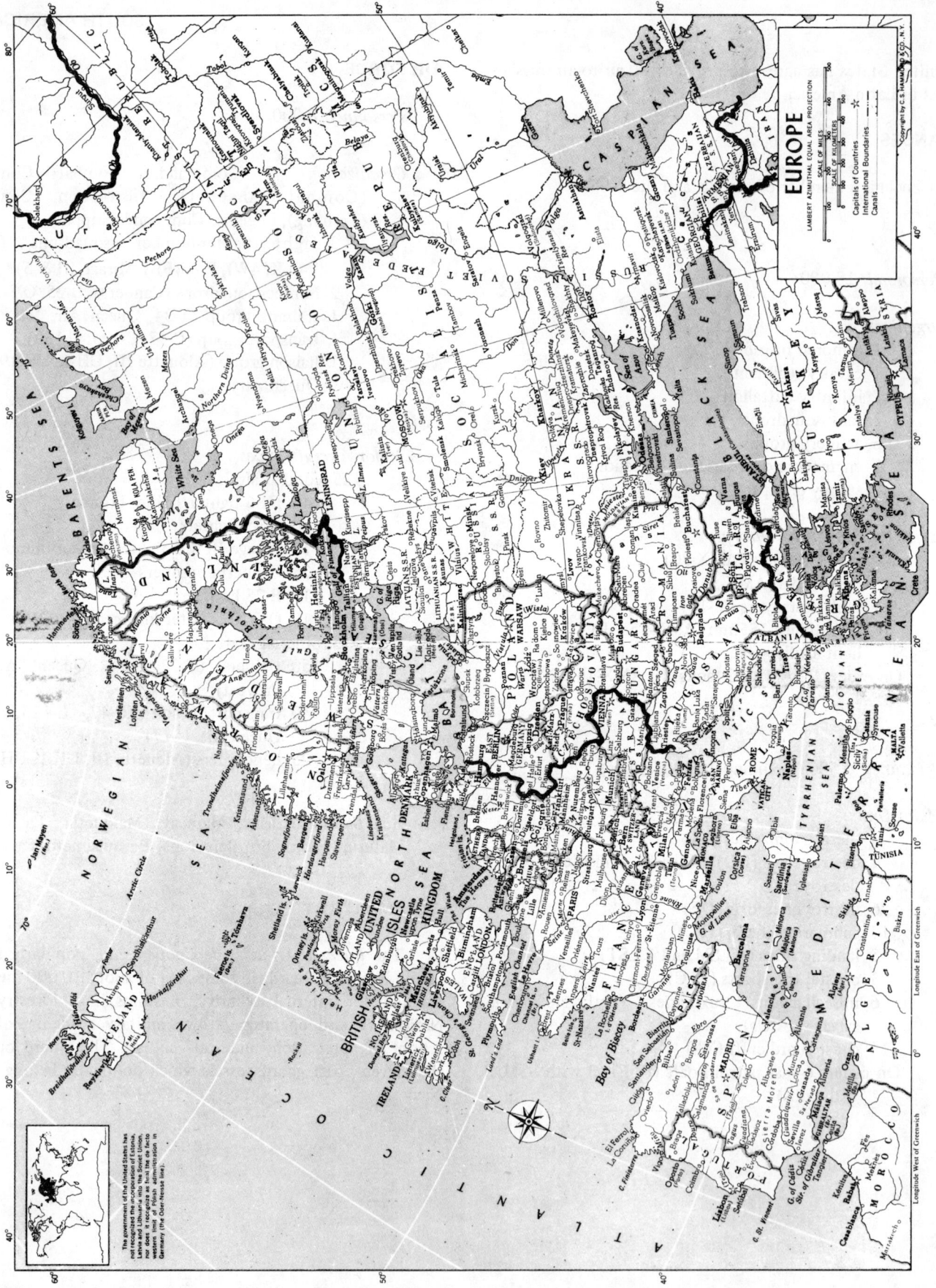

4
WESTERN EUROPE
Regional Survey

MILITARY GEOGRAPHY

Western Europe is a mountainous peninsula from which project a number of other peninsulas, and adjacent to which are a number of large and populous islands. This peninsular-insular geography contributed to the development in early history of a number of isolated, self-contained societies, from which emerged the modern nations of Western Europe. The peninsular-insular geography also stimulated the maritime interest which eventually became a prime factor in Europe's world predominance for more than four centuries.

The tides of war have flowed across Europe generally along the routes most feasible for transport and trade: the rivers, the corridors between mountain ranges, and the coastal lowlands. Principal among these routes have been the Danube basin and the North European Plain.

STRATEGIC SIGNIFICANCE

In addition to the influence of geography, a combination of climatological, demographic, and possibly cultural factors led to the dominant importance of Western Europe in world affairs beginning late in the fifteenth century. This predominance has not entirely disappeared even as the loci of world power have shifted east and west in the mid-twentieth century. Save for the United States and Canada, Western Europe still has the largest collection of highly skilled and educated manpower in the world, has the highest overall standard of living in the world outside North America, has the greatest accumulation of economic and financial power outside the United States, and has the greatest combined military potential aside from the United States and the Soviet Union.

NORTH ATLANTIC TREATY ORGANIZATION

Military rivalries among the nations of Western Europe—most notably between France and Germany—that had for centuries led to recurrent wars, have since World War II dwindled or disappeared in the face of common political and economic problems and the hard destructive and geographical realities of modern war. During the years immediately following that war, Soviet truculence posed a serious threat to the postwar recovery of the nations of Western Europe. American economic assistance through the Marshall Plan helped Western Europe avoid the economic chaos that indigenous and Russian Communists apparently expected would result in internal turmoil and revolution. Full economic recovery in these nations was hampered by fears that Soviet Russia, whose armed strength had increased rather than decreased after the war, would take by invasion what its Communist agents had been unable to subvert from within. Although the United States still possessed a monopoly of nuclear weapons, most Western Europeans feared overt Soviet military aggression that could overrun the militarily impotent nations of Western Europe in less than a week. They recognized the weakness of their own defense efforts, and doubted that America would be able to react in time to prevent a sudden Soviet take-over.

This situation led to negotiations that resulted first in the Brussels Treaty of March 17, 1948, to establish the Western European Union (see below), and that culminated in the establishment of the North Atlantic Treaty Organization (NATO) in a treaty signed April 4, 1949, in Washington, effective August 24, by Belgium, Canada, Denmark, France, Iceland, Italy, Luxembourg, the Netherlands, Norway, Portugal, the United Kingdom, and the United States. Greece and Turkey joined later (February 1952), and Western Germany became a member on May 5, 1955.

The members of NATO agreed to settle disputes by peaceful means, to develop their individual and collective capacity to resist armed aggression, to regard an attack on one as an attack on all, and to take necessary action to repel such an attack under Article 51 of the UN Charter.

The political basis for NATO was somewhat altered in the early 1970s by the development of the spirit of detente between East and West, the growing economic strength of the Western European countries, making them less dependent on the United States, political pressures to cut their defense spending, political pressure in the United States to reduce military forces in Europe, and the tension between the Soviet Union and Communist China, which involved large Soviet forces on the Chinese border. Relations between the United States and other NATO nations were strained by the Arab-Israeli War of 1973, when all but Portugal and the Netherlands refused to assist in rushing aid to Israel. In June 1974 the NATO countries reached agreement on a new Declaration on Atlantic Relations that reaffirmed the original objectives of the Treaty, and restored much of the harmonious facade that had been cracked the previous October.

NATO defense areas are divided into three major commands—Europe, Atlantic, and Channel—with a number of subsidiary commands and a US-Canada Regional Planning Group.

Until 1966 the Supreme Headquarters Allied Powers Europe (SHAPE) was located near Paris, but when France withdrew from the NATO Military Committee, SHAPE moved to a new location at Casteau, Belgium, near Mons. NATO headquarters moved from Paris to Brussels at the same time.

The Allied Command Europe (ACE) defends the territory of all continental European members except France and Portugal, and also that of Turkey, Iceland, Canada, and the United States. The Supreme Allied Commander, Europe (SACEUR), heads this command and also serves as Commander-in-Chief, US Forces Europe (CINCUSFE). At present SACEUR is US General Andrew J. Goodpaster; Deputy SACEUR is British General Sir John Mogg. ACE subsidiary commands are Allied Forces Central Europe (AFCENT), with headquarters at Brunssum, Netherlands; Allied Forces Northern Europe (AFNORTH) with headquarters at Kolsaas, Norway; and Allied Forces Southern Europe, headquarters at Naples. There is also a small air-mobile, air-supported ACE Mobile Force (AMF), combat-ready for deployment to points of strain, especially on the northern and southeastern flanks, on short notice.

AFCENT comprises all land and air forces in the Central Europe Sector (West Germany, Netherlands, Belgium, and Luxembourg; since 1966 France has been excluded), and is commanded by a German general. There are 22 divisions assigned by seven countries (forces of the four continental states plus American, British, and Canadian forces) and about 1,600 tactical aircraft in the command (about 350 of the aircraft are US Air Force fighter-bombers). US and German forces have Sergeant and Pershing SSMs at the corps and army level. There are Hawk and Nike SAM battalions in AFCENT. Within AFCENT are the Northern Army Group (NORTHAG) and the Central Army Group (CENTAG). NORTHAG is composed of all the British, Belgian, and Dutch divisions on the Continent, and four German divisions. These forces are supported by the Second Allied Tactical Air Force, composed of British, Belgian, Dutch, and German air units. CENTAG includes all American ground forces, seven German divisions, and a Canadian battle group and is supported by the Fourth Allied Tactical Air Force (American, German, and Canadian units plus the American Army Air Defense Command).

AFNORTH provides for the defense of Norway, Denmark, Schleswig-Holstein, and the Baltic Approaches and is under the command of a British general. It is composed of most of the Danish and Norwegian land, sea, and tactical air forces, one German division (in Schleswig), two German combat air wings, and the German Baltic Fleet.

AFSOUTH defends Italy, Greece, and Turkey, safeguards communications in the Mediterranean, and is responsible for the Turkish territorial waters of the Black Sea. It is under the command of an American admiral. There have been 14 Turkish divisions, nine Greek divisions, and seven Italian divisions in the command, plus the tactical air forces of these countries. The US Sixth Fleet in the Mediterranean, while under national command in peacetime, is NATO-committed for wartime. Ground defense is divided, under the Southern Command at Naples, and the South Eastern Command at Izmir, Turkey. There is an overall air command at Naples, and a single naval command (NAVSOUTH) under an Italian admiral, also at Naples. For several years, strained relations between Greece and Turkey, mainly over Cyprus, have raised questions about the military effectiveness of these commands. In the serious Cyprus crisis of mid-1974 the Greek government announced its decision to withdraw its forces from NATO. With Greek-Turkish relations near a breaking point future collaboration under NATO seemed doubtful.

The Allied Command Atlantic (ACLANT) extends from the North Pole to the Tropic of Cancer, and from the coastal waters of North America to those of Europe and North Africa. The Supreme Allied Commander, Atlantic (SACLANT), has headquarters at Norfolk, Virginia. Under ACLANT are the Western Atlantic, Eastern Atlantic, and Iberian Atlantic Commands, the Striking Force Atlantic (the nucleus of which is the US Second Fleet), the Submarine Command, and STANAVFORLANT (Standing Naval Force Atlantic—a multinational naval squadron).

The Allied Command Channel (ACCHAN) includes the English Channel and the southern portion of the North Sea. Naval forces are those of Britain, Belgium, and the Netherlands. ACCHAN is commanded by a British admiral with headquarters at Northwood, Middlesex.

NATO air defense is to be supported by the NADGE (NATO Air Defense Ground Environment) system. This is essentially a sophisticated, computerized system for tracking aircraft and correlating target information with locations of interceptor aircraft and missiles, using data supplied by numerous ground radar stations.

OTHER ALLIANCES

Western European Union (WEU). The Brussels Treaty of March 17, 1948, established a 50-year alliance for collaboration in economic, social and cultural matters and for collective self-defense among Belgium, France, Luxembourg, the Netherlands, and the United Kingdom. The obvious principal objective was military: mutual security against feared Soviet-Communist aggression. The defense military aspects of the alliance were merged with NATO when that alliance was created one year later. When France rejected the proposed European Defense Community in 1954, the existence of the WEU provided a useful means of integrating West Germany into the Western Alliance, thus facilitating the end of the Allied occupation of West Germany, its rearmament, and its eventual inclusion within NATO. This was accomplished when

West Germany and Italy adhered to the Brussels Treaty on May 6, 1955. After the breakdown of negotiations for Britain's entry into the Common Market, in 1963, the WEU provided a useful vehicle for continuing meetings between the six members of the Common Market and the UK to take stock of the political and economic situation in Europe. France has recently (1973) urged defense consultation within the WEU, a body in which the United States has no part, and the revitalization of the WEU weapons committee as a privileged forum for European cooperation on arms production. There is, however, an apparent movement within the newly elected (1974) French Government toward a cautious reestablishment of at least some military relations with NATO.

European Communities. Pursuant to the Treaty of Rome of March 25, 1957, the European Economic Community (EEC) was established on January 1, 1958, by Belgium, France, West Germany, Italy, Luxembourg, and the Netherlands (the "Inner Six"). The objective was to move gradually toward integrating and strengthening the economies of the members, and ultimately to move toward political unity.

On July 1, 1967, the EEC, generally known as the Common Market, was merged with two other related organizations with the same membership: the European Coal and Steel Community, established on August 10, 1952, pursuant to the Treaty of Paris of April 18, 1951; and the European Atomic Energy Community (Euratom), which was established on January 1, 1958, pursuant to the Treaty of Rome of March 25, 1957.

In 1960 seven European nations—Austria, Denmark, Norway, Portugal, Sweden, Switzerland and Great Britain—became associated in the European Free Trade Association (EFTA). Finland and Iceland subsequently joined. Two of the members, Great Britain and Denmark, together with Ireland, joined the EEC on January 1, 1973. The seven remaining members joined in signing a treaty at Brussels in July 1972, which effectively merged the two economic groups into a single trading bloc by establishing free trade through a gradual reduction of tariff among the 16 signatories.

A long-standing Warsaw Pact proposal for a European Security Conference was accepted by the NATO and uncommitted nations of Europe in late 1972, following signature of a general treaty to normalize relations between East and West Germany. The first formal meeting of this protracted 35-nation conference was held in Helsinki, in July 1973, and has been meeting intermittently in Geneva since September, 1973. The United States and Canada are participating. A variety of issues concerning relations between Eastern and Western Europe has been discussed, paralleling talks between NATO and the Warsaw Pact on the subject of mutual balanced force reduction (MBFR), which began in Vienna in late January 1973. As of mid-1974 the European Security Conference was reported to be deadlocked on all issues, largely, it appears, because of Soviet refusal to adopt an agreement on human rights proposed by the Western European nations.

While the purposes of these communities are primarily economic, and secondarily political, their military implications are great, as they tend to weld the EEC increasingly into what is in effect the third most powerful economic entity in the world.

RECENT INTRA- AND EXTRA-REGIONAL CONFLICTS

There have been no international armed conflicts in Western Europe since World War II. There have been two instances of internal hostilities, and several of the members have been engaged in conflict or crisis operations outside the region. There have been several crises between Western European nations (individually, or as members of the Western Alliance) and members of the Communist bloc, the most serious being those involving the Western Powers and the USSR in Berlin. In the summer of 1974, Turkish forces landed in Cyprus, following a Greek-engineered coup, in order to prevent a possible union of that strife-torn island and Greece. A list of hostilities, or crises involving military operations, in the last ten years follows:

1964	Intervention in East Africa, at local request (UK)
1964	Intervention in Gabon, at local request (France)
1966	Reinforcement of Zambia (UK)
1967	Intervention in Central African Republic, at local request (France)
1967	Military coup in Greece
1968-date	Intervention in Chad, at local request (France)
1968-date	Defense of overseas territories of Mozambique, Angola, and Portuguese Guinea (Portugal)
1969	UK intervention in Anguilla
1970-date	Violence in Northern Ireland
1974	Military coup in Portugal, followed by moves toward independence and peace in Portuguese overseas territories
1974	Coup in Cyprus, followed by Turkish invasion

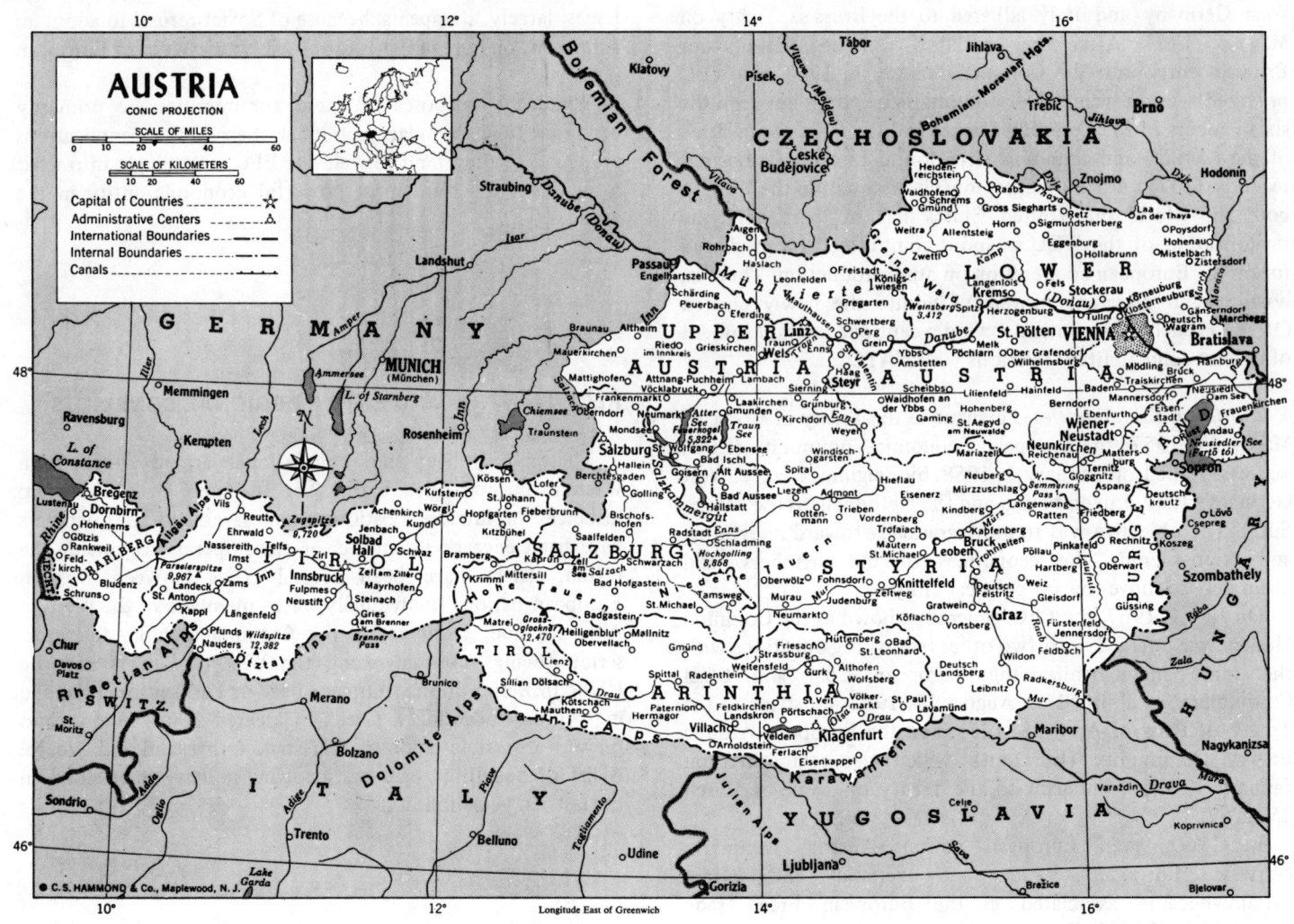

AUSTRIA

Republik Oesterreich
Republic of Austria

POWER POTENTIAL STATISTICS

Area: 32,374 square miles
Population: 7,500,000
Total Active Armed Forces: 52,000 (0.69% population)
Gross National Product: $23.1 billion ($3,080 per capita)
Annual Military Expenditures: $292 million (1.26% GNP)
Iron and Steel Production: 6.8 million metric tons
Fuel Production: Lignite: 3.7 million metric tons
Crude Oil: 2.5 million metric tons
Refined Petroleum Products: 8.4 million metric tons
Natural Gas: 1.9 billion cubic meters
Electric Power Output: 28.8 billion kwh
Civil Air Fleet: 14 jet, 2 piston transports

DEFENSE STRUCTURE

The Federal President nominally controls the armed forces. Supreme administrative and operational authority is actually exercised by the Chancellor through the Ministry of National Defense.

POLITICO-MILITARY POLICY

The Austrian State Treaty, effective July 27, 1955, which ended the post-World War II four-power occupation, specifically provides that in all future time Austria will not join any military alliance and will not permit the establishment of any foreign military base on its territory. Under the treaty Austria is also prohibited from possessing nuclear or other major offensive weapons. Austria declared its permanent neutrality by a law of October 26, 1955.

The armed forces are maintained by conscription. Service is for six months.

STRATEGIC PROBLEMS

Austria has neither the space nor the military force to offer effective resistance against aggression from the north or east; mountainous terrain would probably permit effective defense for a limited time against attack from the south. The Communist Party is weak; internal subversion is unlikely.

MILITARY ASSISTANCE

Between 1955 and 1965 Austria received $100.2 million in US military assistance. Some Air Force training assistance is provided by Sweden.

ALLIANCES

Not permitted by the Austrian State Treaty. Austria is a member of the UN and of EFTA.

ARMY

Personnel: 52,000 (of which 12,000 are regular cadre and 40,000 conscripts; includes Air Defense troops)

Organization:
- 2 corps
    - 3 armored brigades
    - 7 infantry brigades
    - 16 territorial regiments

Major Equipment Inventory:
- 273 medium tanks
    - 120 M-60
    - 153 M-47
- 100 Kuerassier tank destroyers
- 470 Saurer APC
- 108 105mm howitzers
- 38 M-109 self-propelled 155mm gun-howitzers
- 31 155mm SFK M2 howitzers
- 24 155mm howitzers
- 18 130mm Praga V3S rocket launchers
- 301 88mm mortars
- 107 107mm heavy mortars
- 82 120mm heavy mortars
- 44 35mm Oerlikon Super Bat AA guns
- 299 20mm Oerlikon AA guns
- 60 40mm Bofors AA guns

Reserves: Landwehr. An emergency force of full-time guards and reserves, comprising 120 *Grenzschutz* (frontier guards) companies and 140 *Sicherungs* (rear area militia) companies, capable of forming, with the reinforcement of additional reserves, eight *Landwehr* regiments and one independent battalion. There are claimed to be about 500,000 trained reserves available.

AIR FORCE*

Personnel: 3,700 (1,750 regular; 1,950 conscripts)

Organization:
- 3 fighter-bomber squadrons (Saab 105)
- 1 school wing (1 squadron Saab 105, 1 squadron Saab Saphir)
- 1 helicopter wing (6 squadrons, AB-205/206, H-13, Alouette III, Alouette II, S-65).
- 1 transport squadron (L-19, Beaver, Skyvan)
- 1 antiaircraft brigade

Major Aircraft Types:
- 38 combat aircraft (Saab 105 fighter-bombers)
- 113 other aircraft
    - 24 trainers (12 Saab 105, 12 Saab-Saphir)
    - 83 helicopters (23 AB-204, 18 AB-206, 18 H-13, 12 Alouette III, 10 Alouette II, 2 S-65-OE) 24 transports (19 Cessna L-19, 3 Beaver L-20, 2 Skyvan)

Deployment: One 400-man Battalion and one Field Hospital in Cyprus (UNFICYP)

Major Air Bases: Langenlebarn, Hoersching/Linz, Zeltweg, Wiener Neustadt, Algen-Ennstal, and Graz-Thalerhof

PARAMILITARY

Gendarmerie of 12,000.

---

*Austrian Air Units are an integral part of the Army but have been listed separately for comparison.

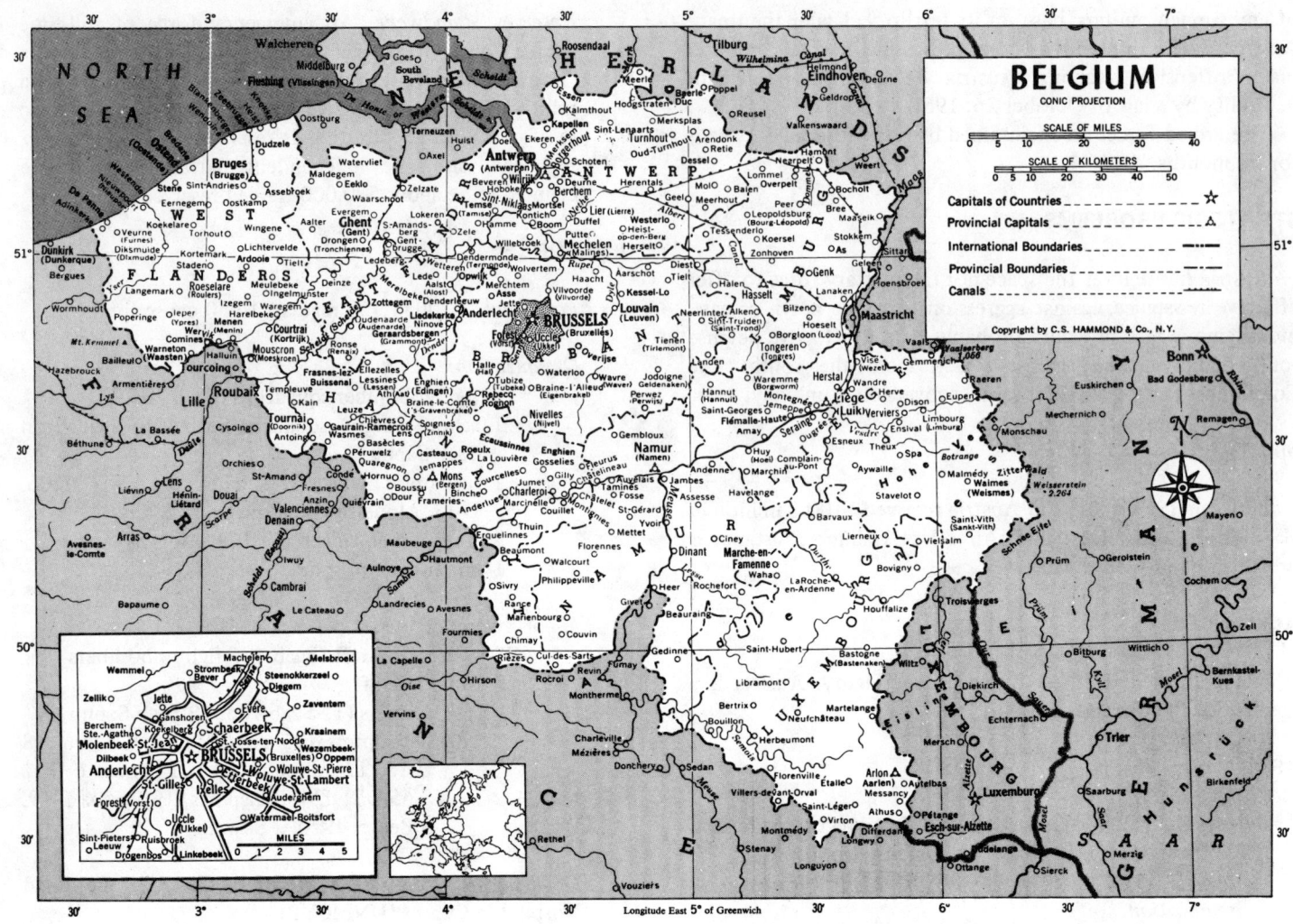

BELGIUM

Royaume de Belgique
Koninkrijk Belgie
Kingdom of Belgium

POWER POTENTIAL STATISTICS

Area: 11,784 square miles
Population: 9,727,000
Total Active Armed Forces: 111,000 (includes Gendarmerie; 1.14% population)
Gross National Product: $35.4 billion ($3,639 per capita)
Annual Military Expenditures: $897 million (2.53% GNP)
Steel Production: 14.53 million metric tons
Fuel Production: Coal: 10.5 million metric tons
  Gas: 2.97 billion cubic meters
  Refined Petroleum Products:* 36.9 million metric tons
Electric Power Output: 35.66 billion kwh
Merchant Fleet: 244 ships; 1.18 million gross tons
Civil Air Fleet: 32 jet, 1 turboprop, 61 piston transports

DEFENSE STRUCTURE

Constitutionally the armed forces are commanded by the King. Overall responsibility for the formulation of defense policy in a parliamentary government is exercised by the Prime Minister and his Cabinet; specific defense decisions are made by the Ministerial Committee of Defense, over which the Prime Minister presides. Implementation of these decisions is the responsibility of the Defense Minister, who is assisted by a military staff system under the direction of the Chief of the General Staff.

*Belgium and Luxembourg.

There are four armed forces—Army, Navy, Air Force and Gendarmerie. There are three elements within the integrated staff echelon of the armed forces: (1) The General Staff, which in turn has two echelons: a conventional, integrated general staff which coordinates the planning of the next echelon of separate Army, Navy, and Air Force general staffs; (2) The Gendarmerie General Staff, responsible for interior order; (3) The Central Administration, to provide administrative support to the operational forces. The operational echelon of the defense establishment includes the principal commands of the four services, the military instruction establishments, and the scientific establishments.

POLITICO-MILITARY POLICY

A traditional policy of neutrality having proved unreliable protection against aggression in two World Wars, since 1945 Belgium has been a leading exponent of collective security. Belgium is a member of the Western European Union established by the Treaty of Brussels in 1948, and was one of the 12 original members of NATO. Belgium's basic defense policy is that of NATO: to prevent war through the deterrent effect of the common efforts of neighbors; if that fails, to defend the common territory by joint military action. The nation's convictions in this regard are demonstrated by the fact that all Belgian armed forces, except those required for internal security, have been fully integrated into NATO forces, and most are deployed in Western Germany under NATO command. Further evidence is the fact that Belgium has provided lodgement for the seat of the NATO Council, and for the principal NATO military headquarters: Allied Command Europe.

Manpower for the armed forces is provided by a combination of long-term enlistment and conscription. Regular enlisted men, with terms of service varying from two to five years, make up about half of the Army, two-thirds of the Navy, and four-fifths of the Air Force. The remainder are conscripts. A new policy announced in 1973 makes it mandatory that Belgian NATO units be all-volunteer. Draftees are to serve six months only, and only on home-guard assignments.

STRATEGIC PROBLEMS

As demonstrated in two World Wars, Belgium is vulnerable to invasion from all directions, with some natural security being provided only by the short seacoast in the northwest and the rugged, forested Ardennes Mountains in the southeast. Some additional defensive capability is provided by lines of the Meuse and Schelde Rivers and many canals, and the potentiality for flooding extensive regions of the western portion of the country. Belgian space is so limited, however, that these natural and man-made obstacles can impose little delay upon the forces of a powerful aggressor. This is adequate reason for Belgium's adherence to the NATO strategic concept.

An internal security problem is created by the ethnic and emotional division of the country between Dutch-speaking Flemings (about 55 percent of the population) and French-speaking Walloons (about 33 percent); (about 11 percent are bilingual). Constitutional reforms in 1971 provided that the ministries be divided equally between the two groups.

The Communist Party is weak and divided, and offers little threat of internal subversion.

MILITARY ASSISTANCE

From 1950 to 1972 Belgium received $1.24 billion in military assistance from the United States. A US Military Assistance and Advisory Group has provided training assistance to the Belgian armed forces in employment of American equipment. Little US military assistance has been received since 1964.

Since 1960 Belgium, at the request of their governments, has provided substantial military assistance to its former colonies: Zaire, Burundi, and Rwanda. While military assistance to Burundi ended in 1973, Belgian military cooperation with Zaire and Rwanda continues, concentrating on military training. This policy is reflected in military assistance expenditures of $7 million for 1974; military missions include 127 Army and six Gendarmerie officers and men for Zaire and 46 Army and six Gendarmerie officers and men for Rwanda; a total of 750 months of military training courses in Belgium for military personnel of Zaire and Rwanda is to be provided; and limited logistical support is to be provided to Rwanda only.

ALLIANCES

Belgium is a member of NATO, of Western European Union, of BENELUX, of the European Common Market, and the UN.

ARMY

Personnel: 71,500

Organization:
- 1 army corps (assigned to the Central European Command of NATO's Allied Command Europe – ACE)
- 4 mechanized or armored brigades, forming 2 divisions (assigned to NATO)
- 1 parachute-commando regiment (one battalion assigned to ACE Mobile Force)
- 2 SSM battalions (Honest John)
- 2 SAM battalions (Hawk)
- 3 helicopter squadrons

1 fixed wing/helicopter mixed squadron
3 infantry battalions for territorial defense (not assigned to NATO)
logistical support units

Major Equipment Inventory:
Leopard and M-47 medium tanks
Scorpion, M-41, AMX-13 light tanks
Striker with Swingfire antitank weapons
M-75, AMX-VTP APCs
105mm, 155mm howitzers
M-109 self-propelled 155mm howitzers
M-44 self-propelled 155mm howitzers
203mm howitzers
M-108 self-propelled 105mm howitzers
On Order:
Scimitar with 30mm Rarden cannon
Samson recovery vehicles
Spartan APC

Reserves: Approximately 120,000 men, organized in two rapidly mobilizable brigades (one mechanized, one motorized), plus independent territorial defense battalions and logistical support units. (About 300,000 additional trained men are available for mobilization.)

NAVY

The Navy is essentially a minesweeping force, earmarked mostly for NATO's Channel Command, partly for coastal minesweeping.

Personnel: 4,500

Major Units:
7 ocean minesweepers/minehunters (MSO)
9 coastal minesweepers/minehunters (MSC)
14 inshore minesweepers (MSI)
2 support and command ships and auxiliaries
6 river patrol boats (PBR)
5 helicopters (S-58 and Alouette III)
10 auxiliaries

Major Naval Base: Ostend

AIR FORCE

All Air Force units except one transport squadron are assigned to NATO Allied Command Europe (ACE).

Personnel: 20,000

Organization:
2 all-weather fighter squadrons (F-104)
5 fighter-bomber squadrons (2 F-104, 3 Mirage 5B)
1 transport wing (1 tactical squadron of C-130, 1 communications squadron of DC-3, DC-6 Pembroke and Falcon 20)
2 SAM wings (8 squadrons; 72 Nike-Hercules; based in West Germany)
1 tactical reconnaissance squadron (Mirage 5 BR)
1 helicopter flight (HSS-1)

Major Aircraft Types:
209 combat aircraft
  90 F-104 fighters
  59 Mirage 5-BA
  24 Mirage 5-BR
  16 Mirage 5-BD
  20 Mirage 5-BR reconnaissance aircraft
200 other aircraft
  12 C-130 transports
   2 Falcon 20 transports
   4 DC-6 transports
   2 C-47 transports
   miscellaneous trainer/support aircraft
  11 HSS-1 helicopters

Air Bases: Beauvechain, Kleine Brohel, Florennes, Brustem, Koksyde, Bierset

PARAMILITARY

National Gendarmerie: 15,000 men with 30 helicopters and light armored cars FN-4 RM62.

CYPRUS

Kypriaki Dimokratia
Kibris Cumhuriyeti
Republic of Cyprus

POWER POTENTIAL STATISTICS

Area: 3,572 square miles
Population: 645,000 (503,100 Greek; 116,100 Turkish)
Total Active Armed Forces: 10,000 man Greek Cypriot National Guard, 5,000 Turkish militia, 2,000-man armed police
UN Peacekeeping Forces (UNFICYP): 4,400
Gross National Product: $699 million ($1,084 per capita)
Annual Military Expenditures: $10.5 million (1.50% GNP)
Electric Power Output: 562 million kwh

Refined Petroleum Products: 620,300 metric tons
Merchant Fleet: 277 ships; 1.5 million gross tons (most use a flag of convenience)
Civil Air Fleet: 2 jet transports

STRATEGIC BACKGROUND

Possession of Cyprus has historically assured to the occupying power control of the Eastern Mediterranean, and in particular of the shores of southern Anatolia and of Syria-Palestine. Typical of the significance of Cyprus as a base for operations on these shores was its seizure by Richard I in 1190 prior to initiating land operations in the Third Crusade. Its value as a base was repeatedly proved by British use in World Wars I and II and in the mounting of the ill-fated Suez expedition of 1956. This value has, if anything, been enhanced by the advent of airpower, and this is one reason Britain retained substantial base areas on the island at the time of granting independence and Commonwealth membership to Cyprus in 1959.

This strategic location undoubtedly has had considerable influence on the obvious concern of the US Government with respect to the disorders in Cyprus, and with respect to Soviet military aid to Cyprus. The establishment of a Soviet foothold on Cyprus would be a serious threat to NATO's position in the Mediterranean as well as to the CENTO defense posture.

There has been endemic unrest and violence in Cyprus for more than 20 years. Formerly a British colony, Cyprus achieved independence in 1960 under a formula which, Britain hoped, would restore tranquility. The predominant Greek majority had long aspired for *enosis* (union with Greece) and in the early 1950s had begun a guerrilla war against the British and the Turkish minority in hopes of achieving this. The Turkish Cypriots opposed *enosis*, and supported continuing British rule, because they feared Greek oppression. Resulting tension between Greece and Turkey nearly split the NATO Alliance.

The Zurich agreement of 1959 — proposed by Britain and accepted by Greece, Turkey, and the Greek and Turkish Cypriots — brought independence to Cyprus in 1960 under terms forbidding *enosis* and safeguarding the security and rights of the Turkish minority. Britain retained two military enclaves at Akrotiri and Dhekelia, with a combined area of 99 square miles. The first President of the new republic was Archbishop Makarios, who had been the principal popular leader in the earlier struggle for *enosis*.

Britain's hopes that the Zurich Agreement would bring peace to Cyprus were soon dashed. Beginning late in 1963, Cyprus was soon engulfed in full-scale civil war, with the opposing Greek and Turkish Cypriot forces receiving none too covert assistance from Greece and Turkey. Establishment of a United Nations force in Cyprus (UNFICYP) in March 1964 resulted only in a temporary and uneasy peace. There were new crises, and new violence, in 1964, 1965, and 1967. After Turkish aircraft intervened in August 1964, President Makarios sought and (in September) received promises of military assistance from the USSR. US pressure on the governments of Cyprus and Greece led to a limitation on this assistance, but considerable Soviet military equipment is believed to have been received. There were continuing crises in 1965 and 1966.

In November 1967, Turkey and Greece again came to the brink of war as violence flared on Cyprus. Mediation by the UN, and primarily by the United States, resolved this crisis in December 1967. Greece and Turkey agreed to withdraw all of their national armed forces on the island (about 10,000 Greek, more than 2,000 Turkish) except for the training contingents of 950 and 650, respectively, provided for in the Zurich Agreement. This withdrawal was completed early in 1968. Internal security remained the responsibility of UNFICYP.

CURRENT MILITARY SITUATION

Discovery that Makarios had secretly purchased arms from Czechoslovakia caused the Greek and Turkish governments to force him to turn them over to the UN in early 1972. Negotiations of the Cypriot factions with constitutional advisers from Greece and Turkey and a UN representative in 1972 seemed to make progress, but the situation was still shaky in July 1974 when a military coup by the Greek-Cypriot National Guard (apparently with the support of Greece)

ousted Makarios. Greek-Turkish relations were already very tense over disputed sovereignty in the eastern Aegean Sea, where oil was discovered earlier in the year. Turkish troops landed on the island and in bitter fighting seized much of the northeast portion of the island. The military junta in Athens backed down and promptly returned the Greek government to civilian control. The foreign ministers of Greece, Turkey, and the United Kingdom met hastily in Geneva, Switzerland, to establish a very precarious ceasefire. The political and military future of Cyprus is extremely uncertain. In late 1974 40,000 Turkish troops remained on the island.

UNFICYP, with a strength fluctuating between 3,500 and 6,000 men, has continued to maintain a force on the island. The national contingents in UNFICYP include small, mostly battalion-sized units, plus supporting elements, from Britain, Canada, Denmark, Sweden, and Finland, under command of an Indian general. Austria provides a 400-man battalion and one field hospital, while Australia provides a small police unit.

Britain maintains in its enclaves on Cyprus a 2,000-man ground force, consisting of two armored reconnaissance squadrons, two infantry battalions and the Headquarters of the Near East Air Force based at Akrotiri, with one squadron of 12 Lightning F3 all-weather fighters, 20 Vulcan medium bombers, one transport squadron of Hercules, and one battalion of Bloodhound surface-to-air missiles. Missions for the bombers include support of CENTO. During the 1974 crisis this force was reinforced to an estimated total of more than 8,000 air and ground personnel.

ALLIANCES

Cyprus is a member of the UN.

GOVERNMENT (GREEK CYPRIOT NATIONAL GUARD) FORCES

Personnel: c. 10,000

Organization: Unknown

Major Equipment Inventory:
- 32 T-34 tanks
- BTR-50P APC
- 40mm Bofors anti-aircraft guns
- artillery pieces (105 and 155mm howitzers, 25-pounder guns)
- 106mm jeep-mounted recoilless rifles
- infantry heavy weapons and small arms
- 6 torpedo boats (P-4) (PT)
- 2 patrol boat gun boats (PGM)
- 2 Agusta-Bell 47G helicopters

TURKISH CYPRIOT FORCES

Personnel: c. 5,000

Organization: Unknown

Major Equipment Inventory:
- 106mm and 75mm recoilless rifles
- infantry heavy weapons and small arms

DENMARK
Kongeriget Danmark
Kingdom of Denmark

POWER POTENTIAL STATISTICS

Area: 16,629 square miles (excluding Faroe Islands and Greenland); Greenland, 840,000 square miles
Population: 5,000,000
Total Active Armed Forces: 30,000 (0.60% population)
Gross National Product: $20 billion ($4,000 per capita)
Annual Military Expenditures: $552.9 million (2.76% GNP)
Fuel Production: Crude Oil: 81,307 metric tons
  Refined Petroleum Products: 10.3 million metric tons
Electric Power Output: 17.2 billion kwh
Merchant Fleet: 1,264 ships; 4 million gross tons
Civil Air Fleet: 35 jet, 16 turboprop, 9 piston transports (exclusive of Danish-owned portion of SAS)

DEFENSE STRUCTURE

The Monarch (Queen Margrethe II) is nominal commander in chief of the armed forces. Civilian control in the conventional parliamentary government of a constitutional democratic monarchy is exercised by the Defense Minister, responsible to the Prime Minister. Full command of the three services rests in the Chief of Defense, the ranking military officer, who, with his Chief of Defense Staff, the Army, Navy, and Air Force Commanders (with appropriate staff), form an integrated Defense Command. The Defense Minister is advised by a Defense Council of the above officers, plus a Chief of Danish Operational Forces.

POLITICO-MILITARY POLICY

For three-quarters of a century prior to World War II Denmark had adhered to a policy of strict neutrality in European power politics. After having been a victim of German aggression in World War II, Denmark espoused the concept of collective security, and was an original member of NATO.

The armed forces consist mainly of conscripted men, serving 12 months, between the ages of 19 and 25; the annual call-up is about 30,000 men. After active service, they may be recalled for refresher training.

STRATEGIC PROBLEMS

Denmark's position astride the entrance to the Baltic Sea makes it one of the most strategically located nations of the world. Its small size and the lack of natural obstacles (save for relatively narrow channels between the islands) make it

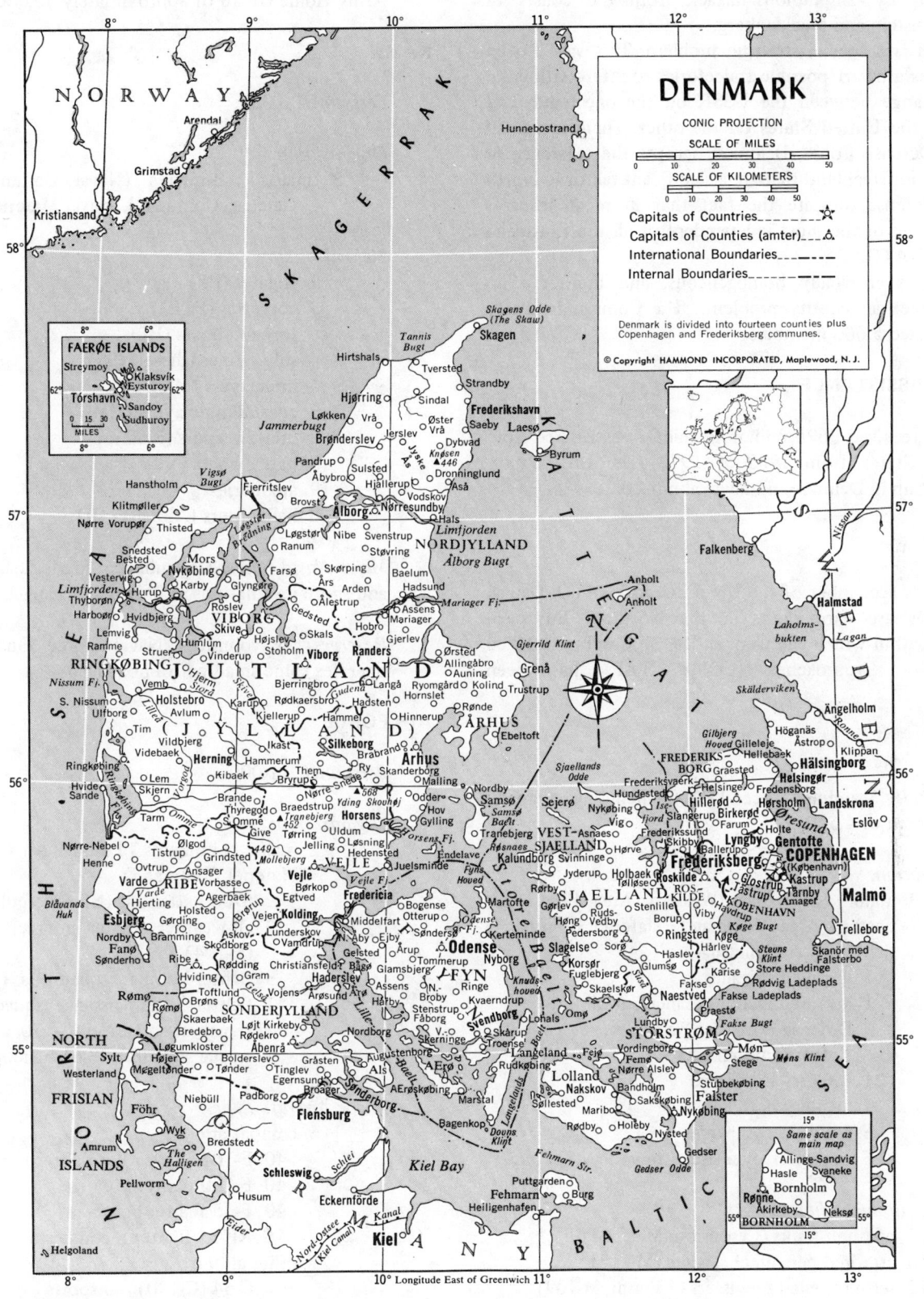

vulnerable to invasion from Germany, both overland through Jutland, and by amphibious attack from the coasts of Schleswig-Holstein and Mecklenberg.

Greenland is a special strategic problem. This vast frozen land mass lies athwart possible trajectories of intercontinental missile exchange between the USSR on the one hand, and Canada and the United States on the other. There is a small Greenland Defense Force; Denmark accepts the existence of the US bases in Greenland that are a significant factor in North American defense, despite the fact that in most respects Denmark is one of the most independent of all the European members of NATO.

Denmark is ethnically homogeneous, and there are no significant internal security problems. The Communist Party has an estimated 5,000 members.

MILITARY ASSISTANCE

Denmark received $625 million in military assistance from the United States from 1950 to 1972. The US Military Advisory Group in Denmark numbers about 20.

ALLIANCES

Denmark is a member of the UN, EEC, and NATO. Danish armed forces are earmarked for the Northern European Command, within which the German-Danish Combined Allied Forces Baltic Approaches (COMBALTAP) has been established.

ARMY

Personnel: Standing force 13,000 including a ready supplement of 4,500

Organization:
    3 major commands (Western Area Command, Eastern Area Command, Materiel Command)
    field army (mobilized)
      5 armored brigades
      1 armored reconnaissance battalion
        Defense Forces of Bornholm
    local defense (mobilized)
     21 infantry battalions
      7 artillery battalions
      6 engineer companies
      6 tank destroyer squadrons

Major Equipment Inventory:
    200 medium tanks (Centurion, M-47, M-48)
    650 armored personnel carriers (M-113)
     72 self-propelled howitzers (155mm, M-109)
     48 light tanks (M-41)
    276 light and medium artillery pieces

Reserves: 65,000 (includes local defense) plus a volunteer Army Home Guard of approximately 50,000

NAVY

Personnel: 6,000

Organization:
    3 major commands (Naval Command, Coastal Defense Command, Naval Materiel Command)

Major Units:
     2 frigates (PF)
     3 corvettes (PCE)
   18 torpedo boats (PT)
     6 submarines (diesel) (SS)
     4 minelayers (MMF)
     3 coastal minelayers (MMC)
     8 minesweepers (MSC)
     8 patrol boats (YP)
   19 auxiliaries
     8 helicopters (Alouette III)

Major Naval Bases: Copenhagen, Frederikshavn, Korsoer, and shore installations at Stevns and Langeland

Reserves: A volunteer Naval Home Guard of 4,000 operates some small patrol boats.

AIR FORCE

Personnel: 11,000

Organization:
    2 major commands (Tactical Air Command, Air Materiel Command)
      2 SAM battalions (Nike-Hercules and Hawk)
      2 all-weather fighter interceptor squadrons (F-104)
      3 fighter-bomber squadrons (F-35, F-100)
      1 fighter reconnaissance squadron (RF-35)
      1 transport squadron (C-130, C-54, C-47)
      1 rescue squadron (S-61 helicopters)

Major Aircraft Types:
  116 combat aircraft
     40 F-104 all-weather fighter interceptors
     40 F-100 fighter-bombers
     20 F-35 fighter-bombers
     16 RF-35 fighter reconnaissance
   21 other aircraft
      5 C-54 (C-130) transports
      8 C-47 transports
      8 S-61 helicopters

Major Air Bases: Karup, Aalborg, Skrydstrup, Vandel, Tirstrup, Vaerloese; on Greenland: Thule, Soendre Stroemfjord, Narsarsuak

Reserves: A volunteer air force Home Guard of 8,000

FINLAND

Suomen Tasavolta—Republiken Finland
Republic of Finland

POWER POTENTIAL STATISTICS

Area: 130,128 square miles
Population: 4,800,000
Total Active Armed Forces: 43,000 (including frontier guards; 0.90% population)
Gross National Product: $12.5 billion ($2,604 per capita)
Annual Military Expenditures: $225 million (1.8% GNP)
Steel and Iron Production: 2.1 million metric tons
Refined Petroleum Products: 9.5 million metric tons
Electric Power Output: 23.5 billion kwh
Merchant Fleet: 390 ships; 1.47 million gross tons
Civil Air Fleet: 21 jet, 1 turboprop, 56 piston transports

DEFENSE STRUCTURE

The President of the Republic of Finland is the commander in chief of the Finnish armed forces, and as the nation's chief executive has considerably more direct personal authority and responsibility for military affairs than does the head of state or of government in most other nations. The Defense Minister has no command authority; his is an essentially administrative position. The armed forces are integrated, and the nation's senior military officer, with the title of Commander of the Defense Forces, is responsible directly to the President. The Prime Minister acts as Chairman of the National Defense Council (comparable to the US National Security Council), which includes the Minister of Defense, four other ministers, the Commander of the Defense Forces, and the Chief of the General Staff.

POLITICO-MILITARY POLICY

Finland's location has forced it to shape its military policy and strategy with primary reference to the Soviet Union. The events of World War II proved conclusively to the Finns that no amount of Finnish valor and military skill can deny Russian might. Thus, Finnish foreign policy is designed to preserve independence, while assuring Russia that (1) Finland is firmly neutral in international affairs, and will not attempt to thwart or to oppose Soviet interests, (2) Finland poses no military threat to Russia, and (3) its defenses are strong enough to make it unlikely that any other power will be able to establish an anti-Soviet base in Finland easily before the USSR can intervene.

Finland's armed forces are limited in size by the 1947 post-World War II peace treaty with the Allied and Associated Powers (USSR, UK, Australia, Canada, Czechoslovakia, India, New Zealand, and the Union of South Africa).

Under the treaty the maximum strength allowed for the Army is 34,400; the Navy is limited to 10,000 tons and 4,500 men; the Air Force cannot exceed 60 combat aircraft and 3,000 men. Among the prohibitions of the treaty are nuclear weapons, guided missiles, submarines, motor torpedo boats, and aircraft with internal bomb-carrying capability. Conscript service is for eight to eleven months. By treaty, no military training may be conducted outside the services.

STRATEGIC PROBLEMS

Finland's principal strategic problem is proximity to the power centers of the USSR. Because of its far northerly location, Finland has traditionally stressed the development of a capability to operate efficiently in cold weather. This capability had much to do with the initial and dramatic successes that the Finns won over the Russians in the early weeks of the 1939-1940 war with the USSR. Finland's defensive capability is enhanced by the obstacles created by the Arctic north, and a vast area of forests and lakes in the east and central portions of the country. The obstacles are less formidable, however, on the direct but narrow approaches to Finland's heartland from the Soviet power center of Leningrad.

ALLIANCES AND MILITARY ASSISTANCE

Finland's bilateral treaties with the USSR specifically exclude it from any foreign alliances and military assistance other than Russian. As a member of the UN, however, Finland has contributed contingents or observers to UN forces or missions in Cyprus, Kashmir, Jerusalem, and Lebanon. Finland is also a member of EFTA.

ARMY

Personnel: 35,000 (about 10,000 are permanent, regular cadre; the remainder are conscripts)

Organization:
    1 armored brigade (about half strength)
    6 infantry brigades (about 35% of full strength)
    8 independent infantry battalions (reduced strength)
    1 field artillery regiment

6 coast artillery battalions
1 AA regiment
4 AA battalions

Major Equipment Inventory:
medium tanks (T-54, T-55, and Charioteer)
light tanks (PT-76)
APCs (BTR-50P)
105mm, 122mm, and 130mm guns
122mm and 152mm howitzers
81mm and 120mm mortars
AA (ZSU-57/2, 35mm Oerlikon, 40mm Bofors, 30mm Hispano-Suiza, and 23mm Soviet)
Vigilant and SS-11 antitank missiles

Reserve Forces: About 150,000 trained reserves; could be increased to over 500,000.

NAVY

Personnel: 2,000

Major Units:
3 frigates (PF; one used as a training ship)
2 fast gunboats, corvettes (PG)
15 fast patrol boats (PTF)
1 fast guided missile patrol boat with Styx SSM (PTFG)
20 patrol vessels/boats (YP)
2 coastal minelayers (MMC)
6 inshore minesweepers (MSI)
12 landing craft utility (LCU)
9 icebreakers (AGB)
16 auxiliaries

Major Naval Bases: Hanko, Helsinki, Turku

Reserves: About 8,000 trained reservists

AIR FORCE

Personnel: 3,000

Organization:
3 regional wings: Hame, Satahunta, and Karjala
3 fighter squadrons (MiG-21, Gnat, Draken, Magister)
1 transport squadron (C-47, Pembroke, Beaver)

Major Aircraft Types:
58 combat aircraft
    42 fighters (12 MiG-21, 12 Gnat Mk I, 18 Draken)
    16 Magister armed trainers/fighter-bombers
133 other aircraft
    10 transports (C-47, Pembroke, Beaver)
    98 trainer aircraft (4 MiG-15, 4 MiG-21, 55 Magister, 35 Safir)
    25 helicopters (AB204, Alouette II, Hound)

Major Air Bases: Dissala, Pori, Luonetjarvi, Parote, Kuopio, Jyvaskyla, Utti, Tampere, Kauhava

Reserves: About 11,000 men

PARAMILITARY

The national police force of 5,000 provides for internal security. There is a frontier guard organization numbering 3,000 men.

FRANCE

La Republique Francaise
French Republic

POWER POTENTIAL STATISTICS

Area: 212,918 square miles (including Corsica)
Population: 52,300,000
Total Active Armed Forces: 573,500 (includes 70,000 Gendarmerie; 1.10% population)
Gross National Product: $217 billion ($4,149 per capita)
Annual Military Expenditures: $9.1 billion (4.2% GNP)
Steel and Iron Production: 41.2 million metric tons
Fuel Production: Coal: 33.0 million metric tons
    Natural Gas: 7.2 billion cubic meters
    Refined Petroleum Products: 122.2 million metric tons
Electric Power Output: 147.8 billion kwh
Merchant Fleet: 1,399 ships; 7.01 million gross tons
Civil Air Fleet: 67 jet, 59 turboprop, 33 piston transports

DEFENSE STRUCTURE

The President of France is the commander in chief of the armed forces. He also presides over the Council of Ministers, the High Defense Council, and the Defense Committee. The Council of Ministers defines defense policy as part of the general national policy. The High Defense Council is the decision-making body for general defense policies within the framework established by the Council of Ministers, and includes the Premier, the Ministers of Foreign Affairs, National Defense, Interior, and Finance, and the General Secretary for National Defense. The High Defense Council advises the Council of Ministers.

The Premier is responsible for overall defense management,

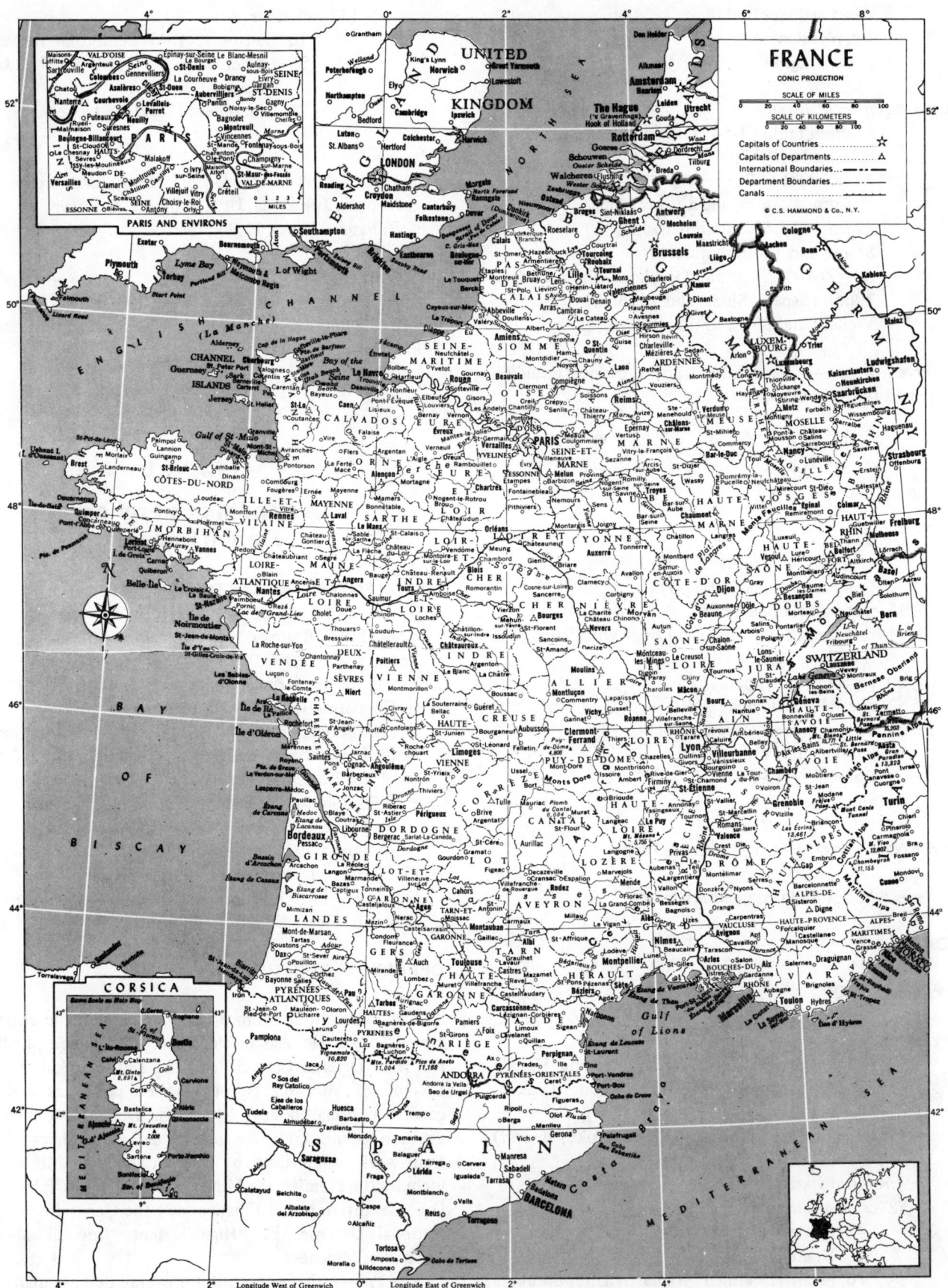

the coordination of defense activities, and the implementation of the decisions of the Council of Ministers and the Defense Council. The Minister of National Defense, who functions as the executive of the Premier, has authority over the three integrated services and is responsible for their preparedness. He is assisted by the Chief of Staff of the Armed Forces and the general staffs of the three services. The French armed forces are organized on the basis of three task-oriented operational systems (the Nuclear Strategic Force, the Forces of Maneuver, and the Territorial Defense Force), each including elements of all three services.

POLITICO-MILITARY POLICY

The structure and missions of the French armed forces reflect the government's basic conviction that for reasons of national security and national prestige France should remain responsible for its own defense, and that it should retain a substantial degree of independence of the two superpowers. The French government also believes that with its own nuclear force France contributes to a more stable international environment. Because of its diminished confidence in the US commitment to invoke its deterrent on behalf of a European ally, France believes that it has to possess its own nuclear forces to deter attack by another power. The French feel, therefore, that their nuclear capability complements the US nuclear deterrent. France hopes that eventually a European security system will evolve, built around the French nuclear force.

The Strategic Force forms France's major deterrent and is capable of attack over intercontinental range. It is projected in three generations. The first generation is fully operational and consists of Mirage IV bombers armed with 100 kiloton nuclear bombs. The second generation, consisting of intermediate range ground-to-ground solid fuel ballistic nuclear missiles stationed in southern France, has recently become fully operational. Four nuclear-powered submarines with Polaris-type missiles will complete the third generation, to become fully operational by 1976. In 1973 the government announced construction in southeastern France of sites for an additional group of intermediate range ballistic missiles equipped with thermonuclear warheads of almost megaton strength. The Strategic Force operates directly under the President.

The Forces of Maneuver have as their mission the containment of a nuclear or conventional attack inside or outside Europe. They include the bulk of the Army, the Navy, and the tactical Air Force units.

The Territorial Defense Forces (DOT) are responsible both for the defense of national territory and for internal security. An Alpine brigade, which is entrusted with the protection of the strategic missile silos in southeastern France, 25 other Army battalions, and gendarmerie units, constitute the core of the DOT. Light air force squadrons support the DOT.

France's independent defense policy in 1966 led to French withdrawal from NATO's military structure, even though it remained a member of the North Atlantic Alliance. France has also retained its membership in the Western European Union. Two French mechanized divisions continue to be stationed in Western Germany under a bilateral arrangement; one independent brigade remains in West Berlin. France also retains nominal membership in SEATO. Despite France's withdrawal from ACE, it cooperated in Mediterranean naval exercises in 1970, and has never left NATO's air defense communications system. As a result of the 1974 elections, France seems to be moving cautiously toward reestablishing closer ties with NATO.

Because of France's determination to establish its own nuclear capability, it refused to sign the Limited Test Ban Treaty. France has continued nuclear and thermonuclear tests at its Pacific test range near Tahiti, despite a call from the International Court of Justice in mid-1973 to stop them.

Economic, military and cultural treaties with former French colonies in Africa maintain France's influence there.

Universal military service in principle, but modified by exception of certain classifications, provides the majority of the armed forces. Active service lasts 12 months and is followed by three and one-half years of availability, with another 12 years of reserve service.

STRATEGIC PROBLEMS

The country's geographic situation gives it a marked contrast of defensive strength and vulnerabilities. The Pyrenees and the Southern Alps, combined with the existence of a determinedly neutral Switzerland, provide protection from land attack on the southern and southeastern frontiers. Although the Rhine from Switzerland to north of Strasbourg is a difficult obstacle, it is not impassable. From the Rhine to the North Sea the northern border is rugged in places and subject to inundation in a few, but is nevertheless demonstrably passable to troops. The ocean borders—Channel, Atlantic and Mediterranean—while they strengthen France's economic position in seaborne trade, are not invulnerable to modern amphibious assault. French realization of this geographic situation goes far to explain the incompleteness of France's separation from the North Atlantic Alliance, despite its insistence both on political independence and on rejection of NATO military command.

The internal political situation is traditionally fraught with dissension among a multiplicity of contending parties. As a result of the 1974 elections no single party has a majority in the National Assembly, but control is exercised by a centrist coalition. However the Communist Party and the Federation of the Left hold nearly a fifth of the seats. In times of international crisis, minor parties have in the past rallied to the national cause but the Communist Party of 400,000 members (the second largest in the West) has the capability of weakening the national effort in the fields of politics, economics, and defense.

In January 1974 the government banned four separatist movements: two rival Breton groups, the Liberation Front of Brittany (FLB-ARB) and the left-wing Liberation Front of Brittany for National Liberation and Socialism (FLB-LNS); the Corsican Peasant Front for Liberation (FPCL); and Basque Enbata. These groups were believed to have foreign support.

Agreement was reached with Spain in January 1974 on the limits of each country's claims to the continental shelf in the Bay of Biscay.

MILITARY ASSISTANCE

The United States provided France with $4.153 billion in military aid from 1950 to 1966, plus $96.6 million in excess military stocks. France has various kinds of multilateral and bilateral defense accords with most of its former African colonies and territories. These arrangements usually call for military aid in the form of equipment and training. Under some of the agreements, the African government can call upon French military intervention in case of an internal or external threat.

French naval, army, and air units participate in joint exercises with indigenous troops in Africa. Some 3,000 French officers and NCOs are serving on secondment or on contract with African armed forces.

The French armament industry has become a major pillar of the French economy, and France now sells arms worldwide.

ALLIANCES

France is a member of the UN, the Western European Union, NATO (limited), SEATO, and the European Common Market. It also has bilateral treaties with most of its former colonies.

ARMY

Personnel: 331,000

Organization:
- 1 Army consisting of 2 Army Corps (5 mechanized divisions, 2 in Germany) plus supporting elements
- 2 Alpine brigades
- 1 parachute division (2 paratroop brigades)
- 1 independent brigade (in Berlin)
- 1 air portable motorized brigade
- 2 motorized infantry regiments
- 2 armored car regiments
- 1 parachute battalion
- 19 infantry battalions (with 120mm mortars)
- 3 regiments SAM (Hawk)

Deployment: France remains responsible for the protection and security of its overseas departments and territories, which have been organized into five defense zones; the Antilles and Guiana zone in the Caribbean (one battalion); the Indian Ocean zone with Headquarters in La Reunion Island (two regiments); the Pacific Ocean zone (divided into two zones, New Caledonia and Polynesia, two battalions); and French Territory of the Afars and Issas (two battalions). Additional units are stationed in independent Africa: Senegal, Chad, Ivory Coast.

Major Equipment Inventory:
- 800 AMX-30 medium tanks
- 800 AMX-13 light tanks (with 90mm guns and 4 SS-11 antitank missiles)
- EBR heavy armored cars
- AML light armored cars
- 500 APCs (AMX-VTT)
- AMX 105mm and 155mm self-propelled howitzers
- AMX twin 30mm self-propelled AA guns
- 155mm field artillery
- 40 fixed wing aircraft
- 550 helicopters (including 130 SA.330 Puma)

Missiles: SSM: Pluton; SAM: Hawk, Crotale, Roland; ATM: Nord SS-11, Entac, Nord/Bolkow Hot, Milan.

Reserves: There are approximately 450,000 trained reservists available for mobilization, organized in 70 infantry battalions and seven armored car regiments. They comprise 27 mobilized infantry regiments.

NAVY

Personnel: 68,500 (includes a Naval Air Force of 11,500 and some 2,500 Marines)

Major Units:
- 2 light aircraft carriers (CVL)
- 1 ASW helicopter carrier (24 helicopters: CVS)
- 1 helicopter carrier (training/Marine Commando: CLG)
- 2 nuclear-powered ballistic missile submarines (SSBN)
- 19 diesel submarines (SS)
- 1 antiaircraft cruiser (CLAA)
- 2 assault landing ships (LSD)
- 2 guided missile frigates (DLG)

5 guided missile destroyers (DDG)
  12 destroyers (ASW, radar picket, and command; DD, DER)
  27 destroyer escorts (DE)
  13 ocean minesweepers (MSO)
  62 coastal minesweepers (MSC)
  15 inshore minesweepers (MSI)
   5 minehunters
  15 coastal escorts (PCE)
   4 patrol boats (PC)
   9 survey ships (AGS)
 180 support ships and service craft
   4 experimental ships
  Entering service or nearing completion: 3 guided missile frigates (C67 type) and 2 nuclear powered ballistic missile submarines (SSBN)

Naval Air Force:

Organization:
  2 fighter-bomber squadrons (Etendard IV-M)
  2 interceptor squadrons (F-8E Crusader)
  1 reconnaissance squadron (Etendard IV-P)
  3 ASW squadrons (Alize)
  5 maritime reconnaissance squadrons (Neptune and Atlantique)
  6 helicopter squadrons (Super Frelon, SH-34, Alouette II and III)

Major Aircraft Types:
  246 combat aircraft:
    90 Etendard IV-M and IV-P fighter-bomber and reconnaissance aircraft
    37 F-8E Crusader interceptors
    58 Alize ASW aircraft
    26 P-2E/H Neptune maritime reconnaissance aircraft
    35 BR 1150 Atlantique maritime reconnaissance aircraft
  300+ other aircraft:
    17 Super Frelon helicopters
    43 SH-34 helicopters
    38 Alouette II and III helicopters
    67 miscellaneous transports
  135+ trainer/support aircraft

Missiles: long-range SSM: MSBS; anti-surface: MM38 Exocet; surface to air: Masurca and Tartar; surface to sea: Malafon; air to air: Sidewinder and Matra D530; air to surface: Nord AS20, Nord AS37 Martel and Nord S210

Major Naval Bases: Brest, Toulon, Cherbourg, Lorient

Major Naval Air Bases: Lann Bihoue, Nimes Garons, Landivisiau, Hyeres

Reserves: About 90,000 trained reservists

AIR FORCE

Personnel: 104,000

Organization:
  Strategic Air Command (CFAS): subject to President's command
    1 IRBM group (2 squadrons of 9 missiles each)
    3 strategic bomber wings (3 squadrons per wing; Mirage IV-A)
    3 tanker squadrons (1 per bomber wing; KC 135 F)
  Tactical Air Command (FATAC)
    2 tactical air commands
    2 light bomber squadrons (Vautour 2B)
   16 fighter-bomber squadrons (1 Mirage III-B, 8 Mirage III-E, 2 Jaguar, 3 F-100 D, 2 Mirage V)
    3 tactical reconnaissance squadrons (Mirage III-R and III-RD)
  Air Defense Command (CAFDA): coordinated by the automatic STRIDA II air defense system
    3 interceptor squadrons (Mirage III-C)
    2 all-weather interceptor squadrons (Vautour 2N) converting to F-1
    5 fighter squadrons (Mystere IV-A, Super Mystere B2)
  Military Air Transport Command (COTAM)
    1 squadron DC-6 and BR-765 Sahara transports
    4 squadrons Nord 2501 Noratlas transports
    1 squadron STOL BR 941 S
    3 squadrons C.160 Transall
    2 mixed squadrons
    4 helicopter squadrons (H-34, Alouette II)
  Air Force Schools Command (CEAA)
  Air Communications Service (CTAA)

Overseas Deployment: 1 squadron of F-100, 1 squadron of A-1Ds and 1 mixed transport squadron of H-34 and Alouette II helicopters and Noratlas transports in French Territory of Afars and Issas

Major Aircraft Types:
  600+ combat aircraft
    60+ Mirage IV-A strategic bombers
    24 Vautour 2B light bombers
    95 Mirage III-C light bombers

160 Mirage III-B, E, and V fighter-bombers
20 Mirage IV-A fighter-bombers
60 F-100 D Fighter-bombers
15 F-100 F fighter-bombers
60 Mirage III-R reconnaissance aircraft
28 Vautour 2 N all-weather interceptors
47 Super-Mystere B 2 fighter-bombers
20 A-1D/E fighter-bombers
15 Jaguar fighter-bombers
1,960 other aircraft
10 KC-135 F tankers
6 DC-6 transports
4 DC-8 transports
160 Noratlas transports
52 Transall C-160 F transports
123 miscellaneous transports
170 helicopters (H-34, Alouette II and III)
1,435 miscellaneous trainers/support aircraft

Missiles: AAM: Matra R-511 and R-530; ASM: Matra Martel, Nord AS-12, AS-20, AS-30, and AS-33; SAM: Crotale; SSM: SSBS (IRBM)

Major Air Bases: LeBourget, Metz, Bordeaux, Aix, Bretigny, Tours, Chartres, Orange, Strasbourg, Cognac, Pau, Reims, Toulouse, Dijon, Nimes, Villacoublay, Limoges, Cambrai, Etampes, Creil

PARAMILITARY

The Gendarmerie of some 70,000 men plus 85,000 more in reserve is administered by the Ministry of the Armed Forces and can augment the regular forces. There is also a Republican Security Force (*Compagnies Republicaines de Securite*) of 17,000 men, under the Ministry of the Interior.

(WEST) GERMANY
Bundesrepublik Deutschland
Federal Republic of Germany

POWER POTENTIAL STATISTICS

Area: 95,974 square miles (includes West Berlin)
Population: 61,700,000 (includes West Berlin)
Total Active Armed Forces: 500,500 (including security and border forces: 0.81% population)
Gross National Product: $243 billion ($3,938 per capita)
Annual Military Expenditures: $9.0 billion (3.7% GNP)
Steel and Iron Production: 70.6 million metric tons
Fuel Production: Coal: 255.2 million metric tons
    Crude Oil: 7.1 million metric tons
    Refined Petroleum Products: 104.5 million metric tons
    Gas: 34.22 billion cubic meters
Electric Power Output: 259.6 billion kwh
Merchant Fleet: 2,826 ships; 8.7 million gross tons
Civil Air Fleet: 121 jet, 3 turboprop, 61 piston transports

DEFENSE STRUCTURE

The President of the Federal Republic as chief of state is the titular head of the armed forces of West Germany; actual control is exercised by the Chancellor (Prime Minister) through the Minister of Defense in typical parliamentary governmental fashion. Under existing law the Minister of Defense is commander in chief of the armed forces in peacetime, the Chancellor in wartime. Parliamentary authority is exercised by a Defense Committee with power to investigate any aspect of military affairs.

There is no overall military command structure in the West German armed forces. The rearmament of West Germany was begun while the nation was still nominally occupied by the Western Allies of World War II. The purpose was to integrate West German forces into the NATO defense structure so that they could participate in the defense of their own country as a part of Western Europe. This philosophy is still the basis of West Germany's defense policy, partly to continue to reassure its allies, and partly as a key element of the determination of modern West Germany to maintain unquestioned civilian control over the armed forces. Thus the West German armed forces can operate effectively only as elements of an integrated, international, NATO army. There is no national General Staff, although a General Staff Corps provides officers for operational headquarters; the senior military officer in the West German defense structure is the Inspector General; there is no West German operational command larger than an army corps or air wing (although German officers can, and do, serve as army and regional commanders and staff officers in the international command structure of NATO's Allied Command Europe).

There are three territorial defense commands—Schleswig-Holstein, North, and South—and six military regions under these commands. The Territorial Defense Organization is under army command but staffed by all three services.

POLITICO-MILITARY POLICY

One of the most important features of the deliberate and carefully structured renunciation of traditional German militarism is the effort to make the armed forces truly democratic without seriously impairing military efficiency. In a series of laws beginning with the initial authorization of German armed forces in 1955, the West German Bundestag (Parliament) has included measures to assure the maintenance

of civilian control and to guarantee the rights of all citizens who are members of the armed forces.

The present German military policy of eschewing nationalistic, aggressive military operations, and of participating in war only as an integral element of an international army is a dramatic reversal of one of the most consistent national policies in history.

Something over half of the manpower of the armed forces (*Bundeswehr*) is obtained through conscription under the compulsory Military Service Law of 1956. The present term of service is 15 months.

STRATEGIC PROBLEMS

The strategic situation that contributed to the development of Germany's former aggressive politico-military policies has not changed fundamentally. Germany's southern frontier is secured by the Alps. In all other directions, however, its frontiers are vulnerable. Its participation in NATO has safeguarded the western frontier, and has provided some protection for the north (although the military weakness of NATO allies Denmark and Norway, combined with Soviet Baltic strength, perpetuates that vulnerability to some extent). Traditional German vulnerability to attack from the east across the North European Plain is exacerbated by the continuing division of Germany, with East Germany and Czechoslovakia occupied by very powerful Soviet forces; this division also has formed West Germany geographically into an elongated shape, north and south, with a narrow waist that permits the peacetime concentration of Soviet armored spearheads less than 100 miles east of the Rhine River. Thus NATO's problem for the defense of Western Europe is essentially how to stop a westward thrust by Soviet forces before they can reach the Rhine; West Germany's problem, within this, is how to contribute effectively to this defense without assuring the devastation of its national territory.

The country's strategic position is affected by the initiatives of former Chancellor Willy Brandt in seeking and obtaining treaties with the USSR and Poland in 1970. In the August treaty with the USSR, both nations mutually renounced the threat or use of force, and affirmed the permanence of the existing boundary between East and West Germany, and the Oder-Neisse boundary of Poland. The Polish treaty affirms recognition of the Oder-Neisse line as permanent and inviolable by either party, and otherwise parallels the USSR treaty.

Simultaneously with these negotiations, the four occupying powers of Berlin (France, the United Kingdom, the United States, and the USSR) held meetings concerning access to Berlin from the West, and the problems of transit between East and West Berlin. One of the provisions of the resulting agreement, signed in September 1971, was that details of German intra-city and intra-Germany transit would be settled between the two Germanies. In December 1972 the two German states signed a treaty normalizing relations. It provided for an exchange of diplomatic representatives. Although West Germany hoped this might lead to reunification East Germany made plain its intention that it would not.

The potential threat to West Germany through the Baltic has led not only to the establishment of special military arrangements with Denmark, through NATO (see NATO and Denmark), but also to the revival of a small but efficient West German Navy. Although there was no naval tradition in Germany prior to the establishment of the German Empire in 1871, the outstanding performance of the German Navy in two world wars has created a rich naval heritage. The size of ships is limited by the Paris Agreements of 1954. In September 1973 West Germany was authorized by the Council of Western European Union to build conventionally-powered submarines up to 1,800 tons (almost twice the earlier limit), to permit greater responsibility for surveillance of the North Sea and the Atlantic Ocean.

West Germany is a homogeneous nation, without any significant minorities that might assist a hostile invader. There is, however, evidence of some perpetuation in a small minority of the German people of the ultranationalistic, reactionary philosophy which brought Hitler to power. How significant this is, and whether, in a period of turmoil, crisis, or economic hardship, the majority of the people might be vulnerable to such a philosophy, or to the opposed philosophy of Communism, is difficult to estimate.

MILITARY ASSISTANCE

Between 1954 and 1965 Germany received $900.8 million in military assistance from the United States, plus more than $200 million in excess military stocks. Germany's economic recovery has rendered further military assistance unnecessary.

West Germany has offered assistance to a number of African countries on both a sales and a grant basis. This has included aircraft and pilot training, patrol craft and naval training, police training and equipment, and military transport.

ALLIANCES

West Germany is a member of three overlapping alliances: the 15-member NATO alliance, the Western European Union (with Britain, France, and Benelux), and a bilateral alliance with the United States. Within these alliances West Germany has undertaken several collaborative projects. The continuing presence of forces of the United States, Britain, Canada, France, and Belgium on German soil, as part of the NATO shield forces, has created an acute shortage of training facilities in Germany. The West German government has reached agreements with Portugal and France whereby the Bundeswehr can send contingents to train on the territory of those NATO partners. Also, joint research and development has been done with NATO allies. Military aircraft have been jointly produced by West Germany and France, and a number of military items have been designed and produced in cooperation with the United States. West Germany was admitted to the United Nations in 1973.

ARMY

Personnel: 327,000 (292,000 for NATO forces; 35,000 in a Territorial Force which is held for rear-area duties, and not assigned to NATO)

Organization:
- 3 army corps
- 12 armored brigades
- 1 armored regiment
- 13 armored infantry brigades
- 3 infantry brigades
- 2 mountain brigades
- 3 airborne brigades
- 15 SSM battalions (Honest John and Sergeant)

Major Equipment Inventory:
- 1,050 medium tanks (M-48A2)
- 2,250 medium tanks (Leopard)
- 250 105mm howitzers
- 75 155mm howitzers
- 432 155mm self-propelled howitzers
- 150 175mm self-propelled guns
- 75 203mm self-propelled howitzers
- 209 multiple rocket launchers
- 500 40mm self-propelled AA guns
- 1,600 APCs (Marder)
- 1,770 APCs (HS-30)
- 3,140 APCs (M-113)
- 1,086 tank destroyers (90mm Kanonpanzer or SS-11 mounted on APCs)
- 150+ light aircraft (mostly Do-27; some OV-10)
- 460 helicopters (UH-1, Alouette II, CH-53, Bell 47)
- 100 SSM Sergeant, Honest John

Reserves: There are approximately 1.8 million Bundeswehr reservists, including all men who have actually served in the Bundeswehr. Of these, 540,000 are available for immediate mobilization. Enlisted reservists are subject to recall up to the age of 45 in peacetime and up to 60 in wartime. Officers and non-commissioned officers are subject to recall at any time up to age 60; those who have been members of the professional regular cadre of the Bundeswehr can be called back up to age 65, regardless of rank. There is a regular reserve training program, part obligatory and part voluntary, which has been only partially implemented to date due to shortages of facilities.

NAVY

Personnel: 35,900 (including 6,000 Naval Air Arm)

Major Units:
- 3 guided missile destroyers with Tartar SAM (DDG)
- 8 destroyers (DD)
- 6 fast frigates (DE)
- 11 coastal submarines (SSC)
- 6 patrol escorts (PF)
- 13 escorts (PCE)
- 28 fast minesweepers (MSC)
- 24 coastal minesweepers (MSC)
- 20 inshore minesweepers (MSI)
- 38 fast torpedo boats (PT)
- 1 landing ship medium (LSM)
- 16 landing craft mechanized (LCM)
- 22 landing craft utility (LCU)
- 83 auxiliaries
- 1 training ship (light cruiser-type)
- 84 F-104/TF-104 (four fighter-bomber/ reconnaissance squadrons)
- 20 BR 1150 Atlantique (2 maritime patrol squadrons)
- 23 helicopters (S-58 for search and rescue; being replaced by 22 SH-3)
- 20 Do-28 liaison aircraft

Under Construction:
- 4 guided missile destroyer escorts (DEG)
- 10 guided missile patrol craft (PTFG)
- 20 fast patrol craft (PG)

Reserves: 36,000 for direct mobilization

AIR FORCE

Personnel: 104,000

Organization:
- 2 tactical air divisions (each with ground attack, reconnaissance, and guided missile wings)
- 2 air defense divisions
- 1 air transport command (2 groups)
- 4 fighter/interceptor squadrons (F-104)
- 10 fighter-bomber close-support squadrons (F-104)

10 light ground attack squadrons (2 normally used for training; G-91)
4 fighter reconnaissance squadrons (RF-4)
6 transport squadrons (Transall)
24 SAM batteries (Nike-Hercules; 9 launchers each)
36 SAM batteries (Hawk; 6 launchers each)
2 SSM wings (Pershing; 36 launchers each)
4 helicopter squadrons (UH-1; Alouette II, H-13)

Major Aircraft Types:
661 combat aircraft
    80 RF-4 reconnaissance aircraft
   252 F-104 interceptors, fighter-bombers
   119 TF-104 fighter trainers (with full combat capability)
   210 G-91 light ground attack aircraft (delivery of 175 F-4F fighter-bombers to begin in 1974)
1,539 other aircraft
   110 Transall transports
     4 Boeing 707-320 transports
   175 miscellaneous transports (C-140, C-47, DC-6, Pembroke, Heron, T-43)
1,000 miscellaneous trainer/support aircraft (Do-27, Do-28, L-4, P-149, T-37, T-38)
   250 helicopters (UH-1, H-13, Alouette II)

Reserves: 87,000 for direct mobilization

PARAMILITARY

In addition to the Territorial Force, and reservists for that force, there are approximately 18,500 Border Police (equipped with Saladin armored cars and nine patrol boats) and 15,000 internal security forces.

GREECE
Hellenic Republic

POWER POTENTIAL STATISTICS

Area: 50,944 square miles
Population: 9,100,000
Total Active Armed Forces: 184,000 (includes 25,000 Gendarmerie; 2.05% population)
Gross National Product: $12.8 billion ($1,407 per capita)
Annual Military Expenditures: $608 million (4.75% GNP)
Refined Petroleum Products: 6.8 million metric tons
Electric Power Output: 10.6 billion kwh
Merchant Fleet: 2,056 ships; 13.1 million gross tons
Civil Air Fleet: 12 jet, 9 turboprop, 13 piston transports

DEFENSE STRUCTURE

The government of Greece was controlled by military officers from 1967 to 1974. Elections in early 1974 confirmed General Phaedon Gezikis as president of an unpopular government. A number of plots and attempted coups resulted in forced retirement of many officers, both senior and junior, in the armed forces, leaving Greece's military organization weak. The government's debilities became apparent during the Cyprus crisis in July 1974, and Gezikis called on Constantine Karamanlis (Greece's most effective statesman since World War II, who had resigned and gone into voluntary exile in 1963, in protest against the turbulent political proclivity) to return and form a civilian government. Gezikis remained as President, but Karamanlis moved toward restoration of democratic government and replacement of junta military appointees.

The three services are integrated under the Ministry of National Defense. Under the Defense Minister is a Commander in Chief, Armed Forces, who heads a staff composed of the Chiefs of Staff of the Army, the Navy, and the Air Force.

POLITICO-MILITARY POLICY

During much of the century-and-a-half existence of the modern Greek state, its military policy has reflected traditional hostility to Turkey, the former occupying power, despite the fact that Greece and Turkey have been allies in NATO. Discovery of oil off the island of Thasos, at the northern end of the Aegean Sea, in early 1974 exacerbated a long-standing rivalry over maritime sovereignty in that area. Tensions between the two nations were already high when the coup d'etat in Cyprus, supported if not engineered by the Greek military junta, brought them to the brink of war in July 1974. With almost 40,000 Turkish troops ashore on the island, the Greek government realized the futility of sending units to attempt to resist them.

In January 1973 US and Greek representatives signed an agreement granting the United States home port facilities for the Sixth Fleet in the Athens area, but the installation was subsequently postponed indefinitely by the Greek government. Karamanlis announced the withdrawal of Greek units from NATO during the crisis in 1974. What effect this would have on US NATO force bases in Greece was not clear.

The armed forces are supported by conscription, with all able-bodied men between the ages of 21 and 50 being liable to

WESTERN EUROPE 95

24 months' service. In the Navy, which has many volunteers, conscript service is 18 months. The annual call-up is about 50,000.

STRATEGIC PROBLEMS

Greece commands a significant geographic position from which to control the eastern basin of the Mediterranean, and consequently the maritime communications to and from the Black Sea and the Middle East. It was because of this that foreign armies invaded Greece in two world wars, and NATO now considers Greece a fundamental link in its defenses of southeastern Europe.

Although the long northern frontier of Greece is largely mountainous, the corridors and natural communications lines are generally perpendicular to the frontier, and thus the mountains do not form an effective barrier to invasion. This is compounded by the narrowness of northeastern Greece. The vulnerability of this frontier was not only amply demonstrated in World Wars I and II; it was successfully exploited by Greece's northern communist neighbors during the Greek Civil War of 1945-1949.

The emotional and political involvement of Greece in the bitter dispute between Greek and Turkish Cypriots brought Greece and Turkey to the threshold of war twice (1963 and 1964) before the military coup in Cyprus in July 1974 resulted in Turkish invasion of the island and caused a military and political crisis in Greece. Weakened by the upheavals and forced retirements of military leaders in recent years, Greece refrained from a military response and sought a solution through the UN, NATO, and meetings of the foreign ministers of Great Britain, Turkey and Greece in Geneva, Switzerland.

MILITARY ASSISTANCE

The original stimulus to the American foreign aid program was provided when the United States decided, in 1947, to replace faltering British military and economic assistance to Greece. This resulted in the Truman Doctrine, followed by the Marshall Plan, and the subsequent US worldwide military assistance programs to underdeveloped Free World nations threatened by Communism. Greece has received a total of $1.7 billion in military assistance since 1950, in addition to about $200 million immediate assistance (mostly economic) provided under the Truman Doctrine in the two previous years. US military assistance to Greece was briefly suspended after the 1967 coup d'etat, but has been resumed.

Under the terms of the Zurich-London Agreements of 1959 Greece is committed to assist (in concert with Turkey) in the establishment and training of the armed forces and internal security forces of Cyprus. This agreement was never fully implemented, and was completely ended by the mid-1974 events in Cyprus.

ALLIANCES

Greece is a member of NATO. It is also a member of the 20-year Balkan Alliance of 1954 with Yugoslavia and Turkey.

ARMY

Personnel: 118,000

Organization:
- 3 corps (2 on northern frontier assigned to NATO)
- 11 infantry divisions (8 under strength)
- 1 armored division
- 1 commando brigade (marines)
- 2 SSM battalions (Honest John)
- 1 SAM battalion (Hawk)

Major Equipment Inventory:
- 250 medium tanks (M-47)
- 270 medium tanks (M-48)
- 50 medium tanks (AMX-30)
- light tanks (M-24 and M-41)
- APCs (M-2, M-59, and M-113)
- 105mm, 155mm and 175mm self-propelled guns
- 105mm, 155mm, and 203mm self-propelled howitzers
- armored cars (M-8 and M-20)
- scout cars (M-3)
- Hawk SAMs
- Honest John SSMs
- 40mm, 75mm, and 90mm AA guns
- 20 light aircraft, helicopters

Reserves: About 350,000 reservists available for mobilization

NAVY

Personnel: 18,000

Major Units:
- 9 destroyers (DD)
- 4 destroyer escorts (DE)
- 7 diesel submarines (SS)
- 2 minelayers (MMC)
- 5 minesweepers (MSO)
- 3 submarine chasers (PC)
- 15 coastal minesweepers (MSC)
- 4 fast patrol boats with Exocet SSM (PTFG)
- 14 torpedo boats (PT)
- 1 landing ship dock (LSD)
- 8 landing ships tank (LST)

6 landing ships medium (LSM)
8 landing craft (LCU/LCT)
13 landing craft mechanized (LCM)
34 landing craft vehicle-personnel (LCVP)
17 auxiliaries

Major Naval Bases: Piraeus, Salonika, Valos, Mitilini

Reserves: About 50,000 trained reservists

AIR FORCE

The 28th (Hellenic) Tactical Air Force is made up of 7 combat squadrons, and 1 transport squadron and has been assigned to NATO's Sixth Allied Tactical Air Force.

Personnel: 23,000

Organization:
6 fighter-bomber squadrons (F-104 and F-84F)
4 day interceptor squadrons (F-5)
1 all-weather interceptor squadron (F-102)
2 reconnaissance squadrons (RF-84F and RF-5)
3 transport squadrons (Noratlas, C-47, C-119, Do-28)
2 helicopter squadrons (Alouette II, Bell 47, AB-204, H-19)
1 ASW/search and rescue squadron (under Navy control; HU-16)
1 SAM wing (1 battalion each of Nike-Ajax and Nike-Hercules)

Major Aircraft Types:
240 combat aircraft
    108 fighter-bombers (36 F-104, 72 F-84F)
    18 F-102A all-weather fighter interceptors
    72 F-5A fighter-interceptors
    30 fighter reconnaissance aircraft (15 RF-5, 15 RF-84F)
    12 HU-16 ASW/rescue aircraft
244 other aircraft
    108 transports (27 C-47, 40 Noratlas, 31 Do-28, 10 C-119)
    36 helicopters (12 Bell 47, 6 AB-204, 10 H-19, 8 Alouette II)
    100 trainer/support aircraft
    38 F-4 fighters on order to be delivered starting in March 1974

Reserves: About 30,000 trained reservists

PARAMILITARY

There is a National Gendarmerie of 25,000 men for internal security. In addition the National Guard of 50,000 organized March 30, 1970, has the duty of ensuring internal order and safeguarding the country from Communist, anarchist, or any other form of hostile action. It is manned by reservists from all three services between the ages of 19 and 50, and is also open to volunteers up to age 60; it is organized on a regional basis, all its members serving a minimum of six months and training on Sundays and holidays.

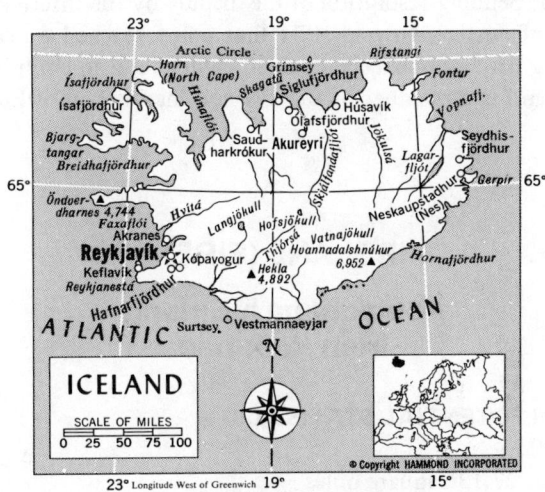

ICELAND
Lydveldid Island
Republic of Iceland

POWER POTENTIAL STATISTICS

Area: 39,768 square miles
Population: 213,000
Total Active Armed Forces: None
Gross National Product: $977.6 million ($4,684 per capita)
Electric Power Output: 1.6 billion kwh
Merchant Fleet: 288 ships; 125,912 gross tons
Civil Air Fleet: 7 jet, 4 turboprop, 4 piston transports

POLITICO-MILITARY POLICIES AND POSTURE

A member of NATO, Iceland maintains no military forces, although there is an internal security police force of about 500 men, and a Coast Guard of five ships and 120 men. Iceland provides its NATO allies with air and radar base sites on its territory; there are 3,300 US Air Force and Navy personnel in Iceland, stationed at the NATO air base of Keflavik. In March 1974 Iceland proposed their removal by mid-1976. The Icelandic government extended its coastal limits for fishing from 12 miles to 50 on September 1, 1972, evoking sharp protests from the governments of Great Britain and West Germany. A "cod war" developed in 1973 as fishermen from both countries ignored the limits. Great Britain responded to harassment by Icelandic patrol craft by sending an unarmed sea-going tug to the area. After several reported incidents between British trawlers and Icelandic gunboats, Britain sent three frigates to the area in May 1973. Incidents continued, and attempts at negotiation through the UN and NATO accomplished little. In October, following an ultimatum by Iceland, Great Britain agreed to withdraw its warships beyond the 50-mile zone and an agreement was reached limiting the catch and the number of ships that could fish in areas close to Iceland, pending resolution of the dispute by the International Court of Justice. In mid-1974 that court reached a decision favoring Britain, but Iceland has threatened not to comply.

Iceland is a member of the UN and the Council of Europe.

IRELAND (EIRE)

Poblacht na h'Eirlann
Irish Republic

POWER POTENTIAL STATISTICS

Area: 27,136 square miles
Population: 3,000,000
Total Active Armed Forces: 13,000 (0.44% population)
Gross National Product: $5.1 billion ($1,700 per capita)
Annual Military Expenditures: $47 million (0.92% GNP)
Fuel Production: Coal: 90,000 metric tons
    Refined Petroleum Products: 2.8 million metric tons
Electric Power Output: 6.1 billion kwh
Merchant Fleet: 90 ships; 174,459 gross tons
Civil Air Fleet: 20 jet and 5 piston transports

DEFENSE STRUCTURE

In a republican, parliamentary form of government, the Permanent Defence Force of Eire (including Army, Air Force, and Navy) is administered by the Minister of Defence, assisted by the Chief of Staff, the Adjutant General, and the Quartermaster General.

POLITICO-MILITARY POLICY

Irish national foreign policy and military policy are traditionally neutral. With respect to the East-West confrontation since World War II, however, Irish policy has been retitled independent, rather than neutral, in view of Ireland's ideological commitment to Western democracy. Implicitly Eire relies upon the armed forces of the United Kingdom and of NATO for its security, and thus maintains armed forces totally inadequate for effective self-defense. In international affairs Ireland has increasingly offered members or elements of its armed forces (recruited from the Reserve force) for peacekeeping activities, almost exclusively through the United Nations.

Under current Irish law, the Permanent Defense Force is limited to a total strength of 13,000 men, and the reserves to 26,000. In May 1973, however, the Defense Minister announced an increase of the army by two battalions, to be stationed at Dundalk and County Donegal, near the border with Northern Ireland. All personnel of the active and reserve armed forces are volunteers; the term of service is three years for the Army followed by nine years in the Reserve, four years in the Naval Service and Air Corps, followed by six years in the Reserve.

STRATEGIC PROBLEMS

The long-standing Irish hostility to Great Britain is perpetuated in large part by the fact that the predominantly Scots-Irish Protestant population of Northern Ireland retains loyalty and allegiance to the British Crown, and refuses to join predominantly Catholic Eire. Recent years have seen repeated incidents of violence, terrorism and bloodshed in Northern Ireland that have increased the tension between Britain and Ireland. The Irish Republican Army, although outlawed, has continued to function, using Ireland as a base. In 1972 the Irish government increased its efforts to curb its activities, arresting many of its leaders and passing a strict law that greatly assisted the police in trying to apprehend IRA members. A rational solution to the internal troubles in Northern Ireland is not in sight, and thus relations between Eire and Britain will necessarily remain tense.

MILITARY ASSISTANCE

Ireland trains officer cadets from Zambia.

ALLIANCES

Ireland is a member of the UN and the EEC. It actively supports UN peacekeeping efforts and maintains an infantry battalion with the UN Force in Cyprus, while officers have served on UN observer teams in Kashmir, Lebanon, the Congo, Palestine, and New Guinea.

ARMY

Personnel: 11,940

Organization:
    7 infantry battalions
    1 tank squadron
    1 armed reconnaissance squadron
    6 field artillery batteries
    1 AA battery

Major Equipment Inventory:
- medium tanks, ex-British
- armored cars, Panhard
- APC, Panhard
- light field artillery, 25-pounder
- Bofors AA guns

Reserves: There are approximately 24,500 volunteers formally enrolled in the Reserve Defense Force.

NAVY (Naval Service)

Personnel: 560

Major Units:
- 1 corvette (PCE)
- 3 fisheries protection ships, ex-British minesweepers (MSC)
- 2 tenders

AIR FORCE (Air Corps)

Personnel: 500

Organization:
- 1 tactical reconnaissance squadron (FR-172, Vampire)
- 1 support squadron (Dove, Alouette III)

Major Aircraft Types:
- 8 FR-172 light ground attack aircraft
- 3 Vampire armed trainers
- 3 Dove transports
- 14 miscellaneous trainer/support aircraft (Provost, Chipmunk)
- 5 Alouette III helicopters
- 3 Magister armed trainers on order

PARAMILITARY

Constabulary and civil police number 3,000.

ITALY

Repubblica Italiana
Italian Republic

POWER POTENTIAL STATISTICS

Area: 116,315 square miles
Population: 54,600,000
Total Active Armed Forces: 503,000 (includes 86,000 Carabinieri; 0.92% population)
Gross National Product: $136.6 billion ($2,502 per capita)
Annual Military Expenditures: $3.87 billion (2.83% GNP)
Steel and Iron Production: 26.2 million metric tons
Fuel Production: Coal: 1.6 million metric tons
  Crude Oil: 1.15 million metric tons
  Refined Petroleum Products: 129.5 million metric tons
Electric Power Output: 126 billion kwh
Merchant Fleet: 1,690 ships; 8.14 million gross tons
Civil Air Fleet: 94 jet, 23 turboprop, 5 piston transports

DEFENSE STRUCTURE

Italy has a parliamentary republican government; the President is the nominal commander of the armed forces. Actual civilian control of the armed forces is exercised by the Cabinet, through the Minister of Defense, who in turn is advised by a Defense Committee, consisting of the Chief of the Defense Staff, the Secretary of State for Defense, and the chiefs of staff of the three services.

POLITICO-MILITARY POLICY

Since its emergence as a great power in the late nineteenth century. Italy has been a member of one of the major European military alliances, but prior to World War II Italian policy was largely opportunistic, with no fixed ideological or regional orientation or commitment. Since World War II, despite the strong political trend toward socialism, and the influence of the most powerful communist party in Western Europe, Italy has aligned itself consistently with the Western European democratic powers, and was a charter member of NATO.

The armed forces of Italy are raised and maintained through conscription. For the Army and the Air Force the term of conscript service is 15 months; for the Navy it is 24 months.

STRATEGIC PROBLEMS

Italy's relatively large population is densely concentrated in the narrow coastal lowlands and river valleys of this mountainous peninsula. Thus its population and industrial centers are particularly vulnerable to air attack, and the homeland of the originator of the concept of modern strategic air bombardment (Giulio Douhet) is perhaps more susceptible to this controversial form of warfare than any other major power.

As demonstrated in World War II, Italy's elongated coast line is vulnerable to hostile amphibious operations. This vulnerability is to some extent offset by the mountain barrier of the Alps in the north, and the central spine of the Apennines, which create effective obstacles to military movement in all directions in the Italian peninsula.

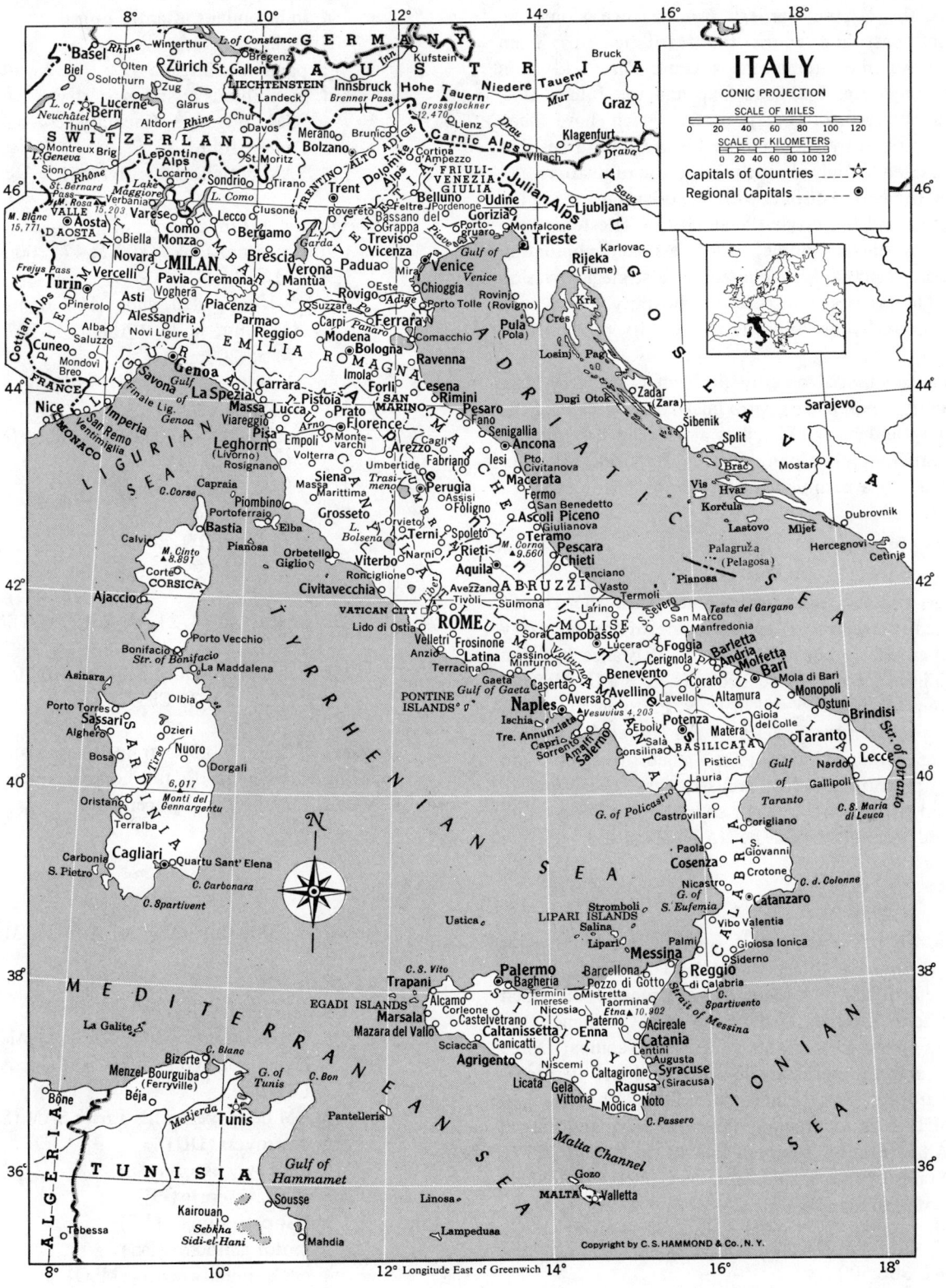

There are three principal and traditional overland invasion routes across the Alpine barrier: from France along the Mediterranean coast and across the Maritime Alps; from Germany and Austria through the Brenner Pass; and from Yugoslavia through the Ljubljana Gap and the Julian Alps. There are a number of other passes which have been successfully exploited by the innumerable invasion forces that have been attracted to Italy through the course of history.

There is an irredentist dispute with Yugoslavia involving the Istrian Peninsula and the major Italian city of Trieste and the Yugoslav city of Rijeka (Fiume), where a mixed population (including about 200,000 Slavs) inhabiting a strategic invasion route region has prompted dispute and hostility in the past, and creates serious defense and internal security problems for Italy.

Italy's greatest internal security problem is the very large Communist Party, comprising approximately 25 percent of the electorate. Italy and its NATO allies are forced to conclude that a substantial number of these would provide direct or indirect support to a communist bloc enemy in the event of hostilities.

MILITARY ASSISTANCE

A bilateral military assistance alliance with the United States has greatly facilitated the equipping of the relatively large Italian armed forces. US military assistance totalled nearly $2.3 billion from 1950 to 1967. There is a US Military Advisory Group of about 35 still in Italy. Partly as a result of the off-shore procurement policies of the United States, and partly through Italian and joint allied research and development projects, Italian industry has been greatly benefitted, and has become a major supplier of American and Italian-designed weapons within the NATO alliance.

ALLIANCES

Italy is a UN member and is one of the four major contributors of military forces to the NATO alliance; Italian forces form essentially the entire force structure of Allied Forces, Southern Europe. Within the NATO alliance the United States maintains in Italy a small combat force headquarters, and the necessary logistical support elements: the South European Task Force, or SETAF. The principal mission of SETAF is to provide nuclear artillery and missile support to Allied Forces, Southern Europe, in Italy. In 1973 the United States opened a submarine base on La Maddalena Island, north of Sardinia.

ARMY

Personnel: 306,500

Organization:

    2 armored divisions* and 1 independent calvalry brigade* with M-47, M-60 and Leopard tanks

*Assigned to NATO

    5 infantry divisions*
    4 independent infantry brigades
    5 alpine brigades
    1 parachute brigade
    1 amphibious regiment
    1 SSM brigade* (including 4 battalions with Honest John)
    4 SAM battalions* with Hawk

Major Equipment Inventory:

    1,200 medium tanks (800 M-47, 200 M-60, 200 Leopard)
    3,300 M-113 APCs
        self-propelled guns (M-7 65mm, M-109 155mm, M-36 170mm, M-107 175mm, M-55 203mm)
        howitzers (105mm, 120mm, 155mm, 105mm pack)
        antitank guided missiles (Mosquito, Cobra, SS-11)
        SSM (Honest John)
        SAM (Hawk)
    On order: TOW, 26 CH-47

Army Aviation:

    220 aircraft (60 L-21, 60 L-19, 100 SM-1019 fixed wing)
    260 helicopters (50 AB-47, 50 AB-204, 50 AB-205, 84 AB-206, 26 CH-47C)

Reserves: About 700,000 trained reservists are available to bring active units to full combat strength, to create new units, or to act as replacements.

NAVY

Personnel: 41,000 (including Air Arm and Marines)

Major Units:

    9 submarines (SS)
    3 GM cruisers with Terrier SAM and ASW helicopters (one with ASROC ASW missiles; CLG)
    3 GM destroyers with Tartar SAM (DDG)
    5 destroyers (DD)
  10 destroyer escorts (DE)
    8 coastal escorts (PF)
    9 fast patrol boats (PT)
    5 motor gunboats (PG)
    4 ocean minesweepers (MSO)
  37 coastal minesweepers (MSC)
  20 inshore minesweepers (MSI)
    2 amphibious transport ships (AKA)
    2 landing ships tank (LST)

1 marine infantry battalion

Naval Aviation:
- 2 squadrons with 30 S-2 aircraft
- 1 squadron with 18 Atlantic
- 60 ASW helicopters (24 AB-204 and 12 A-106 embarked; 24 SH-3D shore based)

Principal Naval Bases: Spezia, Naples, Taranto, Ancona, Brindisi, Genoa, Leghorn, Augusta, Venice

Reserves: 140,000 men available for rapid mobilization.

AIR FORCE

Personnel: 69,500

Organization:
- 6 air regions: headquarters at Rome, Milan, Bari, Padua, Sicily, Sardinia
- 2 fighter-bomber squadrons* (F-104G)
- 2 fighter-bomber squadrons* (F-104S)
- 2 fighter-bomber squadrons* (G-91Y)
- 3 light-attack/reconnaissance squadrons* (G-91R)
- 1 AWX fighter-interceptor squadron* (F-86K)
- 5 AWX fighter-interceptor squadrons* (F-104S)
- 3 fighter-reconnaissance squadrons (RF-104G, RF-84F)
- 3 transport squadrons* (C-119, C-130E; C-119 to be replaced by FIAT G-222)
- 2 transport squadrons (PD-808, Convair 440, DC-6)
- 2 SAR squadrons (HU-16, AB-204 helicopters)
- 12 Nike-Hercules SAM groups*

Major Aircraft Types:
- 366 combat aircraft
  - 150 fighter-bombers (F-104, G-91)
  - 54 G-91 light attack/reconnaissance aircraft
  - 90 F-104 AWX fighter-interceptors
  - 18 F-86K AWX fighter-interceptors
  - 54 fighter reconnaissance aircraft (RF-104, RF-84F)
- 742 other aircraft
  - 106 transports (34 C-130, 40 C-119, 32 G-222)
  - 38 liaison/transports (PD-808, Convair 440, DC-6, P-166)
  - 440 miscellaneous trainers/support (MB-326, G-91, TF-104, P-148, P-166)
  - 158 helicopters (60 AB-204, 90 AB-205, 2 AB-206, 6 AB-47)

*Assigned to NATO

On Order: 20 Agusta S-61B to replace HU-16; 40 F-104

Principal Air Bases: Vigna de Valle, Cageari, Taranto, Milan, Augusta, Grottaligia, Amendola, Alghero, Grossetto, Brindisi, Bari, Ciampino, Licce, Latina, Liriate, Foggia, Raisi, Genoa, Cameri, Pisa, Catania, Albenga

PARAMILITARY

There is an 86,000-man *Carabinieri*. This superbly trained force performs internal security, frontier guard, and military police duties. Because of the insurgency potential in Italy, the *Carabinieri* should not be considered as normally available to reinforce the Army; however, as demonstrated in World War II, the combat potentialities of this corps are probably superior to any comparable number of Army infantry troops. There are 30,000 other security personnel.

LUXEMBOURG

Grand Duche de Luxembourg
Grand Duchy of Luxembourg

POWER POTENTIAL STATISTICS

Area: 999 square miles
Population: 400,000

Total Active Armed Forces: 900 (including Gendarmerie; 0.23% population)
Gross National Product: $1.2 billion ($3,000 per capita)
Annual Military Expenditures: $10.8 million (0.90% GNP)
Iron and Steel Production: 9.8 million metric tons (largest per-capita production in the world)
Electric Power Output: 2.4 billion kwh
Civil Air Fleet: 4 jet, 3 turboprop transports

POLITICO-MILITARY POLICIES AND POSTURE

The government of Luxembourg abandoned its traditionally neutral policy at the close of World War II, and has since been an enthusiastic partner in all Western European mutual security agreements as a member of the Benelux bloc. A member of NATO, Luxembourg maintains only a nominal armed force, composed of one light infantry battalion of 550 men. US military assistance to Luxembourg since 1950 has totalled slightly more than $8 million, most of which was provided in the early 1950s. Military service is voluntary; enlistment is for three years. The Gendarmerie is 350 strong.

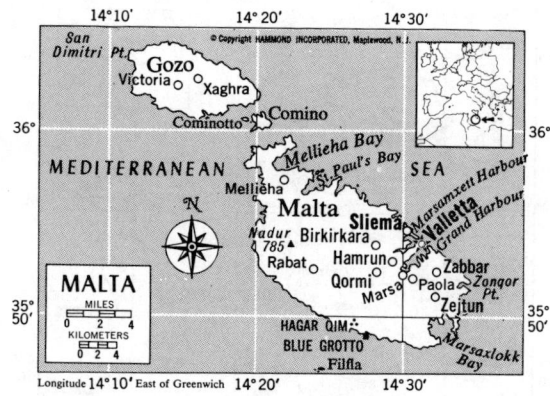

MALTA

POWER POTENTIAL STATISTICS

Area: 122 square miles
Population: 325,000
Total Active Armed Forces: (None (police only)
Gross National Product: $298 million ($917 per capita)
Electric Power Output: 140 million kwh
Merchant Fleet: 23 ships; 34,500 gross tons
Civil Air Fleet: 4 jets (on lease from BEA)

POLITICO-MILITARY POLICIES AND POSTURE

Part of the British Empire and headquarters of the British Mediterranean Fleet since 1814, Malta received independence in 1964 as a parliamentary state within the Commonwealth. Since independence the principal features of Malta's politico-military policies were, until 1971, its continuing close relationship with Britain and its new relationship with NATO. Both stemmed from Malta's strategic location at midpoint in the Mediterranean Sea and between Sicily and North Africa. as well as its important dockyard and several fine harbors. Concurrent with independence, Malta and Britain signed a 10-year Mutual Defense and Assistance Agreement whereby Britain retained the right to station armed forces on Malta, and in return agreed to provide $140 million in financial assistance during the period.

With the election of a Labour parliament in June 1971, Malta denounced the existing treaty and demanded of Britain nearly twice the remuneration for base rights, and increased economic aid. Malta also expelled the headquarters of NATO's Naval Force South, and cancelled the US 6th Fleet visiting rights. The UK accepted the increased base right fee and paid for a half year at the new rate, only to have the Maltese premier demand more. The NATO Council took account of the situation and began negotiations with Malta in January 1972. On March 26, a seven-year defense agreement was signed. It provides for a $37 million NATO rental fee for base rights, a compromise figure. Malta also gained increased economic aid.

No regular military force is maintained, internal security being provided by a 1,200-man police force, equipped with four Bell 47 helicopters.

NETHERLANDS

Koninkrijk der Nederlanden
Kingdom of the Netherlands

POWER POTENTIAL STATISTICS

Area: 14,140 square miles
Population: 13,400,000
Total Active Armed Forces: 113,500 (0.84% population)
Gross National Product: $57.2 billion ($4,269 per capita)
Annual Military Expenditures: $1.04 billion (1.8% GNP)
Steel Production: 5.6 million metric tons
Iron Production: 4.2 million metric tons
Fuel Production: Coal: 2.8 million metric tons
    Crude Oil: 1.6 million metric tons
    Refined Petroleum Products: 118.6 million metric tons
    Gas: 58.4 billion cubic meters
Electric Power Output: 49.6 billion kwh
Merchant Fleet: 786 ships; 3.3 million gross tons
Civil Air Fleet: 93 jet, 15 turboprop, 278 piston transports

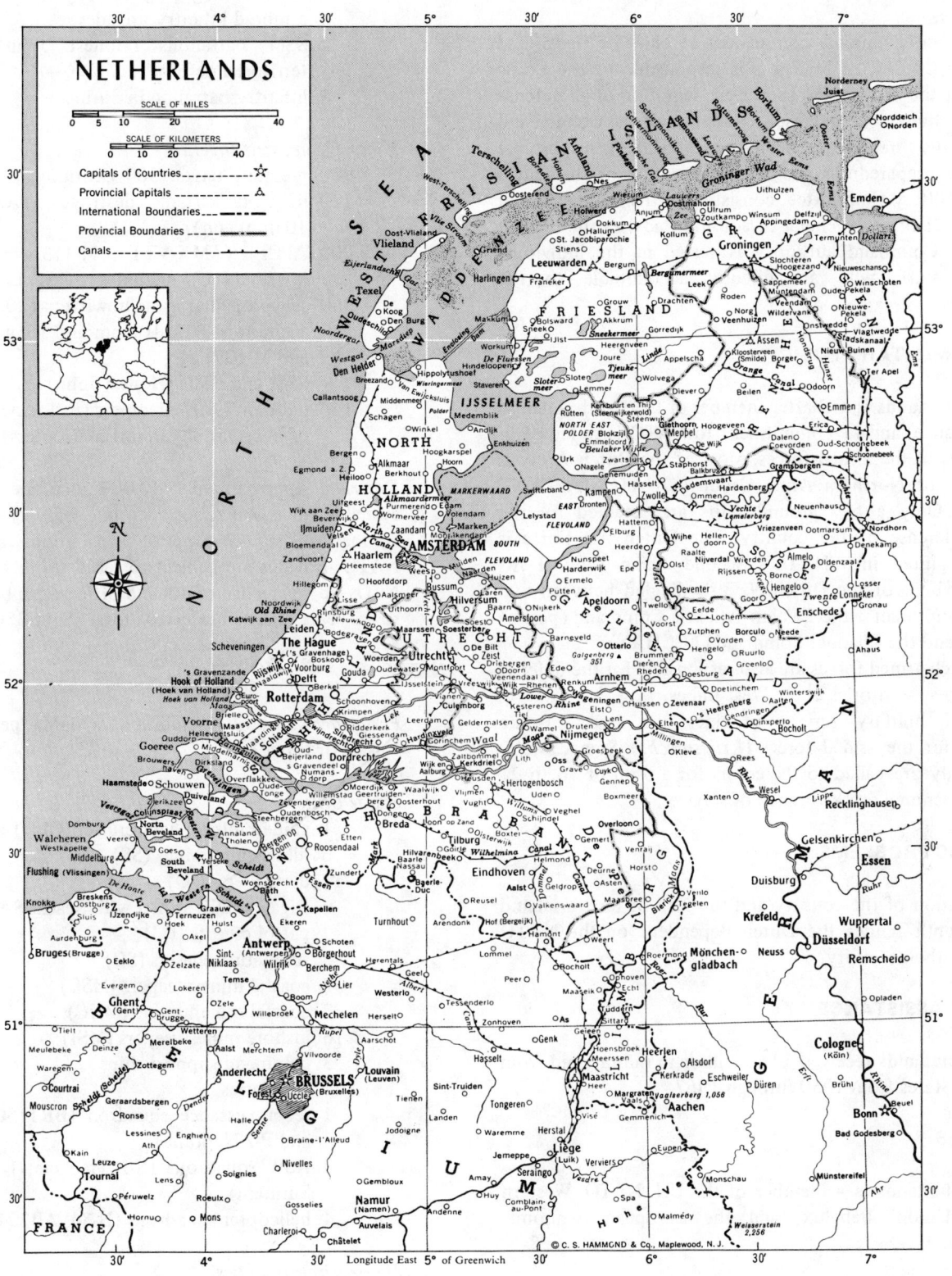

DEFENSE STRUCTURE

The Queen is nominal commander in chief of the armed forces. The Council of Ministers is responsible to the Prime Minister for the preparation and implementation of all defense plans. The Minister of Defense, as member of the Council and assisted by his three service Secretaries of State, is responsible for military preparedness and the organization of the armed forces. A Military Committee, consisting of the three chiefs of staff and a chairman (general or admiral), advises the civilian authorities. Command authority is vested in the individual chiefs of staff, who are directly accountable to the government.

POLITICO-MILITARY POLICY

The Netherlands is a charter member of the North Atlantic Treaty Alliance, and its commitment to NATO is reflected in the missions of the armed forces. Most of the Dutch Army is assigned to the Northern Army Group of NATO's AFCENT Command. Only a few ground units are retained for the territorial defense of the country. The Dutch Air Force is largely integrated into NATO's Second Allied Tactical Air Force. The bulk of the Dutch Navy is divided between two NATO commitments: the Eastern Atlantic Command (part of ACLANT) and the Channel Command (ACCHAN)

The Dutch armed forces are also responsible for the defense of the overseas territories in the West Indies.

Universal military service provides the bulk of the manpower for the armed forces (*Krijgsmacht*). Some 50,000 men annually are called to the colors for a term of 16 to 21 months, depending on the branch of service.

STRATEGIC PROBLEMS

The location of the country and the lack of territorial and air-space depth render the Dutch dependent on the NATO Alliance for their security.

MILITARY ASSISTANCE

The Netherlands received $1.23 billion in military aid from the United States from 1950 through 1967.

ALLIANCES

The Netherlands is a member of the UN, NATO, Western European Union, Benelux, and the European Economic Community.

ARMY

Personnel: 73,000
Organization:
    1 corps (assigned to NATO)
    2 armored brigades
    4 armored infantry brigades
    2 SSM battalions (Honest John) units for territorial defense
    1 infantry battalion in Surinam

Major Equipment Inventory:
  900 medium tanks (500 Centurion, 400 Leopard)
  120 light tanks/tank destroyers (AMX-13 with 105mm gun)
2,000 APCs (AMX-VTT, M-113, DAF-YP-408, M-106, M-577; includes reserves)
  260 self-propelled guns/howitzers (203mm M-110, 175mm M-107, 105mm and 155mm AMX-105 and M-109)
      SSM launchers (Honest John)
  140 light aircraft/helicopters (including 3 squadrons of observation aircraft helicopters)

Reserve: Approximately 40,000 men are immediately available for mobilization into one infantry division plus combat and service support corps troops earmarked for NATO. Privates are subject to recall up to the age of 35; NCOs up to the age of 40; and officers can be recalled up to 45 years. Trained reservists total about 350,000.

NAVY

Personnel: 19,000 (including 2,900 Marines and 2,000 Naval Air Force)

Major Units:
  1 guided missile light cruiser (CLG)
  6 diesel submarines (SS)
12 destroyers (DD)
  6 frigates (DE; armed with Seacat SAMs)
  3 patrol escorts (PC)
  5 submarine chasers (SC)
32 coastal minesweepers (MSC)
  3 coastal minehunters (MHC)
16 inshore minesweepers (MSI)
  3 command support ships
40 auxiliaries
  1 reconnaissance squadron (BR1150 Atlantique and P-2 Neptune)
  3 ASW squadrons (S-2 Trackers; 1 squadron in Surinam)
  4 helicopter squadrons (H-34, AB204)

Major Aircraft Types:
  9 BR1150 Atlantique reconnaissance aircraft (replacing Neptunes)
15 P-2 Neptune reconnaissance aircraft
43 S-2 Tracker ASW aircraft

8   H-34 helicopters
12   Westland Wasp helicopters (carried on DEs)
7   AB204 helicopters

Missiles: SAM: Terrier and Seacat; ASM: Nord AS-12

Major Naval Bases: Valkenburg, Vlissengen, Den Helder

Reserves: About 10,000 reservists (including naval air and Marine personnel)

AIR FORCE

All Air Force units are assigned to NATO

Personnel: 21,500

Organization:
- 2 interceptor squadrons (F-104)
- 5 fighter-bomber squadrons (F-104, F-5)
- 1 reconnaissance squadron (RF-104)
- 1 transport squadron (Fokker F-27)
- 3 light aircraft squadrons (including helicopters; under Army command; Alouette III, L-21, Beaver)
- 20 SAM squadrons (12 Hawk, 8 Nike-Hercules)

Major Aircraft Types:
- 174 combat aircraft
  - 72 F-104 interceptors/fighter-bombers
  - 18 RF-104 fighter reconnaissance aircraft
  - 54 F-5 fighter-bombers
  - 30 F-5 fighter trainers
- 154 other aircraft
  - 12 F-27 transports
  - 70 miscellaneous trainer/support aircraft (L-21, Beaver, C-45, S-11)
  - 72 helicopters (Alouette III)

Major Air Bases: Bilze-Rijen, Deelen, Twenthe, Bolkel, Eindhoven, Soesterberg.

Reserves: About 20,000 trained reservists

PARAMILITARY

The State Police Corps, numbering 4,600, includes water, mounted, and motor police and is under the Ministry of Justice. The Royal Marechaussee (Gendarmerie) number about 3,200 men.

NORWAY

Kongeriket Norge
Kingdom of Norway

POWER POTENTIAL STATISTICS

Area: 149,150 square miles
Population: 4,000,000
Total Active Armed Forces: 35,900 (0.90% population)
Gross National Product: $16.8 billion ($4,200 per capita)
Annual Military Expenditures: $604.8 million (3.6% GNP)
Iron and Steel Production: 2.1 million metric tons
Aluminum Production: 529,000 metric tons
Fuel Production: Coal: 446,000 metric tons
   Crude Oil: 1.6 million metric tons
   Refined Petroleum Products: 6.3 million metric tons
   Manufactured Gas: 29.8 million cubic meters
Electric Power Output: 62.7 billion kwh
Merchant Fleet: 2,814 ships; 21.7 million gross tons
Civil Air Fleet: 10 jet, 8 turboprop, 15 piston transports (exclusive of the Norwegian-owned portion of SAS)

DEFENSE STRUCTURE

Norway is a constitutional monarchy; the King is the nominal commander in chief of the armed forces. Control is exercised, however, by the parliamentary Cabinet, with the Minister of Defense responsible for administering the three independent military services.

POLITICO-MILITARY POLICY

Before World War II Norway adhered to the traditional Scandinavian policy of neutrality. The experience of that war convinced Norwegians that neutrality will not deter an aggressor, and that Norwegian defense policy must be built upon a mutual security alliance, since Norway cannot possibly muster the military strength to defend itself against a major aggressor. Thus Norway has been a wholehearted participant in the NATO alliance but, to avoid offense to its Soviet neighbor (Norway is the only NATO country, except Turkey, with a mutual frontier with Russia), it has consistently refused to allow allied troop units, or bases, or stored nuclear weapons, on Norwegian soil.

NATO maintains a regional headquarters, that of Commander in Chief North (CINCNORTH) at Kolsaas near Oslo. Officers of various NATO nations are represented on the staff. NATO units visit Norway to participate in maneuvers.

Norway has a battalion in the UN force on Cyprus, and furnished a unit for the UN Emergency Force in the Gaza Strip until evacuated in June 1967.

Norway's armed forces are maintained by conscription, with an annual call-up of more than 20,000 young men.

108 ALMANAC OF WORLD MILITARY POWER

Service is for 12 months in the Army, and 15 months in the Navy and Air Force. Most of the Norwegian armed forces are earmarked for AFNORTH (Allied Forces Northern Europe).

STRATEGIC PROBLEMS

Norway's extreme length (its eastern boundary is over 1,600 miles long), the rugged nature of the interior of the country (particularly in the north), and the near total absence of a ground communications network in the north, pose almost insuperable defense problems, particularly near the Soviet border.

Introduction of Soviet submarines into the numerous ice-free fjords would facilitate interdiction of North Atlantic sea lanes, and thus the loss of even northern Norway would represent a severe setback to NATO. In addition to the coastal invasion route from Kerkenes near the Soviet-Norwegian border, a serious threat is posed by the Finnish wedge, a salient of Finland with a good road which stretches close to the coast in the strategic Bardufoss-Tromso-Harstad area. A Soviet offensive on this axis could quickly seize northern Norway.

Problems of defense are compounded by the Arctic climate, and by a deeply indented, sparsely inhabited coastline more than 2,000 miles long, very vulnerable to surprise amphibious attack. The nature of these defense problems was thoroughly demonstrated during World War II.

Near the Soviet Union on the strategic polar route from the US, the archipelago of Spitsbergen (Svalbard) was awarded to Norway in 1920 by an international treaty, which also prohibited establishment of naval or military bases. There are a number of active coal mines on the islands, worked by some 700 Norwegians and 2,000 Russians. Beginning in 1944 Russia sought revision of the treaty to include joint Soviet-Norwegian defense measures. Norway has refused to consider this without the concurrence of all treaty signatories, which has not been forthcoming.

It is believed that there are also extensive oil and gas deposits in the continental shelf of the Barents Sea between Spitsbergen and the Soviet Union. Norway and the USSR have overlapping claims to this area, and negotiations on these claims were to be held between the two governments in the fall of 1974.

MILITARY ASSISTANCE

Since 1950 Norway has received $908.2 million in American military aid. The US Military Advisory Group in Norway numbers about 30.

ALLIANCES

Norway is a member of the NATO alliance. Otherwise it has maintained a strict neutrality in international relations and, as noted above, has to some extent limited its involvement in NATO. Norway is a member of the UN.

ARMY

Personnel: 18,000

Organization:
- 5 regional commands divided into land defense districts
- 2 regimental combat teams (one in north, one in south)
- 4 tank companies

Major Equipment Inventory:
- 80 medium tanks (M-48)
- 78 medium tanks (Leopard)
- 47 light tanks (M-24)
- armored cars (M-8)
- 30 artillery pieces (including M-109 155mm SP howitzers)
- APCs (M-113 and BV-202)
- 40mm AA
- 34 light aircraft (L-4, 0-1)
- 10 helicopters

Reserve: About 160,000 men who will be organized into 11 RCTs, supporting units, and territorial defense forces.

NAVY

Personnel: 8,500 (including 800 coast artillerymen)

Major Units:
- 5 destroyer escorts (DE)
- 15 coastal submarines (SS)
- 5 coastal minelayers (MMC)
- 10 coastal minesweepers (MSC)
- 2 patrol escorts/submarine chasers (PCE)
- 20 gunboats/fast patrol boats (PG/PBF; refitting with Penguin SSM)
- 26 torpedo boats (PT, six with Penguin SSM)
- 7 landing craft (LCT)
- 14 auxiliaries
- coast defense artillery battalions

Main Naval Bases: Haakonsvern, Harstad, Tromso, Trondheim, Bergen

Reserves: 18,000 trained reservists

AIR FORCE

Personnel: 9,400

110 ALMANAC OF WORLD MILITARY POWER

Organization:
- 2 fighter-interceptor squadrons (F-104)
- 5 fighter-bomber squadrons (F-5)
- 1 reconnaissance squadron (RF-5)
- 2 maritime patrol squadrons (P-3 and HU-16)
- 1 transport squadron (C-130)
- 2 helicopter squadrons (UH-1, Bell 47, Sea King)
- 4 SAM battalions (Nike-Hercules)

Major Aircraft Types:
- 141 combat aircraft
  - 38 F-104 interceptors
  - 80 F-5 fighter-bombers
  - 16 RF-5 fighter reconnaissance aircraft
  - 5 P-3 maritime patrol aircraft
  - 2 HU-16 maritime patrol aircraft
- 128 other aircraft
  - 6 C-130 transports
  - 4 Twin Otter light transports
  - 2 Falcon 20 light transports
  - 22 miscellaneous transports
  - 3 PBY patrol/fishing protection aircraft
  - 49 miscellaneous trainer/support aircraft (25 Safir, 20 L-18, 4 Twin Otter)
  - 44 helicopters (UH-1, Bell 47, Sea King)

Reserves: 19,000 trained reservists. Twelve light antiaircraft defense battalions.

Major Air Bases: Stavanger, Bodo, Bardufoss, Andoya (Lofoten Islands)

PARAMILITARY

There is a highly organized Home Guard consisting of 75,000 individuals. Most of them are in Army units, linked to the nation's territorial defense area commands. There are also a few Navy and Air Force Home Guard units. All these are organized in small groups and platoons with specific defense missions in their home localities. Weapons are kept at home, and a relatively high state of readiness is maintained by periodic drills and alerts.

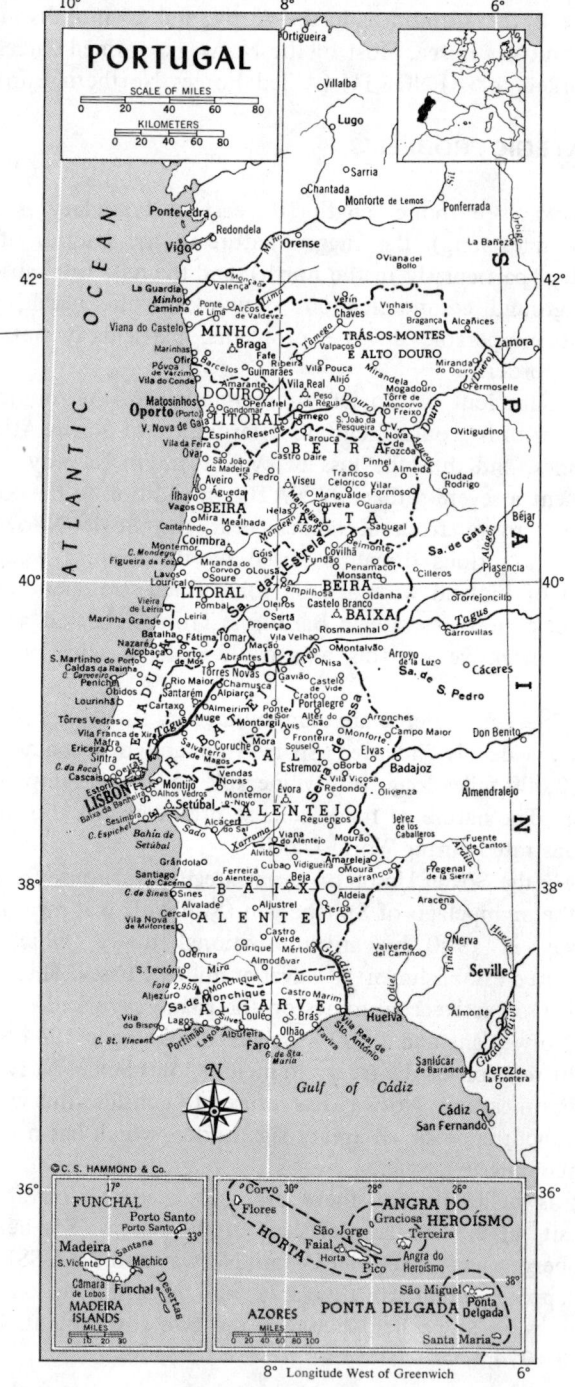

PORTUGAL
Republica Portuguesa
Portuguese Republic

POWER POTENTIAL STATISTICS

Area: 35,553 square miles (including the Azores and Madeira)

Population: 9,200,000
Total Active Armed Forces: 217,000 (2.36% population)
Gross National Product: $10.5 billion ($1,141 per capita)
Annual Military Expenditure: $524 million (4.99% GNP)
Fuel Production: Coal: 253,000 metric tons
  Refined Petroleum Products: 4.4 million metric tons
Electric Power Output: 7.9 billion kwh
Merchant Fleet: 384 ships; 925,793 gross tons
Civil Air Fleet: 18 jet, 2 turboprop, 14 piston transports

DEFENSE STRUCTURE

In April 1974 forty years of civilian dictatorship in Portugal came to an end when the Armed Forces Movement seized the government and installed a seven-man "junta of national salvation." The new President, General Antonio de Spinola, moved immediately to change established orders and procedures throughout the country. The new President is in fact, as well as nominally, the commander in chief of the armed forces, exercising close central direction over the three partly integrated military services.

The Portuguese armed forces are organized within two major joint commands: the Home Command, which includes Continental Portugal, Madeira, and the Azores; and the Overseas Command, which includes all other overseas provinces.

POLITICO-MILITARY POLICY

Portugal has traditionally relied upon its remoteness from the center of Europe, as well as its long-standing alliance with Great Britain (since 1381; now largely nominal) for external security. It is also greatly influenced by events in Spain, its larger neighbor. Thus, the conservative, highly centralized regime of former Prime Minister Salazar (ideologically pro-Franco) remained neutral in World War II but (under some pressures from Britain and the US) nevertheless provided air base rights to the Allies. After World War II the strongly anti-communist Salazar regime brought Portugal into NATO as a charter member.

The armed forces are maintained by conscription; until recently the terms of service have been 24 months for the Army, 36 months for the Air Force, and 48 months for the Navy. In mid-1967, however, due to the pressure of guerrilla warfare in the African colonies, the maximum term for all services was increased to 48 months. Before the Spinola coup many young men emigrated to escape conscription. Another result of the overseas hostilities has been to accept more women volunteers for non-combat military service, in order to make more men available for troop duty.

STRATEGIC PROBLEMS

Portugal determinedly opposed the anticolonial tide of international affairs after World War II. As a result, there has been considerable nationalistic unrest, including extensive guerrilla conflict, in most of Portugal's remaining overseas territories: Angola, Mozambique, Portuguese Guinea, and the islands of Sao Tome and Principe in the African region; Macao (on the Chinese coast near Hong Kong) and Timor (in Indonesia) in the Far East. In 1961 Portugal lost its three small Indian provinces to Indian occupation. Problems of nationalism do not affect two of Portugal's Atlantic island possessions: the Azores and Madeira. The Cape Verde Islands, however, have close ties with Portuguese Guinea. Spinola announced in July 1974 his government's plan to grant independence to the three African colonies promptly, the first probably being Portuguese Guinea, or Guinea-Bissau.

The sudden liberalization of the Portuguese government under Spinola, after so many years of repression, encouraged excesses of liberalism which for a while came closely to anarchy. Spinola and the armed forces have been quietly but firmly re-establishing controls, while endeavoring to avoid the dictatorial measures of the former government. The poverty of Portugal will make it difficult to achieve stability and security without inhibiting the new-found democratic liberties of the Portuguese people.

MILITARY ASSISTANCE

Portugal has received $327.2 million in military aid from the United States since 1950. The present US Military Advisory Group in Portugal numbers about 20.

ALLIANCES

Portugal is a member of the UN and the NATO Alliance. It also has bilateral treaties with the United Kingdom, with the United States, and with Spain. The treaty with the United States provides base rights in the Azores. The Iberian Defense Alliance with Spain provides a convenient NATO link with the Franco government.

ARMY

Personnel: 179,000

Organization:
- 7 regional commands
- 2 infantry divisions (under strength; one subordinated to NATO, the other to joint Iberian defense)
- 21 infantry regiments
- 13 independent infantry battalions
- 13 independent infantry companies
- 7 battalions of cacadores
- 7 artillery regiments (5 light, 2 medium)
- 6 artillery groups
- 5 independent artillery batteries
- 1 coast artillery regiment
- 1 antiaircraft artillery regiment
- 2 independent AA battalions
- 3 independent AA and coastal batteries
- 4 cavalry regiments
- 1 cavalry group
- 5 independent cavalry batteries
- 1 MP regiment
- 2 tank regiments

1 engineer regiment
3 engineer battalions
1 signal regiment
3 signal battalions
1 railway battalion
logistic units

Major Equipment Inventory:
medium tanks (M-47 and M-4)
light tanks (M-41)
armored cars (Humber Mk IV and EBR-75)
scout cars (AML-60)
200 light artillery pieces (mostly 140mm howitzers)

Reserve Forces: There are at least 550,000 trained reserves, available to bring the existing units up to strength, and to create new units in the event of national mobilization.

NAVY

Personnel: 19,500 (including 3,400 in the Marines)

Major Units:
8 frigates (DE)
4 diesel submarines (SS)
9 coastal minesweepers (MSC)
6 submarine chasers/corvettes (SC)
29 coastal patrol vessels (PG)
25 patrol launches (YP)
6 landing craft (LCT)
58 landing craft (LCU, LCM)
12 auxiliaries

Major Naval Base: Lisbon

Reserves: 12,000 reservists (including Marines)

AIR FORCE

Personnel: 18,500 (including 4,000 paratroops)

Organization:
2 light bomber squadrons (B-26 and PV-2)
1 fighter-interceptor squadron (F-86)
2 fighter-bomber squadrons (G-91)
6 COIN flights (T-6)
1 maritime patrol squadron (P-2)
1 transport group (C-47, C-45, DC-6, Noratlas)
1 paratroop regiment

Major Aircraft Types:
133 combat aircraft
6 B-26 light bombers
10 PV-2 light bombers
25 F-86 fighter-interceptors
30 G-91 fighter-bombers
50 T-6 armed trainers
12 P-2 maritime patrol aircraft
306 other aircraft
65 transports (20 Noratlas, 20 C-47, 10 DC-6, 15 C-45)
70 Do-27 light transports
78 trainers (13 T-33, 25 T-37, 40 T-6)
93 helicopters (2 Alouette II, 80 Alouette III, 11 Puma)

Major Air Bases: Montijo, Tanoas, Sintra, Porto, Ota, Alverca, Jacinto

Reserves: Approximately 30,000 reservists, including parachute troops.

PARAMILITARY

There are 9,700 active duty personnel in the National Republic Guard for internal security.

SPAIN

Estado Espanol
Spanish State

POWER POTENTIAL STATISTICS

Area: 194,884 square miles
Population: 34,200,000
Total Active Armed Forces: 366,000 (including Guardia Civil; 1.07% population)
Gross National Product: $45.2 billion ($1,322 per capita)
Annual Military Expenditures: $1.2 billion (2.65% GNP)
Steel and Iron Production: 12.7 million metric tons
Fuel Production: Coal: 13.5 million metric tons
Crude Oil: 140,000 metric tons
Refined Petroleum Products: 38.7 million metric tons
Electric Power: 59.9 billion kwh
Merchant Fleet: 2,279 ships; 3.9 million gross tons
Civil Air Fleet: 117 jet, 21 turboprop, 20 piston transports

DEFENSE STRUCTURE

The *Caudillo* (Leader) of Spain for 35 years has been General Francisco Franco, serving as Chief of State, Prime Minister, and Commander in Chief of the Armed Forces. The armed forces are administered through three separate, independent ministries: Army, Navy, and Air. The principal

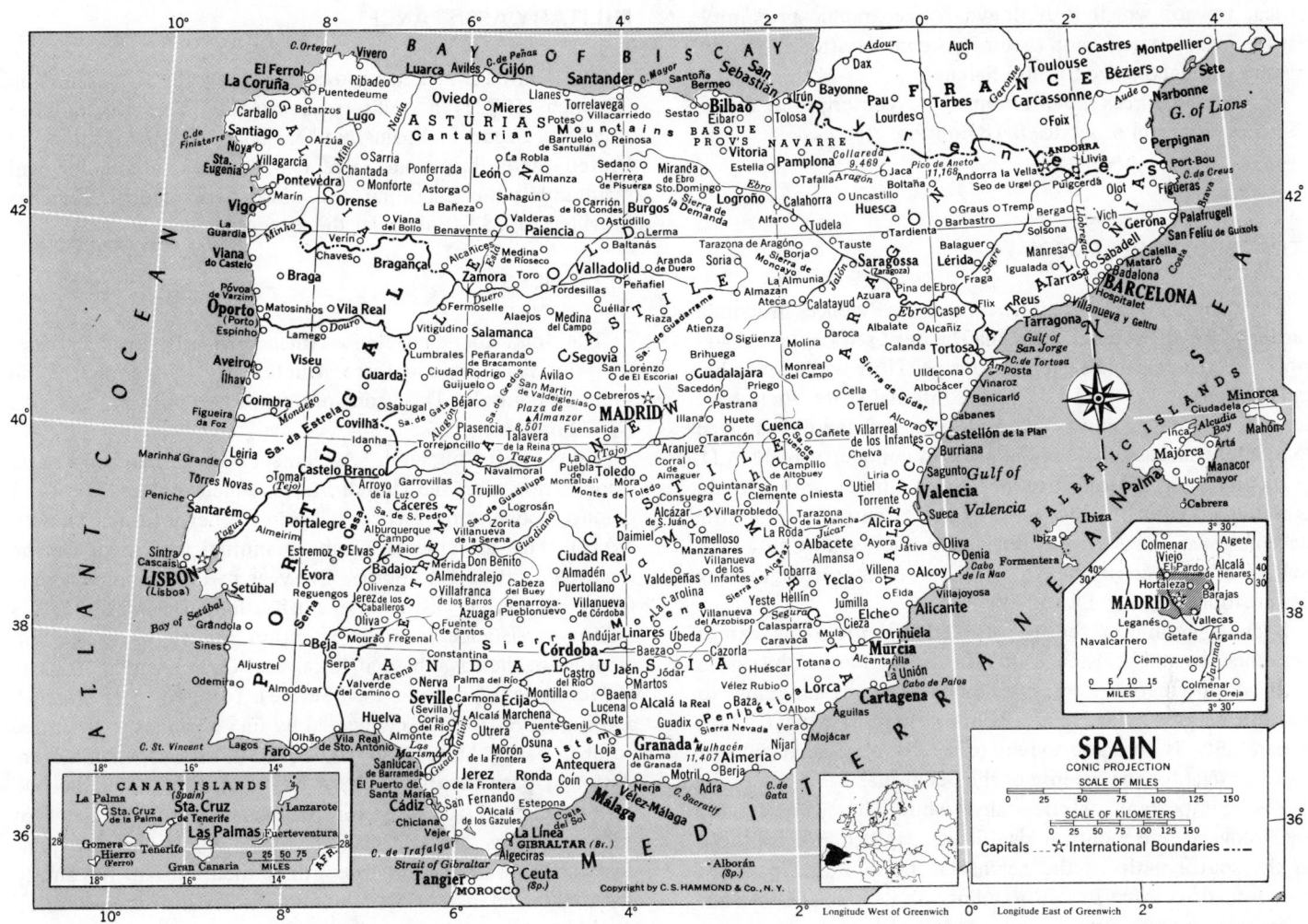

military planning and supervisory agency for all of the armed services is the High General Staff of the Army. The Army is the predominant service.

In 1969 General Franco announced Prince Juan Carlos, grandson of the last King of Spain, as his eventual successor as Head of State. In July 1971, the Prince, aged 33, was named to act for the *Caudillo*, if Franco should be ill or out of the country. On July 19, 1974, the 81-year old general, hospitalized with a serious illness, delegated power to his designated heir for an indefinite period.

POLITICO-MILITARY POLICY

Since the victory of General Franco's Nationalist forces in the Spanish Civil War (1936-1939), Spanish foreign and military policy has been guided by two major objectives that have not always been easy to reconcile: neutrality and anticommunism. Recently, Spanish foreign and military policy has sought to end the isolation in which Spain found itself after World War II, when it was pointedly excluded from the United Nations. In 1955, Spain's long-standing application to the UN was accepted (at the same time as those of 15 other nations). Today, Spain is a member of most major world organizations, and some Western regional ones as well. In 1970 Spain and the European Economic Community (EEC) concluded a preferential trade agreement, and Spain contributes to Western defense through bilateral military cooperation with the United States, but its full integration in the Western economic organization is still opposed in some countries, and Spain is not a member of NATO.

Relations with Eastern Europe also have been strengthened. In 1972 a commercial agreement with the USSR was signed; in 1973 diplomatic relations with the German Democratic Republic (as well as the People's Republic of China) were established. Spain has commercial and consular agreements with most Eastern European countries. It has consistently supported the Arabs in their dispute with Israel, and it maintains generally cordial relations with the countries of

Africa, toward which it is drawn by geographic proximity, history, economics, and security considerations, despite pressures to decolonize Spanish Sahara.

The armed forces are maintained by conscription; for all branches, the term of service is 18 months.

STRATEGIC PROBLEMS

The combination of remoteness and the Pyrenees mountain barrier make the Iberian peninsula the most self-contained and most easily defensible region in Europe. Thus, while Spain has had perhaps more than its share of internal strife, there have been few foreign invasions, and none of these has been completely successful since the Moslem conquest of 711 A.D.

By its geographical location, Spain shares with Britain Gibraltar's control of the western entrance to the Mediterranean Sea. Spain retains footholds at Ceuta and Melilla in Morocco on the African shore, further strengthening this position of control.

Spain's natural defensive strength is to some extent weakened by the existence of Portugal in the southwestern sixth of the Iberian Peninsula; Spain is most vulnerable to invasion across the land frontier with Portugal. This vulnerability is to some extent offset by a bilateral alliance with Portugal for the defense of the peninsula.

Less important strategically, but of considerable psychological and political significance, is Britain's foothold on the southern tip of the peninsula at Gibraltar. Spain has long wished to force Britain to relinquish its base at Gibraltar.

Spain's greatest strategic weaknesses today, as for several centuries, lie in severe internal divisions, of which two are particularly significant: political opposition to the Falangist regime of General Franco, and the Basque separatist movement.

The passage of time, and the institution of severely repressive measures followed by a gradual and seemingly wise relaxation of repression, have done much to heal the bitterness which characterized the Spanish Civil War. Nonetheless, there is apparently still considerable Republican sentiment in Spain, which is to some extent supported by liberal opposition to the conservative dictatorship. Many Spaniards are dissatisfied by slow, and only partial, liberalization of the government. Whether Juan Carlos can remain in power on Franco's death is questionable. A self-styled "democratic Spanish junta," with expatriate members ranging from communists to monarchists, announced in July 1974 the launching of a campaign to restore democratic rule in Spain.

The centuries-old effort of the Basques to achieve autonomy is not in itself a serious threat to the central authority of the Spanish government. Incidents occur from time to time, most significantly the assassination of the Spanish Premier in December 1973.

MILITARY ASSISTANCE

The United States has provided Spain with $627.4 million (through 1972) in military assistance. The US Military Advisory Group in Spain numbers about 60. In addition the United States has made large expenditures in building and maintaining the major air and naval bases which Spain has provided to US forces under the agreement.

ALLIANCES

The Joint Iberian Defense Alliance with Portugal provides for joint planning and force structure for the defense of the Iberian Peninsula. This is one of Spain's two informal ties with NATO nations.

The 1970 bilateral Agreement of Friendship and Cooperation with the United States, which replaced the 1953 defense cooperation accord, is Spain's other informal tie with NATO. This agreement, which by mutual agreement can be renewed in 1975 for another five-year period, is not a formal treaty requiring US Senate ratification. It authorizes US military assistance to Spain in return for the use of certain facilities at the naval base at Rota (near Cadiz), and at air bases at Moron de la Frontera (near Seville), Torrejon (near Madrid), and Zaragoza. Rota is connected by fuel pipelines to the three bomber bases. More than 10,000 US military personnel are stationed permanently at these bases. In July 1974, the two nations cleared the way for renegotiation of US leases of military bases on Spanish territory by issuing a joint declaration of agreement to continue their military ties and to coordinate defense efforts "within the Atlantic framework."

US-Spanish defense relations are overseen by a Joint Committee, co-chaired by the Spanish Foreign Minister and the US Ambassador to Spain. The US National Aeronautics and Space Administration (NASA) and the Spanish National Institute of Aerospace (INTA) jointly operate tracking stations in the Madrid area and the Canary Islands, under an agreement in force until 1984.

ARMY

Personnel: 220,000 (approximately 41,000 overseas, including 20,000 of the volunteer Spanish Foreign Legion)

Organization: 10 military regions (headquarters: Madrid, Seville, Valencia, Barcelona, Zaragoza, Burgos, Valladolid, La Coruna, Ceuta, Melilla) each accounting for one corps
- 1 armored division (cadre form)
- 2 mechanized/motorized infantry divisions (cadre form)
- 2 mountain divisions (cadre form)
- 12 independent infantry brigades

1 armored cavalry brigade
1 high mountain brigade
1 air transportable brigade
1 parachute brigade
2 artillery brigades
1 SAM battalion (Hawk)
various island and colonial garrisons: 8,000 in Canary Islands, 6,000 in Balearic Islands, 27,000 in Spanish Africa

Major Equipment Inventory:
- 365 medium tanks (M-47, M-48)
- 225 light tanks (M-24, M-41)
- scout and armored cars (M-3, M-8, AML-60/90)
- 50 APCs (M-113)
- 105mm, 155mm self-propelled guns
- 200 105mm, 155mm, 203mm howitzers
- 90mm self-propelled antitank guns
- Hawk SAM launchers
- 20 light aircraft (O-1, Do-27)
- 55 helicopters (AB-47, AB-205, AB-206)

Reserves: There are about 600,000 trained reservists in a so-called Home Army, for which weapons and equipment are believed to be incomplete. Some of these would be mobilized to form three infantry divisions in Spanish Africa from cadres now stationed there. The total mobilization capability could man about 40 divisions.

NAVY

Personnel: 47,500 (including 6,000 Marines)

Major Units:
- 1 ASW helicopter carrier (CVS)
- 1 heavy cruiser (CA)
- 23 destroyers (2 with helicopters; DD)
- 14 destroyer escorts/patrol escorts (DE/PF)
- 8 diesel submarines (SS)
- 2 midget submarines
- 6 frigate minelayers
- 12 fleet minesweepers (MSF)
- 16 coastal minesweepers (MSC)
- 3 attack transports (APA/AKA)
- 3 torpedo boats (PT)
- 2 ASW patrol vessels (PC, SC)
- 16 patrol boats and launches (YP)
- 1 landing ship dock (LSD)
- 3 landing ships tank (LST)
- 33 landing ships/craft (LSM, LCT, LCU)
- 43 auxiliaries
- 4 helicopter squadrons (49 helicopters: 10 Hughes 500, 4 Huey Cobra, 6 SH-3, 9 SH-19, 4 AB-204, 16 AB-47)
- 20 other aircraft (Piper light aircraft)

Major Naval Bases: Rota, Mallorca, Cartagena

Reserves: About 190,000 trained reservists, including Marines; no reserve fleet

AIR FORCE

Personnel: 33,500

Organization:
- 3 major commands: Air Defense, Tactical Air, Air Transport
- 5 interceptor squadrons (F-5, F-4)
- 2 fighter-bomber squadrons (Mirage III)
- 2 light bomber squadrons (He-111, being retired)
- 1 ASW squadron (HU-16)
- 1 anti-submarine squadron (P-3)
- 2 transport wings (C-54, Caribou, Azor)

Major Aircraft Types:
- 248 combat aircraft
  - 24 Mirage III EE fighter-bombers
  - 6 Mirage III BE fighter-bomber/trainers
  - 70 F-5 fighters
  - 36 F-4 interceptors
  - 73 HA-200 armed trainers
  - 19 HA-220 ground attack aircraft
  - 17 HU-16 ASW aircraft
  - 3 P-3 anti-submarine aircraft
- 229 other aircraft
  - 50 C-47 transports
  - 14 C-54 transports
  - 17 CASA 212 Aviocar transports
  - 12 Caribou transports
  - 4 C-130 transports
  - 3 KC-97 tankers
  - 1 Convair 440
  - 74 trainer/support aircraft (T-33, T-34, O-1, Do-27, T-6, CASA Azor)
  - 54 helicopters (AB-47, AB-205, AB-206)

On order: 15 Mirage F-1C, 8 AV-8 Harriers

Major Air Bases: Torrejon (Madrid), San Pablo y Moron (Seville), Valencia, Talavera la Real, Sanjurjo (Zaragoza), Valladolid, Tetuan, Palma, Las Palmas de Gran Canaria, Getafe

Reserves: 80,000 reservists

PARAMILITARY

There are 65,000 in the *Guardia Civil*, a highly trained, extremely efficient national gendarmerie; this is a volunteer force with officers assigned from the Army.

The reserve Home Army noted above performs home guard functions.

116 ALMANAC OF WORLD MILITARY POWER

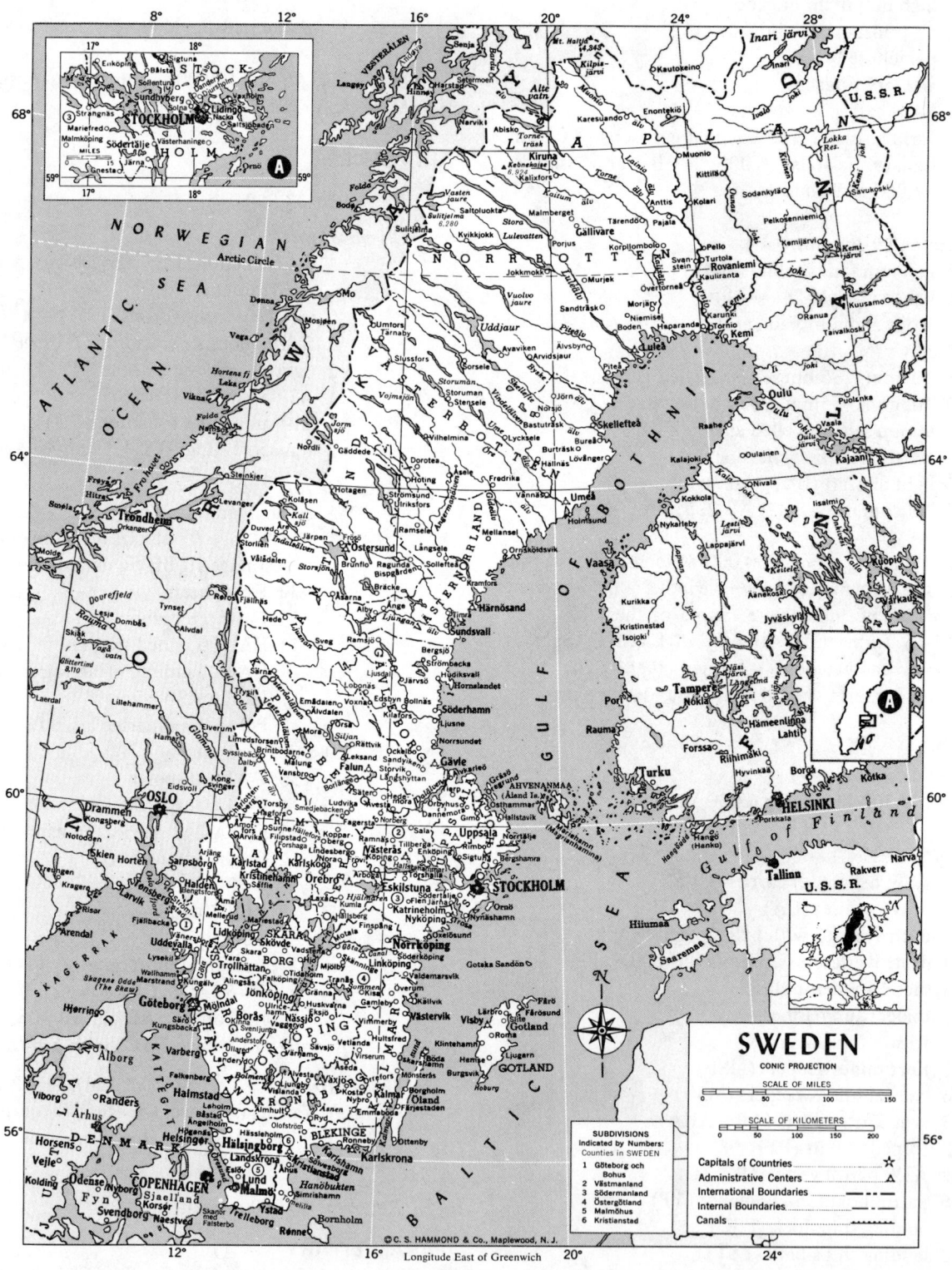

SWEDEN
Konungariket Sverige
Kingdom of Sweden

POWER POTENTIAL STATISTICS

Area: 173,648 square miles
Population: 8,200,000
Total Active Armed Forces: 87,300 (1.07% population)
Gross National Product: $42 billion ($5,121 per capita)
Annual Military Expenditures: $1.84 billion (4.38% GNP)
Steel and Iron Production: 7.84 million metric tons
Iron Ore Production: 33.28 million metric tons
Refined Petroleum Products: 11.8 million metric tons
Electric Power Output: 66.5 billion kwh
Merchant Fleet: 937 ships; 5 million gross tons
Civil Air Fleet: 80 jet, 5 turboprop, 58 piston transports (includes SAS)

DEFENSE STRUCTURE

The King is the supreme military authority of Sweden, but in a limited constitutional monarchy he exercises this responsibility through the Minister of Defense, who is politically responsible to the Prime Minister. Recent administrative changes have strengthened centralized operational and logistical control and surveillance by the Minister of Defense over the three loosely integrated military services (each of which has its own commander in chief). Overall military planning and coordination are performed by an integrated Defense Staff under a Supreme Commander who is responsible to the King through the Minister of Defense.

POLITICO-MILITARY POLICY

Since 1814, Sweden has avoided war through a policy of armed neutrality. Although unequivocally aligned with the Western powers in the bipolar world of post-World War II, Sweden has nonetheless adhered unswervingly to its policy of neutrality, and has refused to join NATO or any other form of military alliance. However, it has economic ties through membership in the European Free Trade Association (EFTA) and a trade agreement with the European Economic Community (EEC). Sweden (unlike Switzerland) came to the conclusion that membership in the United Nations would not compromise this policy of neutrality. Sweden has strongly supported the international police activities of the United Nations, and has contributed individuals and units to most of the UN observer teams or peace-preservation forces; Swedish diplomats and soldiers have played leading roles in many of these activities. Sweden has been critical of US policy in Southeast Asia; in 1969 it recognized the North Vietnamese government and three years later raised its charge at Hanoi to the rank of ambassador.

Sweden relies upon a policy of deterrence as well as neutrality in the preservation of its national security. As a result, for many years the Swedish armed forces have been more powerful, more modern, and better prepared than those of any other secondary power. To give credibility to its avowed determination to resist any aggression as bitterly and as effectively as possible, Sweden has been one of the world leaders in all aspects of military research, development, and production—with the notable exception of offensive nuclear weaponry. Sweden's armament industry is among the largest and most sophisticated of the secondary powers', producing heavy artillery, tanks, warships, high performance jet aircraft, and all the lesser weapons of war.

Typical of Sweden's defensive and deterrence posture has been the development of nuclear bombproof facilities for deter an aggressor, Sweden is probably capable of surviving all but a major nuclear assault, and of launching effective counterblows. There is an operational underground war headquarters; vast quantities of weapons and materiel are stored underground; even the largest warships can take refuge in deep harbors dug thousands of feet into coastal mountainsides; there are similar air facilities cut into inland mountainsides; a number of highways are especially designed for use as runways. Sweden's defense expenditure per capita is by far the highest in Europe, and exceeded in the world only by the United States (and possibly the USSR).

Additional evidence of national defensive determination is the policy of universal compulsory service in the armed forces. Every physically fit male citizen between the ages of 19 and 47 is required to serve in the armed forces. After a period of 10 months' training most of the conscripts are placed on indefinite leave. Thus while theoretically full-fledged members of the armed fforces, they are virtually reservists who are required to undergo periodic refresher training on an elaborate schedule. Administration is on a local, decentralized basis, and the total armed forces of Sweden—approximately 700,000 strong—can be mobilized into combat-ready units in a matter of hours.

STRATEGIC PROBLEMS

Sweden's long Baltic coastline makes it particularly vulnerable to amphibious assault, or devastating bombardment, by the forces of any nation controlling the Baltic. At present the only possibly hostile Baltic nation is the USSR. Because of this vulnerability, Sweden has strongly fortified the island of Gotland, which dominates the Baltic and is an important base for air and naval strike forces. It has a strong coastal defense system.

Thinly-populated northern Sweden, with its long frontier with Finland, is also vulnerable to possible Soviet overland attack, which could quickly drive across the intervening

Finnish territory. Sweden's concerns regarding these two vulnerabilities is reflected in its attitude in opposing fortification and defense of Finland's Aland Islands, which dominate the Northern Baltic and Gulf of Bothnia, and which are disturbingly close to Stockholm and Sweden's heartland. Presumably Sweden is prepared to seize these islands rapidly in the event of war.

MILITARY ASSISTANCE

Sweden has been active in supporting UN peacekeeping operations, furnishing battalion-size units for the UN Emergency Force (UNEF) in Sinai and the Gaza Strip from 1956 to 1967, for the UN Operation in the Congo (UNOC) from 1960 to 1964, and for UN Forces in Cyprus (UNFICYP) from 1964 to date. Truce observers have served in Palestine since 1948, in Kashmir since 1951, in Greece from 1952 to 1954, in Egypt from 1956 to 1967, in Lebanon in 1958, in New Guinea in 1962, and in Yemen in 1963-1964.

While military assistance is not given on a grant basis, training missions have been dispatched to developing nations, notably Ethiopia. Swedish artillery and aircraft are sold widely throughout the world, and technical and training personnel are often provided to purchasers. Sweden favors delivery of foreign aid through multilateral agencies, especially the UN, but also provides bilateral aid to less developed countries.

ALLIANCES

Sweden is a member of the UN, but is involved in no alliances.

ARMY

Personnel:
 12,500 regulars (officers and non-commissioned officers)
 36,500 conscript trainees

Organization:
 6 military regions, each able to operate independently with integrated forces of all services
 16 infantry brigades (cadre only; 5,000-6,000 men each when mobilized)
 8 Norrland brigades (trained and equipped for arctic warfare)
 6 armored brigades (cadre only; 5,000-6,000 men each when mobilized)
 7 artillery brigades (cadre)
 1 parachute training group (cadre)
 6 AA regiments (cadre)
 1 SAM battalion (Hawk)
 engineers, signal, and corps service units

Upon mobilization, these units would form some 100 battalions and a number of independent units (approximately 15 combat divisions). Territorial and local defense forces provide 100 more battalions and 400 to 500 more independent companies.
 1 battalion in Cyprus (UN Forces)

Major Equipment Inventory:
 80 medium tanks (Centurion)
 main battle tanks (Strv-103 or S-tank)
 light tanks (Strv-74; IKV-91)
 SS-11 and Bantam antitank missiles, Carl Gustav and Mini-man antitank weapons
 APCs (Pbv301/302)
 Hawk SAM (1 battalion)
 90mm recoilless guns (jeep-mounted)
 Redeye troop-portable lightweight SAM
 105mm and 155mm guns; 155mm self-propelled guns
 105mm and 155mm self-propelled howitzers
 90 light aircraft (Bulldog, Do-27)
 50 helicopters (AB-204, AB-206)
 AA guns (20mm and 40mm guns; 57mm self-propelled)

Reserves: There are about 600,000 reserves. High priority personnel are mobilizable within 48 hours; most of the balance, within two to three days. There are 100,000 reserves on active duty for from 14 to 40 days.

NAVY

Personnel:
 4,700 naval regulars (mostly officers and petty officers)
 14,000 coast artillery regulars
 7,400 conscripts (Navy and coast artillery)

Major Units:
 8 destroyers (2 with SSM; 4 with Seacat SAM; DD, DDG)
 5 ASW frigate escorts (2 with helicopters; DE)
 26 diesel submarines (SS)
 2 minelayer/submarine depot ships (MM)
 10 mining tenders
 26 small minelayers (MMC; 8 assigned to coast artillery)
 18 coastal minesweepers (MSC)
 20 inshore minesweepers (MSI)
 55 torpedo boats (PT)
 31 patrol boats/launches (YP)

183 landing craft (LCU, LCM, and smaller craft)
 36 auxiliaries
 30 coast artillery battalions (75mm, 105mm, 120mm, 152mm, and 210mm guns, and Rb-08 and Rb-52 [SS-11] SSMs)
 25 helicopters (including Vertol 107 and AB-206)

Reserves: There are 50,000 reserves mobilizable within 48 hours

Naval Bases: Stockholm, Kariskrona, and Goteborg are the bases in the conventional sense; ships and support facilities are dispersed, however, in hardened underground shelters in three base areas: Naval Base East Coast, Naval Base South Coast, and Naval Base West Coast.

AIR FORCE

Personnel: 5,750 regulars (mostly officers and NCOs); 6,400 active duty conscripts; 7,500 conscripts on refresher training

Organization:
 13 wings (2 to 3 squadrons each)
  9 ground attack squadrons (Lansen, Viggen)
 17 all-weather fighter squadrons (Draken)
  2 light attack/fighter squadrons (SK60, Draken)
  4 fighter reconnaissance squadrons (Lansen, Draken)
  4 transport squadrons (2 C-47, 2 C-130)
  1 tow target squadron (Lansen)
  1 communications squadron (SK60, Safir)
  5 training squadrons (Bulldog)
  5 helicopter groups (Vertol 107, AB-204)
  9 SAM squadrons (Bloodhound II; 120 missiles)

Major Aircraft Types:
 550 combat aircraft
  120 Lansen attack aircraft
   45 Viggen attack aircraft
  225 Draken fighters
   40 Lansen reconnaissance aircraft
   40 Draken reconnaissance aircraft
   50 SK60 light attack aircraft
 530 other aircraft
   60 transports (30 C-130, 25 C-47, 5 Pembroke)
  410 trainer/support aircraft (Bulldog, Safir, SK60, Lear jet)
   60 helicopters (21 AB-204, 22 AB-206, 17 KV-107)

Reserves: There are 50,000 reserves mobilizable within 48 hours.

Major Air Bases: Haslo, Ostersund, Ljunghyed, Karlsborg, Satenas, Angelholm, Nykoping, Kalmar, Norrkoping, Soderham, Uppsala, Kallinge, Tullinge, Lulea, Halmstad, Malmslatt

Air Defense Control System: Sophisticated computerized control and air surveillance system Stril 60 (comparable to American SAGE)

PARAMILITARY

There are about one million men and women in local defense organizations. Civil defense service—general defense and factory defense—is compulsory for men and women not serving in the armed forces. Of the total cited above, 90,000 are women with most of the remainder men who are older than 47 years.

SWITZERLAND

Schweiz—Suisse—Svizzera
Swiss Confederation

POWER POTENTIAL STATISTICS

Area: 15,944 square miles
Population: 6,500,000
Total Armed Forces: 620,000 immediately mobilizable (9.3% native population); the civilian militia system envisions no standing army
Gross National Product: $31.4 billion ($4,830 per capita for *total* population)
Annual Military Expenditures: $785 million (2.5% GNP)
Refined Petroleum Products: 5.5 million metric tons
Electric Power Output: 31.6 billion kwh
Merchant Fleet: 32 ships; 199,591 gross tons
Civil Air Fleet: 54 jet, 33 piston transports

DEFENSE STRUCTURE

One of the seven members of Switzerland's Federal Council—the executive department of the republic's government—is the Minister, or chief, of the Federal Department of Defense. He is assisted by a very small military planning staff. Administration is shared by the Federation and the cantons. There is no overall military commander of the Swiss armed forces in peacetime; in time of war or national emergency the two houses of the Federal Assembly (the bicameral parliament) meet to elect a commander of the armed forces, who then becomes the nation's only general officer.

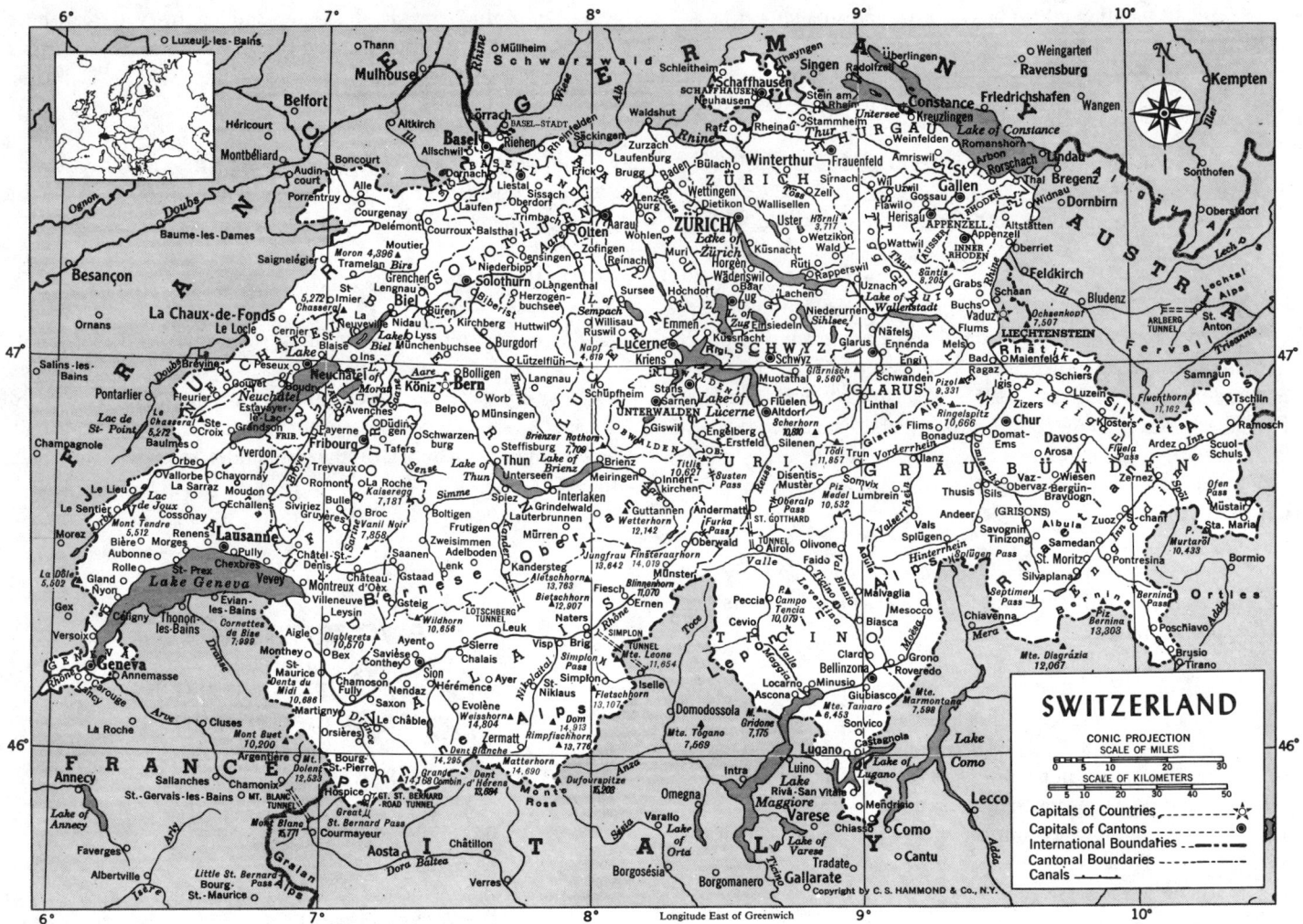

POLITICO-MILITARY POLICY

Since the emergence of the Swiss state in the 13th Century, the nation has traditionally been neutral, although prior to the early 16th Century this was a bellicose independence maintained and supported by the most renowned mercenary soldiery of Europe. Subsequently, and particularly since the early 19th Century, Switzerland has been the most determined and consistently impartial neutral nation in the world.

To support this foreign policy of neutrality Switzerland has in modern times relied upon a completely defensive military policy which eschews a standing military force. The security of the nation is entrusted to a national militia, in which service is universal and compulsory for all physically fit male citizens between the ages of 20 and 50, with officers serving up to age 55. Each class of men reaching age 20 serves for four months in a basic training program, followed by regular refresher training.

There are three classes of military service, according to age: *Auszug* (Elite), ages 20-32; *Landwehr*, ages 33-42; and *Landsturm*, ages 43-50. Men of the *Auszug* are required to serve three weeks per year for refresher training, but after age 28 this is generally excused for all men below the rank of sergeant. The *Landwehr* are called up for two weeks' training every two years; a period of two weeks' refresher training is required for members of the non-commissioned officers of the *Landsturm* soon after they reach the age of 43. Officers and pilots receive more extensive training.

Swiss defensive strategy is based essentially on the concept of deterrence through demonstrated readiness. The entire national militia can be mobilized and ready for battle in mobile operational units and carefully prepared defensive positions within 48 hours. All of the approaches into Switzerland are prepared for demolition, and demolitions are also pre-positioned to destroy vital industrial plants and to block all major defiles within the country. An intensely fortified national redoubt has been prepared in the Alpine interior region of the country, its base areas being the regions of Sargans in the northeast, of the St. Gothard Pass in the center, and of St. Maurice in the southwest. Thus any potential aggressor is on notice that the conquest of Switzerland will be extremely costly, and that the potential prizes and wealth of the country will be destroyed before they can be seized.

The defensive policy and strategy have been sufficiently convincing and formidable to deter all potential aggressors since the time of the French Revolutionary Wars, and were particularly successful in World Wars I and II.

STRATEGIC PROBLEMS

Two of Switzerland's major strategic problems are complementary: lack of space, and the consequent vulnerability of the economic resources of the nation, which are concentrated in the lowlands of northern and western Switzerland. Swiss national military policy and the apparent defensive strategy are probably as well designed as possible to offset these disadvantages within the capabilities of the nation, to wit: the ability to mobilize rapidly the entire trained military manpower of the nation; the pre-planned and pre-positioned demolitions; the apparent determination to withdraw from successive strong defensive positions into the nation's mountain redoubt as a last solution; and the probably deterrent effect of these evidences of determination.

The government is stable, untroubled by major domestic policy problems or significant disaffected elements, and supported by a politically sophisticated electorate in the policy of armed neutrality. However, Switzerland shows some concern about its nearly one million foreigners, the vast majority laborers, coming not only from contiguous countries but also from nearly every Mediterranean nation. By law, whatever their origin, they may not serve in the Army. In any emergency serious enough for mobilization to be considered they could face expulsion from the country.

ALLIANCES

Switzerland belongs to no alliances, and has not joined the UN, but it maintains an observer at UN headquarters and it has joined several UN specialized agencies.

Although much of Swiss foreign trade (about two-fifths of exports and three-fifths of imports) is with the European Common Market (EEC), and although Swiss trade with communist countries is negligible, Switzerland has considered membership in the EEC to be incompatible with its traditional neutrality (and its agricultural interests). In 1973, however, it did sign an agreement which establishes a free trade relationship with the Common Market, and it is a member of the European Free Trade Association (EFTA). It is also a member of the Organization for Economic Cooperation and Development (OECD). The Swiss have a policy they term solidarity, which involves acceptance of a moral obligation to contribute, as a neutral state, to world peace and prosperity by undertaking economic and humanitarian activities such as assistance to developing countries, support for the extension of international law and for the UN specialized agencies it has joined, and the extension of good offices. There are no problems in Switzerland's bilateral relations, which include almost all independent states.

ARMY

Personnel:
1,400-1,500 training force (instructor officers and NCO's)
25,000 conscript trainees (average)
578,000 total mobilizable within 24 hours

Organization:
    4 corps (1 for the Alps, 3 for the plateau region)
    3 mountain divisions (all in the Alpine corps)
    3 mechanized divisions (1 per corps in plateau region)
    6 infantry divisions (2 per corps in plateau region)
      frontier, fortress, and redoubt brigades
      army engineer, communications, and logistics units

Major Equipment Inventory:
   630 medium tanks (Centurion, Pz-61, Pz-68)
   200 light tanks (AMX-13)
1,250 APCs (M-113)
   140 155mm self-propelled gun/howitzers (M-109)
       150mm artillery pieces
       105mm artillery pieces
       81mm and 120mm mortars
       Oerlikon 20mm and twin 35mm AA
       patrol boats (on major lakes)

AIR FORCE

The Air Force is an integral part of the Army, as are the aircraft units included below.

Personnel:
  2,000 training force (instructor officers and NCO's)
  3,000 conscript trainees (average)
42,000 total mobilizable within 48 hours
       (maintenance performed by civilian employees during peacetime, militarized in emergencies)

Organization:
  11 fighter-bomber squadrons (Venom)
   5 fighter-bomber squadrons (Hunter)
   2 fighter-interceptor squadrons (Mirage III)
   1 fighter reconnaissance squadron (Mirage III-R)
   5 support squadrons (helicopter, transport,

trainer, liaison; Alouette II/III, Ju-52, Do-27, Vampire)
- 40 AA artillery batteries
- 2 SAM battalions (Bloodhound 2)

Major Aircraft Types:
- 374 combat aircraft
  - 100 Hunter fighter-bombers
  - 36 Mirage III-S fighter-interceptors
  - 18 Mirage III-RS fighter/reconnaissance aircraft
  - 220 Venom fighter-bombers
- 372 other aircraft
  - 26 transports (Ju-52, Do-27)
  - 250 miscellaneous trainer/support aircraft
  - 96 helicopters (including 86 Alouette II/III)
  - 30 Hunters on order

Major Air Training Bases: Dubendorf, Bayerne, Emmen, Magadino, Sion

TURKEY
Turkiye Cumhuriyeti
Turkish Republic

POWER POTENTIAL STATISTICS

Area: 301,380 square miles
Population: 38,600,000
Total Active Armed Forces: 563,500 (includes gendarmerie; 1.46% population)
Gross National Product: $15.08 billion ($391 per capita)
Annual Military Expenditures: $802 million (5.32% GNP)
Iron and Steel Production: 2.0 million metric tons
Fuel Production: Coal: 13.8 million metric tons
  Crude Oil: 3.4 million metric tons
  Refined Petroleum Products: 11 million metric tons
Electric Power Output: 9.7 billion kwh
Merchant Fleet: 328 ships; 713,767 gross tons
Civil Air Fleet: 16 jet, 7 turboprop transports

DEFENSE STRUCTURE

The President of the Republic of Turkey constitutionally exercises power as a strong executive; he is the actual as well as nominal commander in chief of the armed forces. This responsibility is exercised through the Prime Minister and the Minister of National Defense. The Army is the predominant element of the partially integrated armed forces. The Chief of the General Staff is also Commander-in-Chief of the armed forces.

POLITICO-MILITARY POLICIES

For several centuries Russia has been the principal traditional enemy of Turkey. After the republic was established, following World War I, Turkey followed an essentially neutral policy, in which an important element was rapprochement with Soviet Russia. Soviet domination of the Balkans after World War II brought renewed Russian pressure to obtain control over the Turkish Straits. Despite occasional gestures of friendship on both sides, security from the threat of Russia has been the principal element of Turkish foreign and military policy since 1945. Turkish appeals for support in opposing Russian threats stimulated the enunciation of the Truman Doctrine in 1947, and the beginning of a bilateral alliance with the United States. This same Turkish policy caused Turkey to contribute a highly effective brigade to the UN forces during the Korean conflict and to join the NATO alliance in 1952 and the Baghdad Pact (later the CENTO alliance) in 1955. Recently Turkey has taken steps to normalize its relations with the Soviet Union, without weakening its membership in NATO. In 1973, during the Arab-Israeli confrontation, Turkey made clear both that NATO bases might not be used to ship war material to Israel, and that any Soviet airlift to Arab nations might not traverse Turkish air space.

In 1971, Turkey established diplomatic relations with the People's Republic of China.

The Turkish armed forces are raised by conscription. The term of service is 20 months for all services. The quality of the armed forces is greatly enhanced by a proud national military tradition, and by the toughness, frugality, courage, loyalty, and self-reliance of the Turkish peasants, who make up the bulk of the rank and file. Since World War II, about 30 percent of the annual budget has been for defense.

STRATEGIC PROBLEMS

Turkey's location between the Mediterranean and Black Seas, and between Europe and Asia, is one of the most significant in the world militarily and strategically. Turkey has been the principal obstacle to Imperial and Soviet Russian expansion into the Mediterranean and also to Soviet movement into the oil-rich Middle East. By its participation in the NATO and CENTO alliances, and because of the effectiveness and reliability of the Turkish armed forces, Turkey has become one of the key elements of the chain of mutual security alliances that has manifested misgivings at Communist expansionism since 1947.

The security of the Straits (Bosporus, Sea of Marmara, and Dardanelles) is perhaps the greatest Turkish strategic problem. For 200 years the right of foreign warships to go through them has been the subject of controversy—and of agreements. The Montreux Convention of 1936 allowed Turkey to fortify the Straits, and provided for free passage in peacetime of warships

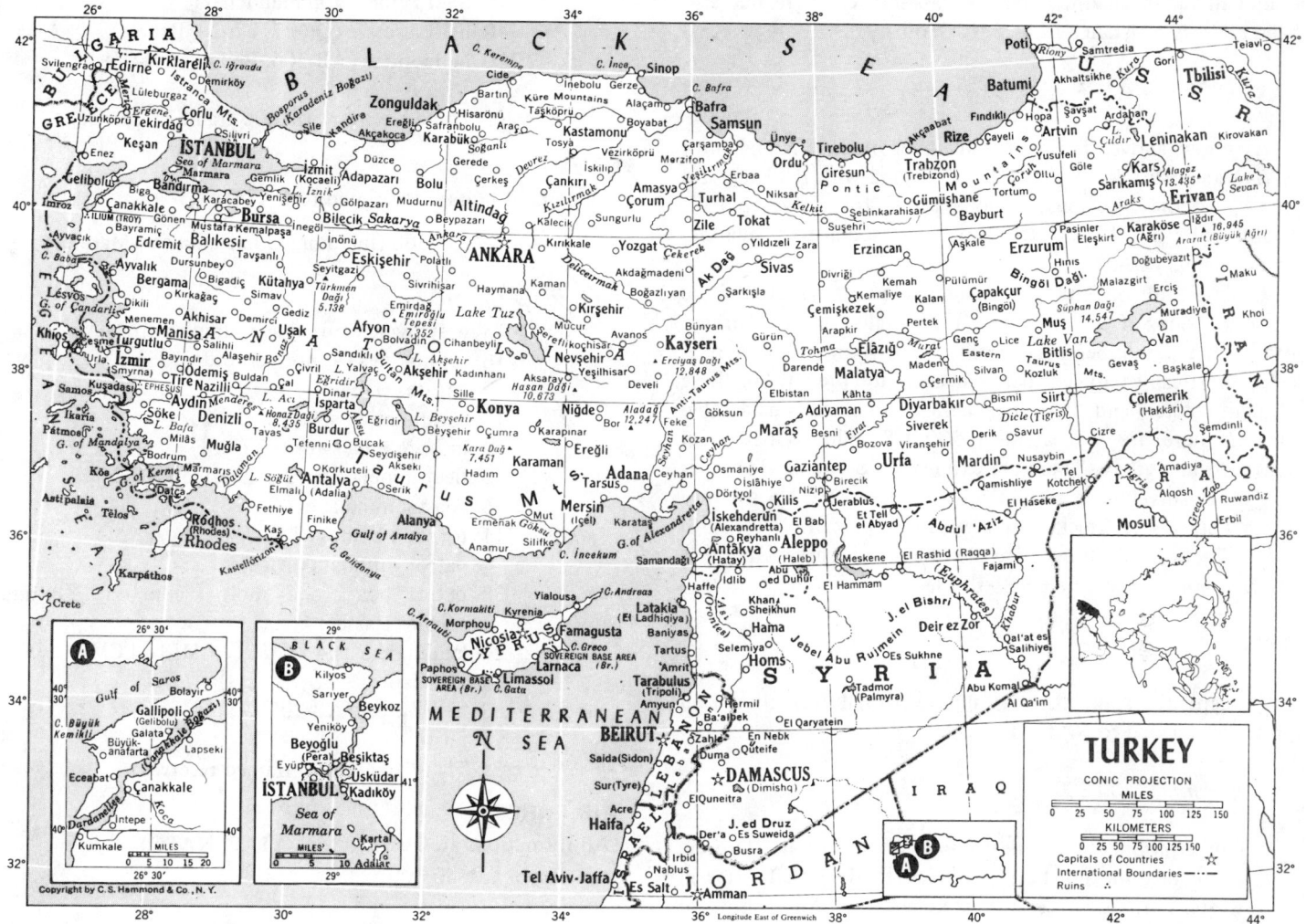

under a certain size, and for closing the Straits in wartime to belligerents so long as Turkey should remain neutral. A related problem is the defense of the small and isolated region in Europe north and west of the Straits. The defense of Turkey's eastern frontiers with the USSR and Iran is facilitated by extremely rugged mountains. A security weakness in this area, however, is the presence of two ethnic minorities: the Kurds and the Armenians.

Turkey's interest in preventing the absorption of Cyprus by Greece is mainly nationalist and emotional, in support of the Turkish Cypriot minority. There is, however, an important strategic aspect of this interest. Despite their joint participation in the NATO alliance, Greek-Turkish enmity has deep and lasting roots, and Cyprus in Greek hands would place Turkey at a significant strategic disadvantage. Thus in 1974, when the status quo in Cyprus was violently upset, an estimated 40,000 Turkish troops were landed on the island. (See Cyprus and Greece.)

Except for the small Armenian and Kurdish minorities mentioned above, and an equally insignificant Greek minority in western Anatolia and European Turkey, the population is quite homogeneous. Communism has had little impact upon the predominantly Moslem people, and despite the low standard of living of most Turks, is not likely to. Leftist disaffection is apparent among university students and intellectuals, however, and has resulted in many riots, bombings, kidnappings and murders. This unrest, partly directed against the presence of American NATO personnel, has created some governmental instability, and in 1971 eleven provinces were put under modified military law.

MILITARY ASSISTANCE

Largely because of Turkey's strategic location, and its military reliability, the United States has provided it with more than $5.0 billion in foreign aid since 1950; of this more than half has been direct military assistance. There has also been military assistance from West Germany.

ALLIANCES

As noted above, Turkey is a member of the UN and both NATO and CENTO. It is a member, along with Pakistan and Iran, of the Regional Cooperation for Development, established in 1964. It also has extensive bilateral arrangements with the United States.

Izmir is a major NATO base and headquarters area, and the main location of a number of US installations in Turkey. Although the number of US military personnel in Turkey is being drastically reduced, partly because the presence of these affluent soldiers and their dependents has caused considerable unrest, there are still about 6,000 US military personnel stationed in Turkey. There are extensive US and NATO radar and other surveillance installations. At least 200 US military aircraft and some Greek combat air units, part of NATO's 6th Allied Tactical Air Force, are also based in Turkey. Izmir is also a major base for the US Sixth Fleet.

ARMY

(Except for some fortress and territorial formations, all units are assigned to NATO.)

Personnel: 400,000

Organization: 3 armies: one in European Turkey, protecting the northern approach to the Straits; one in western Anatolia, concentrated near the Asiatic side of the Straits; and one in eastern Anatolia, concentrated near the Soviet frontier.
- 6 army corps; two for each army
- 1 armored division (M-48 tanks)
- 1 mechanized infantry division
- 12 infantry divisions
- 4 armored cavalry brigades
- 4 armored brigades (M-48 tanks)
- 3 mechanized infantry brigades
- 2 parachute battalions
- 2 SSM battalions (Honest John)

Major Equipment Inventory:
- 1,500 medium tanks (M-47 and M-48)
- light tanks (M-24 and M-41)
- tank destroyers (M-36)
- armored cars (M-8)
- 500+ APCs (M-113 and M-59)
- 105mm and 155mm self-propelled guns
- 105mm, 155mm, and 203mm howitzers
- 40mm, 75mm, and 90mm AA artillery pieces
- SS-11 ATGW
- SSM Honest John launchers
- 40 light aircraft (Do-27, Do-28, Beaver)
- 20 helicopters (AB-206, Bell 47, CH-47)

Reserves: There are over 800,000 trained reservists.

NAVY

(All combat units are assigned to NATO)

Personnel: 38,500 (including 3 battalions of Marines)

Major Units:
- 15 destroyers (1 used as training ship; DD)
- 16 submarines (4 more on order; SS)
- 2 frigates (DE)
- 16 coastal minesweepers (MSC)
- 4 inshore minesweepers (MSI)
- 3 fleet minelayers (2 converted LST; MMF)
- 6 coastal minelayers (MMC)
- 11 torpedo boats (PT)
- 4 patrol gunboats (PGM)
- 38 patrol boats and motor launches (YP and smaller classes)
- 24 landing craft (4 LCU, 2 LCM, 18 LCVP)
- 39 auxiliaries
- 3 helicopters (AB-205; ASW)

Reserves: There are 70,000 trained reserves

AIR FORCE

(All formations are assigned to 6 ATAF, NATO)

Personnel: 50,000

Organization:
- 2 tactical air forces
  - 2 fighter-interceptor squadrons AW (F-102)
  - 2 fighter-interceptor squadrons (F-5)
  - 5 fighter-bomber squadrons (F-100)
  - 2 fighter-bomber squadrons (F-104)
  - 2 fighter-bomber squadrons (F-5)
  - 3 fighter reconnaissance squadrons (RF-84F, RF-5)
  - 4 transport squadrons (C-45, C-47, C-54, C-130, Viscount, Transall)
  - 1 helicopter squadron (UH-1, H-19)
  - 2 SAM battalions (Nike-Hercules; 6 batteries)

Major Aircraft Types:
- 349 combat aircraft
  - 130 F-5 interceptor/fighter-bombers
  - 38 F-104 fighter-bombers
  - 100 F-100 fighter-bombers
  - 36 F-102 AW fighter-interceptors
  - 30 RF-84 fighter reconnaissance aircraft

    15 RF-5 fighter-reconnaissance aircraft
224 other aircraft
    12 C-47 transports
      6 C-45 transports
      3 C-54 transports
    10 C-130 transports
    20 Transall transports
    23 helicopters (UH-1, H-19)
  150 trainer/support aircraft (including T-33, TF-102, TF-104, T-37, T-41, T-42, T-34, T-11, F-100F, and F-5)
On Order: 40 F-4, 42 F-5 Tiger II

Major Air Bases: Izmir, Adana, Bandirma, Diyarbakir, Esluboga, Sivas, Etimesgut, Eskisehir, Yesilkoy, Merzifon, Balikesir.

Reserves: There are 80,000 trained reserves

PARAMILITARY

75,000 National Gendarmerie (3 mobile brigades)
20,000 National Guard

UNITED KINGDOM OF GREAT BRITAIN AND NORTHERN IRELAND

POWER POTENTIAL STATISTICS

Area: 94,216 square miles
Population: 57,000,000
Total Active Armed Forces: 370,000 (including 9,900 non-British; 0.65% population)
Gross National Product: $151.6 billion ($2,161 per capita)
Annual Military Expenditures: $8.1 billion (5.34% GNP)
Steel and Iron Production: 40 million metric tons
Fuel Production: Coal: 149.7 million metric tons
    Gas (manufactured): 20.5 billion cubic meters
    Gas (natural): 19 billion cubic meters
Electric Power Output: 254 billion kwh
Merchant Fleet: 3,785 ships; 27.3 million gross tons
Civil Air Fleet: 246 jet, 83 turboprop, 108 piston transports

DEFENSE STRUCTURE

The Sovereign is the nominal commander in chief of all the armed forces. Actual control is exercised by the Prime Minister and the Cabinet, through the Secretary of State for Defence. Within the Cabinet all defense matters are considered by the Defence and Overseas Policy Committee, which includes the Prime Minister, the Secretary of State for Defence, the Foreign Secretary, the Home Secretary, the Chancellor of the Exchequer, and such others as are appointed by the Prime Minister; the Secretary of State for Defence is responsible to Parliament for carrying out the decisions of this Committee and for administering the Ministry of Defence. His principal assistant in carrying out these tasks is a civil servant, the Permanent Under-Secretary of State for Defence.

Within the Ministry of Defence are the three Service Departments, each headed by an Under-Secretary of State (one each for Navy, Army, and Air Force), although each department retains its individual identity (Admiralty Board, Army Board, and Air Force Board). Directly under the Secretary of State for Defence, and next to him in rank within the Ministry, are two Defence Ministers, one for Administration, the other for Equipment. There is a military Defence Staff, coordinating planning and operations for all of the services; each of the services retains its traditional General Staff (or equivalent); overall defense military planning is directed by the Chiefs of Staff Committee, under the chairmanship of the Chief of the Defence Staff, and with the three service staff chiefs as members. Under the Secretary of State is a Defence Council (of which he is chairman), responsible for exercising the powers of command and administrative control over the largely integrated services. Members of this Council are: Secretary of State, the two Defence Ministers, the three Service Parliamentary Under-Secretaries of State, the Chief of the Defence Staff, the chiefs of the three service staffs, the Chief Scientist, and the Permanent Under-Secretary of State for Defence.

A substantial degree of military integration has been achieved through centralized operational directives to overseas commands, and through assignment of multi-service logistical responsibilities to various functional agencies of the three services; for instance, the Navy is responsible for procurement of petrol, oil, and lubricants (POL).

POLITICO-MILITARY POLICY

In the years since World War II it has been necessary for Britain to make a painful transition whereby policies are necessarily related to the facts of diminished power and wealth, and the consequent situation of diminished influence in world affairs. Nevertheless, residual reservoirs of power are substantial, and Britain is still unquestionably first among the handful of major powers of secondary rank. Its position as leader of the Commonwealth reinforces that status.

Traditionally the most important of Britain's politico-military objectives were: to command the seas surrounding the British Isles; to maintain the European balance of power; to keep open the shipping lanes to Britain to provide food for the people and raw materials for the industry; to protect overseas possessions and to encourage them (since

126 ALMANAC OF WORLD MILITARY POWER

1783) to become self-governing and economically and militarily self-reliant partners within a world-wide British system (formerly called an Empire, more recently a Commonwealth).

Among the most important traditional military policies supporting these objectives were: to undertake whatever military operations were necessary to prevent any major European power from controlling the Low Countries; to maintain a fleet at least as large and as powerful as the combined naval forces of the next two most powerful European maritime nations; to dominate the Mediterranean and the Middle East littoral; to avoid major land force involvement in a European war, but rather to encourage Continental allies to bear the brunt of land operations while Britain bore the major burden of naval and amphibious operations; to maintain major forces overseas, particularly in Asia and the Indian Ocean; to secure and protect overseas possessions and all sources of valuable materials.

It is probable that all of the cited objectives are still valid, within a more limited frame of reference. None of the major traditional policies listed above are fully applicable today, mostly because of Britain's diminished capabilities and resources, and its consequent reduced influence as a world power. Thus its need to protect Britain through seapower requires emphasis on retaining a formal or informal alliance with the United States; its reduced ability to influence Continental affairs, on the other hand, requires more direct involvement on the Continent and provision to Continental allies of substantial evidence of willingness to participate militarily, politically, and economically as an equal partner.

Slowly but inexorably the policies for dominating the Mediterranean, the Middle East, the Indian Ocean, and the rimlands of Southern Asia have been abandoned in the years since World War II. The last vestiges of these policies were the retention of control of the Persian Gulf, maintenance of major military forces at the principal exits from the Indian Ocean (Aden and Singapore), and the retention of other bases in the Indian Ocean. By 1974 even these vestiges of far-flung power east of Suez had been abandoned.

The British withdrawal from Aden was complete in 1968, and the Headquarters Far East Command at Singapore was closed November 1, 1971. It was succeeded by Headquarters ANZUK Force (Australian, New Zealand, United Kingdom). Malaysian and Singapore forces fill out this Five-Power command. The UK furnishes an infantry battalion group on station at Singapore, as well as Nimrod maritime patrol bombers and ASW helicopters. Patrolling the Indian Ocean and Mozambique Channel and the South China Sea are Royal Navy frigates. The RAF maintains staging posts at Masirah and Gan, and the Navy has a base at Hong Kong. The Army has five infantry battalions (three of them Gurkhas) and an artillery regiment there.

Britain relies upon voluntary enlistment to maintain its armed forces. To gain flexibility and attract recruits, volunteers are offered options of early release, on 18 months' notice, provided they serve at least three years, though long-term service is still encouraged.

STRATEGIC PROBLEMS

Britain's greatest strategic problem is its lack of sufficient raw materials to feed the population and to feed the vital industries. It can obtain these raw materials only by sea, and thus is vulnerable to any hostile capability to interfere with its overseas lanes of trade. It is this potential vulnerability that has been the principal determinant of British objectives and British policies since the end of the 16th Century. Next in importance among Britain's strategic problems is its proximity to the continent of Europe, and its vulnerability to attack across the narrow waters of the English Channel and North Sea, and the even narrower waters of the Strait of Dover (22 miles across). This has been the basis of traditional British sensitivity to the possibility that a hostile power could establish dangerous bases in the Low Countries.

Another strategic vulnerability is the concentration of a large population, and of an extensive industrial complex, in a limited area. This vulnerability, which was serious in World War II, has become critical in the era of nuclear-armed missiles. This has convinced the British government and people—despite the changing political complexion of the leadership—that Britain must maintain an effective and convincing deterrent to possible aggression.

Britain has tiny groups seeking independence within both Scotland and Wales, and a comparable, but much more difficult, problem in Northern Ireland. Dealing with the Welsh and Scottish separatists is essentially a police problem, and does not pose any substantial security threat to the United Kingdom. In Northern Ireland, however, approximately one-third of the population of about 1.5 million are Irish Catholics, with strong religious, cultural, and emotional ties with the people of Eire. More than half of the remainder are Scots-Irish in origin and strongly Protestant, anti-Eire, and anti-Catholic in attitude. Feelings run high between these two groups, and are exacerbated by the activities of a group of terrorists—claiming to be members of the outlawed Irish Republic Army, disavowed by the government of Eire—who are seeking to bring about the union of Northern Ireland with Eire by employing urban guerrilla tactics of murder, arson, and bombing. In an effort to control the situation, Britain has employed at times as many as 17 major units of all services on internal security duty in Northern Ireland. The Ulster Defense Regiment, specially created for such duty, is at a strength of about 6,000. Naval units patrol off-shore to intercept arms runners. In 1974 strife between Catholics and Protestants in Ulster continued, acts of violence on both sides increased, and a British attempt to establish a new, joint government failed.

One strategic security problem is the preservation of control over certain overseas territories where British rights or sovereignty are challenged. Most important among these is Gibraltar, which Spain seeks to regain, demanding that Britain renounce the rights gained by the Treaty of Utrecht in 1713. Of less significance are Belize, where British rights are disputed by neighboring Guatemala, and the Falkland Islands, claimed by Argentina.

In 1973 Britain and Iceland became involved in a "Cod War" over fishing rights off Iceland's coasts. After numerous incidents between fishing trawlers and Icelandic gunboats, the British government sent three frigates to the area. Temporary agreement was finally reached in October, limiting catches, numbers of boats and areas in which they might fish. The issue is not resolved, however, since Iceland apparently intends to defy a ruling in favor of Britain by the International Court of Justice.

MILITARY ASSISTANCE

In the sense that it relies to a considerable degree upon the United States for the production of all or parts of many of the most expensive weapons systems, Britain has been the recipient of US military assistance. For the most part, however, American aid has taken the form of making available weapons and equipment for purchase by Britain. A small Military Advisory Group (currently one civilian employee) has been stationed in Britain, and since 1950 a total value of $1.0345 billion (virtually none since 1963) has been provided to Britain by the United States.

Over the years since World War II Britain has provided to other nations far more military aid than it has received from the United States. Most of this assistance has been given to other Commonwealth nations, and mainly to those that have received their independence since 1945.

ALLIANCES

The United Kingdom, a UN member with a permanent seat on the Security Council, is a participant in seven major alliances, and a number of lesser or subsidiary bilaterial alliances.

First, Britain is the leading member of the Commonwealth of Nations. The Sovereign of Great Britain is accepted by all members of this free association of independent states as the Head of the Commonwealth. There is no other tangible link, and the objectives of the members are rarely in full accord with each other. The purposes of the alliance are vague, but generally are economic in practical effect. Nevertheless, there are implied political and military commitments, more demanding upon Britain and the other English-speaking members, perhaps, than on the others. The members of the Commonwealth are: United Kingdom, Canada, Australia, New Zealand, India, Sri Lanka, Ghana, Nigeria, Cyprus, Sierra Leone, Jamaica, Trinidad and Tobago, Uganda, Kenya, Malaysia, Tanzania, Malawi, Malta, Zambia, Gambia, Singapore, Guyana, Botswana, Lesotho, Barbados, Mauritius, Bahamas, Bangladesh, Swaziland, Tonga, Western Samoa, and Fiji. The UK hasseparate defense agreements or understandings with most of these, and provides most with various forms of military assistance.

The United Kingdom is also a member of the three major regional alliances established between 1950 and 1954 to deter threatened Communist aggression in Europe and Asia: NATO, CENTO, and SEATO. Related to NATO is the earlier Western European Union (WEU) which was established by the Brussels Treaty between Britain, France and the Benelux countries in 1948, and has been enlarged by the addition of Italy and West Germany.

Britain in 1971 joined with Malaysia, Singapore, Australia, and New Zealand in the so-called Five-Power Pact for the defense of British Commonwealth interests in Southeast Asia (see Malaysia).

Britain's principal alliance is that with the United States. A special relationship between these two nations has existed since Prime Minister Winston Churchill and President Franklin D. Roosevelt met aboard warships in Argentia Bay, off Newfoundland, in August 1941. Rarely, if ever, have two major powers established so close and cordial a wartime alliance as that which existed between them in World War II. The peacetime relationship that followed is equally unprecedented. America's ties with Canada are perhaps closer than those with the United Kingdom, but the Canadian alliance is one for the defense of the homelands of the participants, one being a major partner and the other a relatively minor one. In the continuing Anglo-American alliance the UK is, perforce, now a junior partner, but nonetheless still a major power, with worldwide interests, influence, and commitments. This alliance between the two major English-speaking nations is perhaps the most powerful force for peace in the world today.

The UK joined the European Common Market on January 1, 1973, without relinquishing its membership in the European Free Trade Association (EFTA), a step which followed the trend of its foreign trade and was widely considered to augur further changes in foreign policy.

ARMY

Personnel: 176,000 (including 8,200 enlisted abroad, and 5,600 women)

Organization:
  Within the United Kingdom:
    United Kingdom Land Forces (Headquarters, Wilton)
      Strategic Command
      Southern Command
      Northern Command
      Western Command

Scottish District (Headquarters, Edinburgh)
Northern Ireland District (Headquarters Lisburn)—Ulster Defense Regiment of 6,000 men (plus other units rotated through Northern Ireland during the continuing disturbances there)

Overseas:
Near East Land Forces (part of Near East Command; Headquarters, Cyprus)
Forces in Far East (now under five-power control, see above)
British Army of the Rhine (BAOR; Headquarters: Munchen-Gladbach)

Operational Units:
12 infantry brigades
49 infantry battalions (6 Gurkhas, equalling 1 brigade)
1 parachute brigade
1 Special Air Service regiment (air-mobile commandos)
12 armored regiments
5 armored car regiments
27 artillery regiments (3 with Honest John SSMs and 203mm howitzers)
14 engineer regiments
10 signal regiments

Deployment:
18 battalions in UK commands (forces in Northern Ireland comprise three brigade headquarters, one armored reconnaissance regiment, one field squadron of Royal Engineers, 17 major units—five of which are redeployed from BAOR). In the latter part of 1971 a battalion of Gurkhas was deployed to the UK.
Strategic Command (three infantry brigades—air portable—and one parachute force of two battalions forming one division, stationed in Strategic Command area; one SAS regiment)
British Army of the Rhine (BAOR) (54,900 men, assigned to NATO)
3 divisions (one corps) plus two artillery brigades
5 armored brigades
1 mechanized brigade
2 armored car regiments

Far East
1 battalion group at Singapore (under ANZUK, Five-Power Pact)
5 infantry battalions (including 3 Gurkha) in Hong Kong
1 artillery regiment in Hong Kong
1 battalion (Gurkha) in Brunei
1 Marine Commando Brigade afloat (1,650 Marines, 200 soldiers, 50 sailors)

Mediterranean
2 infantry battalions on Cyprus (including 1 in UNFICYP)
1 armored car squadron
1 battalion at Gibraltar
2 air portable reconnaissance squadrons (UNFICYP)

Other Detachments
1 brigade in Berlin Garrison (3,200)
1 infantry battalion (less one company) in Belize

Major Equipment Inventory:
about 1,000 Chieftain heavy tanks and Centurion medium tanks (latter being phased out)
armored cars (Saladin and Ferret)
scout cars (Ferret)
APCs (Saracen and Trojan)
Honest John SSM (2 batteries per regiment in three BAOR regiments)
175mm/203mm self-propelled guns/howitzers (with nuclear capability)
5.5 inch howitzers
155mm self-propelled howitzers (M-109 and M-44)
105mm self-propelled howitzers (Abbot)
Vigilant and Swingfire antitank guided weapons
200 light aircraft
190 helicopters

Reserves: The Territorial and Army Volunteer Reserve (volunteer militia) numbers 56,400. Its mission is UK home defense and preservation of law and order in emergency. The Regular Army Reserve of 120,000 comprises men with specific mobilization assignments in war or in situations short of war. An additional 180,000 men, without specific mobilization assignments, belong to the Army General Reserve.

NAVY

Personnel: 83,100 (including 8,000 Royal Marines, Fleet Air Arm, and 3,400 women)

Organization:
Commander in Chief, Fleet (Headquarters, Northwood)
Naval Home Commands
Fleet Air Arm
Royal Marines (four 800-man Commandos with a

brigade headquarters; the balance of the force serving on various duties afloat and ashore)

Major Units:

Operational Fleet:
- 1 aircraft carrier (CVA)
- 2 guided missile cruisers (CLG; Seacat SAM helicopters)
- 2 Commando carriers (LPH)
- 2 amphibious assault ships (LPD)
- 8 guided missile frigates (guided missile destroyers, DLG)
- 3 radar picket destroyers (antiaircraft frigates, DDR)
- 45 escort ships (26 general purpose frigates, 19 ASW frigates, DE)
- 4 radar picket escort ships (aircraft direction frigates; DER)
- 3 fleet ballistic missile submarines (SSBN), 48 Polaris A-3 missiles
- 8 fleet nuclear submarines (SSN; 3 more under construction; a further one ordered)
- 16 diesel submarines (SS)
- 42 coastal and inshore minesweepers (36 MSC and 6 MSI)
- 226 auxiliaries
- 24 attack aircraft (Buccaneer Mk.2) being transferred to RAF
- 72 All-weather fighters (Phantom FG.1 and Sea Vixen Mk.2)
- 120 helicopters (14 squadrons Wessex, Sea King, Wasp, and Whirlwind)
- 40 miscellaneous trainer/support aircraft

Reserve Fleet or Refitting:
- 10 escort ships (9 general purpose and 1 ASW frigate, DE)
- 1 Polaris submarine (SSBN)
- 6 diesel submarines (SS)
- guided missile destroyers (DLG)
- 7 submarines (SS)
- 2 coastal minesweepers (MSC)
- 2 fleet maintenance ships

Major Naval Bases: Portsmouth, Devonport, Chatham, Rosyth, Portland, Gibraltar, Hong Kong.

Reserves: Royal Navy and Marine regular reserves number 26,300, and Volunteer Reserve and Auxiliary forces account for an additional 8,400.

AIR FORCE

Personnel: 110,900 (including 6,000 women)

Organization:

Strike Command: Headquarters: High Wycombe
- 4 medium bomber squadrons (Vulcan Mk-2)
- 3 tanker squadrons (Victor Mk-1)
- 1 strategic reconnaissance squadron (Victor Mk-2)
- 1 photo-reconnaissance squadron (Canberra PR-7)
- 1 electronic reconnaissance squadron (Canberra, Nimrod)
- 3 maritime strike/attack squadrons (Buccaneer Mk-2)
- 6 interceptor squadrons (5 Lightning, 1 Phantom)
- 4 patrol bomber squadrons (Nimrod Mk-1)
- SAM squadrons (Bloodhound Mk-1)
- 10 strategic transport squadrons (2 Britannia, 1 VC-10, 1 Belfast, 1 Comet, 5 Hercules)
- 6 ground attack squadrons (1 Harrier, 2 Hunter, 3 Phantom)
- 3 helicopter squadrons (1 Wessex, 2 Puma)
- 1 light transport squadron (Andover)

Training Command: Headquarters: Brampton
- 17 training/support squadrons

RAF Germany (2nd Allied Tactical Air Force): Headquarters: Rheindahlen
- 2 fighter-interceptor squadrons (Lightning)
- 7 reconnaissance/attack squadrons (3 Harrier, 4 Phantom)
- 2 attack squadrons (Buccaneer)
- SAMs (Bloodhound)
- 1 helicopter squadron (Wessex)

Near East (Air Force) Command: Headquarters: Cyprus
- 1 interceptor squadron (Lightning)
- 2 medium bomber squadrons (Vulcan assigned to CENTO)
- 2 reconnaissance squadrons (Canberra based on Malta)
- SAMs (Bloodhound)
- 1 helicopter squadron (Whirlwind)
- 1 squadron (Hunter) based on Gibraltar
- 1 maritime patrol/ASW squadron (Nimrod) based on Malta
- 1 transport squadron (Hercules, Argosy)

RAF in Far East (under ANZUK, Five-Power Pact force)
- 1 patrol bomber squadron (Nimrod) based in Singapore
- 2 helicopter squadrons, 1 in Singapore, 1 in Hong Kong

Royal Air Force Regiment (Mission: ground defense of airfields, and manning of SAMs)
- 12 squadrons (deployed in UK and overseas)

SAM batteries (Tigercat, Bloodhound, Rapier)

Major Aircraft Types:
- 618 combat aircraft
  - 118 Phantom fighter/attack aircraft
  - 90 Harrier V/STOL attack/reconnaissance aircraft
  - 100 Lightning interceptors (Firestreak Redtop AAM)
  - 100 Buccaneer attack aircraft
  - 35 Hunter fighter-bombers
  - 12 Victor Mk-2 medium bombers (reconnaissance)
  - 41 Nimrod maritime patrol aircraft
  - 50 Vulcan Mk-2 medium bombers
  - 20 Canberra light bombers
  - 12 Shackleton patrol bombers
  - 40 Canberra photo reconnaissance aircraft
- 929 other aircraft
  - 38 Victor Mk-1 tankers
  - 51 strategic transports (Belfast, Britannia, Comet, VC-10, Hercules)
  - 91 light transports (HS-125, Andover, Bassett, Pembroke)
  - 115 helicopters (Whirlwind, Wessex, Sioux, Puma)
  - 565 trainers (170 Chipmunk, 195 Jet Provost, 54 Varsity, 65 Gnat, 40 Bulldog, 19 Dominie, 22 Hunter)
  - 45 miscellaneous support aircraft
  - 24 helicopters (8 Sioux, 16 Whirlwind)

Major Air Bases: Stanmore, W. Raynham, Wattisham, Conningsby, Oldham, Brampton, Linton-on-Ouse, White Waltham, Waterbeach, Bassingbourne, Binbrook, Coltishall, Chivenor, Finningley, Thorney Island, Gaydon, Stradishall, Syerston, Leeming, Oakington, Aclington, Waddington, Cottesmore, Scampton, St. Mawgan, Wyton, Marham, Wittering, Kinloss, Ballykelly, Lindholm, Church Fenton, Lynham, Odiham, Bawtry, Topcliffe, St. Anthan, Benson, Mancy, Shawbury, Boscombe, High Wycombe, Upavon, Brize Norton, Colerne, Abingdon, Fairford, Pitreavie

Reserves: There are approximately 33,000 regular RAF reservists plus several hundred Volunteer Reserve and Auxiliary Force members.

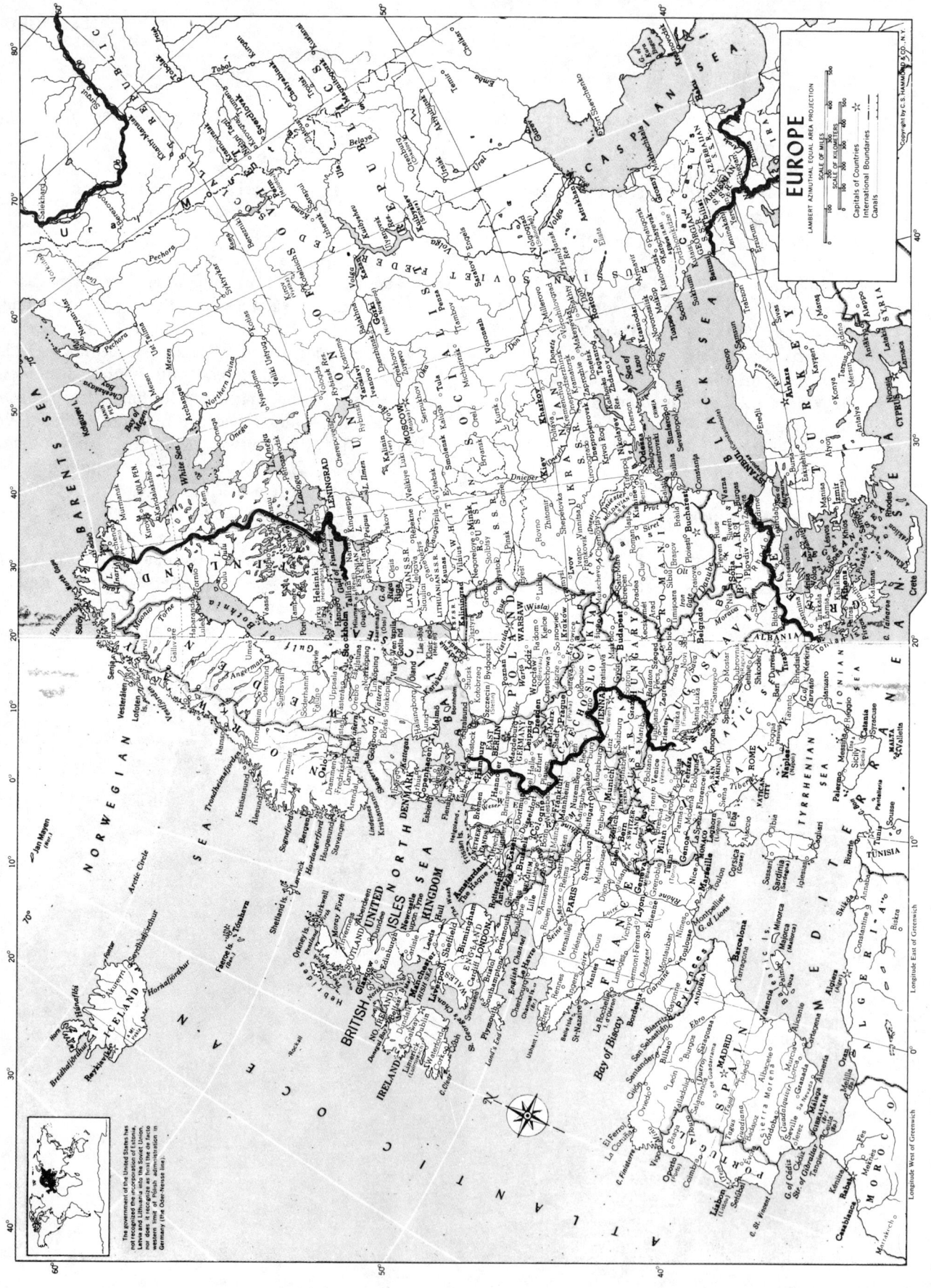

5
EASTERN EUROPE

Regional Survey

MILITARY GEOGRAPHY

Geographically Eastern Europe includes all of Europe east of a line running generally along the Finnish-Soviet border, the Gulf of Finland and the Baltic Sea, and from the southwest corner of the Baltic Sea to the northeast corner of the Adriatic. Politically it comprises all of the European nations with Communist governments. Since the USSR is both the largest state geographically and the most important politically in this region, the coverage of this chapter also includes all Soviet territory in Asia. The non-Communist nations, Finland, Greece, and Turkey, are included in the chapter on Western Europe.

Within this vast region there are three major sub-regions, each with numerous distinct geographical areas. The sub-regions are: North European and Russian plains; the Carpathian-Balkan mountain complex; and Asiatic Russia.

The plains and steppes of North Europe and Russia are characterized by hot, dry summers, and bitterly cold winters. These extremes are only slightly ameliorated in the south by the tempering effect of the nearby Black Sea. In the center of the sub-region, and throughout its northern extent, there are great swamps, seriously interfering with military movement in summer but easily traversed in winter. There are many broad rivers, creating difficult obstacles, generally to east-west movement. There are extensive forests through much of this region. The road net is relatively limited, compared to Western Europe.

The Carpathian-Balkan region is an essentially mountainous peninsula extending southward from the heart of Europe, and cut by the generally broad and fertile Danube basin and a number of smaller river valleys. Inhospitable terrain, shortages of raw materials (and resultant lack of industrialization) and too-numerous independent nations in a relatively small area, all combine to make this the least-developed region of Europe in economic terms. Despite its general ruggedness, two factors have made this sub-region a traditional highway of war: proximity to the westernmost tip of Asia, in the area of the Turkish Straits; and the traversibility of the river valleys, facilitating commerce and other east and west transit, not only across the Straits, but between Central Europe and South Russia.

Soviet Asia includes practically every type of terrain except tropical: rocky and sandy deserts, steppes, tundra, lofty mountains, great expanses of forests, and a varied assortment of temperate zone farming areas. This tremendous region extends across the entire northern half of Asia; even without European Russia of which it is an extension, it comprises the largest single political territory in the world. It includes the bulk of the Heartland area of Sir Halford J. Mackinder's geopolitical concept of political and spatial relationships.

STRATEGIC SIGNIFICANCE

The first, and possibly most impressive, strategic consideration relating to this region is the geopolitical fact noted above. This region is a combination of Mackinder's Heartland and Eastern Europe, and requires consideration of Mackinder's famous thesis: Who rules East Europe commands the Heartland; who rules the Heartland commands the World Island [Eastern Hemisphere]; who rules the World Island commands the World. Whether or not one agrees with its validity, the idea cannot be ignored.

All except two of the countries of Eastern Europe are solidly within the Soviet orbit, and are members of the Soviet-dominated Warsaw Pact (see below). The two exceptions are Yugoslavia and Albania. The extent of Soviet domination over the other six nations of the region (often referred to as Soviet satellites) varies from country to country. There is no question, however, that such domination exists; this was amply reaffirmed by the 1968 invasion and occupation of Czechoslovakia.

The Soviet satellites of East Central Europe are a strategic protective belt, garrisoned by Soviet and satellite ground forces, within which the Soviet advanced air defense system functions. This belt also encompasses some of the formidable defense obstacles noted above, including the Carpathian Mountains, and the Elbe, Oder, and Vistula Rivers. Moreover, politically this belt helps to insulate Russia's population from Western influence, and at the same time affords an advanced base for penetration of Western Europe by Communist intelligence, subversion and propaganda. It also provides an advance base that would be militarily useful in war. It projects the Soviet military frontier 750 miles westward and 400 miles southward from Russia's pre-World War II border. The Rhine would be the first serious natural obstacle in the path of Soviet armies attacking West Germany.

REGIONAL ALLIANCES

Warsaw Pact. This is an alliance of the Soviet Union and six of the other Communist states of East Europe: East Germany, Poland, Czechoslovakia, Hungary, Romania, and Bulgaria. It was established as a 20-year mutual-defense alliance in May 1955 in a conference called at Warsaw in response to the ratification (March 1955) of West Germany's admittance to the North Atlantic Treaty Organization (NATO). Albania was represented at the conference, and was one of the original Pact members. However, Albania has been excluded from all Warsaw Pact activities since 1962, after that nation aligned itself with Communist China in the Sino-Soviet dispute. Albania formally withdrew from the Pact in September, 1968, after the Soviet invasion of Czechoslovakia.

East Germany also participated in the conference, but was not officially admitted to the Pact until 1958, after it became obvious that Communist-bloc pressures would not reverse the rearmament of West Germany.

The Warsaw Pact established a joint command and defense staff for the combined armed forces of the seven participants. This staff is located in Moscow; the Commander in Chief is a Soviet marshal. Each other member of the alliance provides a General Staff mission, headed by a senior officer. The Pact also maintains permanent military staff missions, composed of Soviet officers only, in the capitals of each of the other member nations. There is also a political Consultative Committee, consisting of the foreign ministers of the participating nations, under the chairmanship of the Soviet Foreign Minister. In the terms of the treaty creating the Pact, armed attack in Europe on a member state will oblige all other members to come to its assistance.

Other Alliances. The USSR has 20-year bilateral treaties of friendship, cooperation, and mutual assistance, renewable on expiration, with each of the other members of the Warsaw Pact. These treaties broaden the terms of assistance in war to specify an attack by any state or combination of states, whether in Europe or not. There are similar bilateral treaties among the other members. Additionally there are status of forces treaties with all Pact countries where Soviet troops are stationed.

In 1949 the USSR established the Council for Mutual Economic Assistance (COMECON, or CEMA). Members were the other members of the Warsaw Pact. Albania left in 1961, and Mongolia joined in 1962. Cuba became the ninth member in 1972. It was originally stated to be a consultative, cooperative body to facilitate through joint action the economic development of all, but the USSR soon assumed dominance in all matters. By 1962 no national mid-range (3- or 5-year) plan, nor its annual fulfillment plan or budget, could be put in effect without USSR approval; items and quantities in international trade were virtually dictated, as were the categories of goods to be produced in each country.

RECENT INTRA- AND EXTRA-REGIONAL CONFLICTS

There have been a few major conflicts or incidents within the region involving the use, or threatened use, of armed forces. In addition to the two Berlin crises noted below, there have been several others of only slightly lesser significance. There have also been two major incidents outside the region in which Soviet armed forces have been directly involved. No attempt is made here to assess the extent to which Soviet influence may have been involved, directly or indirectly, in other incidents or conflicts outside the region.

The major incidents are:

1968	Warsaw Pact (less Romania) occupation of Czechoslovakia
1969	Sino-Soviet border engagements along frontiers with Manchuria and Sinkiang (these were only the most publicized of many border incidents since 1961)
1970	Civil disturbances in northern Poland resulting in major changes in Party and Government leadership

Merchant Fleet: 17 ships; 56,523 gross tons

DEFENSE STRUCTURE

The Albanian Armed Forces are under the Ministry of National Defense. The Minister, who is both a senior military officer and a high ranking member of the Albanian Workers (Communist) Party, exercises direct military and administrative control over the military establishment. All of the regular military forces are within the People's Army, although the air force and navy are treated separately because of their distinctive functions and equipment. Designations of rank were abolished in 1966. Position in the military hierarchy is based on responsibilities stipulated in the tables of organization of the armed forces.

About 80% of the military personnel are in the army, and many functions that apply to all of the services are administered by the army. Among them are the Main Political Directorate and the Rear Services (logistics).

Naval units are controlled by the Coastal Defense Command, which is operationally responsible directly to the Ministry of National Defense. The senior naval officer is Commander of Naval Forces, Deputy Commander of Coastal Defense and Deputy Minister of Defense for Naval Affairs. As Deputy Commander of Coastal Defense he coordinates naval operations with those of air defense and ground forces. The mission of the navy is to provide for military security of coastal waters, prevent submarines from approaching the coast, lay and sweep mines, intercept enemy forces, escort convoys, and, together with frontier guard and police, control entries to and exits from the country.

The commander of the Air Force is also a Deputy Minister of Defense. About two-thirds of the air force strength is air defense artillery and missile units. Because the force is small, could not be easily resupplied, has exposed bases, and possesses no appreciable area to retreat into, it could not be expected to contribute significantly to a sustained combat effort.

POLITICO-MILITARY POLICY

Albania has consistently supported Communist China since the first public evidence of the Sino-Soviet split. This has alienated Albania from the rest of Eastern Europe.

Military service is universal. All men of 19 to 35 years of age are liable for two years of compulsory military service in most branches of the Army, and for three years in the Air Force, Navy, and frontier units. Men from 35 to 55 years of age are subject to obligatory military service in the reserve. In the event of mobilization Albania cluld call about 500,000 males between 16 and 50 years old. About 70% are physically fit for military service and about half have had military experience. It is believed that in case of war the Albanian armed forces will revert to guerrilla fighting.

ALBANIA

POWER POTENTIAL STATISTICS

Area: 11,100 square miles
Population: 2,390,000
Total Active Armed Forces: 54,500 (including internal security and border troops; 2.28% population)
Gross National Product: $1.29 billion ($540 per capita)
Annual Military Expenditures: $119.3 million (9.25% GNP)

The People's Republic of China took over the Soviet military assistance role after 1961, introduced its advisers and experts, and started to provide military and economic help. But training methods have remained Soviet. Almost all training manuals have been translated from Russian. Political indoctrination, conducted and supervised by political commissars, is heavily administered in all training programs.

Naval officers are required to have at least some university credits. They receive specialized courses before going to sea. Before 1961 most officers received training in the USSR. Since then some Albanian officers have gone to China for advanced training.

STRATEGIC PROBLEMS

Albania's important strategic position at the southern entrance to the Adriatic, and its weakness and isolation, make it a potential target of any power which would strive for domination over the Adriatic. Thus in 1939 Albania was invaded and subjugated by Mussolini when he decided to turn the Adriatic into an Italian lake.

After Stalin's death in 1953 Albanian-Soviet relations gradually deteriorated to the extent that in December 1961 Khrushchev broke off diplomatic relations with Albania, ended Soviet economic assistance, withdrew Soviet military forces (which included a Soviet submarine base on Sazan Island, near Vlone, garrisoned by some 3,000 Soviet soldiers and reportedly harboring eight Soviet submarines), and excluded it from all meetings of the Warsaw Pact. Albania formally drew from the Pact in 1968.

Historically and linguistically the Albanians comprise a relatively homogeneous nation. The Greeks (in the south) and the Yugoslavs (in the north) are numerically unimportant. In addition, 920,000 Albanians live in southern Yugoslavia, in the autonomous Kosovo-Metohija region where they form a potential source of friction between the two countries.

MILITARY ASSISTANCE

The 1961 diplomatic break with the Soviet Union ended the supply of Soviet arms and equipment, and of spare parts to keep the Soviet tanks and planes running. This situation was alleviated in 1964-1965 when Communist China began to provide spares for the MiG fighters and also furnished 30 Chinese-built MiG-17s. Defense cooperation between Albania and Communist China continues.

ALLIANCES

In September 1968, after the invasion of Czechoslovakia by troops of the Soviet Union and other Warsaw Pact powers, Albania formally withdrew from the Pact. In fact it had not participated since 1961, when Albania sided with Communist China in the Sino-Soviet split. Albania is a member of the United Nations and has an alliance and friendship treaty with the People's Republic of China.

ARMY

Personnel: 35,000

Organization:
    1 tank brigade
    6 infantry brigades

Major Equipment Inventory:
    100 medium tanks (45 Soviet T-34 and T-54, 55 Chinese T-59/62)
    122mm and 152mm guns and howitzers
    SU-76 self-propelled 76mm AT guns
    APCs (BTR-40, BTR-50, BTR-152)
    Snapper antitank missiles
    45mm, 57mm and 85mm antitank guns
    37mm, 57mm and 85mm AA

Reserves: 75,000 to 80,000 trained reservists

NAVY

Personnel: 3,000

Organization:
    Submarine Brigade
    Vlore Sea Defense Brigade
    Durres Sea Defense Brigade

Major Units:
    4 submarines (SS)
    2 fleet minesweepers (T-43 class; MSF)
    6 inshore minesweepers (T-301 class; MSI)
    4 submarine chasers (Kronstadt class; PC)
    36 torpedo boats, patrol craft and gunboats (P-4, P-6, Hu Chwan PTFG)

Naval Base: Sazan

Reserves: Over 5,000 trained reservists

AIR FORCE

Personnel: 4,500

Organization:
    2 fighter interceptor squadrons (MiG-21)
    4 fighter-bomber squadrons (MiG-17/19)
    1 transport squadron (An-2, Il-14)

Major Aircraft Types:
- 80 combat aircraft (Chinese built)
  - 32 MiG-17 fighters
  - 16 MiG-19 fighters (AGM)
  - 32 MiG-21 fighters (Atoll AAM)
- 97 other aircraft
  - 8 Il-14 transports
  - 4 An-2 transports
  - 65 trainers (MiG-15, Yak-11, Yak-18)
  - 20 helicopters (Mi-1, Mi-4)

Missiles:
Sa-2 Guideline SAMs (from China)

Air Bases: Tirane, Sazan, Vlone, Shijak, Kucove

Reserves: About 6,000 reservists

PARAMILITARY

There is a Frontier Guard of 5 battalions, plus 3 battalions in reserve, and a Security Police of 4 battalions. These total about 12,500. Formal paramilitary training is obligatory for all young people.

BULGARIA
Narodna Republika Bulgaria
People's Republic of Bulgaria

POWER POTENTIAL STATISTICS

Area: 42,823 square miles
Population: 8,670,000
Total Active Armed Forces: 193,000 (includes border troops and internal security troops; 2.23% population)
Gross National Product: $12.1 billion ($1,395 per capita)
Annual Military Expenditures: $310 million (2.56% GNP)
Steel and Iron Production: 3.3 million metric tons
Fuel Production: Coal: 27.09 million metric tons
  Oil: 305,000 metric tons
Electric Power Output: 21.02 billion kwh
Merchant Fleet: 148 ships; 703,878 gross tons
Civil Air Fleet: 7 jet, 23 turboprop and 6 piston transports

DEFENSE STRUCTURE

The Minister of National Defense is the commander of the fully integrated Bulgarian armed forces known as the People's Army. He is the highest ranking officer. Under the Ministry of Defense are the General Staff, the Main Political Directorate, the Main Inspectorate of Training, the rear services (logistics), the naval forces, the air and air defense forces, military districts and frontier troops. The Chief of the Main Political Directorate, responsible for political indoctrination of the forces, reports not only to the Minister of Defense, but to the Central Committee of the Bulgarian Communist Party. There are three military districts, with headquarters in Sofia, Plovdiv, and Sliven.

POLITICO-MILITARY POLICY

The internal, foreign, and military policies of Bulgaria follow those of the USSR. Bulgaria's close association with the Soviet Union reflects not only Bulgarian ideological and economic ties with that country, but also traditional Bulgarian friendship for Russia rooted in Bulgaria's struggle for independence in the 19th Century. In 1968 troops took part in the military intervention in Czechoslovakia.

There is compulsory military service for all male citizens. The term of service is two years for the Army and Air Force and three years for the Navy. The treaty of peace signed by Bulgaria in 1947 limits the overall size of its armed forces to 65,000 men. But with Soviet backing, the Bulgarian military establishment has grown beyond the treaty size and now totals 193,000.

STRATEGIC PROBLEMS

Bulgaria shares a dearth of strategic space with the other small Balkan countries. This, combined with other inadequacies of resources, means that Bulgaria cannot play an important role in a major European war.

Otherwise, Bulgaria's principal strategic problems stem from longstanding frontier controversies with its neighbors. Bulgaria shares ancient Macedonia with Greece and Yugoslavia; it has long been a Bulgarian dream to unite all of Macedonia with Bulgaria, a dream which has contributed to a number of wars and incidents over the past century.

Bulgaria also has irredentist claims on the southern portion of Romania's Dobruja — the region lying east of the lower Danube—which was lost to Romania in 1913 as a result of the Second Balkan War. But while relations between Bulgaria and Romania are relatively cool, the Dobruja issue does not seem to be as critical as the Macedonian problem. Relations with Greece and Turkey, members of NATO and historical antagonists, which have been marked by a prolonged tension for many years, have recently improved.

MILITARY ASSISTANCE

Bulgarian armed forces are organized, trained, and equipped along Soviet lines, with the benefit of substantial Soviet assistance.

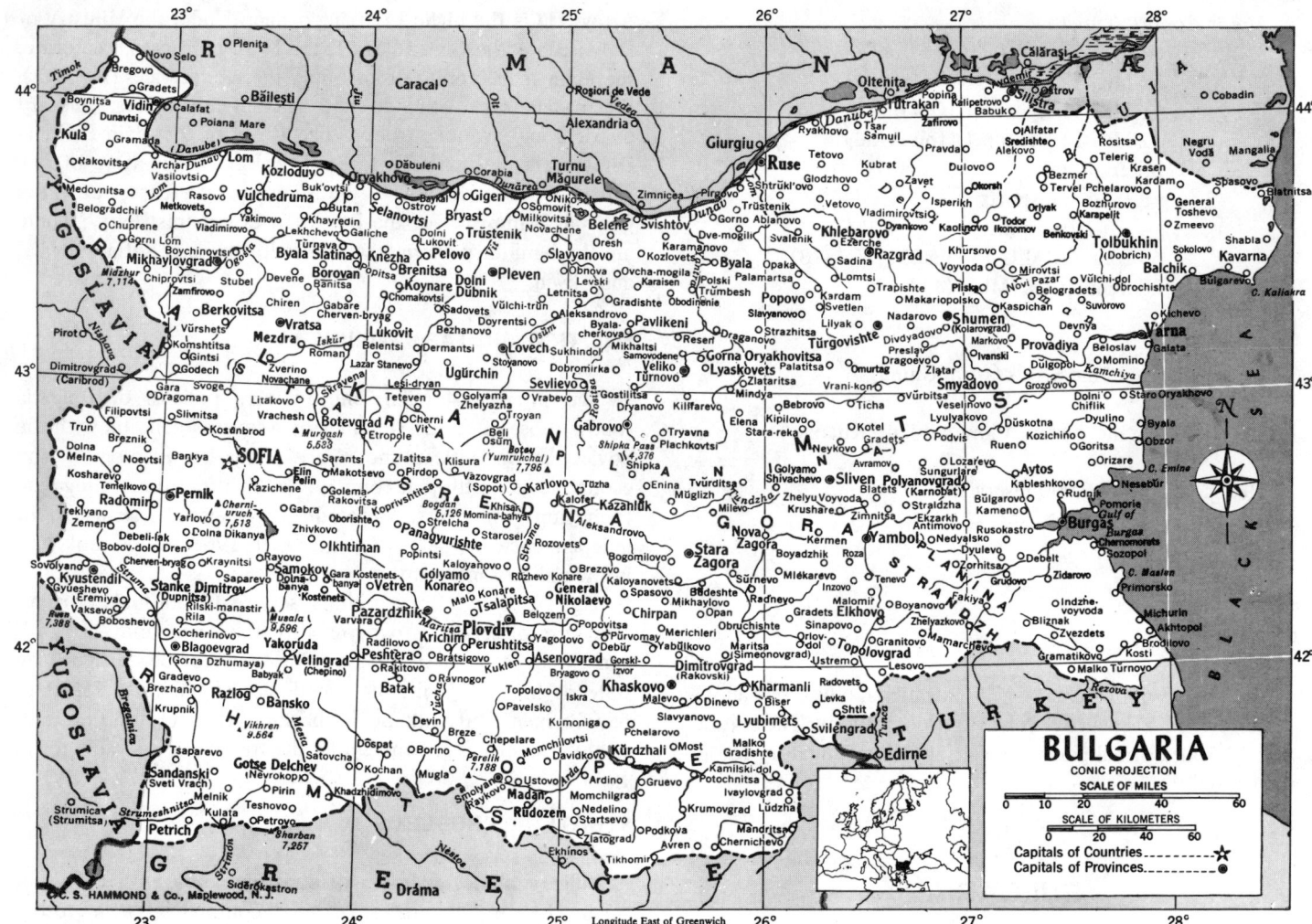

Bulgarian military leaders consider that their forces have adequate quantities of modern equipment. Bulgaria, like all of the other Warsaw Pact countries, has received heavy weapons and more complex equipment from the USSR. Ground forces have Soviet-made artillery, antitank guns and antitank wire-guided missiles, and short range surface-to-surface missiles. There are very few weapons manufactures locally. All combat aircraft are from the USSR.

ALLIANCES

In addition to a 1955 Treaty of Friendship and Mutual Assistance with the USSR, Bulgaria is a member of the Warsaw Pact and the Council of Mutual Economic Assistance (CEMA). It has also signed bilateral treaties of friendship, cooperation and mutual assistnnce with all other members of the Warsaw Pact. It belongs to the United Nations and its specialized agencies.

ARMY

Personnel: 119,000

Organization:

- 3 armies (military regions), with headquarters at Sofia, Plovdiv, and Sliven
- 9 motorized rifle divisions (3 in cadre form)
- 5 tank brigades
- 1 parachute regiment
- 4 AAA regiments

Major Equipment Inventory:

- 30 heavy tanks (JS-3 and T-10)
- 2,000 medium tanks (T-34, T-54, T-55, T-62)
- light tanks (PT-76)
- 1,000+ light, medium, and heavy artillery pieces
- Snapper, Sagger, and Swatter antitank guided missiles
- scout cars (BTR-40P)
- APCs (BTR-50, BTR-60, and BTR-152)
- SAMs (SA-2 Guideline)
- SSMs (Frog and Scud)
- SU-100 and JSU-122 self-propelled guns
- ZSU-57/2 self-propelled AA

Reserves: Over 500,000 trained reservists

NAVY (includes a small Danube flotilla)

Personnel: 9,000

Major Units:

    2 submarines (W class; SS)
    2 destroyer escorts (Riga class; DE)
    8 submarine chasers (2 Kronstadt class; 6 SO-1; PC)
    3 fast patrol boats (PTFG) (with Styx missiles)
    12 torpedo boats (4 Shershen, 8 P-4 class; PT)
    4 fleet minesweepers (T-43 class; MSF)
    6 inshore minesweepers (2 Vanya, 4 T-301 class; MSI)
    24 minesweeping launches (Po-2 class; MSL)
    10 landing craft utility (LCU)
    26 training and service craft

Major Naval Bases: Varna, Burgas

Reserves: About 40,000 trained reservists

AIR FORCE

Personnel: 22,000

Organization:

    12 fighter/interceptor squadrons (MiG-21/19/17)
    6 fighter-bomber squadrons (MiG-17)
    1 light bomber squadron (Il-28)
    3 reconnaissance squadrons (MiG-15, MiG-17, Il-28)
    3 transport squadrons (Il-12/14, Li-2, An-2)
    4 helicopter squadrons (Mi-4, Mi-6, Mi-8)

Major Aircraft Types:

    264 combat aircraft
        44 MiG-21 fighter/interceptors
        36 MiG-19 fighter/interceptors
        152 MiG-17 fighter-bomber/interceptor/reconnaissance
        8 MiG-15 fighter/reconnaissance
        24 Il-28 light bomber/reconnaissance

    208 other aircraft
        10 Il-14 transports
        4 Li-2 transports
        6 Il-12 transports
        8 An-2 transports
        140 trainer/support aircraft (L-29)
        40 helicopters (Mi-4, Mi-6, Mi-8

Air Bases: Sofia, Yambol, Burgas, Balchik, Tolbukhin, Ignatiev, Plovdiv, Karlovo

PARAMILITARY

There are five brigades of border guards, totalling about 18,000 men. There is a security police force of about 25,000 organized in eight regiments. A People's Militia of 150,000 is available for local defense in the event of war.

CZECHOSLOVAKIA

Ceskoslovenska Socialisticka Republika
Czechoslovak Socialist Republic

POWER POTENTIAL STATISTICS

Area: 49,371 square miles
Population: 14,710,000
Total Active Armed Forces: 220,000 (includes border troops and internal security troops; 1.5% population)
Gross National Product: $34.2 billion ($2,325 per capita)
Annual Military Expenditures: $1.84 billion (5.38% GNP)
Steel and Iron Production: 20.14 million metric tons
Fuel Production: Coal: 113.6 million metric tons
    Oil: 191,000 metric tons
Electric Power Output: 47.2 billion kwh
Merchant Fleet: 12 ships, 82,731 gross tons (based on Stettin, Poland)
Civil Air Fleet: 18 jet, 7 turboprop, and 27 piston transports

DEFENSE STRUCTURE

The Czechoslovakian armed forces include ground forces, air forces, frontier forces and internal forces. The President of the republic is commander in chief of the armed forces and titular head of the defense establishment. The Council of Defense, which exercises policy and budgetary control over national defense and security organizations, is nominally responsible to the Federal Assembly, but the Communist Party is in de facto control over its activities.

The armed forces are administered by the Minister of Defense, a high ranking military officer, who is responsible to the Prime Minister, the effective head of the government. Under the Minister of Defense are the General Staff, Inspector General, Main Political Directorate, Main Directorate for the Ground Forces, Main Directorate for the Air and Air Defense Forces, Personnel Directorate, Rear Services, and Frontier and Interior Troops. Organizationally the country is divided into military districts whose headquarters administer ground forces and support units within their boundaries.

140 ALMANAC OF WORLD MILITARY POWER

Effective party domination over the military establishment is assured by placement of high Communist Party officials in positions of control over the Ministry of National Defense. Political officers, under the Main Political Directorate of the Ministry of National Defense, are assigned to all units. The party organization and communist youth groups are also represented at all levels and in all branches of the military services.

The Ground Force, commonly referred to as the army, is by far the largest and most important of the services. Army officers hold most of the higher staff positions, and army support units provide the common services that are required by all branches of the armed forces. Like the chiefs of the other main directorates, the Ground Force commander is a Deputy Minister of National Defense.

After those of the Soviet Union and Poland the Czechoslovak air forces are the largest and the best equipped of the Warsaw Pact members. Air defenses include aircraft detection and surveillance stations, antiaircraft artillery and surface-to-air missile units. Most of the surveillance stations are located on the northwestern and southwestern borders of Bohemia, where they would be the first to spot planes approaching the Czechoslovakian airspace from west and southwest. Antiaircraft artillery is assigned to the defense of military formations or targets that might be attacked by low-flying aircraft. Surface-to-air missile units, because of their better capability against high flying planes, are usually responsible for city and outer perimeter defenses.

The Main Directorate for Rear Services (logistics) procures and distributes most of the weapons, ammunition, military equipment, and other supplies to all components of the armed forces. Uniformity of organization and procedures, and standardization of many items of armament and equipment in the various Warsaw Pact forces, allow easier interchange of materiel.

Until 1965 the frontier forces serving on the country's borders were under the Ministry of Interior. In 1965 they were transferred to the Ministry of National Defense and placed within the armed forces.

POLITICO-MILITARY POLICY

From January to August 20, 1968, a new nationalistically communist government, dominated by Party General Secretary Alexander Dubcek, was drifting away from its former close ties with the Soviet Union toward a form of independent, relatively liberal Communism. Soviet political and military leaders, recollecting the defection of Tito's Yugoslavia in 1948, doubted Dubcek's repeated affirmations of full and complete loyalty to the USSR and the Warsaw Pact. During the night of August 20-21 massive Soviet armed forces moved into Czechoslovakia and quickly established complete military control over the entire country. The invasion forces numbered approximately 500,000 Soviet troops, with East German, Polish, Hungarian, and Bulgarian contingents totalling an additional 150,000 men. On orders from the Czech Government, the greatly outnumbered Czechoslovak armed forces made no organized effort to interfere, although there were some instances of resistance, and a few military and civilian casualties.

Under constant Soviet pressure and continuing occupation by Soviet troops, Czechoslovakia has been forced to give up its reform program and revert to orthodox Communism. The new Czechoslovak leadership signed an agreement with the Soviets which justified the invasion, accepted the Brezhnev doctrine of limited sovereignty, and acknowledged that the stationing of Soviet troops in Czechoslovakia was essential to the security of the country.

Military service is universal. There are two draft calls annually, one in the spring, the other in the fall. The basic tour of conscript duty is two years. Discharged conscripts usually remain on reserve status in various categories until age fifty. Nearly 40 percent of the total force is replaced each year, creating a potential trained reserve of about 1,000,000 men under 35 years of age who have had active service within about 15 years.

STRATEGIC PROBLEMS

As evidenced by the Soviet takeover, as well as the German occupation in 1939, Czechoslovakia's principal strategic problem is its small size, exacerbated by an elongated shape that puts the vital regions of the country within easy striking distance of the frontiers, and provides little opportunity for effective air defense. This vulnerability is only slightly offset by the mountainous nature of the frontier regions on the Polish and German borders.

During the 54-year history of Czechoslovakia there have been divisive tensions between the more numerous, and dominant, Czechs of Bohemia and Moravia and the minority Slovaks of Slovakia. A major issue has been the justified claim of the Slovaks that they have not been adequately represented in the central government. This tension has unquestionably weakened Czech governments in the past, but it is notable that Czechs and Slovaks were united in support of their liberal government at the time of the Soviet invasion of August 1968.

MILITARY ASSISTANCE

Like the other East European communist countries, Czechoslovakia has been the recipient of massive Soviet military assistance. The Soviet Union continues to supply combat aircraft, tanks, heavy artillery and similar weapons. However, Czechoslovakia produces weapons' components and spare parts. The variety of additional complete material items that is locally produced is extensive, ranging from a light wire-guided antitank missile to a jet trainer and cargo aircraft.

The advanced technology and efficiency of Czechoslovakia's arms industry has resulted in Czechoslovakia's playing a leading role in the Communist military assistance program. A substantial proportion of the Communist arms, equipment, and training advisers that have been provided to underdeveloped clients have come from Czechoslovakia.

ALLIANCES

In addition to a mutual assistance Treaty of Friendship with the USSR and all other East European countries, Czechoslovakia is a member of the Warsaw Treaty Organization and the Council of Mutual Economic Assistance. All of her allies (if that is the right term), with the exception of Romania, participated in the 1968 invasion of Czechoslovakia.

Of the Soviet Forces that invaded Czechoslovakia in August 1968 five divisions and other units totaling 51,000 men remained as of the end of 1973. Czechoslovak political and military leaders rationalize that the continued presence of, and requirement for, Soviet troops in their country reflects a joint decision of the Warsaw Pact leadership in response to world and central European instability. A Soviet withdrawal in the foreseeable future can not be anticipated. From the standpoint of the Czechoslovak forces, the accommodation of the large body of Soviet troops in the already marginally adequate military installations creates some inconvenience. In general, relations between Soviet troops and the Czechoslovaks are reasonably good, but resentments surface at times and incidents occur occasionally.

ARMY

Personnel: 145,000

Organization:

- 2 military districts: headquarters: Prague and Trencin
- 3 armies: headquarters: Prague, Brno, and Olomouc
- 4 tank divisions*
- 8 motorized rifle divisions (2 cadre)*
- 1 airborne brigade*

Major Equipment Inventory:

- 100 heavy tanks (JS-3 and T-10)
- 3,500 medium tanks (T-55 and T-62, some T-54 and T-34 models remain)
- light tanks (PT-76)
- scout cars (OT-65 and FUG-1966)
- 2,000 APCs (BTR-50P, OT-62, OT-64, BTR-152)
- 150 152mm self-propelled guns (JSU-152)
- 180 heavy artillery pieces
- 360 medium artillery pieces
- 600 light artillery pieces
- 300 240mm rocket launchers
- 200 antitank guns
- Snapper, Swatter, and Sagger antitank missiles
- ZSU-57/2 self-propelled AA
- 300 AAA guns
- SSMs (Frog and Scud)
- SAMs (SA-2 Guideline)

Reserves: About 750,000 trained reserves

AIR FORCE

Personnel: 40,000

Organization:

- 18 interceptor squadrons (MiG-21/19)
- 12 fighter-bomber squadrons (MiG-17/15, Su-7)
- 6 reconnaissance squadrons (MiG-21, Il-28, L-29)
- 1 transport air division (Il-18, Il-14, An-2, Mi-4, Mi-8)

Major Aircraft Types:

- 575 combat aircraft
  - 200 MiG-21 interceptors/fighter reconnaissance
  - 85 MiG-19 interceptors
  - 60 MiG-17 fighter-bombers
  - 30 MiG-15 fighter-bombers
  - 120 Su-7B fighter-bombers
  - 50 Il-28 reconnaissance
  - 30 L-29 reconnaissance
- 465 other aircraft
  - 65 transports (Il-14, Il-18, Li-2, An-12)
  - 100 helicopters (Mi-1/4/6/8)
  - 300 trainer/support aircraft (including 150 L-29s)

Air Bases: Prague, Kosice, Zatec

Reserves: 90,000 trained reservists

PARAMILITARY

There are approximately 35,000 frontier guards and internal security troops on active duty as well as a 120,000-man volunteer People's Militia.

(EAST) GERMANY

Deutsche Demokratische Republik
German Democratic Republic

POWER POTENTIAL STATISTICS

Area: 41,766 square miles
Population: 17,200,000
Total Active Armed Forces: 201,000 (including security units; 1.17% population)
Gross National Product: $38.8 billion ($2,256 per capita)
Annual Military Expenditures: $2.64 billion (6.8% GNP)
Steel and Iron Production: 7.4 million metric tons
Fuel Production: Coal: 259.2 million metric tons
Electric Power Output: 69.4 billion kwh
Merchant Fleet: 430 ships; 1,016,205 gross tons
Civil Air Fleet: 7 jet and 18 turboprop transports

DEFENSE STRUCTURE

The People's Chamber, a unicameral legislature, is the supreme organ of the state. In practice, the executive branch of the government, consisting of the Council of State and the

---

*One division is full combat stength. The others average 30-70 percent full strength.

EASTERN EUROPE 143

Council of Ministers, is the center of official power. The executive is itself controlled by the ruling Socialist United Party of Germany (Communist Party) and, because of the board overlapping, the same individuals hold power in both party and government. The Council of State is an administrative organ of the People's Chamber operating between the parliamentary sessions. The executive powers granted to the Council of State include, among others, control over the defense and security forces of the country, as well as responsibility for the fundamental decisions regarding defense and security matters. In the administration and organization of military affairs the Council of State is assisted by the National Defense Council.

The National Defense Council serves as directing agency in matters of defense and state security, and exercises control over the Ministry of National Defense. The Minister of National Defense is the highest ranking active military officer. He has several deputies, four of whom serve as chiefs of the Main Staff, Training Directorate, Main Political Directorate and Rear Services Directorate. The commanders of the naval, border, and air defense forces are not at the deputy minister level. The Minister of National Defense has retained direct control over the ground forces. Top area and tactical commanders are responsible directly to the Minister and to the Chief of the Main Staff. The Main Staff also controls several directorates that have functions common to all service branches.

Each of the service branches has its own military school, which offers a university level curriculum and provides the service with the bulk of its officers. Cadets are young men who have completed general or technical secondary schools, or conscripts who have performed well and have been able to meet entrance requirements. Political reliability is the most important factor taken into consideration for the admission to military schools. The Friedrich Engels War College in Dresden, directly under the Ministry of National Defense, provides advanced military and political courses for officers of all services. Senior and midcareer training is made available to a substantial number of East German officers at several of the war colleges and specialized military schools in the Soviet Union.

POLITICO-MILITARY POLICY

East Germany is more rigidly and more directly controlled by Moscow than any of the other East European states (with the possible exception of Czechoslovakia since August 1968).

The task of the armed forces is officially stated to be not only to defend the State, but also to protect the "Socialist achievement." Defending Communist policies and objectives against possible dissidence is thus seen as important as defense of the country. To the extent that the government of East Germany has independent policy objectives, they are essentially negative and defensive. First, and foremost, is the internal security of the regime — since external security is adequately guaranteed by the Soviet occupation forces. Second, the GDR for its own natural purposes, as well as in support of Soviet foreign policy, wishes to establish itself in the eyes of the world, and particularly nearby neighbors, as a sovereign equal of its arch-rival, the Federal Republic of Germany (West Germany), as the legitimate successor to the prewar governments of Germany.

The armed forces are maintained by conscription. The term of service for young men between the ages of 18 and 25 is 18 months for the Army, two years for the Navy and the Air Force. To meet normal peacetime personnel requirements, it is necessary to draft about two-thirds of the 18-year old group. The average conscript has a good educational background and has had enough preinduction military training to make for easy transition to service life. After completion of active duty obligations, all personnel remain in reserve status until the age of 50 and officers until the age of 60. Of some 2,500,000 individuals that are the military-age mobilization potential, most could step into military units with a minimum of basic training.

STRATEGIC PROBLEMS

Because the Soviet Union has clearly assumed responsibility for the external security of East Germany as a geographic component of the Communist bloc, East Germany has little concern or responsibility for strategic planning, save as a minor partner and contributor within the Warsaw Pact. The principal strategic concern of the government, therefore, is to avoid the possibility of political isolation from the sources of its power in Russia. This concern was obviously evident by Ulbricht's attitude during the period prior to the Warsaw Pact invasion of Czechoslovakia in August 1968. Apparently he urged the rulers of Russia to intervene, although it is likely they would have done so without his urging.

MILITARY ASSISTANCE

Like the other East bloc nations, East Germany has received massive Soviet assistance in arms, equipment, and training, and the East German armed forces are organized along Soviet lines. Soviet military advisers occupy key positions in the staff of the Ministry of National Defense, and at lower echelons.

ALLIANCES

East Germany has bilateral treaties of friendship and mutual assistance with the USSR and other East European states, and is also a member of the Warsaw Treaty Organization and of the Council of Mutual Economic Assistance.

As the westernmost area of the Warsaw Treaty Organization East Germany has the strongest concentration of Soviet troops outside the USSR. These forces, called the Group of Soviet Forces in Germany, are among the best in the Soviet military establishment. The Soviet contingent is vastly superior to East German forces in numbers and equipment. Soviet ground forces, about 200,000 strong, are organized into twenty divisions (ten motorized rifle and ten tank) maintained at combat strength. They have over 7,000 tanks, about a quarter of the Soviet army's total tank inventory. Tactical aviation units supporting and providing air defense for the Soviet forces have about 800 interceptors and fighter bombers and several hundred transport planes. The operation of the air warning and air defense systems is a joint Soviet-East German effort.

ARMY

Personnel: 136,000 (90,000 regular army, 46,000 frontier guards)

Organization:
- Border Command (controlling the border troops; organized into brigades and independent regiments)
- 2 mobile army corps (1 tank division, 2 motorized rifle divisions each); headquarters: Leipzig and Mecklenburg
- 2 tank divisions (3 tank regiments, 1 motorized rifle regiment, 1 artillery regiment each)
- 4 motorized rifle divisions (3 motorized rifle regiments, 1 tank regiment, 1 artillery regiment each)

Tank and motorized rifle divisions also have engineer, signal, AA artillery, medical and missile battalions plus rear services, armored reconnaissance and nuclear decontamination companies.

Major Equipment Inventory:
- 100 heavy tanks (JS-3 and T-10)
- 2,200 medium tanks (T-55, T-54, T-34, and T-62)
- 125 light tanks (PT-76)
- Snapper, Swatter, and Sagger antitank guided missiles
- 700+ APCs (BTR-152, BTR-50P, BTR-60P)
- 850 light, medium, and heavy artillery pieces
- ZSU-57/2 self-propelled AA
- SSMs (Frog and Scud)

Reserves: About 250,000 trained reserves

NAVY

Naval Headquarters: Rostock

Schools and Training Facilities: Stralsund
Organized into three flotillas

Personnel: 16,000 (including 3,500, three to four battalions, Marines)

Major Units:
- 4 destroyer escorts (Riga class; DE)
- 15 submarine chasers (Hai class; PC)
- 16 submarine chasers (SO-1 class; PCS)
- 14 guided missile patrol boats (Osa class with Styx SSM; PTFG)
- 16 fleet minesweepers (MSF)
- 25 inshore minesweepers (MSI)
- 70 torpedo boats (PT)
- 34 small patrol craft (YP)
- 18 landing craft
- 30 auxiliaries
- 1 landing force (3,500 Marines)
- 16 Mi-4 helicopters

Major Naval Bases: Rostock, Warnemunde, Sassnitz, Peenemunde, Stralsund

Reserves: No more than 40,000 trained reservists

AIR FORCE

Personnel: 29,000 (including 9,000 antiaircraft troops)

Organization:
- 1 interceptor division (18 squadrons; MiG-21)
- 1 fighter-bomber division (11 squadrons; MiG-19/17, Su-7)
- 1 bomber squadron (Il-28)
- 3 transport squadrons (Tu-124, Il-14, An-2, An-14)
- 2 helicopter squadrons (Mi-1, Mi-4, Mi-8)
- 1 training division (L-29)
- 1 AA division (5 AA regiments and 21 SAM battalions)

Major Aircraft Types:
- 482 combat aircraft
  - 290 MiG-21 interceptors
  - 30 MiG-19 fighter-bombers
  - 30 MiG-17 fighter-bombers
  - 120 Su-7 fighter-bombers
  - 12 Il-28 light bombers

415 other aircraft
- 75 transports (An-2, An-14, Il-14, Tu-124)
- 40 helicopters (Mi-1, Mi-4, Mi-8)
- 300 trainer/support aircraft (L-29, Yak-18, MiG-15, MiG-21)

Major AA Equipment:
- 126 SAM launchers (SA-2 Guideline; 21 battalions)
- 162 AAA guns (57mm and 100mm)

Reserves: There are 45,000 to 50,000 reservists

Air Bases: Eggersdorf, Cottbus, Jacksdorf, Neubrandenburg, Annahutte, Kamenz, Bautzen, Brandenburg-Breis, Marxwald, Odenbruch, Janischwelk-Ost, Drewitz, Dresden, Frankfurt-Oder, Gross-Dollen, Dessau, Vogelsang, Gorlitz, Peenemunde, Preschen, Orewitz.

PARAMILITARY

In addition to *Grenzschutztruppe*, or border troops (included above, under Army), the *Volkspolizei* (People's Police) internal security police number 20,000, and the Transport Police number 8,500. The *Betreibskampfgruppen*, an armed workers' militia organization, trained by the People's Police, and numbering about 350,000, is available for home guard functions.

HUNGARY
Magyar Nepkoztarsasag
Magyar People's Republic

POWER POTENTIAL STATISTICS

Area: 35,919 square miles
Population: 10,400,000
Total Active Armed Forces: 129,500 (including border troops and internal security troops; 1.24% population)
Gross National Product: $16.5 billion ($1,586 per capita)
Annual Military Expenditures: $590 million (3.57% GNP)
Steel and Iron Production: 5.10 million metric tons
Fuel Production: Coal: 27.4 million metric tons
  Oil: 1.96 million metric tons
  Gas: 3.71 billion cubic meters
Electric Power Output: 14.99 billion kwh
Merchant Fleet: 18 ships; 33,061 gross tons
Civil Air Fleet: 5 jet, 8 turboprop and 8 piston transports

DEFENSE STRUCTURE

As in the other East European Communist republics, the armed forces of Hungary are controlled through the interlocking hierarchies of the Communist Party and the Government. The Minister of National Defense is the senior military officer, a member of the Cabinet and of the Defense Council. He exercises administrative control of the air forces and frontier forces. Under the Ministry of Defense are the General Staff, the Main Political Directorate, the Training Directorate, the Directorate of Rear Services, and the Personnel Directorate. The Chief of the Main Political Directorate is Deputy Minister of Defense. He reports to the Party's Central Committee and is responsible for political indoctrination. All military units have deputy commanders for political affairs.

POLITICO-MILITARY POLICY

Hungary's foreign and military policies are largely directed by Moscow. The strict Soviet control established after Russian troops suppressed the Hungarian Revolution of 1956 is beginning to be relaxed. The extent of Soviet influence is evidenced by the fact that, despite obvious reluctance, Hungarian troops participated in the August 1968 invasion of Czechoslovakia by Warsaw Pact forces.

The peace treaty of 1947 restricted the armed forces to ground forces of 65,000 men and an air force of 5,000 men and 90 aircraft (70 combat), and limited their functions to the defense of frontiers. In total disregard of these limitations the numbers were well over these figures in 1973.

The armed forces are maintained by compulsory military service, which begins at age 18. The term of service is generally two years, but can be three years in certain specialist branches.

STRATEGIC PROBLEMS

Hungary, like the other small countries of Eastern Europe, has suffered strategically from the twin liabilities of inadequate size, and location, which resulted in Hungary's present situation as a satellite of Russia. Hungary's freedom of action is still further limited by the presence of 40,000 Soviet troops, the four divisions of the Southern Group of Forces and a Tactical Air Army (referred to as the Soviet Air Force, Hungary), which have maintained strict, although relatively unobtrusive, military control over Hungary since 1956. Soviet ground and air units are based near major Hungarian military installations.

EASTERN EUROPE 147

MILITARY ASSISTANCE

Hungarian armed forces are organized, trained, and equipped along Soviet lines, and with the benefit of substantial Soviet assistance in provision of equipment and training personnel. Soviet control is facilitated by the presence of Russian advisers at several echelons in the Hungarian staff and command system.

ALLIANCES

Hungary has bilateral treaties of friendship and mutual assistance with the USSR and all other East European Communist countries. Hungary is a member of the UN, the Warsaw Pact and the Council for Mutual Economic Assistance.

ARMY

Personnel: 90,000

Organization:

- 4 military districts (Budapest, Debrecen, Kiskunfelegyhaza, and Pecs)
- 2 tank divisions (3 tank regiments, 1 motorized rifle regiment, 1 artillery regiment and support)
- 5 motorized rifle divisions (3 motorized rifle regiments, 1 tank regiment, 1 artillery regiment, engineer, AT, signal)
- 1 airborne regiment
- 1 river flotilla (see Navy)

Major Equipment Inventory:
heavy tanks (T-10 and JS-3)

1,600 medium tanks (T-34, T-54, T-55, and T-62)
  50 light tanks (PT-76)
     armored cars (FUG-A)
     scout cars (OT-65)
     APCs (OT-64, OT-66, and BTR-152)
 400 field artillery pieces
     light artillery rocket launchers
     SU-100 and JSU-122 self-propelled guns
     AA guns
     ZSU-57/2 self-propelled AA
     Snapper, Swatter, and Sagger antitank missiles
     SSMs (Frog, Scud)
  84 SAM launchers (SA-2 Guideline; 14 battalions)

Reserves: There are approximately 100,000 trained reserves

NAVY

There is no Navy as such. The Danube flotilla, part of the Army, has 1,500 men, and gunboats, small minesweepers, and small patrol craft on the river.

AIR FORCE

Personnel: 12,500

Organization:
  1 fighter-interceptor division (10 squadrons; MiG-21/19)
  1 light bomber squadron (Il-28)
  1 fighter-bomber/reconnaissance squadron (MiG-17, MiG-19)
  1 transport squadron (An-2, Il-14, Li-2)
  3 fighter-bomber squadrons (Su-7)
  2 helicopter squadrons (Mi-2, Mi-4, Mi-8)

Major Aircraft Types:
 180 combat aircraft
  84 MiG-21 interceptors
  24 MiG-19 fighter-bombers
  12 MiG-17 fighter-bombers
  48 Su-7 fighter bombers
  12 Il-28 bombers
 146 other aircraft
  10 Il-14 transports
  10 An-2 transports
   6 Li-2 transports
  30 helicopters (Mi-2, Mi-4, Mi-8)
  90 trainers (L-29, Yak-18, MiG-15)

Air Bases: Budapest (3), Miskolc, Pecs, Debrecen, Kiskunfelegyhaza, Nyiregyhaza, Estergom, Szolnok, Kaposvar, Szeged, Dombova, Tokol, Gyor, Papa, Szombathely, Szekesfehervar. Soviet air force units (approximately 300 aircraft) are based at some of these bases.

Reserves: 30,000 trained reservists

PARAMILITARY

The Security Police, some 27,000 strong, includes border guards and internal security forces. Since the revolution of 1956 these units have been under the Ministry of the Interior.

There is a Workers' Militia, about 35,000 strong, for home guard functions.

POLAND

Polska Rzeczpospolita Ludowa
Polish Peoples' Republic

POWER POTENTIAL STATISTICS

Area: 120,756 square miles
Population: 33,400,000
Total Active Armed Forces: 330,000 (including internal security and border troops; 0.99% population)
Gross National Product: $48.6 billion ($1,455 per capita)
Annual Military Expenditures: $2.25 billion (4.62% GNP)
Steel and Iron Production: 20.2 million metric tons
Fuel Production: Coal: 195.2 million metric tons
  Oil: 424,500 metric tons
  Gas: 12.47 million cubic meters
Electric Power Output: 68.87 billion kwh
Merchant Fleet: 606 ships; 1.76 million gross tons
Civil Air Fleet: 7 jet, 23 turboprop and 5 piston transports

DEFENSE STRUCTURE

The governmental structure is similar to that of the USSR, with the government controlled by the communist Polish United Workers' Party. The Minister of Defense is the Commander in Chief of the armed forces, which he controls through the Ministry of Defense and the General Staff. He is responsible to the National Defense Council and the Prime Minister. Ultimate authority over the forces resides in the Politburo, which determines broader policies and fundamental strategy.

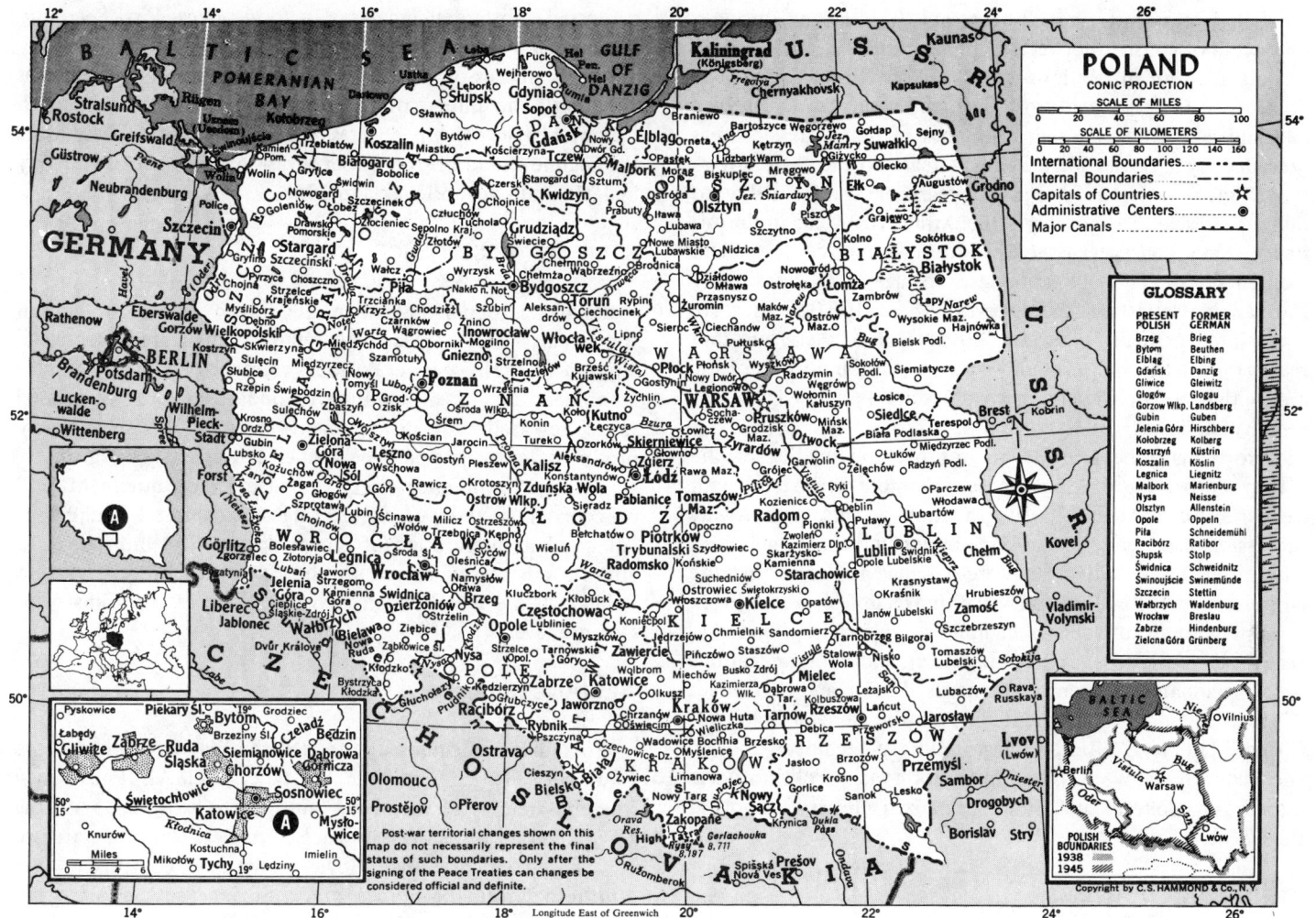

Vice Ministers of Defense are usually the chiefs of the General Staff, Main Political Directorate, Main Inspectorate of Training, and Main Inspectorate of Territorial Defense. Commanders of the navy, air force and air defense force, internal security forces and frontier troops are directly under the Minister of Defense. Ground forces, which are predominant among the three integrated services, are commanded by the Minister himself through the General Staff and the three military districts: the Warsaw Military District with headquarters in Warsaw, the Pomeranian Military District with headquarters in Bydogoszcz, and the Silesian Military District with headquarters in Wroclaw. The divisions located in the western military districts are maintained at a higher state of combat readiness than those in the eastern district.

Party influence is evident at all echelons of the armed forces. Political officers are in all units. Approximately 15 percent of all military personnel (80 percent of officers) are party members.

POLITICO-MILITARY POLICY

Poland emerged from World War II as an independent state but with different boundaries, and in a different political situation, from prewar Poland. The eastern half of the nation (about 70,000 square miles) had been lost to Russia. Poland was compensated for the loss of its eastern provinces by most of East Prussia and all other German provinces east of the Odra-Nissa (Oder-Neisse) line (a total of about 40,000 square miles). Most of the German population of these provinces, some six million, had fled west at the approach of the Soviet Army, and the remainder (several hundred thousands) were deported to Germany after World War II in accordance with the Allied Potsdam agreement of 1945. These new territories were resettled and gradually rehabilitated by Poles from overpopulated central Poland and from the eastern provinces lost to Russia. The Poles consider the territory east of the Odra-Nissa line as "recovered land," historically the cradle of the Polish state but gradually lost and Germanized during a millenium of conflict between Germans and Poles.

Poland's foreign relations closely follow Soviet policy. The Polish-West German treaty of 1970 confirming the Odra-Nissa line and containing mutual assurances of non-aggression was preceded by a Soviet-West German treaty to the same effect.

All men between 19 and 50 years of age are liable to military service: 18 months in the Army, two years in the Air Force, Navy and special services, internal security troops and frontier forces. This obligation after the age of 27 is ordinarily fulfilled by service in the reserves. About 100,000 men are conscripted annually, less than 30 percent of the group that reaches draft age and around 35 percent of the portion of the group that is considered physically suitable and eligible for military service.

Efforts have been made to improve the quality of the officer corps, by making the service more attractive, with better educational qualifications, and improving professionalism and promotion opportunities. Regulations enacted in the middle 1960s were designed to assure that the entire officers corps would have university degrees. From officers schools specializing in military engineering, infantry, armor, air force, rear services (logistics), and communications cadets graduate as second lieutenants. Senior and mid-career officers training establishments include the General Staff War College, Military-Political College, Military-Technical College, and Senior Naval War College. In addition many Polish officers attend War Colleges and other specialized military schools in the USSR.

STRATEGIC PROBLEMS

Lying across the main land routes from Russia to Central and Western Europe, Poland has for centuries been invaded repeatedly from both east and west. The Polish people present an ethnic monolith united by strong nationalism and memories of a great historical past. In their overwhelming majority they are opposed to Russian-communist domination, they are acutely aware of their low standard of living in comparison with the West, and they are strongly anti-Russian because of past and recent injuries inflicted on Poland by Russia (partitions, deportations, the Katyn mass-murder of prisoners-of-war, and Stalin's reign of terror).

In June 1956, serious worker "bread and freedom" riots broke out in the city of Poznan. Polish military units refused to act against these popularly supported riots. The Polish communists understood the seriousness of the situation and publicly admitted their responsibility for the past errors. They promised redress of grievances, increase of salaries, and improvement of the standard of living. By these quick concessions they prevented the spread of rebellion and saved their regime, but traces of unrest remain.

Numerous disorders broke out in Gdansk, Szczecin, Katowice, and elsewhere in December 1970 as workers protested substantial increases in food prices. First Secretary W. Gomulka and other key members of the Politburo resigned, and his successor, Gierek, promised reform. There was apparently no intervention by the Soviet Union. The Polish Communist leadership realizes that an attempt to overthrow the regime would bring a Soviet invasion like those of Hungary in 1956 and Czechoslovakia in 1968.

MILITARY ASSISTANCE

Poland is dependent upon the Soviet Union for certain spare parts and replacements and sophisticated electronic equipment. However, Poland produces much military equipment and is endeavoring to update materiel by a long range research and development program. Polish industry produces tanks, armored personnel carriers, trucks, artillery, small arms, communications and electronic equipment, and miscellaneous items of engineering and chemical equipment. All combat aircraft are of Soviet design. The more modern aircraft are manufactured in the Soviet Union, the rest in Poland. There is a Russian advisory group at the Ministry of Defense level.

ALLIANCES

Poland is a member of the UN, the Warsaw Pact, and the Council of Mutual Economic Assistance (CEMA). It has signed bilateral treaties of friendship and mutual assistance with the USSR and all other Warsaw Pact countries. Under a status of forces agreement, two Soviet divisions comprising the Northern Group of Forces, and a Soviet Tactical Air Army (the 37th) are stationed in Poland. The headquarters of Soviet Forces in Poland is located in Legnica.

ARMY

Personnel: 190,000

Organization:
- 3 military districts (Warsaw, Wroclaw, Bydgoszcz)
- 5 tank divisions (3 tank regiments, 1 motorized infantry regiment, 1 artillery regiment, 9,000 men each)
- 8 mechanized infantry (motorized rifle) divisions (3 motorized rifle regiments, 1 tank regiment, 1 artillery regiment, 11,000 men each)
- 1 airborne division (light weight equipment)
- 1 amphibious division Sea-Land (smaller than motorized rifle division with additional amphibious transport vehicles)
- 30 SAM battalions (SA-2 Guideline and SA-3 Goa)

Major Equipment Inventory:
- 30 heavy tanks (JS-3 and T-10)
- 3,400 medium tanks (T-34 and T-54; Polish-built T-55; some T-62)
- 150 light tanks (PT-76)
- 1,500 APCs (BTR-152, BTR-50P, OT-62, OT-64, BTRM-1967)
- armored cars (FUG-A)
- scout cars (BTR-40P)
- ASU-57, SU-100, JSU-122, JSU-152 self-propelled guns
- 700 light artillery pieces
- 250 medium artillery pieces
- 100 heavy artillery pieces
- ZSU-23/4 and ZSU-57/2 self-propelled AA guns
- 200 SAM launchers (SA-2 Guideline and SA-3 Goa)
- 200 SAM launchers (SA-2 Guideline and SA-3 Goa)
- SSMs (Frog and Scud)
- antitank guided missiles Snapper, Swatter, and Sagger

Reserves: There are approximately 800,000 trained reservists

NAVY

Personnel: 20,000 (includes 1,000 Marines)

Major Units:
- 5 diesel submarines (5 W class; SS)
- 4 destroyers (2 Skory class, 1 British-built, 1 Kotling class with SAMs; DD)
- 12 guided missile patrol boats (Osa class; PTFG)
- 8 submarine chasers (Kronstadt class; PC)
- 18 patrol boats (PGM)
- 20 patrol craft (YP) (frontier guard)
- 20 torpedo boats (P-6; PT)
- 24 fleet minesweepers (MSF)
- 4 coastal minesweepers (MSC)
- 27 minesweeping launches (MSL)
- 20 landing ships (LST/LSMR)
- 10 landing craft (LCT)
- 39 auxiliaries and support ships
- 50 naval aircraft (Il-28 and MiG-17)
- 60 trainer/support aircraft (MiG-15UTI, Yak-11, etc.)
- SSMs for coast defense (Samlet)
- 1 Marine battalion

Naval Bases: Szczecin, Gdansk, Gdynia

Reserves: There are 70,000 to 80,000 trained naval reservists.

AIR FORCE

Personnel: 55,000

Organization:
- 4 bomber squadrons (Il-28)
- 36 interceptor squadrons (MiG-17/19/21)
- 18 fighter-bomber squadrons (MiG-17, Su-7)
- 3 fighter reconnaissance squadrons (MiG-15/17)
- 4 transport squadrons (An-2, An-12, Il-14, Il-18)
- 4 helicopter squadrons (Mi-2, Mi-4)
- 4 training squadrons (Wilga, Iskra, MiG-15)

Major Aircraft Types:
- 765 combat aircraft
  - 50 Il-28 light bombers
  - 150 MiG-21 interceptors
  - 150 MiG-19 interceptors
  - 280 MiG-17 (Polish-built, LiM-5) fighter-bomber/interceptor/reconnaissance
  - 15 MiG-15 (Polish-built, LiM-4) fighter reconnaissance
  - 120 Su-7 fighter-bombers
- 390 other aircraft
  - 50 transports (An-2, An-12, Il-14, Il-18)
  - 40 helicopters (Mi-2, Mi-4)
  - 300 trainer/support aircraft

Air Bases: There are more than 50, some joint Soviet-Polish, others solely for Soviet use.

Reserves: There are about 110,000 reservists

PARAMILITARY

There are 65,000 internal security and border troops (frontier guard), the latter organized into mechanized brigades and operating smaller border patrol boats. In addition organized paramilitary training is conducted by the National Defense League at about 100 training centers. There is also a paramilitary volunteer reserve of citizens militia some half a million strong.

ROMANIA

Republica Socialista Romania
Socialist Republic of Romania

POWER POTENTIAL STATISTICS

Area: 91,700 square miles
Population: 20,900,000
Total Active Armed Forces: 200,000 (including internal security and border troops; 0.96% population)
Gross National Product: $28 billion ($1,340 per capita)
Annual Military Expenditures: $800 million (2.86% GNP)
Steel and Iron Production: 9.02 million metric tons
Fuel Production: Coal: 21.7 million metric tons
  Oil: 13.8 million metric tons
  Gas: 562.5 million cubic meters
Electric Power Output: 38.32 billion kwh
Merchant Fleet: 71 ships; 363,996 gross tons
Civil Air Fleet: 5 jet, 12 turboprop and 2 piston transports

DEFENSE STRUCTURE

As in the other East European Communist states, the armed forces of Romania are controlled by the Communist Party. The military establishment consists of ground, naval, air and air defense, and frontier forces. It is administered by the Minister of Armed Forces, who is responsible to the Defense Council and the Head of State. The Minister, who assumes the highest military rank, has several deputies, including the chiefs of the Main Political Directorate, General Staff, Directorate of Training, and Rear Services (logistics). Commanders of operational commands report directly to the minister. The highest level of tactical organization includes the commands of navy, air force, ground forces, frontier forces, and military districts.

Political indoctrination of the armed forces is the responsibility of the Main Political Directorate. Party and communist youth organizations are at all levels of the forces. Practically all senior officers and the majority of junior officers are Communist Party members.

POLITICO-MILITARY POLICY

Although Romania still follows the Soviet pattern in its

internal affairs, it is the least compliant of the Soviet allies. In June 1958, a status of forces agreement with the USSR, which had allowed the stationing of Soviet forces in Romania, lapsed when Soviet forces left the country. Beginning cautiously that same year Romania adopted a form of nationalistic Communism. Since 1963 Romania has asserted virtual independence of the USSR in its foreign policy, and its membership in the Warsaw Pact is only nominal. In some matters Romania has taken stands in opposition to Soviet policy, as in its continuing friendly relations with Communist China, Albania, and Israel.

The absence of Romanian troops from the Warsaw Pact forces that invaded Czechoslovakia in August 1968 was significant. The Romanians were presumably not considered sufficiently trustworthy allies to be kept informed of the invasion plans. Also, there was considerable speculation throughout the world (not least in Romania) that the Warsaw Pact forces would next invade Romania. It is noteworthy that the Bucharest Government, while continuing to assert its independence, and even making some ostentatious plans for resistance, also strongly reaffirmed its loyalty to Marxism-Leninism.

The limits to Romania's independence are clear. The government believes that complete abandonment of traditional communist economic, political, and social policies, or excessive provocation of the USSR in foreign policy, could bring about a new Soviet occupation.

Military service is universal. Length of service is 16 months in the ground forces and border troops and certain elements of the air force, and two years in the navy and the rest of the air force. Of the nearly 200,000 young men who reach the draft age annually, about 80 percent are physically and otherwise fit to serve. Men released from active duty remain in the reserve and subject to recall. Only those recently discharged are considered trained reserves and could be quickly mobilized and go into action without extensive retraining. There is insufficient emphasis on periodic reserve training to keep the older men up to date on new weapons and tactics.

STRATEGIC PROBLEMS

There are long-standing territorial frictions with three of Romania's four neighbors. In 1940, even before either country was involved in World War II, the USSR annexed Bessarabia and Northern Bukovina from Romania; these annexations were confirmed by the postwar peace treaty. The majority of the populations of these regions is Romanian.

After the breakup of the Austro-Hungarian Empire, under the World War I peace treaties Romania received Transylvania, with a majority population of Romanians. This region, however, had been traditionally Hungarian, and has been a source of trouble and conflict between the two nations ever since.

Less serious is the Dobruja Question with Bulgaria. The southern portion of the Dobruja (the region between the lower Danube and the Black Sea) has a slight Bulgarian majority in its population, but was awarded to Romania after the Second Balkan War in 1913. Bulgaria still aspires to regain this territory (as it did briefly in World War II), but it is not likely to become a source of conflict.

MILITARY ASSISTANCE

All major weapons and heavy equipment are of Soviet design, but because of Romania's independent policies, Romanian armed forces are not the first to receive newer equipment. Romania is attempting to reduce its dependence on the USSR and other Warsaw Pact countries by producing more military materiel within the country. There are no Soviet advisers with the Romanian armed forces, and no Soviet troops are stationed in Romania.

ALLIANCES

Romania is a member of the Warsaw Pact, but is the least active participant in the alliance. The Romanian role in the Council for Mutual Economic Assistance (CEMA) has been relatively inactive. It has consistently avoided agreeing to any multilateral measure which would limit its control over its own economy. Romania has signed bilateral treaties of friendship and mutual assistance with the USSR, all other Warsaw Pact states, the People's Republic of China and Mongolia. It is a member of the UN, and its specialized agencies.

ARMY

Personnel: 130,000

Organization:
- 2 military districts, 3 divisions each, with headquarters at Iasi and Cluj
- 1 independent garrison (Bucharest)
- 2 tank divisions (3 tank regiments, 1 motorized rifle regiment, 1 artillery regiment each)
- 7 motorized rifle divisions (3 motorized rifle regiments, 1 tank regiment, 1 artillery regiment each)
- 1 mountain brigade
- 1 airborne regiment
- 1 artillery division

Major Equipment Inventory:
- heavy tanks (JS-3 and T-10)
- 1,700 medium tanks (T-34, T-54, T-55, T-62)
- 900 APCs (BTR-152, BTR-50P)
- antitank guided missiles Snapper, Swatter and Sagger

154 ALMANAC OF WORLD MILITARY POWER

    heavy assault guns (JSU-152)
    light artillery pieces
    medium artillery pieces
    SU-100 and JSU-122 self-propelled guns
200 AA guns
    SAMs (SA-2 Guideline)
75 Frog SSMs

Reserves: There are approximately 900,000 reserves

NAVY

Personnel: 9,000

Major Units:
- 6 guided missile patrol boats (Osa class; PTFG)
- 6 submarine chasers (Kronstadt and Poti class; PC)
- 8 torpedo boats (P-4 class; PT)
- 4 coastal minesweepers (MSC)
- 22 inshore minesweepers (T-301 class; MSI)
- 12 landing ships (LSM)
- 8 minesweeping launches (MSL)
- 2 training ships
- 30 auxiliaries

Naval Bases: Constanta, Mamaia, Braila

Reserves: 25,000 to 30,000 reserves

AIR FORCE

Personnel: 21,000

Organization:
- 9 interceptor squadrons (MiG-19, MiG-21)
- 9 fighter-bomber squadrons (MiG-17)
- 2 reconnaissance/bomber squadrons (Il-28)
- 3 transport squadrons (An-2, Li-2, Il-12, Il-14)
- 1 helicopter squadron (Mi-2, Mi-4, Alouette III)

Major Aircraft Types:
- 265 combat aircraft
  - 60 MiG-21 interceptors
  - 40 MiG-19 fighter-bombers
  - 120 MiG-17 fighter-bombers
  - 20 MiG-15 fighter-bombers (used primarily for training)
  - 25 Il-28 light bomber/reconnaissance aircraft
- 210 other aircraft
  - 50 transports (An-2, Li-2, Il-12, Il-14)
  - 60+ helicopters (Mi-2, Mi-4, Alouette III)
  - 100 trainer and support aircraft (MiG-15, L-29, etc.)

Air bases: Baneasa, Otopeni, and Popesti-Leordeni (Bucharest area), Tirgusor, Buzau, Zilistea, Galati, Tecuci, Iasi, Bacau, Satu Mare, Oradea, Arad, Timisoara, Brasov, Cluj, Calarasi, Craiova, Constanta, Mamaia.

Reserves: 45,000 to 50,000 trained reservists

PARAMILITARY

There are approximately 40,000 men in border and internal security units plus a volunteer militia and armed workers' organizations numbering up to 500,000 members.

THE SOVIET UNION

Soyuz Sovetskikh Sotsialisticheskikh Respublik
Union of Soviet Socialist Republics

POWER POTENTIAL STATISTICS

Area: 8,600,350 square miles
Population: 251,500,000
Total Active Armed Forces: 3,655,000 (including MVD forces; 1.45% population)
Annual Military Expenditures: $72.9 billion by Western estimates (12.56% GNP)
Steel and Iron Production: 300 million metric tons
Fuel Production: Coal: 655 million metric tons
   Crude Oil: 394 million metric tons
   Refined Oil Products: 344 million metric tons
Electric Power Output: 800 billion kwh
Merchant Fleet: 6,575 ships; 16.2 million gross tons
Civil Air Fleet: at least 350 jet, 800 turboprop and 200 piston transports

DEFENSE STRUCTURE

The Union of the Soviet Socialist Republics is a communist federative state comprising 15 Union Republics with control highly centralized in the government in Moscow. The elective Supreme Soviet is theoretically the supreme body of state authority. The 33-member Presidium, elected by the Supreme Soviet, includes prominent members of the Communist Party

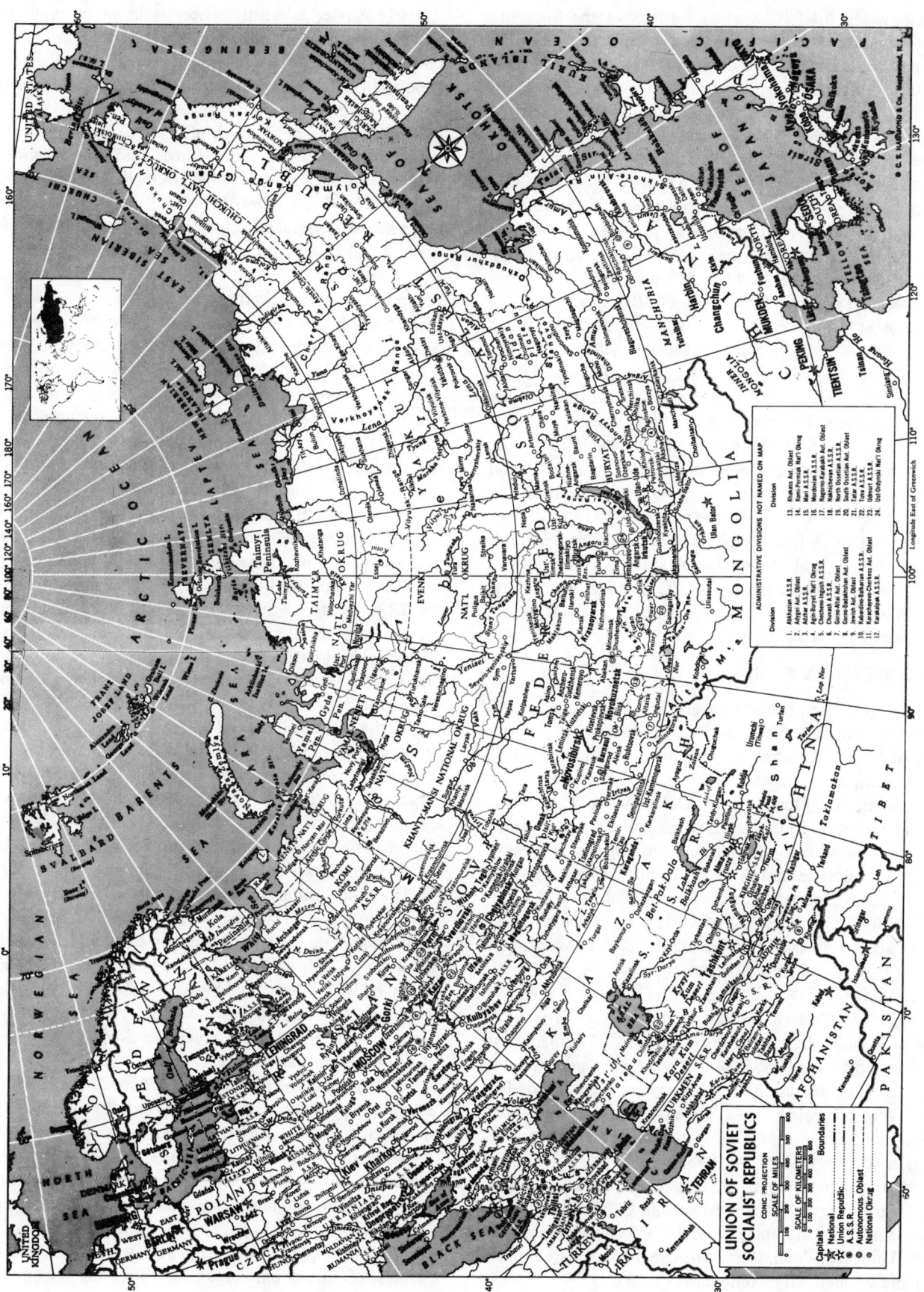

and rules between brief, occasional sessions of the Supreme Soviet; it appoints members of the Council of Ministers, appoints and dismisses the high command of the armed forces, and has authority to decree mobilization.

De facto, the ultimate power in the Soviet system is exercised by the leaders of the Communist Party of the Soviet Union (CPSU). The party imposes its will through the government apparatus. The most powerful policy-making organ in the Communist Party is the Politburo. The Secretariat of the party's Central Committee provides day-to-day executive and administrative direction for the entire party machine. Together, the Politburo and the Secretariat constitute the real seat of power in the USSR.

The Minister of National Defense — who is always a prominent Soviet officer and eminent member of the Communist Party — is the Commander in Chief of the Armed Forces, of which there are five major components: Strategic Rocket Forces, Air Defense Forces, Army, Navy, and Air Force. The General Staff is responsible for operational and strategic planning, intelligence, mobilization plans, and coordination of preparedness of the major components of the Armed Forces. The Chief of the General Staff is a First Deputy Minister of Defense. The Main Political Directorate of the Soviet Army and Navy is responsible for political indoctrination of the armed forces. Its chief is also a First Deputy Minister of Defense and has a direct channel to the Central Committee of the Party.

POLITICO-MILITARY POLICY

The modern communist government of the USSR apparently is following the general expansionist policy which was pursued by Russian governments during the four preceding centuries. But the slogans and rationale are far different from the Czarist imperialism which the Soviet government professes to detest. Expansion of the USSR in the past 35 years has taken the form of establishing vast spheres of influence and a determination to create buffer states that are not only friendly but completely subservient to the Soviet Union. The Soviet invasion of Czechoslovakia in 1968 and its menacing attitude toward Romania and Yugoslavia are dramatic evidence of the Soviet concern over geographic penetrability.

The major question which has divided the USSR from its World War II allies has been the problem of Germany and European security. The USSR would not agree to the Western proposal for the unification of Germany on the basis of free elections, and objected to the remilitarization of West Germany. In response to the admission of West Germany to NATO as a sovereign state in 1955, the Soviet Government announced the conclusion of a 20-year defense alliance (the Warsaw Treaty Organization) between the USSR and its seven European satellites: Albania, Bulgaria, Czechoslovakia, East Germany, Hungary, Poland, and Romania (Albania has since defected and is allied with Communist China).

Early Soviet scientific successes in space exploration and missile development did much to restore Soviet international prestige, so severely damaged by brutal suppression of the Hungarian rebellion. This prestige was further enhanced by Soviet accomplishments during the late 1950s in the improvement and stock-piling of nuclear weapons, modernization of the armed forces, and upgrading of their air defense system against possible strategic nuclear attack.

Meanwhile, on the diplomatic front there have been extensive East-West discussions and negotiations for arms control and disarmament. The Soviet Union refuses to accept any form of effective inspection which would assure compliance with disarmament agreements. Even without inspection, in the open societies of the West, failure to comply would be immediately evident; in the closed Soviet society there would be no fool-proof way to ascertain compliance. Bearing in mind such Soviet activities as the shipment of missiles to Cuba, while denying this was being done, Western diplomatic leaders have been reluctant to accept any terms of disarmament which do not include adequate means of verification. A degree of accommodation of the opposing positions has been arrived at in the treaty and the interim executive agreement limiting the installation of anti-ballistic and offensive long-range missiles (ABMs, ICBMs, and SLBMs) resulting from the bilateral Strategic Arms Limitation Talks (SALT) and signed at Moscow in May 1972. Both documents, while silent on the subject of on-site inspection, state that "national technical means" for verification of compliance with the agreed terms will be employed (see US, Politico-Military Policy).

At the Mutual Balanced Force Reductions (MBFR) talks in Vienna in the fall of 1973, the Warsaw Pack proposed a cut of 20,000 ground and air forces on both sides, followed by cuts of 5% in 1976 and 10% in 1977, in response to NATO's proposed cut of 15% and common ceiling of 700,000 ground forces. When the meetings adjourned in December, both sides were still opposed on all basic principles.

The arms limitation agreements have had little effect on the Soviet buildup of weapons. The USSR is rushing to build additional long-range offensive missiles which will bring the total to 2,359, permitted under the agreement. Four new types of long-range, land-based missiles are being developed. Two are designed to carry multiple, independently-targeted reentry vehicles (MIRV), which the Soviets tested for the first time in the summer of 1973.

In contrast to the rapid buildup of strategic offensive missiles during the past few years the Kremlin has apparently undergone a substantial change in its thinking in regard to the importance of ABM systems. The USSR led the call for serious limitation of ABM systems in the SALT talks. Moscow probably will not construct systems to the limit allowed by the treaty — two sites with 100 launchers each — but will limit itself to one site, Soviet strategy has apparently shifted to a greater offensive emphasis. The Kremlin abandoned active defenses against ballistic missiles because of its inability to develop an effective system. Instead, damage limitation will be accomplished by developing counter-force ICBMs and SLBMs, and by increasing the importance attached to passive defense measures such as urban evacuation and shelter construction, which might successfully attenuate the effects of a nuclear exchange and permit continued operations even under the most adverse conditions.

From analysis of the considerable Soviet professional literature on strategy and military affairs, there are indications that in recent years the Soviets have shifted their military thinking away from total reliance on nuclear deterrence, and that they have evolved their strategy along combined conventional and nuclear lines.

While there has been a reappraisal of the problems of nuclear war there has been no basic revision of Soviet views on war. The debate has had conventional and nuclear phases, but the emphasis has been on balance. A multiple option concept envisages Soviet forces trained for general nuclear war, conventional operations, and operations in which nuclear weapons are employed on a limited scale.

The USSR is still prepared to start a war with simultaneous nuclear attacks (presumably a preemptive first strike) against both the continental United States and Western Europe. The nuclear blow against the United States would be aimed at the annihilation of its nuclear capabilities, smashing of its economy and of its state and military control centers, disruption of communications, and destruction of strategic reserves. The objective of the attack would be to eliminate US capability to deliver a second strike nuclear blow against the USSR, and to prevent American participation in the defense of Europe. The simultaneous nuclear attack against Western Europe would be followed by a massive invasion of Western Europe by Soviet ground forces armed with tactical nuclear weapons, with the objective the seizure of all of Europe.

The introduction of nuclear weapons and missiles has resulted in an extensive weapons research and development program. Groups of experts with high military rank and advanced academic degrees in military and related fields work ceaselessly in all areas of military science. A network of military, scientific, and party leaders controls and guides the drive for new and better weapons. The Supreme Military Council of the Central Committee of the Communist Party controls weapons research and development, providing guidelines to the Ministry of Defense and the Academy of Sciences. Within the Ministry the General Staff is responsible for all military science programs. Its Military Science Directorate supervises and implements the programs, with the assistance of several institutions devoted to military science. Basic research is performed by six directorates, specializing in weapons, missiles, engineering, naval weapons, ships and aircraft. The military effort is also served by the Ministries of Defense Industry, Aviation Industry, and Automotive Industry. Original research for new weapons systems starts in the Academy of Sciences or the Research Institutes of the General Staff. Prototypes are produced from approved designs at one of the plants. After being tested, an accepted prototype is admitted for serial production in one of the plants of the several ministries, depending upon its characteristics. The total development cycle for a complex weapon such as a missile is estimated to take six to eight years. The Soviet military research and development systems spend about $9,000,000,000 annually.

The Soviet law on military service promulgated in 1967 reduced the length of conscripted service, which is universal, to two years for the Army, Air Force, and coastal and border defense units, and three for the Navy and units on coastal patrol vessels. Draftees with advanced education have only a one year obligation. The call up age is 18 years, with inductions in June and December. Compulsory pre-military training is carried out in schools, factories and collective farms by instructors from regular forces, providing many surplus officers with jobs and giving the potential conscript some rudimentary military training.

In an effort to prevent competent young officers from moving prematurely into the reserves, the law sets precise age limits on service, by age, rank and length of service. Marshals, generals of the army, admirals and colonel generals must retire at age 60, lieutenant generals and major generals at age 55, colonels at 50, lieutenant colonels and majors at 45, and captains and senior lieutenants at 40.

Educational requirements for Soviet officers are increasing steadily. More than 50 percent of the officer corps are technicians and engineers. There are 120 specialized military schools and 18 war colleges, with courses lasting from two to six years.

Soviet reinforcement planning allows for rapid mobilization of both reservists and active personnel in training units to bring the understrength divisions (about half the total) to full complement. These units would have to be moved from the interior by rail or road and in many cases it would take some time for them to become operational. Nevertheless the fact that the Soviet Union maintains so many formations, if only as skeletons, and that it has some 60 divisions in Europe alone, means that it can deploy a very large number of combat strength divisions in Central Europe within weeks of mobilization.

The Soviet Army insists on the primacy of offensive action, involving rapid movement by mobile forces to bring a heavy concentration of armor into the enemy rear. This doctrine calls for army units to attack from the line of march and to cover up to 70 miles in 24 hours, operating along independent axes. A Soviet field army holding a sector of 70 to 80 miles would attack on a front of about 30 miles, with divisional attack frontages of about seven miles each.

The overriding impression from a study of Soviet military literature is that the Soviet command is placing increasing reliance on airborne forces which it considers capable of performing strategic missions independently, both in direct relation to the Soviet Union and possibly to protect its interests in more distant areas. In the last decade a great amount of money and time have been spent on developing transport aircraft, assault guns, multiple rocket launchers and other equipment for use by airborne troops. Transport capacity appears to be adequate to move from two to three fully equipped divisions in one lift.

The importance of the Soviet Navy in the Soviet military establishment has been increased by new technological developments, and the extension of Soviet power and interests beyond the land perimeters of the USSR. The navy's prime mission is to counter the direct threat posed by the maritime strike capability of the western nations, and particularly the United States. To counter aircraft carriers and Polaris submarines the Soviet Navy must move out of the confines of its four fleet areas (Northern, Baltic, Black Sea and Pacific) to the high seas. At the same time it must maintain the capability of cooperating with the Soviet Army in coastal areas.

Although the organization of the Soviet Navy has not changed much since the end of World War II the strategic concept for its use is quite different. The cautious stationing of ships along the coast has given way to emphasis on global deployment. Soviet submarines from the Northern and Pacific Fleets are patrolling vast areas of the Atlantic and Pacific Oceans. The fleet in the Mediterranean is showing the Soviet flag and tying up the US Sixth Fleet. There also is intensified Soviet naval activity in the Caribbean, South Atlantic, Indian Ocean, Persian Gulf and the Red Sea. The imminent reopening of the Suez Canal will increase the Soviet naval presence in the waters of the Middle and Far East. The significance of this, both strategically and economically in a world highly dependent upon the flow of oil from these areas, is enormous and will certainly have great impact on US as well as USSR military planning.

STRATEGIC PROBLEMS

The USSR has long and difficult borders. Its western frontier in Europe is crossed by two major natural invasion routes from the west with little or no truly defensive terrain. Maintaining the integrity of the long border across Asia presents overwhelming military and logistic problems.

The geopolitical situation poses threats to the USSR from potential enemies on two fronts, Germany in the west and China in the east. Viewed through Soviet eyes and the perspective of history, the danger of attack from the west cannot be ignored merely because Germany today is different from the nation which twice attacked Russia during this century. Although China currently is militarily weak, its potential is enormous, and there is abundant historic and ideological hostility toward the USSR. The possibility of future cooperation between Japan and China cannot be overlooked by Soviet strategists.

The deteriorating and explosive relationship between the USSR and the People's Republic of China has become an important element in the global balance of power. With the Chinese acquiring operational nuclear weapons, the Soviet strategic problem becomes more significant. Almost all cities and military and industrial complexes in the Soviet Far East and Central Asia are vulnerable to a surprise Chinese attack which could inflict heavy damage. Once the Chinese begin to deploy the new 3,500-mile range missiles they are already producing they will be capable of hitting Moscow and other major centers in European Russia. The Kremlin leaders and the Soviet high command face a difficult choice of strategic alternatives. They can unleash a preventive nuclear strike that would destroy China's nuclear capability and eventually overthrow the anti-Soviet government in Peking, or they can adopt a waiting, no action, policy, which would condemn Russians to live in danger from almost one billion Chinese, whose military strength and hostility is growing rapidly. Today, and in the immediate future, the USSR could attack China with reasonable expectation of destroying Peking's nuclear bases, with little risk of effective Chinese nuclear retaliation. The political damage to the USSR, and to international communism, however, would be enormous. On the other hand, in a few years the military risk of a Soviet preventive strike might be prohibitive.

Although Sino-Soviet war may not be imminent, there is good evidence of preparations for it on both sides of the 4,000-mile frontier. In the past several years the Soviets have expanded their forces in the area from 15 divisions to possibly as many as 50 motorized and tank divisions. This ground force of well over 800,000 men is supported by 75,000 border ground troops, more than 1,000 combat aircraft and the Amur River flotilla. Backing up these conventional forces are a substantial number of missiles with nuclear warheads.

MILITARY ASSISTANCE

The Soviet Union has provided substantial military assistance to all communist-controlled countries in the world, and to unaligned and leftist underdeveloped nations through a combination of sale, loan, and grant. It is estimated that the total value of military assistance provided by the USSR to 35 developing countries in Asia, Africa and the Middle East since 1955 has been at least $8 billion. Of this total, which does not include support provided in the October War of 1973, some 77 percent ($6.2 billion) has gone to the Middle East and Asia. Egypt has received the largest amount — $2.5 billion — with India and Iraq receiving about $1 billion each. Nearly all of the $1.1 billion sent to Southeast Asia went to Indonesia prior to 1966. Africa has received less than $1 billion, $400 million of it going to Algeria. No known military assistance was provided through 1973 to Latin American countries, except for Cuba. In conjunction with the military assistance program, approximately 30,000 military personnel from developing countries have received military training in the USSR since 1955. At present there are in Afghanistan some 200 Soviet military advisers, in Iraq 1,500, in Syria nearly 3,000, in Algeria over 1,000, in Sudan 500, in Yemen Arab Republic 400, in the People's Republic of Yemen 200, in Egypt about 1,000, in the Somali Republic 300, in Ceylon 100, and in India over 150. Cuba has the largest Soviet advisory and training mission among Communist countries, about 5,000 officers and NCOs.

ALLIANCES

In addition to being a member of the UN and the leading member of the Warsaw Pact Alliance, the USSR has bilateral treaties of friendship and mutual assistance with all other communist nations (including the People's Republic of China), with the exception of Albania.

STRATEGIC ROCKET FORCES

Personnel: 350,000

Missile Inventory:
- c. 1600 intercontinental ballistic missiles (ICBMs): 288 SS-9, and 950+ SS-11; 210 SS-7 and SS-8; 100 SS-13. Ranges up to 7,000 miles. There are 91 silos under construction. Most missiles are liquid-fueled, resulting in a delayed reaction time. Some solid-fueled missiles are apparently now being deployed. Protection of launch sites is achieved by "hardening" in massive underground silos and by dispersion. Warhead yields range up to 25 megatons; some missiles have multiple warheads, but are not at this time believed to be independently targeted.
- c. 700 medium range ballistic missiles (MRBMs) and intermediate range ballistic missiles (IRBMs): 100 SS-5 and 600 SS-4. MRBMs have ranges up to 1,000 miles; IRBM ranges are up to 3,000 miles. These are deployed near Soviet land frontiers, and threaten Western Europe, Japan, and China. Most of these are also fixed emplacement, liquid-fueled missiles in hardened sites. These earlier systems will be supplemented, and eventually replaced by mobile, solid-fueled missiles (e.g., SS-14).

AIR DEFENSE COMMAND

Personnel: 500,000; about half in ground units (PVO-Voysk) and half in air operational units (PVO-Strany); ground units are supported by the Army; air units by the Air Force.

Antiaircraft Artillery Equipment:
- light artillery pieces: 23mm and 57mm; for close-in defense 1,000 feet and below. Many of these are self-propelled, on tracked chassis, as the twin-barrelled ZSU-57/2, and the quadruple-barrelled ZSU-23/4.
- medium artillery pieces: 85mm, 100mm, and 130mm; almost completely replaced by surface-to-air missiles.

Surface-to-Air Missiles (SAMs): 10,000: 5,000 SA-2, 5,000 other
- SA-1 Guild*: roughly comparable to the US Nike-Ajax; still deployed around Moscow.
- SA-2 Guideline: a two-stage missile, with a slant-range of 27 miles, intercept capability at altitudes from 1,000 to 80,000 feet. At least four versions exist (one for naval use) and the latest version is believed to have nuclear capability. The SA-2 has been used with ground forces.
- SA-3 Goa: a two-stage missile, intended primarily for low-altitude air defense. Three versions known to exist — one for naval use. Some SA-3 units may be assigned to ground forces air defense; range about 15 miles.
- SA-4 Ganef: twin-mounted on a tracked carrier, for use with ground forces, comparable in capabilities to Guideline but much more mobile.
- SA-5 Griffon: a long-range SAM, also called Tallinn system, thought by some to have a limited ABM capability.
- SA-6 Gainful: triple-mounted on a tracked carrier, probably intended as a low-altitude complement to Ganef with the ground forces.

Anti-Ballistic Missile (ABM):
- Galosh: a multi-stage missile now being deployed around Moscow; 64 launchers have missiles installed. It is presumed to have a range of several hundred miles with a warhead yield of more than one megaton. There are some indications that a more advanced version exists and will eventually replace some or all Galosh presently deployed.

*This and all other code names are assigned by NATO.

Fighter Aircraft:
> 3,000+ defensive interceptor and all weather fighters (MiG-17/19/21/25, Su-9/11, Yak-25/28 and Tu-28; most equipped with air-to-air missiles Alkali, Anab, Ash, Atoll, Awl)

Airborne Warning and Control System (AWACS):
> 10 modified Tu-114 Cleat turboprop transports (codenamed Moss by NATO) carry airborne detection radars to detect and track enemy aircraft while vectoring interceptors toward these targets.

ARMY

The Soviet Army is prepared for both nuclear and conventional war. It is trained to advance on a broad front at high speed. Infantry is provided with covered armored personnel carriers to facilitate advance across radioactive terrain. All major Soviet units are equipped with tactical nuclear missiles, and are also well equipped for offensive and defensive chemical warfare. The conventional fire-power of a Soviet division is comparable to that of a NATO division. Logistics, which was always the weakest point in the Soviet military system, is evidently being improved and adapted to the requirements of high speed advance and the extended range of operations. Soviet organizational doctrine provides for limited numbers of support troops in the divisions, which therefore are dependent on higher echelons for support.

Soviet divisions have three degrees of combat readiness. Category I, 35 to 50 percent of the total, are divisions at, or near full strength. These include the Soviet divisions in Eastern Europe and most of those stationed on the Chinese border. Category II, about one-quarter of the total, are divisions at more than half-strength. Category III, the remaining one-quarter, are divisions at less than half-strength. All divisions have full equipment, but much of it in Categories II and III is in storage. In case of war, the Soviet Army will probably return to the World War II Front (army group) organization, with each front incorporating several combined arms armies, one or more tank armies, a tactical air army, missile and artillery units, airborne troops and special forces.

Major components of a motorized rifle division are three motorized rifle regiments, one medium tank regiment, one artillery regiment, one each rocket artillery, Frog (surface to surface missile), engineer, antiaircraft and signal battalion, a reconnaissance, helicopter, and chemical warfare company, and rear services units. All motorized rifle regiments have been upgraded in firepower and mobility. In addition, within the next few years most, if not all, Soviet divisions will be equipped with the T-62 main battle tank. Total strength is 10,485 men (1,094 officers, 9,391 enlisted), 188 tanks, 308 APCs, 48 howitzers, and 1,350 trucks.

The Soviet tank division consists of three medium tank regiments, one motorized rifle regiment, one each rocket launcher, Frog, antiaircraft, engineer, reconnaissance, and signal battalion, a helicopter company, and chemical warfare and rear services units. Total strength is 8,415 men, 316 tanks, c. 190 APCs, c. 1,300 trucks, and 10 to 15 helicopters.

Each airborne division has three airborne regiments, one artillery regiment, and one each engineer, multiple rocket launcher, signal, antiaircraft, medical, supply and transport, and maintenance battalion. There are also indications that a tactical nuclear missile (Frog) battalion recently became an organic part of the airborne division.

The trend in the Soviet Army seems to be toward further perfection of the mobile striking forces and airborne forces. Operational and logistical exploitation of the helicopter, refinement of command and control, and management of the nuclear and conventional battle, including the concept of the automated battlefield, will increasingly occupy the attention of the Soviet command. There will be qualitative advances in conventional weapons and in the variety of nuclear missiles. Greater attention will be paid to officer training, especially in the technical fields.

Personnel: 1,750,000

Organization:
> 17 military and special military districts
> 102 motorized rifle divisions
> 51 tank divisions
> 7 airborne divisions
> Numerous artillery, engineering, signal, antiaircraft, chemical and missile units

Deployment:
> East Europe
>> 31 divisions: 20 in Germany (Group of Soviet Forces, Germany) including 10 tank divisions; 4 in Hungary (Southern Group of Forces) including 2 tank divisions; 2 in Poland (Northern Group of Forces) including a tank division; 5 in Czechoslovakia (Central Group of Forces); all or most are in Category I, or full readiness status.
>
> European USSR (west of Urals, north of Caucasus):
>> 60 divisions: includes 22 tank divisions: about 28 divisions are in Category II, and 14 in Category III.
>
> Central USSR (Siberia, between the Urals and Lake Baikal):
>> 5 divisions: includes 2 tank divisions; all or most are Category III, below half-strength
>
> Southern USSR (Trans-Caucasus, Turkestan):
>> 28 divisions: includes 4 tank divisions; 2 divisions in Category I; 4 in Category II, and 5 in Category III.

Soviet Far East (east of Lake Baikal):
51 divisions: about 21, including 10 tank divisions, are in Category I, 21 are in Category II; 2 of the 33 Far East divisions are in Mongolia (Soviet Forces, Mongolia).

Major Equipment Inventory:
- 1,500+ heavy tanks (T-10, modification of JS-2/3, with 122mm gun)
- 42,000+ medium tanks (T-62, with 155mm gun, T-54 and T-55, both with 100mm gun)
- 1,500+ light reconnaissance tanks (PT-76, amphibious, with 76mm gun)
- 30,000 APCs (BMP-76, BRDM, BTR-60, BTR-50, BTR-40, BTRM-1967, M-1970, etc.)
- 1,000 heavy artillery pieces (152mm and nuclear capable 203mm; many self-propelled)
- 3,000 medium artillery pieces (122mm and 130mm; many self-propelled)
- 8,000 light artillery pieces (85mm, ASU-85 ATK, and 100mm; many self-propelled)
- 5,000 antitank guns (57mm; some self-propelled ASU-57)
- 4,000 truck-mounted 240mm rocket launchers, multi-barrelled
- 1,000 light AAA pieces (14.5mm, 23mm, 37mm)
- mobile tactical missiles (Scud, Shaddock, Salish, Frog, and Scaleboard; ranges of 15 to 500 miles)
- antitank missiles (Snapper, Swatter, and Sagger

Reserves: At least nine million trained reserves are available for mobilization; of these about 500,000 are probably earmarked to bring Category II and III divisions, and supporting units, up to strength. The remainder are available as replacements and to create new units. Training is reported to be haphazard and inadequate.

NAVY

With over 2,000 units the Soviet Navy ranks as the second largest in the world. The buildup in both scope and strength became obvious in the 1960s when new Soviet naval units started roaming all oceans. With the new Y-class submarines as its mainstay, the Soviet Navy is strong in surface ships, submarines and a naval air force. The Soviet Naval Air Force, except for helicopters, is based on shore.

The Commander in Chief of the Soviet Navy is directly under the Minister of Defense. The line of direct command goes from the Commander in Chief to the fleets, flotillas, Naval Air Force, Naval Infantry, Naval Educational Directorate and the Rear Services.

The Soviet Navy has recently strengthened and reorganized its Naval Infantry (marines) to increase its capability for intervention and amphibious landings. It is well equipped, trained and led. The basic organizational structure of the Naval Infantry is the reinforced battalion (sometimes called regiment). Naval Infantry battalions are organized into brigades of three to five battalions each (comparable to a USMC Regimental Landing Team), an amphibious tank battalion and an amphibious assault unit (engineers and frogmen). Each fleet has at least one brigade.

Personnel: 500,000 (includes Naval Air Force of 100,000 and 20,000 Naval Infantry). About 200,000 are serving afloat.

Organization:
Four fleets: Baltic Sea, Black Sea/Mediterranean, Arctic Ocean/White Sea, Far East (Pacific)

Major Units:
Surface Ships:
- 1 45,000 ton aircraft carrier, *Kiev*
- 27 cruisers (CA, CLG)
    - 9 Kresta class (4 Kresta I and 5 Kresta II) with SS-N-10, (Shaddock) cruise SSMs, SA-N-1 and SA-N-3 (Goa) SAMs
    - 4 Kynda class (same armament as Kresta class)
    - 12 Sverdlov class (2 have SA-N-4 Ganef; 1 has SA-N-2 Guideline SAMs)
    - 2 other cruisers (Chapaev and Kirov class, used mainly for training)
- 2 helicopter carriers, *Moskva, Leningrad,* with SA-N-3 Sams and 20 Ka-25 ASW helicopters each)
- 101 destroyers (DD)
    - 3 Krivak class with SS-N-10 SSCM and SA-N-4 SAM
    - 5 Krupny class with SS-N-1 cruise SSMs
    - 4 Kildin class with SS-N-1 cruise SSMs
    - 15 Kashin class AA and ASW destroyers with SA-N-1 SAMs
    - 3 Kanin class with SA-N-1 SAMs
    - 26 Kotlin class AA and ASW destroyers (9 with SA-N-1 SAMs)
    - 45 Skory class AA and ASW destroyers

130 frigates and destroyer escorts (DL, DE)
258 coastal escorts and submarine chasers (PF, PC, SC)
186 fleet minesweepers (MSO)
121 coastal minesweepers (MLS)
115 Osa class patrol boats with Styx missiles (PTFG)
16 Komar class patrol boats with Styx missiles (PTFG)
301 fast patrol and torpedo boats (PTF, PT)
95 amphibious ships (LS)
139 amphibious craft (LCU, LCT)
1,000 auxiliaries and support ships
numerous minesweepers and trawlers have been modified for gethering electronic intelligence (ELINT)

Submarines:
114 nuclear-powered submarines (SSN)
12 H-II class equipped to fire 3 SS-N-5 IRBMs
3 D class equipped to fire 12 SS-N-8 missiles
34 Y class equipped to fire 16 SS-N-6 missiles
39 C class equipped to fire 8 SS-N-7 cruise missiles, E-I and E-II class equipped to fire 6 to 8 SS-N-3 cruise missiles with a range of about 300 miles
26 N and V class attack submarines
316 conventionally-powered submarines (SS)
24 G class equipped to fire 3 SS-N-4 or SS-N-5 IRBMs
29 J and W class equipped to fire 2 to 4 SS-N-3 cruise missiles
263 B, F, Z, R, Q, and W class attack and training submarines

Submarine deployment
Baltic Fleet: 60
Arctic Fleet: 160 (including about half the missile-equipped submarines)
Black Sea/Mediterranean Fleet: 50
Far East Fleet: 105 (including about half the missile-equipped submarines)
Remainder: deployment not known.

Naval Air Force (all land-based, except for 2 helicopter carriers):
770 combat aircraft
400 Tu-16 Badger bomber/reconnaissance/tankers equipped with ASMs (Kipper or Kelt)
60 Tu-22 Blinder bomber/reconnaissance (Kitchen)
30 Il-38 May maritime reconnaissance aircraft
50 Tu-20 Bear long-range bomber/reconnaissance aircraft; some equipped with a Kangaroo ASM
50 Il-28 Beagle light reconnaissance/bombers
100 Mi-4 Hound and Ka-25A Hormone ASW helicopters
80 Be-12 Mail ASW flying boats (amphibian)
360 other aircraft
210 miscellaneous transport aircraft
150 trainer/support aircraft

Naval Infantry (Marines):
Personnel: 20,000
Deployment: One brigade in each of the four fleets

Reserves: An unknown number of reservists are available to bring the complements of all warships (some below full manning level) to war strength.

Major Naval Bases: Leningrad, Nikolayev, Sevastopol, Molotovsk, Murmansk, Vladivostok, Arkhangelsk

AIR FORCE

Tactical aviation with its ground attack and fighter-interceptor aircraft, light bombers and reconnaissance planes makes up the bulk of the Air Force. It is organized in 12 air armies. Long range aviation with nine air divisions is organized in three air armies, two of which are deployed in Europe and one in the Far East.

The Air Transport Command has over 2,000 transport planes. The largest aircraft in service is the Antonov AN-22 with a maximum range of nearly 6,000 nm, or over 2,500 nm with maximum load of 176,000 lb. Half of the Soviet transport aircraft are made up of An-12 (range 1,800 nm) and Il-18 (range 2,000 nm). Military transport can readily be augmented by nearly 400 Aeroflot (Soviet airline) aircraft, Tu-104s, Tu-114s, Tu-124s, and Tu-134s.

There has been no let-up in the pace of modernization in the Soviet Air Force. About 15 new types of Soviet aircraft have appeared in the past 10 years. In 1973 the USSR built nearly 1,800 planes, half of them fighters, the rest bombers, transports and helicopters.

Personnel: 255,000 (not including Air Defense units)

Organization:
Long-Range Air Force

Intercontinental Bomber Force (Mya-4 and Tu-20)
Medium Bomber Force (Tu-16 and Tu-22)
Tactical Air Force (a Tactical Air Army is based in each of these countries: East Germany, Poland, Czechoslovakia and Hungary)
Air Transport Command

Major Aircraft Types (not including Air Defense units):
- 6,840 combat aircraft
  - 140 strategic bombers
    - 40 Mya-4 Bison* long-range bombers
    - 100 Tu-20 Bear* long-range turboprop bombers (about two-thirds armed with Kangaroo ASM)
  - 700 medium bombers
    - 200 Tu-22 Blinder supersonic bombers (about half with Kitchen ASM)
    - 500 Tu-16 Badger bombers (about half armed with Kelt ASM)
  - 4,000 fighter/fighter-bombers
    - MiG-17 Fresco
    - MiG-19 Farmer
    - MiG-21 Fishbed
    - MiG-23 Flogger
    - MiG-25 Foxbat
    - Su-7 Fitter
    - Yak-25 Flashlight
    - Yak-28P Firebar
  - 2,000 tactical attack light bombers
    - Il-28 Beagle light bomber
    - Yak-28 Brewer supersonic light bomber
- 8,515 other aircraft
  - 50 long-range tankers (converted Mya-4 and Tu-20 bombers)
  - 1,700 short-, medium-, and long-range transports (Il-14 Crate, An-24 Coke, An-12 Cub, An-14 Clod, Il-18 Coot)
  - 15 heavy transports (An-22 Cock)
  - 1,750 helicopters (Mi-1 Hare, Mi-4 Hound, Mi-6 Hook, Mi-8 Hip, Mi-10 Harke, Mi-12)
  - 4,950 miscellaneous trainer/support aircraft
  - 50 tactical reconnaissance aircraft Yak-26 Mangrove

Reserves: There is a highly trained air reserve totaling about 600,000 men. Also, most of the Aeroflot medium- and long-range civil airliners are convertible to military use.

Air Bases: There are about 500 air bases. Of these over 90 are in the Arctic or sub-Arctic regions. About two-thirds of the operational bases are in Europe.

PARAMILITARY

There are approximately 300,000 MVD internal security (125,000) and border troops (175,000); in addition, the Soviet DOSAAF (Volunteer Organization for Support of the Army, Air Force, and Navy) trains the population in basic military skills.

---

*One-syllable NATO code-names are for propeller (piston- or turbine-powered) aircraft; two-syllable names are for pure-jet.

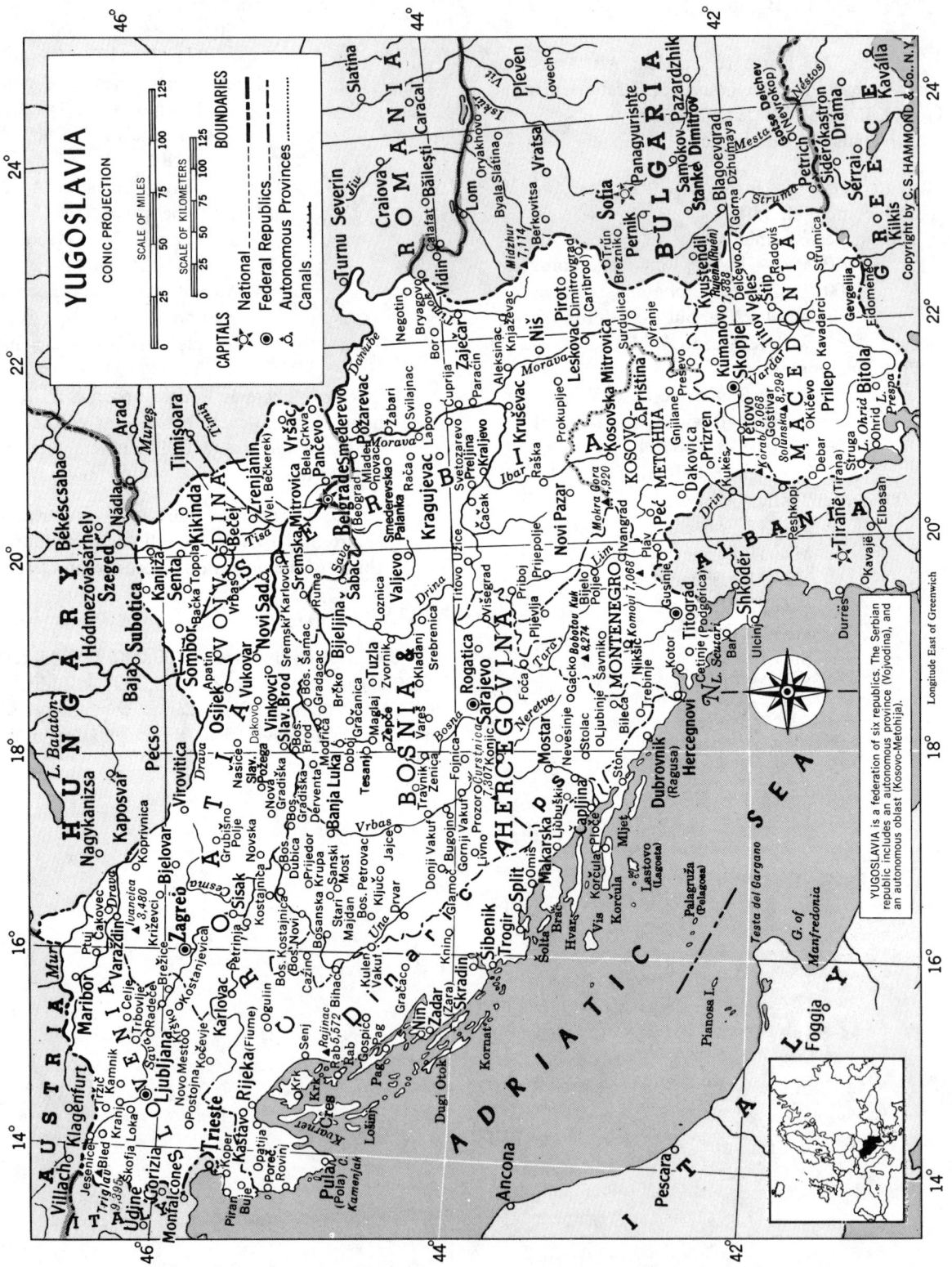

YUGOSLAVIA
Federativna Socijalisticka Republika Jugoslavija
Socialist Federal Republic of Yugoslavia

POWER POTENTIAL STATISTICS

Area: 98,766 square miles
Population: 20,811,000
Total Active Armed Forces: 266,000 (includes Frontier Guards; 1.27% population)
Gross National Product: $16.2 billion ($778 per capita)
Annual Military Expenditures: $875 million (5.4% GNP)
Steel and Iron Production: 5.36 million metric tons
Fuel Production: Coal: 30.9 million metric tons
   Crude Oil: 3.9 million metric tons
   Refined Products: 8.5 million metric tons
Electric Power Output: 29.43 billion kwh
Merchant Fleet: 356 ships; 1.54 million gross tons
Civil Air Fleet: 28 jet and 20 piston transports

DEFENSE STRUCTURE

The Yugoslav League of Communists (Communist Party) controls the government, including all elements of the military establishment, its leaders occupying key positions. The President, Marshal Tito, who heads the Communist Party, is the Commander in Chief of the Armed Forces and the Chairman of the Council of National Defense.

The Department of National Defense and the Federal Secretary for National Defense are responsible for preparing defense plans, organizing and training the armed forces, and organizing and mobilizing human and material resources (including the formation of a guerrilla resistance in the event of invasion). The Department includes an integrated General Staff of the Armed Forces for the Army, Navy, and Air Force.

POLITICO-MILITARY POLICY

Yugoslavia's foreign policy is based on the principle of independence and neutrality. Yugoslavia declares itself a socialist country, but not part of the Communist bloc. It maintains close ties with nonaligned nations and strives to assume leadership of nations outside the Western and Soviet alliance systems.

Since 1948, Yugoslavia's relations with the USSR have followed a fluctuating pattern of tensions and improvements. In recent years they worsened after Yugoslav criticism of the Soviet invasion of Czehoslovakia and improved after the 1971 visit by Soviet Communist Party leader Brezhnev to Belgrade.

At present Yugoslavia maintains friendly relations with most of its neighbors. Relations with Albania have improved since 1971, when Albania and Yugoslavia announced their intention to exchange ambassadors. Bulgaria's irredentist claims to Yugoslav Macedonia had strained relations between the two countries.

Military service is universal. All male citizens between the ages of 19 and 27 are liable for military service. The length of service is 18 months in the Army, Air Force, and Navy. There is compulsory reserve service, for officers up to 60 years of age, and for others up to age 55. Women between 19 and 40 years of age can serve in reserve non-combat activities. Full mobilization could bring the strength of the armed forces to over 1,300,000 men.

STRATEGIC PROBLEMS

In the north and east Yugoslavia borders on neutral Austria and three members of the Warsaw Pact: Hungary, Romania, and Bulgaria. The long border with these nations has few obstacles, and is open to an enveloping invasion in the event of a Soviet-Yugoslav conflict. On all sides Yugoslavia's borders are protected by mountains or the rugged Adriatic Coast.

In order to resist a Warsaw Pact invasion, Yugoslavia probably would need extensive help from the outside. Since it must be assumed that the invaders would use the Ljubljana Gap to seize the port of Rijeka (Fiume) and to sever Yugoslavia's land communication with Italy, communications with the outside world could be maintained only through the remaining Dalmatian ports and through Greece. In view of the presence of strong Soviet naval forces in the Mediterranean, these communications could be kept open only in cooperation with the US Mediterranean Fleet. However, in order to avoid exacerbating relations with Moscow after its invasion of Czechoslovakia, Tito stated publicly that Yugoslavia does not ask for any protection from NATO.

The multinational and multireligious population of Yugoslavia is divided by many old ethnic and religious antagonisms. The independence movement in Croatia is particularly strong and active. However, it is reasonable to assume that, if threatened with foreign invasion, the people will unite for the defense of their country under the leadership of the present government. Mindful of Czechoslovakia's quick subjugation, and of its own historical development of guerrilla combat, Yugoslavia's 1969 national defense law stresses the doctrine of the people in arms and the ignominy of surrender. In conformity with this principle, the Territorial Defense Force is continuously in being, and plans are closely coordinated with the regular forces for instant action in a national emergency.

MILITARY ASSISTANCE

Because of its vulnerable position between NATO and Soviet-bloc nations, and its determination to maintain an independent third world position, Yugoslavia has sought to avoid complete dependence on either group for armaments. This has necessitated a buildup of defense industries which now are able to supply Yugoslavia's needs except for the heaviest and most sophisticated equipment. Light aircraft, tanks, submarines, most artillery weapons, trucks, and small arms are made locally.

After Tito's break with Stalin in 1948, Yugoslavia developed ties with the U.S. and other Western countries and received extensive American military and economic assistance in order to help Tito to preserve independence from the USSR. United States military assistance to Yugoslavia from 1950 to 1965 amounted to $703 million. There has been no American military aid since.

After relations improved with the USSR, Yugoslavia bought Soviet military equipment which has totalled over $200 million in surplus ruble funds.

In its attempt at leadership among third world developing and nonaligned nations, Yugoslavia gains additional leverage by its ability to supply arms from its significant armaments industry to countries who may not wish to depend for armaments on either the Soviet bloc, Communist China, or Western countries. Arms are sold, without grant-aid.

Yugoslavia has consistently supported the peacekeeping efforts of the United Nations. A reinforced battalion was furnished the United Nations Emergency Force in the Gaza Strip of Palestine from 1957 until its withdrawal in May 1967. A small detachment was sent to the United Nations Operations in the Congo.

ALLIANCES

In 1953, before Yugoslavia had built up its defenses with self-help and US military aid, and before NATO and US aid had strengthened the defenses of Greece and Turkey, these three countries signed the Balkan Defense Pact at Ankara, Turkey. This was a five-year treaty of friendship and collaboration which provided for common defensive measures. It was strengthened and extended for 20 years in 1954. Yugoslavia is a member of the United Nations and of its specialized agencies.

ARMY

Personnel: 200,000

Organization: Four army commands with headquarters at Belgrade (First), Skoplje (Third), Zagreb (Fifth), and Sarajevo (Seventh).
    8 army corps
        1 armored division
        9 infantry divisions
        30 independent infantry brigades
        12 independent tank brigades
        1 airborne brigade
        1 Marine brigade

Major Equipment Inventory:
    650 medium tanks (M-4, M-47, T-34, T-54, T-55)
    light tanks (PT-76 and AMX-13)
    APCs (M-3, BTR-50P, BTR-60P)
    tank destroyer/assault guns (SU-100)
    57mm airborne self-propelled guns (ASU-57)
    57mm self-propelled AA guns (ZSU-57/2)
    37mm antiaircraft guns
    antitank missiles (Snapper)
    armored cars (M-8)
    76.2mm mountain guns
    75mm mountain howitzers
    76mm antitank guns
    88mm coast defense guns
    105mm and 155mm howitzers
    155mm guns
    120mm heavy mortars
    81mm and 60mm mortars

Reserves: There are 1,200,000 available for mobilization, some to bring units up to strength, others to expand the 33 brigades to divisions.

NAVY

Personnel: 27,000

Major Units:
    5 coastal submarines (SSC)
    1 destroyer (DD)
    3 subchasers (PC)
    27 patrol vessels (PCF)
    1 minelayer/training ship
    4 coastal minesweepers (MSC)
    20 inshore minesweepers (MSI)
    14 river minesweepers (MSM)
    10 guided missile patrol boats (Osa class; Styx SSM; PTFG)
    35 coast torpedo boats (PT)
    26 auxiliaries and support ships
    30 landing vessels (LC)

Major Naval Bases: Nadar, Sibenik, Split, Dubrovnik, Kotor, Pula.

AIR FORCE

Personnel: 20,000

Organization:
- 2 air corps headquartered at Zagreb and Zemun
- 2 interceptor divisions (2 squadrons of MiG-21, 1 squadron of MiG-19, and 8 squadrons of CF-86E and F-86D)
- 3 fighter-bomber divisions (9 squadrons of F-84G; being replaced by Jastreb and Kraguj light attack and close support aircraft)
- 2 reconnaissance squadrons, one for each air corps (RT-33A and RF-86F)
- 8 SAM battalions (SA-2 Guideline)

Major Aircraft Types:
- 385 combat aircraft
  - 85 MiG-21 interceptors
  - 15 MiG-19 interceptors
  - 100 CF-86E and F-86D interceptors
  - 75 F-84G fighter-bombers
  - 30 Rt-33 reconnaissance/fighter aircraft
  - 40 Jastreb/Galeb light attack aircraft
  - 40 Kraguj close support aircraft
- 402 other aircraft
  - 15 C-47 transports
  - 4 DC-6B transports
  - 15 Il-14 transports
  - 18 Mi-4 helicopters
  - 10 Il-18 transports
  - 40 Whirlwind and Dragonfly helicopters
  - 300 trainer/support aircraft (Aero 2, 3, UTVA-60/66)

On order: 112 SA-341 Gazelle helicopters

Air Bases: Zemun, Ljubljana, Zagreb, Kotor, Titograd, Batajnica, Nis, Sombor, Sarajevo, Pleso, Pula, Nickoic, Mostar, Skoplje, Vrsac, Cerklje, Salusani.

PARAMILITARY

Yugoslavia has a force of 19,000 Frontier Guards under the Ministry of National Defense and a National Police or *Milija* of 163,000. Territorial Defense Units, incorporating armed workers and partisan organizations closely affiliated with the armed forces, probably include virtually every able-bodied adult citizen (accounting for a total strength of up to 3,000,000 men and women by the end of 1972). At the time of the 1968 invasion of Czechoslovakia arms were issued to many of these partisans, and bases in the mountains were stocked with arms and other supplies.

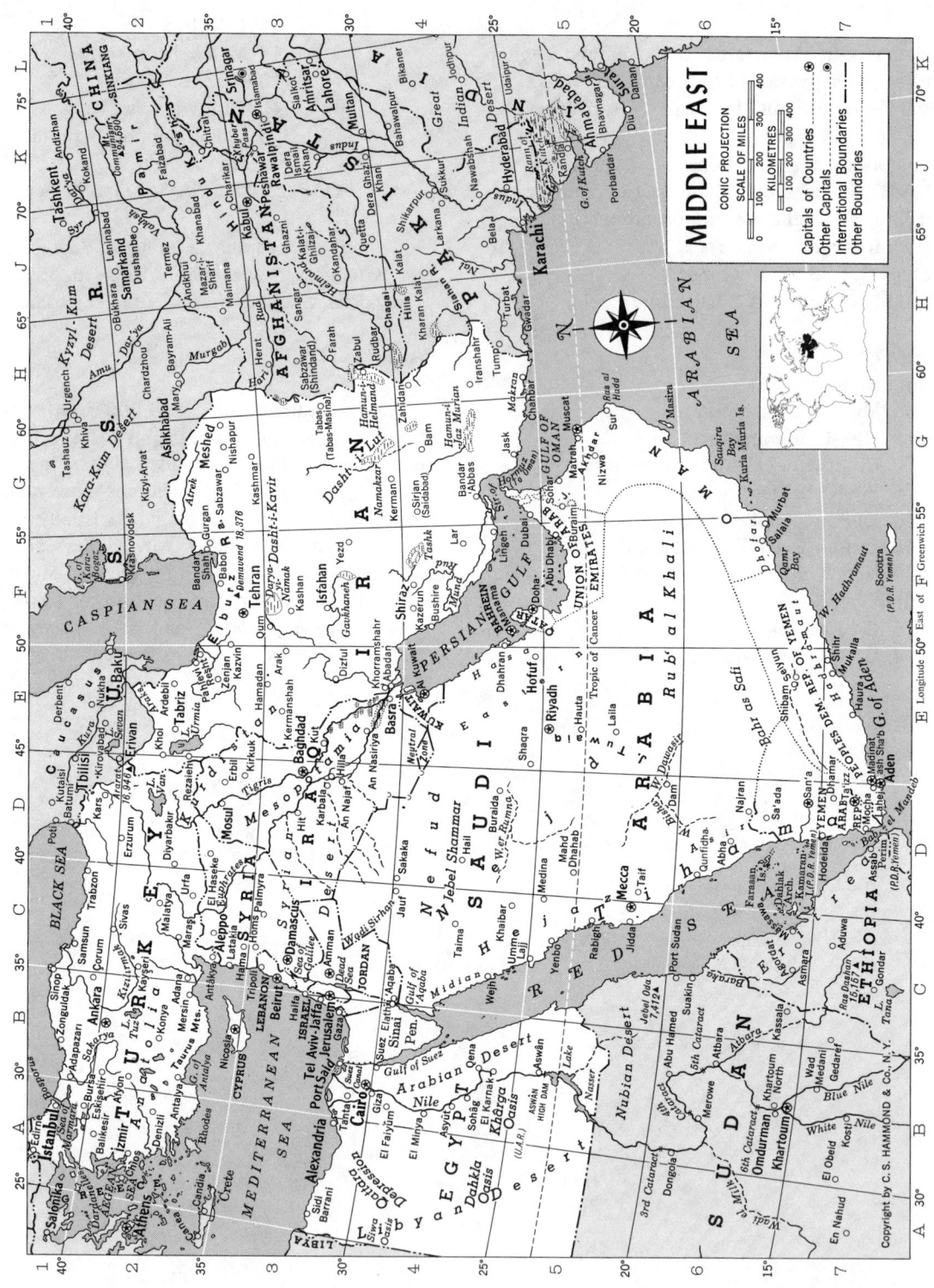

6
MIDDLE EAST
Regional Survey

MILITARY GEOGRAPHY

The political and military realities of the second half of the twentieth century make it desirable to consider together the countries clustered about the shores of three major bodies of water that approach each other near the western extremity of Southwest Asia: the Mediterranean Sea, the Red Sea, and the Persian Gulf. These countries, collectively called the Middle East, include Egypt, Israel, Jordan, Lebanon, Syria, Iraq, Iran, Kuwait, Saudi Arabia, Oman, Yemen (Aden), Yemen (San'a), Bahrain, Qatar, and the United Arab Emirates.

STRATEGIC SIGNIFICANCE

The military and strategic significance of the Middle East is the result of two major geographical factors: its location linking the three major continents of the Eastern Hemisphere, and its fabulously wealthy deposits of oil. Otherwise the region is generally barren, consisting mostly of lightly inhabited deserts, with relatively dense aggregations of people scattered in those regions having sufficient water and arable land to support agriculture.

As the land bridge linking Africa, Asia, and Europe, the Middle East has been the scene of conflict between contending powers from the beginnings of recorded history. The Hyksos and the Egyptians clashed near Megiddo Pass in Palestine c. 1469 B.C.; the Assyrians, Persians, Alexander the Great, the Seleucids, the Ptolemies, and the Romans in turn established hegemony over the area, which became a frequent battleground in the wars of the later Romans and Byzantines against various Persian dynasties. The Moslems overran the region in the seventh century; Crusaders fought Saracens, colonized, and were in turn ejected. After the brief Mongol conquest of the thirteenth century, the Ottoman Turks established an empire that withstood Napoleon's onslaught, only to lose all except Anatolia through the combined pressure of British arms and Arab revolt in World War I. Meanwhile, the building of the Suez Canal (the short rapid route to the Far East from Europe which became the lifeline of the British Empire), and the later discovery of oil in the Persian Gulf area, both ensured the continuing strategic and economic importance of the region.

More recently, the British withdrawal from the Indian Ocean periphery, pipelines from the Persian Gulf oil fields to the Mediterranean coast, super-tankers which can carry oil economically around Africa, and the discovery of oil fields in North Africa, have combined to lessen the importance of the Suez Canal. Nevertheless, right of free passage through the canal was an issue in both the 1956 and 1967 Arab-Israeli wars. The imminent reopening of the canal, which has been closed since the 1967 War, is a consequence of negotiations following the 1973 conflict. This will be both an asset and a source of problems for the United States and the Soviet Union. Strategically the canal has little importance to the United States for US commerce or naval mobility, but considerable importance in the framework of worldwide strategic security. For the Soviet Union the importance is direct. Control or at least access to the Suez Canal would permit the Soviet fleet in the Black Sea and the Mediterranean easy passage to and from the Indian Ocean and the Far East.

A major factor in the strategic picture of the Middle East is the state of Israel, established in 1948 from the British mandate of Palestine that was created from Arab lands after World War I. Arab opposition to Israel's existence has not only flared in four wars in which Israel has fought various of the other nations of the area, and focussed in terrorist groups based in the camps of displaced Palestinians in Lebanon and Syria, but has resulted in involvement of two major powers, the United States and the Soviet Union, on opposite sides. A major objective of international diplomacy is establishment of a political situation agreeable to both the Arab nations and Israel.

US support for Israel, fostered by widespread revulsion at Hitler's treatment of the Jews and the vehement urging of large numbers of Jewish citizens of the United States, is complicated by US dependence on the Arab nations for a portion of its oil supplies. The location of five-eighths of the non-communist world's proven oil reserves in the Middle East has given the Arab nations that control them diplomatic importance disproportionate to their size. The serious interests of both the United States and the Soviet Union in the Middle East make it impossible for either to exert overt pressure on the governments of the oil-rich nations without risking confrontation with the other.

Intense opposition to the Israeli presence is focussed in the Palestine Liberation Organization (PLO), established in 1964 as the executive arm of the Palestinian National Congress and official spokesman for the Palestinian community, and the Palestine Liberation Army, founded in 1970. The latter comprises the four major guerrilla-terrorist groups, al-Fatah,

The Popular Front for the Liberation of Palestine, The Popular Democratic Front for the Liberation of Palestine, and Syria's Sa'iqa, loosely allied under the coordinating leadership of the head of al-Fatah, Yassir Arafat, who also heads the PLO and is recognized as the spokesman for the Palestinian cause.

The combination of the withdrawal of the British from the Persian Gulf area, the entry of the Soviets into the eastern Mediterranean, the oil, with its effect on the economy of previously unimportant Arab states, and the Palestinian question has brought about several potentially dangerous politico-military situations in this area. Iran has started an expensive and extensive buildup of its military capability, having bought the most sophisticated weapons from both the Soviet and western military powers. Iran has been described as considering itself the replacement for Britain in providing the barrier between the Soviet Union and the Persian Gulf area (even with equipment obtained from the Soviet Union, although most recent acquisitions are from the United States). Saudi Arabia has strengthened itself with equipment from Britain, France and the United States. Smaller countries—Jordan, Kuwait, Lebanon, Oman, and the United Arab Emirates—are also building up their forces, with British, French, and US equipment. Egypt, Iraq, Syria, and both Yemens are obtaining equipment from the Soviet Union. Israel has received US aid but has also obtained arms from the French and the British and has captured Soviet material from the Arab states in the Mideast wars. A yet unknown, but potentially extremely complicating, factor in the whole Middle Eastern problem is the introduction of a nuclear capability into Egypt and Israel.

In the October War, also called the Yom Kippur War, which began with attacks by Egypt and Syria on Israel on October 6, 1973, and ended with a ceasefire on October 24, reportedly 15,000 tons of supplies were flown to the Arabs by the Soviets, while 22,395 tons were airlifted to the Israelis by the United States, supplemented by 5,000 tons flown from the United States by the Israeli airline El Al. Both sides also used sealift.

The military strengths of Israel, Egypt, Syria, Jordan, Saudi Arabia and Iraq given here are based upon reported October War losses and replacements at the time of the printing of this book. It is likely that some of these countries are undergoing a buildup to make them stronger in terms of military equipment than shown here. There have been scattered reports of MiG-23, Flogger, and Su-7, Fitter-B, both advanced variable geometry fighter aircraft, being supplied to Syria, and Tu-22, Blinder, supersonic bombers to Iraq. It is too early to evaluate these reports, but if true they reflect a major upgrading of the air capabilities of the two countries.

The increased demand for oil and the determination of the oil-producing countries to control their own resources have given the oil-rich countries of the Middle East an economic power over industrial nations dependent on oil for their energy needs. Recent agreements between the oil companies and the Persian Gulf Arab states allow each country an immediate 25 percent ownership of the oil companies operating in their lands. This is to increase to 51 percent by 1982, and Libya is demanding an immediate 50 percent. Iran is negotiating independently. Control of oil flowing into world markets will be in the hands of oil-producing nations instead of by international oil companies. Because of the October War most of the Arab oil-producing nations restricted crude oil production and embargoed oil shipments to the United States, the Netherlands, and certain other apparent Israeli supporters. Iraq did not reduce production but sold its oil only to those countries that favored the Arab side of the war.

THE ARAB LEAGUE

The Arab League was established shortly before the end of World War II (March 22, 1945) by the governments of Egypt, Iraq, Jordan, Lebanon, Saudi Arabia, Syria, and Yemen. The principal purpose was to prevent Palestine from becoming a separate and independent Jewish state. The League has since been joined by Algeria, Kuwait, Libya, Morocco, Sudan, Tunisia, Yemen (Aden), Oman, Bahrain, Qatar, and the Union of Arab Emirates. Cairo has been the headquarters for the Secretary General of the League, and its official activities and pronouncements have been much influenced by the government of Egypt.

Because of the often divergent, and sometimes hostile, policies of the individual members of the League, it has been able to represent its members in only one unified area of policy and activity: opposition to Israel. Even in this there have been some League members such as Tunisia (openly) and Jordan (covertly) who believe that they should accept and recognize Israel's existence diplomatically as well as practically. Such recognition is not now acceptable, however, to a majority of the members of the League and to their citizens. It is not even clear whether the League could survive if militant hostility to Israel were to be abandoned by its members.

CENTRAL TREATY ORGANIZATION OF THE MIDDLE EAST

The Central Treaty Organization of the Middle East (CENTO) is a successor organization to the Middle East Treaty Organization (METO), which was formally established on November 21, 1955, in Baghdad—and hence was known as the Baghdad Pact. The Middle East Treaty Organization was created to discourage the possibility of Soviet aggression into Southwest Asia; its original members were: Iran, Iraq, Turkey, Pakistan, and the United Kingdom. The United States, while not joining the pact, sent observers to its meetings, provided some financial and secretarial support, and participated in its deliberations.

The Middle East Treaty Organization was reorganized as the

Central Treaty Organization on October 7, 1959, shortly after the withdrawal of Iraq, following its revolution in 1958. Otherwise the membership remains unchanged.

ORGANIZATION OF PETROLEUM EXPORTING COUNTRIES

The Organization of Petroleum Exporting Countries (OPEC) was formed in 1960 by Iran, Iraq, Kuwait, Saudi Arabia, and Venezuela and now includes Algeria, Ecuador, Gabon, Indonesia, Libya, Nigeria, Qatar, and Abu Dhabi of the United Arab Emirates.

RECENT INTRA- AND EXTRA-REGIONAL CONFLICTS

1963-1967	Guerrilla warfare in Aden Protectorate against British forces
1964	Insurrection suppressed in Syria
1965	Partial coup d'etat in Iraq
1966	Coup d'etat in Syria
1967	Third Arab-Israeli War
1967-present	Palestinian guerrilla action and Arab military probes on borders of Israel
1968-present	Guerrilla warfare in Southern Yemen and by Yemeni extremists against Oman
1968	Coup d'etat in Iraq
1969	Border clashes between Saudi Arabia and Southern Yemen
1969	Coup d'etat in Syria
1970	Attempted coup in Iraq crushed
1970	Hostilities in Jordan between Jordanian forces and Arab guerrillas
1970	Coup d'etat in Muscat and Oman; becomes Sultanate of Oman
1970	Coup d'etat in Syria
1970	Syrian invasion of Jordan repulsed
1971	Iran seizes Persian Gulf islands claimed by Arab emirates
1973	Fourth Arab-Israeli War (October War)

ARAB GULF STATES
(Bahrain, Qatar, United Arab Emirates)

POWER POTENTIAL STATISTICS

BAHRAIN

Area: 240 square miles
Population: 212,000
Total Active Armed Forces: 1,100 (.52% population)

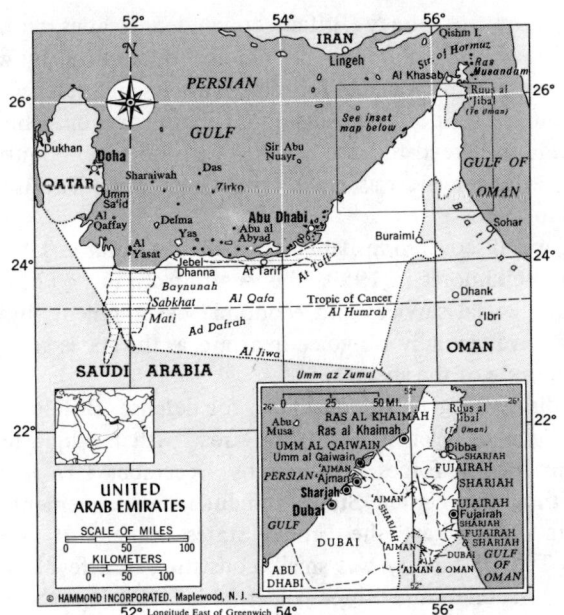

Gross National Product: $120 million ($566 per capita)
Fuel Production: Crude Oil: 3.5 million metric tons
    Refined Products: 12.1 million metric tons
Civil Air Fleet: 2 jet, 3 turboprop, 7 piston transports

QATAR

Area: 6,000 square miles
Population: 115,000
Total Active Armed Forces: 2,000 (1.7% population)
Gross National Product: $200 million ($1,740 per capita)
Fuel Production: Crude Oil: 22.9 million metric tons
    Refined Products: 33,000 metric tons

UNITED ARAB EMIRATES*

Area: 32,000 square miles
Population: 220,000
Total Active Armed Forces: 11,500 (6.4% population)
Gross National Product: $530 million ($2,409 per capita)
Fuel Production: Crude Oil: 58.3 million metric tons
Civil Air Fleet: 2 jet, 6 turboprop, 5 piston transports

POLITICO-MILITARY POLICIES AND POSTURE

The Persian Gulf (Arab Gulf to the Arabs) is vital to Iraq and Iran as their only access to the open sea. It is important to the world because its bordering countries and its offshore waters contain 60 percent of the world's proved oil reserves. On the southern shore of this gulf are the small states of Bahrain, Qatar, and the United Arab Emirates.

*Abu Dhabi, Dubai, Sharjah, Ajman, Umm al Qaiwain, Ras al Khaimah, and Fujairah

To eliminate piracy Britain concluded treaties with the Sheikhdoms and Bahrain in the nineteenth century, by which Britain became responsible for foreign affairs and defense, gave some budget support, and advised on administration, while the Sheikhdoms agreed to have dealings with no other country. A similar arrangement was made with Qatar when Turkish rule ended in 1916.

Oil was discovered in Bahrain in 1932, in Qatar in 1949 and in the Sheikhdoms in 1959. The wealth from this oil has been used for social services and economic development, but the people have virtually no voice in affairs as the states are under absolute rule of the sheikhs.

In discharging its responsibility for defense, Britain kept a joint force of over 9,000 in the area, with headquarters at Bahrain. British forces withdrew by December 1971. At the same time the United States concluded an agreement with Bahrain, which gave the United States home port facilities there. The US facility was small, consisting of a few hundred naval personnel and three older ships. During the 1973 Arab-Israeli War Bahrein unilaterally cancelled the agreement.

Anticipating the British withdrawal, the nine sheikhdoms formed a loose federation in July 1968. Authority was vested in a Council consisting of the nine sheikhs and a Federal Council functioning as both cabinet and legislature. In 1971 the sheikhdoms of Abu Dhabi, Dubai, Sharjah, Ajman, Umm al Qaiwain and Fujairah merged to form a single nation, the United Arab Emirates. The union's government was to be located in Abu Dhabi until a new capital was built on the border of Abu Dhabi and Dubai. It was not until early 1972 that the sheikhdom of Ras al Khaimah, which had originally abstained from joining, finally became the union's seventh member. The state has been admitted to the UN and the Arab League.

The rulers of the United Arab Emirates have absolute power over their own subjects, although the ruler of Abu Dhabi has appointed a cabinet and a national consultative assembly.

In January 1972 Sheikh Khalid of Sharjah was killed in an attempted coup by his cousin, who had been deposed as ruler in 1965. He was replaced by his younger brother.

Bahrain declared its independence from Great Britain on August 14, 1971, and was admitted to the UN on September 21 of that year. Qatar declared independence from Great Britain on September 1, 1971, and was admitted to the UN on September 21. Both states have joined the Arab League. In February 1972, the Prime Minister of Qatar, Sheikh Khalifa bin Hamad al-Thani, deposed his cousin the Emir, Sheikh Ahmed, in a bloodless coup, and began implementing wide-ranging social and economic reforms.

External problems include border disputes and territorial claims. The Qatar-Saudi Arabia border is disputed, and Saudi Arabia also claims portions of Abu Dhabi. Iran, in the past, has claimed Bahrain, but has agreed not to push its claim further. Perhaps the most serious problem facing the new state is subversion and attacks by externally based liberation movements feeding on internal dissatisfaction with authoritarian rule. The Dhofar Liberation Front, backed by radical Yemen (Aden) and the People's Republic of China, is directed against the Dhofar Sheikhdom of Oman, and was expanded in December 1968 to include the Federation as a target. It is now known as the National Front for the Liberation of the Arabian Gulf (NFLAG) and is headquartered in Aden. It also opposes what it considers an Iranian threat to the area.

On November 30, 1971, Iranian troops seized the Persian Gulf islands of Greater and Lesser Tunb and Abu Musa. Ras al Khaimah, claiming the Tunb islands as its own, protested the Iranian action. Abu Musa's takeover was peaceful since accord between Iran and Sharjah had already been reached whereby Iranian troops were to occupy specified areas of Abu Musa while Sharjah authorities retained control over the remainder of the island.

The Union Defence Force of the United Arab Emirates is composed of 1,600 men and is made up primarily of the former Trucial Oman Scouts, turned over to the Union when it was formed. In addition to its equipment of land rovers, mortars and dhows, three Agusta Bell (AB-206 Jet Ranger) helicopters are operated by the Emirate Ministry of Defence in support of the force. In January 1972 the Union Defence Force joined local security forces in Sharjah in putting down the attempted coup. The larger emirates, notably Abu Dhabi, also maintain their own relatively substantial defense establishments.

Abu Dhabi has an army of about 7,500, equipped with 90 Saladin and Ferret armored and scout cars, some artillery and some Vigilant antitank guided weapons. The Navy has three 58-foot and six 41-foot patrol vessels, armed with 20mm antiaircraft guns and machine guns, and manned by 150 men. The Air Force, with 350 men, has 12 Hunter fighter/fighter-bombers, five Alouette III and three Puma helicopters, four DHC-4 Caribou and four Britten-Norman Islander transports, and it has on order 14 Mirage 5 aircraft, reportedly to be operated by Pakistani crews. The other emirates have a total of about 1,600 men in their armies, equipped with Saladin and Ferret armored and scout cars, mortars and land rovers.

Bahrain has a total force of 1,100, equipped with Saladin and Ferret armored and scout cars, antitank guns, mortars, two helicopters and some patrol vessels.

Qatar has an armed force of 2,000, equipped with Saladin and Ferret armored and scout cars, some artillery and mortars, a few armed launches and six Hunter fighter-bombers.

MIDDLE EAST 173

EGYPT

Al Jumhuriyah Misr al'Arabiyah
Arab Republic of Egypt

Gross National Product: $7.6 billion ($206 per capita)
Annual Military Expenditures: $1.6 billion (23.3% GNP)
Fuel Production: Crude Oil: 11.2 million metric tons
　Refined Products: 6.4 million metric tons
Electric Power Output: 7.13 billion kwh
Merchant Fleet: 127 ships; 241,429 gross tons
Civil Air Fleet: 11 jet, 6 turboprop, and 2 piston transports

DEFENSE STRUCTURE

The President of the Arab Republic of Egypt, with strong executive powers, is the supreme commander of the unified armed forces, and presides over the National Defense Council. Under the President there is a single military Commander in Chief of the Armed Forces, who has direct access to the

POWER POTENTIAL STATISTICS

Area: 386,900 square miles
Population: 36,900,000
Total Active Armed Forces: 313,500 (not including security forces; 0.86% population)

President, and is not responsible to the Minister of War, who is the administrative director of the armed forces.

The Commander in Chief of the Armed Forces controls all components of the armed forces and is responsible for organization, training, armament, and combat readiness.

POLITICO-MILITARY POLICY

According to Egyptian military leaders four missions have influenced the design of the Egyptian armed forces: accomplishment of the officially announced military goal of recapturing all territories lost to the Israelis; defense against attempts to impose foreign domination; defense against intra-Arab hostilities or a threat thereof; and control of internal disturbances. Under President Gamal Nasser stress was placed on gaining hegemony, or at least preeminence, over the Arab states of the Middle East and nearby African states.

This apparent objective was pursued in part to obtain access to the income of the rich oil-producing Arab states, in part to secure the headwaters of the life-giving Nile against diversion, and in part to secure strategic positions surrounding Israel. Pursuit of this objective was demonstrated by: Egyptian-sponsored subversion and coup attempts against Libya, Sudan, Saudi Arabia, Iraq and Jordan; by the military occupation of Yemen; and by support of subversion among the Arab populations of Ethiopian Eritrea and the Persian Gulf regions of Iran. After President Nasser's sudden death on September 28, 1970, his successor, President Anwar Sadat, made every effort to insure continuity, and government policy was dominated by the unresolved conflict with Israel.

In the disastrous and humiliating defeat which Egypt suffered at the hands of Israel in three or four days of fighting in June 1967, the Israeli armed forces destroyed seven Egyptian divisions, destroyed or captured 800 tanks, and destroyed approximately 280 aircraft, most of them on the ground. After that war the major objective of Egyptian leaders was rebuilding strength, efficiency, confidence and morale in the armed forces. To that end, Egypt's Communist allies, led by the USSR, provided military aid, both in materiel and in training. Not only was lost equipment replaced, but the forces were reorganized and officers and men were trained to operate the most sophisticated modern hardware.

Egypt's surprise attack on Israel on October 6, 1973, thanks to the interwar buildup achieved immediate but transitory success. Israel's prompt recovery from the initial losses, however, not only reduced the scope of the Egyptian gains, but also was marked by a dramatic Israeli crossing to the west bank of the Suez Canal before the ceasefire of October 24 finally ended the fighting. Since the diplomatic efforts of US Secretary of State Henry Kissinger have achieved a withdrawal of troops by both Egypt and Israel the possibility of a more stable situation on the Egyptian-Israeli border at last seems greater.

Military service is compulsory for all men 18 years and over. University students may postpone their service until they finish school or reach the age of 28. The length of service is one year for university graduates, 18 months for high school graduates, and three years for all others. Enlisted men serve nine years more in the reserves. About 30,000 to 35,000 men are inducted per year, most of them into the army.

There are three officer training schools. The Military Academy in Cairo graduates army line officers and trains naval and air force officers for one year, after which they report to the Naval Academy at Ras al-Tin or the Air Force Academy at Bilbeis.

STRATEGIC PROBLEMS

The population of Egypt is compressed within the narrow Nile River Valley, which comprises only 3.6 percent of its total area, where the population density is over 2,200 per square mile—one of the highest in the world. Thus the population of Egypt, and its productive capacity, are dangerously concentrated, and vulnerable to threat or damage by a hostile foreign power. Although the new Aswan high dam will increase productivity, and will slightly enlarge the arable area of Egypt, it will also be very vulnerable. The performance of the Israeli armed forces in June 1967, and the helicopter-borne commando raid of November 1968 against Nile bridges and power plants, demonstrate that this vulnerability of population and of productive resources could be exploited by Egypt's principal enemy.

The 1967 war also demonstrated the vulnerability of Egypt's principal source of capital—the Suez Canal. The loss of income from the Canal would have ruined Egypt's economy if the oil-rich members of the Arab League had not provided substitute subsidies. However, recent discoveries of oil in the Western Desert may be important even after the Canal is reopened, since modified transportation patterns while it has been closed, and the increasing use of super-tankers (which cannot negotiate the Canal), may greatly reduce the future volume of traffic.

MILITARY ASSISTANCE

Egypt was almost completely dependent upon the USSR, or upon Soviet satellites of the Warsaw Pact, prior to the October War, for military equipment, and for training of its forces in the use of modern equipment. Estimates of total Soviet aid are that over $4.5 billion was received between June 1967 and 1972. Prior to that $1.5 billion had been delivered.

The 20,000-man Soviet mission was expelled from Egypt in 1972. Thereafter the technicians remaining are estimated to have numbered about 1,000. Soviet pilots flew reconnaissance missions from Cairo in MiG-25s. These were primarily high-speed and high-altitude flights over the Sinai Peninsula and other Israeli positions.

ALLIANCES

Egypt is a member of the UN and the Organization of African Unity (OAU). It is the leading member of the Arab League and the principal force behind the United Arab Command, the League's military organization. Egypt is also the predominant member of a three-way military alliance with Jordan and Iraq. It also has joint military command relationships with Sudan, Libya and Syria, and since September 1971 has joined with Libya and Syria in the Federation of Arab Republics. In May 1971 Egypt and the Soviet Union signed a 15-year treaty of friendship and cooperation.

ARMY

Personnel: 276,000

Organization:

    3 armored divisions
    5 infantry divisions
    5 mechanized infantry divisions
  16 artillery brigades
    2 airborne brigades
  20 battalion combat groups

Major Equipment Inventory:

      50 heavy tanks (JS-3 and T-10)
  1,575 medium tanks
        1,300 T-54/55, T-62
          100 T-34
          150 Centurion Mk.3
           25 Sherman
    170 light tanks
          150 PT-76
           20 AMX-13
    150 assault guns (SU-100 and JSU-152)
  1,200 APCs (BTR-40P, BTR-50P, OT-64, BTR-152, BTR-60P)
        K-61 amphibious assault vehicles
  2,200 light, medium, and heavy artillery pieces (122mm, 130mm, and 152mm guns and howitzers, and 160mm mortars) self-propelled AA guns (ZSU-57/2 and ZSU-23/4)
        203mm howitzers
        RPG-7 antitank weapons
        57mm, 85mm, and 100mm antitank guns
      24 SSMs (Frog 3/4)
      25 SSMs (Samlet)
        SSMs (Scud)
        Snapper, Sagger, and Swatter antitank missiles
        SA-7 Grail missiles
    420 vehicle-mounted rocket launchers
        20mm, 23mm, 37mm, 57mm, 85mm, and 100mm AA guns integrated with Air Force interceptors

Reserves: Approximately 600,000 trained reservists

NAVY

Personnel: 14,500 (organized in four commands: Destroyer, Submarine, Minesweeper and Torpedo)

Major Units:

  12 submarines (6 R class; 6 W class; SS)
    5 destroyers (4 Skory class; 1 British Z class; DD)
    3 frigates (British Hunt, Black Swan, River class; DE)
    2 corvettes (British Flower, Bangor class, PF)
  10 fleet minesweepers (6 T-43, 4 Yurka class; MSF)
    2 inshore minesweepers (T-301 class; MSI)
  12 subchasers (SO-1 class; PCS)
  15 guided missile patrol boats (12 Osa, 3 Komar class; PTFG) with Styx SSM
  26 torpedo boats (20 P-6; 6 Shershen class; PT)
  14 landing ships (10 Vydra; 4 SMB-1 class; LS)
    2 auxiliaries

Naval Bases: Ras al Tin, Port Tawficq, Port Said, Mersa Matruh (probably for Soviet use)

Reserves: About 25,000 trained reservists

AIR FORCE

Personnel: 25,000

Organization:

    13 fighter-interceptor squadrons (MiG-21/19)
    20 fighter-bomber squadrons (Su-7, MiG-17)
      1 medium bomber squadron (Tu-16)
      2 light bomber squadrons (Il-28)
      5 transport squadrons (Il-14, An-12, C-47)
  150 SAM battalions (Sa-2, 3, 4, 6)

Major Aircraft Types:

  590 combat aircraft
      200 MiG-21 fighter-interceptors
        60 MiG-19 fighter-interceptors

130 Su-7 fighter-bombers
150 MiG-17 fighter-bombers
20 Tu-16 medium bombers
30 Il-28 light bombers
490 other aircraft
80 transports (40 Il-14, 30 An-12, 10 C-47)
250 trainer/support aircraft (MiG-15, L-29, Saeta)
160 helicopters (Mi-4/6/8, Sea King)

Missiles: 650 SAM launchers (SA-2 Guideline, SA-3 Goa, SA-4 Ganef, SA-6 Gainful)
ASM-5 Kelt carried by Tu-16 bombers
AAm K-13 Atoll carried by fighter-interceptors

Reserves: 35,000 trained reservists

Major Air Bases: Almaza, Cairo West, Bilbeis, Beni Suwayf, Luxor, El Minya, Ras Banas, Hurghada.

PARAMILITARY

The National Guard, a poorly-armed and equipped home guard type force, of 120,000.

IRAN

Keshvare Shahanshahiye Iran
Empire of Iran (Persia)

POWER POTENTIAL STATISTICS

Area: 636,292 square miles
Population: 31,100,000
Total Active Armed Forces: 243,000 (includes Gendarmerie: 0.78% population)
Gross National Product: $14.4 billion ($463 per capita)
Annual Military Expenditures: $1.9 billion (13.2% GNP)
Fuel Production: Coal: 323,000 metric tons
  Crude Oil: 250 million metric tons
  Refined Products: 28.2 million metric tons
Electric Power Output: 7 billion kwh
Merchant Fleet: 77 ships, 181,000 gross tons
Civil Air Fleet: 10 jet and 3 piston transports

DEFENSE STRUCTURE

Iran is a constitutional monarchy with executive power vested in the Shah and a cabinet of ministers appointed by him. The Shah is Supreme Commander of the Armed Forces; he exercises operational control through the Supreme Commander's Staff, a joint staff organization that coordinates the activities of the three services. The Army is predominant among the armed forces and within the joint staff. The Minister of War is not in the chain of command; he is primarily concerned with legislative, budgetary, and fiscal matters.

POLITICO-MILITARY POLICY

Since World War II Iranian policy has been oriented mainly toward the West. In 1955 Iran adhered to the Baghdad Pact, now CENTO. Although ties with the US and the West remain strong, relations with the Soviet Union and the Communist countries of Eastern Europe have greatly improved, and in recent years Iran has adopted a more independent stance in its military and foreign policy.

The bulk of the Iranian armed forces consists of conscripts serving a compulsory two-year period of military service. Virtually all officers and noncommissioned officers are career personnel. There is no organized reserve system.

STRATEGIC PROBLEMS

Iran is strategically located along the Persian Gulf and astride vital land and air routes connecting Asia, Europe, and Africa. Iran is a land-bridge between the countries of East and West Asia and between the Soviet Union and the warm waters of the Indian Ocean. Defense against land attack would be aided by rugged mountain ranges rimming the north and the west and by deserts and lesser ranges to the east.

The country's greatest concerns are the 1,100 miles of common land boundary with the Soviet Union, and what Iran considers the Arab threat to its oil-rich province of Khuzestan in the southwest.

As to the first of these concerns, Iran has had several centuries' experience of intermittent contact and conflict with Russia, which steadily pushed its frontiers southward on both sides of the Caspian Sea, at Iranian expense. The latest such experience was shortly after World War II when Soviet forces occupying provinces in northern Iran departed only as a result of great pressure from the United Nations and the United States.

The second strategic concern is the potential Arab threat. Relationships with Saudi Arabia have on the whole been good, and both countries assisted the Royalist regime in Yemen during the fighting against Egyptian forces (see Yemen). However, disputes have arisen with Saudi Arabia over the division of off-shore oil interests in the Gulf. Iran has in the past stated its claims to Bahrain, but relinquished them when Bahrain, with UN approval, announced its desire for full independence in May 1970. When the British vacated the Persian Gulf, Iran occupied three small islands in the Strait of Hormuj, which it had long claimed.

MIDDLE EAST 177

The right of free passage of ships on the Shatt al Arab formed by the confluence of the Tigris and Euphrates and affording access to the Iranian oil loading ports of Abadan and Khorramshahr, has been in dispute. Iraq was awarded control of the waterway in 1937 by Britain, and Iran now contests this. In the spring of 1969 both sides massed troops in the area as Iranian ships transited the passage as a test case. In 1972 there were border clashes, with Iran blaming Iraq for shooting first. Border disputes in February 1974 produced about 100 casualties.

There no longer appears to be a serious internal security threat. The Shah seems to have been largely successful in his efforts to hasten the modernization of Iran, and to assure that all elements of the population begin to share in the benefits of this program. A large Arab minority in Khuzestan offers a possible target for external subversion. Some Iranian encouragement has in the past been quietly provided to the insurgent Kurdish elements in Iraq. The continuing unstable political situation in Iraq is watched carefully.

MILITARY ASSISTANCE

Military assistance has been provided principally by the United States, which, in the years 1950-1972, furnished $853.7 million in military supplies and equipment. In addition 10,807 men have been trained under the MAP. Three hundred US personnel are stationed in Iran in training and advisory roles. Smaller amounts have in the past been furnished by Great Britain and other countries of Western Europe. As the result of Iran's recent rapid economic growth, grant aid has virtually ceased; Iran is now able to meet its requirements by purchase. Many of these are obtained from the United States; major items include several squadrons of F-4 aircraft.

Iran is seeking to diversify its sources of military supply so as not to be completely dependent upon the United States. In 1966, a $70 million agreement was concluded with Great Britain for the purchase of ships, missiles, and hovercraft; in 1967, a $110 million agreement was signed with the Soviet Union to acquire trucks, armored personnel carriers, and automatic antiaircraft weapons, with repayment to be made initially in the form of consumer goods and later with natural gas. Substantial deliveries have been received on both agreements.

ALLIANCES

Iran is a member of the UN; its only formal alliance is its membership in CENTO. Iran and the United States have entered into a number of military assistance agreements beginning in 1952; in 1959 the two countries signed a bilateral agreement of cooperation. Iran is a member, along with Pakistan and Turkey, of the Regional Cooperation for Development, established in 1964.

ARMY

Personnel: 150,000

Organization:

- 3 corps with headquarters at Kermanshah in the northwest, Tehran in the northeast, and Shiraz in the south
- 3 infantry divisions
- 3 armored divisions
- 4 independent brigades (2 infantry, 1 special forces, 1 airborne)
- 5 divisional artillery groups
- 1 aviation battalion
- 1 SAM battalion (Hawk, Rapier)

Major Equipment Inventory:

- 100 heavy tanks (Chieftain)
- 850 medium tanks (M-47, M-60A1)
- 100 light tanks (M-24)
- 200 armored cars (M-8, M-20)
- 2,000 APCs (M-113, BTR-50, BTR-60)
- AAA (Soviet ZU-23, 57mm, and 85mm, and Bofors 40mm)
- 75mm, 105mm, and 203mm howitzers
- 130mm, 155mm, and 175mm guns
- SAMs (Hawk and Rapier)
- SSMs (SS-11, SS-12, TOW)
- light aircraft (L-18, U-17, O-2, Beagle Pup)
- 95 helicopters (5 H-43, 14 CH-47, 52 AB-205, 24 AB-206)

Equipment on Order:

- 700 Chieftain tanks
- 300 Scorpion light tanks
- 300 Fox armored cars
- TOW antitank missiles (to be deployed with infantry, helicopter and armored units)
- 202 AH-1 gunship helicopters

Reserves: About 500,000 men of prior service fit for duty

NAVY

Personnel: 13,000

Organization:

- 2 fleets: Caspian Sea and Persian Gulf or Southern Fleet (larger). There is no naval aviation or marine corps, but a battalion of naval infantry, used mainly to guard shore installations.

Major Units:

- 3 destroyer (DD; 1 with Seacat SAM)
- 8 destroyer escorts (DE; 4 with Sea Killer, Seacat SAMs)
- 4 patrol craft (YP)
- 10 patrol boats/cutters (PGM)
- 3 patrol launches (YP)
- 4 coastal minesweepers (MSC)
- 2 inshore minesweepers (MSI)
- 3 landing ship, infantry, large (LSIL)
- 4 landing craft (LCU)
- 14 hovercraft (8 SRN-6 and 6 BH-7)
- 5 auxiliaries
- 34 helicopters (4 AB-205, 14 AB-206, 6 AB-212, 10 SH-3)

Equipment on Order:

- 6 turboprop Aero Commander Shrike liaison aircraft
- 4 F-28 jet transport aircraft
- 6 fast patrol boats (PTF) with Exocet SSM

Missiles: Seacat and Seakiller SAMs

Naval Bases: Khorramshahr (major base), Bandar Pahlavi, Bushire, Kharg Island, Bandar Abbas, Chahbahar (tri-service)

AIR FORCE

Personnel: 40,000

Organization:

- 8 fighter-interceptor squadrons (F-4 and F-5)
- 10 fighter-bomber squadrons (F-4 and F-5)
- 2 fighter-reconnaissance squadrons (RF-5

and RT-33)
4 transport squadrons (C-130 and F-27)
1 helicopter squadron of the Imperial Court (5 AB-212)

Major Aircraft Types:
283 combat aircraft
    100 F-4 fighter-bomber/interceptors*
    150 F-5 fighter-bomber/interceptors*
    18 RF-5 fighter reconnaissance
    15 RT-33 fighter reconnaissance
186 other aircraft
    56 C-130 transports
    14 F-27 transports
    25 other transports (C-45, C-47)
    38 trainers (T-6, T-41, U-22)
    16 utility (O-2, U-6)
    37 helicopters (10 AB-206, 5 AB-212, 2 CH-47, 4 H-43, 16 Super Frelon)

Equipment on Order:
    30 F-14 fighters with Phoenix AAM
    141 F-5 Tiger II fighters
    60 F-4 fighters
    44 C-130 transports
    287 Bell 214 utility helicopters (service assignment unknown)
    6 Boeing 707 tankers (for F-14, F-4 and F-5 fighters)
    12 Beech F33C trainers
    3 Aero Commander transports
    2,500 Maverick ASMs
    4 maritime patrol aircraft, Lockheed Orion P-3F (to be assigned to the Air Force)

Air Bases: Tehran, Hamadan, Dezful, Doshen-Tappeh, Mehrabad, Galeh-Marghi, Zahidan, Mashad, Shiraz, Ahwaz, Isfahan, Tabriz, Faharabad, Chahbahar

Reserves: Not over 35,000 men of prior service fit for duty

PARAMILITARY

There are three paramilitary organizations: the Imperial Iranian Gendarmerie, the National Police, and the Resistance Forces. The Gendarmerie of 40,000 men consists mainly of volunteers, and a few conscripts. It is organized into 33 regiments, three separate battalions, one light aircraft battalion, and one naval battalion. Equipment includes 15 armored cars, 30 AB206 helicopters, 29 Cessna-185 light aircraft, and 26 patrol craft. In peacetime the Gendarmerie is under the direction of the Minister of the Interior. In wartime it comes under the Ministry of War. Selected units of the National Police organization may be used for special assignments. The mission of the Resistance Forces is to prepare the people to defend their homes and villages and to cooperate with the armed forces in case of aggression or internal unrest.

IRAQ

Al Jumhuriyah al Iraqiah
The Republic of Iraq

POWER POTENTIAL STATISTICS

Area: 169,925 square miles
Population: 10,800,000
Total Active Armed Forces: 116,500 (including security troops; 1.07% population)
Gross National Product: $3.8 billion ($352 per capita)
Annual Military Expenditures: $440 million (11.6% GNP)
Fuel Production: Crude Oil: 71.03 million metric tons
    Refined Products: 4.2 million metric tons
Electric Power Output: 2.12 billion kwh
Merchant Fleet: 45 ships, 121,000 gross tons
Civil Air Fleet: 3 jet, 3 turboprop and 15 piston transports

DEFENSE STRUCTURE

Since 1968 Iraq has been controlled by the Baath (Renaissance) party, a socialist, pan-Arab group with strong ties to the Soviet Union. The governing body is the 14-member Revolutionary Command Council (RCC); a president, elected by the RCC, is head of state and commander in chief of the armed forces. Real power, however, is in the hands of the RCC vice president, Saddan Hussein Takriti, who is also Assistant Secretary General of the Baath Party. A majority of Baath leaders are military officers.

Following an unsuccessful coup attempt in mid-1973, the Baath Party took a number of constitutional and political steps to broaden its base of support. The Communist Party was recognized as a legal party for the first time. It agreed to join with the Baath Party in a National Progressive Front which all progressive parties, including the aggrieved Kurds' Democratic Party of Kurdistan, were invited to join. The Communists agreed to recognize the privileged role of the Baath Party in the new front, and its exclusive control of the RCC, Army and police.

---

*Interceptors carry Sidewinder and Sparrow AAM, fighter-bombers Maverick ASM.

The Iraqi Air Force is subordinate to the Army, and the Navy operates as an integral, specialized component of the Army.

POLITICO-MILITARY POLICY

In spite of considerable oscillation in national and international policies, traditional Arab-Israeli hostility has kept Iraqi policy consistent in opposition to Israel. One consequence of this policy since 1958 has been to keep the successive military governments more or less aligned with the USSR. Iraq depends on the Soviet Union for military equipment and economic assistance, and in exchange is a staunch supporter of Soviet policy. Iraq contributed armored and air (MiG-21 and Hunter) units to the October 1973 Arab-Israeli war. One air squadron operated from Syria and one from Egypt.

Military service for two years is compulsory for all male citizens over the age of 18; liability for service continues through age 40. More than 70,000 males reach military age annually, more than enough to keep units up to their authorized strengths.

Most commissioned officers are graduates of the Military College at Rustamiyah or the Air Force Flying College at Shaiba air base near Basra. The Army also maintains a staff college for the training of selected Army and Air Force officers for high command and staff positions. Iraqi officers are also sent abroad, primarily to the Soviet Union, for specialized training.

STRATEGIC PROBLEMS

Iraq's major strategic problems are internal. One of the largest producers of crude oil in the world, it has one of the lowest standards of living for the general populace. There is evidence that the present regime is attempting to undertake social, political, and economic reform in efforts to rectify this situation, but thus far these efforts have not been very successful.

Since the independence of Iraq in 1932, the Kurdish minority in the north (now numbering about 1,500,000 people) has been seeking independence or autonomy and has been in a state of hostility toward the central government. The previously low level of violence erupted in 1961 into a civil war that lasted until 1970. On March 11, 1970, an agreement was signed providing that there should be two Iraqi nationalities, Arabs and Kurds; that the Vice President of Iraq should be a Kurd; that Kurds should be given proportional representation in the government; that Kurdish should be the official language in Kurdish areas; and that in four years an autonomous Kurdish region should be set up.

Four years later, in March 1974, a new civil war broke out. Although several of the 1970 pledges had been carried out, the Kurds were dissatisfied with the status of others, and especially with the Iraqi decision to exclude the Kirkuk area, and with it Iraq's richest oilfield, from their promised autonomous region. Takriti gave the Democratic Party of Kurdistan a 15-day ultimatum on March 11, and a mass migration of Kurds from other parts of Iraq to Kurdistan began. Fighting began in the area of the Turkish border and spread to the Irbil, Kirkuk, and Sulaymaniyah areas. Beginning in mid-April, the Iraqi Air Force bombed Kurdish areas.

Iraq occupied border areas of Kuwait in 1973 in an effort to expand its holdings on the Persian Gulf, but later withdrew. The government has announced that Iraq must be a Gulf state, and further border disputes are likely.

Border disputes with Iran are another strategic concern. In the most serious clash of 1974, in February, Iraqi tanks and artillery were used, according to Iran, and Iranian jets and artillery, according to Iraq, with total casualties of about 100 killed and wounded.

MILITARY ASSISTANCE

Until July 1958 Iraq's armed forces were largely British-trained and equipped, although there had been some US military assistance.

After the coup of July 1958 deposed the pro-Western government, USSR arms deliveries began; they have continued under a series of agreements until the present. Early shipments may have been grant aid; more recently Iraq reportedly has paid cash. A total of over $700 million of Soviet arms has been delivered.

Under the US Military Assistance Program, through FY 1968 Iraq received a total of $46.7 million, plus $1.1 million in excess military stocks; 404 students were trained. India has trained all Iraqi pilots on MiG-21 aircraft, and the French Army has trained Iraqi pilots on Alouette helicopters.

ALLIANCES

Iraq is a member of the UN and of the Arab League. It was a charter member of the Baghdad Pact (now CENTO) but withdrew after the coup of 1958.

ARMY

Personnel: 95,000

Organization:
- 2 armored divisions
- 4 infantry divisions (each with 3 regiments, plus an artillery regiment, engineers, and support troops)
- 1 independent mechanized infantry brigade
- 2 heavy AA regiments

Major Equipment Inventory:
- 40+ heavy tanks (JS-3)
- 915 medium tanks (T-54 and T-55; some T-34; 55 Centurion Mk.5)
- 45 light tanks (PT-76)
- 1,200 APCs (BTR-152)
- 300 122mm and 130mm guns
- 100mm antitank guns (SU-100)
- 115 armored cars (AML-60)
- 60 scout cars (Ferret)
- 18 aircraft

Reserves: 268,000 trained reservists

NAVY

Personnel: 2,000

Major Units:
- 3 submarine chasers (SO-1 class; PCS)
- 5 Osa class fast patrol boats with Styx SSM (PT)
- 12 torpedo boats (P-6 class; PT)
- 4 river gunboats (PRG)
- 8 patrol craft (YP)
- 3 auxiliaries

Reserves: Approximately 3,000

Naval Base: Basra

AIR FORCE

Personnel: 9,500

Organization:
- 1 bomber squadron (Tu-16, Il-28)
- 8 fighter-interceptor squadrons (MiG-21/17)
- 5 fighter-bomber squadrons (Su-7, Hunter)
- 4 transport squadrons (Tu-124, An-2, An-12, An-24, Il-14, Heron)
- 4 helicopter squadrons (Mi-4, Mi-8, Wessex, Alouette III)
- 1 trainer/support group (L-29, L-39, Jet Provost)

Note. It has been reported that a small number (estimated to be 12) of Tu-22 bombers are based near Baghdad, flown by Russian pilots.

Major Aircraft Types:
    244 combat aircraft
        100 MiG-21 fighters
        30 MiG-17 fighters
        60 Su-7 fighter-bombers
        36 Hunter fighter-bombers
        8 Tu-16 medium bombers
        10 Il-28 light bombers
    176 other aircraft
        47 transports (2 Tu-124, 12 An-2, 8 An-12, 10 An-24, 13 Il-14, 2 Heron)
        80 helicopters (35 Mi-4, 12 Mi-8, 9 Wessex, 24 Alouette III)
        49 trainer/support (20 Jet Provost, 28 L-29, 1 L-39)

Missiles: SAMs (SA-2, SA-3)

Air Bases: Habbaniya, Shaiba, Kirkuk, Raschid, Basra, Mosul

Reserves: over 18,000 trained reservists

PARAMILITARY

There is one security force mechanized brigade (of 4,000 men), used to reinforce the regular police when major disorders break out, plus miscellaneous security units, totalling about 10,000, and a national guard of about 10,000.

ISRAEL

Medinat Israel
State of Israel

POWER POTENTIAL STATISTICS

Area: 8,017 square miles*
Population: 3,200,000
Total Active Armed Forces: 98,100 regular cadre and conscripts (3% population)**

---

*Does not include territories occupied since June 1967.
**Not including mobilized reserves; the total can be raised to about 300,000 within 48 to 72 hours.

Gross National Product: $6.7 billion ($2,094 per capita)
Annual Military Expenditures: $1.6 billion (23.0% GNP)***
Fuel Production: Crude Oil: 6.1 million metric tons****
    Refined Petroleum Products: 6.3 million metric tons
Electric Power Output: 7.7 billion kwh
Merchant Fleet: 102 ships; 645,585 gross tons
Civil Air Fleet: 13 jet, 9 turboprop transports

DEFENSE STRUCTURE

While the Israeli Defense Force was formally organized in 1948 upon independence, it originated in the Haganah, a Jewish underground defense organization started in the Palestine Mandate in the 1920s. Palmach was its elite combat force of full-time regulars. The transformation of these forces into the IDF reserve and regular components upon independence was conceptually and organizationally simple. Not only had these forces considerable experience in guerrilla warfare against the British and Arabs in Palestine, but they were constantly being joined, especially after World War II, by Jewish veterans of the British, American and other armies, including a number of highly trained and experienced middle to senior level officers. With the popular determination to establish and defend Israel tempered by the modern war experience of others, a highly effective military instrument appropriate to the defense needs of the country was evolved during the early years of independence. The form of these forces emerged from this background, the culture of the population, the strategic position of Israel, the experience of four wars (1948, 1956, 1967, and 1973) and numerous border clashes with Arab regular and irregular forces. Initial Israeli setbacks as a result of Egypt's surprise attack in October 1973, and later Israeli withdrawal from occupied territories as a result of post-war negotiations, have stimulated the widespread misconception that the combat outcome was a draw. Following those initial setbacks, the Israelis established and maintained a combat effectiveness superiority over their opponents at least as marked as in previous wars.

Actual control of the Israeli Defense Forces (IDF) is vested in the Prime Minister and the Cabinet. Direct responsibility for administering the armed forces is exercised by the Minister of Defense. The Chief of the General Staff is also Chief of Staff of the Army and presides over the completely unified Defense Forces. The General Staff directs activities and operations of the combat commands (Navy, Air Force, three territorial commads, the Paratroop Command, and the Armored Command), the Training Command, and NAHAL (Fighting Pioneering Youth, a paramilitary organization).

***This was probably considerably larger in 1973.
****Includes occupied Sinai production.

POLITICO-MILITARY POLICIES

Policies are directed primarily against the threat of Arab nations sworn to destroy Israel. These policies encompass: (1) the defense of Israel by whatever means may be necessary; (2) obtaining peace with the Arab states and their diplomatic recognition of Israel; (3) breaking the Arab economic blockade; and (4) seeking friends throughout the world (among the developed powers as sources of heavy military equipment, among the undeveloped countries to secure their favorable votes on Palestine Questions before the UN, and from all the right of free emigration of their Jews to Israel). Israel has had marked success in all of these policies, except that of obtaining Arab recognition. However, in face of the active Arab threat to its new borders, Israel maintains a crushing defense burden and in reality is a nation in arms. The success of the ceasefire and withdrawal negotiations conducted by Secretary of State Kissinger has provided the Israelis with some hope that this state of siege will not endure forever.

Military service is universal for men and women (except the Arab 10 percent of the population); men 18-29 years of age serve 36 months and unmarried women 18-26 serve 20 months from their 18th birthday. Service in the reserves is required up to age 55 for men and 34 for women.

Israeli Defense Forces comprise a regular professional nucleus of about 25-30,000 with two yearly conscript classes of around 25,000 each for a total of about 75,000 normally on active duty at any one time. This active force has two major elements: (1) a mobilization base (including a training cadre and recruits in training), and (2) first-line- of defense units such as air defense and sea patrols and units along the border.

The senior service school is the Command and General Staff College, a tri-service institution which conducts a 10-month course in general staff operations, technique, and procedures. Many officers are also sent to foreign war colleges for training, mostly to the United States.

The logistical system appears to be adequate and efficient, principally because of the high level of managerial and technical skill of the Israelis and their widescale adoption of modern business machines and methods. An important handicap is the continuing dependence on foreign sources for major items of combat equipment.

In the field, responsibility for logistical operations devolves primarily upon the territorial commanders. They are responsible for arming and equipping reserve forces in their areas and for providing logistical support to all units coming under their control. Supply depots are located at key points to provide arms, equipment, and field rations in the event of mobilization and to furnish base support for combat operations.

STRATEGIC PROBLEMS

Israel's strategic position is characterized by lack of space, and by encirclement by hostile Arab countries. As was clearly illustrated in the October 1973 War, save for the occupied territories, there is no space to afford warning time against air attack and no space to trade for time or in which to maneuver against an invading army. While retention of Golan Heights and the Gaza Strip are strategic necessities, and the Jordan River is the natural boundary for a strategically viable Israel, the ultimate fate of these territories remains undecided, with Israel continuing to occupy them, despite minor adjustments in early 1974.

Regardless of the eventual adjustment of this territorial situation, Israel's strategic position remains essentially the same, although improved. Its industrial area is still only 15 minutes from Egyptian airfields; the Sinai Desert offers little obstacle to armored forces whether based on the east bank of the Canal or poised on the Israeli border.

This situation has led to a strategy based on offensive strikes by closely coordinated modern land, air and sea forces against any threatening Arab forces. Border incidents and infiltrations, as in the past, prompt instant, severe Israeli reaction. Border police and fortified farms along the border provide the tripwire against incursions and are backed up by mobile army units. Surface-to-surface missiles are available as retaliation for any possible Egyptian missiles delivering high explosives against Israeli cities.

A number of factors permit this strategy. First is the high literacy and technical competence of Israeli manpower, plus physical fitness derived through proper nutrition, rural life, and fitness programs. Also contributing is the military experience of the leadership, going back to World War II and enriched by further experience in three successful campaigns against Arab armies. These factors plus the motivation of self-survival have resulted in very high morale and *esprit de corps* in a relatively homogeneous and united population. All of this permits utilization of the most modern weapons, bold, rapid, and sometimes complex maneuvers, and an extremely rapid mobilization.

In addition to the geographical problem, Israeli leadership must cope with several other strategic weaknesses: (1) the increased number of Arab residents resulting from the territorial acquisitions of the June 1967 war form a potential guerrilla base, and presumably provide some assistance to the terrorist guerrillas based in Lebanon and Syria; (2) lack of allies (see below); and (3) inability to date to establish an industrial base adequate to produce the latest weapons such as supersonic aircraft, surface-to-air missile systems, tanks, or heavy artillery. This last deficiency has been partially overcome by the diplomatic expedient of securing modern heavy weapons from the US, which is anxious to keep a Middle East arms balance. Some temporary alleviation has resulted from modernizing obsolescent weapons such as tanks and artillery and from the capture of modern Russian weapons from the Arabs in 1967 and 1973.

MILITARY ASSISTANCE

Israel has received no grant aid military assistance, paying for all of the weapons it imports. Payment is facilitated by a flourishing export economy augmented by substantial US economic aid, sale of Bonds for Israel in the United States, and West German reparations. Pre-1973 purchases include M-48 and M-60 tanks, Hawk surface-to-air missiles, A-4 jet light attack bombers, F-4 jet fighter-bombers, and a computerized air defense radar network. During the 1973 war Israel lost nearly half of its pre-war tank inventory, but American resupply, captured Egyptian (Soviet) tanks, and efficient repair techniques have at least offset these losses. Proportionally smaller aircraft losses have also been offset.

In a bid to win friends Israel operates a modest but wide-spread military assistance program in numbers of undeveloped countries. This consists of gifts of small numbers of Israeli-made weapons and equipment, training both in Israel and in the host country, and advice on both organization and operations. Subjects of training and advice include: infantry, parachute, intelligence and security, navy, air force, border protection, and paramilitary youth organizations. Small or initial programs are grant aid; more extensive programs are paid for by the recipient. Equipment sales include small arms, mortars, military vehicles, and armed jet trainers, all made in Israel.

ALLIANCES

Israel is a member of the UN. During the 1967 hostilities France terminated a previous de facto alliance, in which it had been Israel's source of modern aircraft and heavy weapons. The United States demonstrated in the 1973 war that it will provide Israel with whatever military support is necessary to offset Soviet aid to the Arab countries, in order to maintain a Middle East balance of power.

ARMY

Personnel: 81,500 (21,500 regulars and about 60,000 conscripts); total is 275,000 when fully mobilized

Organizations:
- 4 infantry brigades
- 4 armored brigades
- 1 paratroop brigade
  Regional defense cadres and border guards training Command and reserve cadres (see below)

Major Equipment Inventory:
- 1,700+ medium tanks
  - 425 M-48 Patton (105mm guns)
  - 800 Centurion, Ben Gurion, and Sabra (105mm gun)
  - 100 T-54 and T-55 (105mm gun; Israeli designation TI-67)
  - 175 M-60 medium tanks
  - 200 Super Sherman or Isherman (105mm gun)
      T-62, T-55, T-54 (captured Soviet tanks)
- 150 light tanks (AMX-13 and PT-76)
- 300+ self-propelled artillery pieces (including heavy mortars or 155mm howitzers on Sherman chassis, and 105mm SP howitzers or mortars AMX-13 chassis; 24 M-109 self-propelled 155mm gun-howitzers)
- 400 APCs (M-113)
- 1,200 half-track (M-2 and M-3)
- 50 106mm recoilless rifles (jeep-mounted)
- 50 90mm self-propelled guns
     SS-11 missiles on weapons carriers
- 15 armored cars (AML-90)
     armored cars (Staghound and AML-60)
     Cobra antitank missiles, Swingfire ATGW
- 200 20mm, 30mm, and 40mm AA guns

Reserves: Approximately 200,000 available for immediate mobilization, to activate approximately:
- 15 infantry brigades
- 7 armored brigades
- 3 paratroop brigades

Training: Reserves are called up for training 14 to 31 days per year, plus one day per month; officers and NCOs receive special courses an additional week per year.

Mobilization: Reserves are mobilizable within 48 hours; individuals report to depots where they join their unit cadres, obtain their weapons and equipment, and are ready for operations.

NAVY

Personnel: 4,000 regular and conscripts (8,000 total when fully mobilized); 500 naval commandos

Major Units:
- 3 submarines (SS)
- 2 destroyers (DD, one used as training ship)

9 fast patrol boats (PF; Saar class; each with 5 to 8 Gabriel SSMs)
6 fast patrol boats (PF; Reshef class; each with 7 Gabriel SSMs)
7 torpedo boats (PT)
12 patrol launches (PBR)
11 patrol craft (YP)
9 landing craft (6 LCT, 3 LCM)

Naval Bases: Haifa, Ashdod, Eilat

AIR FORCE

Personnel: 13,000 (12,000 regulars and about 1,000 conscripts; 20,000 total when fully mobilized)

Organization:
- 5 fighter squadrons (Mirage III, Barak, Super Mystere) armed with AAM Shafrir, R-530 Matra, Sidewinder
- 8 fighter-bomber squadrons (F-4, RF-4, Mystere, Ouragan)
- 8 ground attack squadrons (A-4, Vautour)

Note. Fighter-bomber and ground attack squadrons are armed with AGM Bullpup, Shrike, Standard ARM, Rockeye, Walleye and Maverick.

- 4 transport squadrons (C-47, C-130, C-97, Noratlas, IAI Arava)
- 1 helicopter wing (CH-53, AB-205, Super Frelon, Alouette II, Iroquois)
- 1 training wing (Fokker S-11, Magister, Mystere, Ouragan, Mirage)
- SAM battalions (Hawk)

Major Aircraft Types:
- 475 combat aircraft
  - 60 Mirage III fighters
  - 25 Barak fighters
  - 18 Super Mystere fighters
  - 140 F-4, RF-4 fighter-bombers
  - 30 Mystere fighter-bombers
  - 30 Ouragan fighter-bombers
  - 160 A-4 ground attack aircraft
  - 12 Vautour ground attack aircraft
- 254 other aircraft
  - 74+ transports (12 C-47, 12 C-130, 12 C-97, 38 Noratlas, unknown num- Matra, Sidewinder
  - 80 helicopters (12 CH-53, 30 AB-205, 8 Super Frelon, 5 Alouette II, 25 Iroquois)
  - 100+ trainers (Fokker S-11, Magister, Mystere, Ouragan, Mirage)

Missiles: 420 Hawk SAMs and 50 Hawk launchers

Major Air Bases: Lod, Ekron, Hatzerim

PARAMILITARY

Virtually the entire Israeli population, excluding Arabs, is assigned civil defense and home guard duties. Communal farms are well organized for defense with fortifications and stocks of arms and ammunition. Older men, youths and women are well trained to man these positions; many are veterans of the Defense Forces or participated in the guerrilla struggle in Palestine before 1948.

The principal paramilitary force is called NAHAL (Fighting Pioneering Youth), an organization that combines military service with agricultural training. NAHAL's prime military mission is to serve as first line of defense against ground attack along the borders and to prevent infiltration. A secondary mission is to assist and support the army in performing duties in the occupied territories.

JORDAN

Al Mamiaka al Urduniya al Hashemiyah
The Hashemite Kingdom of Jordan

POWER POTENTIAL STATISTICS

Area: 37,737 square miles*
Population: 2,400,000
Total Active Armed Forces: 73,000 (including Gendarmerie; 2.8% population)
Gross National Product: $650 million ($250 per capita)
Annual Military Expenditures: $120 million (18% GNP)
Refined Petroleum Products: 806,000 metric tons
Electric Power Output: 165 million kwh
Civil Air Fleet: 7 jet transports

DEFENSE STRUCTURE

The King exercises principal political and military authority in this constitutional monarchy. He is in fact, as well as nominally, the commander in chief of the armed forces. He exercises his administrative authority generally through the

*Includes West Jordan, approximately 2,185 square miles, occupied by Israel since June 1967.

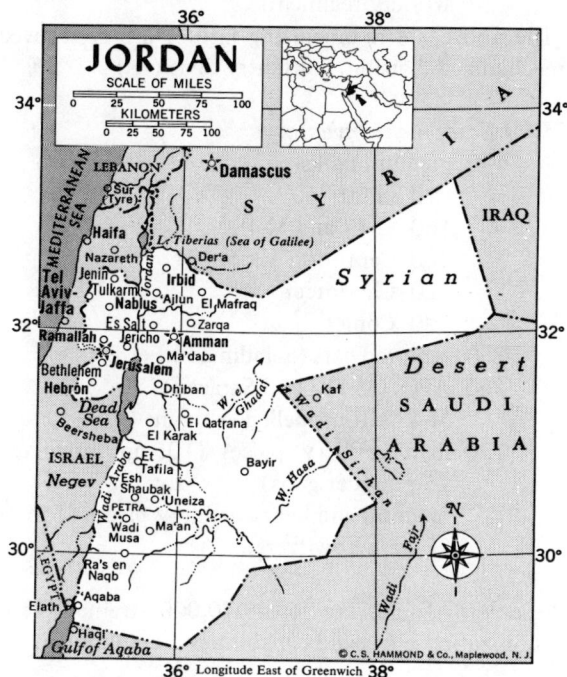

Minister of Defense, but retains a direct, personal command relationship with the command of the Jordan Arab Army (formerly the Arab Legion).

In addition to the Jordan Arab Army, the armed forces include the Royal Air Force and a small Royal Navy, which is an integral part of the Army. The Public Security Force is under the Ministry of Interior, but is operationally subordinate to the Army, and during war is part of the military service.

POLITICO-MILITARY POLICY

Military service is for three years.

Since its establishment as an independent kingdom in 1946, the Hashemite Kingdom of Jordan has been a consistently liberal and pro-Western Arab state. The people share the general Arab hostility toward Israel. Jordan's military policy, like its foreign policy, has been to a considerable degree ambivalent. On the one hand, in company with its Arab neighbors, Jordan's policy is to be ready for defense against possible Israeli aggression while at the same time preparing for an ultimate offensive war to regain occupied territories. On the other hand, Jordan has sought (certainly indirectly, and possibly directly) to reach some sort of accomodation with Israel, probably with the ultimate aim of accepting and diplomatically recognizing Israel's presence in the region formerly known as Palestine, and probably with some compromise sharing of sovereignty over the now-occupied West Bank.

It was this tendency toward accommodation with Israel that was almost certainly responsible for the assassination of the present monarch's grandfather, King Abdullah, the first King of Jordan, in 1951. It has caused considerable internal popular unrest and resentment of the policies of the present king, and frequent threats from more militantly anti-Israeli Arab states, such as Syria, Libya, and Egypt. Although the armed forces, made up largely from the population of East Jordan, are basically loyal to the monarch, they share the traditional anti-Zionist attitude.

British influence is strong in the armed forces, because of the long period of British control. British officers organized and trained the Arab Legion, and British doctrine and staff organization have carried over.

The Army's logistical system is modern and effective. Growing stocks of US arms, equipment, and spare parts, and adoption of US record and maintenance procedures have made it increasingly American in character. All weapons and major equipment for the armed forces are imported.

The most important source of officers is the Royal Military Academy in Amman. It offers a two-year course of military and academic subjects. The Royal Staff College, also in Amman, offers a two-year course for the higher education of selected officers. In addition, the armed forces rely on foreign staff and technical schools for specialized training.

The Bedouin inhabitants of the area east of Amman continue to be the most numerous element in the armed forces, particularly in the infantry armored units. Palestinian Arabs are predominant in the National Guard, technical services, and Air Force.

STRATEGIC PROBLEMS

The principal strategic problem for Jordan is the threat to its viability as a nation as a result of the loss of West Jordan (the richest region of the country) to Israel in June 1967. It is likely that most of this region will be returned to Jordan in some eventual peace settlement, but meanwhile the economic and political strains on Jordan are tremendous.

Related to the problem of the future of West Jordan is the question of the orientation of the total population. Almost half are native inhabitants of West Jordan. Nearly 700,000 are refugees, or children of refugees, from those portions of Palestine that became incorporated in the boundaries of Israel in 1948-1949. Most of the refugees are militant in their hatred of Israel, and in their incitement of Arab action to destroy Israel and to permit them to return to their ancestral homes in an Arab Palestine. With some significant exceptions, the refugees feel little or no loyalty to Jordan or to its monarch. The loyalty and support of the Palestinian Arab inhabitants of West Jordan are only slightly less suspect.

Because of the anti-Israeli militancy of a majority of Jordan's inhabitants, the government was long forced to permit the establishment of guerrilla bases in East Jordan, near the Jordan River, from which raids were periodically mounted against Israel and Israeli-occupied West Jordan. The presence of these bases, and the continuation of the raids provoked

Israel to frequent retaliation, which neither the Jordanian armed forces nor the guerrillas could oppose effectively.

Government attempts to curb guerrilla activities led in 1969 and 1970 to clashes between government forces and Palestinian commandos which resulted, in September of 1970, in complete defeat of the commandos, and reestablishment of government control throughout the country. During this fighting Syrian troops crossed into Jordan, apparently intending to link up with Palestinian commandos and to overthrow the King. They were defeated, however, by combined Jordanian air and armored units; fear of Israeli intervention apparently forced Syria to accept this defeat, and to withdraw from Jordan.

Jordan did not open a front against Israel at their common border during the October 1973 war, but did send Jordanian Army units to fight under Syrian command on the Syrian front.

MILITARY ASSISTANCE

After World War II most of Jordan's military equipment and training was British. At the time of the Lebanon Crisis of 1958 Britain sent troops to Jordan to bolster the King's regime. More recently, to assist in maintaining a semblance of arms balance in the Middle East and to preempt Soviet military aid to Jordan, the United States had provided about $91 million in tanks, artillery, aircraft, and other equipment by the end of 1972. About $5.3 million in excess military stocks have also been provided and 694 students have been trained under the MAP. In early 1969 Jordan purchased $14.4 million of British Tigercat surface-to-air missiles and associated radars for airfield defense. Funds for this and other purchases came from a $100 million yearly subsidy paid by oil-rich Kuwait, Saudi Arabia, and Libya to compensate Jordan for the lost income from West Bank territories occupied by Israel. After King Hussein's crackdown on Palestinian commandos operating from Jordan in 1970, Kuwait and Libya withdrew their subsidies (amounting to $65 million annually), but in October 1973 Kuwait resumed its subsidy, now some $48 million annually.

ALLIANCES

Jordan is a member of the UN and of the Arab League.

ARMY

Personnel: 62,000

Organization:
    4 armored brigades
    7 infantry and mechanized brigades
    1 Royal Guards brigade (mechanized)
    1 AA regiment (Tigercat SAMs on order)
    12 artillery regiments
(The above are re-organizing into: 1 armored division; 1 mechanized division; 2 infantry divisions)

Major Equipment Inventory:
    490 medium tanks
        90 M-60
        160 M-47 and M-48
        200 Centurion Mk.5
        20 Charioteer
        20 Comet
    250 armored cars (Saladin and Ferret)
    500 APCs (M-113 and Saracen)
    M-42 self-propelled AA guns
    130 light artillery pieces (105mm howitzers and 25-pounder guns)
    medium and heavy artillery pieces (155mm and 203mm howitzers)

Reserves: There are over 70,000 trained reservists; mobilization plans and capabilities are unknown.

NAVY

Personnel: 250

Major Units: 8 patrol craft (YP)

Naval Base: Aqaba

AIR FORCE

Personnel: 2,000

Organization:
    4 fighter squadrons (F-104 and Hunter)
    1 transport squadron (C-47)
    1 helicopter squadron (Alouette II, Whirlwind, Scout)

Major Aircraft Types:
    35 combat aircraft
        17 Hunter fighter-bombers
        18 F-104 fighter interceptors
    42 other aircraft
        4 C-47 transports
        8 light transports (Devon, Dove, Herald, Varsity, and Twin Bonanza)
        20 trainers
        10 helicopters (Alouette III, Whirlwind, and Scout)

Equipment on Order:
    30 F-5 Tiger II

Air Bases: Amman, Aqaba, Al Mafraq, Jerusalem (occupied by the Israelis)

PARAMILITARY

Jordan has a 8,750-man Gendarmerie (including the camel-mounted Desert Patrol).

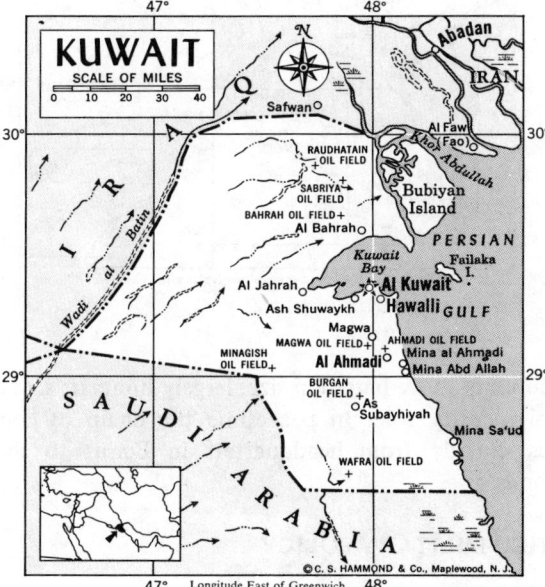

KUWAIT
Dawlat al Kuwait
State of Kuwait

POWER POTENTIAL STATISTICS

Area: 6,880 square miles
Population: 930,000
Total Active Armed Forces: 10,500 (1.1% population)
Gross National Product: $3.65 billion ($3,924 per capita)
Annual Military Expenditures: $100 million (2.73% GNP)
Fuel Production: Crude Oil: 151.2 million metric tons
    Refined Petroleum Products: 19.1 million metric tons
Merchant Fleet: 164 ships; 656,403 gross tons
Civil Air Fleet: 5 jet transports

POLITICO-MILITARY POLICIES AND POSTURE

Kuwait is a constitutional monarchy, but the authority of the monarch (emir) is close to absolute. Formerly a British protectorate, this enormously wealthy tiny kingdom still relies to a large extent upon British protection for its security, and has a defense treaty with the United Kingdom. This was successfully invoked in June 1961, when Iraq threatened invasion and annexation. There is a continuing border dispute with Iraq, which seeks to expand its minuscule Persian Gulf coastline at Kuwait's expense. Iraq occupied some Kuwait territory in 1973, but later withdrew. Saudi Arabia sent 15,000-20,000 soldiers into Kuwait to strengthen its defenses.

Kuwait is a member of UN and the Arab League, and has been a principal source of funds for that organization and for many of its members, particularly since the disastrous defeats of Egypt (to which it gives about $84 million annually), Jordon (to which it gives $48 million annually), and Syria.

ARMY

Personnel: 6,500

Organization:
    1 armored brigade
    2 composite brigades (armored/infantry/artillery)

Major Equipment Inventory:
    50 Vickers Victorious main battle tanks
    20 Centurion main battle tanks
       Saladin armored cars
       Saracen APCs
       Ferret scout cars
       25 pounder artillery
       TOW SSM antitank
       Hawk SAM

Equipment on Order:
    Hawk SAM
    M6 tanks

NAVY (Coast Guard)

Personnel: 500

Major Units:
    18 patrol boats (YP)
    2 landing craft

AIR FORCE

Personnel: 1,500

Organization:
    1 fighter-bomber squadron (Hunter, Lightning)
    1 ground attack squadron (Strikemaster, Jet Provost)
    1 support squadron (C-130, Caribou)

1 helicopter squadron (AB-205, AB-206, Whirlwind)

Major Aircraft Types:
40 combat aircraft
  8 Hunter fighters
 14 Lightning fighters
 12 Strikemaster ground attack
  6 Jet Provost trainer/ground attack
16 other aircraft
  2 Caribou light transports
  2 C-130 medium transports
 12 helicopters (6 AB-205, 4 AB-206, 2 Whirlwind)

Equipment on Order: Jaguar and Mirage fighters

PARAMILITARY

A constabulary of 2,000 men provides internal and border security.

LEBANON

Al Jumhuriyah al Lubnaniyah
The Republic of Lebanon

POWER POTENTIAL STATISTICS

Area: 4,015 square miles
Population: 3,130,000
Total Active Armed Forces: 21,050 (includes internal security forces; 0.67% population)
Gross National Product: $2 billion ($639 per capita)
Annual Military Expenditures: $76 million (4% GNP)
Electric Power Output: 1.36 billion kwh
Refined Petroleum Products: 2.2 million metric tons
Merchant Fleet: 70 ships; 116,571 gross tons
Civil Air Fleet: 23 jet, 5 piston transports

DEFENSE STRUCTURE

Lebanon is a parliamentary republic; the president of the Republic is the commander in chief of the armed forces. The Ministry of Defense has duties largely administrative in nature, and the President maintains direct contact with the Commanding General of the Army, who exercises real leadership and control over the armed forces.

The armed forces follow French patterns in organization, tactics, and staff direction. The organization of the Army, with no units above battalion size, largely limits its scope to an internal security role. In peacetime the chain of command extends directly from headquarters in Beirut to the field commands.

POLITICO-MILITARY POLICY

Lebanon's small size and population are totally inadequate for effective defense against determined aggression. For external security Lebanon relies essentially upon its memberships in the United Nations and the Arab League. Except for a brief period in 1958, largely as a result of Syrian-inspired internal violence, Lebanon's small armed forces have been adequate to maintain internal security. At that time Lebanon asked for, and received, assistance from the United States government, which intervened to restore order and assure national security in the face of a Syrian invasion threat.

The armed forces are composed entirely of volunteers. Enlistments vary from one to ten years, but usually a volunteer is accepted for a five-year period; average reenlistment is also for five years. Most commissioned officers are obtained from the Lebanese Military Academy at Fayyadiyah, near Beirut. The Army maintains several schools, principally for specialist training. Training at the war college level is usually conducted under military assistance programs in Western Europe and the United States.

STRATEGIC PROBLEMS

Although Lebanon is more stable than most of the other Arab states, this has a possibly precarious foundation: a democratic *modus vivendi* between the Christian population (less than 50%) and Moslem population (more than 40%). In times of crisis, as in 1958, that foundation may collapse.

Lebanon has attempted to pursue a moderate policy toward Israel. However, several of the Palestine guerrilla organizations have their headquarters in Lebanon and Lebanon has permitted the establishment on its territory of guerrilla military bases for operations against Israel. Guerrilla and terrorist actions against Israel have brought heavy Israeli reprisals.

MILITARY ASSISTANCE

The French military heritage, dating from the close of World War I, is still strong in Lebanon, and most equipment was French at the time of the 1958 US landing. After that date the United States contributed $10.1 million in military aid and $101,000 in excess military stocks. In addition 1,417 students were trained under the MAP. British and French tanks and aircraft also were purchased. A French military mission has visited Lebanon to survey its defense requirements and offer advice. On August 26, 1971, Lebanon's parliament approved a $52.7 million, five-year defense plan under which $15 million will be spent to purchase Soviet arms for the first time.

ALLIANCES

Lebanon is a member of the UN and of the Arab League, in which it is not a militant member.

ARMY

Personnel: 15,000

Organization:
    2 armored battalions
   10 infantry battalions (one motorized)
    3 field artillery battalions
    2 reconnaissance battalions
    1 commando battalion
    1 AA battalion

Major Equipment Inventory:
  40 Centurion Mk.5 medium tanks
  40 AMX-13 light tanks
  20 M-41 light tanks
     Armored cars (Staghound, AEC Mk.3)
     APCs (M-113, M-706, M-59)
  15 self-propelled AA guns (M-42)
     75mm guns
     122mm, 155mm howitzers

NAVY

Personnel: 200

Major Units:
  5 coastal and harbor patrol launches (YP)
  1 landing craft (LCU)

Naval Base: Beirut

AIR FORCE

Personnel: 1,000

Organization:
  2 fighter/fighter-bomber squadrons (Hunter and Mirage)
  1 transport squadron (Dove)
  1 trainer/support squadron (Chipmunk, Magister, Vampire, O-1)
  1 helicopter squadron (Alouette II/III)

Major Aircraft Types:
  23 combat aircraft
    12 Hunter fighter-bombers
    11 Mirage fighters
  38 other aircraft
     3 transports (Dove)
    25 trainer/support aircraft (Chipmunk, Magister, Vampire, O-1)
    10 helicopters (Alouette II/III)

Air Bases: Beirut (Khalde), Riyaq, Tripoli

PARAMILITARY

The national gendarmerie numbers 4,000 men. Other internal security units total about 850 men. A National Guard of up to 5,000 is planned.

OMAN

Sultanat Oman
The Sultanate of Oman

POWER POTENTIAL STATISTICS

Area: 82,000 square miles
Population: 773,000
Total Active Armed Forces: 7,000 (0.91% population)
Gross National Product: $266 million ($344 per capita)
Annual Military Expenditures: $32 million*
Fuel Production: Oil: 14 million metric tons
Merchant Fleet: 3 ships; 2,013 gross tons

*Has been estimated as high as $60 million.

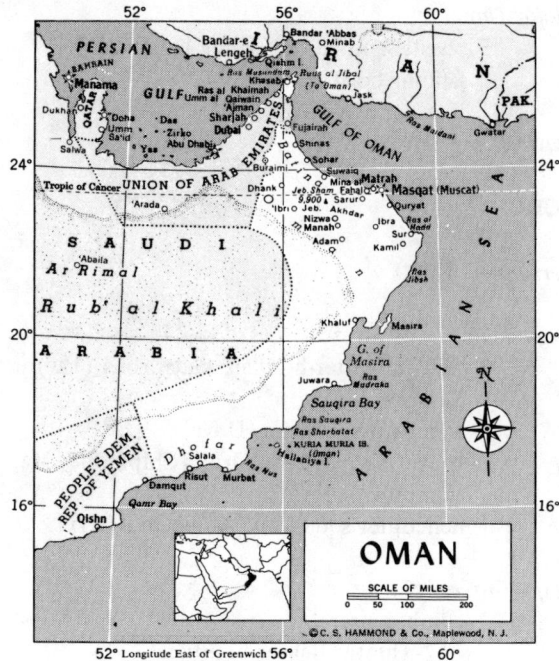

POLITICO-MILITARY POLICIES AND POSTURE

This absolute monarchy (known until 1970 as the Sultanate of Muscat and Oman), while fully sovereign, depends essentially upon the United Kingdom for external security. On July 23, 1970, a coup carried out by the Palace Guard replaced Sultan Said bin Taimur with his son, Qabus bin Said. The new ruler immediately introduced a more modern form of government and sought to hasten the country's development in all fields. The country's name was changed to the Sultanate of Oman to reflect a unity under the new regime. Legislation is still by decree; the sultan rules with the advice of his cabinet.

The Buraymi Oasis, in the undefined border zone of Saudi Arabia, Abu Dhabi and Oman, has been the scene of violent clashes because of Saudi Arabian claims to it. These have abated in recent years, but Saudi Arabia has not officially renounced its claim. Since 1966 internal unrest has been instigated by the Marxist-led Dhofar Liberation Front, operating from Southern Yemen, now Yemen (Aden), and receiving support from China. In mid-1974 the government appeared to be gaining the upper hand, thanks in part to Iranian help.

The island of Al Masirah, important only for its airfield, is claimed by Southern Yemen. Britain maintains a staging airfield there, despite withdrawal in 1971 from most other points east of Suez.

The Sultan of Oman's defense forces are commanded by a British brigadier. Many of the personnel in the forces are mercenaries of various nationalities, personnel seconded from the RAF, and contract personnel hired for maintenance and other technical work by a British organization that has a contract with the Omani government. About a third of the officers in the Sultan of Oman's Air Force (SOAF) are seconded from the RAF. Flying personnel are virtually all non-Omani. The Army is engaged mainly in operations against the Dhofar Liberation Front. The Air Force's role is to support the Army by airstrikes by the Strikemasters and logistical support by the STOL transports. The Army is made up of six battalions that operate throughout the country against insurgents.

Oman is a member of the UN and the Arab League.

ARMY

Personnel: 6,000

Organization:
    6 battalions (composite infantry and armored cavalry)
    1 artillery regiment

Major Equipment Inventory:
    Saladin armored cars
    Ferret scout cars
    Light artillery (75mm howitzers, 25 pounder and 5.5 inch guns)

NAVY

Personnel: 200

Major Units:
    1 corvette (PF, also used as yacht)
    3 fast patrol craft (PTF)

AIR FORCE

Personnel: 500

Organization:
    1 strike squadron (Strikemaster, Beaver)
    1 air support squadron (Skyvan, Caribou)
    1 transport flight (Viscount)
    1 helicopter squadron (AB-205, AB-206)

Major Aircraft Types:
    12 combat aircraft
        12 Strikemaster ground attack aircraft
    39 other aircraft
        13 STOL transports (10 Skyvan, 3 Caribou)
        6 Viscount medium transports
        5 Beaver light transports
        15 helicopters (11 AB-205, 4 AB-206)

Air Bases: Bait-al-Falaj (Muscat), Salalah, Azaiba

Equipment on Order:
- 1 fast patrol craft (PTF)
- 6 Skyvan STOL transports
- 8 BN-2A light strike aircraft
- 4 Strikemasters
- 10 helicopters (5 AB-205, 5 AB-214)

PARAMILITARY

The Sultan of Oman has a gendarmerie of 300.

SAUDI ARABIA
Al Mamlakah al'Arabiyah as Sa'udiyah
The Kingdom of Saudi Arabia

POWER POTENTIAL STATISTICS

Area: 873,972 square miles
Population: 8,400,000
Total Active Armed Forces: 71,000 (including National Guard; 0.85% population)
Gross National Product: $5.3 billion ($631 per capita)
Annual Military Expenditures: $1,200 million (22.7% GNP)
Fuel Production: Crude Oil: 286 million metric tons
   Refined Petroleum Products: 29.1 million metric tons
Electric Power Output: 770 million kwh
Merchant Fleet: 3 ships; 50,369 gross tons
Civil Air Fleet: 7 jet, 5 turboprop, 20 piston transports

DEFENSE STRUCTURE

In this slowly liberalizing, semi-constitutionalized, absolute monarchy, the King is commander in chief of the regular armed forces, and one of his most trusted brothers is the Minister of Defense and Aviation. The King is also the commander in chief of the National Guard, or White Army.

Long-continued use of US materiel and US assistance in training have influenced the thinking of Saudi Arabian military planners. Organization and tactical doctrine are patterned after US models.

POLITICO-MILITARY POLICY

Saudi Arabia's fabulous oil wealth, with proven reserves that could support the present massive production of crude oil for at least 90 years, has placed the nation in a position to influence international alignments and developments particularly in those highly industrialized nations of western Europe that are dependent upon the oil of the Middle East.

The armed forces and the nation's tremendous oil-based wealth are the primary instruments for maintaining Saudi Arabia's position of predominance in the Arabian Peninsula, and for challenging the position of Egypt as the leading member of the Arab League. However, even the rivalry with Egypt is subordinated to Saudi Arabia's support of the solid Arab front of hostility to Israel. At the time of the Arab-Israeli War of June 1967, Saudi Arabia sent its contingent of 20,000 troops to Jordan rather than support either Egypt or Syria. In the 1973 war, Saudi Arabian units were sent to aid the Syrian Army.

Some observers believe that the King's interest in his paramilitary National Guard is evidence that he has some doubts as to the complete loyalty of the regular armed forces. If so, this may be due to concern lest the exposure of his Western-trained Army officers to democratic and liberal thinking might cause them to be restive under a regime that is only slowly relaxing the semi-medieval restrictions of traditional Arab society. It is possible, also, that he might have concern lest the military officers be attracted to leftist pan-Arabism. In any event, the National Guard, or White Army, has been strengthened in recent years, and in any internal crisis could be counted upon to give full support to the reigning Saud family.

All armed forces service is voluntary, and recruits enlist for a three-year term. Recruiting for the regular forces is done on a nationwide basis. The White Army, in contrast, is recruited on a tribal or area basis, and units stationed at various posts are recruited from tribes in those areas.

Most younger military officers are graduates of the Royal Military College (Academy) in Riyadh, which offers a three-year course in academic and military subjects; graduates of technical schools may also obtain commissions. The Army School Command directs a system of service schools. For advanced training, Saudi Arabia sends its officers to war colleges in the United States and Great Britain.

STRATEGIC PROBLEMS

Rivalry with Egypt led Saudi Arabia to the brink of war in Yemen during the period 1962-1967. Saudi Arabia supported the deposed Imam of Yemen in civil war against the newly established Republic of Yemen, now Yemen (San'a), which was in turn supported by Egypt. Under financial pressure from Saudi Arabia, Egypt withdrew its support of the Republic of Yemen after the disastrous war with Israel in June 1967. In June 1970, Saudi Arabia recognized the Republic of Yemen, thereby ending an estrangement between the two countries that had lasted for eight years.

The states to the south and southeast, Southern Yemen, now Yemen (Aden), and the Sultanate of Oman, are also generally hostile to Saudi Arabia. One ameliorating factor for

194 ALMANAC OF WORLD MILITARY POWER

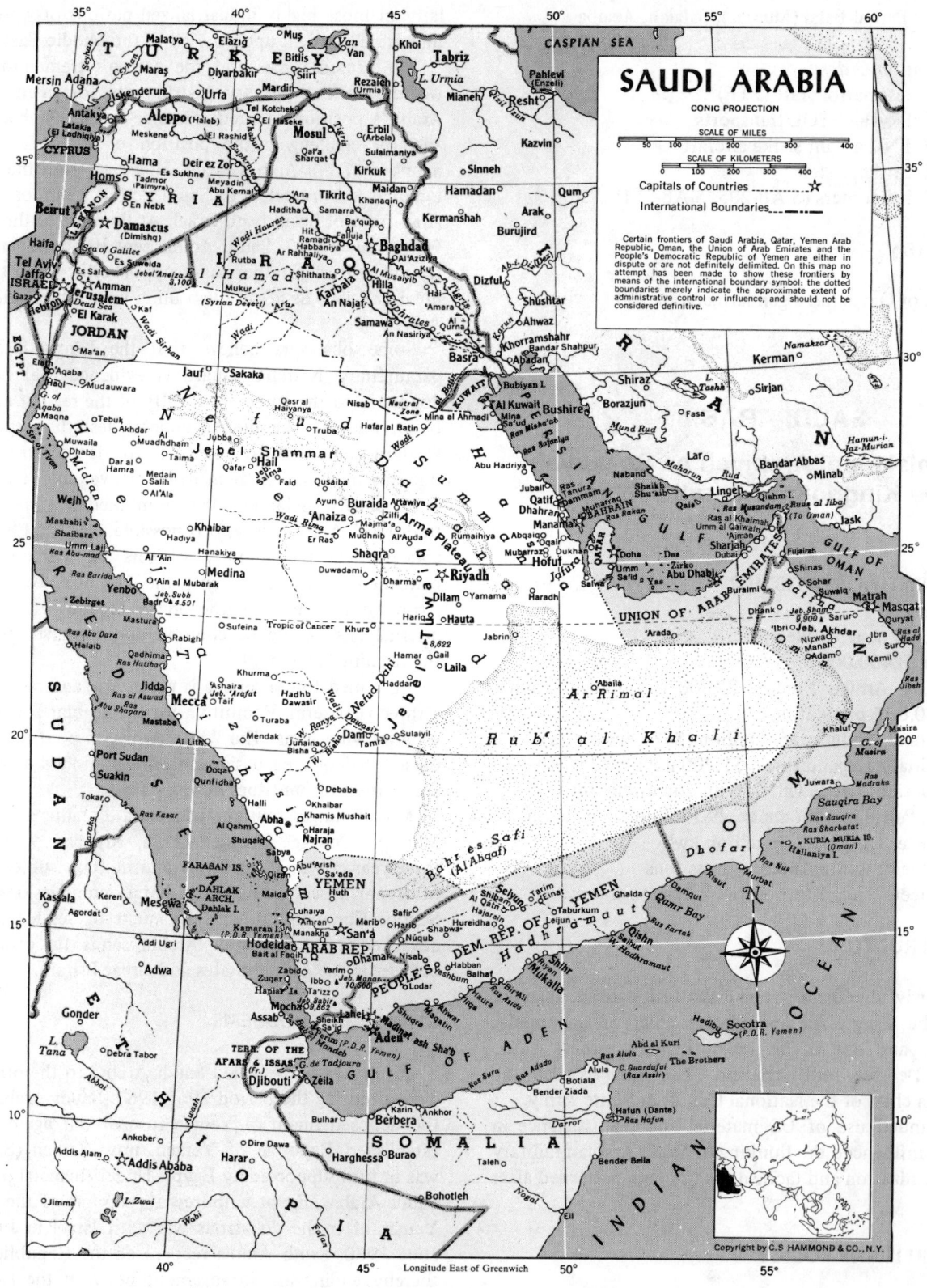

Saudi Arabia is that Communist-influenced Yemen (Aden) is also hostile to Oman. Intermittent hostilities with Oman and Abu Dhabi (one of the United Arab Emirates of the Persian Gulf) over the possession of the Buraymi Oasis have subsided, but Saudi Arabia's claim is not formally relinquished and could come into dispute again.

MILITARY ASSISTANCE

Saudi Arabia is the principal contributor to an annual subsidy being paid to Egypt by the three wealthiest Arab states (Saudi Arabia, Kuwait, and Libya) to maintain the Egyptian economy while the Suez Canal remains closed as a result of the Arab-Israeli War of June 1967. Substantial financial support is also being provided to Jordan.

Saudi Arabia is a major recipient of US military assistance, having received $36.1 million, from 1950-1972, and $589,000 in excess stocks of defense materials, and 1,290 students having been trained under the MAP. Training is provided also in the United Kingdom, and a large US training mission is maintained in Saudi Arabia.

ALLIANCES

Saudi Arabia is a member of the UN and of the Arab League.

ARMY

Personnel: 35,000

Organization:
- 4 infantry brigades
- 2 tank battalions
- 6 artillery battalions (3 of these are AA)
- 10 SAM batteries (Hawk)

Major Equipment Inventory:
- 30 main battle tanks (AMX-30)
- 55 medium tanks (M-47)
- 65 light tanks
    - 35 M-41
    - 30 AMX-13
- 200+ armored cars (AML-60 and AML-90, M-6, and M-8)
- scout cars (Ferret)
- antitank missiles (Vigilant)
- light artillery and AA

NAVY

Personnel: 1,000

Major Units:
- 1 patrol gunboat (PGM)
- 3 fast torpedo boats (PTF)
- 33 small patrol boats (YP)
- 8 Hovercraft (SRN-6)
- 2 rescue launches

Naval Bases: Jidda, Dammam

AIR FORCE

Personnel: 5,000 (There are about 2,000 contract personnel from BAC, training maintenance personnel and doing contract maintenance on the aircraft and technical equipment of the Saudi Air Force.)

Organization:
- 3 fighter squadrons (Lightning, F-5)
- 2 operational training squadrons (F-86, T-33)
- 2 basic training squadrons (Strikemaster)
- 1 primary training squadron (T-41)
- 2 transport squadrons (C-130)
- 2 helicopter squadrons (AB-205, AB-206)
- 1 Royal flight (AB-205, C-140)

Note: The Strikemaster, F-86, and T-33 have a combat capability for ground attack, and F-86s were used as such against the Yemeni.

Major Aircraft Types:
- 116 combat aircraft
    - 20 F-5 fighters
    - 34 Lightning fighters
    - 30 Strikemaster trainer/ground attack
    - 32 F-86, T-33 operational trainer/ground attack
- 67 other aircraft
    - 15 C-130 transports
    - 2 C-140 VIP transports
    - 8 T-41 trainers
    - 42 helicopters (2 Alouette III, 24 AB-205, 16 AB-206)

Equipment on Order:
- 68 fighters (30 F-5, 38 Mirage III)
- 12 KC-130 tankers
- 30 Sea King and Commando helicopters
- 10 Strikemaster trainer/ground attack
- Unknown number improved Hawk SAM

Air Bases: Dhahran, Riyadh, Jidda Taif, Medina, Tabuk, Yanbu

PARAMILITARY

The National Guard, or White Army, consists of approximately 30,000 tribal levies. Its mission is internal security. It is equipped with a number of armored cars and antitank weapons. Senior commanders are chosen from among trusted members of the royal family.

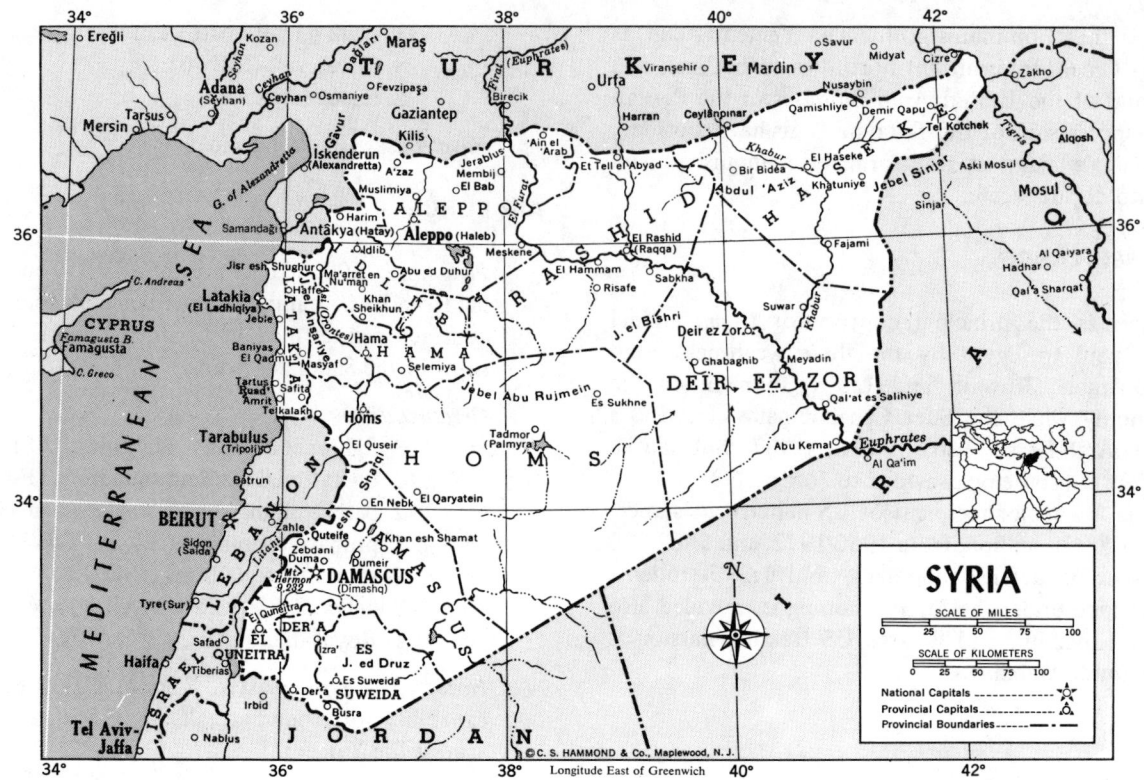

SYRIA

Al Jumhuriyah al' Arabiyah as-Souriyah
Syrian Arab Republic

POWER POTENTIAL STATISTICS

Area: 71,498 square miles
Population: 6,800,000
Total Active Armed Forces: 140,300 (including security forces; 2.06% population)
Gross National Product: $1.98 billion ($298 per capita)
Annual Military Expenditures: $209 million (10.6% GNP)
Fuel Production: Crude Oil: 6.5 million metric tons
  Refined Petroleum Products: 2.2 million metric tons
Electric Power Output: 947 million kwh
Merchant Fleet: 7 ships; 1,659 gross tons
Civil Air Fleet: 4 jet, 4 piston transports

DEFENSE STRUCTURE

The present government of Syria is dominated by the relatively conservative, nationalist, faction of the Baath Party, which replaced the more leftist progressive wing of the party by bloodless coup in November 1970. (The Baath Party also rules Iraq.) The President, General Hafiz al Assad, is also both premier and defense minister, and controls the armed forces. A general staff organization patterned after that of the French army has been retained, but it is changing rapidly to fit the Soviet model.

POLITICO-MILITARY POLICY

Syria is one of the most militantly anti-Israeli states of the Arab League. Syrian harassment of Israel—by long-range artillery fire and by fedayin raids—was a major cause of the Arab-Israeli War of June 1967. Syria openly supports the Palestinian terrorist organizations.

In August 1970, Syria opened a vitriolic radio campaign against Jordan, in protest against the Jordanian crackdown on Palestine commandos in that country. Soon after that a Syrian military force intervened in Jordan, but was defeated and driven out. In August 1971 Syria, alleging artillery shelling across its border against Syrian villages, severed diplomatic relations with Jordan, despite Jordan's denial and counterclaims of harassment by guerrillas based in Syria. Relations have since been restored.

Hostility to Israel is the only consistent theme in the recent history of this exceedingly unstable nation, which has suffered nine successful revolts or coups d'etat since independence in 1945, and has been wracked by even more numerous unsuccessful revolts or violent upheavals in the same period. During these years Syria has been aligned both with and against most of the other members of the Arab League, has been united politically with Egypt in the United Arab

Republic, and has at times been close to political or military union with both Iraq and Jordan.

In April 1971 Syria agreed to join Egypt and Libya in the Federation of Arab Republics, but the Federation never became a reality (see Libya).

Two major objectives preoccupied Syria's government during the early 1970s: the recovery of the Golan Heights and other territory occupied by Israel in the Six-Day War, and the restoration of what is now Israel to the Palestinian Arabs. During the period 1967-1973, Syria accumulated arms and equipment from Communist nations and continuously urged other Arab nations to prepare for a holy war against Israel.

Syria has maintained a close relationship to the USSR since 1954, and has received substantial Soviet economic and military aid (over $1 billion).

Military service is compulsory. Upon completion of his tour of duty the soldier becomes a member of the reserve for 18 years, after which he reverts to inactive reserve status. The manpower for recruitment of about 15,000 to 20,000 men each year is selected from some 60,000 youth who reach military age during the induction year.

Most of the officers receive their training in one of three military schools: the Military Academy in Homs, the Naval Academy in Latakia, and the Air Force Academy located at Nayrab air base in Aleppo. All three academies conduct a two-year course leading to a commission. For advanced military training Syrian officers are sent to war colleges abroad, mostly to the USSR and other communist countries. Selection for service academies as well as for war colleges abroad are made from those who pass the required entrance examination, and are staunch supporters of the Baath Party and the regime.

STRATEGIC PROBLEMS

When Israel occupied the high ground of southwestern Syria, in the Al Quanaytira area, in the closing hours of the June 1967 war, Damascus, capital of Syria, became virtually indefensible against a determined Israeli assault. By the time of the October 1973 war, Syria had strongly fortified the approaches to the capital. After some minor early successes in that war, however, the Syrian Army was outclassed by the Israelis, and despite these fortifications lost more territory between the Golan Heights and Damascus. On balance, the Syrians performed more creditably than in previous wars. As a result of postwar negotiations, under American auspices, Syria regained this lost territory and a small portion of that lost in 1967 around Al Quanaytira. The Israelis also surrendered a small strip for a demilitarized zone occupied by a UN force.

Two major pipelines cross Syria from Iraq and Saudi Arabia to terminal points on the Mediterranean coasts of Lebanon and Syria. This puts Syria in a position to control a highly critical source of fuel oil for Western Europe. It also means that Syria must always consider the possibility that in a variety of circumstances hostile powers might undertake action to seize, or destroy, or neutralize these pipelines.

MILITARY ASSISTANCE

The bulk of the modern and heavy equipment of all of the Syrian armed forces has been provided by the USSR. Most of the equipment lost in the brief hostilities against the Israelis in 1967 and 1973 was replaced. On the eve of the October 1973 war, there were over 3,000 Soviet military and technical advisers in Syria. Soviet officers serve as advisers with all Syrian combat units. Apparently they actually exercised command over some units in the 1967 and 1973 wars with Israel. They may also have been present with the force invading Jordan in 1970.

ALLIANCES

Syria belongs to the UN and the Arab League. It has a mutual defense agreement with Egypt.

ARMY

Personnel: 130,000

Organization:
- 2 armored divisions
- 3 mechanized divisions
- 2 infantry divisions
- 1 parachute battalion
- 5 commando battalions
- 7 artillery regiments (including 6 AAA companies)
- 20 SAM battalions
- SSM

Major Equipment Inventory:
- 35 JS-3 heavy tanks
- 900 T-62 medium tanks
- 800 medium tanks (T-54/55, T-34)
- 100 PT-76 light tanks
- 900 APC (BTR-50, BTR-152)
- 1,200 artillery pieces (122mm, 130mm, 152mm guns)
- 100 self propelled guns (SU-100)
- 165 AA guns (37mm, 57mm, 85mm, 100mm)
- 200 SAM launchers (SA-2 Guideline, SA-3 Goa, SA-6 Gainful, SA-7 Grail)
- RPG-7 Attack weapons
- 16 Frog SSM

NAVY

Personnel: 2,000

Major Units:
- 2 fleet minesweepers (T-43 class; MSF)
- 3 sub chasers (PC)
- 8 guided missile patrol boats (2 Osa class, 6 Komar class, with Styx SSMs; PTFG)
- 17 torpedo boats (P-4 type; PT)

AIR FORCE

Personnel: 10,000

Organization:
- 8 fighter squadrons (MiG-21)
- 8 fighter-bomber squadrons (MiG-15/17, Su-7)
- 2 transport squadrons (C-47/Li-2, Il-14, Il-18)
- 3 training/support squadrons (L-29, Pa-31)
- 2 helicopter squadrons (Mi-1/4, Mi-6, Mi-8, Ka-25)

Major Aircraft Types:
- 369 combat aircraft
  - 4 Il-28 light bombers
  - 200 MiG-21 fighters
  - 165 fighter-bombers (45 Su-7, 100 MiG-17, 20 MiG-15)
- 127 other aircraft
  - 27 transports (7 C-47, 3 Li-2, 12 Il-14, 5 Il-18)
  - 45 trainer/support (L-29, Pa-31)
  - 55 helicopters (10 Mi-1/4, 6 Mi-6, 30 Mi-8, 9 Ka-25)

Note: There have been reports of Su-7 variable-geometry fighter-bombers and MiG-23 variable-geometry fighters, given by the USSR to Syria.

Air Bases: Damascus, Hamah, Dumayr, Palmyra, Sahles, Sahra, Rasafa, Aleppo, Sayqat, Blay, Khalkhalah, Masiriyah

Reserves: about 8,000 trained reservists

PARAMILITARY

Organized, standing internal security forces are: Gendarmerie, 5,000; Internal Security Camel Corps, 1,500; Civil Police, 1,800. A People's Army, reportedly about 150,000 men, is a home guard militia organization.

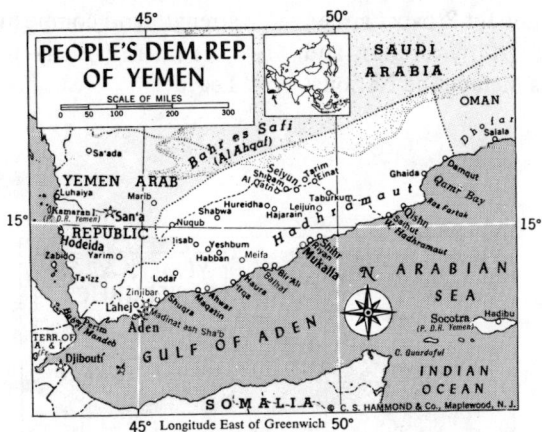

YEMEN (ADEN)
People's Democratic Republic of Yemen
Southern Yemen

POWER POTENTIAL STATISTICS

Area: 112,000 square miles
Population: 1,475,000
Total Active Armed Forces: 10,500 (0.71% population)
Gross National Product: $140 million ($95 per capita)
Annual Military Expenditures: $6 million (4.3% of GNP)
Refined Petroleum Products: 3.7 Million metric tons
Electric Power Output: 194 million kwh
Merchant Fleet: 5 ships; 1,417 tons

POLITICO-MILITARY POLICIES AND POSTURE

British efforts to prepare the combined colonial regions of Aden and the South Arabian Protectorate for an orderly transition to independence in 1968 were frustrated by a combination of anticolonial nationalism and internal dissension among the various segments of the population. Terrorism and counterterrorism against each other and against the British by the Egyptian-backed Front for the Liberation of Occupied South Yemen (FLOSY) and the indigenous National Liberation Front (NLF) caused the British to withdraw earlier than they had originally intended. With the National Liberation Front generally successful in the internal disorders, Britain recognized this group as the basis of an independent government and granted independence on November 30, 1967. The president is head of state and supreme commander of the armed forces.

The port of Aden, and its strategic location at the southern exit of the Red Sea, gives to Southern Yemen a strategic importance which its small size, weak economy, and unstable government would not otherwise warrant. Only one percent of the region is arable. The communist-influenced government is hostile to Saudi Arabia and to Oman.

Throughout 1968 government troops fought with FLOSY adherents and remaining dissidents in the former sheikhdoms north and northeast of Aden, in a generally successful campaign to establish government authority over the entire country. Defensive operations were also conducted against alleged Saudi Arabian incursions across the ill-defined border. In October 1971 army and air force units attacked targets in Yemen (San'a), and relations between the two nations continued strained, to the point that in October 1972 open warfare erupted. The conflict ended the same month with a cease-fire arranged by the Arab League. Both sides agreed to a union of the two Yemens, to be formed within 18 months. The proposed merger encountered many difficulties. In May 1973 border clashes between the two countries erupted again.

An arms agreement with the Soviet Union was signed in 1968. Substantial deliveries of Soviet equipment are reported, including 12 MiG-17 fighters and possibly some MiG-21 fighters. There are foreign military technicians and instructor-advisers present in Southern Yemen who have been reported as Soviet and also as Cuban. Early in 1971 Communist China established a military mission in Aden staffed by several dozen officers. China's $55 million aid program has centered largely on construction of a military road from Aden to Mukalla. The island of Socotra, off the Horn of Africa, harbors a Soviet naval base, and Aden is regularly visited by Soviet naval ships.

The Army numbers about 10,000, organized in ten infantry and two armored car battalions. It was developed upon independence from the former Federal Regular Army (Aden Protectorate Levies), the Eastern Protectorate's Hadhrami Bedouin Legion, and the Mukalla Regular Army; all British and Royalist oriented personnel have been removed and replaced by politically reliable NLF members.

A Navy of about 150 men operates three inshore minesweepers (MSI), two subchasers (PCS, SO-1 type), and 15 patrol craft (YP). The Air Force of about 350 men operates 12 MiG-17 fighters, five Strikemaster and eight Jet Provost armed trainers, four C-47 transports, six Beaver utility aircraft, and six Bell 47 helicopters. Paramilitary units include the National Security Police and the NLF Party Militia of unknown strength and composition.

Yemen (Aden) is a member of the UN and the Arab League.

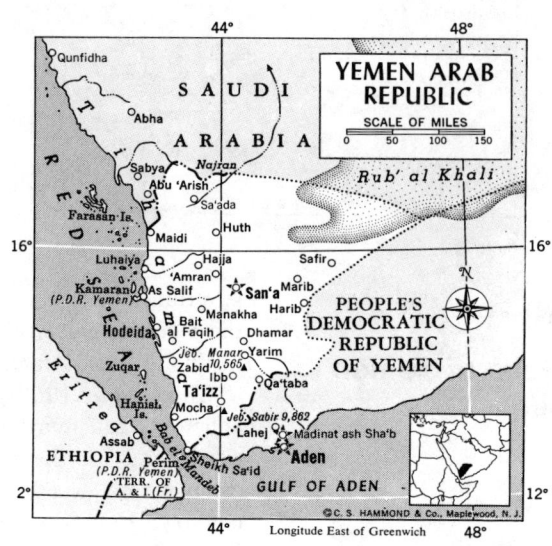

YEMEN (SAN'A)

Al Jumhuriyah al'Arabiyah al Yaminiyah
The Yemen Arab Republic

POWER POTENTIAL STATISTICS

Area: 75,000 square miles
Population: 6,500,000
Total Active Armed Forces: 40,000 including tribal levies; (0.61% population)
Gross National Product: $600 million ($92 per capita)
Annual Military Expenditures: $15 million (2.5% GNP)
Merchant Fleet: 4 ships; 2,844 gross tons
Civil Air Fleet: Yemen Airways Corporation operates scheduled passenger, cargo, and charter flights internally, but the numbers of aircraft are unknown

POLITICO-MILITARY POLICIES AND POSTURE

The revolution which began as a military revolt against Imam Muhammad al-Badr in 1962 ended successfully in 1969, after withdrawal of troops of both the Arab Republic of Egypt and Saudi Arabia. In March 1970 an agreement was reached with Saudi Arabia, calling for reconciliation of all tribes and factions, and the return of all exiles (except the Imam and his family). Saudi Arabia recognized the Yemen Arab Republic and promised economic aid.

Under a 1971 constitution there is a Consultative Assembly, partly elected and partly appointed by the president of the Council. The Assembly elects the 3-5 member Presidential Council, which in turn elects one of its members its president.

The strategic significance of Yemen derives from the fact that its border with Southern Yemen runs just inside the entrance to the Red Sea. It contains some of the most arable lands of the Arabian Peninsula along its coast and on the seaward mountain slopes.

Army and air force units of Southern Yemen—now Yemen (Aden)—attacked Yemen in October 1971, but with little effect. Relations between the two countries remain strained. In October 1972 the recurring border incidents between People's Democratic Republic of Yemen (Southern Yemen) and the Yemen Arab Republic flared into open warfare. A ceasefire was arranged the same month under the auspices of the Arab League, and both sides agreed that union of the two countries would be implemented within 18 months.

In addition to economic aid promised by Saudi Arabia at the time of the 1970 agreement, Yemen received substantial financial aid and food following a disastrous drought and resulting famine at the end of that year, from the World Food Program of the UN, Iraq, Kuwait, and the United States. Soviet advisers, who had arrived in Yemen with UAR troops in 1962, were unpopular under the new Yemeni government, and left soon after the Egyptian withdrawal in 1967. Chinese Communist engineers, who built a road from San'a to Al Hudaydah, have remained in the country as a military engineer unit, working on other projects.

The army numbers about 10,000 men; some of the officers have been trained in Egypt and the USSR. Equipment is Soviet. It includes at least 30 T-34 medium tanks, 50 SU-100 assault guns, 70 BTR-40 armored personnel carriers, 50 76mm guns, 100 antiaircraft guns of various calibers, 12 MiG-17 fighters, 16 Il-28 light bombers, and some Il-14 and C-47 transports, Mi-4 helicopters and Yak-11 armed trainers. A small naval force operates a few patrol craft (YP) at the main port of Al Hudaydah. Some 20,000 tribal levies may be considered a potential reserve.

Yemen is a member of the UN and most of its specialized agencies. It is a member of the Arab League.

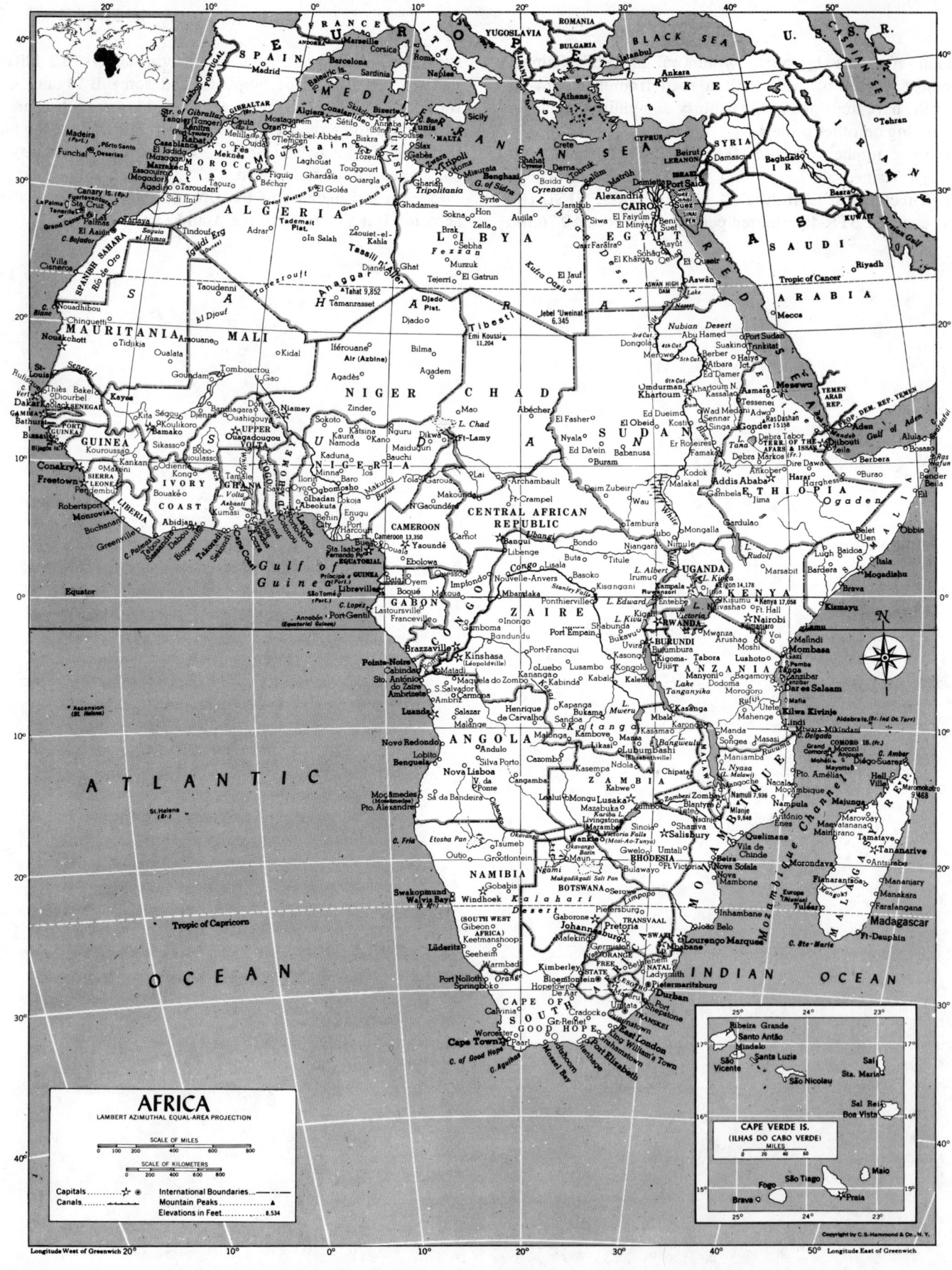

7
AFRICA
Regional Survey

MILITARY GEOGRAPHY

Largely colonial before 1960, largely independent thereafter, Africa is characterized by rich natural resources, inadequate economic development, increasing overpopulation in relation to food production in many areas, widespread and disruptive tribal differences, and friction engendered by the Organization of African Unity and indigenous black nationalists against several countries in southern Africa controlled by white minorities. These conditions have resulted in internal tensions, disorders, military coups, civil wars, and overt and covert military support of insurgencies against the white-dominated regimes as well as against moderate governments maintaining close ties with former colonial rulers.

Vast—measuring 4,000 miles by 4,000 miles along its greatest dimensions—Africa is divided for this discussion into four disparate regions: North Africa, the Horn of Africa, Equatorial Africa, and Southern Africa. Egypt, geographically a part of North Africa, is included in the chapter on the Middle East.

In North Africa civilization is mostly concentrated in a narrow coastal strip along the Mediterranean and Atlantic shores. Most of the littoral, as well as the interior, is desert in Egypt and Libya. In Tunisia, Algeria and Morocco the coastal regions are relatively fertile and enjoy a typical Mediterranean climate, but are backed by mountains and interior deserts. In the 8th Century this region served as a base for Arab penetration into Europe and, although separated from the rest of Africa by the formidable Sahara Desert, for expansion of Arab trade and Islamic religion and culture into trans-Saharan Africa. The countries of North Africa gained their independence after World War II, and recent significant oil discoveries promise to provide them funds for future economic development.

The Horn of Africa consists of the Abyssinian massif, bisected by the Great Rift Valley, containing the headwaters of the Blue Nile, and the surrounding arid coasts of the Red Sea, Gulf of Aden, and Indian Ocean. The Christian Ethiopian Empire from its mountain fastness was able to defend itself successfully against waves of Moslem invaders and against all colonialists except Italy (1935-1941). For half of its external trade it depends on a railroad which reaches the sea through a French-ruled Moslem land, and recently it has been under renewed pressure from its own lowland Moslem population and the surrounding Moslem states.

Equatorial Africa is the savannah and forest area between the southern borders of the Sahara and the temperate and arid areas of Southern Africa. Both coasts are uninviting, with few natural harbors, and largely swampy terrain between the coast and the African escarpment, which begins 50 to 100 miles inland. Most river navigation stops at this point. Exceptions are the Senegal, Gambia, and Niger rivers, which are navigable 300 to 500 miles from the sea. Also, once above the Congo rapids, 80 miles from the sea, there are over 7,000 miles of river transportation routes in use. The forbidding coastal features inhibited exploration and colonial penetration of the central African plateau for centuries, and still inhibit the development of the interior and the exploitation of its vast mineral resources. The jungle-covered lowlands and Congo basin are bordered on north and south by savannah plains.

The interior of Southern Africa is also in large part guarded by the African escarpment. The savannah uplands of Angola, Zambia, Rhodesia, Malawi, and northern Mozambique give way to the Southwest Africa Deserts, the Kalahari desert of Botswana, and the lowland savannah of central and southern Mozambique. East-west railroads running through the Portuguese overseas territories of Angola and Mozambique serve the landlocked, mineral-rich interior states. South of this area to the Cape of Good Hope lies prosperous, developed, but racially divided, South Africa.

STRATEGIC SIGNIFICANCE

Most of Africa, surrounded on all sides by water since the 100-mile Suez isthmus was cut by a canal a century ago, has always been isolated from the rest of the world. North Africa since prehistoric times has been closely tied to events in Southern Europe and the Middle East and has influenced and been influenced by their civilizations. However, Africa south of the Sahara was effectively isolated until the mid-19th century except for coastal trading posts and an occasional explorer.

Africa has become a cold war area of contention. Former colonial powers try to maintain special military and economic relationships with their former colonies. The Soviet Union, Communist China, and radical African states attempt political subversion, economic penetration, and military influence, while the United States tries to offset these moves through economic assistance and limited selective military aid. Political repercussions of Arab-Israeli conflict extend into Africa as

Algeria, Egypt, and Libya try to exert their influence over lands to the south, while Israel campaigns politically to block these moves with military advice and to win the 30 independent African votes in the UN by technical assistance programs. Recently President al Kadhafi of Libya has made vigorous efforts, with some limited success, to persuade black African states to break relations with Israel.

Throughout newly independent black Africa friction and minor conflicts are constantly caused by the fact that boundary lines of the new nations are legacies from colonial Africa and do not follow tribal and ethnic divisions. The African nations, separately and jointly (through the Organization of African Unity), have set out on a course of nation building that puts national territory and unity ahead of ethnic ties. In general, African nations have exercised restraint in assisting or encouraging dissident ethnic elements in other states, even when ethnic loyalty might influence them to do so, both because they are vulnerable to the same kind of threat and because they are committed to the preeminence of the nation concept.

North Africa's coastal strip was a route of conquest for Carthaginian, Roman, Vandal, and Arab armies in the distant past, and for Allies and Axis during World War II. Commerce in the Mediterranean has always been subject to interdiction from North Africa, and more than one invasion of Europe has been mounted from its shores, the latest being in 1943 and 1944. North Africa in turn has been equally vulnerable to invasion and colonial penetration from Europe and the Middle East. Recently the Soviet Union has established a continuing naval presence in the Mediterranean seeking the possibility of outflanking NATO, and of gaining control of the world's richest oil reserves by winning the Arab world of North Africa and the Middle East. To some extent related to the growing Soviet presence is the fact that today North Africa is a base for the propagation of Arab radical socialism to the rest of Africa, a phenomenon comparable to the historical southern movement of Islam along the trans-Saharan trade routes.

Northeast Africa is a bastion flanking the Red Sea and Gulf of Aden, overlooking the narrow waters between the two. The Strait of Bab el Mandeb has from pre-history provided a short sea passage between Arabia and Africa. Western-oriented Ethiopia and the French Territory of Afars and Issas provide valuable air bases and ports from which influence can be exerted in Arabia and part of Africa, and from which movements into South Asia and the Indian Ocean can be staged. Because of the strategic location of the Horn, both the Soviet Union and Communist China have attempted to exert offsetting influence both through subversion and by economic and military aid in Somalia and Sudan. A parallel effort has been made by the Arabs, with Egypt and Syria taking the lead.

Southern Africa guards the historic sea routes between east and west, which are of increased importance while the Suez Canal is closed. The white-dominated regimes of Southern Africa are the target of liberation movements supported by most other African states (particularly the radical ones), the communist world, and many sympathizers in the West. The Portuguese territories of Angola, Portuguese Guinea, and Mozambique as well as independent Rhodesia, with their less developed economies, very small white minorities, and proximity to insurgent bases, are particularly vulnerable. Well-developed South Africa, however, is separated from the Soviet-armed North African power centers of Algeria and Egypt by 4,000 miles of power vacuum and non-viable lines of communications.

The countries through which runs the Sahelian climate-vegetation strip—the southern fringe of the Sahara Desert—have suffered several years of failed rains, culminating in 1973 in the worst drought of recorded African history. The countries most severely affected—Chad, Niger, Mauritania, Upper Volta, Mali, and Senegal—have been hampered by generally primitive transportation and governmental administration systems in distributing famine-relief aid. The famine holds potentialities for serious damage to, or even destruction of, the nomadic life patterns of large segments of the populations, a decrease in the measure of internal power held by the nomadic groups, increased unemployment and other urban problems as nomads are forced into the cities, coups d'etats triggered by dissatisfaction with governmental relief efforts, and temptations to intervention by outside powers in drought-weakened countries. Similar effects are also seen in Ethiopia.

REGIONAL ALLIANCES

Arab League. (See also Middle East Regional Survey.) The states of North Africa, plus the Sudan, are members. League affairs are directed mainly toward the Middle East and its influence is of little consequence in the rest of Africa.

The Maghreb. (Arabic for The West.) The Arabs and Berbers of Morocco, Algeria, Tunisia, and Libya have thought of their region as an entity from early times. This was reflected at the 1958 Tangier Conference which resulted in establishing a short-lived secretariat of the Arab Maghreb. Achievement of the immediate goal of a consultative assembly and eventual federation was prevented by border disputes and Algerian radical nationalism, which did not accord either with Moroccan conservative monarchism or Tunisian moderation. Subsequent consultations have had no tangible results, but have kept open channels of inter-government communications and cooperation on regional matters of interest.

Organization of African Unity (OAU) was formed in 1963 through the efforts of the leaders of Nigeria, Ethiopia, and Guinea and was the culmination of earlier efforts to form a broad-based continental organization. All African countries are members except South Africa and Rhodesia. The charter prescribes non-interference in the internal affairs of states, observance of sovereignty and territorial integrity of members, peaceful settlement of disputes, condemnation of political assassination and subversive activities, non-alignment with power blocs, and emancipation of the white-ruled African territories. The latter goal has resulted in formation of the OAU Liberation Committee, which has a planning staff and budget. It recognizes and supports the various liberation movements directed against the white-dominated regimes. Committee members are: Algeria, Egypt, Ethiopia, Guinea, Nigeria, Senegal, Somalia, Tanzania, Uganda, Zaire and Zambia. In January 1973, the committee issued a Declaration on African Liberation calling for an increased effort to remove the colonial and white minority regimes still in Africa.

The OAU succeeded in arbitrating the Algerian-Moroccan border war of 1963 and in helping Tanzania replace with African troops the British troops which had quelled its 1964 army mutiny. However, it was ineffective in assisting the Congo (Kinshasa), which is now Zaire, during its rebellion in 1964-1965, in resolving the Nigerian-Biafran civil war in 1969, in reconciling various rival liberation movements, or in successfully prosecuting a war of liberation in Southern Africa or Rhodesia. Following an allegedly Portuguese-inspired mercenary raid on Guinea, in December of 1970, the OAU Defense Commission was instructed to study the establishment of a common Army. Nothing seems to have come of this.

The British Commonwealth in Africa was to have been a community of common economic interests and mutual defense objectives. British assistance to the East African states in suppressing army mutinies in 1964, and a show of force against Somali insurgents in support of Kenya in 1965, underscored this policy. However, the ability of the Commonwealth's African states to force out South Africa, Tanzania's break with Britain over Rhodesia, and reaction to British equipment sales to South Africa, indicate declining British influence over its former territories. The affiliation remains, however loose, as one of mutual interest based on historic ties, and has relevance to mutual defense in the absence of action by broader international organizations.

Common Organization of Africa and Mauritius (OCAM) was formed in 1965 as an outgrowth of earlier attempts at cooperation between French-speaking states, including the African and Malagasy Union and the Regional Council of France, Ivory Coast, Niger, and Dahomey. Aside from political and economic motives, the prime factors were establishment of a common front to meet Ghana's subversive activities, Chinese Communist infiltration and subversion, and endemic chaos in the Congo (now Zaire). OCAM's influence has recently sharply declined; Congo and Zaire withdrew from membership in 1972, and Cameroon, Chad, and the Malagasy Republic withdrew in 1973. The future of the organization now appears to lie in economic cooperation rather than political or military action. Most OCAM members have bilateral defense treaties with France which ensure their immediate internal and external security when threatened beyond their means to cope, and these so far have not been affected in the cases of those states that have withdrawn from OCAM. The 10 current OCAM members are Central African Republic, Dahomey, Gabon, Ivory Coast, Mauritius, Niger, Rwanda, Senegal, Togo, and Upper Volta.

West African Economic Community (CEAO) was established in a treaty signed in June 1972 by seven West African states, all former French colonies. In April 1973, six of these countries—Ivory Coast, Mali, Mauritania, Niger, Senegal, and Upper Volta—agreed to ratify and implement the treaty by January 1, 1974. Dahomey signed the 1972 treaty but later chose observer status. The purpose of the group, which is not a customs union, is the promotion of regional economic development. Most of the CEAO countries have recently suffered severe economic and human problems as a result of famine.

Sahara Group. A loose grouping of Algeria, Mali, Mauritania, and Niger was set up in April 1973. Not established by treaty, the group took as its first goal the construction of the 216-mile Algerian portion of a projected trans-Sahara highway.

The East African Community (EAC), made up of Kenya, Uganda, and Tanzania, grew out of the British colonial East Africa High Commission and was established by treaty in 1967. The EAC countries form a single trade unit; the organization operates and develops railways, ports, airways, and other communications systems.

Conseil de l'Entente is a political-economic regional grouping comprising Dahomey, Ivory Coast, Niger, Togo, and Upper Volta. The emphasis is on economic cooperation, and especially on a common fund used for capital development projects.

Organization of Petroleum Exporting Countries (OPEC). Three African countries—Algeria (exporting 1.1 million barrels a day), Libya (2.3 million), and Nigeria (2.1 million)—are members of OPEC. See Middle East regional survey for discussion of this organization.

INTRA- AND EXTRA-REGIONAL CONFLICTS

1963-1968	Somalia-Kenya border clashes
1964	Army mutinies in Tanzania, Kenya and Uganda suppressed by British troops and loyalist elements
1964	Military coup attempt in Gabon put down by French troops
1964	Revolt by Lumumbist gendarmes in Congo (K)
1964-1965	Communist support of Simba revolt in Congo (K)
1964	Revolt in Mozambique
1965	Military coups in Algeria
1965	Military coup in Congo (K)
1965	Military coup in Dahomey
1965	Army mutiny in Burundi
1966	Military coup in Upper Volta

1966	Unsuccessful Army coup attempt in Sudan; attempted counter-coup suppressed
1966	Military coup in Burundi
1966	Military coup in the Central African Republic
1966	Military-police coup in Ghana
1966	Military coup in Nigeria in January, counter-coup in May
1967	Attempted coup by mercenaries and Kantangese in Congo (K)
1967	Military coup by junior officers in Dahomey
1967	Military coup in Togo
1967	Algerian and Sudanese support for UAR (Egypt) on Suez Canal front
1967-1970	Nigerian civil war (attempted secession of Biafra)
1968	French assistance to Chad in maintaining internal security
1968	Military coup in Mali
1968	Army and police coup in Sierra Leone
1968	Army coup in Congo (B)
1969	Military coup in Libya; monarchy overthrown
1969	Military coup in Sudan
1970	Mercenary and dissident invasion of Guinea (Portuguese supported) fails
1971	Coup in Uganda
1971	Rebellion in Malagasy Republic suppressed
1971	Unsuccessful rebellion in Morocco
1971	Coup in Sudan; counter-coup within three days restored original leadership
1971	Border skirmishes between Tanzania and Uganda
1971	Attempted coup in Chad; relations broken with Libya
1972	Military coup in Ghana
1972	Intertribal violence in Burundi
1972	Military takeover in Malagasy Republic
1972	Military coup in Dahomey
1972	Brief invasion of Uganda by dissident Ugandans from Tanzania
1973	Bloodless coup in Rwanda
1973	Abortive Hutu attempt to seize power in Burundi, followed by extensive reprisals

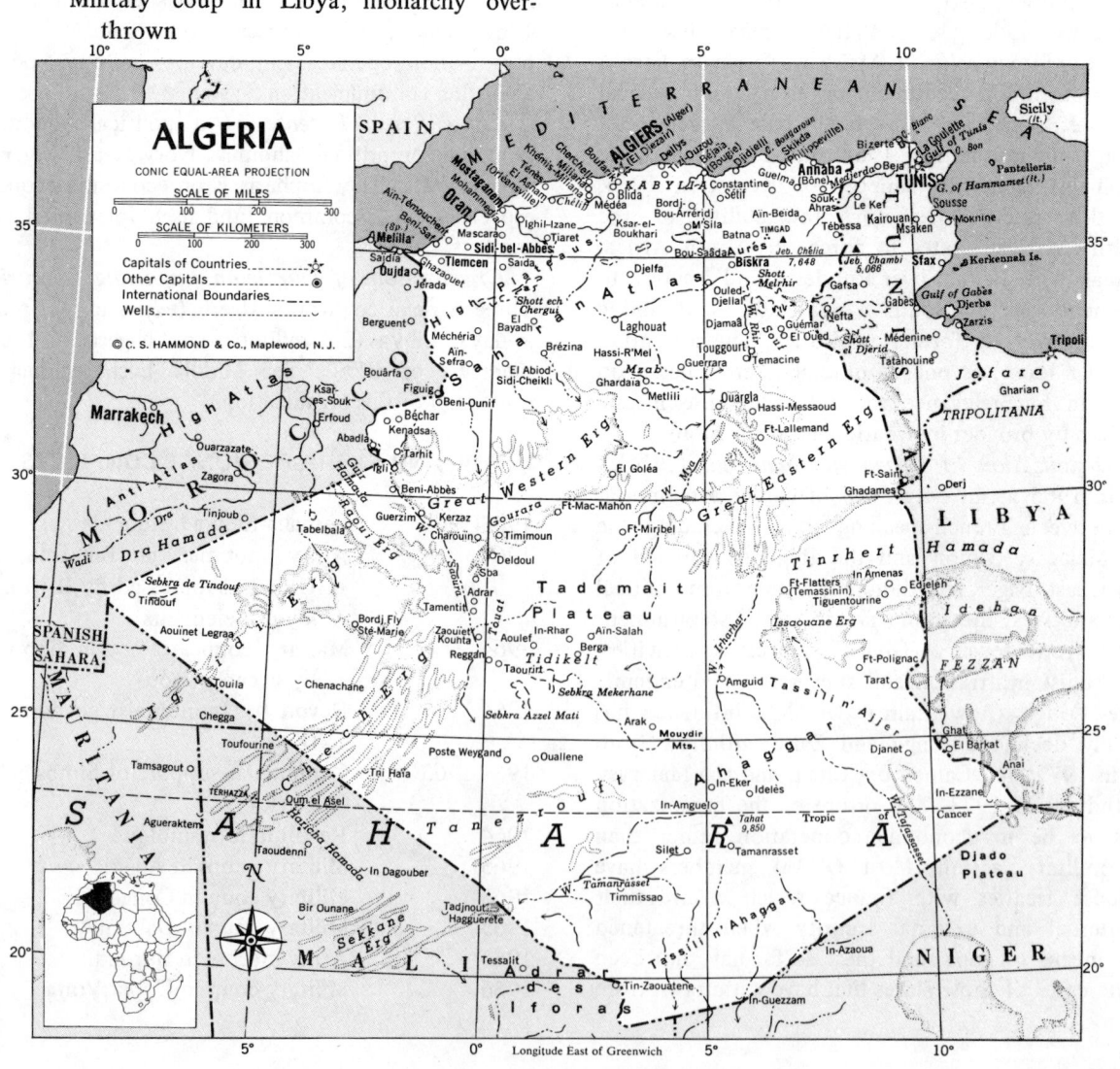

ALGERIA

El Djemhouria El Djazairia Demokratia Echaabia
Algerian Democratic People's Republic

POWER POTENTIAL STATISTICS

Area: 919,591 square miles
Population: 14,150,000
Total Active Armed Forces: 63,000 (including Gendarmerie; 0.42% population)
Gross National Product: $5.4 billion ($366 per capita)
Annual Military Expenditures: $100 million (1.85% GNP)
Fuel Production: Crude Oil: 43.8 million metric tons
  Refined Oil: 2.79 million metric tons
  Gas: 2.985 billion cubic meters
Electric Power Output: 1.71 billion kwh
Merchant Fleet: 17 ships; 56,523 gross tons
Civil Air Fleet: 7 jet, and 9 turboprop transports

DEFENSE STRUCTURE

The President of the Revolutionary Council is the chief of state and the supreme commander of the armed forces. A Higher Council of Defense includes the President, the Ministers of National Defense, Interior, and Foreign Affairs, Chairman of the Committee of National Defense in the National Assembly, and two other members designated by the President. In practice, Colonel Houari Boumedienne, who seized power by a military coup in June 1965, occupies both the positions of President and Minister of National Defense and deals directly with commanders of the armed forces, known collectively as the *Armee Nationale Populaire* (ANP) or National People's Army. The General Staff, under a Chief of Staff, is responsible for organizational, mobilization, budget, and employment planning of the four services: Army, Navy, Air Force, and National Gendarmerie.

The Ministry of National Defense includes a Political Commissariat responsible to the Political Bureau of the nation's single party, the *Front de Liberation Nationale* (FLN). There are Party cells at all levels of the armed forces.

POLITICO-MILITARY POLICIES

Algeria's foreign policy is one of extreme revolutionary idealism abetted by cautious opportunism. Algeria actively and tangibly supports wars of national liberation throughout Africa, and in Palestine, against regimes that it considers reationary, imperialistic or racist.

These policies—combined with an abiding hostility to its more conservative neighbor, Morocco, and the need to maintain internal security against dissident groups—have led to a relatively high rate of defense expenditures. Originally the ANP was maintained by voluntary enlistments with calls for volunteers always oversubscribed. However, in April 1968 the Government decreed two years of compulsory service for all 19-year olds. Also in November 1967 military training was instituted in high schools and universities.

STRATEGIC PROBLEMS

Support for external wars of national liberation has led to the establishment of guerrilla training bases in Algeria and to the establishment of personnel and logistic pipelines to the scenes of conflict. Internal resources plus Chinese, Cuban, and Soviet aid have filled the pipelines. This aid doubtless will continue to the degree that Algeria desires to employ it.

Locally, Algeria feels hemmed in between liberal, Western-oriented Tunisia and conservative, also Western-oriented, Morocco. While both these countries provided sanctuary for the FLN and external elements of its National Liberation Army (ALN) during Algeria's war of national liberation against France (1954-1962), they have not been as cooperative or sympathetic since. Algeria apparently supports dissident elements in both countries and Morocco probably supports Berber dissidents in the Kabyle and Aures mountains of Algeria. Moreover, much of the border between Algeria and Morocco, which passes through an area rich in raw materials, was never precisely defined by the French. Moroccan-Algerian border clashes in 1962 and the fall of 1963 erupted into serious fighting in late October 1963; the ANP, still a guerrilla-type force, was defeated by the smaller Moroccan professional army. Members of the OAU mediated the dispute, and the frontier areas were demilitarized. The dispute was formally ended by agreements signed at the OAU annual meeting of 1972.

Tunisia claims the oil fields at Edjele and surrounding portions of the Algerian Sahara. Tunisia has an advantage since the pipeline carrying oil from the Edjele fields runs through Tunisia to the port of Sekhira. The dispute is not currently active.

Internally Algeria is beset by military, ideological and ethnic divisions. During the war of independence the "internal" ALN of about 60,000 fought the French while the "external" ALN of 30,000 to 40,000 of better equipped and trained troops remained in Tunisia and Morocco. The external ALN entered Algeria upon independence and, with the addition of only 10,000 of the internal army, became the ANP, leaving 50,000 or more former insurgents, mostly Berbers, dissatisfied. This resulted in two abortive revolts immediately after independence in 1962.

Boumedienne's coup of 1965 was the result of his concern about the dangerously unrealistic socialism and revolutionary interventionism of President Ben Bella. Boumedienne's somewhat more moderate policies have been opposed by doctrinaire extreme left idealists, including many Berbers and former members of the "internal" army. Dissidence still exists in the Berber mountain areas.

MILITARY ASSISTANCE

After independence Algeria fell heir to much French equipment. After the defeat by Morocco in 1963 the Soviet Union immediately made a loan of $100 million for arms to strengthen Algeria's defense. By mid-1971 this is believed to have reached a total of over $300 million. It is not known what proportion is a loan and what is grant aid. All classes of weapons were received: tanks, artillery, APCs, surface to air missiles, jet fighters and bombers, and submarine chasers and guided missile patrol craft. Three thousand Algerian officers have been trained in the Soviet Union and about 1,000 Soviet military instructors are in Algeria. Because of Soviet control of spare parts Algeria is reported to have second thoughts about increased Soviet influence coupled to increased military aid.

Communist China aided the FLN with arms and training during the war for liberation. Since independence it has trained Algerian ground officers and pilots in China, conducted guerrilla training for dissidents from other African countries in Algeria, has provided arms for African insurgents which are transshipped through Algeria, and begun to supply arms and training for an Algerian People's Militia. Communist Cuba has also participated in the guerrilla training in Algeria.

After Algeria's independence, a bilateral treaty permitted France to maintain several atomic test and space rocket launch sites, various civil aviation facilities, and the large modern naval base at Mers-el-Kebir. The French withdrew in 1967-1968 but continue to occupy the small airfield of Bou Sfer, near Mers-el-Kebir, until 1977. About 300 French airmen are there and the field serves for observation of activities at Mers-el-Kebir and as a staging field for the support of French forces in Central and West Africa. France is believed to have retained the right to deny use of its former bases to any power except France and Algeria until 1977. This would serve legally to deny their use to the Soviet Union with its increased naval presence in the Mediterranean. France has a training mission with the National Gendarmerie and has equipped it with armored cars mounting anti-tank guns, machine guns, and other equipment. Algeria, in 1969, ordered 28 Fouga Magister armed jet trainers (these are refurbished ex-Luftwaffe aircraft).

Algeria's support for wars of liberation has included delivery of arms to the Congo (Kinshasa) rebels in 1964 and to others, and the training of insurgents in the guerrilla training center in Algiers. Palestinian guerrillas are also trained. In the June 1967 war Algeria sent a battalion of troops and a squadron of MiG-21s to assist Egypt. While the ground unit did not see action, it was reported that six of the jet fighters were lost to the Israelis (two or three when they landed at an Israeli occupied airfield in the Sinai). Two thousand Algerian troops remain in Egypt.

ALLIANCES

Algeria is a member of the United Nations, the Organization of African Unity (OAU) and a member of the OAU Liberation Committee, which sponsors insurgent movements against the white and colonial regimes of Southern Africa. A member of the Arab League, Algeria vies with Egypt for leadership by the volume of its pronouncements against Israel and "reactionarry" regimes, and actively supports the Arab conflict with Israel. Algeria also maintains membership in the Maghreb, and is a member of OPEC.

ARMY

Personnel: 55,000

Organization:
- 4 motorized infantry brigades (with some armor)
- 3 independent tank battalions
- 50 independent infantry battalions
- 5 independent artillery battalions
- 12 companies of desert troops
- 1 paratroop brigade
- AA troops
- engineer troops

Major Equipment Inventory:
- 400 medium tanks (T-34, T-54/55)
- 50 light tanks (AMX-13)
- 50 assault guns (SU-100) SP
- 10 assault guns (JSU-152) SP
- 350 APCs (BTR-152)
- 300 artillery pieces (140mm and 240mm rocket launchers, 85mm guns, 122mm and 152mm howitzers)
- AA guns (57mm, 85mm, 100mm)

Reserves: Perhaps as many as 100,000 men are experienced veterans of the ALN and post-independence ANP, and this number will be at least maintained as classes of conscripts pass through their two-year army training.

NAVY

Personnel: 3,500

Major Units:
- 2 fleet minesweepers (T-43 class)
- 6 submarine chasers (SO-1 class; PCS)
- 1 coastal minesweeper (MSC)
- 3 guided missile patrol boat (Osa class; PTFG) (4 Styx SSM)
- 6 guided missile patrol boats (Komar class; PTFG) (2 Styx SSM)

14 torpedo boats (P-6 class; PT)
1 trawler
(possibly for intelligence collection; Sekstan class)
6 patrol vessels (20 tons each)

Major Naval Bases: Mers-el-Kebir, Oran, Arzew, Algiers, La Senia, Philippeville, Bone

Reserves: About 9,000 trained reservists.

AIR FORCE

Personnel: 4,500

Organization:
9 fighter/fighter-bomber squadrons, MiG-15/17/21)
2 light bomber squadrons (Il-28)
2 counterinsurgency (COIN squadrons (Magister)
2 transport squadrons (An-12, Il-18)
4 helicopter squadrons (Mi-1, Mi-4, Hughes 269, SA-330 Puma)
1 (or more) SAM battalion (SA-2 Guideline)

Major Aircraft Types:
198 combat aircraft
52 MiG-21 fighters
28 MiG-17 fighter-bombers
60 MiG-15 fighter-bombers
28 Magister armed trainers (COIN) (ex-Luftwaffe)
30 Il-28 light bombers
156 other aircraft
58 transports (An-12, Il-18)
50 helicopters (Mi-1, Mi-4, Hughes 269, SA-330 Puma)
48 training aircraft (T-28, Magister)

Missiles: 40 SAMs (SA-2 Guideline)

Major Air Bases: Dar-el-Beider, Maison Blanche, Boufarak, Paul-Cazelles, Marine, Oukar, Biskra, Algiers, Oran, Sidi-bel-Abbes. There are 30 additional medium airfields and 20 minor ones.

Reserves: About 3,000 reservists

PARAMILITARY

The French-trained and -equipped National Gendarmerie numbers about 8,000 and is equipped with heavy weapons up to armored cars mounting cannon (about 50 AMLs).

After the 1962 military coup the People's Militia (about 30,000 Chinese-armed and -trained party leftists) was abolished and it is doubtful that it has been re-established.

FRENCH FORCES

1 infantry company (Legionnaires); 1 Air Force detachment

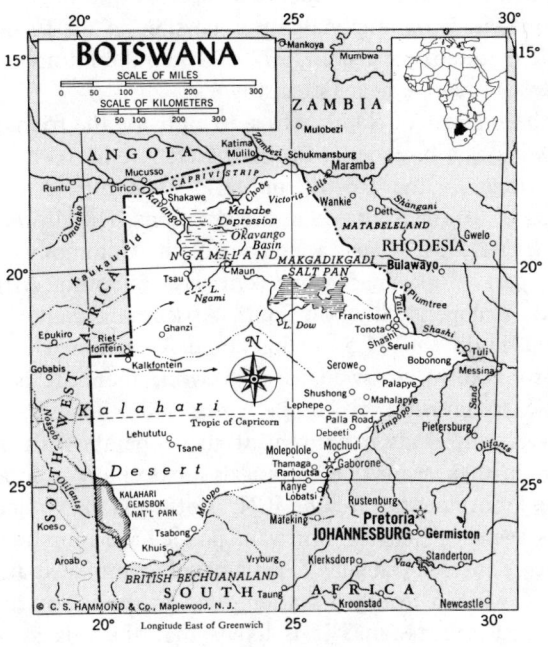

BOTSWANA

Republic of Botswana

POWER POTENTIAL STATISTICS

Area: 220,000 square miles
Population: 669,000
Total Active Armed Police Forces: 1,100 (0.16% population)
Gross National Product: $70 million ($105 per capita)
Annual Police Expenditures: $1.2 million (1.7% GNP)
Civil Air Fleet: 1 turboprop transport

POLITICO-MILITARY POLICIES AND POSTURE

The elected President is chief of state, head of government, and commander in chief of the armed force. The police, the only armed force, is directly controlled by the Minister for Home Affairs who, like the other cabinet members, is appointed by the President from the Legislative Assembly.

210 ALMANAC OF WORLD MILITARY POWER

Formerly the British Protectorate of Bechuanaland, Botswana became independent in 1966. The last British troops left a year later. Botswana's defense then depended upon its British-officered police force, now about 1,100 strong, on whatever collective security might be afforded by membership in the UN, the Commonwealth, and the OAU, and on its continued good relations with Rhodesia and South Africa.

Botswana's politico-military policies are dictated by its economic backwardness and its location between South Africa and Rhodesia. Most of its income is derived from livestock shipped to South Africa. The UK subsidizes one third of its meager budget. Economic viability is possible in the future as the result of the discovery in 1967 of a 33 million-ton copper and nickel ore reserve near Francistown.

It is the interest of South Africa to cultivate the friendship of Botswana as a basis for a future *modus vivendi* with other black nations to the North, and also as a buffer against incursions of insurgents based in those nations. The alternative is an unfriendly Botswana, a member of the Commonwealth. For its part Botswana, while critical of South African apartheid, is dependent upon South Africa as a market and dependent upon the $1.5 million annually returned by the 40,000 to 60,000 Botswanans who work there. It is also vulnerable to invasion by South Africa and Rhodesia. As a result, Botswana finds it convenient to cooperate with these neighbors in their security efforts against externally supported liberation movements. In the UN, Botswana has rejected sanctions against Rhodesia. Botswana police have apprehended numerous Tanzania-trained, Zambia-based communist-armed Southwest African insurgents attempting to reach Southwest Africa through Botswana. It is likely that there is at least informal cooperation with the South African police.

Despite its weak economy, Botswana is fairly stable. The people are mostly Bantu in closely related tribal groupings. The party in power is moderate. Three minor opposition parties are all left-wing, Pan-African, and have ties with the African nationalist parties of South Africa, but have little popular support.

BURUNDI

Republic of Burundi

POWER POTENTIAL STATISTICS

Area: 10,739 square miles
Population: 3,615,000
Total Active Armed Forces: 1,950 (includes Gendarmerie; 0.05% population)
Gross National Product: $210 million ($58 per capita)
Annual Military Expenditures: $970,000 (0.46% GNP)
Electric Power Output: 15 million kwh

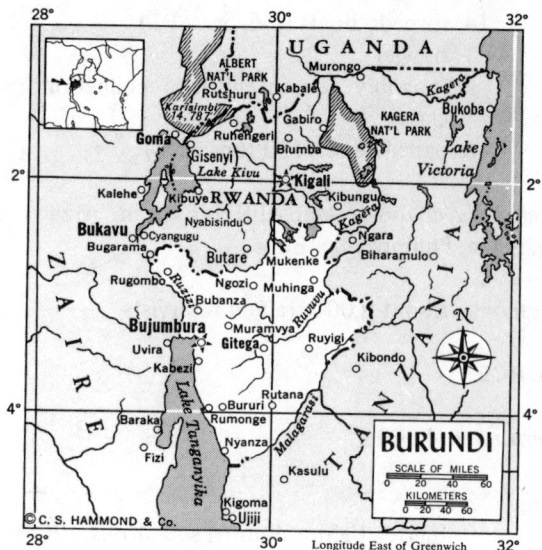

POLITICO-MILITARY POLICIES AND POSTURE

Colonel Michel Micombero, who had previously been Premier, Minister of Defense and commander of the 950-man army, deposed the King in November 1966 and declared himself President. He continues to hold the portfolios of Defense and Interior and rules through a National Revolutionary Council composed entirely of Army officers. The eight provinces are ruled by military governors.

The Army is trained and advised by Belgium. About 40 Belgian officers are in Burundi. Evidence of Chinese Communist efforts to support subversion in Burundi and neighboring Rwanda and Congo (K)—now Zaire—led Burundi to break diplomatic relations with China in 1965. Because of this attempted subversion, the governments of the Congo (K), Rwanda, and Burundi signed a security agreement in mid-1966. Under this agreement, Zaire has trained a number of Burundi paratroopers.

Ethno-tribal divisions in Burundi have been a source of internal security problems and led in 1965, and again in early 1972, to widespread massacres. The Nilotic Tutsi (Watusi) tribe, comprising about 15 percent of the population, has traditionally ruled over the much more numerous peasant Bantu Hutu (Bahutu) tribe. The Tutsi are further divided into Big Tutsi, including the royalty and high government officials who tend to be moderate and conciliatory toward the Hutu, and the Little Tutsi, who tend to be leftist and anti-Hutu. President Micombero comes from this extremist group. In October 1965 Hutu officers in the army and gendarmerie, aided by some Tutsi soldiers and police, staged an abortive coup. Hutu in the countryside also rose and massacred several thousand Tutsi, and bloody reprisals by the Tutsi followed. In March 1972, young King Ntare V, deposed by Micombero in 1966, was allowed to return to Burundi, but was arrested and, in April, was killed during an attempt by monarchists to free him and overthrow the government. An estimated 20,000 people, most of them Tutsi, were killed in the uprising, and an estimated 100,000 Hutu were killed in the suppression of the uprising and the reprisals that followed. Zaire sent troops to assist the government in suppressing the uprising.

In May 1973 there was another abortive Hutu attempt to seize power, opened by Hutu raiders from Tanzania and Rwanda, and followed by the killing of 10,000 or more Hutu. The Army numbers about 950, organized as an infantry battalion. The strength of the Gendarmerie is about 1,000. In March 1967 the Gendarmerie was incorporated into the National Army, and the President took over the functions of the Chief of Staff of the Army. Burundi is a member of the United Nations and the Organization of African Unity.

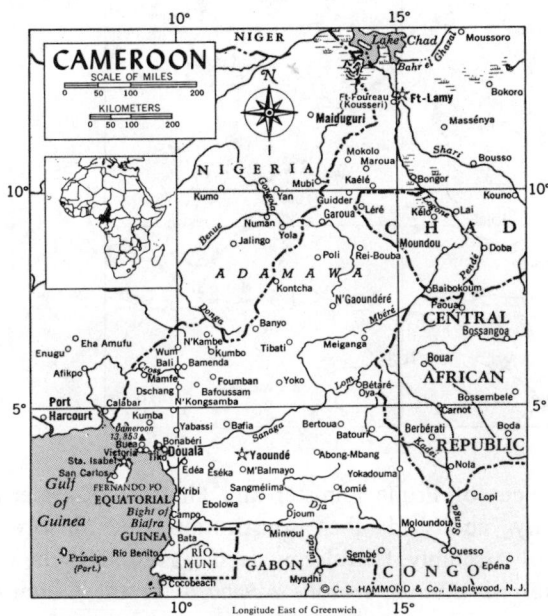

CAMEROON

Republique Federale du Cameroun
Federal Republic of Cameroon

POWER POTENTIAL STATISTICS

Area: 183,591 square miles
Population: 5,836,000
Total Active Armed Forces: 9,500 (includes Gendarmerie and Mobile Police; 0.16% population)
Gross National Product: $1.2 billion ($206 per capita)
Annual Military Expenditures: $19.0 million (1.58% GNP)
Electric Power Output: 1.02 billion kwh
Merchant Fleet: 13 ships; 2,334 gross tons
Civil Air Fleet: 2 jet transports and 3 piston transports

POLITICO-MILITARY POLICIES AND POSTURE

The President is chief of state and commander of the armed forces. This command is exercised through a Minister of the Armed Forces. Although officially nonaligned in the world ideological struggle, Cameroon is Western-oriented. Cameroon was established in 1961 from former British Cameroon and the much larger and more populous French Cameroun. The French portion, upon independence in 1960, retained close ties with the French Community and entered into certain thus-far unpublished mutual defense arrangements and a technical military assistance arrangement with France. These continued following the unification of the two Cameroons. In late 1973, however, Cameroon was negotiating for revisions in its cooperation agreements with France that would end its patron-protege relationship with the former ruling country and would establish normal state-to-state relations.

Cameroon's main strategic problem since its independence is related to the maintenance of internal security against the efforts of a communist insurgent group sponsored, trained and supplied by Communist China and the radical African states. This is the *Union des Populations du Cameroun* (PUC), which has maintained a low-key insurgency with a strength of about 1,200. It has some bases in the mountains, but by 1968 its activities had been reduced to occasional hit and run raids from the sanctuary of Congo (Brazzaville). Its leader was captured, tried, and executed in 1971.

A potential for internal instability is inherent in the ethno-religious diversity of the people. There are about 200 tribes speaking 24 major languages. In the north, where the Moslem 15% of the country's population is concentrated, the Fang and Fulani tribes predominate. One third of the population, mainly the southern Bantus, profess Christianity and the remainder are animist. The core of the leftist insurgency comes from the Bamileke, about 20 percent of the population, in the central highlands area. So far the north-south split on ethno-religious grounds, so prevalent in West African states, has not manifested itself.

French military assistance has continued since 1960 at a rate of about $7 million annually. Until recently, French officers commanded Cameroonian units while others trained, staffed and performed technical services. A small instructor-adviser detachment continues to work with the military and police forces. Training of Cameroonian officers and NCOs is conducted in France, also. Between 1960 and 1964 some 10,000 French troops were in Cameroon, assisting the government against the insurgency. The troops have been evacuated, except for the training detachment.

The United States in 1962-1963 provided $249,000 military assistance and $1,000 in surplus equipment.

Cameroon, which withdrew in 1972 from the French-oriented OCAM, is a member of Organization of African Unity (OAU), and the United Nations. It has also withdrawn from *Air Afrique*, French-backed and shared by

OCAM nations, and now has its own successful Cameroon Airlines.

Cameroon's relative stability, in a region plagued by military coups, is perhaps due to a military balance of power. There is a Gendarmerie of 3,000 men and a mobile police force (the Cameroonian Guard) of 2,000 in addition to an Army of 4,000. All three forces are said to watch each other jealously and all are under close observation by the President's own special security police. The Army is organized as three infantry battalions, an armored car company, and engineer and support companies. There is a Navy of 200 men, operating two 75-ton patrol boats (YP), one 46-ton patrol boat (YP), and four landing craft (LCVP). The Air Force of 300 operates six Magister armed jet trainers, one C-47 transport, four light aircraft and two Sud SA-1221 Djinn helicopters. There are airbases at Batouri, Douala, Foumban, Garoua, Kaele, N'Gaoundere, Maroua Salak. Port Pouet, Yaounde, Tiko.

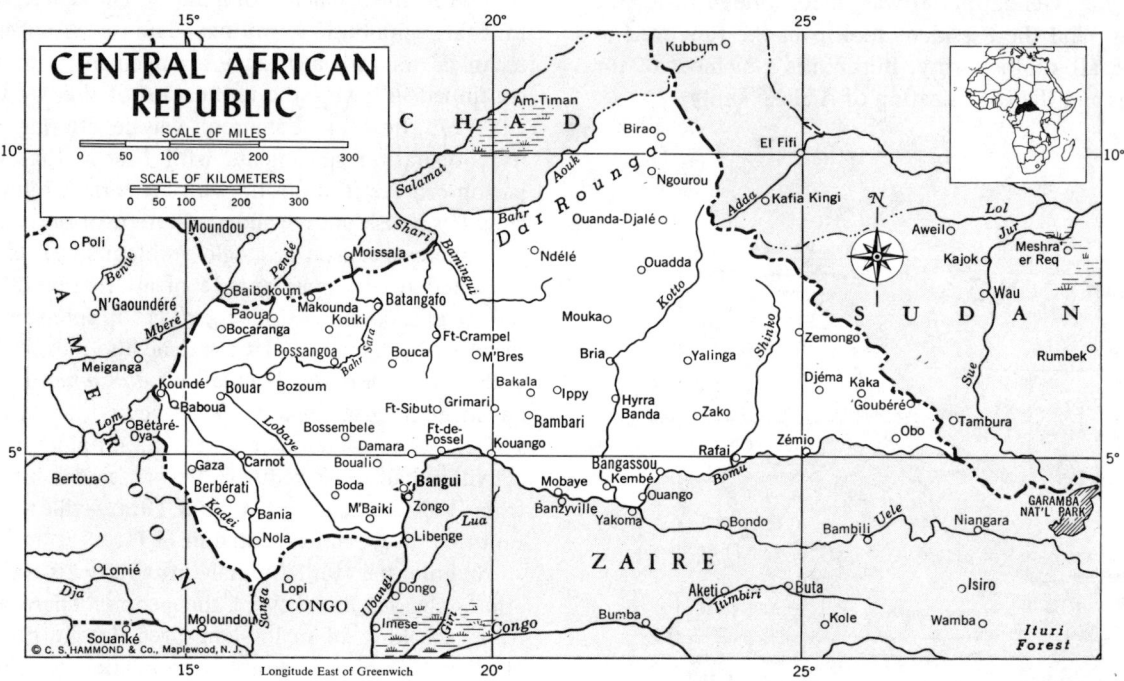

CENTRAL AFRICAN REPUBLIC

Republique Centrafricaine

POWER POTENTIAL STATISTICS

Area: 241,313 square miles
Population: 1,637,000
Total Active Armed Forces: 2,000 (including paramilitary; 0.12% population)
Gross National Product: $220 million ($134 per capita)
Annual Military Expenditures: $6 million (2.7% GNP)
Civil Air Fleet: 2 jet, 1 turboprop, 1 piston transport

POLITICO-MILITARY POLICIES AND POSTURE

President Bokassa, former Chief of Staff of the Army, deposed his predecessor on January 1, 1966, and also assumed the offices of Prime Minister and Minister of Defense. He promptly abolished the Constitution and dissolved the National Assembly. He rules by decree, assisted by the Council of Ministers. Among reasons advanced for the military coup were economic stagnation, discovery of vast uranium ore deposits in which France was much interested, Army-Gendarmerie rivalry, and growing Chinese Communist influence. Bokassa broke diplomatic relations with Peking and publicized Chinese Communist plans for increased control.

Upon independence from France in 1960, the CAR signed a defense agreement with France which included internal security matters, base rights, transit and overflight privileges, and military assistance. Ubangi veterans of the French Army formed the CAR Army. French officers were seconded as instructor-advisers. France has furnished equipment as well as training, has kept garrisons at Bangui and Bouar, and in November 1967, at the request of the President during a governmental crisis, deployed a paratroop company to the Bangui airfield.

The CAR is a member of the UN, the OAU, the OCAM, the French-sponsored Equatorial Defense Council, and the Union of Central African States (UEAC)

The United States furnished $200,000 in vehicles and other equipment in 1962 under an internal security assistance program.

Israel has assisted the CAR to establish a youth organization on the lines of its own, a paramilitary organization for pioneering new agricultural settlements, and a preliminary training and indoctrination organization. Several thousand youths have passed through the training programs given by a team of 20 Israeli officers.

The Army consists of 700 men, organized as an infantry battalion with a supporting engineer company. The equipment includes French EBR-75 armored cars and EBR-ETT armored personnel carriers. The Air Force of 100 men operates ten A-1 Skyraider attack aircraft, two C-47, ten Noratlas and ten AL-60 transports, and ten Sikorsky H-34 and Alouette II helicopters. Air bases are Bangui, Bouar, Bambari, and Berberati. There is a Gendarmerie with a strength of 500 and a *Garde Republicaine* of 700 men.

CHAD
Republique du Tchad
Republic of Chad

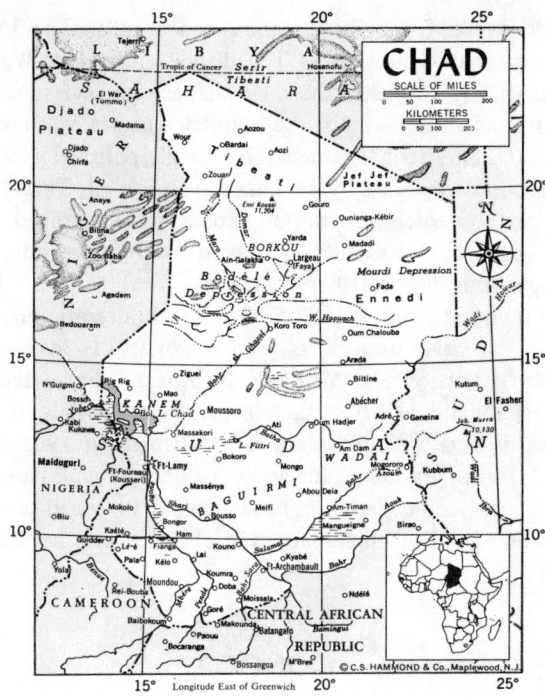

POWER POTENTIAL STATISTICS

Area: 495,752 square miles
Population: 3,791,000
Total Active Armed Forces: 1,950 (including Gendarmerie; 0.05% population)
Gross National Product: $300 million ($79 per capita)
Annual Military Expenditures: $8.0 million (2.66% GNP)
Electric Power Output: 15 million kwh
Civil Air Fleet: 5 piston transports

POLITICO-MILITARY POLICIES AND POSTURE

The President of the Republic is also Prime Minister. Control of the armed forces is exercised through a Minister of Defense.

Upon independence from France in 1960 the army was formed from Chadian veterans of the French Army. It inherited a stock of French arms and equipment, and a bilateral military technical assistance agreement provided additional equipment and some 500 French officers and men as instructor-advisers. This agreement, similar to those executed between France and other former African colonies, provides also for French assistance in maintenance of internal security, base rights, and transit and overflight privileges. The French Army continued to control northern Chad until 1965, and under the agreement France maintains a reinforced infantry battalion at Fort Lamy which has been used for intervention—at the request of the governments concerned—in Congo (Brazzaville) in 1963, Gabon in 1964, and in Chad itself in 1968. The strength of French troops stationed in Chad was reduced in June 1971 to about 900 officers and men, apart from advisers attached to the Chad Army. French military assistance has amounted to about $1.2 million yearly. Chad is a member of the UN, the OAU, the Equatorial Defense Council, and the Union of Central African States (UEAC). It withdrew from the OCAM in 1973.

Chad is faced with the same north-south split along lines of race, religion, and living patterns that threatens the domestic tranquility of many Sudanic African countries. The sedentary animist and Christian people of the south accepted education and training from the French, and have controlled the government since independence. The nomadic Moslems of the north retain their traditional ways under feudal leaders and maintain close ties with kinsmen in Libya and Sudan. There was serious insurgency in the northern and central regions from 1963 to 1968, leading the president in August 1968 to request and obtain military assistance from the French Government to put down the rebellion. In August 1971 the Chadian government broke diplomatic relations with Libya after a foreign-inspired coup attempt failed to oust President Francois Tombalbaye.

French influence in Chad suffered as a result of French intervention in the rebellions of the 1960's. Not only were the French resented by the insurgents and their sympathizers in the north; the Chadian government also resented French pressure for administrative reform and made the French scapegoats for the government's own actions. In September

1973 President Tombalbaye announced a cultural and social revolution that would stress Tchaditude and reject Western, and specifically French, values. He changed his own first name to Ngarta, and the name of the country's capital was changed from Fort Lamy to N'Djamena. The single political party was abolished and replaced by an Executive Council. Thus far no military or strategic reorientation appears to be involved.

The Army of 1,200 men consists of two infantry battalions and supporting light artillery batteries. There is an Air Force of 200 men with five A-1 Skyraider attack aircraft, one C-47 and ten Noratlas transports, ten Sikorsky H-34 and ten Alouette II helicopters. Air bases are Abeche, Fada, Largeau, Fort Archambault, N'Djamena, Mongo, Moudou, Pala, Bongor.

There is also a Gendarmerie of 550 men. In 1965 it was planned, with French assistance, to recruit and train six brigades of Gendarmerie to be stationed in the disaffected areas. The extent of implementation of this plan is not known.

CONGO

Republique Populaire du Congo
People's Republic of Congo

POWER POTENTIAL STATISTICS

Area: 134,749 square miles
Population: 982,000
Total Active Armed Forces: 4,800 (includes Gendarmerie; 0.48% population)
Gross National Product: $233 million ($237 per capita)
Annual Military Expenditures: $6 million (2.6% GNP)

POLITICO-MILITARY POLICIES AND POSTURE

Congo is governed by an eight-man National Revolutionary Council which seized power from the constitutional government in August 1968. The Council is headed by President Marien N'gouabi, a former Army Captain who led the coup.

At the time of independence from France in 1960 the Army was formed from French African units. A mutual defense agreement provides for French assistance in internal security, base rights, and provision of arms and training. The Army has been involved in the political unrest that has plagued the republic since 1963. The latest Army seizure of power resulted from military concern about growing communist influence in the government and the creation by the government of a Presidential Guard cadred by 100 Cuban negroes and of a Cuban-trained people's militia known as the Youth of the National Movement of the Revolution, or the *Jeunesse*. The Army demanded that this rival military force be incorporated in the Army. When left-wing dissidents opposed the transfer, violence broke out in July and August 1968. In the ensuing conflict over 450 of the *Jeunesse* were killed. The coup was the result of an internal power struggle, exacerbated by deep-rooted tribal rivalries, rather than of political ideology; the political orientation of the present military government is still leftist. In 1970 President Marien N'gouabi put down two attempted coups against his regime. N'gouabi charged that Congo (Kinshasa; now Zaire) supported the rebels, but cordial relations between Brazzaville and Kinshasa were reestablished later in the year. Constant maneuvering for power continues among various factions formed largely on the basis of tribal loyalties, army unit loyalties, and orientation toward China or the Soviet Union. There were unsuccessful coup attempts in 1972 and 1973.

Under its leftist governments, Congo has been a base for radical and communist subversion in Africa since 1963. Instructor-advisers from communist countries and the radical African states (Soviet Union, China, Cuba, Algeria, Egypt, and formerly Ghana) came to Congo to train not only the *Armee Nationale Populaire*, but also the exiled insurgents from surrounding African countries who had taken refuge there.

The Army has a strength of about 3,000 and consists of two infantry battalions (one parachute-commando), a support battalion containing armored cars, artillery, anti-aircraft, anti-tank, and combat engineer units, a communications company, and a transportation company. French weapons are being replaced with more modern Soviet and Chinese equipment. Service is voluntary and for two years. The Navy numbers about 200, with a patrol craft (YP) at Pointe Noire and 12 river patrol craft (PBR) on the Congo and Oubangui Rivers. The Air Force is also about 200 strong and operates two C-47 transports, two liaison aircraft, and three helicopters. Air bases are at Brazzaville, Dolisie, and Pointe Noire.

There is a People's Militia (under the command of the Army), and a Gendarmerie of 1,400 in 20 companies.

Congo is a member of the UN and OAU. It withdrew from OCAM in 1972.

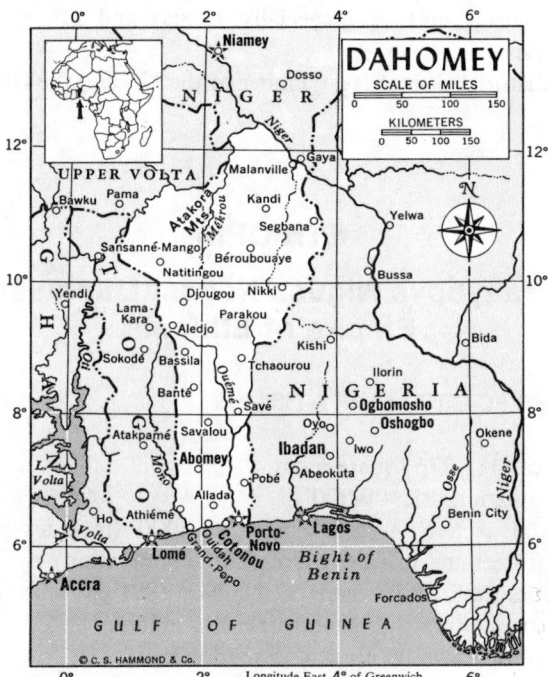

DAHOMEY

Republique du Dahomey

POWER POTENTIAL STATISTICS

Area: 43,383 square miles
Population: 2,900,000
Total Active Armed Forces: 3,060 (includes Gendarmerie; 0.10% population)
Gross National Product: $235 million ($81 per capita)
Annual Military Expenditures: $4 million (1.7% GNP)

POLITICO-MILITARY POLICIES AND POSTURE

On October 26, 1972, an Army junta headed by Major (now Lt. Colonel) Mathieu Kerekou seized power. Control of the country is now firmly in the hands of President Kerekou and his Military Revolutionary Government of Dahomey (MRGD). Kerekou quashed a coup attempt in February 1973. He has forced out the senior officers who aided him in his 1972 coup, and is attempting to broaden his base of support by establishing a 67-member National Revolutionary Council (September 1973), setting up local councils, and bringing young intellectuals and younger officers into government.

Dahomey received its independence from France in 1960; initially, its armed forces comprised former soldiers in the French Army. Upon independence, a defense agreement was signed which provided for French assistance in maintaining internal security, base rights, and arms and training. In 1962 the United States furnished token military assistance of $62,000 which included some vehicles, motor launches, and police equipment. Israel has given some military vehicles and has helped establish and train a National Service Corps (which begins with six-months military training followed by a year of agricultural service) and a National Youth Movement. Dahomey is a member of the UN, OAU, OCAM, and the *Conseil de l'Entente*.

Dahomey's weak economy and dense population cause dependence on France for an annual budget subsidy of about $10 million. Internal security problems have come mainly from tribal-regional divisions among politicians, civil servants, and the Army. Three power centers exist: Abomey in the southwest, Porto-Novo in the southeast, and the politically and economically undeveloped north. There were six presidents in the first turbulent decade of independence, with the Army playing the principal role in their selection and ousting. At the time of Kerekou's 1972 coup, the country was being governed under a May 1970 charter that called for rotation of the presidency every two years among members of a presidential council, and one transfer of power had taken place peacefully. There have recently (1973) been announcements that a constitutional convention will be held within a year, but no action has been taken.

The Army numbers about 1,750 men, organized into three infantry battalions. Voluntary enlistments are for 18 months. Arms and equipment are mainly French and include a few armored cars. There is no navy, but about 100 army personnel man three patrol carft used for port control at Cotonou. The Air Force, part of the army, is 110 men strong, and operates one C-47 transport, one light transport, two liaison aircraft and one Alouette II helicopter. There is a Gendarmerie of 1,200 men organized into eight companies.

EQUATORIAL GUINEA

POWER POTENTIAL STATISTICS

Area: 10,833 square miles (10,040 Rio Muni, 779 Fernando Po, 14 minor islets)
Population: 300,000
Total Active Armed Forces: 1,000 (includes Gendarmerie)

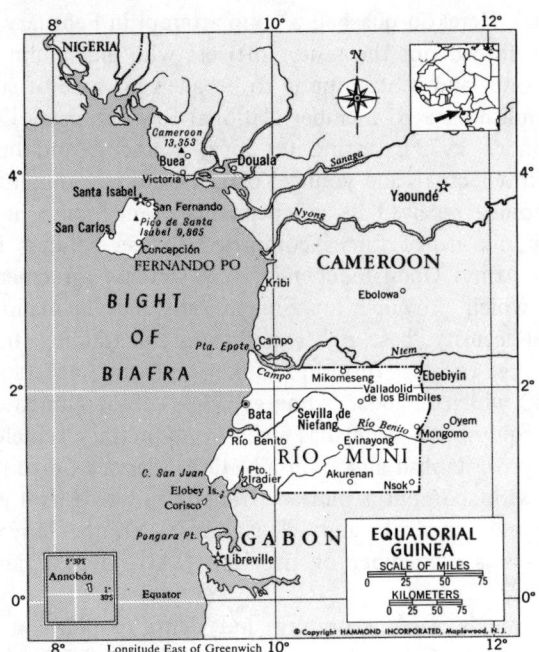

Gross National Product: $60 million ($200 per capita)
Annual Military Expenditures: $200,000 (est.) (0.33% GNP)
Electric Power Output: 11 million kwh
Civil Air Fleet: 2 piston transports

POLITICO-MILITARY POLICIES AND POSTURE

Spanish colonies since 1778, the island of Fernando Po and mainland Spanish Guinea (Rio Muni) received independence as Equatorial Guinea on October 12, 1968. Included in Fernando Po are adjacent islets and the island of Annobon, and in Rio Muni the island of Corisco, Islas Elobey and adjacent islets.

Before independence Fernando Po's strategic location, combined with the presence of 40,000 Ibos (Biafrans) on the island, and Spain's permissive policies, had caused the island to become an air base for arms and food flights to Biafra in the Nigeria-Biafra civil war (1967-1970).

Before Spain granted independence Nigeria had contemplated annexation or purchase of Fernando Po. Also, Cameroon had claimed both Fernando Po and Rio Muni, and Gabon had claimed Rio Muni. Since independence Cameroon and Gabon have each renounced these claims, contingent on a like restraint by the other. In 1972 Gabon occupied two tiny disputed islands, ostensibly over a fishing dispute and probably as a part of an attempt to extend its territorial waters; the presence of offshore oil is suspected in this area. Equatorial Guinea charged invasion and both called on the UN for help. Gabon withdrew, and the matter is now quiescent.

The minority, but wealthier, Bubis of Fernando Po fear diversion of their island's economic resources to development of poorer Rio Muni, whose population is predominantly of the Fang tribe.

Equatorial Guinea's currently depressed economy is based on cocoa, coffee, and timber, grown on large plantations that were formerly worked by imported Nigerian labor. The departure of most of the Nigerians after disputes over wages and working conditions has sharply cut production of all crops, reducing timber production to near zero.

Spain contributes substantially to Equatorial Guinea's economy both through subsidies and as a trading partner; 80% of the country's trade is with Spain.

The armed forces have received training from Spain, some communist countries (especially China) and other African countries.

Equatorial Guinea is a member of the UN and the OAU.

ETHIOPIA

Yaityopya Nigusa Nagast Manguist
Empire of Ethiopia

POWER POTENTIAL STATISTICS

Area: 471,776 square miles
Population: 25,900,000
Total Active Armed Forces: 53,000 (includes security forces and frontier guard; 0.20% population)
Gross National Product: $2.1 billion ($81 per capita)
Annual Military Expenditures: $41 million (1.95% GNP)
Electric Power Output: 455 million kwh
Merchant Fleet: 23 ships; 45,903 gross tons
Civil Air Fleet: 4 jet and 19 piston transports

DEFENSE STRUCTURE

The Emperor, Haile Selassie I, has been the hereditary constitutional monarch since 1931, with full sovereignty vested in his person as chief of state and head of government. He is commander in chief of each of the three armed services and may determine their size and organization. The limitations on his authority, minimal until 1974, have greatly increased, with the balance of power shifting to leaders of the armed forces. The armed services are administered by a Ministry of National Defense. The Minister is an Army general nominally appointed by the Prime Minister, who is appointed by the Emperor.

POLITICO-MILITARY POLICY

When dramatic change finally came to Ethiopia in the spring of 1974, it was triggered not by the separatist

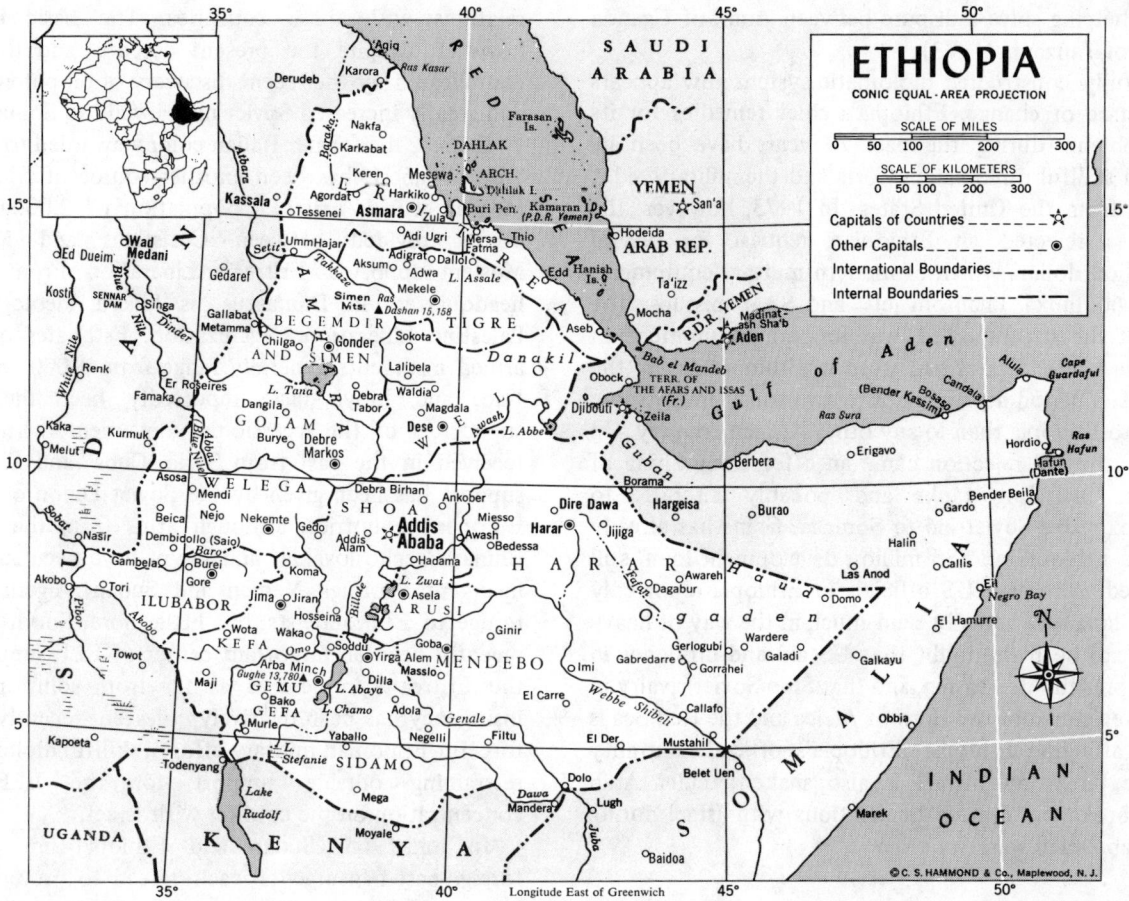

movements that have long threatened the heterogeneous nation, but rather by inflation following a famine (1973) that was apparently unnecessarily devastating because of mismanaged relief efforts. There were strikes and riots in Addis Ababa in late February over the cost of living, and a week later (February 26) the army's 2d Division took control of Asmara, Ethiopia's second largest city. The troops' grievances were unrelated to Asmara's location in Eritrea or the Eritrean Liberation Front; spokesmen for the Army rebels demanded higher pay, better fringe benefits, and the dismissal of many cabinet members. They were joined by most other units of the armed forces, with the 4th Division taking control of Addis Ababa.

The prime minister resigned, there were numerous cabinet changes, and the Emperor announced pay increases for the armed forces, but unrest continued. A general strike, pay demands by priests, student protests, and scattered peasant uprisings were followed by more concessions from the Emperor. By mid-1974 the Army was controlling the government, and the emperor had been shorne of most of his power.

Ethiopia has a long tradition of independence broken only by brief Italian conquest (1935-1941). This tradition is perpetuated by a current posture of nonalignment. Ethiopia supports the UN and the principle of collective security. In implementation of this policy it has contributed to UN forces in Korea (1951-1953) and the Congo (1960-1964). It has also taken a lead in the African unity movement, was a founder of OAU, and built the OAU headquarters in Addis Ababa.

Independence has been maintained over the centuries against neighboring enemies by the relative inaccessibility of the high (6-10,000 feet) central plateau. For more than a millenium Ethiopia's traditional enemies have been Arabs and other Moslems who surround it on three sides.

Diplomacy has been used with great efficacy by Ethiopia, and specifically by Haile Selassie. The Emperor developed a good personal relationship with Nasser, and Ethiopia now maintains generally good relations with the Arab countries. The Emperor has made numerous useful state visits during recent years, including one to Peking in 1971. He has firmly established Ethiopia as an African state, despite ethnic, religious, and historical separateness. He has also repeatedly acted successfully as a mediator, most recently helping bring improved relations between Senegal and Guinea (1972), helping end the conflict between north and south in Sudan

(1972), and helping solve a dispute between Amin of Uganda and Nyerere of Tanzania (1973).

This carefully constructed diplomatic system now appears to be in a state of change. Ethiopia's chief remedies for its strategic problems during the past 20 years have been its intensive and skillful diplomatic efforts and the military aid it has received from the United States. In 1973, however, the United States rejected an Ethiopian request for several hundred million dollars worth of modern military equipment, including M-60 tanks, Phantom jets, and SAM missiles. The request, if of the size reported, was for more equipment, in cost, than the United States had given to Ethiopia during the past 20 years, a period during which it gave considerably more military aid to Ethiopia than to any other African country. On the heels of the US rejection came an offer from China of heavy arms, including tanks and possibly aircraft, to counteract extensive Soviet aid to Somalia. China has already (1971) made Ethiopia an $85 million development loan, still largely unused. Although US officials in Ethiopia reportedly doubt that China will actually send much in the way of heavy arms, there can be little doubt that US aid and influence in Ethiopia are steadily decreasing, and that Sino-Soviet rivalry in the key strategic area of the Horn of Africa and the Red Sea is increasingly affecting Ethiopia. Ethiopia's official neutrality between the Arabs and Israel is also shaken; under Arab pressure, it broke off diplomatic relations with Israel during the 1973 Arab-Israeli war.

STRATEGIC PROBLEMS

Ethiopia's principal strategic problems are: internal ethno-religious and socio-economic tensions, and encirclement by largely hostile Arab and Moslem neighbors.

The aging Emperor rules over a heterogeneous nation split along both ethnic and religious lines. There are some 40 different tribes, mostly of Semitic or Hamitic origin. The ruling Amharas and Tigreans of the highlands comprise 40 percent of the population and are mostly Coptic Christians; the coastal and lowland peoples of various origins are mostly Moslems. Concentration of power and wealth in the Amharas has aroused jealousy among others.

There is continuing friction with Moslem neighbors, especially over the Somalian question and Eritrea. Half a million Moslem Somalis live in the Ogaden region of Ethiopia, which adjacent Somalia claims. In the early and middle 1960s there were numerous border clashes between Ethiopian and Somalian Army and police forces along this border, complicated by traditional movements of Somali nomadic herdsmen across the poorly defined frontier. Somalia's growing arsenal of communist arms from Egypt, the Soviet Union and China posed a serious threat to Ethiopian territorial integrity and stimulated its further military buildup. In early 1968 Somalia renounced its former irredentist policy against Kenya, Ethiopia, and French Somaliland, and sought friendly relations with these countries. The basic issues remain, however, despite the present detente, and they have been complicated by the recent discovery of oil potential in Ogaden and greatly increased Soviet military aid to Somalia.

Eritrea, the former Italian colony awarded to Ethiopia after World War II, has been another source of friction with the Moslem world. Eritrea's population of 2,000,000 is almost evenly divided between Christians and Moslems. The Moslem-supported Eritrean Liberation Front (ELF), with headquarters in Damascus, is linked ideologically to the Palestine Liberation Organization. Estimates of numbers of armed insurgents generally range from 1,000 to 2,000. Syria, Iraq, and Libya have reportedly been the chief recent supporters of the secessionist movement, with ELF training received in the past from Syria, Cuba, and China. No open support has been given by the Soviet Union or other Eastern European countries, although arms from the Soviet Union, China, Czechoslovakia, and Egypt have been smuggled to the insurgents through Yemen and Sudan. Algeria has provided refuge to ELF activists, but little more. Southern Yemen has recently been an important center of ELF support. Although the Eritrean problem is as far from solution as ever, the insurgency has been relatively quiescent recently, as a result of forceful Ethiopian military efforts, skillful diplomacy aimed at restraining outside support for the ELF, and Arab concentration on the conflict with Israel.

In mid-1965, Sudan and Ethiopia—both coping with foreign-based insurgents—each agreed to prevent its territory being used for any activity harmful to the national interest of the other. (Similar agreements have since been discussed with Kenya, Uganda, and Tanzania.) There has been considerable friction periodically since 1965, but Sudan has now withdrawn support from the ELF and moved the approximately 20,000 Eritrean refugees in Sudan farther from the Ethiopian border. Ethiopia has also made constructive diplomatic moves, and the situation is now relatively stable.

The only railroad linking the Abyssinian plateau with the sea runs to the port of Djibouti in French Somaliland (now the French Territory of the Afars and the Issas). The security of this access to the sea is vital to Ethiopia. The Afar and Danakil tribes indigenous to this territory are closely related to Ethiopian tribes, but the Issas are Somalis, and Somalia has claimed the territory. A possible confrontation was deferred by a 1966 plebiscite of bona fide residents of French Somaliland who voted overwhelmingly to remain under French dominion. But if Somalia, or any potentially hostile regime, were to obtain control of Djibouti, Ethiopia would be likely to act on the bases of strategic necessity and ethnic kinship with a portion of the population.

Military service in Ethiopia is voluntary and is a profession sought by the warrior Amharas and Tigreans.

MILITARY ASSISTANCE

Historic ties, a desire to maintain a certain balancing

neutrality among foreign military influences, and the realities of the world power struggle, have shaped Ethiopia's acceptance of several forms of military assistance. The British, who drove out the Italians in 1941, conducted military training from 1947 to 1951, and are still active in training and advising the Navy. Sweden helped organize and train the Air Force, organized a cadet school in 1946, and helped establish the office of the Chief of Staff of the Imperial Armed Forces in 1956. France, India, Israel, and Norway have helped train the Navy. Prior to rupture of diplomatic relations Israeli advisers conducted special infantry training, and provided advisers for the Frontier Guard and the Commando Police. West Germany has provided equipment for police field units. India has helped with training of the Imperial Bodyguard and the Military Academy. Most of this assistance is by contract, paid for by Ethiopia.

Military assistance from the United States, since 1953, has been considerably more substantial. It has comprised armament, equipment, and supplies of all kinds, worth $163 million through 1972, and the training of about 3,000 Ethiopians in the United States. Recently the rate of US assistance has been about $10-$12 million annually, and this is the amount expected through fiscal year 1974. Through 1972 some $8.4 million worth of excess American military stocks was furnished. The United States has provided this armament in the conviction that it contributes to stability in the Horn of Africa, and in consideration of Ethiopian permission, by a 1953 agreement, to operate the Kagnew Communications Station at Asmara, in Eritrea. US advisers have recently been phased out of sensitive positions in the Ethiopian government, however, and there is in general a gradual US withdrawal from Ethiopia in progress.

The Kagnew station, said to be the world's largest high frequency radio relaying and receiving station, was established in 1942 to insure strategic communications to the Middle East and South Asia. It includes elements of the US space communications and tracking system as well as receivers to monitor Soviet rocket tests and strategic communications. Some other African countries, as well as some Ethiopians, have objected to this US presence as inconsistent with Ethiopia's professed nonalignment. It has been a source of irritation for both Ethiopia's external relations and its domestic politics. In October 1970, the US State and Defense Departments disclosed an unpublicized agreement with Ethiopia (made in 1960) to equip and train the 40,000-man Ethiopian army and to oppose any threats to Ethiopia's territorial integrity. In exchange, the US was authorized to expand Kagnew Station. Recently, the use of earth satellite communications has made the Kagnew station less essential to the US than it was earlier, and it is being phased out.

For its part, Ethiopia has provided pilot and supporting aviation training for students from other African countries including Sudan, Kenya, and Nigeria.

ALLIANCES

Ethiopia is a member of the UN and the OAU. In 1963, in response to armed incursions of Somali nomadic tribesmen across the borders of both countries, Ethiopia and Kenya concluded a treaty of mutual defense, directed against Somalia.

ARMY

Personnel: 40,000

Organization:
- 4 infantry divisions (each of 3 brigades of 3 battalions; 8,000 men per division; 1 division is the Imperial Bodyguard)
- 4 artillery battalions
- 5 antiaircraft batteries
- 1 armored battalion
- 1 airborne (parachute) infantry battalion
- 2 combat engineer battalions
- 8 training battalions
- 1 armored car squadron

Major Equipment Inventory:
- 70 tanks (M-41 and M-24)
- 50 APCs
- 50 armored cars (AML-245, M-9, M-20)
- 50 105mm howitzers, 155mm guns
- 6 helicopters UH-1
- AA guns

NAVY

Personnel: 1,500

Organization:
- Coastal Patrol Force
- Diving Section (parachutists and attack-divers)
- Marine Corps

Major Units:
- 1 coastal minesweeper (MSC)
- 1 training ship (ex-AVP)
- 4 patrol launches (YP)
- 5 patrol gunboats (PGM)
- 4 landing craft mechanized (LCM)

Naval Bases: Massaua, Asab

AIR FORCE

Personnel: 3,000

Organization:
- 1 bomber squadron (Canberra)
- 2 fighter/fighter-bomber squadrons (F-5, F-86)
- 2 COIN squadrons (Saab 17A/B, T-33, T-28)
- 1 transport squadron (C-119, C-54, C-47, Dove)

Major Aircraft Types:
- 48 combat aircraft
  - 15 F-5 fighters
  - 12 F-86 fighters
  - 8 Saab 17A/B COIN aircraft
  - 9 T-33, T-28 armed trainers
  - 4 Canberra light bombers
- 82 other aircraft
  - 30 transports (C-54, C-47, Dove, Il-14, C-119)
  - 30 Saab 91 Safir trainers
  - 8 T-28 trainers
  - 14 Alouette II/III, Mi-8, UH-1 helicopters

Military Air Bases: Debre Zeit, Bishiftu, Jijiga, Harar

PARAMILITARY

The National Police Force is about 28,000 strong with 4,000 of these committed against the insurgency in the province of Eritrea, as are the 3,000 special Commando Police. The Frontier Guard numbering some 1,500 men patrols the Somalia border against the incursions of the *shifta* (gangs of bandits).

FRENCH TERRITORY OF THE AFARS AND ISSAS

Territoire Francais des Afars et des Issas

POWER POTENTIAL STATISTICS

Area: 8,880 square miles
Population: 97,000
Total Active Armed Forces: 4,400 (4.53% population)
Gross National Product: $60 million ($619 per capita)
Civil Air Fleet: 5 piston transports

POLITICO-MILITARY POLICIES AND POSTURE

Former French Somaliland, while having a measure of local self-government, is subject to France in matters of foreign affairs and defense through a resident High Commissioner.

The Territory's strategic problems are a combination of significant location and internal ethnic divisions. Located at the Indian Ocean entrance to the Red Sea, it is a trade crossroads, entrepot, and refueling point, and also a base for air transport between Europe, East Africa, Arabia, and India. This strategic position assures French influence in the Middle East and East Africa. Additionally, the Territory's modern port, Djibouti, is connected by rail to Addis Ababa, the capital of Ethiopia, and half of that country's external trade travels by this route. Ethiopia, therefore, has a vital interest in the Territory. To date control by France has been acceptable to the inhabitants of the Territory. Continued French sovereignty appears very important to the stability of the Horn of Africa, discouraging conflict between Ethiopia and the states that surround it, and preventing Arab control of the straits between the Gulf of Aden and the Red Sea.

Internally, the indigenous population is about equally divided between the Afars, related to the Ethiopian Danakil tribe, and the Issas, a Somali tribe. However, the Somali presence is artificially increased by an influx of tribesmen seeking jobs in the more prosperous territory. On this ethnic basis, Somalia has claimed the Territory. In response, Ethiopia claimed that the area was part of its 19th Century empire. Both would probably attempt to enforce these claims by arms should France withdraw. It is to avoid this, as well as for strategic reasons, that France has maintained its colonial position. In a referendum on March 19, 1967, the electorate voted 60 percent for continued association with France. Most of this majority were Afars; many Issas, who otherwise might have constituted a majority, were barred from voting because they were considered transients from Somalia. Predictably, this decision, and consequently the election results, became controversial and resulted in riots by the nationalist Issa *Parti Mouvement Populaire*. Order was restored by 7,000 Garde Mobile troops from France. Although quiet for the time being, the Issa independence movement provides a potential for future internal conflict related to a confrontation between Ethiopia and Somalia.

The Territory's economy, development, and defense are subsidized by France at the rate of about $30 million yearly. Summarized below are the military elements of the French armed forces stationed in the Territory.

ARMY

Personnel: 3,600

Organization and Equipment:
- 1 mixed regiment
- 1 infantry regiment (Foreign Legion)
- 1 artillery regiment
- AMX-13 light tanks
- Ferret scout cars

NAVY

Personnel: 300
Equipment:
- 2 minesweepers
- some landing craft

AIR FORCE

Personnel: 500

Organization and Aircraft Types:
    1 squadron of A-1s
    1 transport squadron with Noratlas piston transports and H-34 and Alouette II helicopters

PARAMILITARY

There is a Gendarmerie of 500, headed by French Gendarmes, and including 400 locally recruited auxiliaries.

GABON
Republique Gabonaise

POWER POTENTIAL STATISTICS

Area: 103,100 square miles
Population: 500,000
Total Active Armed Forces: 1,350 (includes Gendarmerie; 0.27% population)
Gross National Product: $310 million ($620 per capita)
Annual Military Expenditures: $3 million (estimated; 0.96% GNP)
Fuel Production: Crude Oil: 6.3 million metric tons
    Refined Products: 927,000 metric tons
Electric Power Output: 98 million kwh
Civil Air Fleet: 15 piston transports

POLITICO-MILITARY POLICIES AND POSTURE

The President of this parliamentary democracy is both chief of state and Premier. Currently he is also Minister of National Defense, thus combining in one person the commander in chief and civilian administrator of the armed forces.

Upon independence from France in 1960, Gabon entered into a series of mutual defense and military assistance agreements with France relating to internal security, base rights, transit and overflight privileges, and military assistance. In February 1964 the internal security agreement was implemented when a military coup led by dissatisfied junior officers of the Army and Gendarmerie sought to depose the regime in power. A reinforced French regiment was flown in, with fighter support from bases in Dakar and Brazzaville, crushed the revolt, and restored the government.

Gabon is rich in raw materials: timber, petroleum, iron, manganese, and uranium. This, together with foreign technical assistance and investment, and relative stability, has permitted one of the highest per capita incomes in Africa. France's nuclear program is largely dependent upon uranium from Gabon.

In 1972 Gabon seized two tiny offshore islands claimed by Equatorial Guinea, as part of Gabonese efforts to extend the country's territorial waters to 100 miles; oil deposits are suspected in the disputed area. Equatorial Guinea charged invasion, and both sides appealed to the UN. The matter was peacefully settled and Gabon withdrew, but the potential for conflict remains.

Gabon is a member of the UN, OAU, OCAM, the Equatorial Defense Council, and the defense agreement of the African and Malagasy Union in 1961.

The Gabonese Army was formed in 1960 around a nucleus of French Army veterans. France has continued to supply arms and equipment and instructor-advisers. French military assistance costs about $800,000 annually. The Army numbers 600 and is organized as a two-company infantry battalion. Service is voluntary and for one year. The Navy has 100 men and a small patrol craft (YP) based at Libreville and Port Gentil. The Air Force of 50 operates one C-47 transport, three liaison aircraft, and four Alouette II helicopters. There are international airports at Libreville and Port Gentil. The Gendarmerie has a strength of about 600, including 60 French officers and NCOs. French forces in Gabon consist of 400 army personnel, including a paratroop company.

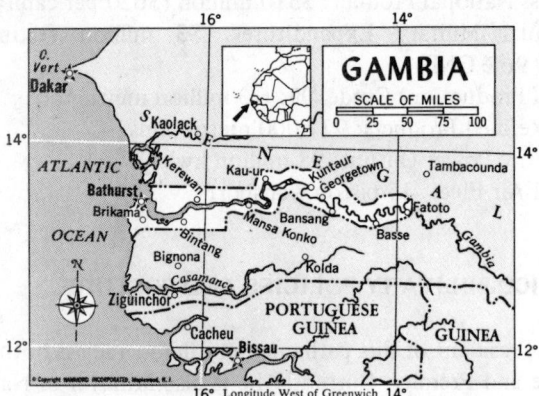

THE GAMBIA

POWER POTENTIAL STATISTICS

Area: 4,467 square miles
Population: 380,000
Total Active Armed Forces: 170 (Police Field Force; 0.04% population)
Gross National Product: $40.0 million ($105 per capita)
Electric Power Output: 7.4 million kwh

POLITICO-MILITARY POLICIES AND POSTURE

The Gambia was granted independence by Britain in 1965; in April 1970 it was proclaimed a republic within the Commonwealth with the president/prime minister as head of state. With no formal armed forces, there is no Defense Minister.

The Gambia, a 300-mile strip along both banks of the Gambia River, is bounded on all sides except the river mouth by Senegal. Because of this unusual geographical relationship, as well as tribal and religious (Moslem) affinities, very close ties are maintained with Senegal, including a mutual defense pact and joint economic development of the Gambia River Valley.

Because of its strategic position in the bulge of West Africa, its deep water port at Bathurst, and nearby Yendum airport, The Gambia was a port of call for Allied naval convoys during World War II and a US air stop for flights to the Middle East.

The Gambia is a member of the UN, the OAU, and the British Commonwealth of Nations. An agreement with Britain provides for police and paramilitary training, advisers, and equipment. The defense agreement with Senegal provides for a joint Defense Committee with a permanent Secretariat, and Senegalese assistance in training any Gambian military unit should it be required.

The Gambia has no armed forces as such. Within the 580-man British led and trained police force is a Field Force of 170 men and two British officers, which operates as a mobile military company.

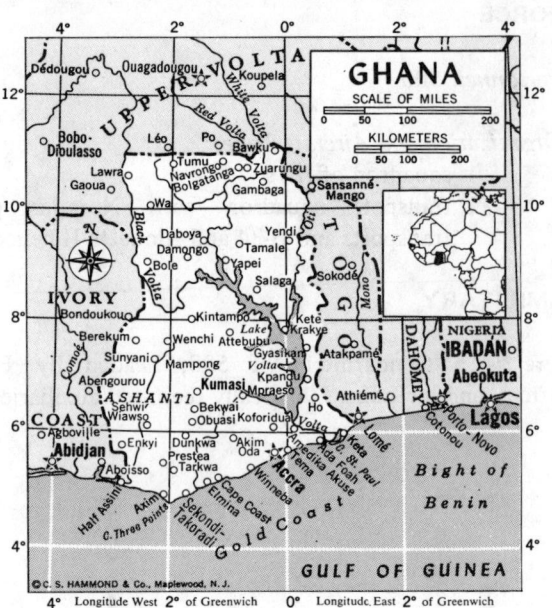

GHANA

Republic of Ghana

POWER POTENTIAL STATISTICS

Area: 92,100 square miles
Population: 9,900,000
Total Active Armed Forces: 18,600 (0.18% population)
Gross National Product: $2.62 billion ($290 per capita)
Annual Military Expenditures: $49 million (1.87% GNP)
Refined Petroleum Products: 1.0 million metric tons
Electric Power Output: 2.93 billion kwh
Merchant Fleet: 74 ships; 166,183 gross tons
Civil Air Fleet: 2 jets, 3 turboprop and 1 piston transports

POLITICO-MILITARY POLICIES AND POSTURE

After the ousting and exile of Ghana's dictatorial President Nkrumah in 1966 by a military coup, the country was ruled for three years by a seven-man National Liberation Council. Following promulgation of a new constitution, civilian rule was restored in September 1969 but was ended in January 1972 by a bloodless coup led by Colonel Ignatius Acheampong. The military junta withdrew the Constitution, dissolved Parliament, and established a National Redemption Council as the governing body. The new government has moved leftward, restoring relations with Guinea and increasing contacts with communist countries. A coup attempt was suppressed in July 1973.

The Ghanaian armed forces were formed upon independence in 1957 from the Gold Coast Regiment of Britain's Royal West African Frontier Force. Initially most of the officers and many NCOs were British. In 1961, however, these 200 seconded British officers and NCOs were dismissed by the Nkrumah government, and military assistance began to be accepted from other sources. However, a British Joint Services Training Team remained and Ghanaian cadets continued to be trained at Sandhurst.

Up until the 1966 coup, the Soviet Union had given an estimated $10 to $50 million in military aid including ground arms and ammunition, aircraft, training of cadets in Russia, and training of Nkrumah's Presidential Guard regiment. When the Presidential Guard resisted the February 1966 coup, eleven Russian instructor-advisers were reportedly killed.

Pilot training has been conducted in Ghana by Indians, Israelis, and Canadians and in Britain and Italy. US military assistance from 1950-1972 amounted to $235,000. In addition, 138 students have been trained in the US under the MAP. Pakistan has provided limited training assistance, arms have been purchased from New Zealand and Australia, and aircraft from the Soviet Union (only civil aircraft for Ghana Airways), Italy, and Canada. Yugoslavia assisted in the construction of a naval base.

Ghana possesses strategic mineral wealth which, with effective management, could ensure a viable economy and place it among the economic leaders of Africa. It exports over 450,000 tons of manganese ore and 270,000 tons of bauxite yearly. The 750,000 kw Volta hydroelectric power project, completed before Nkrumah's overthrow, has permitted an increased production of refined aluminum. Oil deposits have been discovered recently, and gold and industrial diamonds are mined in significant quantities. Nkrumah left the country with heavy foreign debts, most of which the new government has repudiated or declared a moratorium on. The loss of foreign credit, the government's nationalization of foreign assets, and extremely high prices for food are elements of a very serious economic situation.

Ghana is faced by substantial internal and external threats. Insurgency potential is inherent in tribal divisions and among some 1,500 government employees discharged since the 1966 coup. The main external threat comes from Guinea, which gave sanctuary to Nkrumah. However, even before his death in 1972, his host Sekou Toure had lost enthusiasm for the projected invasion and counter revolution.

Ghana is a member of the United Nations, the British Commonwealth of Nations, and the Organization of African Unity.

ARMY

Personnel: 16,500

Organization:
- 2 Brigade Groups (3 infantry battalions each with support troops of reconnaissance, artillery, engineers, transport)
- 1 paratroop battalion

Major Equipment Inventory:
- Saladin armored cars (British)
- Ferret scout cars (British)
- 76mm guns (USSR)
- infantry crew served and individual weapons (USSR and British)

Reserves: 500 Army Volunteer Force; 2 reconnaissance squadrons

NAVY

Personnel: 1,000

Major Units:
- 2 corvettes (PC)
- 1 coastal minesweeper (MSC)
- 2 inshore minesweepers (MSI)
- 2 seaward defense vessels (SC)
- 3 patrol boats (YP)
- 1 training ship
- 1 maintenance repair craft

Reserves: 200

AIR FORCE

Personnel: 1,100

Organization:
- 1 fighter-bomber squadron (MB-326B)
- 2 transport squadrons (Otter, Caribou, Heron)
- 1 communication/liaison squadron (Beaver, BN-2A)
- 1 helicopter squadron (S-58 Wessex, Hughes 269 Osage, Whirlwind)
- 1 training squadron (Bulldog)

Major Aircraft Types:
- 6 combat aircraft
  - 6 MB-326GB fighter-bombers
- 44 other aircraft
  - 19 transports (7 Otter, 8 Caribou, 3 Heron, 1 HS 125)
  - 19 communication/liaison (11 Beaver, 8 BN-2A)
  - 6 trainers (Bulldog)

Air Bases: Accra, Takoradi, Kumasi, Temale

GUINEA
Republique de Guinee

POWER POTENTIAL STATISTICS

Area: 94,925 square miles
Population: 4,200,000
Total Active Armed Forces: 8,450 (includes Republican Guards and Gendarmerie; 0.20% population)
Gross National Product: $417 million ($99 per capita)
Annual Military Expenditures: $17.8 million (4.26% GNP)
Merchant Fleet: 9 ships; 15,538 gross tons
Civil Air Fleet: 5 turbo prop, 3 piston transports

POLITICO-MILITARY POLICIES AND POSTURE

Since independence from France in 1958 President Sekou Toure has headed a strongly centralized one-party government. As chief of state he commands the armed forces through the Minister of the People's Army.

At the time of independence Guinea chose not to remain a member of the French Community; as a result all French interests were withdrawn and no French military assistance was provided. At that time some 22,000 Guineans were serving in the French armed forces. Of these 10,000 elected to remain with the French and 12,000 were demobilized. All French military equipment and stores were removed, leaving Guinea with no military force except an ill-equipped Gendarmerie. Guinea claims that its request to purchase 500 small arms from the US was turned down. Communist bloc assistance began in March 1959, and a year later a Soviet military mission arrived. Since March 1960 Soviet arms shipments are said to have exceeded $15 million. Upon the base of the French-trained Gendarmerie and French Army veterans selected for political reliability, an Army of 2,000 men was formed. Additional military aid has been received from Communist China and Cuba. In 1960 Guinea sent a battalion for six months with the UN Operation in the Congo.

Having rejected French ties, Guinea has supported the overthrow of the governments of those former French African colonies which do maintain close relationships with France: Ivory Coast, Upper Volta, Central African Republic, Cameroon, Dahomey, and Senegal. As one of the radical bloc of African states, Guinea has provided sanctuary and training for exile insurgent groups from some of these countries as well as from Ghana, Portuguese Guinea, and Angola. The Soviet Union, China, and Cuba have aided this effort with funds, training, and arms, while Guinea has reexported its surplus Soviet arms to insurgent groups active elsewhere in Africa. A Guinea-Sierra Leone mutual defense pact, negotiated in 1970, was invoked by the Sierra Leone government in March 1971, when its overthrow was threatened; Guinean troops responded, and about 200 are still stationed in Sierra Leone.

Guinea's mineral wealth assures a substantial future economic potential and considerable strategic importance, despite its current poor economic situation. Almost one-half of the world's known reserves of bauxite are in Guinea, and about 1.5 million metric tons a year are being exported. A 200 million-ton deposit of iron ore also exists and about 700,000 metric tons a year are exported. Gold and diamonds are mined in significant quantities, and oil has been discovered.

Guinea's strategic position in the bulge of West Africa led the Soviet Union to undertake a project to expand Conakry's airport to take the largest jets. But Guinea denied the Soviet request for permission to use the field for flights to Cuba during the October 1962 missile crisis. The denial was probably as much due to the December 1961 dismissal of the Soviet ambassador for subversive activities as it was to Guinea's declared nonalignment. Soviet arms aid ceased during this period. However, there was a rapprochement in 1965, and Soviet aircraft, torpedo boats, and fishing trawlers have since been received. During the period of Guinea's coolness toward the Soviet Union, West Germany instituted a $2.5 million military aid program for the training and equipping of three engineer companies and for building military roads and communications.

Due to economic stagnation and tensions arising from President Toure's one-man rule, there is a substantial potential for insurgency. Perhaps as many as 1,000,000 Guineans have moved to neighboring countries, mostly in search of jobs. Opposition parties have been established by these expatriates in Paris, Dakar, Freetown, and Abidjan. In the Ivory Coast, 5,000 have formed the Guinean National Liberation Front and are cooperating with Guinean expatriates elsewhere. The Army and police are said to be dissatisfied with alleged government mismanagement; there is also a coup potential within radical elements of Toure's *Parti democratique de Guinee*. These are members of the Cuban-trained and Chinese-armed People's Party Militia, who believe that Toure's nonalignment betrays the revolution. On November 22, 1970, an anti-Toure force of about 300 men landed from four ships and attacked Conakry, capital of Guinea. After three days of fighting the invaders and their local supporters were defeated. Guinea accused Portugal of sponsoring and manning the invasion. Portugal denied these charges. A UN Security Council mission, after investigating Toure's charges, accused Portugal of being actively involved in the attempt to overthrow Toure.

From 1950 through 1972 the United States provided $902,000 in military assistance and excess defense materials, and trained four students in the US.

Guinea's Army of 5,000 is organized into five infantry battalions supported by an armored battalion, an artillery battalion, and three engineer companies. Military service is compulsory for two years, although not all eligible men are called up. Equipment includes Soviet T-34 tanks, a few BTR-152 armored personnel carriers, 100mm antitank guns, 122mm howitzers, and 14.5mm ZPU-1 antiaircraft machineguns. The Army, however, has been diverted largely to civic action type tasks, major diversions which must adversely affect combat efficiency. Reserves number about 15,000.

The main combat units of the 150-man Navy are six Soviet P-6 torpedo boats (PT) received in 1967. There are also two small patrol craft (YP) for port and river security and two landing craft (LCVP). Ports are Conakry and Kakande.

The Guinean Air Force numbers about 800 men. Some Soviet transports, Il-14, Il-18, and An-14 have been received. There are also eight MiG-17 fighters and Soviet Yak-18 piston primary trainers and L-29 and MiG-15 jet trainers.

There is a 900-man Gendarmerie. The People's Militia, some 5,000 men from the Party youth organization, was formed in 1966 officially to shield Guinea against invasion, but generally assumed to be a counterforce against the possibility of an Army coup. Units are assigned to the main population centers and have actually taken over internal security tasks from the Army. Republican Guards number 1,600 men.

Guinea is a member of the United Nations and the Organization of African Unity.

IVORY COAST

Republique de Cote d'Ivoire

POWER POTENTIAL STATISTICS

Area: 124,503 square miles
Population: 4,637,500
Total Active Armed Forces: 6,400 (includes Gendarmerie; 0.13% population)
Gross National Product: $1.82 billion ($392 per capita)
Annual Military Expenditures: $28.8 million (1.58% GNP)
Merchant Fleet: 36 ships; 82,316 gross tons
Civil Air Fleet: 8 jet and 1 piston transports

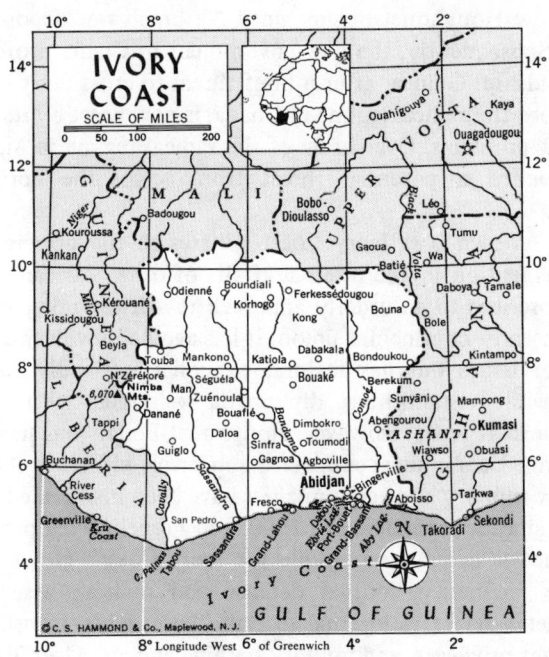

POLITICO-MILITARY POLICIES AND POSTURE

The elected President is head of government, as well as chief of state; he is commander in chief of the armed forces and is currently also Minister of Defense. President Houphouet-Boigny, one of Africa's most distinguished statesmen, is assisted in military and paramilitary matters by a Minister of the Armed Forces. Youth and Civic Service. There is constitutional separation of powers between the elected Executive, the National Assembly, and the Judiciary.

The country is committed to a paramilitary civic action effort in support of nationbuilding. The *Service Civique* and a youth organization promote literacy, modern agricultural methods, basic technical skills, health and sanitation, and social services. The armed forces, however, have not been performing a civic action role. Military service is compulsory but selective, six months in the Army or two years in the *Service Civique*.

Ivory Coast has enjoyed relative internal stability since its independence in 1960. Several cabinet ministers and Army officers were arrested in 1963 for plotting against the government, but there have been no overt rebellious acts. President Houphouet-Boigny is a member of the Baoule tribe, largest in the country, and other tribes fear its domination. Should the President die in office, transfer of power is likely to be contested. Another potential source of trouble is the fact that about one-quarter of the population are recent immigrants from neighboring states, attracted by the burgeoning economy.

There appears to be no significant external threat. The radical leaders of Ghana and Guinea were evidently plotting to overthrow Houphouet-Boigny until Nkrumah was deposed in 1966. Subsequently, the new government in Ghana professed its friendship. Guinea, after a brief threat to cross Ivory Coast to restore the radical regime in Ghana, is now beset by its own internal problems. Overthrow of the radical regime in Mali in 1968 ended a potential threat from across the northern border.

For its own part Ivory Coast adheres to the principle of nonintervention in the internal affairs of other African states and subscribes to an orderly approach to African unity rather than an early continental union. It has avoided involvement in cold-war issues but has maintained policies friendly to the West while establishing diplomatic relations with some communist regimes. However, Houphouet-Boigny has strongly condemned communist-supported subversive efforts in Africa.

Close military and economic ties have been maintained with France since independence in 1960, and French developmental assistance is largely responsible for Ivory Coast's growth and relative prosperity. Mutual defense and military assistance agreements relate to internal security, base rights, transit and overflight privileges, and military training and aid. Over 30,000 Frenchmen are in Ivory Coast in business and in advisory posts. Of these, 140 French military men are on training assignments with the armed forces, 400 are on civic action projects, and 350 guard the principal airport at Abidjan. In September 1967 France and Ivory Coast held joint amphibious exercises. French armed forces in Ivory Coast number 600 organized in a regimental combat group. An armored car squadron from the group is on detachment in Niger.

The United States provided $60,000 in military aid through 1972. Israel has had a training mission in Ivory Coast since 1963 with the *Service Civique*, and with a women's army unit.

Ivory Coast is a member of the UN and OAU, and was instrumental in furthering the discussions that led to forming the OCAM in 1965. It is a member of the *Conseil de l'Entente* with Niger, Upper Volta, Dahomey, and Togo, and in 1961 entered into a mutual defense pact with Niger and France. In 1966 it entered into an agreement of mutual friendship and defense with the new government of Ghana.

The Army numbers 4,000 and is organized into three infantry battalions, one armored squadron, one reconnaissance squadron, one paratroop company, two artillery batteries with 105mm howitzers and 40mm AA guns, and one engineer company. Reserves number from 12,000 to 15,000 men. Equipment is French and includes five AMX-13 light tanks, armored cars, and infantry heavy weapons. The 100-man Navy operates two small landing craft (LCVP) and three patrol boats (PGM) of 75-235 tons. The largest is armed with eight SS-12 missiles. Seaports are Abidjan, Sassandra, Tabou, and a new port in the southwest, San Pedro. The 300-man Air Force operates seven light transports (four Broussard, one C-45, one Falcon, one Aero Commander), three C-47 transports, five helicopters (four Alouette II and one Puma), and some trainers. Principal airfields are at Port Bouet (Abidjan), Bouake, Man Daloa, Sassandra, Korhogo, Tabou, and Odienne.

The Gendarmerie is 2,000 strong. The *Service Civique* and the youth organization receive military training, but their strengths and the extent to which they are armed are not known. There is reputed to be an armed militia of loyal Party militants created for the purpose of ensuring an orderly transfer of power within the Party in the event of the President's death. Its strength is not known.

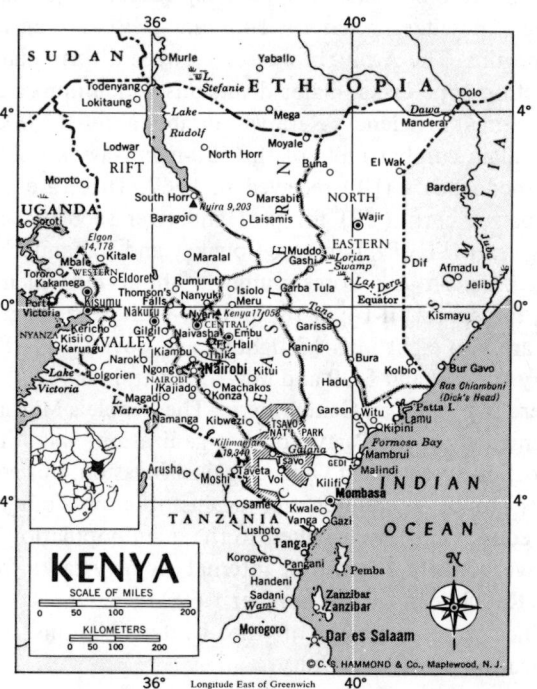

KENYA

POWER POTENTIAL STATISTICS

Area: 224,960 square miles
Population: 12,400,000
Total Active Armed Forces: 9,020 (including internal security forces; 0.07% population)
Gross National Product: $2.0 billion ($161 per capita)
Annual Military Expenditures: $27.5 million (1.37% GNP)
Refined Petroleum Products: 2.5 million metric tons
Electric Power Output: 556 million kwh
Merchant Fleet: 23 ships; 21,857 gross tons
Civil Air Fleet: 4 jet, 8 turboprop, 37 piston transports

POLITICO-MILITARY POLICIES AND POSTURE

The President is commander in chief of the armed forces, which he controls through the Minister of Defence. The armed forces are integrated under the Commander of the Army, who is also Commander, Kenya Military Forces. He reports directly to the Minister of Defence without intermediate joint staff organization.

The Kenyan Army grew out of three battalions of the former King's African Rifles, at the time of independence in 1963. Africanization of the Army proceeded much faster in Kenya than in neighboring Tanganyika and Uganda. However, British officers still held top command positions in January 1964, when a strike or mutiny occurred at the headquarters of the 11th Battalion of the Kenya Rifles near Nakuru in protest against continued British presence and also against inadequate pay. At the request of President Jomo Kenyatta, British forces intervened to suppress the outbreak. Kenyatta disciplined the mutineers with long prison sentences, and intensified on-going efforts to develop a modern force with professional, non-political elan.

Kenya relies on a voluntary recruitment program for its armed forces; because of ample manpower it is able to be rigidly selective. The Kenyan Army enjoys a standard of health and education considerably higher than that existing in the country as a whole. Service is for nine years.

The foremost defense problem facing Kenya today is that posed by separatist elements among some 300,000 Somali peoples who are presently living in the northeastern section of Kenya. Since independence Kenya has been concerned about Somali ambitions to establish a Greater Somalia embracing parts of Kenya and Ethiopia. Kenya's 1963 defense treaty with Ethiopia stems from this fear. (On June 9, 1970, the border with Ethiopia was delineated and accepted by both countries.) A State of Emergency was proclaimed in the area in 1963, and until 1968 there was almost constant irregular conflict on the Kenya-Somali frontier. The recent establishment of better relations between Kenya and Somalia has decreased the danger of war; however, many Somali insurgents (known as *shiftas*) are operating without the sponsorship of the Somalia government, and remain a threat to Kenya's internal security.

There is some potential for insurgency. It is contained, however, by the large and professional Kenya Police. Tribal unrest has increased since the 1969 assassination of one of Kenya's leading statesmen, Tom Mboya, by a member of the majority Kikuyu tribe. Nevertheless, the 1969 election was quiet. In June 1971, a small group of alleged conspirators was sentenced to imprisonment for attempting to overthrow the government. The Chief of the Defence Staff was dismissed for having been implicated in the conspiracy.

Upon independence the Kenyan Army, already equipped by Britain, was given $9.8 million in additional arms and equipment plus another $23.8 million in military assets, mainly installations. To establish a Navy with patrol craft, Britain has provided a base at Mombasa, training, and $3.64 million in equipment. Over 300 British military men continue on duty with the Kenyan armed forces in a training role. Kenyans receive training in Britain. Joint training exercises of British and Kenyan units are held annually in Kenya. By a 1964 agreement Britain granted Kenya $140 million in development and military aid.

In addition to British assistance, Kenya has received aircraft from Canada, and Kenyans have been trained in Bulgaria, Ethiopia, and Israel. In 1964 some members of KANU, the majority party, were reported to have received military training in Eastern European Communist countries and others to have had guerrilla training in Communist China.

Kenya is a member of the UN, the British Commonwealth, the OAU, and the East African Community. A 1964 agreement with Britain permits the British Army to train in Kenya and the RAF and RN to use Kenyan bases.

The Army of 6,300 is organized as four infantry battalions, one parachute company, a support battalion, and one armored reconnaissance platoon. Equipment includes Saladin armored cars and Ferret scout cars; 81mm and 120mm mortars and 120 recoilless rifles. There is a Navy of 300 men operating three patrol boats (PGM). The Air Force of 620 men has six BAC 167 Strikemaster light jet attack aircraft, two C-47, seven Beaver and six Caribou transports, five Bulldog trainers and five Bell 47 helicopters. Major air bases are at Eastleigh (Nairobi), Nanyuki, Embakasi, Nyeri, Mombasa, and Kisumu.

The 11,500-man police force is the largest and best equipped in East Africa. Approximately half perform internal security functions; the force is well trained in riot control and includes an air unit and constabulary-type General Service Units (1,800 men).

LESOTHO

Kingdom of Lesotho

POWER POTENTIAL STATISTICS

Area: 11,719 square miles
Population: 1,100,000
Total Active Police Forces: 900 (0.08% population)
Gross National Product: $80 million ($73 per capita)
Annual Police Expenditures: c. $1.2 million (1.5% GNP)
Civil Air Fleet: 6 piston transport

POLITICO-MILITARY POLICIES AND POSTURE

Lesotho, the former British protectorate of Basutoland, became independent in 1966. The Paramount Chief, or King, is constitutional monarch; the Prime Minister is leader of the majority in the National Assembly and thus head of the

has generally been unfruitful, although some diamonds are mined and exploration continues for oil and additional diamond deposits. The only other prospect for earning additional foreign exchange is the Malibamatso (formerly Oxbow) hydroelectric project. It would generate 250 million kwh of power annually, which, along with badly needed water, could be sold in South Africa. Relations between South Africa and Lesotho are currently so cool, however, that no price for the water can be agreed upon, or even discussed; World Bank financing is in abeyance until this problem can be settled.

Government. A power struggle between these two shortly after independence revealed basic factional and ideological divisions within the country. In January 1970, the Prime Minister, Chief Jonathan, suspended the constitution and announced a state of emergency, arresting the leaders of the opposition party and placing the King under house arrest. After a majority of the College of Chiefs refused to depose the King, the King was given permission to leave for the Netherlands. He returned after six months and took a new oath to abstain from involving the monarchy in politics. Chief Jonathan, in addition to being Prime Minister, holds the positions of Minister of Defense, Internal Security, and Internal Affairs. Despite membership in the UN, the British Commonwealth, and the OAU, the nation's external security is completely dependent on friendly relations with South Africa, by which it is totally surrounded.

Both the UN and Britain have warned South Africa not to attempt to annex Lesotho. Nevertheless, Lesotho could be effectively and easily blockaded by South Africa and could offer little assistance to punitive measures directed against any insurgent movements based there. Accordingly, as early as 1965, before independence, attempts to use Lesotho as an insurgent base were broken up by the Government, and political refugees from South Africa were expelled. Despite Lesotho's open criticism of *apartheid* its policy of cooperation with South Africa was continued with little prospect for change.

Lesotho is also dependent on South Africa economically: as a source for all imports, as a market for its exports of livestock and animal products, and as employer for 200,000 workers who send home $3 million annually. Lesotho originally received one-half its annual budget, which totalled about $15 million in 1972-73, from Britain, but recent revenue increases, largely from Lesotho's share in the South Africa Customs Union pool, have made possible a balanced budget. Britain still contributes capital development funds. Mineral exploration

LIBERIA

Republic of Liberia

POWER POTENTIAL STATISTICS

Area: 43,000 square miles
Population: 1,650,000
Total Active Armed Forces: 4,200 (0.25% population)
Gross National Product: $460 million ($279 per capita)
Annual Military Expenditures: $3.1 million (0.67% GNP)
Refined Petroleum Products: 530,000 metric tons
Electric Power Output: 502 million kwh
Merchant Fleet: 2,234 ships; 44.44 million gross tons (most of these are foreign owned and registered under the Liberian flag as a convenience)
Civil Air Fleet: 2 piston transports

POLITICO-MILITARY POLICIES AND POSTURE

Governmental structure is patterned on that of the United States, the President being commander in chief of the armed forces. Control is exercised through a Minister of National

Defense who directs the Chief of Staff of the Army and the Coast Guard Commander.

Government power is centralized. President William Richard Talbert took office in June 1971 following the death of W.V.S. Tubman, who had been president for 25 years. The Honorables, some 25,000 to 50,000 descendants of Afro-American colonizers from the United States, allegedly dominate political and economic affairs, at the expense of the interior tribes. This provides a potential for instability. Alleged governmental corruption, indebtedness, and lack of economic development despite rich iron and rubber resources, are further causes of unrest.

Liberia's strategic position in the bulge of West Africa resulted in an agreement on March 31, 1942, giving the United States the right to construct, control, operate, and defend airports in Liberia for the duration of the war. Under this agreement, Robertsfield near Monrovia was developed as a link in an air route from the US to the Middle East by way of Brazil.

The US Military Aid Program from 1950 through 1971 has given Liberia $7.9 million in arms and equipment; a small Military Assistance and Advisory Group helps with the training of the Liberian forces. From 1950 through 1972 485 Liberian military students were trained in the United States under MAP. An agreement signed in 1959 provides for consultation if either Liberia or the United States is attacked or threatened.

Liberia is a member of the UN and OAU and has taken the initiative in encouraging pan-African cooperation. Liberia provided a small battalion to the UN Operation in the Congo from mid-1960 to mid-1963. In 1968 Liberia contributed funds to the Liberation Committee of the OAU for support of militant nationalists in Southern Africa and the Portuguese territories.

The army, known as the National Guard, is 4,000 strong, organized into three infantry battalions, one engineer battalion, and a heavy weapons support company. Equipment includes a few armored cars and light artillery pieces and two trainer and two transport aircraft. The naval force is the Coast Guard with 200 men operating one patrol gunboat (PGM), two patrol craft (YP), the Presidential yacht, and some landing craft. Principal ports are Monrovia and Buchanan. There is no air force, but the airports of Robertsfield and Spriggs Payne are near Monrovia.

The armed forces are maintained by voluntary enlistment. However, a law rendering male citizens liable for military service between the ages of 16 and 45 years is used to maintain the Militia. This paramilitary force, perhaps 20,000 strong, is organized in two divisions, each with two brigades of four regiments. It is lightly armed and used mainly for security in the interior and in border areas.

LIBYA

Al Jumhuriyah al Libiyya al Arabiyah
Libyan Arab Republic

POWER POTENTIAL STATISTICS

Area: 679,536 square miles
Population: 2,110,000
Total Active Armed Forces: 24,000 (1.1% population)
Gross National Product: $4.3 billion ($2,037 per capita)
Annual Military Expenditures: $140 million (3.25% GNP)
Fuel Production: Crude Oil: 107.6 million metric tons
  Refined Products: 435,700 metric tons
Electric Power Output: 456 million kwh
Merchant Fleet: 13 ships; 5,932 gross tons
Civil Air Fleet: 7 jet, 5 turboprop and 10 piston transports

DEFENSE STRUCTURE

The constitutional monarchy was overthrown September 1, 1969, by a "Captain's coup" which deposed the king and established a Revolutionary Command Council (RCC) as the sole holder of power. A republican constitution decreed in December set up a cabinet in which the coup leader, Captain (self-promoted to Colonel) al Kadhafi, President of the RCC, is both Prime Minister and Defense Minister, and thus commander in chief of the armed forces. There is no provision for a representative assembly, elected or otherwise; hence military budgets are by decree.

POLITICO-MILITARY POLICIES

The coup signaled an immediate change in the former kingdom's relatively moderate stance within the Arab League. The RCC lost no time in announcing that it was in full support of Egyptian President Nasser's anti-Israel policies and that it planned to achieve a socialist society.

Kadhafi has become something of a leader in inter-Arab affairs, pushing for the use of oil to exert stronger pressure on the United States and other Western powers to stop support of Israel. With promises of economic aid he has also persuaded five black African states (Uganda, Niger, Chad, Mali, and Burundi) to break diplomatic relations with Israel. Kadhafi's long-term potential for Arab and African leadership has been diminished, however, by his growing reputation for unpredictable and sometimes imprudent statements and action.

Kadhafi's position within Libya also appears to have deteriorated. In spring 1974 the Revolutionary Command Council relieved him of "political, administrative, and traditional" duties, leaving him as commander-in-chief of the armed forces and ostensibly giving him additional time for

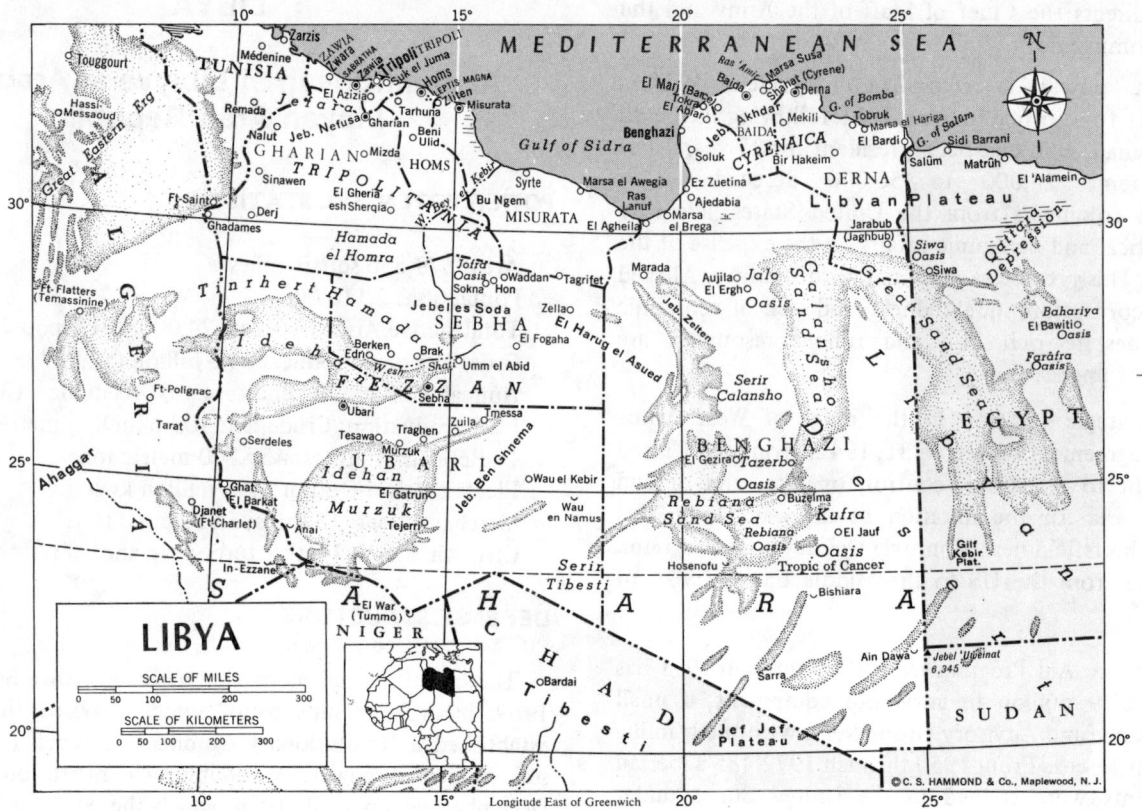

"ideological and mass reorganization" work. Premier Abdel Salaam Jallud, who took over Kadhafi's relinquished duties, has a reputation for pragmatism and a relatively good relationship with President Sadat of Egypt. The full significance of the shift is not yet known.

As early as September 17, 1969, Libya began to cut former economic and military aid ties with the US and UK. By mid-December an agreement was made with the British for return to Libyan control by March 30, 1970, of their bases at Tobruk and al Adem, and the withdrawal of the training mission at Benghazi. At Wheelus AFB (US) near Tripoli, training of Libyan personnel had ceased in September, and in December agreement was reached that the base be turned over by June 30, 1970. Also in December was announced the cancellation of a contract for furnishing, installing, and training operators for a complete British surface-to-air missile system, with radar and all ancillary elements, at a reported cost of over $420 million.

In late 1969 Libya turned to France and the Soviet Union for military assistance. France agreed to sell 110 Mirage 5 aircraft with Mach-2 speed; by the end of 1973 about 80 of these had been delivered. (The contract is said to include the sale of certain electronic equipment and an unannounced number of tanks.) Arms shipment from the USSR began in July 1970.

Libya's strategic importance is principally due to its oil resources. Since 1959, when the first wells were brought in, it has climbed to fourth place in the Mediterranean-Middle East area, after Iran, Saudi Arabia and Kuwait, and has exceeded each of them as a supplier to West Europe. Far-reaching concessions were obtained from foreign companies exploiting Libyan oil resources when these companies were threatened by the RCC, in March 1971, with the prospect of nationalization.

British Petroleum's Libyan operations were nationalized in December 1971, and in May 1973 Kadhafi demanded 100% control of the three largest oil operations in Libya, all of them largely American owned. The following month he nationalized outright a smaller American-owned operation.

Kadhafi has pushed hard for a Federation of Arab Republics, made up of Egypt, Syria, and Libya. According to plans that all three countries had agreed to, the Federation would be governed by a Presidential Council composed of the three presidents, and would have a joint military command. In referendums held in September 1971 the citizens of all three countries voted to form the Federation. It has never been formed, however, and the idea is now dormant and possibly moribund, as a result of Sadat's growing distrust of Kadhafi, mutual animosities between Libyans and Egyptians, and a general feeling among governmental leaders in the countries involved that the plans make radical changes too fast.

A much more quickly aborted merger that would have joined Libya and Tunisia was announced in January 1974; the announcement was followed in a few days by the dismissal of the Tunisian foreign minister who had helped push the merger. Earlier Tunisian acquiescence in Kadhafi's merger plans had apparently been achieved only because of Tunisian President Bourguiba's failing mental and physical strength.

There have been two opportunities for the RCC to show its stability against counter-subversion. The Council reported in December 1969 that it had suppressed an attempted counter-coup led by its Defense and Interior Ministers. A cabinet shake-up resulted in Colonel al Kadhafi taking the portfolio of Defense and his deputy taking that of Interior. In June 1970 the government announced that it had crushed a new plot headed by the nephew of the ousted King Idris.

MILITARY ASSISTANCE

The reversal of military policy noted above has stopped all military aid from the United States and Britain. Libya had received, from 1950 through 1972 $16.2 million from the United States. In addition 470 Libyan military students had been trained under the MAP, 429 of them in the US. Pilots and naval cadets are trained in Greece.

The purchase of French aircraft entails provisions for French instruction of pilots and mechanics. The Libyan dearth of pilots and technically trained manpower, combined with the three-year stretch-out of plane delivery, will postpone the realization of a modern air force for the immediate future. France states that the contract precludes the transfer of planes to a third party. The conditions of Soviet aid are unclear.

ALLIANCES

Libya is a member of the UN, the Arab League, the OAU, the Maghreb, and the OPEC.

ARMY

Personnel: 20,000

Organization:
- 4 armored battalions (British-equipped)
- 5 infantry battalions (British-equipped)
- 3 artillery battalions (US-equipped)
- 2 AA battalions

Major Equipment Inventory:
- 6 Centurion medium tanks
- 115 T-54/55 and 15 T-34 medium tanks
- 40 armored cars (Saladin) and scout cars (Ferret and Shorland)
- 150 APCs (Saracen, BTR-60, M-113)
- 150 105mm and 155mm howitzers, 122mm guns
- 100 antitank missiles (Vigilant and Swingfire)
- 12 helicopters (AB206, Bell 47G, Alouette)
- 40mm AA guns (Bofors)

NAVY

Personnel: 2,000 (including Coast Guard)

Major Units:
- 1 fast frigate (DEG), 6 Seacat SAM
- 1 patrol gunboat (PGM)
- 2 inshore minesweepers (MSI)
- 3 fast patrol boats (PTF), 8 SS-12 SSM
- 8 patrol boats (YP)
- 2 auxiliaries

Naval Base: Tripoli; ports at Benghazi, Darnah, Tobruk and Burayqah

AIR FORCE

Personnel: 2,000

Organization:
- 1 fighter squadron (F-5)
- 2 fighter-bomber squadrons (Mirage)
- 1 transport squadron (C-47, C-130)

Major Aircraft Types:
- 88 combat aircraft
  - 80 Mirage
  - 8 F-5 fighters
- 62 other aircraft
  - 26 transports (9 C-47, 1 C-140, 16 C-130)
  - 15 jet trainers (3 T-33, 12 Magister)
  - 21 helicopters (9 Super Frelon, 7 Alouette II/III, 2 AB-206, 3 OH-13)

Missiles: SAMs (Thunderbird and Rapier)

Air Bases: Wheelus and Idris (Tripoli), Benina (Benghazi), El Adem, El Awai

Note: Total order for Mirage 5s is as follows: 58 single-seat ground attack, 32 single-seat fighter-bomber, 10 single-seat reconnaissance, and 10 two-seat trainers. Of these about 80 had been delivered by the end of 1973.

PARAMILITARY

A paramilitary force of elements loyal to the new regime has been organized. Its composition and strength are unclear.

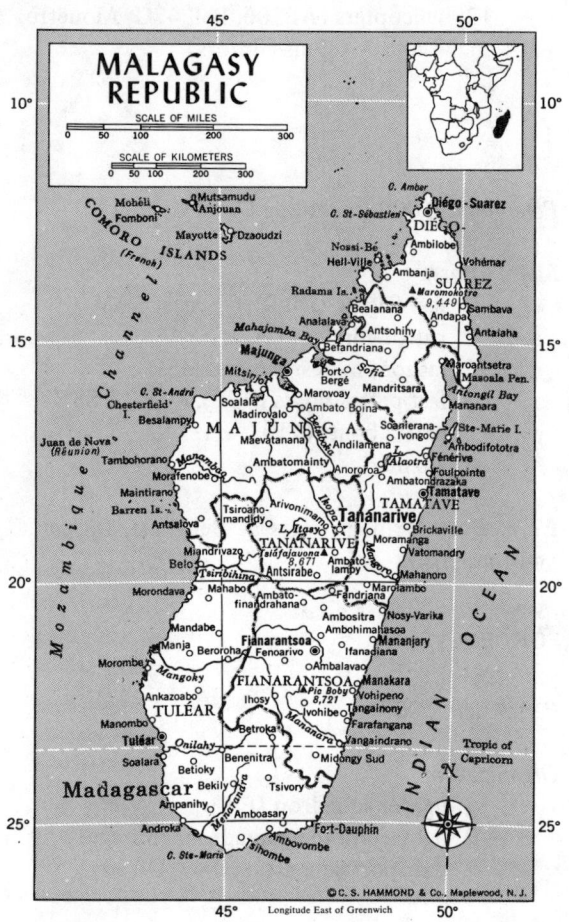

MALAGASY REPUBLIC
Republika Malagasy

POWER POTENTIAL STATISTICS

Area: 228,000 square miles
Population: 7,500,000
Total Active Armed Forces: 8,700 (includes Gendarmerie; 0.11% population)
Gross National Product: $1 billion ($133 per capita)
Annual Military Expenditures: $13.8 million (1.38% GNP)
Refined Petroleum Products: 601,700 metric tons
Electric Power Output: 152 million kwh
Merchant Fleet: 48 ships; 52,162 gross tons
Civil Air Fleet: 3 jet, 6 turboprop, 16 piston transports

POLITICO-MILITARY POLICIES AND POSTURE

In May 1972, student protests triggered extensive rioting and arrests that led to a transfer of power to General Philibert Ramanantsoa, Army Chief of Staff. A referendum in October gave Ramanantsoa full control of the country, with military rule to be maintained for five years.

Upon independence in 1960 the Malagasy Republic concluded mutual defense and military assistance agreements with France which provided for aid in maintaining internal security, for base right, transit and overflight privileges, and military training and aid. Under the agreements France retained the headquarters of Overseas Zone 3 (Indian Ocean) and a garrison of about 2,500 men at the Diego-Suarez naval base, plus detachments at Ivato and Antsirabe. The Malagasy Republic signed an agreement with France in June 1973 under which all 4,000 French troops remaining in the country would be phased out. All ground troops were to have left by September 1973, and the naval base was to be closed in two years. French military assistance has amounted to about $12.5 million annually, but the future of this assistance is uncertain. West Germany has also provided military assistance including 30 light military vehicles and the training of seamen in Germany. Israel has trained 500 security police and provided their weapons. The United States has furnished about $200,000 worth of equipment for the Gendarmerie and police.

Before the 1972 coup the policies of the Malagasy Republic were generally pro-West. The new government has been more strongly anticolonial and independent, breaking several ties with France, and also breaking diplomatic relations with South Africa. The Malagasy Republic is a member of the UN and the OAU, but although it lies only 250 miles off the southeast African coast, its population is mainly of Malay descent, and its interest in African affairs has been slight. It withdrew from OCAM in 1973. It also withdrew from the franc zone, issuing its own currency.

There is internal friction between the Protestant highland peoples of Malay stock and the Catholic coastal peoples of mixed Malay, African, and Arab background. The government is endeavoring to unify these divergent groups. A more serious potential danger to internal stability lies in tensions resulting from the slow economic growth rate coupled with a high birth rate.

All male citizens are subject to 18-month conscription either for military or for civic service. The Army is 4,000 strong and organized into two mixed regiments (each consists of four infantry companies), one paratroop company, one reconnaissance squadron, one engineer unit, one artillery battery, and headquarters and support units. The Navy of about 200 men operates one 250-ton patrol vessel (PGM), one training ship, one tender, and one company of Marines. The Major naval base is Diego-Suarez with ports at Tamatave, Majunga, Tulear, Nossi-Be, Fort Dauphin, and Manakara. The Air Arm has 400 men and operates three C-47, three Flamant, and seven Broussard transports, five helicopters (Bell 47 and Alouette II/III) and some trainers. Main air bases are Arivoniamamo (Tananarive), Ivato (Tananarive), Diego-Suarez, Fort Dauphin, Tamatave, Majunga, and Tulear. There is a Gendarmerie numbering 4,100 men.

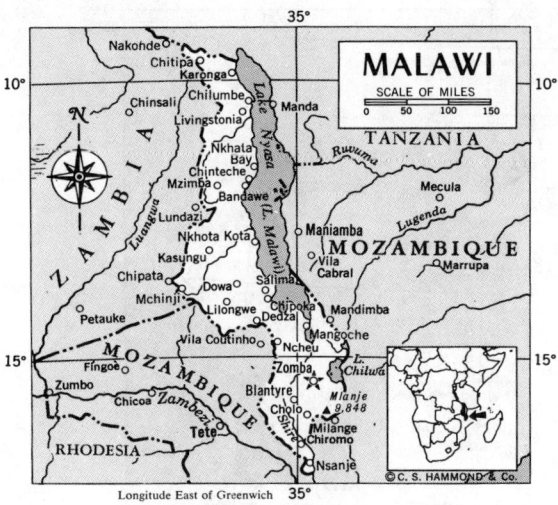

MALAWI

POWER POTENTIAL STATISTICS

Area: 45,747 square miles
Population: 4,800,000
Total Active Armed Forces: 1,200 (0.02% population)
Gross National Product: $330 million ($69 per capita)
Annual Military Expenditures: $1.5 million (0.45% GNP)
Electric Power Output: 144 million kwh
Civil Air Fleet: 1 jet, 4 turboprop, and 2 piston transports

POLITICO-MILITARY POLICIES AND POSTURE

Malawi, a member of the British Commonwealth, is a republic governed by a President who dominates a one-party parliament, and who is the commander in chief of the nation's armed force. Malawi's strategic problems are two-fold: maintaining internal and external security against dissidents at home and abroad, and preventing Malawi from becoming a base for liberation movements directed against white-dominated southern Africa.

Although nominally nonaligned, the government of President H. K. Banda has in recent years severed relations with Communist China, Egypt, and Ghana, and established relations with South Africa and Portugal. Although a member of the OAU, Malawi advocated realism in expectations of African unity, and restraint in achieving Pan-African aims. President Banda's official visit to South Africa in 1971 and President Fouche of South Africa's visit to Malawi in 1972 were the first official visits exchanged by South Africa and any independent black African state.

In 1964 several dissident ministers fled the country and fomented a liberation movement among the 20,000 Malawians working in Tanzania. This movement received support from Algeria, Egypt, Cuba, and Communist China, and was provided sanctuary and bases in Tanzania and Zambia. From these latter neighboring countries, raids against Malawi have been mounted periodically, but the rebels have gained little support from the population and have been quickly rounded up.

For export of its agricultural produce and import of essential goods, landlocked Malawi depends upon rail traffic from the port of Beira in Mozambique and road traffic from Rhodesia across a portion of Mozambique. South Africa has provided a loan to build an additional rail link to the line running to the port of Nacala in Mozambique. Communications by road exist with similarly landlocked Zambia and with Tanzania, but these are tenuous, longer, and do not have the capacity of the routes through Mozambique and Rhodesia. Some 200,000 Malawians work in Rhodesia and 80,000 in South Africa, remitting part of their wages to families at home. This represents a significant contribution to the national income which could be terminated at any time by the host countries.

Thus Malawi is mainly dependent economically on three white-dominated neighboring countries. This reality has shaped the policy of Malawi toward white Southern Africa. However, despite efforts of Malawian security forces, minor elements of Mozambique and Rhodesian liberation movements have made use of Malawi for sanctuary and infiltration.

Malawi's borders were determined by colonial fiat and do not match either ethnic divisions or old tribal boundaries. Based on ethnic realities and tribal history—and also probably as a counterirritant to Tanzania's and Zambia's support for Malawian dissidents—Dr. Banda has laid claim to three districts in Tanzania and to three districts in Zambia. However, no efforts appear to be in progress to force these claims.

Malawi was formerly dependent upon Britain for about 40 percent of its budget, but Britain and Malawi agreed in 1972 to terminate budgetary assistance. Some 50 British officers and NCOs are seconded to Malawi in both command and training posts, but they are being replaced as fast as Malawian officers become trained and qualified. The Army, some 1,200 strong, consists of the 1st Battalion Malawi Rifles, plus supporting services, three patrol craft (YP) on Lake Nyasa, and an air unit. The air unit operates two HS-748 Andover and two Britten-Norman BN-2 aircraft. Airfields are Blantyre-Limbe, Lilongwe, Mzimba, Mzuzu, and Karonga.

The Young Malawi Pioneers, a youth organization, is believed to have paramilitary functions and the League of Malawi Women augments the security services.

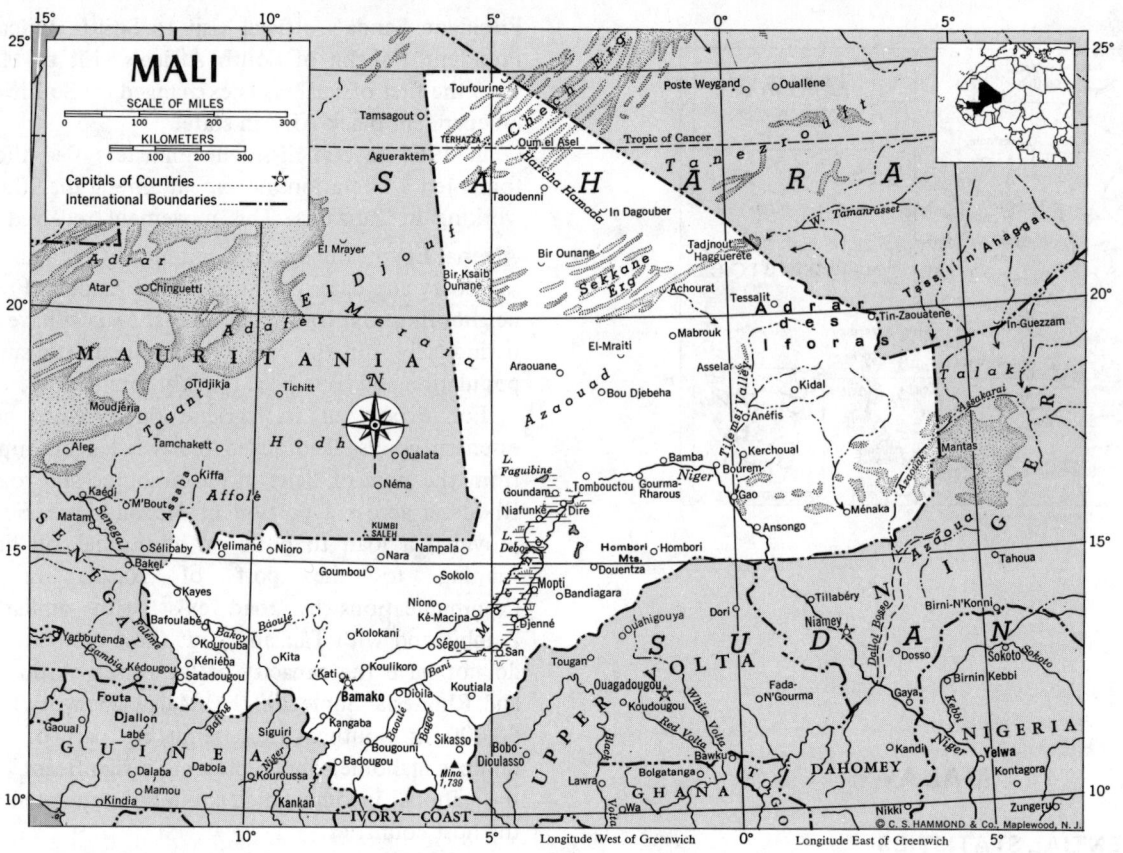

MALI
Republique du Mali

POWER POTENTIAL STATISTICS

Area: 478,652 square miles
Population: 5,500,000
Total Active Armed Forces: 5,140 (including Gendarmerie; 0.09% population)
Gross National Product: $333 million ($61 per capita)
Annual Military Expenditures: $5.0 million (1.5% GNP)
Civil Air Fleet: 1 jet, 2 turboprop, and 1 piston transports

POLITICO-MILITARY POLICIES AND POSTURE

In June 1960 the French colonies then known as the French Sudan and Senegal became independent as the Federation of Mali. Two months later Senegal withdrew from the Federation and the former French Sudan proclaimed itself the Republic of Mali on September 22, 1960. Under a leftist government Mali severed its ties with France and remained outside the French Community. Ruinous economic policies and the growing power and truculence of the Popular Militia, military arm of the President and the Party, led to a military coup d'etat by a group of young officers in November 1968.

The new National Military Committee, headed by a lieutenant, who became head of state and of the government, established a government of military officers and civilian notables. Orientation, while remaining leftist, is much less doctrinaire and more in the national self-interest than previously. Relations with the West have been improved, and nonalignment in international affairs is the stated national policy. In March 1971 an attempted coup failed, and the alleged leaders, including the first vice-president, were dismissed from the army and arrested.

Mali is a member of the UN and the OAU. It contributed a 575-man infantry battalion to the UN's Congo force for four months in 1960. The new regime has not rejoined the French Community or sought membership in the OCAM.

Between 1961 and 1971 Mali received over $20 million in military assistance from the Soviet Union. This included MiG-17 fighters, T-34 tanks, armored personnel carriers, artillery, military vehicles, small arms, training in the Soviet Union, and a Soviet military mission in Mali. Until the 1968 coup, Communist China armed and trained the Popular Militia. In 1964, the United States sent a military mission to Mali to train engineer units for civic action and in 1966 to train a paratroop company; about $2.9 million in American military assistance was provided from 1961 to 1972, and 73 military students have been trained under MAP.

Tribal divisions are not so serious in Mali as in many other African countries since about 60 percent of the population is from the Mande tribe. The Berber Tuaregs have traditionally opposed the central government authority and police action against them is occasionally necessary, but they comprise less than five percent of the population.

The Army has a strength of about 3,500 and is organized into three infantry battalions, one paratroop company, and service support units. Equipment is largely Soviet. There is a river patrol force of about 40 men operating three patrol craft (YP) on the Niger River. The Air Force has about 400 men and operates six MiG-17 jet fighters, two MiG-15 jet fighter-trainers, two C-47 transports, two Il-14 transports, two Broussard liaison aircraft, and two Mi-4 helicopters. Air bases are at Bamako and Gao with other fields at Mopti, Kayes, Nioro, Tombouctou, and Yelimane. There is a Gendarmerie of 1,200.

MAURITANIA

Republique Islamique de Mauritanie

POWER POTENTIAL STATISTICS

Area: 397,683 square miles
Population: 1,300,000
Total Active Armed Forces: 1,000 (0.08% population)
Gross National Product: $200 million ($154 per capita)
Annual Military Expenditures: $8 million (4% GNP)
Iron Ore Production: 8.6 million metric tons
Merchant Fleet: 4 ships; 1,681 gross tons
Civil Air Fleet: 1 turboprop, 4 piston transports

POLITICO-MILITARY POLICIES AND POSTURE

The President of the Republic commands the armed forces through an appointed Minister of Defense. The National Assembly passes upon the defense budget submitted by the Minister.

The Army was formed from Mauritanian-manned French Army units upon independence in November 1960. The following year mutual defense and military assistance agreements were signed with France which provided for help in maintaining internal security base rights, transit and overflight privileges, and military aid and training. All French troops were withdrawn by January 1966. French military aid has been received at the rate of about $1.2 million per year.

There are both external and internal threats to Mauritania's security. Morocco claims all of Mauritania on dubious historical grounds. In 1957, when it was announced that Mauritania would receive independence, an irregular force calling itself the Moroccan Army of Liberation was raised in Morocco—though disavowed by the Moroccan government. This group raided into Mauritania in an attempt to foment a popular uprising and unite the two countries. The incursion was quickly suppressed by French troops. Morocco has neither renounced its claim nor recognized Mauritania. Further, both countries claim Spanish Sahara, which is situated on the African coast between them. Should Spain withdraw (it has ceded its enclave of Ifni to Morocco) this could precipitate a crisis between Morocco and Mauritania. In the event of conflict, Mauritania's miniscule army would be no match for Morocco's much larger modern force.

Mauritania's eastern border with Mali was under dispute until largely settled in favor of the latter in 1968. However, this still vaguely defined border remains a potential source of irritation.

The most important of a number of relatively minor internal tensions is the ethnic division between the Arabic speaking Moorish-Arab-Berber majority (80 percent of the population) and the black minority. Proportionally more blacks than Arabs sought an education during the French regime, and these tend to get positions in government and business, where they can effectively oppose trends toward Arabic control of government administration.

Substantial natural resources provide most of Mauritania's foreign exchange earning. There are several iron ore deposits, and a large copper ore reserve has been discovered. The fishing industry has great potential and is being developed to a catch of 250,000 tons per year. Trawlers are built in France and smaller fishing craft are built locally.

Mauritania is a member of the UN and OAU. In 1965 it withdrew from the French-oriented OCAM and adopted a policy of nonalignment. In June 1973 the franc was replaced by the gold-backed ouquiya. To demonstrate its solidarity with the Arab world at the time of the June 1967 Arab-Israeli War, it broke diplomatic relations with the US; they were resumed in December 1969.

The Army numbers 900 men and is organized into a parachute-commando company, several mechanized reconnaissance squadrons, an artillery battery, and a camel corps. Equipment is French, including light artillery and EBR-75 armored cars. Military service is voluntary and is for two years. There is no navy as such but four small patrol craft (2 PGM, 2 YP) are operated at Port Etienne for port control and customs. The Air Force has a strength of about 100 and operates one C-47 transport, two Broussard utility aircraft, and six light trainers. Airfields are at Atar, Nouakchott, Port Etienne, Fort Gouraud, Fort Trinquet, Akjoujt, Kaedi, Rosso, Kiffa, and Aioun-el-atrous.

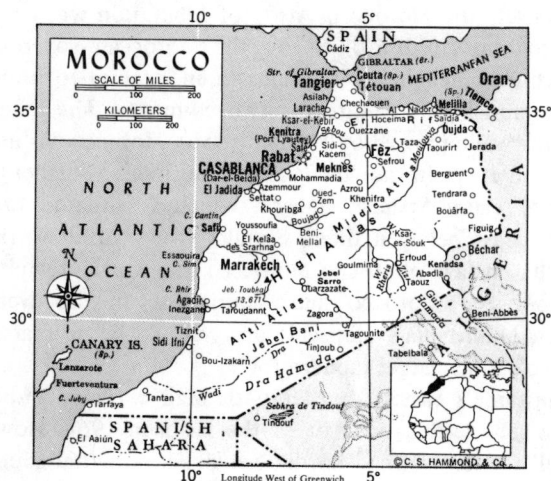

MOROCCO

Al-Mamlaka Al-Maghrebia
Kingdom of the West

POWER POTENTIAL STATISTICS

Area: 174,471 square miles
Population: 17,400,000
Total Active Armed Forces: 59,750 (includes security forces; 0.45% population)
Gross National Product: $4.2 billion ($241 per capita)
Annual Military Expenditures: $116.9 million (2.78% GNP)
Iron Ore Production: 388,000 metric tons
Fuel Production: Coal: 474,000 metric tons
  Crude Oil: 28,000 metric tons
  Refined Products: 1.98 million metric tons
Electric Power Output: 2.1 billion kwh
Merchant Fleet: 39 ships; 46,907 gross tons
Civil Air Fleet: 6 jet transports

DEFENSE STRUCTURE

In this constitutional monarchy the King rules as well as reigns. Despite such trappings of democracy as a bicameral legislature and a Prime Minister, the King dominates the government and has on occasion assumed the Premiership. He is Chief of the General Staff and Supreme Commander of the Royal Armed Forces (FAR). A general, appointed by the King, acts as Minister of National Defense and coordinates the armed forces, Gendarmerie, Royal Police Force, and the Auxiliary Force. Another general, Army Chief of Staff, acts as the King's Adjutant in his role as Chief of the General Staff. A Military Cabinet advises the King on defense matters. The King personally appoints trusted officers to key posts.

The nation is divided for defense into three military zones and one independent sector: Littoral Zone with headquarters at Casablanca, Central Zone with headquarters at Meknes, Independent Sector with headquarters at Marrakech, and the Saharan Zone controlled from the overall headquarters at Rabat. Upon independence in 1956 the Army was formed mainly from Moroccan veterans of the French and Spanish colonial armies, with the further addition of about 5,000 former guerrillas of the Moroccan Army of Liberation.

POLITICO-MILITARY POLICIES

Morocco has followed a policy on non-alignment in East-West relations and of moderation with regard to the burning issues of the Pan-Arab movement. These policies, as well as a dispute over mineral-rich portions of southwestern Algeria claimed by Morocco, together with the heavy arming of Algeria by the Soviet Union, have resulted in tensions between Morocco and Algeria. Morocco has suspected Algeria of aggressive intentions. With a stronger warlike tradition than Algeria, Morocco is confident of success in any campaign fought on near equal material terms, as demonstrated in the brief frontier war of October 1963. However, subsequent Soviet assistance to Algeria has given that nation a four-to-one advantage over Morocco, which has sought additional military aid from the US with a view to reducing Algeria's preponderance to a less overwhelming two-to-one. The stated objective has been a deterrent capability to defend effectively for a few days until the UN can act or friendly powers intervene. In January 1969 Algeria's President Boumedienne and Morocco's King Hassan II concluded a Treaty of Solidarity and Cooperation, apparently upon the initiative of the former. In May 1970, agreement was reached on demarcation of the disputed frontier. These conciliatory moves should dampen tensions between the two countries, although some basic issues remain.

Morocco's own irredentism is far from defensive. One of many ancient Moroccan empires included what is now southwestern Algeria, Spanish Sahara, Mauritania and parts of Mali. The King, both on this basis and in his role as hereditary religious leader of this region, lays claim to these territories for Morocco (although the agreement with Algeria apparently modifies these claims). It is likely that Morocco's moderate King would not continue to assert such claims were it not for pressures from the extreme rightist *Istiqlal* party.

The Army is 80 percent Berber in composition, but most officers are urban Arabs. The ranks were filled by volunteers until 1966 when a Royal decree prescribed conscription of all 18-year-olds for 18 months' service.

In July 1971 an abortive revolt led by a small group of dissident Army officers attempted to topple the King's government. Leading the attack on the King's summer palace were two of his most trusted officers. A total of nine of the country's fifteen generals died as a result of the revolt (including loyal and dissident officers killed during the revolt, and several executed later). An Army cleanup followed, with anti-royal elements purged from the officer corps. The King has promised to eliminate the cause of the uprising by attacking corruption and launching a program of social and economic reforms. In August 1972 another apparent plot against the monarchy, led by the Minister of Defense, was revealed after two Air Force jets fired on the King's plane. The plot was immediately suppressed.

Despite its relatively moderate stance toward Israel, Morocco contributed men and tanks for the 1973 war. Several contingents of Moroccan troops—perhaps 5,000 in all— and some tanks, were sent to Syria on Soviet ships in the spring and summer of 1973.

STRATEGIC PROBLEMS

As both an Atlantic and a Mediterranean power occupying one side of the strategic Straits of Gibraltar, Morocco's strategic situation is significant. Its Western orientation and its location on the fringe of Europe, yet behind a water barrier, led to the US-French agreement to establish four US Strategic Air Command advanced B-47 bomber bases in French Morocco in 1951. These were continued after independence, but abandoned in 1963 as a result of a change in Moroccan policy, and the phase-out of the B-47. Morocco's strategic location will unquestionably continue to attract the interest and attention of major powers.

The conservative monarchy is anathema to leftists and radical Arab elements; its economic problems, as well as the regime's moderate stand on Israel and other Arab issues, provide ample excuses for subversive attempts. Internal unrest is currently Morocco's most serious strategic problem.

In 1968 Spain ceded to Morocco the small enclave of Ifni. Morocco still claims barren, sparsely-populated Spanish Sahara. Profitable exploitation of fishery resources and possibly the world's largest phosphate deposit, may cause Spain to be more reluctant to part with this territory. Further, this Spanish colony is also claimed by Mauritania.

While Morocco recently has not pressed its traditional claims to Mauritania and parts of Mali, these have not been withdrawn and provoke a certain degree of nervousness on the part of these former portions of the ancient Moroccan empire. However, only in the event of extensive internal disintegration in these poverty-stricken countries is Morocco likely to attempt to make good these claims.

An incident with Spain occurred in January 1973 over Moroccan extension of territorial waters from 12 to 70 miles; there was an exchange of fire between Spanish and Moroccan naval ships just six miles off the Spanish coast. A fishing agreement between the countries expired December 31, 1972, and even while it was in effect there had been numerous seizures of Spanish ships. In March 1973 Morocco claimed that Libya had trained two small guerrilla bands that entered southern Morocco, carried out attacks, and were subdued. Neither of these incidents appeared to have serious consequences.

MILITARY ASSISTANCE

At independence France turned over some $40 million in military equipment; Spain also contributed a significant amount. Spain has since further contributed by training Moroccan officers. French military aid and arms sales continued to 1966 when it was terminated, except for the continued training of 200 officers.

Soviet military assistance began in late 1960. Finding Algeria more willing to cooperate in return for arms, the Soviets soon stopped aid to Morocco, but in October 1966 they sold Morocco spare parts for the aircraft, tanks, and artillery previously provided. Total Soviet grants and sales have amounted to nearly $20 million. In 1968 through a barter exchange with Czechoslovakia for $16 million in primary products, Morocco obtained 80 reconditioned T-54 tanks.

From 1956 through 1972 the US provided $38.8 million in military assistance. Excess military stocks provided through 1972 totalled an additional $4.0 million. In early 1967, following a visit to the United States by the King, $14 million additional assistance was promised and delivery began on F-5 jet fighters and antitank weapons. A substantial US military mission was established. Military sales from 1967 to 1972 amounted to $30 million, and 2,000 students have been trained under MAP.

ALLIANCES

Morocco is a member of the UN, the OAU, the Arab League and its Unified Military Command, and the less formal Maghreb (Northwest Africa) grouping. In support of UN peacekeeping operations Morocco sent a brigade to the Congo from August 1960 to March 1961.

After the 1963 cancellation of the air base agreement with the United States, the Americans retained a major communication center at Kenitra. About 1,700 US military personnel are stationed there.

ARMY

Personnel: 52,000

Organization:
- 1 armored brigade
- 3 motorized infantry brigades
- 1 light security brigade
- 1 parachute brigade
- 12 independent infantry battalions
- 4 artillery groups
- 1 mortar battalion
- 3 desert cavalry groups
- 2 camel corps battalions

Major Equipment Inventory:
- 120 medium tanks (T-54)
- 120 light tanks (AMX-13)
- 40 half tracks (M-3)
- 95 APCs (Czech-built)
- 75 self-propelled guns and howitzers (SU-100, M-56 Scorpion, and AMX-105)
- 80 armored cars (AML-245, EBR-75, and M-8)
- 100 light artillery pieces (75mm and 105mm howitzers, 76mm, 85mm, and 105mm guns, 37mm and 100mm AA guns)
- 6 helicopters (Alouette II/III)

Reserves: About 160,000 trained reservists.

NAVY

Personnel: 1,500

Major Units:
- 1 frigate (DE)
- 1 subchaser (PC)
- 2 patrol gunboats (PGM)
- 12 patrol boats (YP)
- 1 landing craft (LCU)
- 1 yacht (training ship)

Naval Bases: Casablanca, Safi, Agadir, Kenitra, Tangier

Reserves: About 2,000 men

AIR FORCE

Personnel: 4,000

Organization:
- 1 fighter squadron (F-5)
- 2 attack squadrons (Magister)
- 1 transport squadron (C-47, C-119)
- 1 utility-liaison squadron (Broussard)
- 2 helicopter squadrons (AB-204/205, H-34, OH-13, HH-43)

Major Aircraft Types:
- 56 combat aircraft
  - 24 F-5 fighters
  - 32 Magister armed trainer/light attack aircraft (mostly ex-Luftwaffe)
  - (12 MiG-17 fighter-bombers in storage)
- 177 other aircraft
  - 11 C-119 transports
  - 10 C-47 transports
  - 21 utility-liaison aircraft (Broussard)
  - 60 helicopters (AB-204/205, H-34, OH-13, HH-43)
  - 75 trainers (T-6, T-28)

Air Bases: Sale (Rabat), Meknes, Marrakech, Nouasseur; other fields at Fez, Ville, Agadir, Khouribga, Anfa (Casablanca), Larache, Sidi Slimane, Ben Guerir, Boulhout, Solon, Oujda, Kenitra

Reserves: About 5,000 trained reservists

PARAMILITARY

There are 2,250 Gendarmerie plus 20,000 auxiliaries. The Gendarmerie maintains two mobile security battalions and mans posts spread over the country. The Royal Guards are basically palace guards at the King's various residences. The function of the auxiliaries is unknown. All are subordinate to the Defense Ministry, except the palace guards, the traditional Senegalese.

NIGER

Republique du Niger

POWER POTENTIAL STATISTICS

Area: 489,206 square miles
Population: 4,243,000
Total Active Armed Forces: 3,400 (includes Gendarmerie; 0.08% population)
Gross National Product: $380 million ($90 per capita)
Annual Military Expenditures: $4.0 million (1.05% GNP)
Production of Uranium Oxide: 867 metric tons (5th in world)
Electric Power Output: 20 million kwh
Civil Air Fleet: 2 piston transports

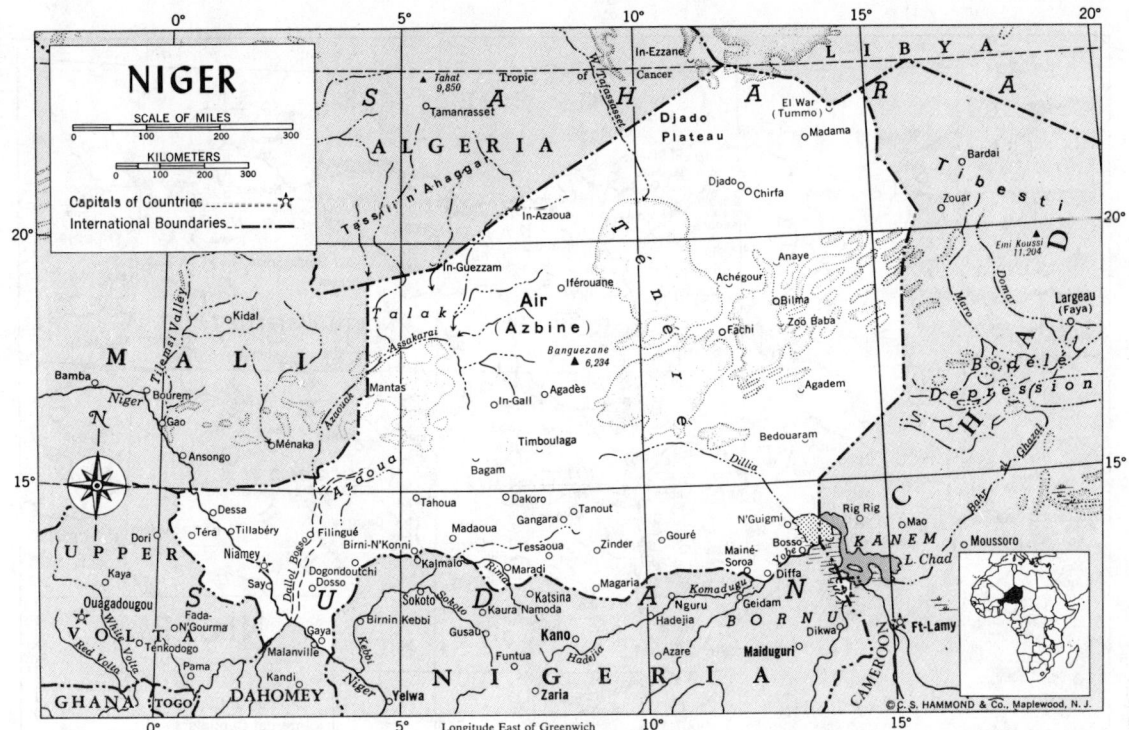

POLITICO-MILITARY POLICIES AND POSTURE

Constitutional government fell victim in April 1974 to the Sahelian drought, which has been especially severe in Niger. A military coup, led by Lt. Col. Seyni Kountie, seized control from Hamani Diori, who had served competently as president since 1960, dissolved the National Assembly, and outlawed all political activity. Although Kountie laid the whole blame for the former government's fall on its allegedly inadequate response to the famine, the press reported speculation that France had played a covert role in the overthrow, in order to maintain its highly privileged position in the exploitation of Niger's high-grade uranium mines, a position that was threatened by Diori's skilled efforts to gain a greater share of uranium revenues for Niger. There is no evidence of French collusion, however, and the new Niger regime has asked for the removal of remaining French troops, something the previous regime had not done. The new regime also appears to be continuing the policy, initiated by Diori, of entering into mineral-exploration agreements with non-French organizations.

The President, who was elected under a one-party system, was also Minister of Defense and of Foreign Affairs and commander in chief of the Armed Forces.

Niger is the terminus of two trans-Saharan caravan and motor routes from Algeria. One military problem is the protection of these routes from the occasional bandits among the nomadic tribesmen in the north.

Former President Diori had been probably the most successful leader of the region in containing internal dissidence; the leaders of the new government, lacking his skill and experience, may have more difficulty. With a low per capita income, a high birth rate, and the tensions between Negro and Berber peoples common to northern sub-Sahara Africa, Niger can expect continuing socio-economic tensions. The country's large high-grade uranium ore deposits and large iron deposits not only make Niger strategically significant, but can be expected eventually to provide income to more than offset current budget deficits, and perhaps to ameliorate internal tensions.

Niger is a member of the UN, the OAU, and the OCAM. Upon independence it entered mutual defense and military assistance agreements with France covering base rights, transit and overflight privileges, and military training and equipping. It also entered into a quadripartite defense agreement with France, Dahomey, and Ivory Coast; and joined the *Conseil de l'Entente*, a political-economic grouping of Dahomey, Ivory Coast, Togo, and Upper Volta. France still maintains a training mission, and a French armored company is stationed at Niamey.

The Army is about 2,000 strong and is maintained by selective two-year conscription. It is organized into five infantry companies, one armored car company, and a para-commando platoon. The Air Force has a strength of about 100 and operates four Noratlas transports, one C-47 transport, and three Broussard utility aircraft. Air bases are Niamey, Zinder, Agadez, Tahoua, and Maradi. There is a river patrol with two PBR on the Niger River operating from Niamey. The Gendarmerie has a strength of 1,300.

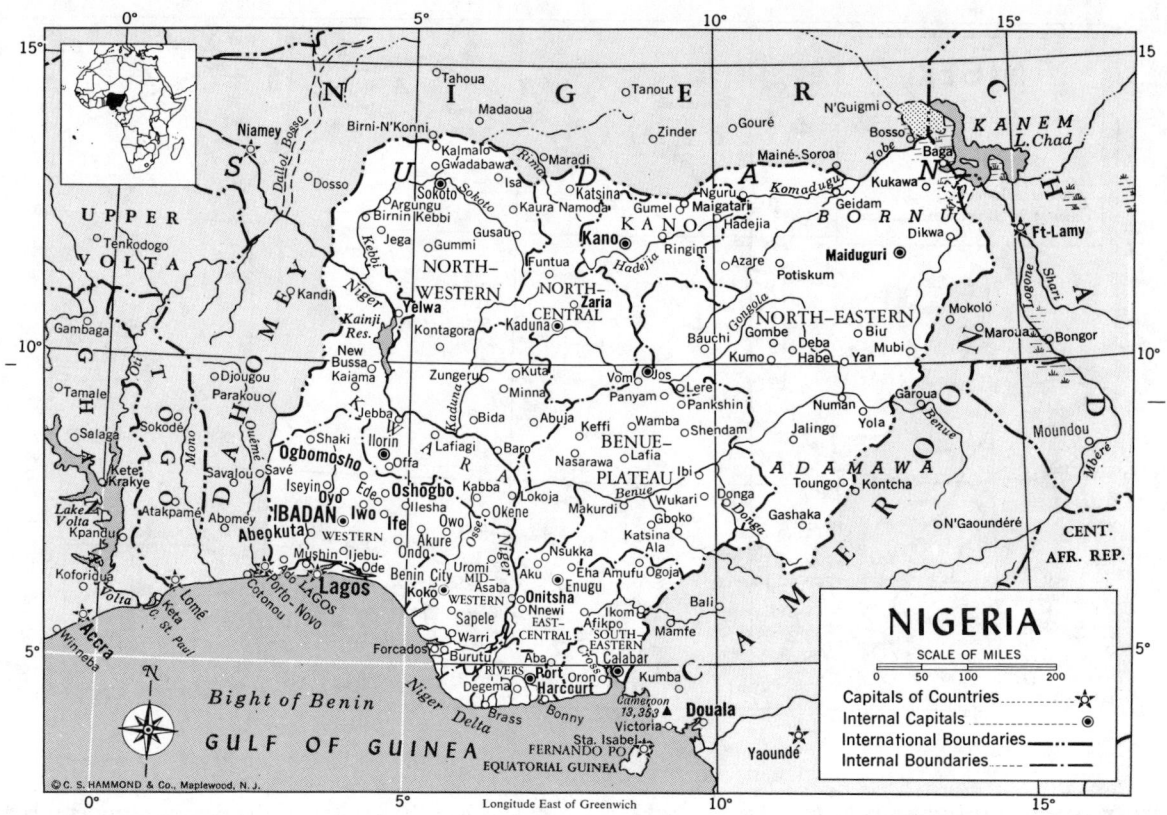

NIGERIA

Federal Republic of Nigeria

POWER POTENTIAL STATISTICS

Area: 356,669 square miles
Population: 69,524,000
Total Active Armed Forces: 106,000 (0.15% population)
Gross National Product: $9.1 billion ($131 per capita)
Annual Military Expenditures: $300 million (3.29% GNP)
Fuel Production: Crude Oil: 89.8 million metric tons
    Refined Products: 2.2 million metric tons
Electric Power Output: 1.81 billion kwh
Merchant Fleet: 56 ships; 99,226 gross tons
Civil Air Fleet: 4 jet, 5 turboprop and 14 piston transports

DEFENSE STRUCTURE

A federal republic and member of the British Commonwealth, Nigeria, following the termination of its civil war in 1970, remains under the Federal Military Government which conducted the war against the Biafran secession. At the head of this government is a Supreme Military Council under Major General Yakubu Gowon, the Commander in Chief of the Armed Forces. The Council controls all government, including military affairs, by decree, the Constitution having been in abeyance since the troubled period of 1966, which preceded the hostilities of the civil war. The chiefs of staff of the three services are members of the Council, which has a general staff modelled on the British system.

POLITICO-MILITARY POLICIES

Nigeria has made an excellent economic and psychological recovery from the civil war, and is now resuming the leadership role in Africa that is suggested by its size, economic resources and military establishment.

Upon independence from Britain in 1960 the Army was formed from Nigerian elements of the Royal West African Frontier Force. At the time 25 percent of the officers were Nigerian; the rest were seconded from the British Army. As a result of increased officer training in Britain, Canada, Australia, India, Pakistan, Israel, Ethiopia, and in US university ROTC, the last British officers were relieved in 1966.

The original civilian government of the shaky, ethnically divided Federation was overthrown in a military coup in January, 1966. The new head of government and about half of the Army officers were Ibos—a progressive tribe of southeastern Nigeria, constituting about 12% of the population, whose energy and education had given them leadership in Nigerian business and government far out of proportion to their numbers. Tribal resentment of Ibo influence, combined with widespread political unrest resulted in a counter-coup in July, which triggered nation-wide attacks against Ibo government officials and businessmen. Growing alienation from the rest of Nigeria led the Ibos of the Eastern Region to secede from Nigeria in May 1967. The Federal Government refused to permit this. A long, bloody, civil war followed, in which the Federal Government finally overcame desperate Ibo resistance in January 1970. The rebel leader, General Ojukwu, fled to Ivory Coast, where he was granted asylum.

During the civil war the Nigerian forces expanded from 12,000 to over 180,000 with consequent dilution of trained leaders. However, after nearly three years of combat, and with substantial modern equipment resources, they now include one of the more powerful, and certainly more experienced, light infantry armies in Africa. Despite expressed fears at releasing large numbers of men upon the civil economy, the forces have been reduced without apparent severe disruption. Military service is voluntary. Immediately after victory, the Nigerian Federal Government under Major General Gowon proclaimed a policy of reconstruction, rehabilitation, and reconciliation. Gowon repeatedly expressed a hope of returning the country to constitutional government before 1976, but there have been no recent signs that this will be done, and the population seems generally well satisfied with the military government and with popular General Gowon. Relations between the Ibos and the rest of the population have improved. The most important factor in this recovery is oil. With an output of about 2.3 million barrels a day, Nigeria had become the world's eighth largest oil producer by fall 1973. Nigeria's oil became even more important with the Arab oil embargo of 1973-1974, and Nigerian oil revenues are expected to increase fourfold over 1973 to at least $8 billion in 1974. The government is allocating large amounts to reconstruction of the Ibo areas, construction of roads, railroads, and airports, and aid to agriculture.

Nigeria is also using its new power, with moderation, in foreign affairs. General Gowon is now chairman of the OAU, the Nigerian oil minister is head of the OPEC, and Nigeria has taken the lead in African trade negotiations with the European Economic Community. Nigeria has also proposed a new West African economic community which, unlike the current CEAO, would comprise both French- and English-speaking nations; this would presumably strengthen Nigeria's regional leadership role at the expense of French influence in West Africa. Although northern Nigeria has suffered some damage during the current drought, the country's own resources have been adequate to provide relief. Nigeria has given famine-relief aid to the Sahelian states and has made development loans to Dahomey, Chad, and Niger.

STRATEGIC PROBLEMS

There are few significant issues that might create tension with neighboring states. Nigeria can apparently look forward to a period of easy, unaggressive regional leadership. Its main strategic problem is avoidance of the kind of internal conflict that so recently devastated the nation.

The defeated Ibos, now somewhat reduced in numbers through casualties and non-combat military and civilian deaths, are not likely again to attempt to secede. However, they do remain the most progressive, energetic, and educated segment of the population, and the oil fields in the Eastern Region will tend to provide resources and incentive to their more rapid advancement and development. The Yorubas of the Western Region, some 15 million people, may again become jealous of the Ibos, as may the somewhat less educated and more warlike Moslem Hausa-Fulanis of the Northern Region, some 10 million in number. A fair and popularly accepted realignment of internal administrative subdivisions needs to be sought. A root cause of the troubles preceding the civil war was a too sudden and arbitrary attempt by the military government of January to July 1966 to abolish all internal boundaries and regional administration in the name of national unity, an act which in fact served to decontrol traditional rivalries and hatreds. Therefore, caution is needed in drawing new boundaries and, especially, time must be found to select and train fair and competent administrators. These conditions appear to be understood by the Federal Military Government.

At present, more serious internal problems than inter-tribal rivalries appear to be urban blight, agricultural depression, and the increasing gap between the extremely wealthy beneficiaries of Nigeria's new economic riches and the great number of Nigerians living in poverty. As indicated above, some governmental efforts are being made to attack these problems.

MILITARY ASSISTANCE

After independence, Britain provided arms, naval craft and navy training, with two ships being supplied by the Netherlands. West Germany trained the Air Force, and Italian trainers, German liaison aircraft and French transports were purchased. The US granted $1.5 million in military assistance from 1960 through mid-1972, and trained 462 students under MAP.

During the civil war, many countries kept to a hands-off policy, but Britain, the Soviet Union and, for a time, France responded to cash offers for needed arms. From Britain came armored cars, artillery, small arms, and ammunition. The Soviet Union and Czechoslovakia sent jet fighters and transport aircraft. The US reduced its military assistance to military medical training only, but renewed assistance after hostilities ceased.

ALLIANCES

Nigeria is a member of the UN, the Commonwealth, OAU, and OPEC. In support of UN peacekeeping operations Nigeria provided a two-battalion force for the UN operation in the Congo from December 1960 to June 1963, and one battalion thereafter to June 1964.

ARMY

Personnel: 100,000

Organization:
- 3 infantry divisions
- 3 reconnaissance regiments
- 3 artillery regiments

Major Equipment Inventory:
- 20 armored cars (AML-60/90)
- 150 armored cars (Saladin)
- scout cars (Ferret)
- APCs (Saracen)
- light artillery (25-pounder gun, 76mm gun, 105mm howitzer, 122mm gun/howitzer)

Reserves: Over 100,000 battle-trained men

NAVY

Personnel: 3,000

Major Units:
- 1 frigate ASW (DE)
- 2 corvettes (DE)
- 3 fast patrol boats (PT, P-6 type)
- 6 subchasers (SC)
- 1 landing craft (LCU)
- 2 survey ships
- 1 tug

Reserves: Possibly 2,500 having war service

Naval Bases: Lagos, Calabar

AIR FORCE

Personnel: 3,000

Organization:
- 1 light bomber squadron (Il-28)
- 2 fighter-bomber squadrons (MiG-17)
- 1 light ground attack squadron (L-29)
- 1 training group (P-149, Bulldog)
- 1 transport group (C-47, Do-27, F-27)
- 1 helicopter squadron (Whirlwind and Alouette II)

Major Aircraft Types:
- 36 combat aircraft
  - 20 MiG-17 fighter-bombers
  - 10 L-29 armed trainer/light ground attack aircraft
  - 6 Il-28 light bombers
- 60 other aircraft
  - 6 C-47 transports
  - 6 F-27 Friendship transports
  - 20 Do-27/28 utility aircraft
  - 8 helicopters (Whirlwind and Allouette II)
  - 20 trainers (P-149, Bulldog)

On Order: 3 Navajo and 4 new helicopters to be used for search and rescue manufactured by Messerschmidt-Bollkow-Blohm, BO-5

Reserves: Over 4,000 with wartime service

Air Bases: Lagos, Kaduna, Ikeja, Maiduguri, Kano

PORTUGUESE AFRICA

Portuguese Africa includes three entities: Angola, Mozambique, and Portuguese Guinea. An amendment to Portugal's Constitution in 1952 changed the status of these regions from colony to Overseas Province, with each considered an integral part of the Portuguese Republic. The central government in Lisbon administers the provinces through the Overseas Ministry; local authority is exercised in each by a provincial Governor General. In June 1971 Portuguese constitutional reforms granted greater autonomy for the African provinces—allowing local legislation and local administration, and authorizing the raising of revenue from a budget drafted and approved by locally elected assemblies.

In spring 1974, frustration over the long and costly fighting in Portuguese Africa brought down the authoritarian government of Portugal. A military coup by younger Portuguese officers brought to power General Antonio de Spinola, himself a veteran of the colonial wars and the author of a recent book urging autonomy within a Portuguese federation for Portugal's African possessions. In August Spinola announced his government's intention to grant immediate independence to the African territories.

Portuguese Army, Navy and Air Force units are occasionally transferred among the three African Overseas Provinces to meet changing requirements. Thus the composition of forces as shown below changes from time to time.

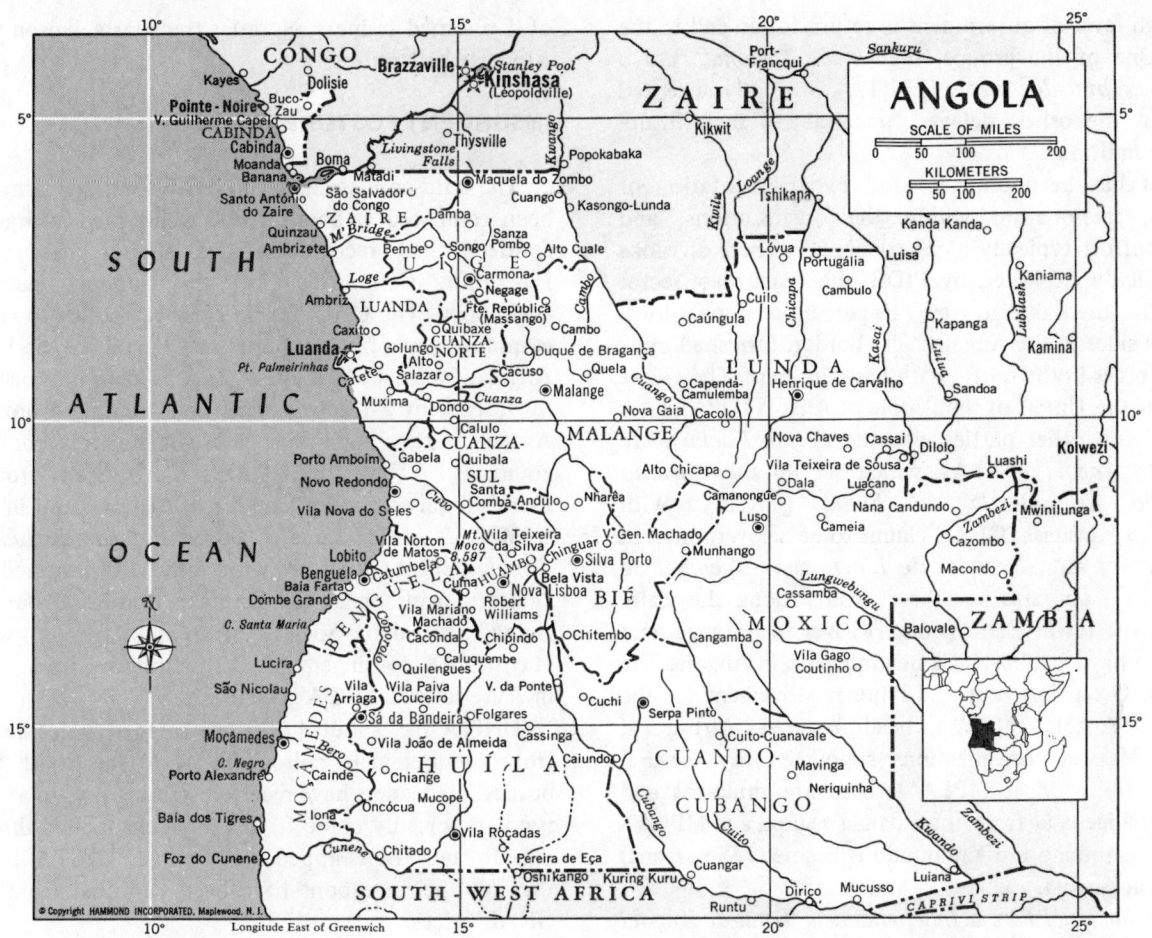

ANGOLA

POWER POTENTIAL STATISTICS

Area: 481,351 square miles
Population: 6,100,000 (includes 300,000 Europeans)
Total Active Armed Forces: 60,000 (0.98% population)
Gross National Product: $1.67 billion ($274 per capita)
Annual Military Expenditures: $25 million provincial funds plus an estimated $35 million from Portugal
Production of Iron Ore: 5.8 million metric tons
Fuel Production: Crude Oil: 7.1 million metric tons
  Refined Products: 501,800 metric tons
Electric Power Output: 644 million kwh
Civil Air Fleet: 10 piston transports

STRATEGIC BACKGROUND

Angola is the largest Portuguese African possession, strongest economically, and most firmly held by Portugal. Its population is about 95 percent black and five percent European. Most of the blacks live by subsistence agriculture, despite rich natural resources. Angola is the world's third largest producer of coffee, and also produces significant amounts of oil and iron ore. The Benguela railroad serves the Katanga province of Zaire as well as Zambia for the export of their copper and to transport their import requirements. First class harbors exist at Luanda, Lobito, and Mocamedes. Recent oil discoveries in the Cabinda enclave are expected to result in sufficient additional production to more than supply the entire Portuguese currency bloc. With peace, Angola could be economically viable and make significant contributions to the Portuguese economy. However, at present, despite a favorable growth rate, development is limited by insurgency, by lack of capital, by shortage of skilled workers, and by poor transportation.

CURRENT MILITARY SITUATION

President Antonio de Spinola's government promised the Angolans a referendum in 1975 to decide between complete independence and a loose federation with Portugal, and the junta-appointed Governor General, General Silvino Silverio Marquez, offered the three guerrilla groups that have been operating in Angola for many years complete amnesty and a place at a high level of government in return for an end to the insurgency. One of the groups, the *Uniao Nacional Para a Independencia Total de Angola* (UNITA), promptly accepted the offer, but the others delayed, uncertain of their future under those conditions.

The revolt has been characterized by fragmentation of organizations, factionalism within the organizations, and dispersion of effort typically along tribal lines. These divisions have been quickly exploited by PIDE, the Portuguese secret police. Initially, the Bakongo tribe (10 percent of population), living on both sides of the Angola-Zaire border, furnished most of the rebel forces in the north, with bases in Zaire. They were affiliated with the Union of the People of Angola (UPA), later consolidated with other parties into the *Frente Nacional de Libertacao de Angola* (FNLA), which set up the *Governo Revolucionario de Angola no Exilio* (GRAE). With headquarters in Kinshasa, GRAE claims to be a government in exile. Its military arm, *Exercito de Liberatacao Nacional de Angola* (ELNA), operates on three fronts along the Zaire border, from the lower Zaire (Congo) River to Katanga, and has claimed to have established a headquarters in Angola. The principal rival group has been the Popular Movement for the Liberation of Angola (MPLA), headquartered in Lusaka, Zambia, a Marxist organization supported by several communist nations. Most MPLA leaders are mulattos and Kimbundu intelligentsia from the Luanda region, and MPLA's main strength is among the Kimbundu tribesmen (25 percent) in north central Angola.

The *Uniao Nacional Para a Independencia Total de Angola* (UNITA), a 1964 offshoot of GRAE, operates from within Angola opposite Zambia. The movement is based on the Ovimbundu tribe (33 percent) and the smaller Chokwe, Lwena, and Luchazi tribes in the east central and southern areas.

MPLA and GRAE were formerly fiercely and violently opposed to each other and to UNITA, but in 1972 they combined to form the Supreme Council for the Liberation of Angola; UNITA was not invited to join, according to UNITA leaders, even though they asked to do so. The cooperation of the two groups does not appear to have been very successful.

GOVERNMENT MILITARY POSTURE

Metropolitan Portuguese forces in Angola, in a joint command, number about 45,000 supplemented by 15,000 locally recruited African troops. In addition, there are numerous paramilitary units including police and *voluntarios*, or auxiliaries, who are often demobilized soldier settlers. Probably all able-bodied males of the 300,000 Portuguese residents are armed, trained, and have designated emergency duties. Small Navy patrol craft guard the coast against infiltration from the sea, while the Air Force of over 100 aircraft provides direct air support to ground units. In addition to a squadron of Fiat G-91 jet fighter-bombers there are units of T-6 armed trainers, Noratlas transports, liaison aircraft, and Alouette helicopters.

INSURGENT POSTURE

The hard-core strength of GRAE's military arm, ELNA, has been estimated at about 5,000 well-armed insurgents. GRAE formerly had recognition and support from the OAU's Liberation Committee, but this support has now been withdrawn. The OAU has no clear-cut policy toward the new, combined organization, Supreme Council for the Liberation of Angola; President Mobutu of Zaire is known to be cool toward it. It currently receives arms and training from the radical African states who in most cases got the arms from communist countries. A base for GRAE's northeastern front exists in Zaire's Kwango district, and for its eastern front in Katanga.

MPLA's armed force, *Exercito Popular de Liberatacao de Angola* (EPLA), operates with about 1,000 armed men on an "eastern front" near the Zambian border. Groups have been trained abroad by Soviet, Cuban and Algerian instructors. In May 1974 a contingent of 112 instructors from China arrived in Zaire to train MPLA guerrillas.

UNITA has about 1,000 guerrillas at bases inside Angola, from the Benguela railroad south to the South West Africa border. Its leaders have received training in China; its arms and funds reportedly come from China, channelled through Dar es Salaam and transshipped via Zambia. UNITA leaders claim that all their weapons have been captured from MPLA and GRAE forces.

MOZAMBIQUE

POWER POTENTIAL STATISTICS

Area: 303,073 square miles
Population: 8,980,000 (includes 120,000 Europeans)
Total Active Armed Forces: 45,000 (0.50% population)
Gross National Product: $2 billion ($223 per capita)
Annual Military Expenditures: $25 million provincial funds plus an estimated $50 million from Portugal
Fuel Production: Coal: 300,000 metric tons
    Refined Petroleum Products: 796,300 metric tons
Electric Power Output: 558 million kwh
Civil Air Fleet: 3 jet and 3 turboprop transports

STRATEGIC BACKGROUND

Despite vigorous efforts by the new Portuguese government to make peace with insurgent forces, the principal rebel group, FRELIMO (*Frente de Liberatacao de Mocambique*), has refused to accept a cease-fire on terms of independence and free elections. FRELIMO demands immediate independence

CURRENT MILITARY SITUATION

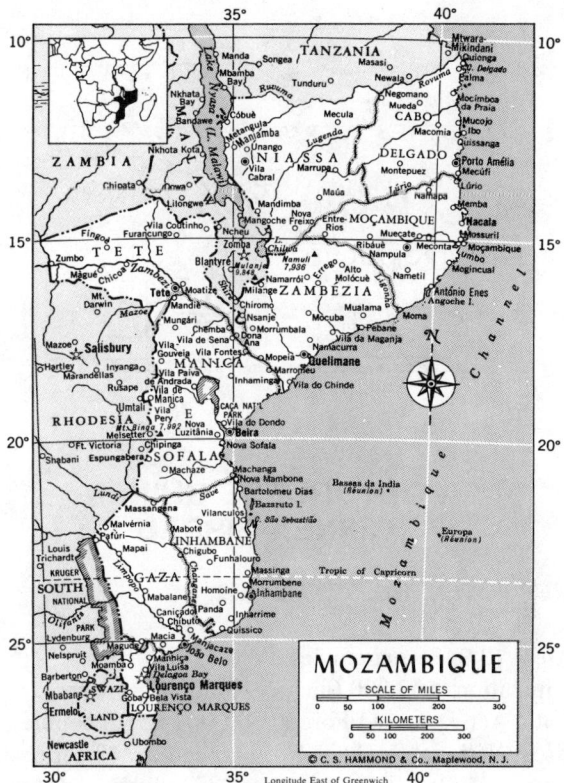

FRELIMO began military operations in 1964 from training bases in southern Tanzania, under the leadership of a cadre trained in Algeria. Most of the rebels are recruited from the fierce Makonde tribe living on both sides of the Tanzanian border in the northeast. On the northwest border the Nyanje tribe also has been recruited to the rebel cause. In the two northern districts, Cabo Delgado and Niassa, FRELIMO controls perhaps 50 percent of the countryside. More recently it opened a new area of operations in the Tete district along the Zambian border, and incursions are also mounted from Malawi. All told it controls about five percent of Mozambique territory. FRELIMO policy prohibits terroristic acts against the population. It claims to have a functioning governmental structure inside Mozambique.

A rival movement, opposed to FRELIMO's strategy, is the *Comite Revolucionario de Mocambique* (COREMO). It is a coalition of a number of minor parties and factions organized in 1965, with headquarters in Lusaka. COREMO's strategy is to train and then infiltrate cadres to all areas of Mozambique to build a clandestine politico-military organization in preparation for a massive country-wide uprising and establishment of a leftist government. There are a number of other groups claiming a following in the liberation movement, but these are of little significance.

Since 1964, when the situation in Angola became fairly stabilized, Portugal has been operating energetically against the Mozambique insurgents. During 1970 and 1971, Portuguese forces in Mozambique concentrated against FRELIMO rebels, mainly in the districts bordering Tanzania. According to Portuguese government sources, more than 700 rebels were killed, 200 were captured, and almost 7,000 surrendered. More recently, however, the rebels have been making increasingly bold attacks, hitting the railroad from Beira to Rhodesia at least six times in early 1974, and raiding farther and farther south. FRELIMO has continued, and even intensified, its attacks since the 1974 change of government in Lisbon.

Despite general UN disapproval of Portuguese colonial policy, Portugal has had no difficulties in purchasing essential combat and support weaponry. Informal arrangements for coordination of security operations, and mutual support if required, exist with Rhodesia and South Africa. Landlocked Malawi, dependent on Mozambique for access to the sea, cooperates in making insurgent operations from its territory difficult.

Tanzania openly supports the rebels, but its border is clearly marked by the Ruvuma River. The Portuguese, while threatening, have not yet struck rebel bases north of the river. Rebels also operate from Zambia, possibly with tacit official approval, although the situation is ambiguous. The border is undefined by natural features and has been crossed frequently by Portuguese ground patrols and aircraft in hot pursuit of rebel bands. Inevitably Zambian villages are hit and Zambians

with transfer of power directly to itself. Communist China is believed to be encouraging FRELIMO in this stand. Most of the black population of Mozambique (more than 98% of the total) is engaged in subsistence agriculture. Export of agricultural products provides income, as do remittances of migrant labor, and transit shipments from inland regions (Malawi, Rhodesia, and South Africa's Transvaal) by railroad through the ports of Nacala, Beira, and Lourenco Marques. A 360 million-ton iron ore deposit has been discovered in the north; petroleum and other mineral exploration has been accelerated. Exploitation of mineral discoveries is expected to improve the economic situation; so too will sale of hydroelectric power to South Africa from the Cahora Bassa dam project under construction on the Zambezi River. Guerrilla attempts at sabotage have been contained, and completion is expected in 1974. Meanwhile, a serious adverse balance of payments continues.

The Portuguese established trading posts in the early 16th Century and control over the entire area was achieved by the end of the 19th Century. However, priorities elsewhere in the empire held back development until the 20th Century. Development was on a small scale until the 1961 revolt in Angola alerted Portugal; belated economic and social reforms were at once begun. Underground nationalist movements had existed for some time, and in 1962 the more prominent of these united as FRELIMO with headquarters in Dar es Salaam.

killed. Zambian protests have been loud, and to date Portuguese replies have been conciliatory and reparations have been offered.

GOVERNMENT MILITARY POSTURE

A Military Commander in Chief directs all operations, under the Governor General and through Army, Navy, and Air Force Commanders and the Director of Police.

Regular Portuguese forces number about 45,000, with 15 to 25 percent being black. There are numerous paramilitary units of police, armed Portuguese settlers, and biracial local militia. The fortified villages are garrisoned by a militia of intervention of 10,000.

Navy patrol and landing craft guard the coast against infiltrations; these transport and land troops in coast and river areas. Two patrol craft armed with 22mm guns are operated on Lake Malawi to prevent infiltrations down the lake from Tanzania or across from Malawi. A new naval patrol base is at Porto Amelia; rear naval bases are at Beira and Lourenco Marques.

The Air Force giving direct air support to the ground units includes a squadron of Fiat G-91 jet fighter-bombers and units of B-26 light bombers, T-6 armed trainers, Noratlas transports, liaison aircraft and Alouette helicopters. Airfields are Lourenco Marques, Beira, Lumbo, Porto Amelia, Ngamba, and Palma on the coast; Umtamba and Mwidumba in the northeast; Porto Arroio in the northwest; nine new jet fields inland; Vila Cabral, Maniamba, Marrupa, and Nova Freixo in the northwest; Fingoe and Tete in Tete district; Mueda in the Cabo Delgado district; and Dona Ana and Mocuba in the Zambezia district.

INSURGENT POSTURE

FRELIMO claims about 15,000 armed trained men. OAU's Liberation Committee recognizes and supports FRELIMO, and has given the liberation of Mozambique top priority over other movements in Africa. FRELIMO is said to have received financial support from sympathizers in the West, while its arms come from communist countries. Rear training bases are at Kongwa and Bagamoyo in central Tanzania and a number of forward bases lie just behind the Ruvuma River border in southern Tanzania. Three, staffed with Communist Chinese instructors, are Mbamba Bay, Songea, and Machingwea; others staffed by Tanzanian army and police are Newala, Tunduru, Masasi, Kitangari, Mingoyo, Mtwara, and Lindi. In 1966 the military headquarters was displaced forward from Dar es Salaam into Mozambique where FRELIMO now says 80 percent of the basic and small-unit training is conducted.

Details of COREMO's military forces are unknown.

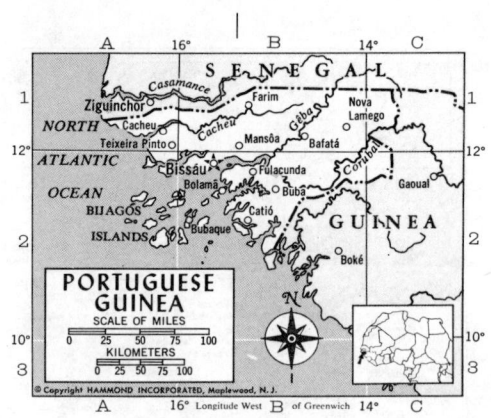

PORTUGUESE GUINEA
GUINEA-BISSAU

POWER POTENTIAL STATISTICS

Area: 13,948 square miles
Population: 563,000 (includes 3,000 Europeans)
Total Active Armed Forces: 30,000 (4.55% population)
Gross National Product: $140 million ($248 per capita)
Annual Military Expenditures: $35 million
Electric Power Output: 3.5 million kwh
Civil Air Fleet: 7 piston transports

STRATEGIC BACKGROUND

Portugal maintained trading posts on the coast from the 15th to the 19th Centuries but did not consolidate the interior until the early 20th Century. The economy is mainly agricultural and there is a $5 million annual trade deficit. The territory thus has little value to Portugal except as a link in the sea and air routes to Angola and Mozambique and as a prestige symbol.

Strategically, Portuguese Guinea (called Guinea-Bissau by its insurgents and by the considerable number of foreign states that have recognized its independence) occupies a significant position in the bulge of West Africa close to central Atlantic sea lanes, and a relatively short distance by air to Brazil. The province has close ties with Portugal's Cape Verde Islands, 600 miles to the northwest, which occupy a comparable strategic position in the Atlantic.

CURRENT MILITARY SITUATION

Revolt by a native liberation movement began in mid-1962; this escalated to full-scale guerrilla warfare in 1963. By the end of 1966 an apparent stalemate had been reached, with the rebels holding at least half of the countryside and the Portuguese holding the fortified towns and cities as well as a number of entrenched military posts in the hinterland supplied by helicopter. In late 1973, the rebel organization—African Independence Party of Guinea and Cape Verde (PAIGC)—claimed to control three-fourths of Portuguese Guinea. It is said to have achieved considerable success in developing political, social, and economic infrastructure in the areas it controls. In the summer of 1972 PAIGC held elections in those areas, and it was preparing to declare the independence of PAIGC-controlled territory when, in January 1973, Amilcar Cabral, PAIGC's leader, was assassinated. The Portuguese denied responsibility for the assassination, and most informed observers seem to support this denial. Direction of PAIGC was taken over by a triumvirate of leaders who are considered more militant than Cabral. The independent Republic of Guinea-Bissau was proclaimed on September 24, 1973; it has been recognized by more than half the members of the UN and has joined the OAU. Portuguese officials, however, ridicule PAIGC claims to control a major portion of the country's territory and to have established a functioning government and economy.

The Balante tribe (30 percent of the population) provides most of the rebel activists and support. Conversely, the Moslem Fulani tribe (20 percent) living in the northeast have remained loyal to the Portuguese and have been heavily armed for self-defense. The Government has established over 400 fortified villages among the Fulani and other loyal tribes. As a result of rebel terrorism, as much as Portuguese oppression, about 10 percent of the population are refugees in Senegal.

The rebel movement has achieved far greater success than those in Angola or Mozambique, and Portuguese presence and interests are vastly less. The rebels are steadily building up strength in the interior and eventually might muster sufficient force to defeat the Portuguese militarily everywhere but in the coastal enclaves. Should Portugal withdraw from Guinea, a Portuguese-speaking PAIGC cadre could be made available to export its more viable ideology and revolutionary technique to the other Portuguese possessions, with possible disastrous results for Portugal. Meanwhile, the insurgency drags on as Portugal alleges that the Soviet Union has recently doubled its support of the rebels with the ultimate hope of thereby securing a base on the Guinea coast or in the Cape Verde Islands.

GOVERNMENT MILITARY POSTURE

Portugal's current commitment is estimated at about 30,000 including locally recruited troops and paramilitary units. A number of navy patrol and landing craft are used along the coast and up rivers. A squadron of 12 Fiat G-91 light jet fighter bombers and a squadron of T-6 armed trainers, 12 DO-27 Skyservant liaison aircraft, and Alouette helicopters operate from Bissau's international airport and interior strips. The Portuguese military high command claimed significant progress in fighting the insurgents in 1970. Severe fighting, mainly in the areas bordering Senegal and the Republic of Guinea, was reported during 1971 with heavy losses on both sides.

INSURGENT POSTURE

PAIGC was formed in 1956 and outlawed in 1959. It established headquarters in Conakry, Guinea, and a base training camp at Kindia in Guinea. Support in money, arms, and training has been received from the Liberation Committee of OAU, Algeria, Morocco, Guinea, Senegal, Cuba, Communist China, the Soviet Union, and East European communist countries. In May 1971 several hundred Cuban advisers arrived in Senegal to train PAIGC forces. They were stationed in the PAIGC camp at Cumbamory in Senegal. According to Portuguese sources each operational guerrilla unit is now led by a Cuban officer.

PAIGC fighting forces are organized on the classic three levels of guerrilla warfare: local part-time guerrillas who harass and form an intelligence network, a militia for local defense, and a mobile fully armed force. The latter element is thought to number 6,000 men. Most of the top leaders received training in China. Arms include communist small arms and mortars and Czech and East German antiaircraft machineguns.

A rival group, the Front for the Liberation of an Independent Nationalist Guinea (FLING), is headquartered in Senegal and does not sponsor active subversion inside Guinea. However, it claims to be more representative of the people, as PAIGC leadership is largely from the Cape Verde Islands. In light of the support shown to Guinea-Bissau the prospects of its gaining control in the area are slight.

RHODESIA

POWER POTENTIAL STATISTICS

Area: 150,820 square miles
Population: 5,690,000 (260,000 whites)
Total Active Armed Forces: 11,000 (includes security police; 0.2% population)
Gross National Product: $1.50 billion ($264 per capita)
Annual Military Expenditures: $30.5 million (2.03% GNP)
Iron and Steel Production: 970,363 metric tons
Fuel Production: Coal: 3.33 million metric tons
Electric Power Output: 6.41 billion kwh
Civil Air Fleet: 7 turboprop and 16 piston transports

DEFENSE STRUCTURE

Until November 11, 1965, Rhodesia was a self-governing British colony. On that date under a Unilateral Declaration of Independence (UDI), the British Governor was replaced by an Officer Administering the Government as chief of state and

248 ALMANAC OF WORLD MILITARY POWER

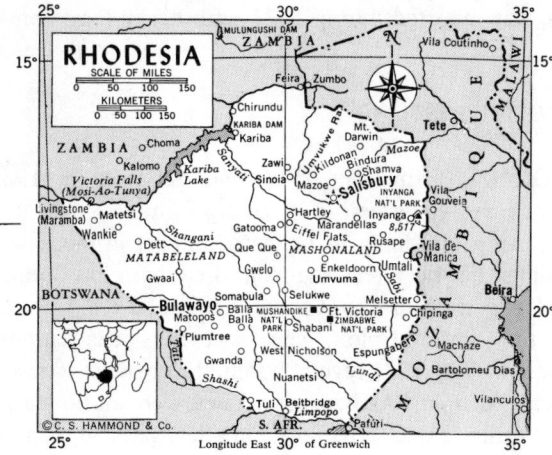

commander in chief of the Rhodesian Defense Forces. The head of government is the Prime Minister, in a traditionally British parliamentary government, and the armed forces are administered by a Minister of Defence. In May 1970 Rhodesia declared itself a republic.

POLITICO-MILITARY POLICY

The central policy of the current government is the maintenance of control by the white population, who comprise about five percent of the total population. The government has been undeterred by refusal of Britain and the UN to recognize its independence, by the resultant economic sanctions against it, and by infiltrations of armed insurgents (from exiled liberation organizations). Defying Britain and the UN, and declaring a state of emergency, Rhodesia has been forced to readjust its economy, apparently with little hardship. Local industry has been built up, the armed forces and police have been increased, and close cooperation in economic and defense matters has been established with South Africa, Botswana, Malawi, and Portuguese Mozambique.

All white males serve for one year in the armed forces followed by three years in the part-time Territorial Force. From this they pass to the class A and B reserves. Virtually all white males are in either the Defence Force reserve or the police reserve. Blacks comprise less than one-third of the regular forces and two-thirds of the police. Those blacks that are in military and police forces are recruited from the Fort Victoria area where the local tribes are hostile to all other tribes. Few blacks are believed to be in the reserves.

STRATEGIC PROBLEMS

Rhodesia's strategic problems derive from its independent policy and the UN's and indigenous nationalists' reactions against it. Negotiations have continued sporadically with Britain in an attempt to work out a mutually satisfactory political solution. In November 1970 Britain revealed that it had reached an agreement with Rhodesia whereby Britain would introduce legislation to confer independence upon Rhodesia as a republic and would commend this legislation to the British Parliament, on the understanding that an amendment to the Rhodesian constitution would provide for unimpeded progress to majority rule and would safeguard against racial discrimination. Large-scale violent demonstrations by Rhodesian Africans against British reconciliation with the Rhodesian government led to Britain's rejection of the treaty in May 1972.

There are two outlawed nationalist liberation organizations: Zimbabwe African People's Union (ZAPU) and Zimbabwe African Nationalist Union (ZANU). They have been outlawed and maintain headquarters in Dar Es Salaam, with training centers and bases elsewhere in Tanzania, and invasion bases in Zambia. In 1967 these two became allied with a similar South African organization, African National Congress (ANC), and the three cooperate in training and operations. ZAPU and ZANU are believed to have several thousand men in training in Tanzania, the Soviet Union, Communist China, Algeria, Egypt, and Cuba. Infiltrators killed or captured have all carried the latest arms of Soviet or Chinese manufacture. Most recent reports indicate that ZANU is now by far the most effective of the insurgent groups; it operates largely in northeastern Rhodesia, presumably in cooperation with the Mozambique group FRELIMO. The African National Council, formed in December 1971, formally presented the African's case against British-Rhodesian reconciliation to a visiting British commission in 1972.

Rhodesia's borders are protected on three sides by friendly nations: Mozambique, South Africa, and Botswana. The first two are informally allied with Rhodesia in defense against African liberation movements, and the third cooperates out of practical necessity. It is the fourth side—the 400-mile Zambezi River border with Zambia—through which the liberation movement attempts to infiltrate. The Rhodesian government has acknowledged that some infiltrators can be expected to get through and perform their missions of subversion, terrorism, and destruction. Despite the thinly defended border, Rhodesian Defence Forces and Police, assisted by South Africa police units, have been quite successful in inflicting severely disproportionate casualties on the infiltrating bands and in rounding up the survivors. There was widespread terrorism in Rhodesia in 1973, however. In January 1973 Rhodesia closed the Zambia border, except for copper shipments, to put pressure on Zambia to control anti-Rhodesian guerrillas. Rhodesia offered to open the border the following month, but Zambia refused to ship copper through Rhodesia during the period when the border was closed and refused to ship anything after the offer to open it was made.

In the larger picture of Southern Africa defense, Rhodesia must be considered a forward position for South Africa and a flank protection for Mozambique. Fully recognizing this, South Africa and Portugal have assisted Rhodesia economically and militarily. In the event of a serious invasion of Rhodesia active military support by these two neighbors is to be expected. Although many African nations have called for an invasion, either by an African alliance or by Britain, the African nations are too weak and disunified militarily, and Britain is committed to a policy of peaceful coercion.

MILITARY ASSISTANCE

Except for a few Canadian and French aircraft, all arms and equipment received before UDI were British. After UDI Britain declared not only an arms embargo but full economic sanctions as well. This action was followed by almost all members of the UN. The sole notable exceptions were Portugal and South Africa, but between them these two countries produce or have access to almost every type of military equipment that Rhodesia could require. South Africa very probably has been supplying Rhodesia's increased defense needs since 1965.

ALLIANCES

While no formal defense agreement with either South Africa or Portugal is known to exist, there appear to be informal working arrangements on defense matters of mutual concern.

ARMY

Personnel: 3,400

Organization:
- 3 brigade headquarters (see Reserves)
  - 2 infantry battalions (one with Ferret scout cars)
  - 1 artillery battery
  - 1 Special Air Service squadron (parachute commandos)

Major Equipment Inventory:
- 20 scout cars (Ferret)
- light artillery (25-pounder)

Reserves: There are 3 brigade establishments or headquarters, two of which are based on the regular infantry battalions cited above. The Territorial Forces referred to below would be used to bring these brigades up to strength:
- 8,400 Territorial Force
  - 4 infantry battalions (subordinated to the 3 brigade headquarters)
- 25,000 Reserve Force
  - command headquarters and supporting units
  - 8 infantry battalions
  - 1 artillery battery

AIR FORCE

Personnel: 1,200

Organization:
- 2 fighter-bomber squadrons (Hunter and Vampire)
- 1 light bomber squadron (Canberra)
- 2 armed reconnaissance/training squadrons (AL-60, AM-3C, Provost)
- 1 transport squadron (C-47)
- 1 helicopter squadron (Alouette III)

Major Aircraft Types:
- 58 combat aircraft
  - 12 Hunter fighter-bombers
  - 12 Vampire fighter-bombers
  - 10 Canberra light bombers
  - 6 AL-60, 6 AM-3C armed trainers
  - 12 Provost armed trainer/reconnaissance aircraft
- 19 other aircraft
  - 4 vampire trainers
  - 3 Canberra trainers
  - 4 C-47 transports
  - 8 Alouette III helicopters

Air Bases: New Sarum (Salisbury), Thornhill (Gwelo), Cranbourne, Bulawayo, Umtali

Reserves: Territorial and Reserve personnel are assigned; numbers not known.

PARAMILITARY

The active police force is some 6,400 strong and has armored cars. It is trained and organized for counterinsurgency. The police reserve numbers 28,500.

RWANDA
Republique Rwandaise
POWER POTENTIAL STATISTICS

Area: 10,169 square miles
Population: 3,900,000
Total Active Armed Forces: 2,500 (0.06% population)
Gross National Product: $210 million ($54 per capita)
Annual Military Expenditures: $3.5 million (1.66% GNP)
Electric Power Output: 48.1 million kwh

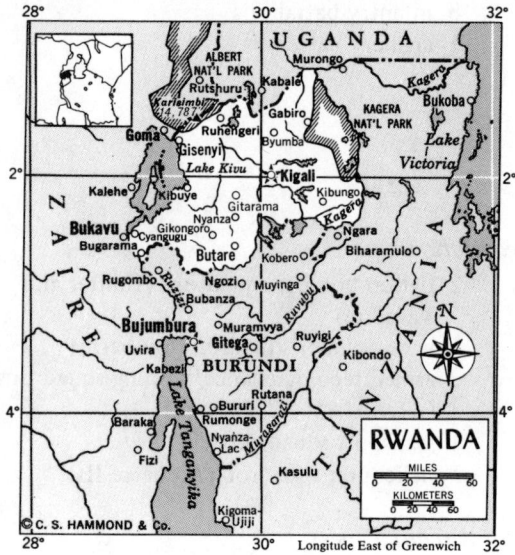

POLITICO-MILITARY POLICIES AND POSTURE

The elected President is commander in chief of the armed forces, exercising this authority through the Minister of National Guard and Police, a military officer. Legislative and budgetary power is shared by the Executive with the National Assembly. Foreign policy is Western-oriented, in part because of Chinese Communist subversive activities.

Rwanda's internal and external strategic problems revolve around a major ethnic division, exacerbated by its central location among neighbors with similar internal security problems. The population is 13 percent Hamitic Tutsi (Watusi) and 86 percent Bantu Hutu. The exceptionally tall-statured Tutsi were a dominant feudal cast ruling their Hutu serfs until the UN-supervised elections of 1961, which the Hutu won. This resulted in violence, and over 160,000 Tutsi fled to neighboring countries. In 1963, 3,000 Tutsi—supported by Chinese agents in Uganda—invaded Rwanda, but were defeated by the National Guard and police in a series of skirmishes. The attempt was repeated in late 1966 by some 2,000 Tutsi armed and trained by Chinese Communist agents in Burundi, with the same result. Burundi then broke relations with Communist China, and a security agreement was entered into between Zaire, Burundi, and Rwanda to preclude further such subversive activities. However, Burundi has a similar ethnic situation with the Tutsi minority in control, and recent tribal warfare in Burundi has brought an influx of Hutu refugees to Rwanda. In early 1973 there were reports of Hutu attacks on Tutsis in Rwanda, with 600 of the latter fleeing to Uganda. Hutu raiders from Rwanda briefly invaded Burundi in May. A bloodless coup in July 1973 brought to power Major General Juvenal Habyalimana, a Hutu like his predecessor; he has indicated that there will be no fundamental policy changes. Rwanda's internal problems are exacerbated by a high population density and high birth rate, combined with a nonviable economy; its yearly budget deficit is made up by Belgium.

With its own dissident ethnic refugees living and plotting in neighboring countries, and with similar refugees from these surrounding countries seeking sanctuary in Rwanda, cooperation and understanding among all of these countries is essential. Rwanda apparently cooperates to some extent with Burundi on mutual security matters growing out of this ethnic dissidence, and with bordering Zaire, Uganda, and Tanzania on matters of refugees, insurgents, and mercenaries. Rwanda is a member of the UN, the OCAM, and the OAU.

Belgian troops withdrew shortly after Rwanda's independence in July 1962, although Belgian military equipment and about 30 instructor-advisers have remained Belgian military assistance has continued at the rate of about $250,000 yearly. Diplomatic relations with China were reestablished in November 1971, and China provided technical assistance for a highway and several agricultural projects.

The National Guard numbers 2,500 and is organized into two infantry battalions, an armored car unit, and supporting elements. The air unit of the National Guard operates two C-47 transports and two Dornier Do-27 liaison aircraft. There are three AM-3C aircraft on order.

SENEGAL

Republique de Senegal

POWER POTENTIAL STATISTICS

Area: 76,124 square miles
Population: 4,200,000
Total Active Armed Forces: 7,500 (including Gendarmerie; 0.17% population)
Gross National Product: $870 million ($207 per capita)
Annual Military Expenditures: $18.0 million (2.06% GNP)
Electric Power Output: 800 million kwh
Merchant Fleet: 39 ships; 16,280 gross tons
Civil Air Fleet: 3 piston transports

POLITICO-MILITARY POLICIES AND POSTURE

The elected President determines and directs national policy, appoints the cabinet and senior military officials, and is commander in chief of the armed forces. He controls the military through a Minister of Armed Forces. The Chief of Staff of the Army is also Commander of the Gendarmerie.

Senegal professes a policy of nonalignment in international affairs. Relations with Portuguese Guinea are strained, however, because of Senegal's support for nationalist guerrillas based in Senegal, who often cross the border and attack

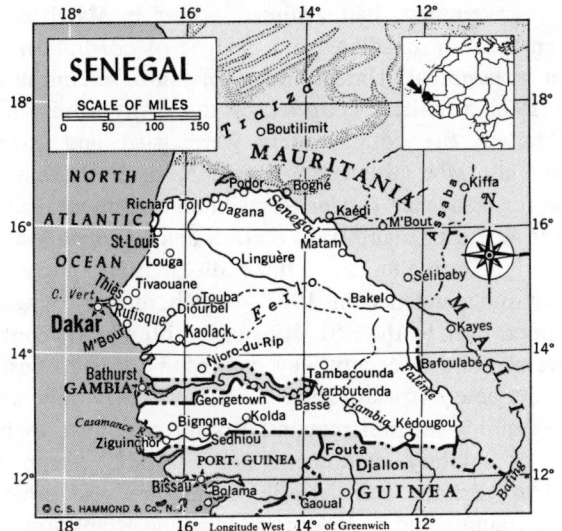

Portuguese forces. Close ties are continued with France, and also are maintained with The Gambia, an enclave within Senegal, with agreements for cooperation in defense and foreign affairs. Senegal supports regional federation and cooperation and is active in the UN, OAU, and OCAM.

Senegal has remained fairly stable internally since independence in 1960, and since the split with Mali a few months later. Disturbances in 1962, 1967, and 1968 were put down effectively by the armed forces and the police. However, there are considerable internal economic difficulties, exacerbated by the high population growth rate. There is a multiplicity of tribes, but ethnic conflicts appear minor; the fact that 80 percent of the population is Moslem has a stabilizing influence.

Senegalese were considered among the best fighting troops of the old French Colonial Army. It was from these veterans that the Senegal armed forces were formed upon independence. Some 10,000 additional Senegalese veterans of the French Army could be considered a potential reserve.

Shortly after independence mutual defense and military assistance agreements were signed with France, which included an internal security agreement, base rights, transit and overflight privileges, and military training and equipment grants. Dakar remained headquarters for French *Zone d'Outre-Mer I*, and a French garrison, now 2,000 men, remains there. In addition to providing a ready unit for deployment anywhere in Africa, this force guards the airfield and certain key installations. It would also be available to assist the government in maintaining internal security under existing agreements. French Forces consist of the following: Army (1,200), 1 mixed regiment; Navy (500), 2 coastal escorts; Air Force (300), 6 Noratlas transports.

Since the initial outfitting with French arms and equipment, Senegal's armed forces have received military assistance from the United States in the amount of $2.8 million from 1961 through 1972 plus $11,000 in excess military stocks.

The armed forces are maintained by selective compulsory service of 24 months. The 5,500-man army is organized into three infantry battalions of five companies each, an engineer battalion, a field artillery battery, a light antiaircraft battery, supporting services, and a mobile force which serves as a general reserve. The mobile force consists of an armored car company, two parachute companies, two commando companies, a motor transport company, and a signal company. Equipment includes French light artillery, AML-245 and M-8 armored cars, and individual and crew served weapons.

The 200-man naval force has coast guard and river patrol and transport missions. It operates one patrol gunboat (PGM), with eight SS-12 SSM, one patrol boat (SC), two patrol boats (YP), and two landing craft mechanized (LCM). The former French naval base at Dakar has extensive modern facilities.

The Air Force is 200 strong and operates ten aircraft in support of the Army: four C-47 transports, four Broussard liaison aircraft, and two Bell 47G helicopters. Airfields are at Yoff (Dakar), St. Louis, Tambacounda, Ziguinchor, Thies, and Kedougou.

There is a National Gendarmerie of 1,600 men.

SIERRA LEONE

POWER POTENTIAL STATISTICS

Area: 27,925 square miles
Population: 2,800,000
Total Active Armed Forces: 2,450 (including constabulary; 0.09% population)
Gross National Product: $490 million ($187 per capita)
Annual Military Expenditures: $3 million (0.61% GNP)
Iron Ore Production: 2.4 million metric tons
Refined Petroleum Products: 300,400 metric tons
Electric Power Output: 197 million kwh
Merchant Fleet: 8 ships; 1,795 gross tons
Civil Air Fleet: 2 piston transports and 1 jet operated by British United Airways for Sierra Leone Airways

POLITICO-MILITARY POLICIES AND POSTURE

Sierra Leone was granted independence by Great Britain in 1961, and became a sovereign republic within the British Commonwealth in April 1971. The Sierra Leone parliament, called the House of Representatives, is a unicameral body. The majority party leader is the Executive President, who is both head of state and of government; he is also Minister of Defence. There is a Vice President and Prime Minister who is charged with general supervision of all ministries. In 1961 the Sierra Leone Battalion of the Royal West African Frontier

Force became the nucleus of the Royal Sierra Leone Military Forces (RSLMF). In 1971 the RSLMF was renamed the Republic of Sierra Leone Military Forces.

Sierra Leone's policy is characterized by nonalignment. Sierra Leone condemns *apartheid* in South Africa, supports self-determination for Portugal's African territories, and advocates the use of force by Britain to depose the white regime in Rhodesia. Implicitly, for defense against possible external aggression, the nation depends upon collective security and protection by Britain and the United States. Sierra Leone is a member of the UN, the British Commonwealth, and the OAU. It contributed a rifle company to the UN Operation in the Congo for 14 months in 1962 and in 1963. Modest military and police forces are maintained to insure internal security and prevent infiltrations.

Sierra Leone is strategically significant for its excellent harbor in the West African bulge and its mineral wealth. The natural harbor at Freetown is one of the finest in West Africa, with anchorage for more than 200 ships of unrestricted draft. Diamonds are a major export (1,955,011 carats valued at over $61 million exported in 1970) as are iron ore (2 million tons annually) and bauxite (200,000 tons annually). There is also a 30 million-ton reserve of titanium oxide exploited at the rate of 100,000 tons annually.

Serious internal security problems stem from political and ethnic disputes. The two principal tribes, the Temne in the north and the Mende in the south, are generally opposed politically in the two major parties. The Creoles, descendants of freed African slaves from the British West Indies who founded the colony, have recently allied with the Temne in a new government which in 1968 overthrew the existing military government with the assistance of Army and police NCOs. The military government had assumed power in March of 1967 after an election deadlock and charges of corruption in the civilian government. Unrest and suspicion have continued. In March 1971 a military coup led by the Army Commander in Chief failed; the coup leaders were tried and executed. Immediately after the coup, Prime Minister Stevens asked Guinea for assistance (under terms of an agreement reached in 1970) in restoring stability to Sierra Leone. Guinea responded by sending airborne units and three MiG fighters.

Upon independence in 1961, British military equipment was turned over to the RSLMF, and British officers continued for several years to occupy key command and staff positions. With complete Africanization of the RSLMF only a small British training mission remains. Britain continues to be the source of military equipment and RSLMF personnel are trained in Britain and Nigeria. Israel has also conducted military training and in 1966 assisted in the establishment of a military academy for officer cadets and youth movement leaders.

The RSLMF is 1,850 strong, organized in an infantry battalion, an armored car squadron, a signal squadron, supporting services, and a harbor and coastal patrol unit. The latter unit of about 50 men operates with a patrol boat (YP) and two harbor launches. Acquisition of a patrol gunboat is planned. There is a combined Army/Police organization (AM/POL) for land and coastal patrol.

The regular police force of about 2,000 includes a special constabulary of 600. There is a special police in industrial areas of about 300 and each chiefdom has its small police force. Sierra Leone recently acquired two Saab MFI-15 light trainer aircraft.

SOMALIA

Al-Jumhouriya As-Somaliya
Al-Democradiya
Somali Democratic Republic

POWER POTENTIAL STATISTICS

Area: 246,155 square miles
Population: 3,000,000
Total Active Armed Forces: 22,750 (including security troops; 0.75% population)
Gross National Product: $190 million ($63 per capita)
Annual Military Expenditures: $9.0 million (4.7% GNP)
Electric Power Output: 70 million kwh
Merchant Fleet: 148 ships; 873,209 gross tons
Civil Air Fleet: 2 turboprop and 5 piston transports

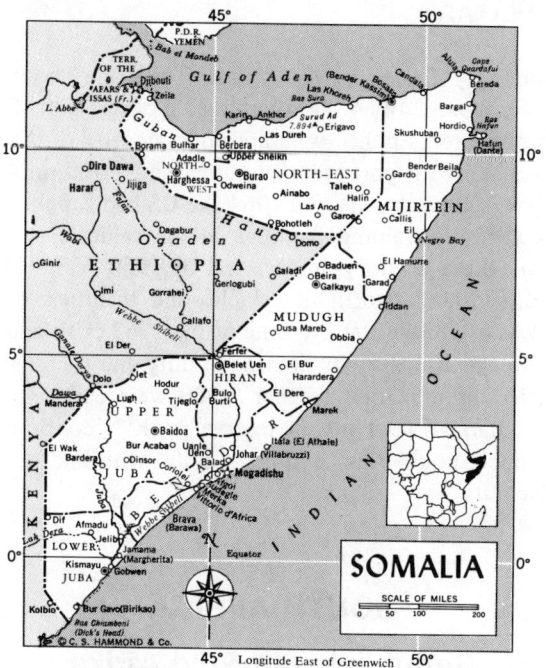

POLITICO-MILITARY POLICIES AND POSTURE

In October 1969, following the assassination of the President, the army and police seized power. A Supreme Revolutionary Council was established, the National Assembly and Cabinet were dissolved, political parties were abolished, the constitution suspended, and the Prime Minister arrested.

The new regime announced that it would support all liberation movements in countries under colonial rule, as well as those in illegally occupied territory. This particularly refers to about 1,000,000 Somalis living in Ethiopia, Kenya, and the French Territory of the Afars and the Issas. Although Somalia proclaimed a policy of nonalignment in foreign relations, its foreign policy has been consistently anti-Western and pro-Communist. Somalia supports the Arab cause in the Arab-Israeli conflict.

The Somali people are made up of separate clan-families that are an important focus of loyalty. The Issas of the French territory of the Afars and Issas, for example, are such a Somali clan-family. The Darod clan-family is the largest, and most Somalis living in Kenya and Ethiopia belong to this group; Darods within Somalia have especially advocated unification of all Somalis in one nation-state, and when Darods have held top government positions, unification has generally been pushed most strongly.

The fact that the Somalis are a nomadic people, and that many of them live in Somalia and also in Kenya or Ethiopia during the same year, further complicates the matter of Somalian nationality.

In 1963 Somalia rejected a joint US-Italian military aid proposal as too small to liberate the Somalis outside the country. It turned instead to the Soviet Union and received a $32 million loan with the objective of raising a 10,000-man army; the Soviets trained the army. It is estimated that later additions raised the amount loaned to $55 million. Up to 1967, when the previous government stopped its arms buildup, it is believed that Somalia received about 40 aircraft, 150 armored vehicles, antiaircraft and field artillery, and quantities of vehicles and infantry weapons. The port of Berbera, 150 miles from the strategic strait of Bab el Mandeb was modernized by the Russians to handle ships up to 10,000 tons and provided with radar. The Soviets have apparently built an airfield in the interior with SAM-2 missile sites around it. After the 1969 military coup, Soviet military assistance to Somalia increased considerably, and several hundred Soviet officers serve as military advisers and technicians.

Somalia is useful to the Soviet Union as a base on the Red Sea. The Soviet-built facilities at Berbera, Kismayu (used by Italian submarines during World War II), Mogadishu, and other ports appear to be far beyond anything needed or usable by Somalia. The Soviet Defense Minister paid a four-day visit to Somalia in February 1972.

Military assistance has also been received from other countries. Egypt supplied 12 torpedo boats, training aircraft, and light arms for Somali guerrillas. Sudan trained staff officers, cadets, and signal and engineer NCOs. Somali soldiers were also trained in the USSR, People's Republic of China, Egypt, Italy, Iraq, and Syria. The United States, Italy, and West Germany supplied equipment and training for the police and a commando battalion. This assistance was suspended in 1970.

In addition to Somalia's strategic location at the Horn of Africa, it achieved further strategic significance in early 1968 with the discovery by UN geologists of what may be one of the world's largest deposits of uranium ore. The ore is close to the surface and susceptible to economical strip mining methods. This discovery and its exploitation is of great importance in the light of increasing world demands for nuclear fuel.

Communist China signed an economic aid agreement with Somalia in 1970 that provided about $125 million in projects including road building, agriculture, and fisheries.

Agreements ending conflict along the Somali borders, at least temporarily, were signed with Kenya in 1967 and Ethiopia in 1968; a policy of relative detente and relaxation of Somali irredentism has been continued by the military regime since 1969. Somalia still remains committed to eventual unification, and also serves as a refuge and base for Somali liberation groups and for other liberation groups operating in Ethiopia.

Military service is voluntary; but all students over 18 years of age are required to undergo military training.

ARMY

Personnel: 13,000

Organization:
- 9 mechanized infantry battalions (700 men each)
- 4 tank battalions
- 1 commando battalion
- 2 field artillery battalions
- 2 heavy AA battalions
- 3 light AA battalions

Major Equipment Inventory:
- 220 medium tanks (T-34, T-55)
- 250 APCs (BTR-40, BTR-50, BTR-152)
- 100 guns and howitzers (76mm guns, 122mm howitzers, 100mm radar controlled AA guns, 37mm AA guns, 14.5mm automatic AA cannon)

NAVY

Personnel: 250

Major Units:
- 6 patrol gunboats (USSR Poluchat type) (PGM)
- 12 fast torpedo boats (P-6 type) (PT)
- 1 Komar class fast rocket torpedo boat (PT with Styx SSM)

AIR FORCE

Personnel: 2,500

Organization:
- 2 fighter squadrons (MiG-15, MiG-17)
- 1 light bomber squadron (Il-28)
- 1 transport squadron (An-24, An-26)
- 1 helicopter unit (Mi-4, Mi-8)

Major Aircraft Types:
- 36 combat aircraft
  - 12 fighters (MiG-17)
  - 12 fighters (MiG-15)
  - 12 light bombers (Il-28)
- 66 other aircraft
  - 19 transports (3 An-2, 12 An-24/An-26, 4 C-47)
  - 12 helicopters (Mi-4, Mi-8)
  - 35 trainers (Piaggio P-148, Yak-11, MiG-15)

Major Air Bases: Hargesia, Mogadishu

PARAMILITARY

Paramilitary forces are significant. There are about 7,000 police composed of 4,000 National Police, 500 Finance Guards or customs police who are under control of the armed forces probably for port security duties, and 2,500 rural police or *Illaloes*, a constabulary. To 1964 the US had supplied $1.57 million worth of training, facilities, radios, vehicles, and patrol boats for these security forces, and in 1968 West Germany supplied $750,000 worth of vehicles and facilities. A Home Guard was established at the time of the 1967 crisis and 3,000 men were called up for six months of duty and training. Upon completion of this tour another 3,000 were called up while those discharged went into a reserve pool. If continued, the reserve pool should now number 12,000 with another 3,000 on active duty.

SOUTH AFRICA
Republiek van Suid-Afrika
Republic of South Africa

POWER POTENTIAL STATISTICS

Area: 790,261 square miles (including South West Africa)
Population: 23,746,320 (including South West Africa; 3,900,000 whites)
Total Active Armed Forces: 47,600 (includes anti-terrorist police; 0.22% population)
Gross National Product: $21.7 billion ($820 per capita
Annual Military Expenditures: $583.2 million (2.68% GNP)
Iron and Steel Production: 21.6 million metric tons
Uranium Oxide Production: 5.069 metric tons
Fuel Production: Coal: 58.4 million metric tons
  Refined Petroleum Products: 11.4 million metric tons
Electric Power Output: 52.9 billion kwh
Merchant Fleet: 255 ships; 511,190 gross tons
Civil Air Fleet: 34 jet, 3 turboprop, and 64 piston transports

DEFENSE STRUCTURE

Under a combined presidential-parliamentary system the President, elected by a bicameral Parliament, is chief of state and nominally commander in chief of the South African Defence Force (Suid-Afrikaanse Weermag). Actual power is vested in the Prime Minister, head of the majority party in Parliament, who controls the Defence Force through a Minister of Defence. Due to South Africa's internal security situation a Ministry of Police (since combined into a Ministry of Interior and Police) was established in 1966; the Prime Minister for a time held the portfolios of both that ministry and the Ministry of Defence.

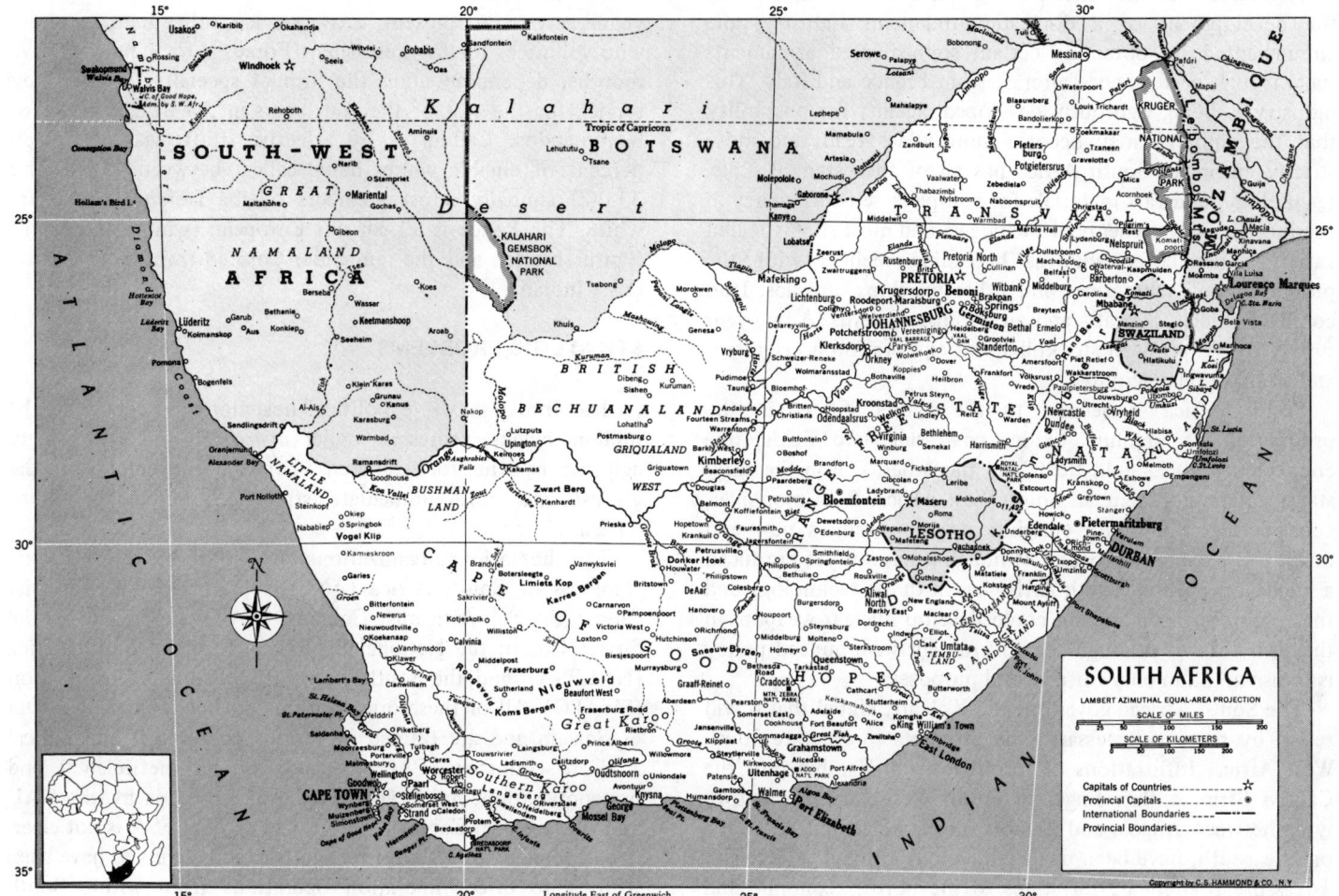

The Defence Force consists of the Permanent Force of professionals, the Citizen Force of part-time soldiers, and the Kommando Force of a home guard nature. The Permanent Force and the Citizen Force have ground, sea, and air components, while the Kommandos have ground and air units. The Defence Force has an integrated organization under a Commandant-General. Under him are Chiefs of Staff of the Army, Navy, and Air Force, and an Adjutant-General, a Quartermaster-General, and a Surgeon-General whose functions are essentially administrative. For operations, service components are integrated under a Commander Joint Combat Forces, who reports to the Commandant-General.

POLITICO-MILITARY POLICY

South Africa's basic social policy of *apartheid* (separation of white and black races in most activities and stringent restriction of the civil rights of blacks) has caused most of the nation's strategic problems. These in turn have necessitated a series of responsive policies.

The threat of foreign-based black liberation movements, the potential for revolt among the black two-thirds of the population, the UN arms embargo endorsed by most nations, the bellicose calls for invasion by the black African states, and action in the UN and the International Court of Justice to remove South West Africa (Namibia) from under South Africa's authority, have all resulted in positive acts and policy statements.

To deter external attack and internal revolt, provisions for defense have been strengthened and a state of siege proclaimed. Defense capability is based upon a rapid mobilization of the highly trained Citizen Force to augment the small Permanent Force. Emphasis has been placed upon mobility and striking power for all permanent and mobilized units. Kommando units were increased, given more intensive training, and provided with modern weapons. Physical security of key installations has been increased with fences, guard towers, lighting, and the like. Internal security matters are the subject of top-level coordination between SADF and the Police. The 1971 defense budget was increased about 20 percent over the previous year and was several times that of 1960.

The effects of the arms embargo have been attenuated by the development of a domestic armaments industry, and circumvented by obtaining certain sophisticated armaments such as high performance aircraft from France and Italy. This industry is being vigorously developed, against the possibility that the embargo may become more widespread, and more strictly enforced. South Africa has all of the essential skills, technology, and raw materials for complete self-sufficiency in production of armaments of the largest and most sophisticated variety. This potentiality is becoming reality, with the production of submarines and other warships, missiles, land combat vehicles, aircraft, and air defense systems. A two-year supply of oil has been stockpiled, oil exploration accelerated, and a tanker fleet acquired.

South Africa is second to the United States in the production of uranium oxide, possessing two fields, one connected with its gold fields and the other, still in the early stages of development, in South West Africa. It is, moreover, constructing a uranium enrichment plant using a new and much less expensive process. Although it has not yet produced a nuclear explosion, South Africa has both the technology and the resources to do so, and could develop nuclear weapons in the near future, although the government's announced policy is to use uranium only for peaceful purposes.

The South African government has clearly stated that it will resist, by force if necessary, any attempts to separate South West Africa. Infiltrations of terrorists from Zambia into the Caprivi Strip, a thin finger of South West African territory lying between Angola and Zambia on the north and Botswana on the south, have been dealt with promptly and effectively. To assure friendly buffer states to the north, economic and military support have been given to northern neighbors, particularly Rhodesia and the Portuguese territories of Angola and Mozambique. Normal relations are also offered the neighboring black African states, and are enjoyed by Botswana, Lesotho, Swaziland and Malawi. These states cooperate with South Africa, Rhodesia, and Portugal in security matters.

South Africa has announced that it will fight the terrorists wherever the opportunity is offered. It has made good this offer in Rhodesia and, if needed, can be expected to do so elsewhere. It has also stated that it will hit back at countries providing bases and sanctuaries for the terrorists. To date the situation has not become desperate enough to warrant such retaliation, but there is little doubt that South Africa has the will to do this, should it seem necessary

The Communist Party was declared illegal in South Africa in 1950. Despite strong disapproval of South Africa's internal policies, the US and Britain find it convenient to collaborate with South Africa against any external communist threat to Southern Africa and its approaches. In this connection South Africa has assumed the mission of assisting in keeping open the Cape of Good Hope sea routes in the event of general war.

Citizens from 17 to 65 years of age are liable for military service on call, and those 17 to 25 are liable for up to four years' service. At present, active service, other than for those who volunteer for the Permanent Force, is for nine or twelve months, depending upon the arm of specialty, followed by service for the rest of the four years in the Citizen Force or Kommandos. Call-up is by selective draft with about 80 percent of eligible whites being called, between 25,000 and 33,000 annually. Most members of the Defence Force are white. The Police is 50 percent European (white) 45 percent Bantu (black), and the remainder Colored (mixed) or Asiatic (East Indian).

STRATEGIC PROBLEMS

The threat to white political hegemony posed by the 14 million blacks, repressed under *apartheid* and increasingly agitated by the foreign-based liberation movements, is the gravest and most immediate strategic problem for South Africa.

The liberation organizations are: the African National Congress of South Africa (ANC), supported by Communist China; the Pan-Africanist Congress (PAC), supported by the Soviet Union; the National Liberation Front of South Africa (NALFSA), and the South West Africa People's Organization (SWAPO). All of these organizations are headquartered in Dar es Salaam and are trained in various communist and radical African countries. PAC, because of its inefficiency and noncooperation, has been denied further funds by the OAU and outlawed in Zambia. The future of NALFSA is not clear; it has applied to OAU for recognition and claims to have been formed to direct liberation operations from within South Africa; the others are supported by the OAU Liberation Committee. ANC and SWAPO coordinate their activities and cooperate with the Rhodesian movements, ZANU and ZAPU, as well. They have bases in Tanzania and Zambia, and have trained some 2,000 terrorists. Most of the political resistance to South African rule over South West Africa comes from a small but politically sophisticated Herero tribe who occupy the land in the center of the territory.

As internal dissatisfaction has caused a tightening of security measures in South Africa, infiltrations across northern borders have led to the establishment of forward defense by the Defence Force. This has included intensive operations in the Caprivi Strip, support of Rhodesia with police units, building a jet airbase and holding large-scale maneuvers near the Rhodesian border, and cooperation and unspecified assistance to Portuguese territories and Botswana.

In the light of white South Africa's determination and socio-economic viability, as well as constant and efficient attention to security measures—as opposed to the disunity and military weakness of the rest of Africa—combined with the operational and logistical difficulties of getting at South Africa, it is difficult to see how the liberation movements can be more than an irritation over the next few years. Over the longer term, however, the picture can well be different, with almost inevitable white relaxation of restrictions as the blacks gain more education and economic strength. This will result in increasing viability of internal black anti-regime forces. Eventually it would appear that white South Africa must seek a satisfactory accommodation with its black citizenry, or else risk serious, and probably disastrous insurgency.

South Africa's position at the southern tip of the African continent controls sea lanes from the Atlantic to the Indian Ocean and the Far East; these have an increased importance whenever the Suez Canal or the Mediterranean is closed. The former British naval base at Simonstown, near Capetown, to which Britain retains use rights, has the biggest and best equipped drydock and dockyard between Europe and Singapore. With Britain's withdrawal of nearly all forces east of Suez, and the entry of Soviet fleet units into the Indian Ocean, South Africa anticipates an eventual threat to its sea flanks and is strengthening its defense forces by acquiring more coastal craft and helicopters, by establishing a submarine base to accommodate three submarines constructed in France, and by opening a new maritime headquarters at the Cape. A reconstructed naval base at Durban was opened in 1971.

MILITARY ASSISTANCE

Until the arms embargo in 1963, some ground force weapons, ships, and most aircraft were purchased from Britain, with some aircraft coming from the US. Since the embargo France has sold over $100 million in arms to South Africa, including Mirage III jet fighters with air-to-surface missiles, helicopters, transports, AMX tanks, and AML armored cars, and three Daphne class coastal submarines. Italy has sold MB-326 armed jet trainers and components and tools with which to build 300 more. West German scientists and firms are reported to be helping to build nuclear reactors and to develop guided missiles. Under an agreement concluded in June 1971, French designed Mirage III and F-1 jet fighters will be built under license in South Africa. Total US military sales 1970-72 equal $3.15 million.

In addition to the police assistance mentioned, South Africa is probably furnishing arms and military advice to Rhodesia. Advice and cooperation in security matters is also extended to Portuguese territories, Malawi, Botswana, Lesotho, and Swaziland. Historically South Africa has been aligned with the West, fighting as a member of the Commonwealth with the allies in World Wars I and II, participating in the Berlin Airlift in 1948, and sending a fighter-bomber squadron to the UN Command in the Korean War from September 1950 until the armistice in 1953.

ALLIANCES

South Africa keeps its membership in the UN although it has withdrawn or has been expelled from some of the specialized agencies. When it became a republic in 1961 South Africa withdrew from the Commonwealth.

South Africa has no openly formal alliances with Rhodesia or Portugal, stating these are not necessary between good neighbors. However, the South African Prime Minister has expressed a willingness to send troops whenever and wherever they are asked for. In 1967 the South African and Portuguese defense ministers met in Lisbon and proclaimed a common objective to pursue resolutely the defense of their positions in Africa.

The United States under a joint agreement maintains three space tracking stations in the vicinity of Pretoria. One is operated by the Department of Defense; the other two by NASA.

Under the Simonstown Naval Base Agreements of 1955 and 1961, the South African Navy cooperated with the Royal Navy and provided base facilities in return for assistance in arms procurement. Under a revised agreement, Britain has withdrawn Royal Navy units stationed at the base, and the two countries will jointly command the base. The British government is legally obligated under terms of the Simonstown Agreement to supply the South African government with a number of Westland Wasp helicopters to equip three frigates supplied earlier, as well as spare parts to keep the ships operational.

ARMY

Personnel: 32,000 (10,000 regular and 22,000 Citizen Force)

Organization: eleven territorial commands: Western Province, Eastern Province, Natal, Orange Free State, Western Transvaal, Northern Transvaal, Witwatersrand, North West Cape, South West Africa, South Western Districts, and Walvisbaai Commands. Within these commands, there are training units and full-time force units, the permanent staff being formed by members of the Permanent Force. Combat arms of the Permanent Force are organized into battalions with smaller units for supporting services. Similar Citizen Force units are rapidly mobilizable and combine with Permanent Force units into brigades and task forces.

Major Equipment Inventory:
- 240 medium tanks (Centurion Mk.5, M-4, and Comet)
- light tanks (AMX-13)
- 550 armored cars (Staghound, AML-60, AML-90)
- 200 scout cars (Ferret)
- APCs (Saracen)
- light and medium artillery
- antiaircraft artillery

Reserves: About 205,000, including 23,000 in organized Citizen Force units, and 75,000 Kommandos.

NAVY

Personnel: 4,600 (3,350 Permanent Force, 1,250 Citizen Force in training)

Major Units:
- 2 destroyers (DD, with Wasp ASW helicopters)
- 6 frigates (DE, 3 with Wasp ASW helicopters)
- 3 submarines (SS; French-built Daphne class)
- 1 escort minesweeper (PF/MSF)
- 10 coastal minesweepers (MSC)
- 5 seaward defense craft (SC)
- 5 patrol boats (YP)
- 1 fleet replenishment ship (AOE)
- 9 auxiliaries

Naval Bases: Simonstown, Capetown, East London, Port Elizabeth, Durban, Walvis Bay

Reserves: 4,750 trained reserves in Citizen Force

AIR FORCE

Personnel: 8,000 (5,000 Regular, 3,000 Active Citizen Force)

Organization:
Strike Command
- 3 fighter/fighter reconnaissance squadrons (Sabre, Mirage)
- 2 strike reconnaissance squadrons (Canberra, Buccaneer)

Maritime Command
- 1 maritime patrol squadron (Shackleton)
- 1 short range patrol, fish surveillance (Piaggio P-166)
- 1 ASW flight (Wasp helicopters on destroyers and frigates)

Transport Command
- 1 long range transport squadron (C-130, C-160)
- 2 transport squadrons (C-47, DC-4)
- 1 VIP transport squadron (Viscount, C-47, HS-125)

Light Aircraft Command
- 4 helicopter squadrons (Alouette III, Puma, Super Frelon)
- *6 refresher training squadrons (MB-326 Impala, T-6)
- *2 forward air controller squadrons (Cessna A-185)
- *12 air commando squadrons, civil auxiliary (light civil aircraft)

Training Group
Primary, basic, advanced weapons training, multi-engine, helicopter schools (T-6, Impala, C-47, Alouette II/III, Vampire)

Maintenance Group

Major Aircraft Types:
- 114 combat aircraft
  - 48 Mirage, fighter/fighter reconnaissance
  - 20 Sabre fighters
  - 9 Canberra strike reconnaissance
  - 15 Buccaneer strike reconnaissance
  - 8 Shackleton maritime patrol
  - 9 P-166 Albatross short range maritime patrol (9 P-166 on order)
  - 5 Wasp ASW helicopters (7 Wasp on order)
- 651 other aircraft
  - 54 transports (7 C-130, 9 C-160, 23 C-47, 5 DC-4, 1 Viscount, 4 HS-125, 5 Do-27)
  - 40 army support (FAC) (Cessna 185, AM-3C)
  - 76 helicopters (40 Alouette III, 20 Puma, 16 Super Frelon)
  - 421 training aircraft, primary, basic, multi engine, advanced weapons, helicopter (170 T-6, 200 Impala, Vampire)

Missiles: Matra R-530, Aerospatiale AS-30, ASM, Cactus all weather SAM, Sidewinder, AIM.

Air Bases: Swartkop (Pretoria), Waterkloof, Langebaanweg Cape, Rooikop, Dunnottar, Lyttleton, Ysterplatt, Bloemspruit, Bloemfontein, Pretoria, Durban, Capetown, Germiston, Port Elizabeth, Pietersburg, Potchefstroom

Reserves: The Citizen Air Force is organized into eight squadrons operating Impala and T-6 armed trainers and C-47 transports.

PARAMILITARY

The National Police numbers about 32,700 (one-half white) and has reserve of 12,000 (all white). An anti-terrorist police force of 3,000 is equipped with 430 riot trucks, 80 Saracen APCs, and heavy infantry weapons.

The Kommandos, or militia with an essentially home guard function, number about 75,000 and are organized into infantry, armored car, and air units.

---

*Active Citizen Force (ACF) squadrons.

AFRICA 259

SUDAN

Jamhuryat es-Sudan al-Democratia
Democratic Republic of the Sudan

POWER POTENTIAL STATISTICS

Area: 967,491 square miles
Population: 17,400,000
Total Active Armed Forces: 40,100 (including frontier and national police; 0.23% population)
Gross National Product: $2 billion ($115 per capita)
Annual Military Expenditures: $174 million (8.7% GNP)
Refined Petroleum Products: 1.1 million metric tons
Electric Power Output: 392 million kwh

Merchant Fleet: 14 ships; 35,502 gross tons
Civil Air Fleet: 2 jet, 8 turboprop, and 1 piston transport

DEFENSE STRUCTURE

The President of the Republic is commander in chief of the armed forces. He is currently also Prime Minister. The Second Vice-President is presently Defense Minister. Under the Defense Ministry is the Headquarters of the Armed Forces, which controls six regional commands—Northern, Eastern, Central, Western, and Southern Commands, and the Khartoum Garrison.

POLITICO-MILITARY POLICY

The British-officered Sudan Defense Force became the Sudan Armed Forces upon independence in 1956. Following the Arab-Israeli War of 1967, Sudan dropped its policy of neutrality in world affairs for one of active support of Arab opposition to Israel and its supporters. To demonstrate this policy a contingent of 2,000 troops is maintained on the Suez Canal, and relations with Britain and the United States were severed.

Sudan has supported the UN in its peacekeeping efforts, having sent an infantry battalion for the first nine months of the UN Operation in the Congo, 1960-1961. Sudan advocates self-determination for the black peoples now under white-dominated regimes in southern Africa, and opposes African regimes which it considers reactionary. Evidence of the latter policy was support of rebels against the Mobutu government in the Congo (now Zaire) in 1964-1965.

Enlistment in the services is voluntary; there are more candidates than vacancies. Since a 1955 revolt of Negro units from the southern provinces, they have not been enlisted, nor have Nile Valley villagers. The forces thus are composed mainly of nomadic tribesmen.

STRATEGIC PROBLEMS

Sudan has long been considered a natural bridge between the Arab world and Black Africa. Psychologically, this concept has reduced significance at this time after more than a decade of internal conflict between the Arab north and the Negro south.

Although the sources of the Nile River, which gives life to Egypt, lie in Ethiopia and Uganda, most of its course passes through Sudan. Increasing amounts are being diverted for various irrigation schemes, and potentially Sudan could control it totally and reduce the flow to Egypt to a trickle. For this reason Egypt, or powers occupying Egypt, have historically sought to dominate the Sudan.

Sudan is divided ethnically and religiously between some ten million Arabic-speaking Moslems in the northern six provinces and about four million Negro animist and Christian peoples in the southern three provinces. For generations the poorer southerners have felt oppressed by the more developed and politically dominant northerners. From 1958 until early 1972 most of the south was in armed revolt, seeking autonomy. The revolt resulted in at least a half-million deaths and a quarter-million refugees in the five countries bordering the south. The revolt was ended by an agreement of March 1972, creating South Sudan as an autonomous region.

In July 1971 the government was temporarily overthrown by a group of left-wing officers. The coup was communist-inspired and the powerful Communist Party of Sudan came out in open support of the new regime. Lasting only three days, the new regime was toppled by military forces loyal to the President, General al Nemery. The coup leaders were arrested, tried, and executed. A purge of the Communist Party followed; its Secretary General was arrested, convicted and executed. The Party was outlawed and its members went into hiding or were arrested. The coup's failure was a setback for Soviet policy in the Sudan. Soviet-Sudanese relations became strained and Sudan sought closer relations with Peking and the West; however, several hundred Soviet military advisers remained in the country.

MILITARY ASSISTANCE

In 1956 Britain left sufficient weapons and equipment to outfit the small armed forces then planned. Small British army and air training missions continued in Sudan through 1966. Naval training has been conducted in Britain and Yugoslavia. Air training has been conducted in Egypt, Britain, Ethiopia, Yugoslavia, and West Germany. Aircraft have been obtained from Britain, the Netherlands, Switzerland, and Egypt. Military training has been provided by Britain, the United States, Ethiopia, Pakistan, and India. Small arms, artillery, and vehicles have been purchased from West Germany and armored cars from Britain and the United States. From 1956 through 1972 the US has provided $700,000 worth of military aid and trained 125 students under the MAP.

Following the 1967 change of policy toward the West, Sudan has accepted large quantities of military aid from the Soviet Union, Czechoslovakia, and Yugoslavia. The Soviet program alone has amounted to about $150 million. Soviet and Czech contributions included tanks, armored personnel carriers, artillery, and jet aircraft, as well as training missions. This has represented the Soviet Union's first significant military assistance effort in sub-Saharan Africa. Since 1971, Communist China has made large loans for development purposes and has offered to supply Sudan with arms and with spares for Soviet weapons. In 1972 an agreement was reportedly signed under which the Chinese would provide training for the Sudanese Army.

Sudan has provided training for Somalian staff officers, officer cadets, and signal and engineer NCOs. It is also alleged to have given sanctuary and training to Chadian and Eritrean dissidents, and to have allowed arms shipments to the Eritreans and to rebels against Zaire government.

ALLIANCES

Sudan is a member of the UN, the OAU, and the Arab League.

ARMY

Personnel: 35,000

Organization:
    6 infantry brigades
    1 independent infantry battalion
    1 armored brigade
    3 artillery regiments

1 parachute regiment
5 AA battalions
1 engineer regiment

Deployment: Two thirds of the Army has been in the three southern provinces. One unit (2000 men) is with the Egyptians on the Suez Canal.

Major Equipment Inventory:
- 100 T-54/55 medium tanks (50 each)
- 20 T-34 medium tanks
- 20 T-62 light tanks
- 95 armored cars (Saladin and M-706 Commando)
- 200 APCs (BTR-40, BTR-152, and Saracen)
- 60 scout cars (Ferret)
- 55 25-pounder guns
- 40 105mm howitzers
- 122mm guns and howitzers
- 20 120mm mortars
- 80+40mm (Bofors) and 37mm and 85mm (Soviet) AA guns
- SAMs (Sa-2 Guideline)

NAVY

Personnel: 600

Organization: Coastal Patrol unit at Port Sudan: River Patrol unit on Nile River

Major Units:
- 2 patrol gunboats (PGM), 190 tons
- 4 patrol gunboats (PGM), 100 tons
- 3 auxiliaries
- 2 landing craft

Naval Bases: Port Sudan, Khartoum

AIR FORCE

Personnel: 1,500

Major Aircraft Types:
- 46 combat aircraft
  - 16 MiG-21 fighters
  - 15 MiG-17 fighter-bombers
  - 15 Jet Provost ground attack aircraft
- 66 other aircraft
  - 4 F-27M Troopship transports
  - 5 An-24 transports
  - 6 An-12 transports
  - 3 Pembroke light transports
  - 8 PC-6A light transports
  - 10 Mi-8 helicopters
  - 30 trainers (Provost and others)

Air Bases: Khartoum, Malakal, Juba, Atbara, Geneina, El Obeid, El Fashir, Wad Medani, Dongola, Merowe, Waw, and Port Sudan.

PARAMILITARY

There are 2,000 Frontier Police and 1,000 civil police.

SWAZILAND

POWER POTENTIAL STATISTICS

Area: 6,704 square miles
Population: 500,000
Total Active Police Forces: 1,100 (.22% population)
Gross National Product: $110 million ($247 per capita)
Iron Ore Production: 3.1 million metric tons
Fuel Production: Coal: 130,000 metric tons
Electric Power Output: 90 million kwh
Annual Military and Police Expenditures: $1.9 million (1.72% GNP)
Civil Air Fleet: 4 piston transports

POLITICO-MILITARY POLICIES AND POSTURE

As a constitutional monarch within the British Commonwealth, the King is chief of state with a Prime Minister heading the government. The Prime Minister is appointed by the King from the Parliament and exercises executive authority.

Swaziland's independence, granted by Britain in 1968, depends upon collective security and strict neutrality. Bordered by Mozambique on one side and South Africa on the others it has cooperated with the police of both of these white-controlled countries in running down insurgents who attempt to use Swaziland as a refuge.

Swaziland depends on Mozambique and South Africa both as markets for agricultural exports and as sources of manufactured goods. Furthermore, a railroad running through Mozambique to the port of Lourenco Marques is the only means of marketing its mineral exports, which provide economic viability and a relatively high (for Africa) GNP per capita. Swaziland is the world's fifth largest producer of asbestos. Coal and tin are also mined.

A potential for internal dissension exists in the distribution of land and the new mineral and industrial wealth. About 40 percent of the land is owned by the few thousand Europeans and Eur-Africans. These same people generally are the investors in new enterprises of the burgeoning economy.

Another potential problem of internal and external security stems from dissent among the blacks of South Africa and the active insurgency underway in Mozambique. While the government of Swaziland is against *apartheid* and in favor of self-determination, its weakness and dependence place it on the horns of a policy dilemma.

Swaziland is a member of the British Commonwealth, the UN and the OAU.

In addition to a police force of 600 men, and the new 500-man army, the King has a force of 4,000 Swazi warrior-retainers. However, they probably do not possess modern weapons and so would have limited use as a paramilitary force until armed and trained.

Swazi Air Limited, with 35 pilots and a number of piston transports and light aircraft, provides internal transportation and connections with world air routes.

TANZANIA

United Republic of Tanzania

POWER POTENTIAL STATISTICS

Area: 364,943 square miles
Population: 14,500,000
Total Active Armed Forces: 11,600 (0.08% population)
Gross National Product: $1.6 billion ($110 per capita)
Annual Military Expenditures: $39.2 million (2.45% GNP)
Refined Petroleum Products: 819,800 metric tons
Electric Power Output: 396 million kwh
Merchant Fleet: 11 ships; 18,218 gross tons
Civil Air Fleet: 5 piston aircraft

DEFENSE STRUCTURE

The Tanzanian armed forces differ greatly from the defense establishment in other formerly British nations, largely as a result of the extensive remodeling of the Army undertaken by President Nyerere following a mutiny in January 1964. Civilian control is exercised directly by the President, although nominally all defense matters are under the jurisdiction of the Office of the Second Vice-President. The First Vice-President of Tanzania (who by the terms of the Tanganyika-Zanzibar merger in April 1964 is also the President of Zanzibar) is also the nominal head of the Zanzibar portions of the armed forces. The Chief of Staff theoretically commands the entire military establishment, which has been named the Tanzanian People's Defence Forces (TPDF). In practice, the senior officer on Zanzibar commands the island portion of the TPDF.

POLITICO-MILITARY POLICY

At present, due to the small size of the TPDF, and the large supply of available manpower, no conscription is necessary. Enlistments are for a two-year term. Tanzania also has a nonmilitary National Service Corps, which is obligatory for all male high school and college graduates from the ages of 18 to 35. After the disbanding of the mutinous Tanganyika Rifles in 1964, the bulk of the recruits for the TPDF were obtained from the National Service Corps. At present there are no formal reserve forces, although the surplus of manpower, coupled with the government's desire to involve the citizenry actively in nationbuilding, has led to several tentative efforts in that direction. In March 1965 the Tanzanian Parliament approved plans to create Field Force Units in each region and to give members of the Police Force, Prison Service, National Service, and the Youth League of the Tanganyika African National Union (TANU) full military training with modern weapons. (TANU is the only legal political party in mainland Tanzania.)

Tanzania's foreign policy is nonaligned in international affairs, seeking friendly relations with all reciprocating countries. The notable exception in Tanzania's insistence on majority rule by the Africans of Southern Africa and disapproval of any African country which is unduly influenced by the white Southern African regimes or by outside powers. In furtherance of the goal of African unity, Tanzania belongs to: (1) the OAU, and to its Liberation Coordinating Committee for which it provides a headquarters in Dar es Salaam, and (2) the East African Community, for which it also provides a headquarters at Arusha. Further, it allows sanctuary, training bases, and arms shipments for various liberation movements and exile groups. After the military coup in Uganda overthrew President Obote in January 1971, relations between Uganda and Tanzania became strained. Obote took refuge in Tanzania, and his claims have been supported by President Nyerere. There was a brief invasion of Uganda by Obote supporters based in Tanzania in 1972, but it was quickly suppressed.

STRATEGIC PROBLEMS

Although Tanzania has been spared the sort of tribal dissensions which have created severe internal security problems elsewhere in Africa, the geopolitical position of Tanzania, and its policy objectives, have caused it to become a logical haven for guerrilla bands dedicated to overthrowing the white regimes in the south of the continent. Their presence could provoke retaliation from white African governments. Tanzania has objected to reconnaissance flights over its territory by Portuguese aircraft from neighboring Mozambique. Sporadic incidents along the Ruvuma River, boundary between Tanzania and Mozambique, have also occurred.

Tanzania's neutral policy, and its need for development and military assistance, have caused it to seek and accept aid from all quarters. Communist China has responded to Tanzanian receptiveness with substantial aid grants. China appears to be trying to gain a foothold in this country, which borders on eight other African nations, and which serves as a base for numerous liberation movements. The Chinese have completely built, equipped, and staffed a police college at Moshi, have established a joint shipping line with two ships, have trained and equipped the marine police force, and have established propaganda outlets by building and operating a 50-kilowatt radio broadcasting station as well as a university bookstore and student center. Construction of the planned 1,116 mile Tanzania-Zambia railroad (from Kapiri Mposhi to Dar es Salaam, begun on October 16, 1970), will ensure the presence of over 13,000 Chinese in Tanzania and Zambia for seven to ten years. These Chinese technicians and workers are all members of the railway engineering and signal corps of the People's Liberation Army and have received basic military training. Both Chinese and Cubans are training the freedom fighters of the various liberation movements whose camps are in the area to be traversed by the railroad. It would be easy to turn these against the Tanzanian government, or to train indigenous malcontents secretly should the government lean the wrong way.

There are few dangerous ethnic, political, or economic divisions among the Tanzanian people. A plethora of over 120 tribes, none large or powerful enough to constitute an independent political threat to the federal government, has actually served to minimize ethnic differences among the African population. The Arab, Asian, and European populations are too small to constitute a threat to established order. The religious divisions between Moslems, Christian and native religionists are more significant, but at present show no signs of leading to disorders.

MILITARY ASSISTANCE

Arms and training are received from a number of foreign countries, thus avoiding over-dependence on any foreign power. Israel, China, West Germany, and Canada have helped train the Air Force and have furnished aircraft. The Netherlands, Indonesia, and West Germany have provided naval training; West and East Germany and Communist China have provided patrol boats. China has trained and equipped the police and Israel has trained police paratroops. The initial provision of arms was British, but this ceased when Tanzania temporarily broke diplomatic relations in 1965 over Rhodesia. Since then China and the Soviet Union have provided most military equipment. China has been sending increasing amounts of equipment for the TPDF, including two squadrons of MiG-17s (24 aircraft), 28 light and medium tanks, 32 guns and howitzers, an undisclosed number of AA guns, and light arms. In 1971 the Chinese began building a naval base at Dar es Salaam, and China has recently completed a military airfield near Morogoro. Tanzanian sailors and officers as well as pilots and technicians are receiving training in China.

Although sympathetic to the various Southern African liberation movements, it is not known whether or not Tanzania provides direct military assistance. It does provide sanctuary and training, and allows rebels to base and train and receive arms from China in Tanzania. Also its monetary contributions to the OAU's Liberation Coordinating Committee helps support these movements.

ALLIANCES

Tanzania is a member of the UN, the British Commonwealth, the OAU, and the East African Community.

ARMY

Personnel: 10,000

Organization:
- 4 infantry battalions
- 1 artillery battalion
- 1 tank company

Major Equipment Inventory:
- 14 T-69 light tanks
- 16 T-59 medium tanks
- 15 APCs (BTR-152)
- scout cars (BTR-40)
- 20 25-pounder guns
- 76mm Soviet artillery pieces (light)
- Chinese mortars
- 122mm howitzers

NAVY

Personnel: 600

Major Units:
- 6 patrol boats, ex-Chinese Shanghai type (PGM)
- 2 motor torpedo boats, ex-Chinese P-6 (PT)

AIR FORCE

Personnel: 1,000

Major Aircraft Types:
- 24 combat aircraft
  - 24 MiG-17 and MiG-19 fighters (acquired from China; to equip two squadrons)
- 48 other aircraft
  - 11 transports (1 An-12, 5 DHC-3, 4 DHC-4, 1 HS-748)
  - 12 trainers (7 P-149, 5 PA-28-140)
  - 25 utility/liaison

Air Bases: Dar es Salaam, Morogoro, Tabora, Zanzibar

PARAMILITARY

Members of the National Service, Prison Service, Tanzanian Youth League, Police, and other uniformed government employees receive military training and are considered available for paramilitary duties or to expand the Army. The Police, under the Minister for Home Affairs and with a strength of 8,350, includes a 120-man paratroop company and a marine police unit with four patrol boats (YP). Ports patrolled by the Marine Police are Dar es Salaam, Zanzibar and Mtwara.

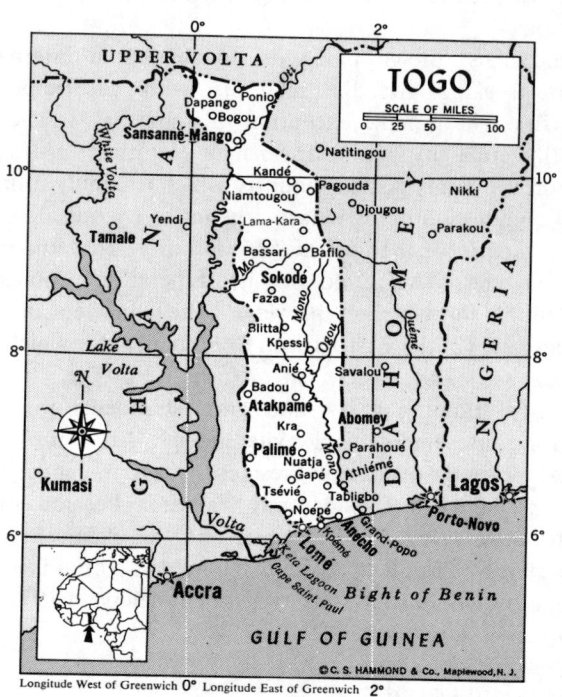

TOGO

Republique Togolaise
Togolese Republic

POWER POTENTIAL STATISTICS

Area: 21,900 square miles
Population: 2,000,000
Total Active Armed Forces: 2,350 (including Gendarmerie; 0.11% population)
Gross National Product: $270 million ($135 per capita)
Annual Military Expenditures: $3.0 million (1.11% GNP)
Electric Power Output: 30 million kwh
Civil Air Fleet: 2 piston transport

POLITICO-MILITARY POLICIES AND POSTURE

The President, as both chief of state and head of the government, is also Commander in Chief of the armed forces and Minister of Defense. The current military ruler, General Eyadema, has consolidated these positions with those he held formerly: Chief of Staff of the Togolese Armed Forces and Commander 1st Battalion Togolese Infantry.

Since independence from French rule in 1960, Togo has maintained close relations with France including a defense agreement, the details of which remain unpublished, as well as agreements for staging, transit, and overflight privileges, and military assistance. Togo is a member of the OCAM and *Conseil de l'Entente*. Togo maintains a policy of nonalignment, and is a member and strong supporter of the UN and a member of the OQU.

Since a military coup in 1967, rule is by decree and ordinance, although a new constitution is being drafted, and a return to civilian government is promised.

Potential ethnic conflict exists between the culturally dominant coastal tribes, particularly the Ewes, and the poor but more warlike northern tribes, particularly the Cabrais, who provide the best soldiers for the Army. The economy, formerly agricultural, has become diversified by exploitation of a 70 million-ton phosphate deposit. Recently discovered are a 550 million-ton deposit of high-grade iron ore and large deposits of limestone and bauxite.

The 1,000 man Army is organized into one infantry battalion, a reconnaissance unit with armored cars, an engineer unit, a band, and supporting elements. Weapons, equipment, and training are French. The Navy with 250 men operates three patrol gunboats (PGM), one offshore patrol, and one river gunboat (PGR). The Air Force has about 100 men and operates one C-47 transport, two Broussard liaison aircraft, and two Alouette helicopters. There is an international airport at Lome and four airstrips in the interior. Paramilitary forces include a Gendarmerie of 1,000 men.

TUNISIA

Al-Djoumhouria Attunusia
Republic of Tunisia

POWER POTENTIAL STATISTICS

Area: 63,378 square miles
Population: 6,000,000
Total Active Armed Forces: 27,650 (includes Gendarmerie; 0.52% population)
Gross National Product: $2.06 billion ($375 per capita)
Annual Military Expenditures: $23 million (1.61% GNP)
Iron Ore Production: 872,047 metric tons
Fuel Production: Crude Oil: 4.1 million metric tons
    Refined Products: 1.1 million metric tons
Electric Power Output: 768 million kwh
Merchant Fleet: 23 ships; 28,268 gross tons
Civil Air Fleet: 5 jet and 1 turboprop transports

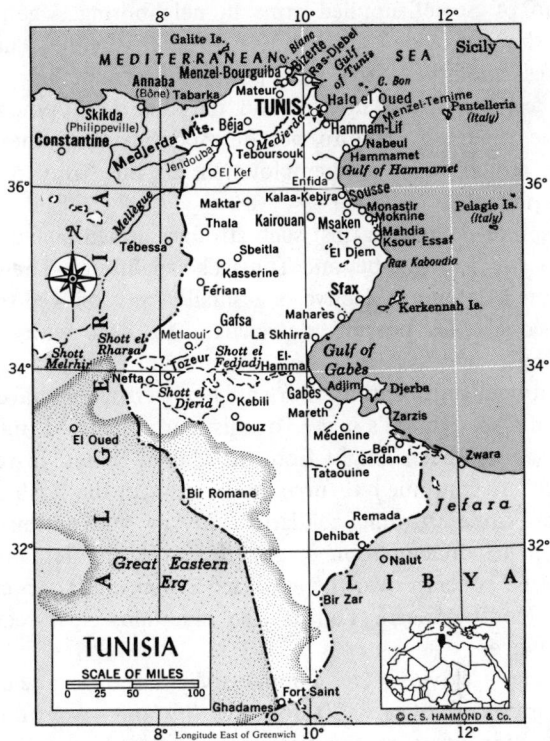

DEFENSE STRUCTURE

A strong President of a one-party political system is chief of state, head of the government, and commander in chief of the armed forces. He appoints his Cabinet, including the Minister of Defense, through whom he administers the armed forces. The Tunisian National Army (TNA) was formed upon independence in 1956 with key positions going to reliable party and resistance movement (*fallagha*) members, although most of the troops were Tunisian veterans of the French Army. The naval and air arms are small adjuncts of the TNA and subordinated to it.

Tunisia's announced, and then aborted, merger with Libya (January 1974) added to concern about the present mental competence of President Habib Bourguiba, a revered figure who led the country to independence in 1956 and has since provided strong and constructive leadership.

POLITICO-MILITARY POLICY

Tunisia has consistently supported policies of moderation in international affairs and collective security through international organizations, particularly the UN. To this end, in 1960 a brigade was sent to the UN Operation in the Congo.

In its attempt to bring reason and moderation to the Arab side in the dispute with Israel, Tunisia has become the target of ideological and subversive attacks from the radical Arab states. These external threats, given greater emphasis by the buildup of Soviet-supplied arms in neighboring Algeria and Libya, have provided an incentive for strengthening Tunisia's defenses, modifying the past policy of channelling scanty resources into social services and national development. To increase readiness, and to permit modernization, there has been a reduction of past employment of the Army on civic action projects.

Absolute defense against such strongly armed neighbors as Algeria and Libya is beyond Tunisia's capabilities. Therefore, the stated defense objective is a small Army of well-trained professionals to provide deterrence, to deal with minor incursions, and so to delay any major attack that an international organization or friendly powers would have time to come to Tunisia's aid. To this end increased military assistance has been sought from the United States. In return, Tunisia has continued to urge moderation in the Arab-Israeli conflict (while affirming solidarity with the Arab nations), did not join in condemnation of America's role in Vietnam, and has voiced concern over the increased Soviet military presence in the Mediterranean. Tunisia also maintains close relations with France.

Military service is compulsory, although selective. Conscription is at age 20 followed by one-year of active service, nine years in the first reserve, and 15 years in the second reserve.

STRATEGIC PROBLEMS

Tunisia's strategic problems stem from its location, the possibility of an attack by radical neighbors, and internal dissent sparked by external subversive efforts as well as its own faltering economy. The naval base at Bizerte, and the port of Tunis, permitting control of the narrow waters between Tunisia and Sicily, make Tunisia's location as strategically significant today as it was in World War II. Tunisia's proven oil reserve of 60 million tons is significant.

Formerly strained relations with Algeria have improved. In January 1971 a treaty of friendship and cooperation was signed between Tunisia and Algeria, and in May a joint military commission completed a final delineation of the frontier. The dispute over the El Borma oil field was resolved in favor of Algeria. However, sources of tension remain on such issues as Tunisia's moderate stand on Israel. Similar tensions exist with Libya, and Tunisia is thus uncomfortably positioned between two radical Arab states. More serious to the Tunisian regime have been frequent subversion attempts by Algerian, Libyan, Syrian, and Egyptian agents. These are probably aided by some leftist elements among Tunisian youth, opposed to the regime's conservatism. The current lack of economic growth, combined with a high birth rate—which are causing the country to fall behind in the race for modernization—also provoke unrest. Following the death or retirement of benevolent dictator President Bourguiba, these pressures could result in a possibly violent change to a more radical government.

MILITARY ASSISTANCE

Extensive French training and equipment continued after independence. Sweden provided training aircraft and pilot instruction in 1960-1961 on a sales basis, as did Italy in 1965-1966. Britain also has sold some arms to Tunisia. A 1961 military assistance treaty with Egypt was apparently never implemented.

From 1960 onward the United States has been the major supplier of arms, all on a grant aid basis. Between 1960 and 1972 $31.4 million in arms was furnished. In this same period about $2.0 million of excess military stocks was provided and 455 were trained under the MAP. In 1968 a formal Military Assistance and Advisory Group was established in Tunis. Aid has included training with US forces in West Germany and the United States, modernizing the infantry weapons of the Army, and the beginning of an air defense system.

ALLIANCES

Tunisia is a member of the UN and the OAU. Although a member of the Arab League, Tunisia has frequently boycotted its meetings because of differences with League policies which preclude the possibility of peace with Israel. Tunisia is also a member of the moribund Maghreb Consultative Committee and has tried to advance cooperation among the four Northwest African states, but with little success.

ARMY

Personnel: 20,000

Organization:
    6 infantry battalions
    1 Sahara patrol group
    1 mixed armored battalion
    1 artillery group
    1 commando battalion

Major Equipment Inventory:
    20 light tanks (M-41 and AMX-13)
    20 armored cars (Saladin and M-8)
    105mm self-propelled guns
    155mm guns
    40mm AA guns (Bofors)

Reserves: About 25,000 trained reservists

NAVY

Personnel: 1,900

Major Units:
- 1 corvette (PCE)
- 1 sub chaser (PC)
- 6 patrol boats (YP)
- 4 patrol gunboats (PGM)
- 7 patrol boats (PCF)
- 1 tug

Naval Bases: Tunis, Bizerte

Reserves: about 3,000

AIR FORCE

Personnel: 750

Major Aircraft Types:
- 20 combat aircraft
  - 12 F-86 fighters
  - 8 MB-326 armed trainers/ground attack aircraft
- 37 other aircraft
  - 3 Flamant light transports
  - 12 T-6 trainers
  - 14 Saab 91 trainers
  - 8 Alouette II helicopters

Air Bases: Tunis (El Aouina), Monastir, Bizerte, Gabes, Sfax, Djerba

Reserves: about 2,500 trained reservists

PARAMILITARY

A Gendarmerie of six battalions totals 5,000. There is a National Guard of 5,000.

UGANDA

POWER POTENTIAL STATISTICS

Area: 91,134 square miles
Population: 10,462,000
Total Active Armed Forces: 9,850 (including security police; 0.09% population)
Gross National Product: $1.50 billion ($143 per capita)
Annual Military Expenditures: $20 million (1.33% GNP)
Electric Power Output: 817 million kwh
Merchant Fleet: 1 ship; 5,510 gross tons
Civil Air Fleet: 7 piston transports

POLITICO-MILITARY POLICIES AND POSTURE

The present government, led by President Idi Amin, came to power in January 1971 through a military coup. The former president, Milton Obote, took refuge in Tanzania, where he has received support from President Nyerere. Clashes between Ugandan and Tanzanian forces along the border followed Amin's takeover, and relations between the two countries have been strained since then.

The present Ugandan armed forces were formed from the former King's African Rifles (KAR), the British colonial army in East Africa, upon independence in 1962. The manpower requirements are easily met by voluntary enlistment.

Most armed forces officers were British until January 1964. At that time the mutinies in Tanganyika and Kenya were duplicated by Ugandan mutineers. Although the uprising was quelled with British assistance, the Army was eventually successful in gaining its demands—immediate Africanization of the officer corps, a new battalion, and pay increases. Since then Army influence has increased, culminating in the 1971 coup.

Bagandan separatist sentiment is the most pressing of tribal disputes in Uganda. However, the new government is popular among the Baganda.

There are recurrent border troubles caused by more than 250,000 refugees from Rwanda, Zaire, and Sudan. Frequent attempts of militant refugees to infiltrate their own countries create severe problems of border surveillance. Neighboring governments, especially Sudan, have threatened to cross the Uganda border for retaliatory strikes against refugee insurgent bases.

In August 1972 President Amin ordered all Asians, about 48,000 people, to leave the country, but under pressure from Tanzania he limited the expulsion to those 25,000 Asians holding British or other foreign passports. There was at this time an invasion by supporters of former president Milton Obote from Tanzania, but it was quickly snuffed out by Amin.

Scattered guerrilla activity was reported early in 1973. Reports indicated some guerrillas were followers of Obote, while some belonged to a group called Front for National Salvation (FRONASA), said to oppose Obote's return. Amin also made charges, in February, against Luo tribe members in Kenya, and seemed to threaten the 50,000 Luos of Uganda with expulsion. The charges and threats were later retracted. In March 1974 Amin survived with ease a 15-hour coup attempt by troops who were Christian members of the Lugbara tribe, led by a brigadier from Amin's own Kakwa tribe.

Uganda is a member of the UN, OAU, and the British Commonwealth.

Initially training and equipment for the armed forces were supplied by the British. In recent years Israeli military assistance has been extensive; however, early in 1972 the Israeli military mission was expelled. In 1973, 300 Ugandan soldiers received training in Libya. Aircraft have been received from Israel, the Soviet Union, and Czechoslovakia. Light weapons may have been furnished by the Soviet Union, Czechoslovakia, and Communist China. The Ugandan Army is 8,550 strong, organized as two brigades of four infantry battalions each, plus supporting armored cars, two border guard battalions, one mechanized battalion, one parachute/commando battalion, and one artillery regiment. Equipment includes five M-4 medium tanks, 16 Ferret scout cars, 20 BTR-40 and 152 and 12 OT-64B APCs. The Air Force, 500 men, operates seven MiG-15/17 fighters, four P-149 trainers, one Caribou transport, six AB-205, two AB-206, two Scout and seven Russian-made Mi4 helicopters in addition to eight Magister and 12 L-29 Delfin trainers, six C-47 transports, and seven liaison aircraft. The main air bases are at Gulu, Kampala and Entebbe.

The General Service Units (GSU) of the police number 800 men, trained for riot control. Under the Ministry of Interior they have remained a genuinely multi-tribal force, still conditioned by the apolitical standards of the British civil service. The police air wing currently operates three helicopters, a Twin Otter, and several other aircraft.

UPPER VOLTA

Republique de Haute-Volta

POWER POTENTIAL STATISTICS

Area: 105,869 square miles
Population: 5,491,000
Total Active Armed Forces: 3,050 (including National Guard; 0.05% population)

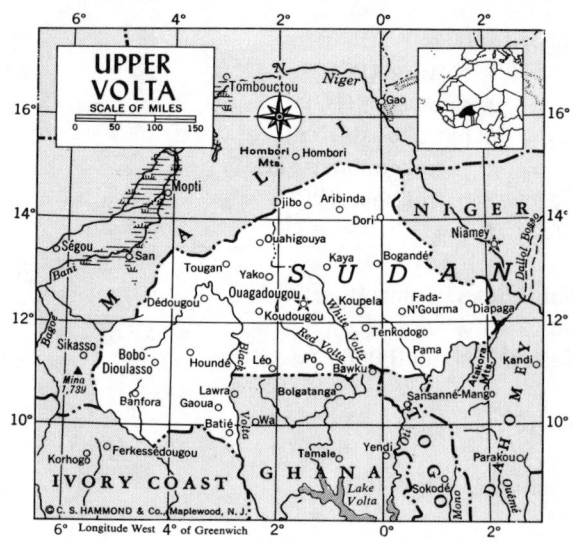

Gross National Product: $340 million ($62 per capita)
Annual Military Expenditures: $4.0 million (1.17% GNP)
Electric Power Output: 18.6 million kwh
Civil Air Fleet: 3 piston transports

POLITICO-MILITARY POLICIES AND POSTURE

The current president achieved his position by a military coup in January 1966. A new constitution was approved by a national referendum in June 1970. Under this constitution the President of the Republic continues to be, for a transitional period of four years, the senior officer in the Army. Thereafter the President is to be elected by direct universal suffrage; one-third of the Cabinet is to consist of military men. The armed forces of Upper Volta are administered through the Minister of Defense.

Upper Volta has maintained close relations with France since independence in 1960, although it did not join the French Community. Staging, transit, and overflight privileges were accorded France and there is a military assistance agreement for arms, equipment, and training. For defense Upper Volta relies essentially on whatever collective security can be provided by its memberships in the UN, OAU, OCAM, and *Conseil de l'Entente*. Within the *Conseil* Upper Volta has cooperated with Ivory Coast and Niger in mutual internal and external security problems.

In 1966 and 1967 the Army easily suppressed abortive countercoup attempts by supporters of the ousted politicians. Ethnic divisions do not threaten stability. The dominant Voltaic Mossi comprise about one-half the population. The Mandingo tribes are next in importance, with smaller proportions of Fulani, Haussa, and Tuareg tribesmen. Islam has made little penetration and most of the people retain their animist beliefs or have been converted to Christianity.

Upper Volta's stability is threatened by its faltering

agricultural economy and its growing population. There are important mineral deposits—manganese, copper, tin ore, limestone, bauxite, and graphite—but these are not being exploited because of the high cost of a 712-mile trip to the coast.

Prior to and just after independence, during the period 1957-1961, France furnished military instructors and $18 million in equipment. Another $25 million was provided for administration of veterans affairs and military pensions for the 200,000 Voltaic veterans of French service. These veterans represent a pool of trained manpower as well as a potential pressure group. Shortly after independence the United States provided $77,000 for military equipment to be used in Army civic action projects and trained 24 students under the MAP. Israel has also furnished some police training and police advisors.

Military service for two years is compulsory by law but the armed forces are kept up to strength by volunteers. The Army numbers 1,500 and is organized as one infantry battalion, an armored car reconnaissance squadron, a paratroop company, and an engineer company. The Air Force is 50 strong and operates one C-47 transport, and one Aero Commander 500B light transport, and two Broussard liaison aircraft. Major air bases are Ouagadougou and Bobo-Dioulasso. There is a National Guard, or gendarmerie, of 1,500.

ZAIRE*
Formerly Congo (Kinshasa)
Republique de Zaire
Republic of Zaire

POWER POTENTIAL STATISTICS

Area: 905,559 square miles
Population: 23,380,000
Total Active Armed Forces: 46,000 (excluding Internal Security Police and Gendarmerie; 0.19% population)
Gross National Product: $2.18 billion ($93 per capita)
Annual Military Expenditures: $85 million (3.89% GNP)
Fuel Production: Coal: 102,000 metric tons
Electric Power Output: 3.19 billion kwh
Merchant Fleet: 7 ships; 39,317 gross tons
Civil Air Fleet: 7 jet, 8 turboprop, and 27 piston transports

*The name was adopted in 1971. It is an early (1484) Portuguese transliteration of a Bantu word meaning "big river", and is a name for the Congo River.

DEFENSE STRUCTURE

President Joseph Mobutu, former Army Commander in Chief, who seized control of a government torn by internal dissension in November 1965, is also Prime Minister and Minister of Defense. He controls the Armed Forces through the Military High Command, a council of senior commanders.

POLITICO-MILITARY POLICY

Policies have centered on building a competent and loyal military force with help from the Western powers, securing the borders against the infiltration of arms and agents by Communists and other dissidents, preventing secession, and extending government control throughout the land.

Despite past attempts of radical African states at subversion in Zaire, it joins them in supporting the Southern African liberation movements and actively supports the Angolan nationalist groups by according recognition and allowing their bases to be located in Zaire.

The armed forces are maintained by voluntary enlistment.

STRATEGIC PROBLEMS

Dominating central Africa, and rich in copper, cobalt, uranium, and other minerals, the Congo—as Zaire was called in the colonial era—was a prize that fell to Belgium in the late 19th Century. Since independence (1960) it has been a target for communist subversion. The secession of mineral-rich Katanga was an attempt by the Katangans (apparently with Belgian encouragement) to salvage the mining area from the chaos which for several years engulfed the rest of the country. The Katanga secession and a serious army revolt were put down by a four-year occupation of much of the country by a UN peacekeeping force of 15-20,000 troops. Concurrently a massive UN and Western training and technical assistance program sought to prepare the Congo for self-government and self-defense.

After the UN forces withdrew in 1964, the northeast Congo erupted in communist-led tribal warfare. Russian and Chinese arms were delivered via Sudan; an insurgent cadre was trained in the radical African states and communist countries, and foreign communist agents (including Cubans) were active in the rebel leadership. With the help of white mercenary commandos, who were supported by a mercenary air force (reportedly US-sponsored) the rebellion was suppressed by 1965. Subsequent brief revolts in 1966 and 1967 were suppressed. Scattered instances of tribal and religious violence have been promptly brought under control.

That Zaire has survived a decade of almost uninterrupted threats and violence is a tribute both to the determination of the Mobutu government and the patience and support of the UN and the West. Since 1967 there have been minor outbreaks of tribal and religious violence which were quickly brought

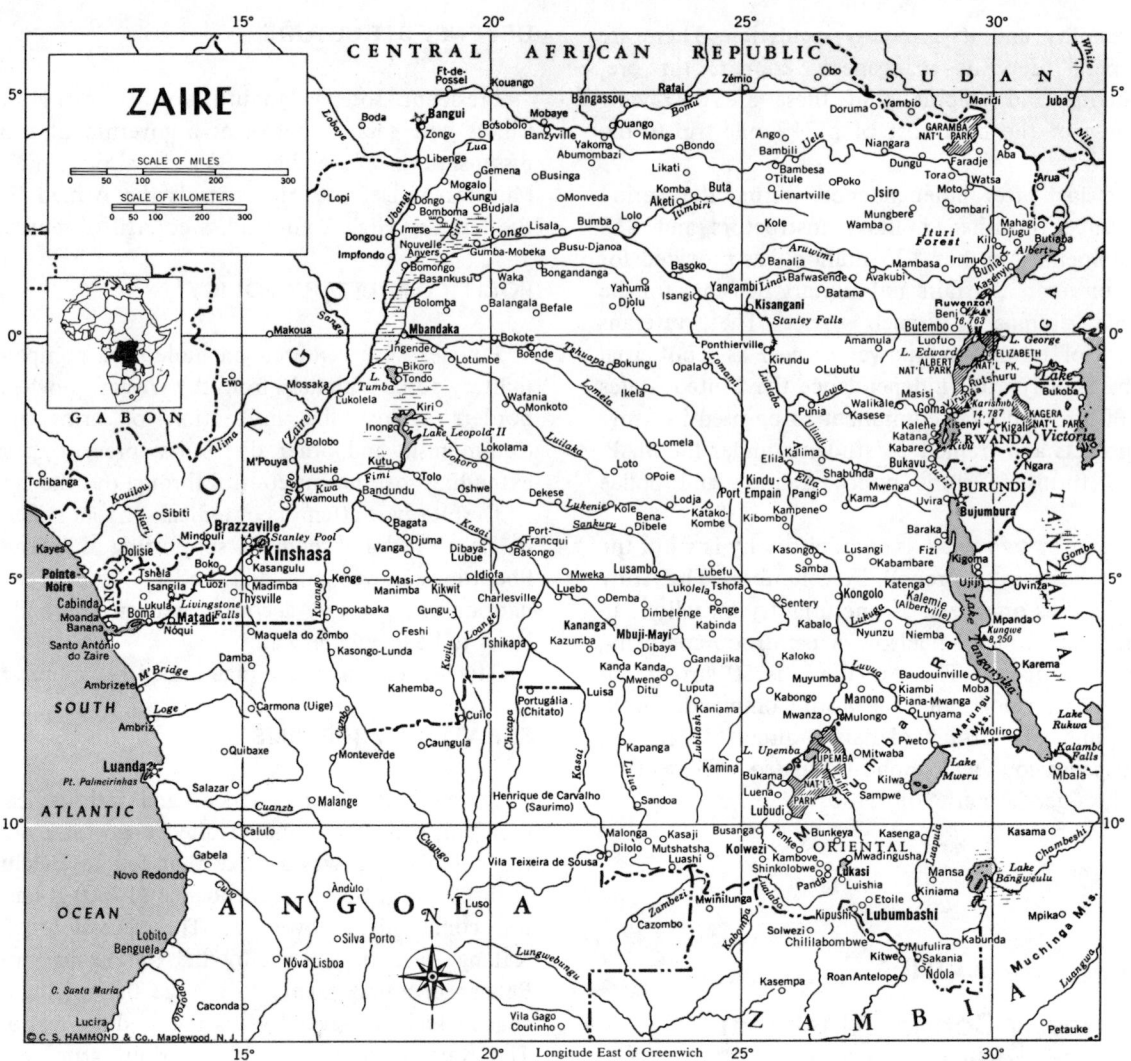

under control. Development of the economy and governmental functions continues and appears to be succeeding. In 1970 the most serious continuing external danger was ameliorated, if not resolved, by renewal of diplomatic ties with its neighbor, Congo (Brazzaville). The possibility of retaliation by Portugal for support to the Angolan rebels continue to pose a problem of border security despite the rapprochement with Brazzaville.

MILITARY ASSISTANCE

After the UN had put down the army revolt and the Katanga secession, the government invited, through the UN, six nations to assist in rebuilding the armed forces as an effective force for internal security and defense of the borders. Belgium has trained the ground forces, Italy the air force, Norway the naval element, Israel the paratroop-commandos, Canada the communications and transport units, and the United States has provided supply and administrative support. The United States, which had paid half the $500 million cost of the UN intervention, contributed $26.3 million in military assistance from 1964 through 1972 and over $1.7 million in excess military stocks through 1971. Under the MAP 541 have been trained. Italy's initial contribution was about $5 million. Belgian aid has been slightly over $1 million a year, and some 500 Belgian adviser-instructors work with the army. Nigeria has assisted in police training. An organization known as WIGMO (Western International Ground Maintenance Organization, alleged to be a US instrument) has kept the government's aircraft in operation and provided the pilots, mostly Cuban exiles. During the 1967 revolt Ghana helped ease the pilot shortage by sending pilots to fly armed trainers.

ALLIANCES

Zaire has no alliances other than military aid agreements with countries named above. It is a member of the UN and the OAU. It withdrew from OCAM in 1972.

ARMY

Personnel: 45,000

Organization:
- 1 parachute division
- 6 brigades
- 6 parachute battalions
- 12 infantry battalions
- 1 heavy weapons battalion
- 4 commando battalions
- support units

Major Equipment Inventory:
- 10 medium tanks
- scout cars (Ferret and M-3)
- 80 armored cars (AML-60 and AML-90)
- light artillery pieces

NAVY

Personnel: 150

Major Units:
- 1 river gunboat (PGR)
- 6 patrol boats (YP)

AIR FORCE

Personnel: 850

Organization:
- 2 air groups
  - 3 light ground attack squadrons (T-6, T-28D, Magister, MB326GB)
  - 1 light reconnaissance squadron (Pembroke)
  - 3 transport squadrons (C-54, C-47, Caribou)
  - 1 light transport squadron (Dove, C-45, Heron)
  - 2 helicopter squadrons (Alouette II/III, Bell 47, SA-330 Puma)
  - 2 training squadrons (SF-260M, T-6)
  - 2 logistic support squadrons (C-46, Caribou, C-130)
  - 1 liaison squadron (Do-27/28, Auster)

Major Aircraft Types:
- 44 combat aircraft
  - 8 T-28D armed trainers
  - 10 T-6G armed trainers
  - 9 Magister armed trainers
  - 17 Aermacchi MB326GB light ground attack aircraft
- 103 other aircraft
  - 4 Pembroke reconnaissance aircraft
  - 2 C-54 transports
  - 2 C-130 transports
  - 10 C-47 transports
  - 6 C-46 transports
  - 4 Caribou transports
  - 11 light transports
  - 6 liaison aircraft
  - 12 SIAI-Marchetti SF260M trainers
  - 8 T-6 trainers
  - 4 L-29 Delfin trainers
  - 34 helicopters (Alouette II and III, Bell 47, and Puma)

Major Air Bases: Kinshasa, Kisangani, Lubumbashi, Luluabourg, Mbandaka, Kamina, Likasi, and Kolweze

PARAMILITARY

There is a civil police force of 21,000, about half trained for internal security. The police operate a small water patrol force in three locations: in the Zaire estuary from Matadi to the sea, on the Zaire River where it forms the border with Congo (Brazzaville), and on Lake Tanganyika.

There are six National Guard and seven Gendarmerie battalions of unknown strength.

ZAMBIA

Republic of Zambia

POWER POTENTIAL STATISTICS

Area: 290,724 square miles
Population: 4,700,000
Total Active Armed Forces: 7,600 (including internal security forces; 0.16% population)
Gross National Product: $1.99 billion ($423 per capita)
Annual Military Expenditures: $20 million (1% GNP)
Fuel Production: Coal: 623,000 metric tons
Electric Power Output: 1.2 billion kwh
Civil Air Fleet: 3 jet, 4 turboprop transports

POLITICO-MILITARY POLICIES AND POSTURE

Since independence in October 1964, Zambia has been governed by a strong presidential form of government. The President is commander in chief of the Zambia Defence Force and controls it through the Minister of Defence. Legislative responsibility for implementation of defense policy and for budgeting is shared by the President and Parliament.

Zambia is a member of the UN, the Commonwealth, and the OAU. It is nonaligned in international affairs, but is a proponent of majority rule by Africans in Southern Africa.

While opposing Rhodesia's Unilateral Declaration of Independence (UDI) in 1965, and its white-dominated government, Zambia is economically dependent on Rhodesia and so maintains a formal but tenuous relationship, frequently punctuated by mutual recriminations. Zambia is implementing plans to reduce this dependence by developing its own hydroelectric power sources and coal mines, building an oil pipeline from Dar es Salaam and, in conjunction with Tanzania, has accepted Communist China's offer to build a railroad from Dar es Salaam to Kapiri Mposhi in Zambia. The first track of the new line was laid in October of 1970 and it is due for completion in 1974, 18 months ahead of the original schedule. The railway's great benefit to Zambia will be in moving its copper exports, greatest in the world, to port without dependence on white-controlled Rhodesia, Angola, or Mozambique. The Soviet Union has repeatedly offered armaments, but the offers have been turned down on the grounds that this action would turn Zambia into an ideological battleground between East and West.

In 1965, despite sympathy for Southern African liberation movements, because of fear of reprisals Zambia forbade use of its territory for their military training or for transshipment of arms to the south. However, because of its large size, rugged terrain, and small armed forces and police—and particularly its geographic location—Zambia has to some extent become a forward base and sanctuary for freedom fighters of liberation organizations generally headquartered in Tanzania.

Zambia is traversed by the only convenient land routes for the northern-based Southern African liberation movements to get to Rhodesia, South Africa, and Southwest Africa, Similarly, Angolan and Mozambique liberation guerrillas operate on both sides of the border, and Portuguese counter-insurgency forces occasionally cross the ill-defined frontier in hot pursuit. Zambia is realistically apprehensive about violation of its territorial integrity by counter-insurgency forces, or even the possible retaliatory occupation of portions of Zambia, and so Zambian police reluctantly attempt to inhibit guerrilla activity. Following incidents near the border, Rhodesia closed its Zambia border in January 1973; copper from Zambia was to be permitted to cross despite the closure. Rhodesia then offered to open the border early in February 1973, but Zambia both refused to ship copper through Rhodesia before the February reopening and refused to ship anything after the reopening. Determined not to be dependent on Rhodesia, it used longer routes that avoided Rhodesia. Zambia received $50 million in grants and low-interest loans after a UN appeal in March, with Communist China, Canada, the United States, and West Germany among those contributing most.

Completion of the pipeline and railroad through Tanzania to Dar es Salaam, the development of coal and hydroelectric

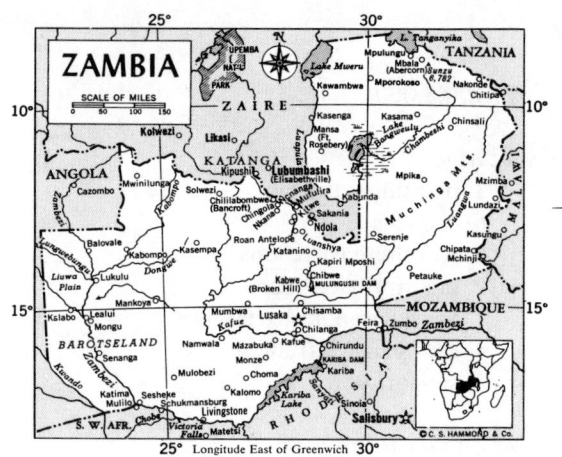

power to reduce dependency on Rhodesia, and expansion and improvement of its Defence Forces and police will enable Zambia to abandon its current reluctant policy of neutrality.

Financing of the Defence Force and concurrent economic expansion are permitted by Zambia's copper wealth. This, and the concomitant economic growth and social services it provides, have made for relative political stability. The 70,000 whites in government posts, industry, and trade are closely watched; they are not yet a divisive factor, although considered a potential danger.

Upon independence British military equipment in Zambia was turned over to the Defence Force, and additional equipment has since been granted or sold by Britain. Until recently the recruiting of white officers and NCOs was permitted by Britain, which made up deficiencies by secondment from the British Army and Royal Air Force. Training of Zambian personnel, including officer cadets, has been conducted in Britain, Canada, and Ireland. Israeli instructor-advisers are working with the police Special Branch (counterintelligence). However, Zambianization of the Defence Force has become a matter of national policy. In 1970, the British commander of the Zambian Army was replaced by a Zambian. In 1971 fifteen British officers in the Zambian Defence Force were dismissed and ordered to leave the country. Their positions were taken over by Zambians.

Military service is voluntary. The Zambian Army consists of about 4,500 troops organized into one brigade of three infantry battalions and one reconnaissance squadron; other units are one artillery battery, one engineer company, and one signal company. Equipment includes 30 Ferret scout cars and sixteen 105mm howitzers and Rapier SAMs. There are 2,000 reserves in two Territorial infantry battalions and special detachments.

The Air Force of 1,000 operates 24 combat aircraft, four Jastreb, 12 MB326 light ground attack, and eight SF-260 armed trainers. There are also two Galeb and six Chipmunk trainers, two C-47 and four Caribou transports, six Beaver and two Pembroke communication/liaison aircraft and three AB-205 helicopters. On order are 22 more AB-205 helicopters and six more MB326 light ground attack aircraft. Air bases are at Lusaka, Livingstone, Kalabo, Broken Hill, Ndola, Abercorn, Kasama, Mpika, Luwingu, N'changa, and Chingola.

The police forces total at least 6,250 and have taken on increasingly paramilitary characteristics. Among such units are the 1st and 2nd Mobile Police Battalions of 750 men each and four Police Strike Force companies of 150 men each.

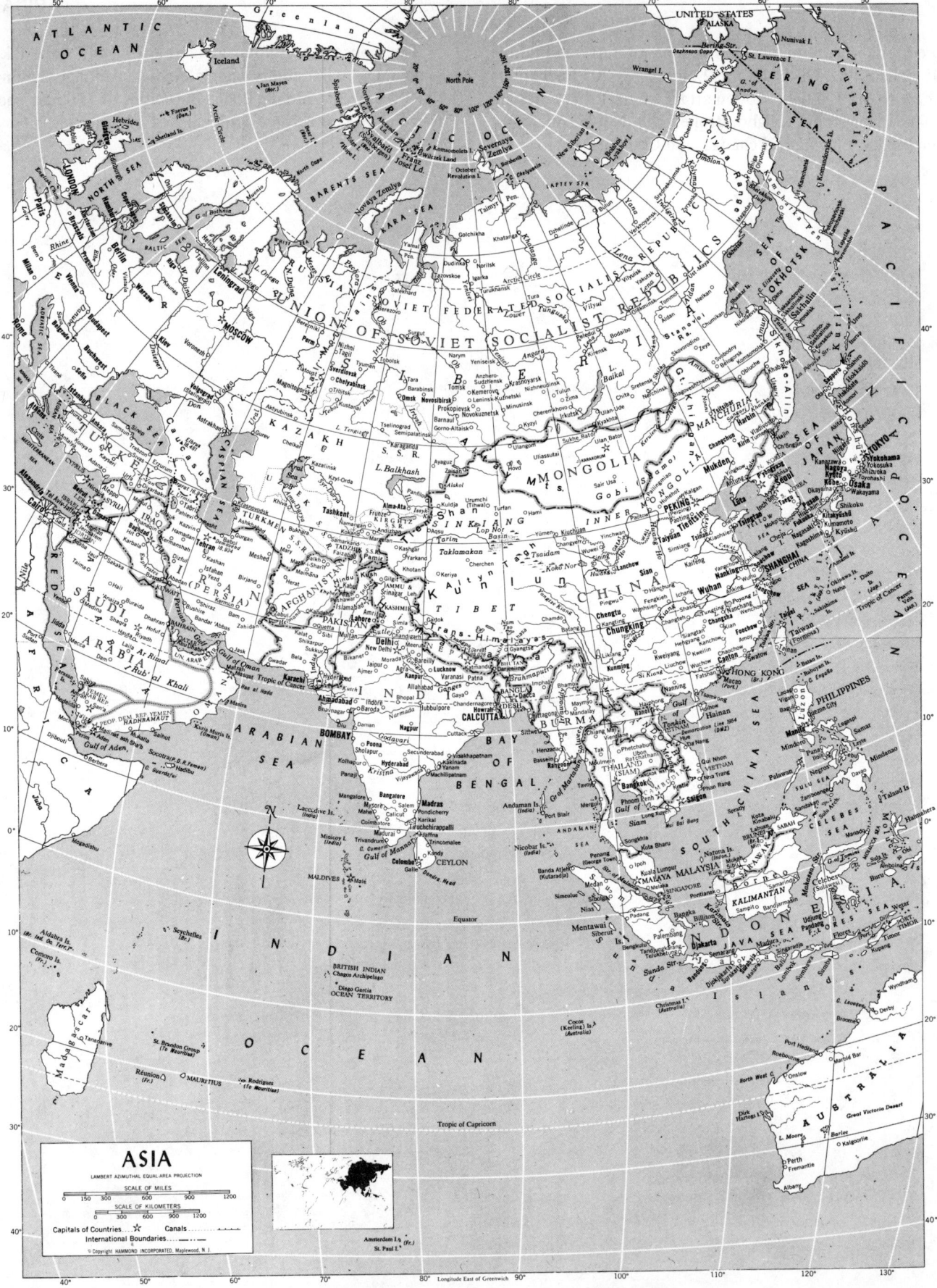

8

CENTRAL AND EAST ASIA

Regional Survey

MILITARY GEOGRAPHY

This region comprises Mongolia, the Koreas, Japan, and China. Russian territories in East and Central Asia are excluded from this consideration; they are discussed in the section dealing with the Soviet Union as a whole. The discussion of China for political reasons is divided into two parts: that dealing with the People's Republic of China, which rules mainland China (including Tibet), and the Republic of China, which controls only Taiwan and a few minor islands off the coast of China.

This region includes some of the most densely populated and some of the most sparsely populated areas in the world. Dense populations are to be found in the river valleys of China and on the islands of Japan. Sparse populations eke out existence in the vast expanse of mountains north of the spine of the Himalayas, and in the broad deserts of the Gobi and Sinkiang.

The coastal and island regions have a monsoon climate quite similar to that found in South and Southeast Asia, although not so precisely patterned and predictable. Little of the monsoon moisture reaches the steppes and deserts of Central Asia, however, because of the intervening Himalayas to the south, and the mountains of China to the east.

STRATEGIC SIGNIFICANCE

China's access to the open sea is blocked to the south by the rimland states of South and Southeast Asia. To the east this access to open sea is also impeded, even though not so rigidly blocked, by the island chain extending from the southern tip of Kamchatka Peninsula to the southern tip of the Malay Peninsula.

China is not vulnerable from the lands to the south; there has never been a major successful overland invasion of East or Central Asia from that direction. However, China—like the rest of mainland East Asia—is vulnerable to invasion by seapowers controlling all or a significant portion of the chain of East Asian islands. This vulnerability, however, is to a large degree superficial because of the great difficulty which a maritime nation would have exerting military power inland through regions in which mountains and large rivers form serious military obstacles, and in which vast populations defy easy control.

To the north and west, however, there are fewer military obstacles and smaller populations. In these areas the tides of conquest have often shifted rapidly and far. Usually these tides have reflected the extent to which the regime controlling eastern and central China could extend its power further inland. In some instances, however, exceptionally powerful Central Asian regimes (most notably that of Genghis Khan) have been able to seize the initiative from China in a positive manner, rather than merely as a reflection of Chinese weakness. Thus, until relatively modern times, the military history of East and Central Asia has been largely that of the fluctuations of power between China proper and evanescent—and usually nomadic—regimes of the lands to the north and west.

In the age of technology, however, the nomads of Central Asia suffered from insuperable disadvantages, and gradually succumbed to pressures of Russia from the north and west, and China from the south and east. More recently, the amazing technological progress of Japan, interrupted only briefly by defeat in World War II, has brought that island kingdom to a position of pre-eminent industrial power in the region, while still retaining a potential military capability that was to some degree evidenced in the Russo-Japanese War, in the various pre-1941 Japanese invasions of China, and even in its ill-fated aggressions of World War II.

The role of nuclear weapons in the area is increasingly important. Japan, with its high concentration of industry and population, is extremely vulnerable. The People's Republic of China, poised between the two nuclear superpowers, protects itself by conciliating one and by deploying its modest nuclear resources against the other in a way that threatens to permit some measure of effective retaliation.

REGIONAL ALLIANCES

There is no major regional alliance relating to this area. There are, however, a number of relevant bilateral alliances and mutual security pacts, and there is in effect one major international alliance as a result of United Nations declarations and actions regarding Korea. The major alliances are listed below:

United Nations Support for the Republic of Korea. This stems directly from the United Nations Declarations of June 1950. Active combat participants in the Korean War were: Australia, Belgium, Canada, Colombia, Ethiopia, France,

Greece, Luxembourg, Netherlands, New Zealand, Thailand, Turkey, Union of South Africa, United Kingdom, United States. Non-combatant participants were: Denmark, India, Italy, Norway, Sweden.

Sino-Soviet Treaty of Friendship, Alliance and Mutual Assistance (February 1950)

Sino-Mongolian Mutual Assistance Treaty (May 1960)

Sino-North Korean Mutual Assistance Treaty (July 1961)

United States Bilateral Mutual Assistance Treaties with: Republic of China (March 1955), Republic of Korea (November 1954), and Japan (January 1960)

Soviet-Mongolian Mutual Assistance Treaty (1936, 1946, 1966).

RECENT INTRA-AND EXTRA-REGIONAL CONFLICTS

Two of the three most important wars since the end of World War II have taken place in this region: the Chinese Civil War and the Korean War. One other important but brief conflict took place along the frontiers of the region between China and India in 1962. It is perhaps significant that the People's Republic of China (Communist China) was involved in all three of these wars. A list of all recent major hostilities, or crises involving military operations in the region follows:

1963-date	Intermittent border violence along Sino-Soviet frontiers
1968	Seizure of USS *Pueblo* by North Korean naval forces
1969	North Korea downs US aircraft over Japan Sea
1973	Soviet Union intensifies intrusions into Japanese airspace; sends naval task force down Taiwan Strait
1974	January: People's Republic of China takes Paracel Islands from South Vietnam forces
1974	February: People's Republic of China takes position in Spratley Islands, also claimed by Republic of China and Republic of Vietnam

CHINA, PEOPLE'S REPUBLIC OF
Chung-hua Jen-min Kung-ho Kuo

POWER POTENTIAL STATISTICS
Area: 3,691,501 square miles (including Tibet)
Population: 825,000,000-875,000,000
Armed Forces: 3,250,000 (including security and border troops; .38% of population)
Gross National Product: $128 billion (1971; $151 per capita)
Annual Military Expenditure: $12.8 billion (10% GNP)
Steel Production: 43 million metric tons
Fuel Production: Coal: 325 million metric tons Crude Oil: 23 million metric tons
Electric Power Output: 70 billion kwh
Grain Production: 230 million metric tons
Merchant Fleet: 290 ships; 1.6 million gross tons
Machine Tools (units): 50,000
Civil Air Fleet: 30 jet, 18 turboprop and 70 piston transports

DEFENSE STRUCTURE

The armed forces of Communist China (all services being integrated within the People's Liberation Army—PLA) are controlled and administered by a Ministry of National Defense. This is one of the major administrative organizations under the State Council, which is the principal governmental executive authority (under the overall authority of the National People's Congress). There is a National Defense Council, whose approximately 100 members actually have little responsibility but much prestige. Real authority over the armed forces is exercised by the Central Committee of the Communist Party (CCP), through its Politburo, with operating direction provided by the Military Commission of the Party Central Committee, consisting of the Party Chairman and five to seven other ranking members of the Party. The office of Chairman of the Republic is vacant.

The Ministry of National Defense (MND) is organized along relatively conventional military headquarters lines, with overall staff coordination exercised by three departments: the General Staff Department, the General Logistics Department, and the General Political Department. The last lost much of its power during the Cultural Revolution but has reappeared as an important force. Specific operational functions are administered by a number of staff directorates, which include: Armored Force, Artillery Force, Engineer Corps, Railway Engineer Corps, Signal Corps, Navy, Air Force, and Air Defense Command. A Second Artillery Corps, of which little is known, may be the nuclear weapons command. Under MND headquarters are the operating forces. The Scientific and Technological Commission for National Defense is under the direct control of the Minister of Defense, but is not under the operational control of the Chief of Staff of the PLA, who (subject to the authority of the Minister of Defense) exercises military command authority over the operation forces.

POLITICO-MILITARY POLICY

The People's Liberation Army serves both domestic and foreign policy. The unique history of the PLA as an "army of

CENTRAL AND EAST ASIA 277

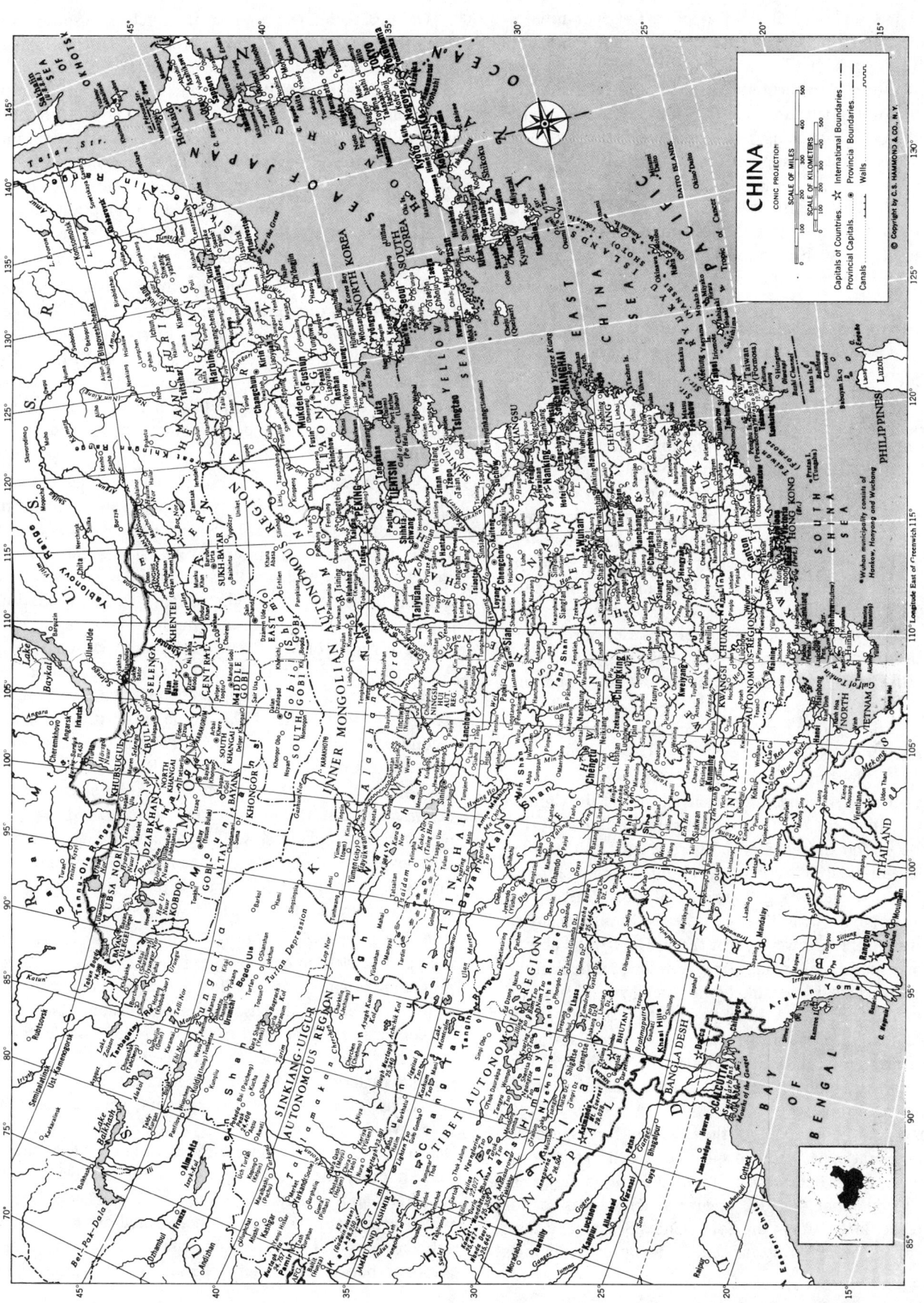

the people" has endowed it with a broad range of interior functions which may be aggregated in the "three supports and two militarys" slogan that had wide currency during the Great Proletarian Cultural Revolution: "Support the left, support industry, support agriculture; exercise military control, give military and political training." In effect, such slogans cover activities as disparate as suppression of near-mutiny, as in Wuhan in July 1967; containing the more violent elements of youth or party activities, as was often the case in the Cultural Revolution; assumption of control over industry and political organs; and activity such as growing a good part of its own subsistence and helping local farmers in their work. At varying levels of intensity, depending on surrounding conditions, the Army has been extolled as a model for the whole populace. The PLA is, in actuality, the army of the party rather than the army of the poeple. Struggle for actual control of this political instrument is at the center of much of the recurring turbulence that appears in the PRC.

In more straightforward exterior functions, the PLA has the task of supplying the military component of a shifting national strategy. From 1968 onward, after the Soviet Union exercised what it described as the "right" of Socialist States to intervene by force, as in the invasion of Czechoslovakia, the PRC's immediate concerns have focused increasingly on its 4,500-mile border in the north. The Russians, for their part, have increased their propaganda activity and their physical presence on the other side of the border. A series of relatively small but sharp encounters in the period March-August 1969 highlighted the level of tension wherever troops faced one another.

The conventional force structure and deployment of the PLA illustrates a realistic response to threat perceptions. The forces are being developed primarily as effective instruments for making the cost of conventional action against the Chinese homeland too high for the prospective gains, whether by the Soviet Union or the United States. There is little effort going into the development of substantial airborne or amphibious capability, further suggesting that large offensive efforts are not contemplated at this time. The steady improvement of capability does imply, however, that the PRC might be able to take significant military action over its borders, particularly in Southeast Asia. This is not likely, in the light of support, expressed or implied, by the super-powers to those neighbors, and Chinese fear of a two-front war. Any physical action to "liberate" Taiwan is unlikely at this time. This is reinforced by the often expressed conviction that reunion will come about without the use of force.

In January and February 1974 the PRC sent forces into the Paracel and Spratley Islands, displacing South Vietnamese units. Some observers believe that potential oil resources are at issue; others think that the PRC might use these locations for tracking Soviet fleet units in the South China Sea. In any case, this style of offensive overseas action is new to Peking's behavior.

The PRC is a late-comer on the nuclear weapons scene and lacks the resources to mount a program that could in any way hope to match those of the United States and the Soviet Union. Consequently Peking's nuclear weapons policies have been directed to achieving maximum impact in both the political and military fields. On the political side the PRC asserts that it will never be the first to use these weapons. The Chinese program is celebrated as encouragement for the poorer countries of the world and as protection for them. Proliferation of nuclear weapons is regarded as desirable in breaking the nuclear monopoly of the great powers.

On the military side, the program has involved some 15 tests, including one underground and one missile-borne. (The missile is believed to have a range of six thousand miles.) The types tested lead to the conclusion that the PRC policy looks primarily to deterrence of the Soviet Union by deploying weapons that can reach targets in metropolitan Russia. This probably represents the best use that can be made of limited resources.

The Chinese ICBM continues to be the subject of much speculation. In July 1973 a large device was sighted at the test installation. Bigger than the Soviet's SS-9, it was reported to be the vehicle for the intercontinental weapon that the PRC has yet to test (although a 2,000-mile rocket firing was thought by some to be a reduced-range trial). Installations that might be associated with tracking have been reported on the northern slopes of Mt. Everest and on the east coast of Africa. An instrumented ship of some 12,000 tons has been reported in the Indian Ocean. Peking launched two earth satellites in April 1970 and March 1971. Some authorities think that the second used solid fuel. In early 1974 the Chairman of the US Joint Chiefs of Staff said that the PRC had several hundred nuclear-armed IRBM and MRBM. At the same time, US defense authorities were reported to have said that the PRC program was moving slower than expected and there would not be a missile capable of reaching the continental United States until 1976 or 1977 and 10 to 25 such weapons would not become available until 1979-80.

Current strategic policy is reflected also in conventional weapons development programs. For ground forces the programs for enhanced mobility and firepower clearly relate to a more effective defense against invasion. The air force concentrates on high performance air defense fighters and a relatively small number of bombers capable of delivering nuclear weapons on Asian and some Russian targets. The navy is adding submarines and destroyers, gaining some modest offensive capabilities, but only incidental to the quest for better defense. All these programs are added burdens to nuclear costs and must be prosecuted with close attention to resources and money. Some of the major new items upon which effort appears to be concentrated are nuclear-powered submarines, hydrofoil patrol boats, missile firing destroyers, armored personnel carriers, fighter aircraft (mach 2, 50,000 feet), and across-the-board communications and electronics gear.

In deference to the egalitarian, revolutionary concepts of Maoist Communism, there are no ranks or grades within the PLA. No titles are employed, other than to designate each individual by the function he performs, as Soldier-Fighter Li, Squad Leader Ch'en, Company Commander Wu, Army Commander Lin, etc. The continuing emphasis on the need to eliminate bureaucrats and officials who exploit their positions for personal gain or comfort suggests that the privileges of rank are still sought and exercised.

There is a political officer in all tactical units, down to and including the company. In conformity with the relationships established by Mao Tse-tung during the Chinese Civil War, the authority of the political officer is superior to that of the tactical unit commander.

Beginning at age 18 every Chinese citizen is liable to military service, up to a total of four years. In practice only a small proportion of the six to seven million young people who become eligible for military service are actually conscripted; selection is done only after a careful screening of all eligible for conscription. Service in the Army is usually for two years, in the Navy for four years, and the Air Force for three years.

STRATEGIC PROBLEMS

The Great Proletarian Cultural Revolution was a device created by Mao Tse-tung to give Chinese youth a revolutionary experience (however synthetic), to uncover and put out of office or reeducate those party officials who had lost their revolutionary zeal, and to purge those officials suspected of trying to capture the Chinese revolution and lead it down the "capitalist road." From August 1966 until the Ninth Party Congress in April 1969, the country was torn by physical and verbal clashes between the numerous groups that appeared. The Red Guards—militant, activist young radicals—swept over the country, doing violence and destruction on a vast scale. The PLA was introduced to support the left, but at times the troops seemed to support more conservative causes. New Revolutionary Committees, dominated by the military, took over Party functions at all levels, as well as the operation of industry and economic affairs generally. Schools closed, production slowed, and the PRC withdrew from exterior contacts almost completely. There was an open rebellion by military authorities in Wuhan in July 1967. Thousands all over China were killed, beaten, and reviled. By the late summer of 1968 the tide was slacking and the young people were put under restraint.

The Ninth Party Congress, held in April, 1969, marked the apparent end of the more visible aspects of the Cultural Revolution. The PLA emerged as the single entity capable of functioning effectively in national affairs. The extreme left was segregated, the activist young were sent down to the countryside for education and training, literally by the millions, and the effort was begun to rebuild the party after its deliberate destruction. Provincial party and special municipality committees were formed. While there were some notable exceptions, it was overwhelmingly true that the new bodies were dominated by the military and military commissar types who had made up the revolutionary committees of the Cultural Revolution period. The new Party constitution named Lin Piao as Mao's successor. Major changes appeared when schools reopened and production began to return to normal. 7 May schools undertook the retraining of cadres, teachers, and administrators.

Almost simultaneously with the Ninth Party Congress, the tension between the PRC and the Soviet Union began to move steadily to the foreground. The armed clashes that took place, although significant, were really tokens of a much wider split that involved old territorial aims, doctrinal differences, and the leadership of the communist world and the less developed countries. There have been efforts to deal rationally with these problems, but the buildup of military power has continued along both sides of the borders. Some estimates of Soviet strength there go as high as one million troops, with nuclear and conventional weapons appropriate to that number.

The Soviet threat naturally evoked a military response from Peking. Further, Chou En-Lai came to effective power as Premier and either made the first move toward improved relations with the United States or moved to accept American initiatives very quickly. From that point onward, the PRC moved rapidly back into the wider world. Peking replaced the Republic of China (Taiwan) as the Chinese representative in the UN on October 25, 1971. President Nixon visited Peking in February 1972. An exchange of liaison officers has made intercourse between Washington and Peking much broader and more open, and Secretary of State Kissinger has made six trips to the PRC. Japan has recognized the PRC and is engaged in working through a number of thorny problems flowing from this act. Over 90 nations now have accorded full diplomatic recognition to Peking. In terms of relations and interests in the outer world, the leaders have made a massive change of direction and effort. The new relations between the United States and the PRC most certainly have required new calculations of power balances and prospects. Peking has changed its style and under carefully controlled conditions entered into substantial overseas trade activities. It would be wrong to think, however, that Peking is undergoing some major change of heart. This shift is tactical. It was to the PRC's interest to reduce tension with one of its two super-power opponents. For a number of reasons, including the real US desire to get out of Vietnam and to begin the reductions explicit in the Nixon Doctrine, the United States was a better candidate. The choicest epithets are now reserved for the Soviets, but the United States gets its share of castigation for "imperialism" and associated qualities. It is a question of Peking's perceptions of menace and priority of response.

While the exterior view of the PRC was brightening, strange events were occurring within. In September 1971 a number of prominent military personages disappeared. In addition to Lin Piao, the Minister of Defense and designated successor to Mao, there were the Chief of Staff of the PLA; the Political Commissar of the Navy; the Commander of the Air Force; and the Director of the General Logistics Department. Only Lin Piao has been accounted for. He is reported dead, killed in an attempt to flee the country after an attempt to assassinate Chairman Mao was thwarted. Of the others there is no word, nor have replacements been named.

In August 1973 the Tenth Party Congress was held and a new constitution approved. Chou En-lai felt called upon to rationalize dealings with an erstwhile enemy (the United States) in terms of revolutionary tactics. Military people were still prominent in the Congress but some reduction in military office holders took place. There was a general atmosphere of ideological debate and compromise over the right style of dealings and relations with the imperialists (the US) and social imperialists (USSR). There have been some indications of the possibility of efforts to mend the quarrel with Moscow, but the search for conciliation with the Soviets is not openly popular.

The recent sharp attacks on Confucius and his social theories have coincided with increasingly vocal exhortations to new revolution. In a move still not clearly understood, eight of the eleven powerful military region commanders were transferred in the closing days of 1973. Mainland China could be poised on the edge of another cultural revolution whose style and intensity cannot yet be identified.

China's greatest strategic problem would seem to be the maintenance of a screen of security from attack by the outside world, particularly from the north, while indulging in interior activities that could at any moment become destabilizing and require sizable intervention by the armed forces to quell interior disturbances.

Continuing resistance of Tibetans to the Chinese Communist occupation has caused the Chinese to maintain a harsh, repressive rule. Several Tibetan tribes persist in waging low-scale guerrilla warfare. The Chinese are also engaging in ethnic absorption through forced migration of Han Chinese. The Soviet Union has done what it can to exacerbate and arouse the ethnic minorities along its borders, particularly in Sinkiang. Local dissidence poses a problem for the Chinese authorities, but it is probably not serious.

Despite evidence of modest improvement in basic areas, the staggering problem of moving China into the modern world of industrialized nations remains. Eighty percent of the people live on 15% of China's total land and make their living from labor-intensive agriculture. Seventy-five percent of disposable personal income goes for such basic items as food, clothing, and shelter. China will for a long time have to face the huge problem of generating investment capital from a primitive base. The military budget, even though it represents 10% of GNP, does not afford the resources to produce the quantities of military equipment, conventional and nuclear, that would be needed if China wanted to assert itself as an effective military power beyond its own borders in an aggressive fashion.

China has at times been unable to produce enough food to provide adequate sustenance to its vast population. In times of poor crops, the result has been widespread famine. Despite some improvement in agricultural and distribution methods in recent years, the population of China is estimated to be growing at a rate of increase greater than the rate of increased agricultural yields. The government has asserted an interest in birth control, but a total solution to this food-production population problem seems not yet to be in sight.

Under the strictly directed economy, China has made substantial economic progress, with industrial production and the gross national product rising sharply. However, in absolute terms, these increases were less than the economic gains being made at the same time in many of the more economically developed powers, and substantially less than either the Soviet Union or the United States. Thus, China's economic planners have had some very difficult decisions to make in the allocation of resources to support the national objectives. High priority seems to have been given to the weapons industry, with some emphasis on improved aircraft and the nuclear program.

Another great strategic problem is to persuade Soviet leaders that should Russia attack, China will use its limited array of nuclear weapons against targets in Russian territory, and that this loss and destruction would offset whatever Soviet gains might be expected from the devastation of mainland China.

The PRC seems to have satisfied itself that the United States will honor its commitment to come to the assistance of the Republic of China on Taiwan against any attempt to take that island or the offshore islands by force, but that the US will not support Taiwan in offensive operations against mainland China. Also, despite various kinds of economic and military assistance to North Vietnam, Peking carefully refrained from any armed involvement in the war in Vietnam.

Chinese refusal to accept the British-imposed McMahon Line of 1914 has resulted in continuing tension with India, punctuated by full-scale hostilities in October 1962. Having achieved a significant military success, and having occupied the areas claimed by China, Chinese troops halted their advance voluntarily, although there seems to have been no way that the demoralized Indian forces could have prevented their descent into the plains of North India. Since that time, however, the Indians have strongly reinforced and improved their forces along the disputed frontier, and the prospect for trouble there is always present. In 1965 Chinese activities along the border were directed to assist Pakistan in its fight with India, but achieved little. The Indians kept six very good mountain divisions in the high passes during the Bangladesh War in

December 1971. This, together with the ominous Soviet presence in the north, limited China's support of Pakistan to some weapons and verbal support. It is very important to the PRC to maintain control over the Aksai Chin region, through which runs the road connecting Sinkiang and the southern frontier.

MILITARY ASSISTANCE

Soviet military aid to the PRC has long since stopped. Peking does not buy military equipment abroad, although there are rumors of an impending discussion of purchase of civilian-configured helicopters from an American manufacturer. It has recently been reported from London that there is an arrangement being worked out for the provision of Rolls-Royce Spey turbofan aircraft engines to the PRC.

China, on its part, provides military assistance to selected clients, including legitimate ones such as Albania, Pakistan, Yemen, Cuba, Tanzania, Zambia, North Korea, and North Vietnam. Rebels and insurgents like the groups in Palestine, Dhofar, and Jordan get arms, training and money. Pakistan has been granted an assistance credit reported to be some $300 million, which includes one-for-one replacement of the Bangladesh losses. A military jet airfield will soon be in service to support the 20-odd MiG-17s and -19s given to Tanzania. Tanzanian forces have also been given ground weapons and patrol gunboats and a number of Chinese advisers.

The PRC tries to maintain a position that competes with that of the Soviet Union or, in some cases, the United States, within the limits imposed by relatively slender resources. The Chinese effort has had mixed results: participation in Indonesian affairs was disastrous for the Communist party there and for Chinese influence; some of the lower-key actions in Africa and the Middle East have at least maintained some influence and show a budding potential.

ALLIANCES

Despite the bitterness of China's ideological split with Soviet Russia, neither nation has repudiated their 30 year Treaty of Friendship, Alliance and Mutual Assistance of February 14, 1950. It is likely that the terms would be invoked, and probably honored, if either nation were to become engaged in overt hostilities with the US. Otherwise the treaty is probably meaingless. Similar bilateral treaties with North Korea and Mongolia have comparable status, since both of these nations have supported the Soviet Union in the ideological split. There has been, however, some indication that the new PRC line in foreign relations has produced a significant move toward closer and warmer ties with North Korea. The tenth anniversary of the treaty between the two countries was celebrated with great intensity.

The only nation with which the PRC appears to have any kind of effective alliance is Albania. This alliance might have some limited usefulness in harassing Soviet or American shipping from sea or air in the event of war with either. There have been some reports of excavations in Albania that might be the start of positions for missiles trained on Russia. Actually, the arrangement has little real significance.

ARMY

(In this and the following sections the figures used represent a rough average from several sources. The PRC does not publish useful information on this subject. This is equally true with respect to deployments.)

Personnel: 2,550,000 (including railway engineer troops)

Organization:

- 11 Military Regions (each usually having 2 or 3 military districts; generally there is one army in each military district)
- 30 armies (equivalents of Western army corps; usually 2 or 3 divisions each; 3 artillery regiments; plus, sometimes, armor and cavalry units)
- 120 infantry divisions* (6 independent; the other 114 are in the 30 armies)
- 5 armored divisions
- 3 cavalry divisions
- 2 airborne divisions
- 1 mountain division (in Tibet)
- 20 artillery divisions (component regiments are normally attached to infantry divisions and include AT and AA units as well as field artillery)
- 11 railway engineer divisions
- 17 independent artillery regiments
- 5 independent AT artillery regiments
- 30 independent AA artillery regiments
- 5 independent armored regiments
- 67 independent engineer regiments
- 2 independent signal regiments
- 34 independent motor transport regiments

Deployment: Divisional strength is believed to be by military regions as follows (including all types except artillery divisions): (It is possible that more troops from Southern and Eastern areas have been moved to the north, raising the number of divisions there by 5 to 10.)

Sinkiang - 5 divisions
Shenyang (Manchuria) - 16 divisions
Peking - 17 divisions
Tsinan - 5 divisions

*Average 12-14,000 in strength; armored, cavalry and airborne divisions are slightly smaller.

Nanking - 8 divisions
Foochow - 9 divisions
Wuhan - 14 divisions
Lanchow - 11 divisions
Chengtu (including Tibet) - 10 divisions
Canton (including Hainan) - 17 divisions
Kunming - 5 divisions

From time to time there is evidence of the formation of special mission-oriented task groupings and activity. Observers on Taiwan say that there has been extensive airfield improvement and expansion of infrastructure in the coastal area across the Strait, as well as an active rotation and training program for air units. A South Seas Command based on Canton, Kunming, and Hainan Island has also been reported.

North Vietnam and Laos: There were over 15,000 railway engineer troops (1 railway engineer division) and some construction engineer troops in these two countries at one time, but this number has been reduced.

Major Equipment Inventory:

          JS-2/3 heavy tanks
          T-34 medium tanks
1,200+ T-59 medium tanks (Chinese-made copies of Soviet T-54)
          T-60 amphibious tanks
          T-69 light tanks
          APCs (Chinese designed and built)
          light, medium, and heavy artillery pieces
1,200+ AA guns
          SAM launchers (SA-2 Guideline)
          SSM launchers

Reserves: China claims to have a civilian militia of 200,000,000, which is practically the entire working force of the nation. These include about 125 million men and 75 million women. Most of these apparently are ordinary militiamen (men between 30 and 50, and women between 16 and 50) few of whom probably have any weapons training, and for whom few weapons and little equipment are available. There are perhaps 5,000,000 "backbone militiamen", carefully selected men between the ages of 16 and 30, who apparently receive annual training, and for whom weapons and equipment are probably in adequate supply in terms of Chinese equipment standards. Backbone militia units, up to battalion strength, are mobilizable for internal security tasks and as a source of reserve manpower for the PLA. Theoretically the entire militia force is mobilizable in division strengths, each division having an indefinite number of regiments, and each regiment including one backbone militia battalion. In practice, it is likely that ordinary militia units would be mobilized only for emergency home-guard type duties.

NAVY

Personnel: 180,000 (including 16,000 Naval Air Force and 28,000 Marines)

Organization:

  3 fleets:
    North Sea Fleet, approximately 240 craft, about 19% of total navy strength, from Yalu River to Lien Yuen Kang;
    East Sea Fleet, approximately 700 craft, about 57% of total navy strength, from Lien Yuen Kang to Chao An Wan;
    South Sea Fleet, approximately 300 craft, about 24% of total navy strength from Chao An Wan to Hainan.
  3 escort squadrons (one per fleet)
  4 landing craft squadrons (two for East Sea Fleet)
  2 submarine squadrons (none for South Sea Fleet)
  4 minesweeper squadrons (two for East Sea Fleet)
  2 torpedo boat squadrons (North Sea Fleet)
  2 auxiliary ship squadrons (1 divided between North and South Sea Fleets)
  6 naval air divisions
  1 independent naval air regiment
  10 marine units, 4 amphibious tank units (size unknown; may be amphibious-trained Army troops)
  10 coast artillery regiments

Major Units:

  1 ballistic missile submarine (G class; SSB)
  39 submarines (W and R class; SS)
  3 coastal submarines (S-1 and M-V class; SSC)
  8 destroyers (4 Gordy class; 4 new construction with SSM)
  8 destroyer escorts (DE)
  11 escorts (PF)
  20 submarine chasers (Kronstadt class; PC)
  35 missile patrol boats (Osa and Komar class; PTFG)
  21 fleet minesweepers (20 T-43 class, 1 Bathurst class, MSF)
  6 coastal minesweepers (MSC)
  215 torpedo boats (80 P-6, 70 P-4, 65 hydrofoil)

225 patrol gunboats (Shanghai class; PG)
 50 fast patrol craft (Swatow class; PTF)
 21 landing ships, tank (LST)
 13 landing ships, medium (LSM)
 16 landing ships, infantry, large (LSIL)
 10 landing craft, utility (LCU)
 12 river gunboats (PRG)
408 auxiliaries and miscellaneous service craft
300 MiG-15/17 fighters
100 Il-28 light bombers
 20 Tu-4 medium bombers
    trainer/support aircraft
    helicopters
    (Total: about 500 shore-based naval aircraft)

Major Naval Bases: Tsingtao, Lushan, Taku, Shanghai, Huangpu, Chou Shan, Amoy, Foochow, Whampoa, Changkiang, Tsamkong.

Reserves: There are about 350,000 trained naval reservists.

AIR FORCE

Personnel: 220,000 (including about 90,000 in air defense units)

Organization:
 20 fighter and fighter-bomber divisions (3 air regiments per division, 3 squadrons per regiment)
  6 bomber divisions
  1 transport division (sufficient airlift for about 2 infantry regiments)
  5 independent air regiments
    trainer/support units and helicopter squadrons
 32 independent AA artillery regiments (1,000 + AA guns)
  9 radar regiments
    miscellaneous service and support ground regiments

Major Aircraft Types:
3,060 combat aircraft
 1,000 MiG-19 fighters
 1,500 MiG-15/17 fighters
   300 MiG-21/F-9 interceptors
    10 Tu-4 medium bombers
   100 Tu-16 medium bombers
   150 Il-28 light bombers
1,050 + other aircraft (including approximately 350 aircraft of the Civil Air Bureau)
  450 transports (An-2, Il-12/14, Il-18)
  300 helicopters (Mi-4, Alouette III)
  300 MiG-15 trainers, trainer/support aircraft
      SS-4 IRBMs (supplied by USSR)
      SA-2 Guideline SAM

Major Air Bases: There are a total of 170 air bases and airfields, of which half are jet capable, and within 745 kilometers of Taiwan. First-line fighter/interceptor bases; Luchiao, Foochow, Tenghai; second-line fighter/interceptor bases: Tsaochiao, Liencheng, Pingtan; third-line fighter/interceptor bases: Hungchiao, Chienchiao, Changsha, Hsincheng, Nanhai; other bases include: Shenyang, Peking, Nanking, Canton, Sian, Kwangchan, Kunming, Wuhan, Chengchow, Lhassa.

Reserves: There are about 500,000 trained air reservists.

PARAMILITARY

There are about 300,000 security and border troops. The latter are organized into 19 infantry-type divisions and 30 independent regiments permanently stationed in the frontier areas, in addition to the regular divisions deployed in the associated military regions.

The People's Armed Police is now referred to as a public security force. The civilian militia has a claimed strength of 200 million, but its effective element is probably no greater than seven million.

CHINA, REPUBLIC OF (TAIWAN)

Chung-hua Min-kuo
Republic of China

POWER POTENTIAL STATISTICS

Area: 13,887 square miles
Population: 15,135,000
Total Active Armed Forces: 500,000 (3.03% population)
Gross National Product: $9.39 billion ($467 per capita)
Annual Military Expenditures: $700 million (7.45% GNP)
Steel and Iron Production: 1,250,000 metric tons
Fuel Production: Coal: 4.5 million metric tons
  Crude Oil: 123,000 metric tons
  Refined Petroleum Products: 8.3 million metric tons
Electric Power Output: 15.17 billion kwh
Merchant Fleet: 316 ships; 1.3 million gross tons
Civil Air Fleet: 8 jet, 12 turboprop, and 37 piston transports

DEFENSE STRUCTURE

The President of the Republic of China (ROC), Generalissimo Chiang Kai-shek, is commander in chief of the armed forces, but the day-to-day operation of the forces is now entrusted to younger men. The services are not integrated, but are centrally administered through a Ministry of Defense and coordinated operationally by a General Staff somewhat similar to the US Joint Staff. The Chief of the General Staff exercises a dual function. He is Chief of Staff to the President in command and operations as well as Chief of Staff to the Defense Minister in administration. The President's son, Chiang Ching-kuo, who is considered by many to be his most likely successor, is now Premier.

POLITICO-MILITARY POLICY

While the eventual return to the mainland is the central goal of the Nationalist leaders, the prospects for a classical invasion decrease. The Taipei government now emphasizes the capability of fast-moving elements that could reach the mainland and cooperate with anti-communist or non-communist elements there in rising against the Peking government. This would take place in a time of turbulence and internal strife on the mainland and would be the first step in the reunion of all China under Nationalist leadership. Meantime, attention goes to the assurance of economic progress and the maintenance of strong armed forces which, while they now seem oriented on effective defense, would be able to act offensively under proper conditions. The defense costs and commitments displayed testify to the realism of the Nationalist view. (It is noteworthy that, despite this burden, Taiwan — making good use of US economic assistance — has prospered economically in the last two decades, and no longer requires American economic aid.) An essential secondary objective of ROC military policy is to secure and stabilize the Taiwan Straits area as its contribution to the Chinese-American mutual security treaty.

After having survived the ravages of World War II—in which China's manpower losses were exceeded only by Russia, Germany, and Japan—the National Government was defeated by the Chinese Communist armies in a bitter civil war (1945-1949), fled to Taiwan, and was displaced in mainland China by the People's Republic of China. Social, political, and psychological factors, as well as serious military errors and reverses, contributed to this defeat. A major objective of military policy has been to correct these shortcomings. With substantial US military assistance and advice, particularly since 1953, it appears that this effort has been to a large degree successful.

The strength of the armed forces is maintained by conscription with military service being mandatory for all male citizens over the age of 19. Service is for two years. The percentage of those of mainland origin in the armed forces is steadily decreasing, although they still dominate in the higher ranks. The majority of the troops, particularly in the lower officer and enlisted ranks, is now of Taiwan origin. The growing prosperity and rapid industrialization in Taiwan are making it more difficult to interest youth in the service as a career, whether they be of mainland or of local birth. The government is coping with this problem in good part by the maintenance of a well-trained and readily available reserve, which now has more than one million members.

STRATEGIC PROBLEMS

It is evident to the ROC that it cannot return to mainland China without massive foreign support and assistance, or without a chaotic breakdown of the central Chinese Communist regime. It has been made clear that the United States will not provide support for any such offensive operations, although the US Government has officially announced its determination to preserve the independence and integrity of Taiwan from communist aggression. Even if mainland China should fall into turmoil that might support hope of a successful action, it is doubtful that the US would provide the kind of economic, logistical and other support that would probably be essential for such an invasion.

The determination of the ROC to retain its control over the islands of Quenoy and Matsu, immediately adjacent to the shores of the mainland, has posed a major strategic problem to the government. Despite repeated and protracted bombardments, and numerous threats of communist offensives against these islands, effective land and air defensive measures, plus American support, have enabled the ROC to retain these footholds. The fact that the ROC controls one province of

China (Taiwan) and parts of another (Quemoy and Matsu are in Fukien province) has considerable political significance in the context of the unresolved civil war. The islands also have some strategic value, particularly Quemoy, which controls Amoy and traffic in that part of the coastal area. It would be extremely difficult to use Amoy as a mounting area for an assault against Quemoy or the main island of Taiwan. There is no such thing as absolute invulnerability, but the cost of action against either target would be extremely high for the attacker.

There is now the additional factor of Communist nuclear weapons. Their use would change the prospects absolutely, since the destruction of only a few targets would severely cripple Taiwan. But, first, the retaliatory power of the United States would have to be reckoned with; second, such action might very well trigger some Soviet move in the north, and a two front war is a nightmare to Peking. As an intangible influence there is also the question of how the Communists would view the use of nuclear weapons against their brethren on Taiwan whose "liberation" is their avowed purpose.

MILITARY ASSISTANCE

Since 1950 the United States has provided $2.85 billion in military assistance to the ROC. A US Military Mission has been stationed on Taiwan since 1951, to assist the Chinese in their utilization of American military equipment provided under the Military Assistance Program. Taiwan has given some support to others, but on a modest scale.

ALLIANCES

The only alliance of the ROC is the mutual security treaty with the United States. Under related bilateral agreements, several US Air Force units are based on Taiwan, and base facilities are also provided for the US Seventh Fleet. The US Navy's Taiwan Strait patrol has been discontinued and the level of support now required for an occasional ship visit is small. Apparently the United States has also provided U-2 high-altitude reconnaissance aircraft for surveillance of mainland China. Normally the US military presence on Taiwan has consisted of several hundred men, mostly in the MAAG and the Taiwan Defense Command, and in some communications activities. The Vietnam War brought a sizable logistic support effort to Taiwan, involving at the peak about 9,000 men. The number is now being reduced slowly, in accordance with President Nixon's promise that the force would be decreased with the relaxation of tension in the area. This element, mostly Air Force, now numbers 7,000.

The United States declined offers of military participation in the war in Vietnam, as it did in the Korean War. However, several civic action units worked in South Vietnam, assisting the government in various aspects of rural development.

In October 1971, the Republic of China was expelled from the UN, and its seat was taken by the People's Republic of China. Since that time, a majority of the nations formerly recognizing Taipei have switched their relations to Peking. The US is the only major nation now having the full range of relations.

ARMY

Personnel: 390,000 (including 60,000 on Quemoy and 20,000 on Matsu)

Organization:
- 4 armored brigades
- 12 infantry divisions
- 6 light divisions
- 4 special forces groups
- 2 airborne brigades
- 3 armored cavalry regiments
- 1 SSM battalion (Honest John)
- 2 SAM battalions (Hawk and Nike-Hercules)
- 1 SAM battery (Nike-Hercules)

Major Equipment Inventory:
- 480 medium tanks (M-47 and M-48)
- 500 light tanks (M-24 and M-41)
- tank destroyers (M-18)
- APCs (M-113)
- SSMs (Honest John)
- SAMs (Hawk and Nike-Hercules)
- 66 helicopters (50 UH-1, 7 H-34, 9 KH-4)
- 10 PL-1 trainers
- 105mm, 155mm, and 203mm howitzers
- 155mm guns
- AA guns (40mm and up)

Reserves: Approximately one million trained reserves are available, as are required weapons and equipment when mobilized.

NAVY

Personnel: 35,000

Major Units:
- 16 destroyers (DD)
- 16 destroyer escorts (DE)
- 3 escorts (PCE; converted MSF)
- 11 submarine chasers (PC)
- 12 submarine chasers (SC)
- 1 escort transport (APD)
- 15 coastal minesweepers (MSC)
- 2 inshore minesweepers (MSI)
- 1 minelayer (converted MSF)
- 1 gunboat (PGM)

    4 torpedo boats (PT)
  46 patrol boats (YP)
  21 auxiliaries and support ships
  21 landing ships, tank (LST)
    1 landing ship, dock (LSD)
  15 landing ships, medium (LSM)
    5 landing ships, infantry, large (LSIL)
  30 landing craft (LCT, LCU)
    3 landing ships, support, large (LSSL)
    2 amphibious force flagships (converted LST)

Major Naval Bases: T'ai-nan, T'ai-tung, Chi-lung, Tso-ying, Penghu

Reserves: About 60,000 trained reservists

AIR FORCE

Personnel: 80,000

Organization:
    8 fighter-bomber squadrons (F-100, F-5)
    4 fighter interceptor squadrons (F-104)
    2 fighter-reconnaissance squadrons (RF-101, RF-104)
    1 ASW squadron (S-2)
    1 SAR squadron (HU-16, PBY)
    1 transport wing (C-46, C-47, C-119, C-123, Boeing 720)
    1 helicopter wing (H-13, H-19, Hughes 500, UH-1)
    1 trainer/support wing (PL-1, PL-2)

Major Aircraft Types:
  279 combat aircraft
      190 fighter-bombers (90 F-100, 100 F-5)
        63 F-104 fighter-interceptors
        17 fighter-reconnaissance aircraft (4 RF-101, 13 RF-104)
         9 S-2 ASW aircraft
  294 other aircraft
      141 transports (40 C-46, 50 C-47, 40 C-119, 10 C-123, 1 Boeing 720)
        10 SAR aircraft (6 HU-16, 4 PBY)
        46 helicopters (10 H-13, 7 H-19, 6 Hughes 500, 23 UH-1)
      100 + trainers and support aircraft (PL-1, PL-2, and others)

Major Air Bases: Taipei, Hsinchu, Tao-yuan, T'ai-chung, Chiai, T'ai-nan, Ping-tung; Kung-k'uang (USAF).

Reserves: About 130,000 trained reservists.

MARINE CORPS

Personnel: 36,000

Organization: 2 divisions

Reserves: 65,000 to 70,000 trained reservists

PARAMILITARY

There is a militia numbering about 175,000.

JAPAN
Nippon, Nihon

POWER POTENTIAL STATISTICS

Area: 142,871 square miles
Population: 107,500,000
Total Active Armed Forces: 260,000 (authorized; 0.24% population)
Gross National Product: $321 billion ($2,986 per capita)
Annual Military Expenditures: $3.53 billion (1.1% GNP)
Steel and Iron Production: 163.2 million metric tons
Fuel Production: Coal: 33.4 million metric tons
    Crude Oil: 713,000 metric tons
    Refined Petroleum Products: 211.5 million metric tons
    Gas: 5.9 billion cubic meters
Electric Power Output: 379 billion kwh
Merchant Fleet: 9,433 ships; 34.9 million gross tons
Civil Air Fleet: 103 jet, 32 turboprop, 6 piston transports

DEFENSE STRUCTURE

The Japanese Empire is a constitutional monarchy, with a parliamentary government. The Prime Minister exercises supreme civilian authority over the armed forces — which in Japan are referred to collectively as the Self Defense Force. He does this through the Japan Defense Agency, which is directly under his office and is not a Cabinet Ministry. Otherwise, the Director General of the Japan Defense Agency functions like a Minister of Defense in other governmental organizations. There are formal Party and Cabinet bodies that examine and act upon major military proposals, and there is a central, integrated military staff, serving the Director General, to coordinate the plans and operations of the three otherwise independent Self Defense Forces.

POLITICO-MILITARY POLICY

Japan's basic military policy is to assure its independence and territorial integrity by the maintenance of forces solely for

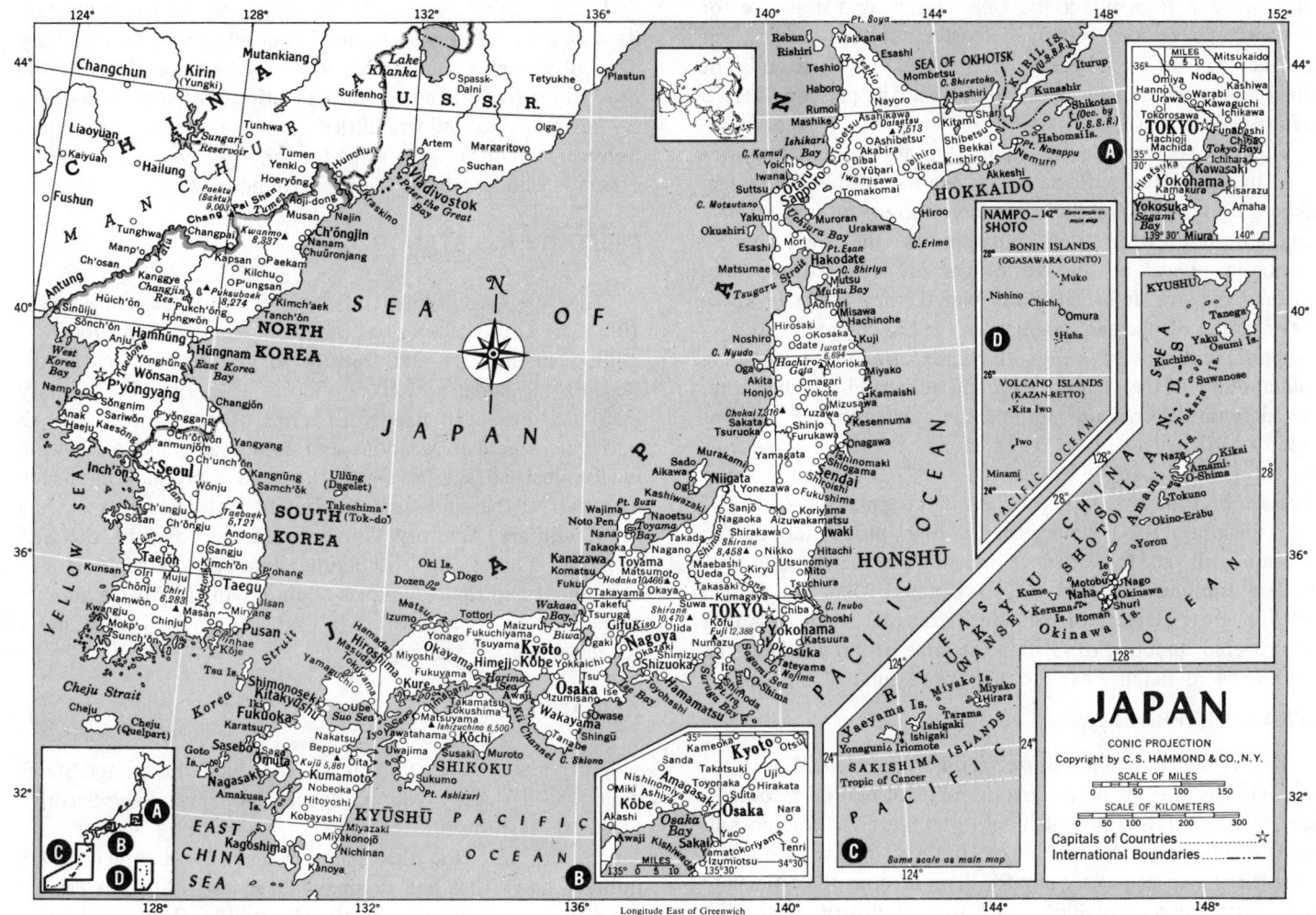

defensive purposes, relying strongly on its firm mutual security treaty with the United States, ratified in 1960 for a period of ten years, after which either side could denounce it with one year's notice. This is a reflection of the Constitution of May 1947, which rejected war or the threat or use of armed force as instruments of national policy. This constitution was approved by the American occupation authorities, under General Douglas MacArthur. It also quite clearly represented the views of a majority of the Japanese people in the immediate years after World War II.

In July 1950, when American forces in Japan had been greatly reduced by movement to Korea, General MacArthur authorized the establishment of a National Police Reserve of some 75,000 men. In 1952, when the Japanese-United States Treaties became effective, the force was reorganized to include a 110,000-man National Self Defense Force and a Maritime Self Defense Force of some 9,000. From these beginnings, and with much debate at every step, the Japanese Defense Agency has grown to its present size.

The members of the Self Defense Force are considered to be civil servants; there is no separate military legal authority such as is found in the armed forces of practically every other nation in the world. Crimes or offense committed by Japanese military men are tried in civilian courts.

There is no conscription, which is further evidence of the firmness of Japanese intentions to avoid anything that could be construed as militarism. Enlistment in the Self Defense Force is entirely voluntary. Military service is not the most attractive prospect for the young man in a nation where, for some time, there were seven job openings for every high school graduate. Only a very small proportion of the civilian population has had any military experience since World War II.

Consistent with the general policy pattern, and also reflecting experience as the only nation to have suffered atomic attack, Japan has consistently refused to consider the development of nuclear weapons. Japanese scientists however, are active in research for the use of nuclear energy for peaceful purposes. The emergence of a nuclear capability in Communist China has forced some reexamination of weapons policy in Tokyo. There have been some tentative suggestions that Japan might find it legal under the Constitution and desirable for defense to have some purely defensive nuclear weapons, but this idea has not gained great support. The final decision is not likely to be made soon, and will depend in part on the US involvement in East Asia.

The Japanese people are ambivalent about military power as an instrument of national policy. On the one hand they feel some disquiet over the fact that their current influence is not commensurate with their position as the third largest economic power in the world. On the other hand, they suffered massive defeat in World War II, they uniquely know the meaning of nuclear weapons, and in the climate of today's weapons and power arrays they perceive the frightening vulnerability of their supply lines and homeland. Furthermore, low defense expenditure permits the application of most of Japan's GNP to maintain the phenomenal rate of growth of the economy. Japan's four-year (1972-1976) defense program plans an expenditure of $16 billion, a rate greatly in excess of past spending. It is stated that a high proportion of the increase will go to the development and construction of modern equipment and advanced weapons of Japanese design, with no great increase of personnel strength. Japan feels that an expected doubling of GNP in the same period will keep the percentage of defense expenditure approximately unchanged.

STRATEGIC PROBLEMS

Today, as during and before World War II, Japan's greatest strategic weakness is its poverty in material natural resources. Save for coal, Japan is dependent upon imports for almost all of the raw materials required for its mighty industrial complex. Japan can easily pay for them through the efficiency and production capability of that industry, but the vulnerability to foreign interference cannot be eliminated.

The world-wide energy crisis has had particularly heavy impact on Japan, relying as it does on oil imported from Arab nations for 42% of total requirements, and on imports in general for 99.7% of consumption, which, in 1972, amounted to 47.5 million metric tons. In addition almost all of the iron and copper needs of Japanese industry come by sea. Although Japan responded quickly to Arab demands for support in their quarrel with Israel, and has been rewarded with some assurance over supply, the steep rise in price threatens Japan's economic position. And Japan remains vulnerable to future Arab demands. Alternate sources and American sharing have yet to be tested.

Another vulnerability is the concentration of the Japanese population and of the industrial complex. This concentration was a major factor in the successful American strategic bombing of Japan in 1945. The Japanese heartland is within easy range of air bases and missile bases in Siberia, North Korea, and Communist China, to say nothing of missile submarines in the waters surrounding the Japanese islands. Japan's recent installation of a comprehensive air defense system can only partially offset this severe vulnerability.

If Japan should decide, in the proximate future, to increase its armed forces drastically, and to develop a nuclear military capability, such a course could sincerely be reconciled with the need for adequate deterrent strength to offset the nation's severe strategic vulnerabilities. Such a course of action, however, would be worrisome to many people — Japanese and others — who remember the background of World War II.

MILITARY ASSISTANCE

Since the establishment of the first Police Reserve Force in 1950, the United States has provided Japan with nearly $900 million in military aid, mostly in the form of weapons. Because of Japan's well developed economy, US military assistance has been mainly in terms of permitting Japan to purchase American weapons and equipment, and to develop local industrial facilities for the continued production of such material. At the same time, the United States has maintained a small Military Advisory Group in Japan, to assist the Self Defense Forces in becoming familiar with American equipment and the techniques of employing it. Also, a number of Japanese military men have been sent to the United States for schooling and training.

ALLIANCES

Japan's only foreign alliance is that with the United States under the ten-year Treaty of Mutual Cooperation and Security of 1960. It provides not only for US military assistance to Japan, but also for the maintenance of a number of US military bases that had originally been established as part of the US occupation of Japan after World War II. In 1970 Japan announced its intention to continue the treaty in force indefinitely. The question of Okinawa was deferred until 1971, when a treaty was signed calling for the reversion of the Ryukyus to Japanese sovereignty by 1972. Under its terms, the US retains certain bases. Nuclear weapons have been withdrawn, not to be replaced without consultation between the two parties.

ARMY (Ground Self Defense Force)

Personnel: 180,000

Organization:

- 5 army areas; 2-4 divisions per army; headquarters at: Sapporo, Sendai, Tokyo, Itami (near Osaka), Kumamoto
- 12 infantry divisions (7,000-9,000 men per division)*
- 1 mechanized division
- 1 airborne brigade

*The Fourth Defense Buildup Plan (1972-76) calls for the mechanization of four of these divisions, all to remain in Hokkaido.

3 independent artillery brigades
1 helicopter brigade
5 independent engineer brigades
1 signal brigade
1 SSM battalion (Honest John)
3 SAM battalions (Hawk)

Major Equipment Inventory:
- 1,000 light and medium tanks (M-24, M-41, M-4, M-47, and Type 61)
- 650 APCs (M-113, Type 60, SU, and SX)
- 64 heavy artillery pieces (203mm howitzers)
- 250 medium artillery pieces (including 155mm self-propelled guns)
- 580 light artillery pieces (mostly 105mm howitzers)
- self-propelled AT guns (SS-4 twin 106mm recoilless rifles)
- 50 AAA pieces
- SSMs (Honest John)
- SAMs (Hawk, Nike-Hercules, Nike-Ajax)
- 140 light aircraft (LM-1, LM-2, O-1, T-34)
- 252 helicopters (50 OH-6, 40 H-13, 90 UH-1, 28 H-55, 42 V-107)

Reserves: There are approximately 30,000 trained, organized reservists.

NAVY (Maritime Self Defense Force)

Personnel: 38,300

Organization:
- 5 regional maritime districts (see Bases, below)
- Fleet Escort Force
- Fleet Air Force
- Air Training Command

Major Units:
- 35 destroyers (2 with Tartar SAM; DD)
- 23 destroyer escorts (DE)
- 17 submarines (SS)
- 20 submarine chasers (PC)
- 3 coastal minelayers (MMC)
- 39 coastal minesweepers (MSC)
- 10 minesweeping boats (MSB)
- 7 torpedo boats (PT)
- 3 landing ships, tank (LST)
- 1 landing ship, medium (LSM)
- 42 landing craft, mechanized (LCM)
- 6 landing craft, utility (LCU)
- 93 auxiliaries
- 55 S-2 ASW patrol aircraft (3 squadrons)
- 73 P-2 patrol bomber/ASW aircraft (4 squadrons)
- 10 PS-1 ASW flying boats
- about 100 trainer/support aircraft (KM-2, Beech King Air)
- 75 helicopters (Vertol 107, H-34, OH-6, UH-1, SH-3); 4 squadrons, one of which is for minelaying

Major Naval Bases: Mutsu, Yokosuka, Maizuru, Kure, Sasebo

AIR FORCE (Air Self Defense Force)

Personnel: 41,700

Organization:
- 3 Regional commands: Northern Air Command, Central Air Command, Western Command
- 4 fighter-bomber squadrons (F-86)
- 3 fighter-interceptor squadrons (F-86)
- 7 fighter-interceptor squadrons (F-104)
- 1 fighter-interceptor squadron (F-4)
- 1 fighter-reconnaissance squadron (RF-86)
- 1 transport wing (YS-11, C-46)
- 4 training wings (T-34, T-1, F-86, T-33)
- 1 rescue wing (T-34, MU-2, S-62, V-107)
- 5 SAM battalions (Nike-Hercules)
- Base Air Defense Ground Environment System (BADGES): a centralized, computerized air defense system with 4 command centers and 24 radar stations.

Major Aircraft Types:
- 470 combat aircraft
  - 246 fighters (26 F-4, 220 F-86)
  - 206 F-104 fighter-interceptors
  - 18 RF-86 fighter-reconnaissance aircraft
- 551 other aircraft
  - 61 transports (13 YS-11, 48 C-46)
  - 414 trainers (57 T-1, 187 T-33, 107 T-34, 63 F-86)
  - 15 MU-2 light transport/utility
  - 61 helicopters (27 UH-1, 8 S-62, 16 V-107, 10 H-19)

Equipment on Order: F-4, RF-4 aircraft

Major Air Bases: Tachikawa, Matsushima, Hofu, Tsuiki, Handa, Hamamatsu, Chitose, Miho, Miyazaki, Komaki, Iruma, Huakuri, Komatsu, Naha (Okinawa)

COAST GUARD (Maritime Safety Agency)

Personnel: 11,500

Major Units:
- 87 patrol vessels
- 42 patrol craft
- 169 coastal craft
- 26 surveying vessels
- 26 tenders

KOREA, NORTH

Choson Minchu-chui Inmin Konghwa-guk
Democratic People's Republic of Korea

POWER POTENTIAL STATISTICS

Area: 46,557 square miles
Population: 14,500,000
Total Active Armed Forces: 436,000 (includes 35,000 security troops; 3% population)
Gross National Product: $4 billion (estimated: $276 per capita)
Annual Military Expenditures: $900 million (22.5% GNP)
Steel and Iron Production: 4.36 million metric tons
Fuel Production: Coal: 24 million metric tons
Electric Power Output: 13.3 billion kwh
Merchant Fleet: 11 ships; 51,000 tons
Civil Air Fleet: 9 piston transports

DEFENSE STRUCTURE

The communist leader of North Korea, Premier Kim Il-Sung, has ruled since 1945. He exercises all real power; he heads both the government and Party apparatus and is also the Supreme Commander of all the armed forces. He is assisted by seven Vice Premiers, one of whom is also Minister of Defense.

The Ministry of Defense consists of a General Staff, the Main Political Administration (for troop indoctrination), Forces Inspectorates (artillery, engineer, armor, etc.), Navy, Air Force, and Rear Service Administration (logistics). All top Defense Ministry chiefs are members of the Korean Labor Party (KLP) Central Committee. North Korea is divided into military districts, each headed by a commander and his deputy for political affairs. Nearly all officers in the armed forces are Party members. Thus centralized KLP control is assured at all levels of the military organization.

POLITICO-MILITARY POLICY

For more than two decades the DPRK's overriding aim has been to overthrow the anti-communist government of South Korea (the Republic of Korea) and to unify the country under a communist government. The DPRK came close to achieving this after invading the South in the summer of 1950, but was soon overrun itself until the Chinese Communists intervened in the autumn. The armistice of July 1953 set a demarcation line approximating the original 38th parallel artificial boundary of 1945. To date, no final peace treaty has been signed officially ending the Korean War.

Since 1956, the DPRK has indicated an ambition to direct its own policies free of either Russian or Chinese Communist control. Fifteen years of harsh austerity controls and ruthless industrialization have brought the DPRK near this goal. Today North Korea is no longer totally dependent economically upon Soviet Russia. However, the DPRK is still dependent on both of its major allies for military and other support. The Pyongyang regime has steered a cautious course through the Sino-Soviet dispute, and currently is pursuing a policy of friendly non-alignment with both communist giants.

Despite a professed policy of peaceful liberation of the South, it is clear that the North Koreans are unable to attract the Southerners, who were disillusioned by communist cruelties in the Korean War. Pyongyang's increased self-confidence and militancy have been displayed in guerrilla raids, in stepped-up incidents in the Armistice line's demilitarized zone, in the January 1968 commando attempt to assassinate the ROK President, and in the seizure of the USS *Pueblo* off North Korea's coast a few days later, and the shooting down of an American EC-121 electronic reconnaissance aircraft well outside territorial waters on April 15, 1969.

The North no longer has the overwhelming military superiority which it possessed in 1950. Even so, it was reported to be making significant redeployments toward the 38th parallel in early 1974. These activities included new barracks and troop units in them, forward airfields and aircraft shelters, and naval installations. The incident rate along the border continues high and the talks between the two Koreas, hailed as promising in 1972, have not so far produced any significant easing of tension.

The armed forces are maintained by conscription. All young men are required to serve three years in the Army or four years in the Navy or Air Force.

STRATEGIC PROBLEMS

The DPRK's basic strategic problem is its geographic proximity to a highly-armed and hostile non-communist nation (the Republic of Korea, South Korea, which regards the North Korean government as an illegal occupier of half of the Korean peninsula). The DPRK is within easy striking range of powerful US aircraft stationed in Japan and Okinawa, as well as nearby aircraft in the ROK. North Korean factories, hydroelectric plants, and population centers are highly

CENTRAL AND EAST ASIA 291

concentrated, and such targets are well-known to opposing intelligence. The DPRK railroad and road system is highly vulnerable to air attack. The long east and west coasts necessitate maintenance of an active patrol force.

The DPRK faces a continuing strategic and military problem in walking a diplomatic tightrope between the feuding communist giants who share its northern borders. The DPRK needs Russian backing to discourage incursions from Red China, which touches most of its northern boundary, as well as to provide economic and military support. Friendly relations with the contiguous Chinese People's Republic, which once came to North Korea's rescue, are equally vital. The DPRK still depends on the back-up of nearby Chinese troops in a renewed war with South Korea, for North Korea's population is less than half that of the ROK, and its army, although supported by a stronger air arm, remains numerically inferior.

MILITARY ASSISTANCE

The principal supporter of the DPRK's large military organization and of its growing economy has been the Soviet Union. Due to this aid, the DPRK was able to mount its nearly successful attack upon the ROK in June 1950. The Soviet Union was also chiefly responsible for rebuilding the DPRK's war-shattered economy and military strength following the July 1953 armistice. Since then, Communist China, which supplied almost a million-man army in the war, has also contributed significantly to DPRK military armaments, although China is incapable of providing the heavy support received from the USSR

When North Korea began openly supporting Chinese policy in 1963, Soviet Premier Khruschev cut off military and economic aid, which included fuel and parts for the Soviet-supplied MiG jet fighters and Ilyushin bombers. But in 1965, when the DPRK changed its pro-Peking position and drew closer again to the USSR, military aid was renewed and increased, including the supply of anti-aircraft missiles.

ALLIANCES

On July 6, 1961, the DPRK signed a ten-year military aid treaty with the Soviet Union, and a similar 1961 agreement was made with Communist China. In March 1967 another DPRK-USSR defense and aid agreement was signed.

ARMY

Personnel: 360,000

Organization:
- 2 armored divisions
- 20 infantry divisions
- 5 independent infantry brigades (probably mechanized or partly mechanized)
- 5 independent armored regiments
- special commando groups (15,000 men)
- 20-25 SAM battalions (SA-2 Guideline)

Major Equipment Inventory:
- 850 medium tanks (T-34, T-54/55, T-59)
- 150 light tanks (PT-76)
- 200 self-propelled guns (SU-76, SU-100, ZSU-57/2)
- 6,000 other mortars and light, medium, and heavy artillery pieces (up to 152mm guns)
- 2,000 AAA pieces
- 900 APCs (BTR-40, BTR-152, BA-64)
- 300 SAMs (SA-2 Guideline)

Reserves: Approximately 1,000,000 trained reservists.

NAVY

Personnel: 11,000

Major Units:
- 3 submarines (W class; SS)
- 6 guided missile patrol boats (Komar class with Styx SSM; PTFR)
- 8 guided missile patrol boats (Osa class with Styx SSM; PTFG)
- 10 fleet minesweepers (2 T-43, 8 Fugas class; MSF)
- 24 inshore minesweeping boats (MB)
- 18 submarine chasers (SC)
- 4 patrol boats (Shanghai class; PTF)
- 43 torpedo boats (USSR P-4 type; PT)
- 11 patrol gunboats (PGM)

Major Naval Bases: Chinnamp'o (west coast), Wonsan (east coast)

Reserves: About 15,000 reservists

AIR FORCE

Personnel: 30,000

Organization:
- 1 light bomber division (Il-28)
- 1 interceptor division (MiG-19/21)
- 2 fighter-bomber divisions (MiG-15/17, Su-7)

Major Aircraft Types:
- 605 combat aircraft
  - 70 Il-28 light bombers

90 MiG-21 interceptors
20 MiG-19 interceptors
25 Su-7 fighter-bombers
60 MiG-15 fighter-bombers
340 MiG-17 fighter-bombers
195 other aircraft
75 transports (An-2, Li-2, Il-12, Il-14)
20 Mi-4 helicopters
100 trainer/support aircraft (Yak-11, Yak-18, MiG-15, Il-28)

Major Air Bases: Pyongyang, Pyongyang East, Taechon, Wonsan, Pyong-ni, Viji, Sunan, Sinuiju, and Saamcham

Reserves: About 40,000 trained reservists

PARAMILITARY

There are 35,000 security forces and border guards. A people's militia claims an additional strength of 1,250,000.

KOREA, SOUTH
Taehan Mik-guk
Republic of Korea

POWER POTENTIAL STATISTICS

Area: 38,022 square miles
Population: 32,848,000
Total Active Armed Forces: 634,250 (1.93% population)
Gross National Product: $9.1 billion ($277 per capita)
Annual Military Expenditures: $464 million (5.1% GNP)
Steel Production: 472,000 metric tons
Fuel Production: Coal: 12.8 million metric tons
  Refined Petroleum Products: 13.2 million metric tons
Electric Power Output: 10.5 billion kwh
Merchant Fleet: 337 ships; 940,000 gross tons
Civil Air Fleet: 11 jet, 12 turboprop transports

DEFENSE STRUCTURE

The Republic of Korea (ROK) has a strong presidential form of government. The ROK President is the constitutional commander of the nation's armed forces; he also heads the State Council (cabinet) which is the highest administrative organ and includes the Minister of National Defense.

The President is assisted by the National Security Council, of which he is chairman and which includes the Prime Minister, the Ministers of National Defense, Economic Planning, Foreign Affairs, Home Affairs, and Finance, and the Director of the Central Intelligence Agency. The Chairman of the Joint Chiefs of Staff also participates in NSC meetings. General control over the armed forces is exercised by the Joint Chiefs of Staff, who are administratively responsible to the National Defense Minister.

POLITICO-MILITARY POLICY

The current primary objective of the Republic of Korea (ROK) is to maintain its independence in the face of an ever-present invasion threat from Communist North Korea. The second major goal is to overthrow the North Korean regime (Democratic People's Republic of Korea), regarded as the illegal occupier of the north, and reunite the Korean peninsula under the South Korean government. The first policy is strongly supported by the United States. The United Nations, who are pledged to defend the ROK from aggression, also support Korea's peaceful reunification under UN-supervised free elections, but not by force.

However, any such peaceful reunification seems precluded in the foreseeable future. North Korea's independence and military strength are supported by both the Soviet Union and the People's Republic of China. The military establishments of North and South Korea, backed up by alliances with the world's greatest powers, are poised in an uneasy deadlock which neither dares break. The first indication of a possible reduction in tensions was provided by high level discussions between representatives of the two Korean governments in July 1972. The momentum of these talks has slowed, for a variety of reasons, all rooted in the almost total distrust that each side feels for the other. Any immediate results of such talks are unlikely.

Meanwhile, South Korea seeks to increase its military and economic strength and decrease its dependence on the United States. The 1968 North Korean attempt to kill the ROK President, the capture of the US intelligence ship *Pueblo*, and the shooting down by North Korean aircraft of a US EC-121 aircraft over international seas on April 15, 1969, caused a rapid remodernization of the Sough Korean and American Forces defending the ROK, especially the neglected air arm. The ROK also benefitted from its contribution of 50,000 troops in Vietnam, which resulted in increased US aid and promises of profitable reconstruction in South Korea.

The control of all aspects of political activity in the ROK is becoming increasingly severe. The kidnapping from Japan in August 1973 of Kim Dae Juk, a political opponent of President Park's, and the subsequent refusal to permit him to go to the United States for an academic appointment, created unfavorable reactions among the ROK's friends. The sense of outrage in Tokyo has had unsettling influence on the progress of affairs between those nations.

Military service is compulsory for all physically fit adult males. After completing service (33 months for Army and Marines, 36 months for Navy and Air Force), the individual is automatically a member of the reserve force.

STRATEGIC PROBLEMS

South Korea's chief strategic vulnerability is the proximity of all ROK targets, including concentrated industries and population centers, to air attacks from North Korea, Communist China, and the Soviet Maritime Provinces. Second is the vulnerability of South Korea to ground infiltration or attack from the north. The ROK has taken energetic steps against continuing North Korean infiltration and sabotage, including special counter-insurgency forces, intensive coastal patrols and a home guard militia. In view of the strong anti-communism of most South Koreans, and their general support of the ROK government, there is no likelihood of indigenous guerrilla warfare arising in the South. With the continued US military commitment and the maintenance of a strong ROK defense structure, the chances of an all-out attack from Pyongyang are slight. Should the Korean War be renewed, there is little possibility of either side mounting a quick, knockout blow.

Economically, South Korea suffers from a severe shortage of natural resources upon which to build a viable industrial base to support its dense population and one of the world's largest military organizations. South Korea remains largely dependent upon the United States for both military and domestic needs. The artificial division of the Korean peninsula in 1945 left the South with the agricultural, unindustrialized part of the country and the less educated and more unskilled part of the population. Yet South Korea cannot even feed her own people and must import food, although the government is planning for agricultural self-sufficiency. Labor unemployment and underemployment remain serious and growing problems. The ROK also has a severe annual balance of payments gap. US economic aid amounted to some $4.7 billion worth of goods, equipment, and technical training from 1946-1968.

MILITARY ASSISTANCE

The ROK military forces are totally dependent on US aid. American military assistance from 1946-1972 amounted to $3.42 billion. The US has recently improved the weapons of the ROK armed services and enlarged and updated the ROK Air Force, which is still far weaker than that of North Korea. In addition, when a US division was recently withdrawn, $200 million in arms and equipment were turned over to the ROK.

The US maintains military advisory groups in Korea which equip and train all four ROK services. Most of South Korea's military units are under operational control of the United Nations Command, which is Korea's senior military headquarters. The UN Commander is also the Commanding General of the US Eighth Army, which has one infantry division, 38th Artillery Brigade (Air Defense), 4th Missile Command (surface-to-surface), and various support units in Korea, numbering 43,000 Americans. More than 100 up-to-date US jets are stationed on five Korean airfields, with at least another 100 in Japan and B-52 bombers in Okinawa. The US Seventh Fleet periodically has a carrier task force patrolling Korean waters.

ALLIANCES

The continuing ROK-US alliance is embodied in the Mutual Defense Treaty of November 1954, which provides that the parties will consult with each other if threatened by external attack. The pact also states that an armed attack on the Pacific territories controlled by either signatory would be dangerous to the security of the other.

Soviet and US opposition has kept both Koreas out of the United Nations. The ROK is a member of the Asian and Pacific Council (ASPAC), the Economic Commission for Asia and the Far East (ECAFE), the Food and Agriculture Organization of the United Nations (FAO), and the World Health Organization (WHO). The ROK also helped found the Asian Nations Anti-Communist League.

ARMY

Personnel: 560,000

Organization:
- 2 armies
- 19 infantry divisions
- 2 armored divisions (M-48 and M-60; additional armor is found in infantry divisions)
- 80 artillery battalions (most with infantry divisions)
- 1 SSM battalion (Honest John)
- 3 SAM battalions (2 Hawk, 1 Nike-Hercules)
- cadres for 10 divisions

Major Equipment Inventory:
- 750 medium tanks (mostly M-48, some M-47, some M-60)
- APCs (M-113)
- light tanks (M-24 and M-41)
- armored cars (M-8)
- 1,200 howitzers (105mm and 155mm)
- 203mm howitzers
- mortars
- SAMs (Hawk, Nike-Hercules)
- SSMs (Honest John)

Reserves: There is a trained manpower pool of approximately 1,500,000 men. These are being organized into a militia force for home defense. Currently available for mobilization are personnel and equipment for four tank battalions and ten infantry divisions.

NAVY

Personnel: 16,750

Major Units:
- 5 destroyers (DD)
- 3 destroyer escorts (DE)
- 4 patrol escorts (PF)
- 11 patrol escorts (PCE)
- 4 submarine chasers (PC)
- 2 submarine chasers (PCS)
- 9 patrol boats (ex-CGC)
- 12 coastal minesweepers (MSC)
- 6 high speed transports (APD)
- 8 landing ships, tank (LST)
- 11 landing ships, medium (LSM)
- 1 landing ship, medium, rocket (LSMR)
- 13 auxiliaries

Major Naval Bases: Chinhae, Pusan, Inchon

Reserves: There are 30,000 to 35,000 trained reservists.

AIR FORCE

Personnel: 24,500

Organization:
- 5 fighter-bomber squadrons (F-5, F-4)
- 1 fighter-interceptor squadron, All Weather (F-86)
- 5 fighter-bomber squadrons (F-86)
- 1 reconnaissance squadron (RF-86)
- 2 transport groups (C-46, C-47, C-54)
- 1 training group (PL-1, PL-2, O-1)

Major Aircraft Types:
- 228 combat aircraft
  - 80 F-5 fighter-bombers
  - 18 F-4 fighter-bombers
  - 100 F-86 fighters
  - 20 F-86 all weather fighter/interceptors
  - 10 RF-86 reconnaissance aircraft
- 140 other aircraft
  - 30 transports (C-46, Aero Commanders, C-47, C-54)
  - 90 trainer/support aircraft (T-28, T-33, PL-1, PL-2, O-1)
  - 20 helicopters (H-19, UH-1N, UH-1, KH-4)

Major Air Bases: ROK: Saechon, Chinhae, Osan, Chongju, Taegu, Suwon, and about 10 small strips; USAF: Seoul, Kimpo, Pusan, Kunsan, Kananung, Pohang, Chunchon, Pyong-taek, Hoengson

Reserves: There are 35,000 trained reservists.

MARINE CORPS

Personnel: 33,000

Organization:
- 1 division (3 brigades)
- 2 independent brigades

Reserves: About 60,000 trained reservists

PARAMILITARY

In addition to the militia force (see above, Army, Reserves), civilians are also being formed into local counterespionage and defense units (based on Israel's example and with Israeli advisors).

MONGOLIA

Bugd Nayramdakh Mongol Ard Uls
Mongolian People's Republic

POWER POTENTIAL STATISTICS

Area: 604,247 square miles
Population: 1,400,000
Total Active Armed Forces: 47,000 (including about 18,000 border guards and security police; 3.36% population)
Gross National Product: $840 million ($600 per capita)
Annual Military Expenditures: $30 million (3.57% GNP)
Fuel Production: Coal: 84,000 metric tons
  Crude Oil: 10,000 metric tons
Electric Power Output: 516 million kwh
Civil Air Fleet: 3 turboprop, 3 piston transports

DEFENSE STRUCTURE

As in all Communist countries, military forces are controlled by the Party. Control is accomplished by individuals holding dual membership in corresponding Party and Government positions. A Central Committee conducts Party affairs; its Secretariat handles organizational, executive, and administrative work through functional departments, one of which is the military department. On the government side, two-thirds of the Council of Ministers are also Central

Committee members. The Council of Ministers exercises general guidance in defense matters and the organization of the armed forces; under it the Ministry of Defense is concerned with the detailed organization of defense matters. Usually, as at present, the Minister of Defense is also Commander of the Mongolian People's Army (MPA). In addition, he is a member of the Party's Central Committee.

POLITICO-MILITARY POLICY

Mongols have always been warriors; from the days of Genghis Khan in the 13th Century, military service has been universal for all males, and Mongolia's territorial militia organization has been the basis for national administration. This military attitude was somewhat attenuated from the late 16th to early 20th Centuries when Tibetan Buddhism and Chinese suzerainty tended to reduce the Mongols to passivity. More recently the revolutionary fervor of Communism, and the threats of Japanese imperialism in the 1930s and 1940s, and of Chinese Communist imperialism since 1960, have restored a considerable war-like spirit among the Mongols. Today, by the Constitution, military service in the Mongolian People's Revolutionary Army is considered "a fundamental and honorable duty of all citizens." Active service for two years is compulsory and universal.

All units of the Mongolian People's Army have political officers and communist party organizations on the Soviet army model. From the founding of the MPR the Army has been considered an important vehicle for modernizing Mongolian society through the promotion of literacy, health measures, technical training, patriotism, and political consciousness. More recently, the Army has been heavily engaged in construction work at the new industrial complex of Darkhan.

STRATEGIC PROBLEMS

Mongolia's strategic situation is characterized by its buffer state role, giving defensive depth to the Soviet Union's central Siberia against an irredentist China. China has not given up claim to Mongolia based on the suzerainty of the Manchu Dynasty. This claim is rejected by Mongolia, which asserts that allegiance was to the Manchus, not to China. Should China expand into sparsely populated Mongolia, Soviet communications (Trans-Siberian Railroad) to its Pacific coast would be within close range (100 miles) of an unfriendly frontier.

Mongolia is obliged to guard some 2,500 miles of Chinese border and to provide forces to ensure internal security, with a large area and the lowest population density of any country in the world. Mongolia can accomplish these defense tasks against a serious threat only with outside help. Thus Soviet troops entered the MPR in 1932 to assist in putting down a counter-revolution and remained until 1956, first because of the Japanese threat and then to help maintain internal security. They returned in the early 1960s after the Sino-Soviet split. Mongolia provides forward defensive positions for Soviet military units, and areas for forward deployment of Soviet missile forces. China complained in 1973 about the addition of more Soviet troops.

The rigorously-controlled existence in a communist state is the antithesis of the free nomadic life previously enjoyed by the Mongols. This, combined with an abortive Pan-Mongol movement, and the preference of some Mongolians for China over Russia, caused some dissension in the 1920s and early 1930s, resulting in repressions and repeated purges. However, the Mongols, now enjoying one of the highest living standards in Asia, appear to have become resigned to modernization under Communism, and are committed to alignment with the Soviet Union; little likelihood for serious insurgency is seen. Communist China, however, continues to employ the MPR's Inner Mongolian cousins for harassment, reconnaissance and subversion along the Sino-Mongolian border.

MILITARY ASSISTANCE

The money value of military training and equipment received from the Soviet Union is not known, nor is the proportion between grant aid and sales. However, the amount over the years has been considerable; the Soviet Union is the MPR's sole source for arms and training. Training missions and technical assistance have been continuous since 1921.

The MPR sent troops to assist the North Koreans during the Korean War, and has been providing aid to North Vietnam.

Soviet SA-2 missile units guard the key communications hub of Choibalsan in eastern Mongolia, and Soviet medium range ballistic missile units are farther east near the Manchurian border where they can cover greater areas of China and US military installations in South Korea and Okinawa. Soviet Forces, Mongolia, are estimated to comprise one army, with supporting units, including 10,000 military engineers.

ALLIANCES

An alliance of friendship and mutual defense with the Soviet Union was signed in 1936. It has been periodically renewed since, the latest renewal being for 20 years in 1966. This pact provides for assistance in the event of attack by a third party. Under it Soviet and Mongolian forces fought the Japanese in the 1930s and 1940s; Mongolia sent horses, food and winter clothing to the Soviet Union during World War II. There are also mutual defense agreements with other communist countries in the Soviet orbit. Mongolia is not a Warsaw Pact member, but is a member of COMECON. (See Eastern Europe, Regional Survey.)

ARMY

Personnel: 28,000

Organization:
    2 infantry divisions (including armor units)
    1 (or more) SAM battalions
       cadres for reserve units

Major Equipment Inventory:
  140 medium tanks (T-34, T-54/55)
   10 SU-100 self-propelled guns
   90 APC (BTR-152 and BTR-60)
      antitank missiles (Snapper)
      130mm howitzers, 152mm gun/howitzers
      SAMs (SA-2 Guideline; at least 1 battalion)

Reserves: Probably personnel for one mechanized infantry division in cadre form. Most adult males have had military service; about 10%, or perhaps 30,000, could be quickly mobilized.

AIR FORCE (a component of the Army)

Personnel: 1,000

Major Aircraft Types:
   10 MiG-15 fighter-bombers
   10 helicopters (Mi-1 and Mi-4)
 400+ transport and training aircraft (An-2, Il-12/14, An-24, Li-2, Yak-11/18, MiG-15)

Air Bases: Ulan Bator, Sayn Shanda, plus 12 or more airstrips throughout the country.

PARAMILITARY

There are four battalions of security police and two to five battalions of frontier guards with a total strength of about 18,000.

There is a Mongolian Society for the Promotion of the Army, founded in 1961, with 100,000 members between the ages of 18 and 35. It is a pre-military training organization on the lines of the Soviet DOSAAF (Voluntary Society for Cooperation with the Army, Aviation, and Fleet). There is also a Labor Defense Association which is a communist workers' militia of armed factory workers.

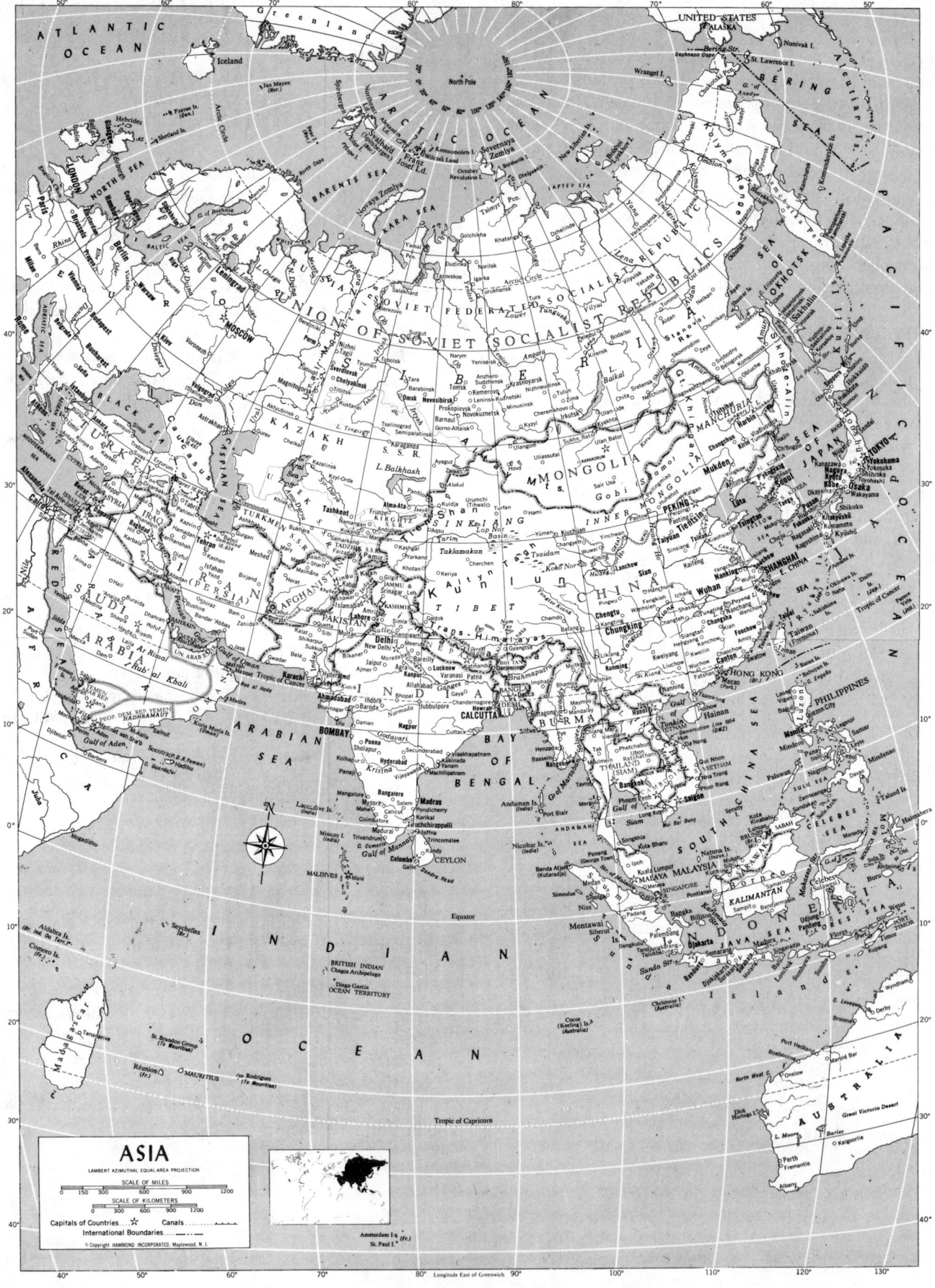

9

SOUTH AND SOUTHEAST ASIA

Regional Survey

MILITARY GEOGRAPHY

South and Southeast Asia comprise, in combination, the southern rimland of the vast Central Asia heartland. These are the regions of Asia most vulnerable to Western-based seapower, and thus were particularly affected by the expansion of Europe in the 16th through the 19th Centuries.

Both South and Southeast Asia are peninsular subcontinents. Isolated from the rest of Asia, and from each other, by lofty mountain ranges, they have had largely independent developments. Yet even before the advent of the Europeans there were important maritime contacts between these two regions, both militarily and economically. The preponderant influence came from the larger, older, and more powerful society of the Indian subcontinent. Thus it was in Southeast Asia that the earliest important meetings of Chinese and Indian cultures took place, because Chinese influence had also been exerted on Southeast Asia both by sea and overland from earliest historical times.

Also common to South and Southeast Asia is the climatological influence of the Indian Ocean and South China Sea, as reflected in the monsoon seasons. The alternating prevailing winds, and wet and dry seasons caused by the monsoon climate have not only greatly affected agricultural and social development, they have also exercised a dominating influence on patterns of war, trade, and conquest, on land as well as on sea.

South Asia is here considered to include the following nations: Afghanistan, Pakistan, Nepal, Bhutan, India, Sikkim, Bangladesh, and Sri Lanka. Southeast Asia includes: Burma, Thailand, Laos, Cambodia, the Vietnams, Singapore, Brunei and Malaysia. The Philippines and Indonesia, which are often considered as Southeast Asian nations, are for geographical reasons included in the South and Southwest Pacific region. It is recognized, of course, that geopolitically Indonesia is closely linked with Southeast Asia, sharing with Malaysia control of the Malacca Strait, through which passes massive seaborne commerce, including 80% of Japan's oil.

STRATEGIC SIGNIFICANCE

The nations of South and Southeast Asia block access to the Indian Ocean from East and Central Asia. This is facilitated by the towering mountain system that extends almost without a break from the Caucasus nearly to the Gulf of Tonkin. This barrier continues southeastward into the Southwest Pacific due to the geographical juxtaposition of the peninsulas of Southeast Asia and the Malay and Philippine archipelagos.

No nation or combination of South or Southeast Asian states has ever been strong enough to contemplate seriously a career of conquest north of the Himalayas. There have, on the other hand, been a number of instances in history when empires of Central or East Asia have been strong enough to conduct extensive campaigns of conquest in these southern rimlands. Never, however, have these forays from the north had more than transitory success, or provided the invaders with a permanent outlet to the Indian Ocean. This has been primarily due to the difficulties of supporting military operations or occupation forces across the Himalayas or over the jungled Himalayan foothills of Southeast Asia.

It is perhaps significant that the only nations that have ever dominated the Indian Ocean (Portugal and Great Britain) did so only after they had gained footholds for bases on, and achieved effective control of, the seacoasts of South and Southeast Asia, and of the straits connecting the Indian Ocean with the Southwest Pacific Ocean. In this connection, the Soviet Union, in pursuing its expanded naval policy, is routinely showing its flag in the Indian Ocean. Soviet Fleet units visit many ports in the area and westward to the Middle East. There are frequent reports of special base arrangements or other accomodation by some of the nations in the area. There is a growing rivalry in the Indian Ocean area and the US Navy seeks to offset the Soviet presence (and better access from the Black Sea and Mediterranean when the Suez Canal reopens) by making improvements in the facilities on the island of Diego Garcia.

The net effects of India's entry into the nuclear club, by exploding an atomic device on May 18, 1974, cannot yet be measures. It is, however, an event with far-reaching political implications, changing the strategic map of Asia.

ALLIANCES

American efforts to establish a mutual security alliance for Southeast Asia were initiated after the 1954 Geneva Conference confirmed the expulsion of France from its Indochina colonies. The pact creating the Southeast Asia Treaty Organization (SEATO) was signed on September 8, 1954, and came into effect on February 19, 1955; its purpose was to provide for collective defense and economic cooperation in Southeast Asia, and to protect the weak nations of former French Indochina (Vietnam, Cambodia, and Laos) from aggression. The signatory powers were Australia, France, New Zealand, Pakistan, the Philippines, Thailand, the United Kingdom and the United States. Headquarters of SEATO was established in Bangkok. Theoretically patterned after NATO, SEATO has been relatively helpless and ineffective due to three major factors: lack of widespread support among Southeast Asian nations fearful of angering Communist China; skillful exploitation of differences within SEATO and Southeast Asia by the Communist powers; and French indifference and opposition. Nevertheless, the treaty provided a basis for the support and active combat involvement of the United States and most of the other signatory powers, in response to North Vietnam's aggression against South Vietnam. As matters now stand, the SEATO Treaty is the only military guarantee that Thailand has.

Through a meeting of Commonwealth countries concerned, and at the initiative of the UK, a five-power pact came into existence in November 1971, when Britain's Far East Command was dissolved. Members are the UK, Malaysia, Singapore, Australia and New Zealand. Malaysia and Singapore furnish the bulk of the force, while the UK, Australia and New Zealand contribute token, or rotating, forces in peacetime. Australia plans to withdraw its troops, but insists it is firm in honoring its commitments. The headquarters of the ANZUK Force is located in Singapore and is commanded by an Australian admiral.

Five nations of the area—Indonesia, Malaysia, Philippines, Singapore, and Thailand—are members of the Association of Southeast Asian Nations (ASEAN), a regional organization established in 1967 to promote economic and political cooperation and mutual defense and security as well.

RECENT INTRA- AND EXTRA-REGIONAL CONFLICTS

1953-date	Viet Minh invasion of Laos; unaffected by 1961-1962 Geneva Conference
1953-date	Sporadic civil war and insurgency in Laos
1954-date	Naga insurgency in northeastern India
1956-date*	Vietnam War
1962-date	Dispute (without hostilities) between Malaysia and the Philippines over ownership of Sabah (N. Borneo)
1963-1966	Sporadic hostilities between Indonesia and Malaysia
1965	Beginning of active US combat involvement in Vietnam war
1965	India-Pakistan border hostilities in Rann of Kutch, and later in Kashmir and the Punjab
1970	Coup in Cambodia
1970-date	Cambodian involvement in Vietnam War
1971	Unsuccessful revolt in Ceylon
1971	Internal violence in East Pakistan
1971	India-Pakistan war; East Pakistan declares independence as Republic of Bangladesh
1973-74	Coups in Thailand; overthrow of military leadership and following civilian regime
1974	PRC forces take over Paracel Islands, defeating SVN garrison; take over parts of Spratleys

*This might more properly be called the Indochina War. Following US withdrawal in January, 1973, fighting continues between North and South Vietnam, in Cambodia and in Laos.

AFGHANISTAN
Republic of Afghanistan

POWER POTENTIAL STATISTICS

Area: 253,861 square miles
Population: 18,300,000
Total Active Armed Forces: 86,000 (0.47% population)
Gross National Product: $1.6 billion ($87 per capita)
Annual Military Expenditures: $35.6 million (2.23% GNP)
Fuel Production: Coal: 136,000 metric tons (there are large reserves of natural gas and probably of oil; production has been negligible)
Electric Power Output: 325 million kwh
Civil Air Fleet: 2 jet and 6 piston transports

DEFENSE STRUCTURE

Following a coup deposing the king in July 1973 Lieutenant General Mohammad Daud Khan was elected President and Premier by the military men who conducted the coup. He exercises his function of commander in chief through the Minister of Defense (who is currently a soldier). The Afghan Air Force is independent, but subordinate to the Army.

POLITICO-MILITARY POLICY

The principal traditional military policy of Afghanistan has been defense against larger and more powerful nations to the north and south. There appears little trace of the centuries-old hostility with Persia (Iran).

The armed forces are recruited by conscription, all men between the ages of 22 and 45 being liable to two years' service, and liable to reserve duty until age 42.

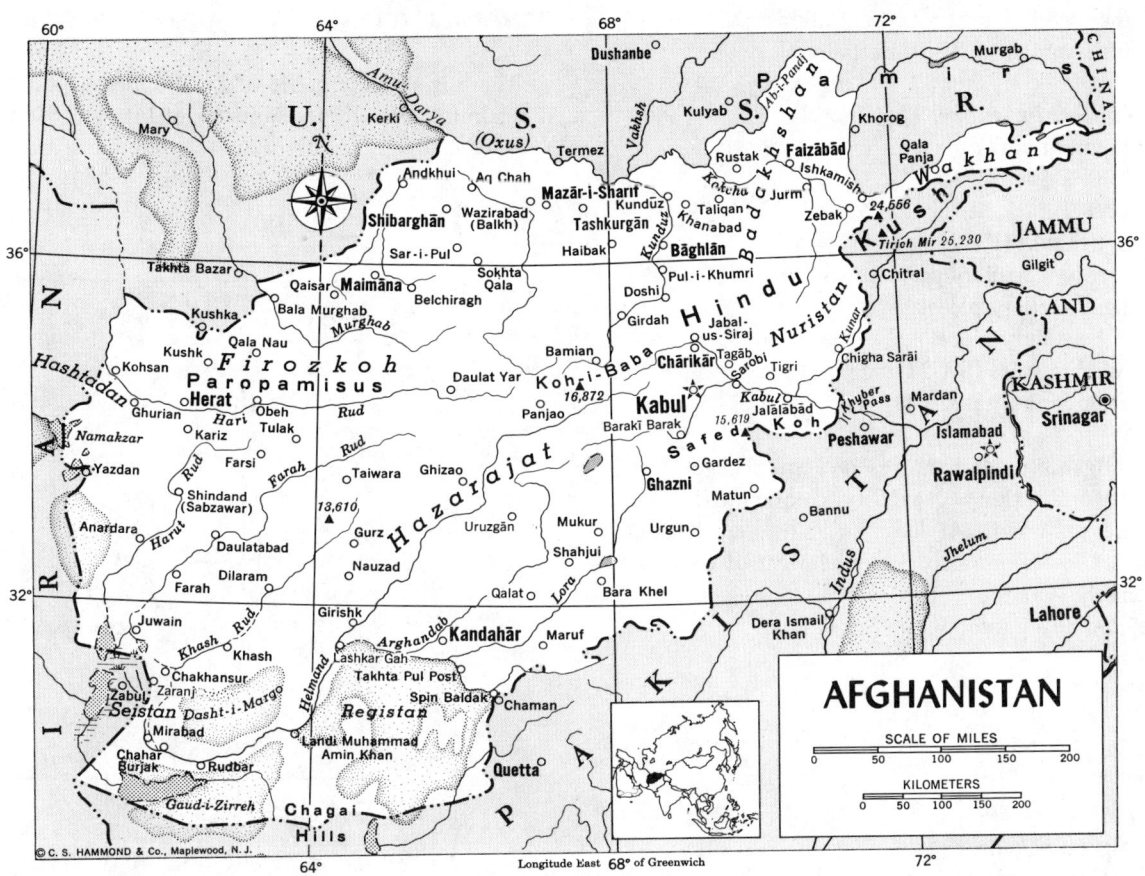

STRATEGIC PROBLEMS

Relations between Afghanistan and Pakistan have been strained since 1947, when Pakistan achieved independence. The Afghans believed that when Britain abandoned its Indian colonies, Afghanistan should have received the substantial territories along the Northwest Frontier which were annexed by Britain as a result of the several Afghan wars. At the least, Afghanistan demanded that this region—now part of Pakistan—be made into an autonomous state, called Pushtunistan. There has been some amelioration of the situation in recent years, but flare-ups do occur and the possibility of war remains. Occasional depredations within Pakistan by frontier Afghan tribes (probably not sponsored by the Afghan government) have added to that possibility.

During most of the 19th Century and the early decades of the 20th, Afghanistan was threatened by Russian expansion in Central Asia. It is probable that only British warnings to Russia prevented absorption of Afghanistan into the Russian Empire. In recent years, relations with Soviet Russia have been cordial.

MILITARY ASSISTANCE

Afghanistan has received over $260 million in military assistance from Russia since 1954, in the form of equipment and training support and advice. Many officers are trained abroad, particularly in Russia, but also in Turkey. Afghanistan received $4.4 million in military assistance from the US from FY 1950 through FY 1972; in addition, 319 students have been trained in the US under the MAP.

ALLIANCES

Afghanistan is a member of the UN and several related specialized agencies. Except for the military assistance agreement with the USSR, it is not a member of any alliance or regional political grouping.

ARMY

Personnel: 80,000

Organization:
    3 army corps, based regionally (Kabul, Kandahar, Gardez); General Reserve (Kabul)
    1 armored division
    2 infantry divisions
    1 mechanized brigade (Royal Bodyguard)

10 independent motorized battalions
10 independent infantry battalions

Major Equipment Inventory:
- 200 medium tanks
  - 100 T-34
  - 100 T-54
- light tanks (PT-76)
- 36 medium artillery pieces
- 108 light artillery pieces
- AA artillery pieces
- SAM missiles (SA-2 Guideline)
- Snapper antitank missiles

Reserves: Organized, trained reserves number at least 250,000. Mobilization capability, equipment, and function are unknown. At least an additional 200,000 men in tribal levies are also available. Most of these are unquestionably fierce fighters, but organization, discipline, and heavy weapons are negligible.

AIR FORCE

Personnel: 6,000

Organization:
- 2 fighter squadrons (MiG-21)
- 2 fighter-bomber squadrons (Su-7)
- 5 fighter-bomber squadrons (MiG-17)
- 3 light bomber squadrons (Il-28)
- 1 transport squadron (Il-14, Il-18, Twin Otter)
- 1 helicopter squadron (Mi-1, Mi-4)
- 1 support squadron (Yak-11, Yak-18, MiG-15, An-2, Anson)

Major Aircraft Types:
- 170 combat aircraft
  - 30 MiG-21 fighters
  - 25 Su-7 fighter-bombers
  - 70 MiG-17 fighter-bombers
  - 45 Il-28 light bombers
- 84 other aircraft
  - 30 transports (2 Il-18, 25 Il-14, 3 Twin Otter)
  - 24 helicopters (Mi-1, Mi-4)
  - 30 trainer/utility (Yak-11, Yak-18, MiG-15, An-2, Anson)

Major Air Bases: Kunduz, Mazar-i-Sharif, Kandahar, Jalalabad, Sherpur, Gazni, Gardez, Herat, Bagram, Shindand

Reserves: 12,000 to 15,000 trained reservists

PARAMILITARY

There is a gendarmerie of 21,000 men for internal security; it is administered by the Ministry of Internal Affairs.

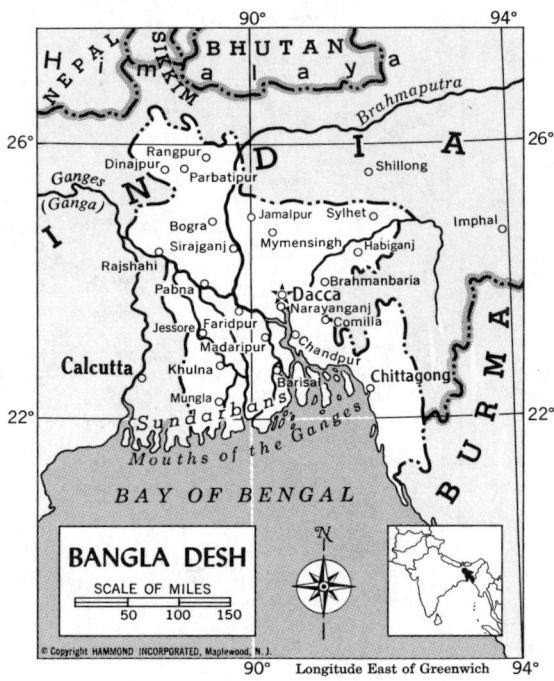

BANGLADESH
Bengal Nation

POWER POTENTIAL STATISTICS

Area: 55,126 square miles
Population: 83,400,000
Total Active Armed Forces: approximately 16,350 (0.02% population)
Gross National Product: $5 billion ($60 per capita)
Military Expenditures: $81 million (1.6% GNP)
Refined Petroleum Products: 817,500 metric tons
Steel Production: 177,000 metric tons

POLITICO-MILITARY POLICIES AND POSTURE

Under the Provisional Constitution the President is titular Head of State. Control of the government and of the armed forces is exercised by the Prime Minister, Sheikh Mujibur Rahman, who is also Minister of Defence.

At the core of the Army are two former Pakistan Bengali infantry regiments, which at the time of the 1971 civil war almost to a man declared for Bangladesh and retreated to India, where they were brought back to strength by enlisting members of the *Mukti Bahini* (liberation Army), a guerrilla force that was operating both within Bangladesh and from Indian territory. These regiments and the Bengali guerrillas reentered the country with Indian forces in December 1971 and participated in the victory over Pakistan. The *Mukti Bahini* were ordered disarmed before February 1, 1972. They are expected to furnish men for a militia force. India has offered training for the Bangladesh Army.

The problems of the poor, overpopulated nation are stupendous. The government is attempting to create political, military, and economic organizations on the ruins left by bitter civil and international war. A source of future trouble are the Bihari (fanatical Moslem refugees from India's Bihar province in 1947) who adhered to the Pakistan forces in the civil war, and have been accused of massacring thousands of Bengalis. They themselves experienced considerable ruthless retaliation from the Bengalis after the war.

The government's solution to its formidable economic problems is nationalization. The principal cash and export products are raw and processed jute, hides and skins, and tea; all production facilities were neglected or damaged during the wars. Rice, a staple of diet, had never recovered from the typhoon and floods of 1969, and heavy imports are required. On top of these disasters is the problem of reabsorbing more than 9,000,000 refugees who escaped to India, and other millions whose homes were destroyed. For this Bangladesh appealed for massive foreign aid. It is unlikely that the country will be able to support more than minimum military forces to maintain order in the near future.

The nation has received massive assistance from others. Prisoner exchange and settlement of other problems with Pakistan have moved forward with much obvious Indian support. Pakistan's recognition of Bangladesh has eased the situation on the subcontinent generally.

ARMY

Personnel: 15,000

Organization:
     5 infantry brigades (each with 3 battalions)
     1 artillery brigade
     engineer and signal corps support troops

Major Equipment Inventory: believed to be equipped with Soviet arms and equipment

NAVY

Personnel: 850
     3 100-foot armed river steamers
     1 patrol boat Soviet Poluchat type (YP)

Naval Bases: Chittagong, Kulna, Dacca

AIR FORCE

Personnel: 500

Organization:
     1 fighter squadron (MiG-21)
     1 helicopter squadron (Alouette III, Wessex, Mi-8)
     1 transport squadron (An-24, An-26, F-27, Yak-40)

Major Aircraft Types:
     12 combat aircraft
          12 MiG-21 fighters
     17 other aircraft
          6 transports (1 An-24, 2 An-26, 2 F-27, 1 Yak-40)
          11 helicopters (6 Alouette III, 3 Mi-8, 2 Wessex)

Note: 3 Sabre Mk 6 and 1 T-33 grounded; no spare parts.

Airbase: Tezgaon (Dacca)

BHUTAN

Druk-Yul
Kingdom of Bhutan

POWER POTENTIAL STATISTICS

Area: 18,147 square miles
Population: 854,000
Total Active Armed Forces: 4,000 (0.47% population)

Gross National Product: $64 million ($75 per capita)
Annual Military Expenditures: Unknown

POLITICO-MILITARY POLICIES AND POSTURE

An autocracy, Bhutan is ruled by a hereditary King, although concepts and forms of representative government have been established.

Bhutan is located in the Himalayas, between China's Tibet Autonomous Region on the north, India's Assam Province on the south, India's North East Frontier Agency on the east, and Sikkim on the west. Bhutan was isolated, although maintaining relations with Manchu China, until signing a treaty with Britain in 1910 which provided for British guidance in foreign relations.

Upon Indian independence in 1947, India continued Britain's role; this was ratified by treaty in 1949. Bhutan can import arms from India, but there is to be no transshipment. India pays Bhutan a yearly subsidy of about $100,000.

Mountain passes crossing Bhutan and connecting Tibet and India give it considerable strategic value to China and India. Beginning in 1958 China renewed claims to large tracts of Bhutanese territory as part of Tibet.

In June 1974 the government announced that it had broken up a plot to assassinate the 18-year-old King Jigme Singye Wangchuck on the eve of his coronation. The takeover of the nation was the only reason cited. It was rumored that the plot was related to making a base for Tibetan action against China.

Because of the Chinese threat, India is providing military assistance. Bhutan's army, trained by Indian Army officers, numbers about 4,000 regulars and 15,000 militia. Military service is obligatory for all males; liability extends from age 18 to 50.

India is building four new roads north into the interior, which would be essential to the forward deployment of Indian troops. Bhutan's first airfield, at Paro, was recently completed with Indian aid.

BRUNEI

Intruding into the Malaysian state of Sarawak is the small (2,226 square miles) sultanate of Brunei, with a population of about 140,000, a gross national product of $150 million, and an annual production of crude petroleum of 9.1 million metric tons. Brunei refused to join the Federation of Malaysia in 1963, after an abortive revolt over the possibility, and is a member of the British Commonwealth. The British 6th Gurkha Battalion is stationed there, at Brunei's expense, and the Sultan maintains the Royal Brunei Malay Regiment. The Regiment's Air Wing has eight Iroquois helicopters and one transport. Brunei's naval forces include a 96-foot fast (57-knot) patrol boat with eight SS-12 missiles on two launchers, three 62-foot coastal patrol boats, each with two machine guns, three 47-foot armed launches, each with two machine guns, a 6-knot hovercraft, SRN-6, and 25 armed river boats. Purely for functional and defense purposes, Brunei's armed forces present no strategic threat to Malaysia. (For map, see Malaysia.)

BURMA

Phidaungsu Myanma Nainggandaw
Union of Burma

POWER POTENTIAL STATISTICS

Area: 261,789 square miles
Population: 29,800,000
Total Active Armed Forces: 143,600 (0.48% population)
Gross National Product: $2.9 billion ($97 per capita)
Annual Military Expenditures: $120 million (4.14% GNP)
Fuel Production: Crude Oil: 1.0 million metric tons
    Refined Petroleum Products: 1.1 million metric tons
Electric Power Output: 474 million kwh
Merchant Fleet: 40 ships; 54,877 gross tons
Civil Air Fleet: 1 jet, 8 turboprop, 6 piston transports

DEFENSE STRUCTURE

By the military coup d'etat of March 2, 1962, the previous parliamentary form of government was abolished and replaced by a Revolutionary Council of 14 military officers. The Council Chairman is Defence Forces Chief of Staff, General Ne Win, who thus also acts as chief of state, head of the government, and Minister of Defence. In this four-fold role he is advised by the Council Executive Committee of senior officers.

The integrated Defence Services Staff is dominated by the Army. Vice Chiefs of Staff for Army, Navy and Air Force administer their respective service affairs. Control of units in the field is exercised through the appropriate Vice Chief of Staff to five army area commands and three naval regions. Two naval regions, Arakan and Tenasserim, correspond to the army's Northwest and Southeast Commands, respectively, while the third naval region, Irrawaddy, overlaps several commands. Operational control in the field is unified.

POLITICO-MILITARY POLICY

Burma's salient policy is neutrality and non-alignment, seeking security through support of the UN. This policy is

complicated by Burma's stategic position, its economic and cultural ties to the Indian sub-continent and to the West, and its 1,300-mile border with Communist China.

Thus Burma must placate China while avoiding any close involvement with it which would alienate either its Western or Soviet bloc friends. Likewise, placation of China requires avoidance of close military or political ties with China's rivals or enemies. This influences the degree of foreign presence in Burma, the sources of its assistance in economic development and overt military aid, and its voting in the UN on questions affecting China.

Although Burma is a federalized union, it is dominated by the majority Burmans (75% of the population). This dominance is resented by many of the minority populations, mostly hill tribesmen, living in five semi-autonomous states.

The consequences of the two basic policies of international non-alignment and domestic centralization have in large part been responsible for a third policy: maintaining large armed forces and incurring large defense expenditures with little in the way of external support, and despite a weak economy. Priority has been given internal security rather than defense against external threats. Therefore the Army is largely light infantry battalions, the Navy a coastal and river patrol and landing force, with the Air Force structured for ground support.

Although the Defence Services are maintained at strength by voluntary enlistments of two years, a National Service Law prescribes conscription of all citizens between 18 and 45, and physicians, engineers, and technicians to age 56. This ensures adequate manpower in an emergency and the availability of scarce skills at all times.

STRATEGIC PROBLEMS

Burma's geographical location, separating Southeast Asia from the Indian sub-continent and providing access to the Indian Ocean from southwest China, caused it to be a major theater of operations in World War II. This strategic location is just as important today.

China has a relatively easy invasion route from Yunnan Province across northern Burma to India's Assam province, and is reputedly subverting Naga tribesmen on the Indo-Burma border. China also wishes to control the Kunming-Lashio-Rangoon road and rail route (the Burma Road of World War II fame), which would link southwest China to the sea. India is said to have a tacit understanding with Burma over joint defense of the Assam-northern Burma area in the event of a Chinese invasion.

From shortly after independence to the present, Burma has been plagued with a variety of insurgencies, domestic communist, ethnic minority, and external Chinese Nationalist. These various groups may still number as many as 20,000 armed men, but factionalism has precluded fully coordinated action against the government. The most serious threat comes from exiled Burman dissidents in the National Liberation Council (NLC) based in Thailand. Under the leadership of former Premier U Nu, the NLC provides an armed nucleus for a potential national uprising. Within Burma the so-called White Flag Communists have been supported by the People's Republic of China (PRC) for some time. They are able to field battalion-size units armed with automatic weapons, artillery, and rockets. The insurgent forces in the north, some 8,000 to 10,000 strong, control 10,000 square miles of territory. It has been reported that Chinese troops have been moved from Laos into North Burma. The problem for the government is compounded by interior economic and social problems and external support for various insurgent groups.

MILITARY ASSISTANCE

Upon achieving independence from Britain in 1948 Burma was provided with equipment for its three services. More British equipment has been added by purchase or grant through the years. A British training mission served until 1953 and special schooling in England has continued. Training has also been received in India and Israel.

During the early insurgencies, shortly after independence, India provided quantities of arms and ammunition and the US provided patrol boats. Later Israel presented small quantities of small arms and heavy infantry weapons.

An amunition and sub-machinegun factory was established with Italian assistance, a rifle factory with West German help, and a naval dockyard with Yugoslav advice. Yugoslavia also sold or gave ten river gunboats, and quantities of 120mm mortars, 75mm pack howitzers, and World War II German MG-42 machine guns.

The largest amount of military assistance has come from the United States through a unique military sales agreement concluded in 1958, and still in effect, which enables Burma to purchase equipment with its own soft currency. The total amount bought under this agreement is $80 million. In addition 794 students have been trained under the MAP. The equipment is known to include jet fighters, helicopters, gunboats, and landing craft and is believed also to include quantities of heavy weapons and transportation, communications, and engineering equipment.

ALLIANCES

Burma is a member of the UN. It rejected membership in the British Commonwealth but has joined a number of international consultative and economic organizations, including the Colombo Plan Council. It is a member of no mutual defense or collective security alliance but advocates collective security through the UN. There are some arrangements with the PRC, including border agreements. Burma sent a small staff detachment to the UN Operation in the Congo in 1960.

ARMY

Personnel: 130,000

Organization: 5 area commands (Central, Eastern, Southeast, Southwest, and Northwest)
  11 brigades (territorial task forces within the area commands)
   100 infantry battalions
   2 armored battalions
   2 artillery battalions
   1 engineer battalion

Major Equipment Inventory:
  medium tanks (Comet, M-4, Sherman)
  armored cars (Humber)
  scout cars (Ferret)
  light artillery pieces (25-pounder guns, 105mm, 75mm howitzers)
  medium artillery pieces (155mm howitzers)

NAVY

Personnel: 6,250 (includes 800 Marines)

Organization: 3 naval regions (Irrawaddy, Arakan, Tenasserim)

Major Units:
  1 escort frigate (British River class; PF)
  1 escort minesweeper/minelayer (British Algerine class, MSE)
  2 corvettes (PCE)
  6 support gunboats (LCG)
  43 river gunboats (PGR)
  18 patrol gunboats (PGM)
  7 motor gunboat/patrol boats (CGC)
  5 torpedo boats (PTFG)
  1 coastal transport (APC)
  8 landing craft, mechanized (LCM)
  1 landing craft, utility (LCU)
  2 survey vessels

Naval Bases: Monkey Point, Seikyi, Sinmalaik, Sittwe (Akyab), Moulmein, Mergui, and Bassein.

AIR FORCE

Personnel: 6,600

Organization:
  3 fighter-bomber squadrons (T-33, T-37, Provost)
  1 transport squadron (C-45, C-47, Otter)
  1 helicopter squadron (Alouette III, Huskie, Sea Knight, Sioux)

Major Aircraft Types:
  60 combat aircraft
   20 armed jet trainer/ground attack (15 T-37, 5 T-33)
   40 armed piston trainer/ground attack (Provost)
  94 other aircraft
   27 transports (6 C-45, 15 C-47, 6 Otter)
   27 helicopters (8 Alouette III, Huskie, Sea Knight, Sioux)
   40 utility/liaison aircraft (including 10 U-17)

Air Bases: Mingaladon (Rangoon), Meiktila (2), Hmawbi, Mandalay, Myitkyina, and Kengtung

PARAMILITARY

The People's Police Force numbers 10,000 and is under the Minister of Home Affairs. Armed village defense and local militia exist under the aegis of the Burma Socialist Program Party (BSPP).

CAMBODIA

Khmer Republic

POWER POTENTIAL STATISTICS

Area: 69,898 square miles
Population: 7,800,000
Total Active Armed Forces: 184,400 (2.36% population)
Gross National Product: $970 million (estimate; $124 per capita)

Annual Military Expenditures: $291 million (30% GNP)
Electric Power Output: 128.3 million kwh
Merchant Fleet: 2 ships; 1,880 gross tons
Civil Air Fleet: 1 jet and 7 piston transports

DEFENSE STRUCTURE

Control of the Khmer Armed Forces is vested in Marshal Lon Nol, who is at once President, Prime Minister and Commander in Chief of the armed forces, of which the Army is by far the predominant service. There is a Chief of Staff and a General Staff. It is difficult to trace the chain of command further.

POLITICO-MILITARY POLICIES

The current politico-military policy of Cambodia is in marked contrast to that of the former Chief of State, Prince Norodom Sihanouk, who was deposed in March 1970. Sihanouk's declared policy of neutralism brought him to tolerate the establishment of several North Vietnamese divisions in eastern Cambodia near the South Vietnam border, and to permit the supply of these troops and the Viet Cong of South Vietnam via extensions of the Ho Chih Minh Trail, routes up Communist-controlled waterways of the Mekong delta, and by sea from the west coast of Cambodia. He determinedly avoided expanding the weak Cambodian army or opposing the encroaching forces other than by unheeded diplomatic representations to the Soviet Union and Communist China.

After the March 1970 coup the new regime demanded the withdrawal of North Vietnamese and Viet Cong elements from Cambodia. They responded with military action against the regime, thus automatically extending the Vietnam War to Cambodia. Marshal (then General) Lon Nol promptly recalled reservists and former soldiers, and called on all men aged 18 to 40 to volunteer for the army. He also closed the western ports to all ships supplying the hostile forces. In late May, martial law was decreed, and a month later general mobilization was ordered, whereby all citizens between 18 and 60 are required to perform military or other service in the national interest, and the requisitioning of property and financial resources was authorized. The economic efficacy of this decree is unclear, but it did result in large increases in the army—larger than could be adquately trained before being exposed to combat. The nation became the Khmer Republic in October.

Under US pressure there has been some measure of reform in the interest of broadening the political base. Lon Nol now shares some of his power, there is a new premier, and a new cabinet with members from several groups. The internal political, military, and economic situation is not encouraging, and Cambodia's future is uncertain.

STRATEGIC PROBLEMS

In 1970 Cambodia lost all control of five northern and northeastern provinces and the northern parts of two others northeast of Tonle Sap—in general the northeast half of the country. In addition much of the territory along the southern border with South Vietnam is at least intermittently occupied by the NVA/VC. Even in the remainder of the country government control is often only nominal because, though greater in numbers, the partially trained Cambodian troops are unable to prevent enemy infiltration. Highway 4, from Phnom Penh to Kompong Som (formerly Sihanoukville) has been cut and blocked several times, and the capital itself has been attacked by mortar and rocket fire. In such efforts the enemy is aided by relatively small numbers of native Communists, the *Khmer Rouge*.

South Vietnamese efforts have helped Cambodia by defeating the invaders near the border, sometimes alone and at others in conjunction with Cambodian troops. South Vietnamese troops have also convoyed supply trucks on Highway 4, assisting in breaking through roadblocks. From among the numerous ethnic Cambodians long resident in southwest Vietnam, troops have been raised, trained and equipped by the US Army. Some 2,000 have been sent to Cambodia, where they have proved to be effective fighters. Others were similarly trained in southern Laos from among Cambodian refugees from the northern provinces. Fighting within the country continued through 1973 and into mid-1974, with the government suffering serious reverses in the first half of 1974.

The Cambodian strategic position is precarious and strongly dependent on foreign aid to procure the time to raise its army's fighting capabilities. Direct military assistance by the United States was halted in mid-1973 by Act of the US Congress.

MILITARY ASSISTANCE

From 1955 to 1963, when Cambodia terminated U.S. aid, America supplied $91.4 million in military assistance (and $309.6 million in economic aid). The U.S. resumed military aid in 1970, to the extent of $218.8 million, and quantities of captured Russian and Chinese weapons, ammunition and equipment taken from the NVA/VC. In 1963 Cambodia accepted its first Communist aid: fighter aircraft from the USSR. Military equipment and economic assistance were received from communist countries—notably the Soviet Union and Communist China—but ceased with the overthrow of Prince Sihanouk. A total of 36,038 Cambodian students have been trained by the United States under the MAP.

ALLIANCES

Cambodia is a member of the UN; it is not a member of any formal military association. Diplomatic relations with Thailand and the Republic of Vietnam, severed in the early 1960s, were resumed in 1970.

ARMY

Personnel: 175,000

Organization:
- 200 infantry and commando battalions
- 1 armored car battalion
- 1 tank regiment
- 3 parachute battalions

Major Equipment Inventory:
- light tanks (M-24, AMX-13)
- armored cars (M-8 and M-20)
- scout cars (M-3)
- APCs (BTR-40 and BTR-152)
- 36 M-109 self-propelled 105mm howitzers
- 105mm howitzers (French)
- 76mm and 122mm guns (Soviet)
- light and medium AA guns and field artillery (Soviet, French, and Chinese)
- 10 Cessna 0-1 liaison aircraft

NAVY

Personnel: 1,600 (includes 150 Marines)

Major Units:
- 2 patrol vessels (PC)
- 2 support gunboats (LSIL and LCI)
- 2 torpedo boats (PT)
- 6 patrol boats (YP)
- 4 landing craft (EDIC and LCU)
- over 30 small patrol craft

Major Naval Bases: Ream, Chran Changvar (Phnom Penh), Kompong Som

AIR FORCE

Personnel: 4,000

Organization:
- 1 jet ground attack squadron (T-37)
- 1 turbo-prop ground attack squadron (AU-24)
- 2 piston ground attack squadrons (T-28, C-47 gunships)
- 1 helicopter ground attack squadron (UH-1 gunship)
- 1 transport squadron (C-47)
- 2 helicopter squadrons (UH-1, Alouette III, Mi-4)
- 1 utility liaison squadron (Beaver, O-1, An-2)

Major Aircraft Types:
- 103 combat aircraft
  - 24 T-37 jet ground attack aircraft
  - 14 AU-24 turbo-prop ground attack aircraft
  - 51 T-28 piston ground attack aircraft
  - 6 C-47 gunships
  - 8 UH-1 gunships
- 110 other aircraft
  - 37 helicopters (24 UH-1, 10 Alouette III, 3 Mi-4)
  - 18 C-47 transports
  - 20 utility/liaison aircraft (Beaver, O-1, An-2)
  - 35 trainers (GY-80, Magister)

Major Air Bases: Seam Reap, Battambang, Pochentong (Phnom Penh)

PARAMILITARY

About 150,000 lightly armed police and home guard type units.

INDIA

Bharet
Republic of India

POWER POTENTIAL STATISTICS

- Area: 1,266,596 square miles
- Population: 600,400,000
- Total Active Armed Forces: 1,074,000 (includes Border Security Force; 0.18% population)
- Gross National Product: $63.4 billion ($105 per capita)
- Annual Military Expenditures: $2.4 billion (3.79% GNP)
- Steel and Iron Production: 12.9 million metric tons
- Fuel Production: Coal: 69.1 million metric tons
  - Crude Oil: 7.7 million metric tons
  - Refined Petroleum Products: 19.6 million metric tons
- Electric Power Output: 58.9 billion kwh
- Merchant Fleet: 412 ships; 2.65 million gross tons
- Civil Air Fleet: 27 jet, 31 turboprop, 13 piston transports

DEFENSE STRUCTURE

The President is the Supreme Commander of the Armed Forces. Actual responsibility for national defense rests with the Cabinet, presided over by the Prime Minister, assisted by the standing Defence Committee, and advised by the top level National Defence Council. The Minister of Defence is head of the defense organization and is responsible to Parliament and the Prime Minister for the administrative and operational control of the armed forces and for implementation of the Government's defense policy. There are three services—Army, Navy, and Air Force—each under its own chief of staff.

310 ALMANAC OF WORLD MILITARY POWER

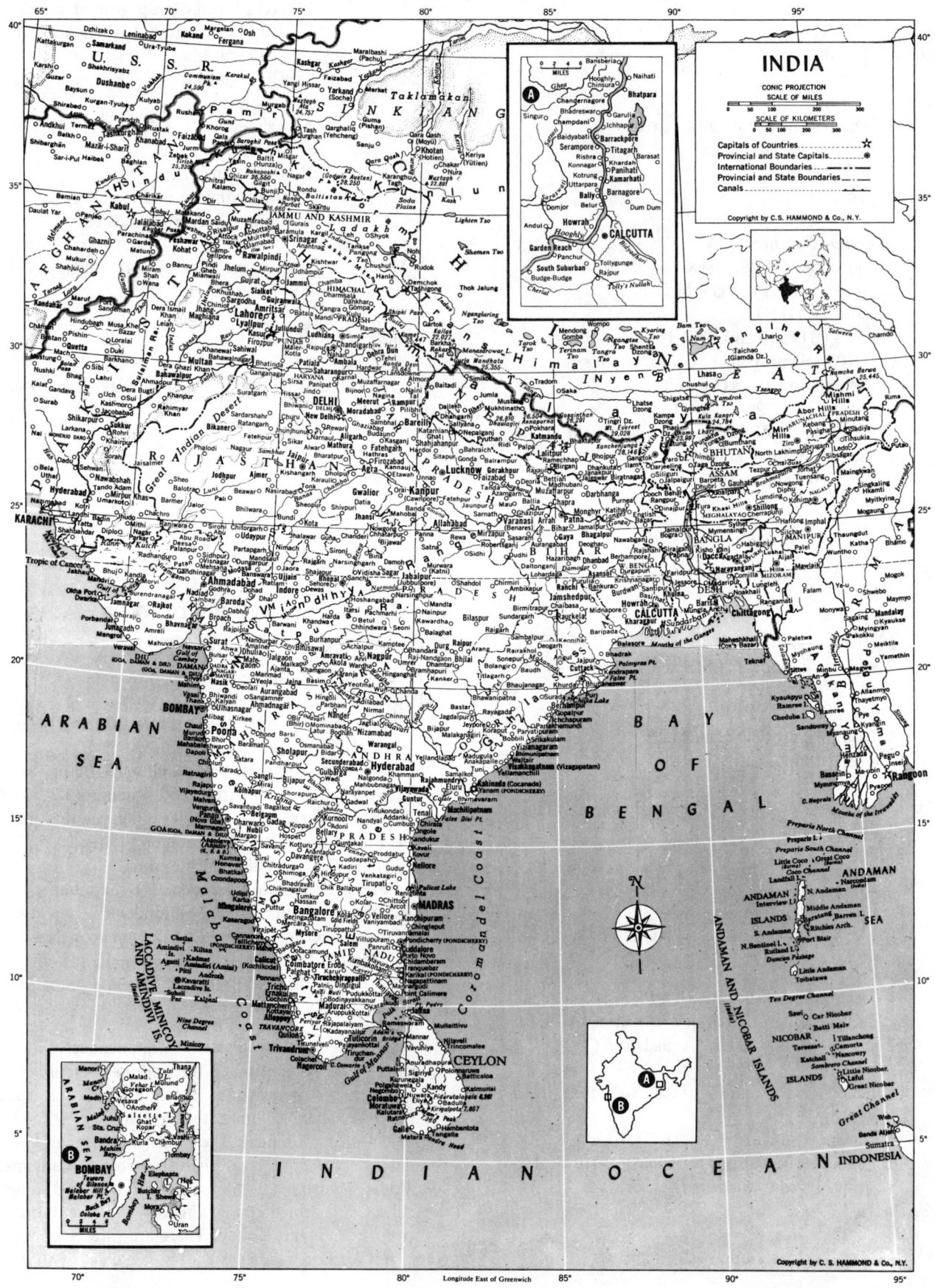

POLITICO-MILITARY POLICY

India's international stance since independence in 1947 had been nonalignment in the East-West confrontation until a 1971 mutual assistance treaty with the USSR, and strained relations with the United States in regard to the 1971 war with Pakistan, altered this traditional policy. Save to the extent they have been related to India's troubles with Pakistan, India has consistently supported and participated in UN peace-keeping functions.

Despite its hitherto determined neutralism and peaceful protestations, India's other policies have been to some extent responsible for a series of small wars and three serious armed confrontations. Since independence India has firmly resolved (1) to maintain its boundaries as drawn in colonial days and by the 1947 partition, (2) to hold Jammu and Kashmir against Pakistan's claims, (3) to unify and rule its diverse population, and (4) to eliminate remaining foreign enclaves along its coast. Small scale guerrilla warfare interspersed with major hostilities against Pakistan has been taking place in Jammu and Kashmir since 1949. The Portuguese enclaves, including Goa, were seized in 1961. Naga and Mizo tribesmen along the border with Burma have been in revolt since the early 1960s, apparently aided and abetted by both Pakistan and Communist China. Border incidents with Communist China, beginning in 1958, culminated in October 1962 in major hostilities in Ladakh and a successful limited objective Chinese offensive in the North East Frontier Agency.

The defeat by China caused a complete reappraisal of Indian defense policy and a massive buildup of its armed forces and defense industries. The armed forces were nearly doubled in size. For the first time, military aid was sought from the United Kingdom, United States, and (mainly since 1965) the USSR. MiG-21 fighters are being produced under a Soviet license. The first was delivered to the Air Force in February 1973. A tank, based on the Chieftain main battle tank, is being manufactured with British assistance.

This buildup, resulting from the confrontation with China, may well have stimulated Pakistan's 1965 efforts to gain Kashmir before India became too powerful. For a time, British and US military aid were withheld from both parties, with India turning to the Soviet Union, and Pakistan to Communist China. While India's military buildup was primarily intended to deter Chinese aggression, it thus developed also into an arms race with Pakistan. That race was undoubtedly ended for the foreseeable future by India's 1971 victory in a two-front war with Pakistan, resulting from Indian support of the Bengali rebels in what has become Bangladesh.

Faced with a nuclear-armed China across the Himalayas, and with the tremendous expense of developing its own nuclear deterrent, India's policy is to keep its options open. This includes rejection of the Nuclear Non-Proliferation Treaty, and continued nuclear and delivery-system research and development, as well as construction of domestic (i.e., without foreign controls of nuclear fuel) reactors. On May 18, 1974, India fired an underground nuclear device of some 10-15 kilotons yield. Indian officials and defense intellectuals claimed that this test was directed toward the peaceful use of nuclear explosions for such purposes as mining and massive earth-moving. International reaction was skeptical and, in some cases, outraged. It remains to be demonstrated just what future course India will follow, but it is clear even very early that a substantial shift in Asian power balances is likely.

Service in the Indian Armed Forces is voluntary for a term of 10 to 15 years, depending upon the degree of technical training required, followed by five or three years in the reserve.

STRATEGIC PROBLEMS

India's primary problem is the reconciliation of defense needs that consume over 40 percent of the budget and over three percent of the GNP, with the insatiable demands for developing the economy of a poor country in the midst of a population explosion. While expenditures are heavy, the Indian defense effort appears to be the minimum acceptable on a risk basis.

The Himalayan defensive barrier covering India's northern border is complicated by the existence of the three independent Himalayan states in the center of the frontier. Direct passes from Tibet run through Nepal and Bhutan, and the two most important, Nathu and Cho, through Sikkim. A mere 60 miles south of these latter passes is the Siliguri Neck, a strip of India between Sikkim and Bangladesh through which run the land communications from central India to oil-rich Assam and the strategic North East Frontier Agency. A collective security agreement was in effect in Nepal until 1969 and India has special treaty rights in both Bhutan and Sikkim. Nepal has recently built up its army. The army of Bhutan has been strengthened with Indian help, and Indian troops are stationed in Sikkim. Roads and airfields have been built in all three.

The World War II route from India to China through north Burma—the Ledo and Burma Roads—is another potential invasion route. An understanding apparently exists between India and Burma on arrangements for mutual defense of this area.

Nagaland is in the rugged mountain frontier region between Upper Assam and northern Burma, and just to the south is the home of the Mizo tribes. Both are in revolt against Indian sovereignty, demanding full autonomy. They have several thousand armed insurgents, and the Nagas receive training and weapons from China. Arms are packed across north Burma from Yunnan Province. India has had 36,000 troops deployed against these insurgents and is pursuing a fullfledged counterinsurgency campaign of political compromise and reconciliation, rural redevelopment, and civic action, as well as direct military force.

Communist-led disorders throughout India, on the rise in recent years, pose further threats to internal security. Communist strength is particularly great in South India and among poverty-stricken city dwellers.

With Chinese airfields in Tibet relatively close to Indian cities, while Chinese cities are remote from Indian airbases, India's air defenses have been extensively overhauled. An air defense radar and command control system has been installed with US help; Soviet MiG-21 interceptors and SA-2 Guideline surface-to-air missiles provide the active defense.

MILITARY ASSISTANCE

Soviet military assistance began about 1960, and accelerated after 1965. All classes of arms, tanks, artillery, aircraft, and ships, as well as production facilities, have been delivered. The total value by early 1969 was estimated at about $1.2 billion. Terms were sales on long term credit repayable in Indian currency or commodities. Indian military personnel are trained in the Soviet Union, and there are several hundred Soviet officers in India.

US aid under the Military Assistance Program amounted to $98.3 million from 1950 through 1967, but only $3 million since that time. Since 1962 both the United States and Great Britain have provided substantial aid in grants and on favorable credit terms. US aid was mainly in transport aircraft, air defense detection and control equipment, and light weapons for mountain operations. The agreement was for $200 million, but only $85 million had been delivered by the September 1965 Indian-Pakistan War, when deliveries were stopped.

India provided military aid to Burma in the form of small arms and ammunition during Burma's first wave of insurgency in 1950. India has also provided military advisers to, and accepted military students from, a number of Asian, Middle Eastern, and African countries.

ALLIANCES

India is a member of the UN and the British Commonwealth. In August 1971 a treaty of Peace, Cooperation and Friendship with the USSR was made, which contains clauses calling for consultation in case of attack or threat thereof by a third party.

ARMY

Personnel: 860,000

Organization: 4 commands (Eastern: headquarters, Calcutta; Western: headquarters, Simla; Central: headquarters, Lucknow; Southern: headquarters, Poona)

  1 armored division (another armored division is being formed)
  5 independent armored brigades
 14 infantry divisions
 12 mountain divisions
  6 independent infantry brigades
  1 or 2 parachute brigades
 20 AAA groups

Major Equipment Inventory:
medium tanks
   200 Centurion Mk.5/9
   500 Vijayanta (Indian-designed and -built
    26 M-47 (captured from Pakistan in 1965)
   250 M4A3E8 Sherman*
 1,000 T-54/55
light tanks
   140 AMX-13
   150 PT-76
    50 M3A1 Stuart*
APCs (OT-62, Mk.2/4A)
   350 armored cars (Daimler and Humber)
 3,000 artillery pieces (mostly 25-pounders, but including 350 100mm and 140 130mm Soviet-built guns)
SAM
SS-11 and Entac antitank missiles
    95 liaison aircraft (HS-748, Auster, Krishak)
    22 helicopters (Lama, Alouette III)

Reserves: At least 100,000 (includes 44,000 in the Territorial Army). Mobilization plans and procedures are not known.

*These older weapons are probably being retired from first line units.

NAVY

Personnel: 24,000

Organization: The Indian Fleet and 3 naval area commands, headquartered at Bombay, Cochin, Vishakhapatnam (East Coast)

Major Units:
  1 aircraft carrier (CVS/CVL)
  4 submarines (F class; SS)
  2 light cruisers (CL)
  6 destroyers (DD, DDE)
 24 frigates (including 3 with SAM Seacat, 8 ex-Soviet Petya type, 4 being built; DE)

4 coastal minesweepers (MSC)
4 inshore minesweepers (MSI)
8 missile boats (Osa type with Styx SSM; PTFG)
21 patrol craft (PC)
1 landing ship, tank (LST)
3 landing craft (2 Polocny class, 1 LCT)
13 auxiliaries
74 Sea Hawk fighter-bombers (2 squadrons)
12 Alize ASW aircraft (1 squadron)
25 Alouette II and III helicopters
24 Sea King helicopters
HS-748 maritime reconnaissance)
51 trainer aircraft (HT-2, HJT-16, Hughes 300)

Naval Bases: Bombay (including Jamnagar and Lonavaia), Cochin (including Calicut and Coimbatore), Calcutta (including Vishakahapatnam), Goa (including Dabolim), Port Blair.

AIR FORCE

Personnel: 90,000

Organization: 5 commands (Western, Central, Eastern, Training, and Maintenance)

- 4 light bomber squadrons (Canberra)
- 8 fighter/interceptor squadrons (MiG-21 with Atoll AAM)
- 8 fighter/interceptor squadrons (Gnat)
- 6 fighter-bomber squadrons (Su-7)
- 3 fighter-bomber squadrons (Marut)
- 6 fighter-bomber squadrons (Hunter)
- 2 fighter-bomber squadrons (Mystere IVA)
- 1 maritime reconnaissance squadron (Constellation)
- 1 photo reconnaissance squadron (Canberra)
- 12 transport squadrons (C-47, C-119, An-12, Il-14, HS-748, Otter, Caribou)
- 1 communications squadron (Tu-124, HS-748, VIP flight)
- 8 helicopter squadrons (Mi-4, Mi-8, Alouette III, HH-52, SA-315)

Major Aircraft Types:

- 896 combat aircraft
- 86 Canberra light bombers
- 440 fighter/interceptors (220 MiG-21, 220 Gnat)
- 354 fighter-bombers (145 Su-7, 60 Marut, 32 Mystere IVA, 117 Hunter)
- 8 Super Constellation maritime reconnaissance aircraft
- 8 Canberra photo reconnaissance aircraft
- 898 other aircraft
- 229 transports (60 C-47, 60 C-119, 3 Tu-124, 34 An-12, 30 Otter, 15 Caribous, 27 HS-748)
- 423 trainers (20 Su-7, 8 MiG-21, 10 Canberra, 35 Vampire, 20 Hunter, 130 HT-2, 155 Kiran, 15 Chipmunk, 30 T-6)
- 246 helicopters (50 Mi-4, 50 Mi-8, 130 Alouette III, 10 HH-52, 6 SA-315)

Missiles:

- 20 SA-2 Guideline sites, SAM
- 40 Tigercat SAM

Reserves: These consist of the Regular Reserves (former regular Air Force personnel), the Air Defense Reserves (personnel in civil aviation) and the Auxiliary Air Force of 7 squadrons of Harvard and Vampire trainers.

Air Bases: The Air Force operates from 60 airfields oriented mainly to the northwest and the northeast.

PARAMILITARY

The Border Security Force numbers 100,000 men organized as light infantry. Civil police throughout the country total some 550,000.

The National Volunteer Force (Lok Sahayak Sena) gives elementary military training to segments of the population at large with no liability for active military service.

LAOS

Royaume de Laos
Kingdom of Laos

POWER POTENTIAL STATISTICS

Area: 91.400 square miles
Population: 3,200,000
Total Active Armed Forces: 120,150 total (3.75% population; 55,150 Royal Lao Forces; 45,000 Pathet Lao. 20,000 Meo irregulars, supporting Royal Lao Forces
Gross National Product: $230 million ($72 per capita)
Annual Military Expenditures: $21 million (9.13% GNP)
Electric Power Output: 16.1 million kwh
Civil Air Fleet: 1 turboprop, 7 piston transports

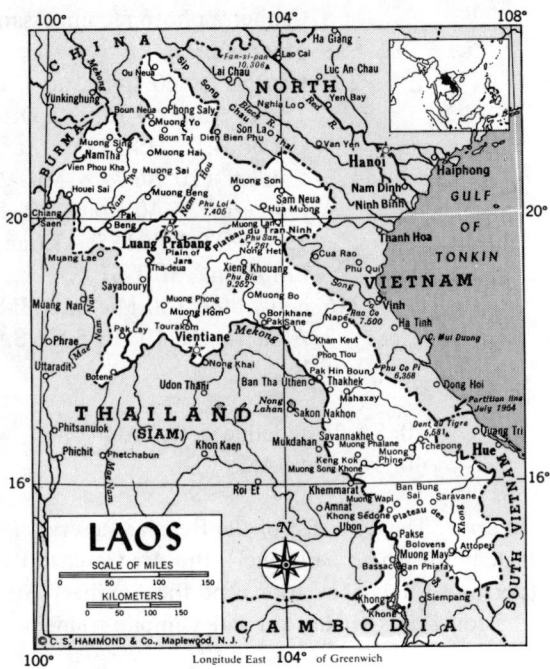

STRATEGIC BACKGROUND

In 1949 this former French colony was granted independence within the French Union as the United Kingdom of Laos. Internal opposition soon developed under the leadership of communist-oriented Prince Souphanouvong, who organized the Pathet Lao (Free Lao) movement. Early in 1953, Viet Minh troops, and Pathet Lao forces organized in Vietnam, invaded eastern Laos to plunge the nation into civil war.

Two multi-nation conferences at Geneva, co-chaired by the UK and USSR, one in 1954 and a later one in 1962, produced compromise agreements, but neither was long successful in checking the Pathet Lao rebellion, supported by Communist North Vietnam troops. The international guarantees of Laotian independence and neutrality given as part of the 1962 agreement were violated in less than three months by renewed attacks by Pathet Lao and NVN forces.

CURRENT MILITARY SITUATION

American military assistance has been provided in unspecified amounts, including support, reportedly by the Central Intelligence Agency, of about 20,000 Meo tribesmen as irregulars. The scope of the conflict broadened in 1971 when troops from both Thailand and South Vietnam crossed their respective borders into Laos to attack Communist forces. North Vietnam extended its participation by operating aircraft in Laotian airspace, by moving SAM units into the country along with large amounts of AA guns, and by sending in more regular units of its army to support Pathet Lao forces. In late 1971 NVN-Pathet Lao forces overran the Tranvinh Plateau (including the Plaine des Jarres) and they now control Luang Prabang and well over half of the Laotian countryside. In April 1974 a new coalition government was finally formed as a result of a February 1973 peace agreement, related to the settlement between the United States and North Vietnam the previous month. Under the terms of that agreement all American military forces had been withdrawn by mid-1974. More than 20,000 North Vietnamese troops, however, seem to have remained in northern Laos, in defiance of the agreement. The power situation is reflected in the preponderance of Pathet Lao influence and presence in the new organs of government. Meantime, the economic situation is deteriorating and the immediate future is not promising.

A military road from China through Laos to the Mekong toward the Thai border is virtually complete. Built by 20,000 Chinese railway and engineering construction troops, it has been protected by Chinese AA units.

Under the Military Assistance Program from FY 1950 through FY 1967 $346.7 million was provided to Laos. In addition 34,623 students were trained under the MAP.

ROYAL LAO ARMY

Personnel: 52,600 regular forces

Organization:
    24 mobile infantry battalions
     1 parachute battalion
    33 garrison infantry battalions
     1 artillery regiment (4 batteries)

Major Equipment Inventory:
    light tanks (M-24 and PT-76)
    armored cars (M-8)
    scout cars (M-3)
    APCs (BTR-40 and M-113)
    60 artillery pieces (105mm and 155mm howitzers, heavy mortars)
    19 light aircraft (O-1)

ROYAL LAO NAVY

Personnel: 400

Organization: 4 river squadrons

Major Units:
    17 gunboats
     4 landing craft

ROYAL LAO AIR FORCE

Personnel: 2,150

Major Aircraft Types:
- 90 combat aircraft
  - 75 T-28 armed trainers
  - 5 T-6 armed trainers
  - 10 AC-47 gunships
- 80 other aircraft
  - 20 T-28 trainers
  - 10 C-47 transports
  - 10 Beaver and Aero Commander light transports
  - 16 trainer/support aircraft (U-17, T-41)
  - 24 helicopters (Alouette II and III, UH-19, H-34)

PARAMILITARY

Paramilitary units total 40,000 men, including 20,000 Meo irregulars, who are apparently well armed, equipped, and effective.

PATHET LAO

Personnel: 45,000 (approximately)

Organization: Battalions organized from companies; details unknown

Major Equipment Inventory:
- light tanks (PT-76)
- scout cars (BTR-40)
- 105mm howitzers

Foreign Support: About 75,000 regular North Vietnamese troops operate in the northern provinces and in the eastern area of the southern provinces. The Pathet Lao and North Vietnamese are in control of the entire eastern half of Laos, including the Plaine des Jarres and the frontier with Vietnam.

MALAYSIA

Federation of Malaysia

POWER POTENTIAL STATISTICS

Area: 128,727 square miles
Population: 11,800,000
Total Active Armed Forces: 62,590 (including security police; 0.53% population)
Gross National Product: $4.63 billion ($392 per capita)
Annual Military Expenditures: $243 million (5.25% GNP)
Fuel Production: Crude Oil: 4.4 million metric tons
  Refined Petroleum Products: 6.4 million metric tons
Rubber Production: 1.325 million metric tons
Tin Production (concentrates): 75,000 metric tons
Electric Power Output: 3.7 billion kwh
Merchant Fleet: 99 ships; 149,304 gross tons
Civil Air Fleet: 7 jets, 9 turboprop, 12 piston transports

DEFENSE STRUCTURE

This federated monarchy, with 13 separate component states, is a member of the British Commonwealth, and has a parliamentary form of government. The commander in chief is the elected Paramount Ruler. The services are independent, but are closely coordinated by the Armed Forces Council, under the chairmanship of the Minister of Defence.

The armed forces are maintained by voluntary recruitment.

STRATEGIC PROBLEMS

The two most formidable strategic problems are internal; a latent ethnic division between Malays and Chinese; and the danger of a revival of Communist insurgency, exacerbated by the ethnic split.

Approximately 36 percent of the population are Chinese; about 45 percent are Malay; the remainder are mostly Indian and Pakistani in origin. While the Chinese hold much of the nation's wealth, political power is jealously preserved by the Malays, who are exceedingly suspicious of the Chinese. This ethnic split erupted into serious rioting in mid-1969, resulting in well over one hundred deaths and the declaration of a State of Emergency which lasted until February 1971.

During the Communist insurgency in Malaya, from 1947 to 1960, most of the insurgents were Chinese. The remnants of the insurgents, including a handful of recruits, have taken refuge in the remote mountainous jungles along the Thailand-Malaysia border. There, aided by lack of complete coordination between Malaysian and Thai armed forces and police, and with support from Peking, they have maintained themselves, awaiting an opportunity to move either south or north. If they move south, they may attain the overt or covert support of some of the Chinese population of Malaysia. Upon establishment of full diplomatic relations with the People's Republic of China in June 1974 Malaysia received assurances that China views the rebel problem as internal to Malaysia, to be solved as the Malaysian government sees fit.

Although former difficulties with Indonesia have been settled, there is a continuing state of low-level insurgency in Malaysian Borneo, dating back to Indonesian subversion in the early 1960s. Sabah is also a source of latent diplomatic controversy with the Philippines, which claims the province (see Philippines). This is not likely, however, to lead to war. The general dissatisfaction of the people of the Borneo states with the Malaysian government has been lessened through such measures as the constitutional amendment of 1971, which gave the inhabitants of East Malaysia equal status with the Malays of West Malaysia.

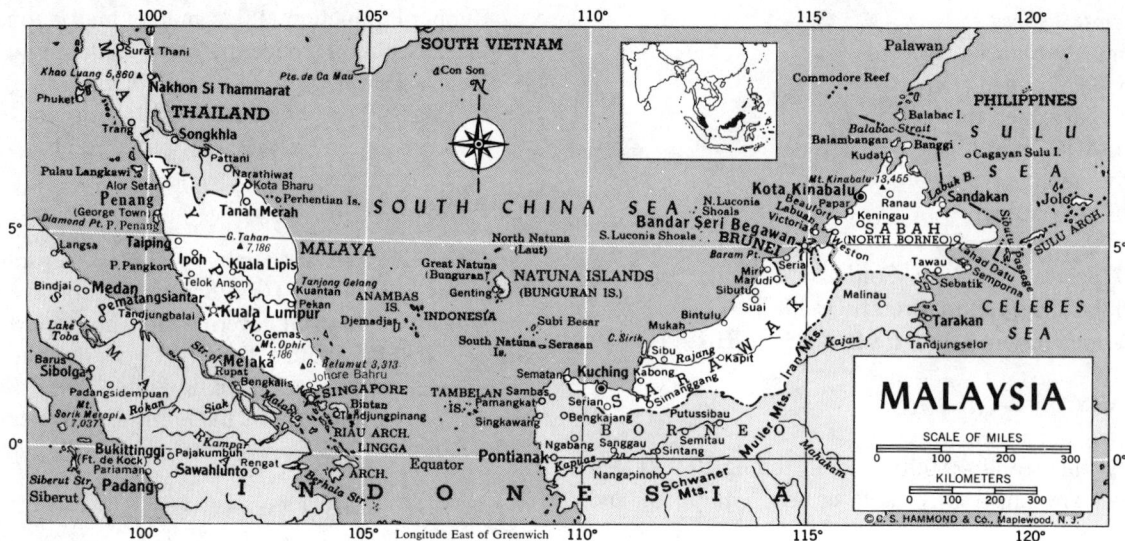

Now that most British forces have been withdrawn, Malaysia bears the brunt of the responsibility for its own defense. As a signatory in 1971 of the five-power defence pact (with the UK, Australia, New Zealand, and Singapore) Malaysia contributes the largest single contingent of forces. In addition, New Zealand and the UK have small contigents in Malaysia.

MILITARY ASSISTANCE

Britain has now terminated the substantial military assistance provided after Malaysia's independence. British contributions of forces to the five-power defence pact arrangement have eased Malaysian concern about a complete British pull-out, as earlier planned. To some extent Australia is filling Britain's former role. Both Britain and Australia have had small ground forces cooperating with Malaysian counter-insurgent forces in Borneo.

Although not formally allied with the United States, Malaysia has strongly supported American assistance to South Vietnam in the Vietnamese war, and has provided training facilities (operated by British personnel) and other assistance to the republic of Vietnam in its prosecution of that war. In return the United States has provided $1.3 million in military aid and has trained 333 students under the MAP.

ALLIANCES

Malaysia is a member of the British Commonwealth, the Anglo-Malaysian Mutual Defence Treaty, and a signatory of the five-power defence pact. It is also a member of the Association of South East Asian Nations (ASEAN).

ARMY

Personnel: 43,000

Organization:
- 7 infantry brigades
- 24 infantry battalions
- 3 reconnaissance regiments (Ferret scout cars, Commando V150 APC)
- 3 artillery regiments (105mm howitzers)
- 1 Special Service unit

Major Equipment Inventory:
- scout cars (Ferret, 100 Commando V150 APC)
- 32 105mm howitzers

Reserves: There are approximately 45,000 trained reservists in the Army Volunteer Forces (national militia). The militia units are prepared to take the field at short notice, either beside the regular forces, or for home defense.

NAVY

Personnel: 5,090

Major Units:
- 2 destroyer escorts (DE; 1 with Seacat SAMs)
- 6 coastal minesweepers (MSC)
- 2 inshore minesweepers (MSI)
- 8 fast patrol missile boats (4 with SS12 SSM, 4 with Exocet SSM; PTF)
- 25 patrol gunboats (PGM)
- 2 auxiliaries
- 20 landing craft (LCM, LCP)
- 24 police launches (YP)

AIR FORCE

Personnel: 4,500

Organization:
- 1 fighter squadron (Sabre)
- 1 ground attack squadron (CL-41G)
- 4 transport squadrons (Caribou, Herald, Dove, Heron, Cessna 310)
- 4 helicopter squadrons (S-61, Alouette III)
- 1 training squadron (Chipmunk, Bulldog, Provost)

Major Aircraft Types:
- 37 combat aircraft
  - 17 Sabre fighters
  - 20 CL-41G ground attack aircraft
- 154 other aircraft
  - 8 Herald transports
  - 14 DHC-4 Caribou transports
  - 36 light transports (Heron, Dove, Cessna 310, HS-125)
  - 16 S-61A helicopter troop carriers
  - 25 Alouette III helicopters
  - 55 trainers (Chipmunk, Provost, Bulldog)

On Order: 16 F-5 fighters

Major Air Bases: Kuala Lumpur, Ipoh, Paya Lebar, Labuan, Kuantan, Alor Star, Gong, Kedak

PARAMILITARY

There is a field police force, some 10,000 men in 14 companies with the primary mission of maintaining internal security.

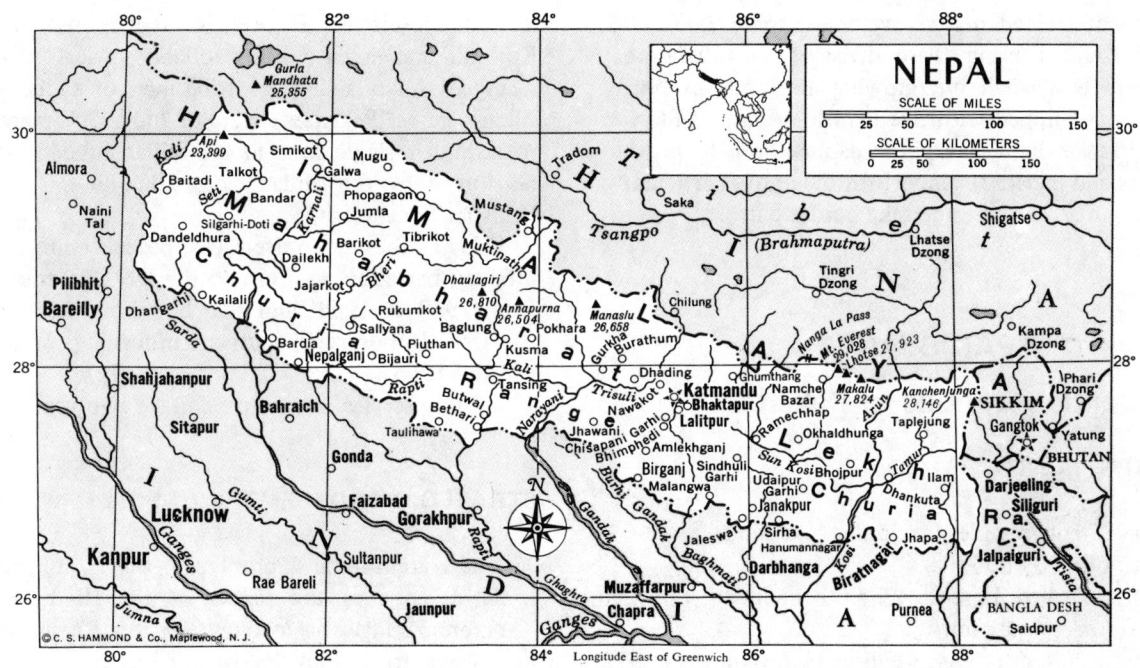

NEPAL

POWER POTENTIAL STATISTICS

Area: 54,362 square miles
Population: 12,000,000
Total Active Armed Forces: 20,000 (0.16% population)
Gross National Product: $920 million ($77 per capita)
Annual Military Expenditures: $7.1 million (0.77% GNP)
Electric Power Output: 31 million kwh

Civil Air Fleet: 5 turboprop, 7 piston transports

POLITICO-MILITARY POLICIES AND POSTURE

The renowned, and possibly the most important, resource of this small Himalayan kingdom is its fierce Gurkha manpower. For more than a century Gurkha regiments were prominent in the British Indian Army, with a combat potential proportionately much greater than their numerical ratio within that rmy. In 1947 upon the partition of British India into India and Pakistan and the division of the army between the two new countries, India retained six Gurkha regiments while the British kept four as the Brigade of Gurkhas, thus perpetuating a great military tradition. Both governments are permitted to recruit Gurkhas in Nepal, and India has subsequently raised another regiment.

Nepal, situated between two major powers, must maneuver and placate to survive. It formerly had a collective security agreement with India, with whom it has substantial defense, political, and economic ties. These included supply of arms and training. However, in June 1969 Nepal cancelled the mutual security agreement and called for withdrawal of Indian troops, but accepted Indian aid in training officers and men. Cordial relations are maintained with Great Britain, the United States, Communist China, and the Soviet Union. All of these have provided Nepal with varying forms of economic assistance, that of the United States being the most significant. Britain and the United States also have provided military assistance. The United States gave $1.9 million through 1972 and trained 27 students under the MAP.

The regular Nepalese army of about 20,000 men (mostly Gurkhas), is organized as two understrength divisions. A militia reserve of trained military veterans, some 25-30,000, can be mobilized to bring these divisions to full combat strength. There is a small but growing air force, currently about 500 men, equipped with five British aircraft—2 Skyvan and 3 Twin Pioneer light transports; its mission is to provide reconnaissance and logistical support for the army, particularly for internal security, and to undertake border patrol.

PAKISTAN

Islamic Republic of Pakistan

POWER POTENTIAL STATISTICS

Area: 310,403 square miles (excluding Kashmir)
Population: 68,300,000
Total Active Armed Forces: 423,000 (including Frontier Corps; 0.62% population)
Gross National Product: $4.9 billion (approximately; $72 per capita)
Annual Military Expenditures: $407 million (8.31% GNP)
Fuel Production: Coal: 1.25 million metric tons
  Crude Oil: 450,740 metric tons
  Refined Petroleum Products: 4.1 million metric tons
  Gas: 3.5 billion cubic meters
Electric Power Output: 2.0 billion kwh
Merchant Fleet: 131 ships; 532,637 gross tons
Civil Air Fleet: 11 jet, 7 turboprop transports

DEFENSE STRUCTURE

The present government is federal and presidential in form, under a new constitution promulgated early in 1972. A Ministry of Defence administers the armed forces, which consist of a separate Army, Navy, and Air Force, plus paramilitary border units. The president holds the positions of Minister of Defence, Foreign Affairs, and Interior. There is a direct line of authority from the Minister of Defence to the commanders of the three separate armed services.

POLITICO-MILITARY POLICY

Pakistan's politico-military policy is largely centered on its confrontation with India over Kashmir and its long-standing fear that India, unreconciled to the 1947 partition of the subcontinent, may try to regain control of Pakistan. It was this apprehension, rather than fear of the Soviet Union and Communist China, that apparently impelled Pakistan into the SEATO and CENTO pacts in a search for allies, and that later caused acceptance of military assistance from Communist China and the Soviet Union after a US arms embargo instituted in 1965 during the India-Pakistan Kashmir War. The continuing confrontation with India, and rival claims to Kashmir, resulted in Pakistan's direct sponsorship of the Azad Kashmir movement, and probably covert support for the insurgent Mizo and Naga tribesmen of India's Manipur and Assam states. Pakistan's fears of India's ultimate intention to reestablish a single state in the Indian subcontinent have been reinforced by the Indian victory in the 1971 war over East Pakistan/Bangladesh.

Pakistan has supported UN peacekeeping operations; an infantry battalion was sent to the UN Operation in the Congo from 1960 to 1964, and two battalions were contributed to the UN Temporary Executive Authority in West New Guinea in 1962-1963.

Military service is selective and for two years.

STRATEGIC PROBLEMS

The traditional problem that concerned British India—defense of the passes of the Hindu Kush and the Karakoram ranges against invasion by Russia or China—does not seem to bother Pakistan. Rather, Pakistan's strategic problems are fear of invasion by India seeking to reunite the subcontinent, and the desire to bring Kashmir, with its predominantly Muslim population, into the Republic.

Concern for these problems has led to a disproportionately large defense establishment, two short but intense wars, numerous border skirmishes, and support of an insurgency in Kashmir. Seen in this context, Pakistan's close relationship with China, and presumed support for Mizo and Naga tribesmen in northeastern India, appear as diversions designed to pin down Indian troops distant from the strategic Punjab core of Pakistan.

Endemic political, economic and social problems have

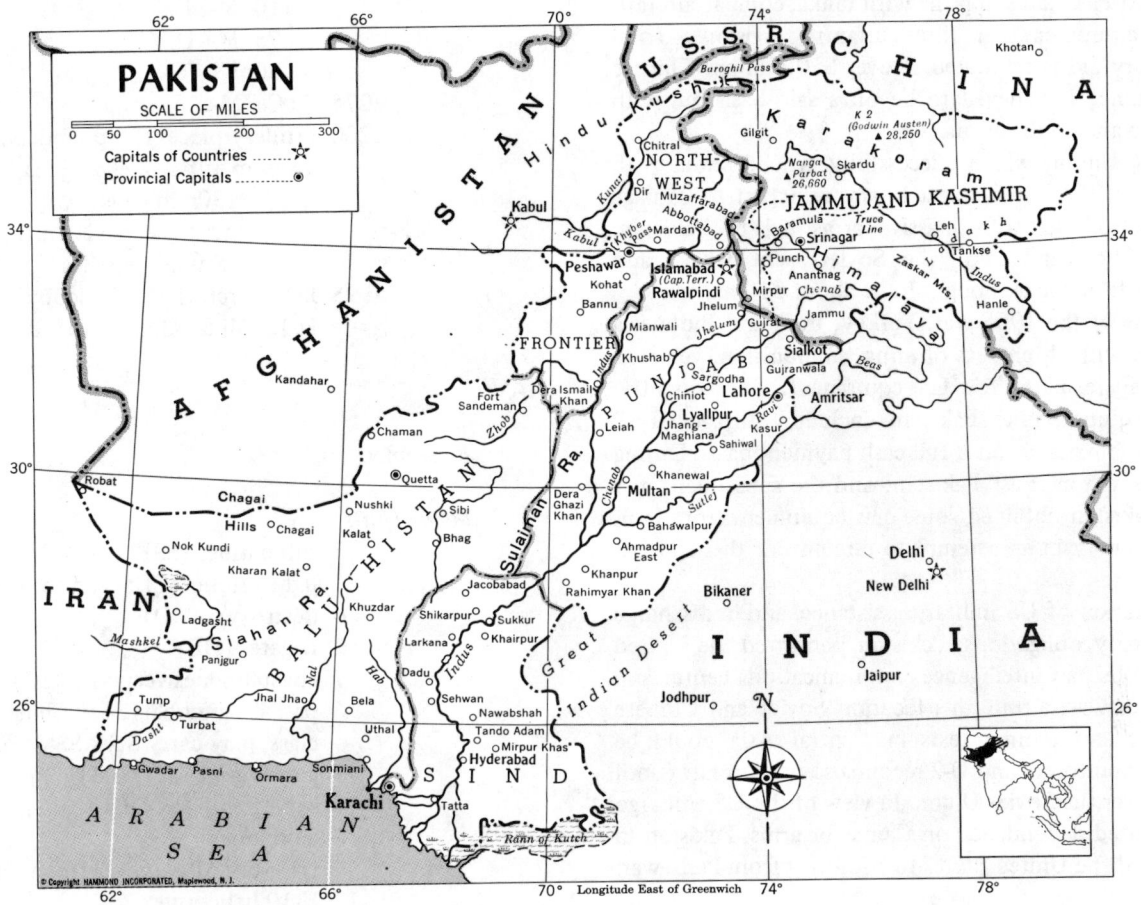

plagued Pakistan since independence in 1947. Only part of this was due to tensions between East and West Pakistan, separated by 1,100 miles, and united only by a common Moslem religion. These problems led to military dictatorship under Marshal Ayub Khan in 1958. His successor, General Yahya Khan, resigned on December 20, 1971, following the defeat by India, which stimulated nationwide demonstrations. He was succeeded by Z.K. Bhutto, who thus became the first civilian to head the government since 1958. Bhutto moved swiftly to eliminate some of the more senior military and to inaugurate a policy of conciliation. This included recognition or establishment of better relations with left-tending nations, withdrawal from the UN Commission in Korea and from SEATO. On July 10, 1973, the National Assembly approved a resolution allowing recognition of Bangladesh when this proved to be in the national interest. The intention to do so was announced on February 22, 1974.

The border with Afghanistan, which bisects the territory inhabited by the Pushtun tribes, has been in dispute. Afghanistan claims all of Pushtunistan and advocates self-determination for Pushtuns. There was a spate of Pushtun raids across the border which was finally closed by Pakistan from 1961 to 1963. Relations between the two countries have been correct since, but the division of the warlike Pushtun continues on the old Northwest Frontier and could again result in local conflict (see Afghanistan). There was armed rebellion in Baluchistan in January 1973 and government troops were used against the rebels.

India's nuclear explosion was understandably disturbing to the government of Pakistan, which has announced its intention to pursue its own interests in the nuclear field.

MILITARY ASSISTANCE

From independence in 1947 until 1954 equipment was British. Following Pakistan's adherence to regional security arrangements sponsored by the United States, $681.3 million in American military aid was received from 1950 to 1973, and 4,279 were trained under the MAP. In September 1965 both Britain and the United States imposed arms embargos against both Pakistan and India. Britain lifted the embargo in March 1966, and the United States lifted it for spare parts only. This precluded the replacement of the large numbers of tanks lost during the brief 1965 war with India. Pakistani efforts to obtain substantial quantities of US equipment by deals with Iran and with NATO nations have been blocked by Indian diplomacy and US disapproval.

After that war Communist China responded almost

immediately to Pakistan's appeals with tanks, combat aircraft, and enough equipment for three infantry divisions. Total Chinese military aid is estimated at over $50 million. Chinese military assistance is believed to be on a sale basis but with favorable price and credit terms.

The Soviet Union, which successfully wooed India with arms after the 1962 Chinese attack, was reluctant to damage this new relationship with massive arms aid to Pakistan. However, in 1966 and 1967 the Soviets sent trucks and helicopters. Total value is thought to be about $10 million.

At the time of the 1965 war, Turkey, Iran, and Indonesia aided Pakistan with shipments of arms, ammunition, vehicles, aircraft and spare parts for US equipment. Subsequently, France sold equipment to Pakistan—including Mirage III-EP fighters, and submarines—on a full cash payment basis. During the 1971 civil war in East Pakistan, and the subsequent war with India, Pakistan obtained some new equipment from Iran, Jordan, and Turkey in an attempt to circumvent the US arms embargo.

In consideration of US military assistance, and in discharge of CENTO treaty obligations, Pakistan permitted the United States to establish an intelligence-communications center and airbase at Peshawar. From this location Soviet and Chinese space, missile, and atomic tests in Central Asia could be conveniently monitored, and U-2 reconnaissance aircraft (until 1960) flown over the Soviet Union. In view of the US embargo and the increased dependence on China for arms, Pakistan in late 1968 asked the United States to withdraw from Peshawar.

ALLIANCES

Pakistan is a member of the UN and the Commonwealth. It has withdrawn from SEATO, and its membership in CENTO has become largely nominal.

ARMY

Personnel: 365,000 (including 25,000 Azad Kashmir troops)

Organization:
- 2 armored divisions
- 14 infantry divisions
- 1 independent armored brigade
- 1 air defense brigade

Major Equipment Inventory:
- 750 medium tanks
  - 75 T-54
  - 45 T-55
  - 300 T-59
  - 305 M-47, M-48
  - 25 M4A3E8 Sherman
- 205 light tanks
  - 110 M-24
  - 75 M-41
  - 20 PT-76
- 275 APCs (M-113)
- 1,200 artillery pieces (25-pounders, 105mm and 155mm self-propelled guns, Soviet 130mm guns
- AAA pieces (20mm)
- antitank missiles (Cobra)
- 95 light aircraft and helicopters (O-1, H-19, H-13, Mi-8, Alouette III, Beaver)

NAVY

Personnel: 10,000

Major Units:
- 3 submarines (SS)
- 1 light cruiser (CL; used for cadet training)
- 4 destroyers (DD)
- 2 frigates (DE)
- 7 coastal minesweepers (MSC)
- 6 patrol gunboats (ex-Chinese Shanghai class; may carry Styx SSM; PGM)
- 1 patrol gunboat (PGM)
- 1 survey ship (ex-DE)
- 7 auxiliaries
- 4 HU-16A Albatross patrol aircraft
- 3 H-19 helicopters

Naval Base: Karachi

Reserves: 5,000 to 6,000 trained reservists

AIR FORCES

Personnel: 18,000

Organization:
- 2 light bomber squadrons (B-57)
- 7 fighter-bomber squadrons (Sabre)
- 2 fighter-bomber squadrons (Mirage III, Mirage 5)
- 7 fighter squadrons (MiG-19, F-6)
- 1 fighter/interceptor squadron (F-104, F-5)
- 2 reconnaissance squadrons (RB-57, Mirage III, RT-33)
- 2 transport squadrons (C-47, C-130, Falcon 20)
- 1 helicopter squadron (Alouette III, H-13, H-19, H-43, Mi-6)

(A medium bomber squadron is phasing in; Tu-16)

Major Aircraft Types:
- 347 combat aircraft
  - 12 Tu-16 medium bombers
  - 20 B-57 light bombers
  - 156 fighter-bombers (112 Sabre, 16 Mirage III, 28 Mirage 5)
  - 138 fighters (10 F-104, 120 MiG-19/F-6, 8 F-5)
  - 21 reconnaissance aircraft (2 RB-57, 15 Mirage III, 4 RT-33)
- 169 other aircraft
  - 24 transports (C-47, C-130, Falcon 20)
  - 100 trainers (T-6, T-37, T-33, Mirage III, B-57)
  - 45 helicopters (Alouette III, H-13, H-19, H-43, Mi-6)

Missiles: MiG-19 and F-6 carry Sidewinder AAM
Mirage III and Mirage 5 carry R530 AAM and AS30 ASM

Air Bases: Peshawar, Kohat, Mauripur, Samundri, Deigh Road, Risalpur, Sargodha, Gilgit, Chitral, Malir, and Miramshah

Reserves: About 9,000 trained reservists

PARAMILITARY

The Frontier Corps numbers 30,000 hill tribesmen of the Northwest Frontier and guards the borders with Iran and Afghanistan.

SIKKIM
State of Sikkim

POWER POTENTIAL STATISTICS

Area: 2,818 square miles
Population: 204,760
Total Active Armed Forces: 300 (0.15% population)
Gross National Product: $25.2 million (estimate; $123 per capita)
Annual Military Expenditures: Unknown

Sikkim is nestled between Nepal on the western side, Bhutan on the eastern, and India on the southern. It is ruled by a hereditary Chogyal, or Maharaja, and is a protectorate of India. It is not a member of the UN. Under terms of a 1950 treaty, India handles all foreign affairs and defense matters and has the right to station troops anywhere in Sikkim (there are presently two Indian divisions there). Indian advisers permeate Sikkim's administration and all top police officers are seconded from the Indian police. Following unrest and civil violence in Sikkim, India took over administrative control in August 1973. One of Sikkim's problems is ethnic rivalry. Seventy-five percent of the people are Nepal Hindus. The remainder are Lepcha or Bhutia people.

India's interest in Sikkim derives from the strategic passes which link Tibet to India. These are traversed by traditional trade routes, and since the Indo-China war of 1962 both sides have built motor roads up to the 14,400-foot Natu and Jelep Passes, three-and-one-half miles apart. China claims this area, and border clashes occurred at the passes in 1963, 1965, 1967, and 1968. Should China seize these passes it would be possible, by a strike 50 miles southward, to reach the plains of the Ganges-Bramahputra basin. India is the primary source of aid to Sikkim's armed forces, which consist of a 300-man Indian-officered palace guard and a militia of two companies. There are 4,000 Sikkimese serving in the Indian Army, stationed in India. India has built strategic roads into the country and an airfield at Gangtok.

SINGAPORE
Republic of Singapore

POWER POTENTIAL STATISTICS

Area: 225.6 square miles
Population: 2,300,000
Total Active Armed Forces: 16,000 (0.76% population)
Gross National Product: $2.8 billion ($1,217 per capita)
Annual Military Expenditures: $240 million (8.69% GNP)
Electric Power Output: 1.64 billion kwh
Merchant Fleet: 281 ships; 870,513 gross tons
Civil Air Fleet: 14 jet, 2 turboprop transports

POLITICO-MILITARY POLICIES AND POSTURE

Singapore seceded from Malaysia in August 1965. Responsibility for Singapore's external security has since been borne primarily by Great Britain, and secondarily by Malaysia. After the 1967 UK announcement that all British forces would be withdrawn in 1971, Singapore began taking energetic fiscal and administrative steps to increase its armed forces. Conscription has been initiated, with all males above the age of 19 being liable to military service for two to three years.

Singapore (along with Britain, New Zealand, Australia, and Malaysia) is a participant in the five-power defense pact signed in 1971 which replaced the British sole responsibility for defense of the area. British, Australian and New Zealand army,

322 ALMANAC OF WORLD MILITARY POWER

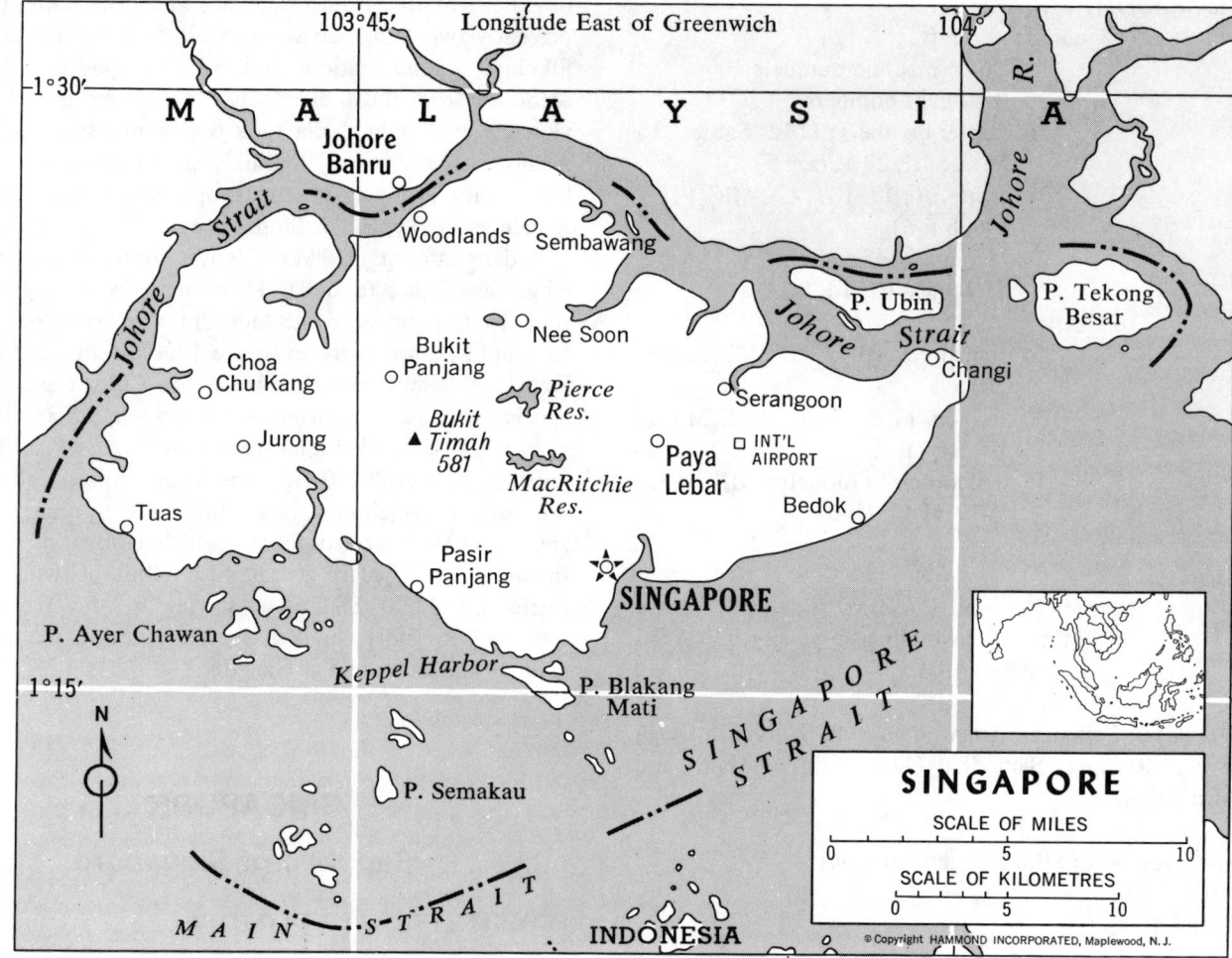

navy and air units have been stationed in Singapore on rotation, but the Australian contingent is being withdrawn. Canberra says, however, that its commitment to ANZUK remains firm.

The government of Singapore tries to maintain cordial relations with all nations and to do business with any legitimate patron.

The Singapore armed forces are made up of an Army, a Navy and the Singapore Air Defence Command (Air Force).

ARMY

Personnel: 16,000

Organization:
  3 brigades, composed of
    9 infantry battalions
    1 armored regiment
    2 artillery battalions
    1 engineer battalion
    1 signal battalion

Major Equipment Inventory:
  60 AMX-13 light tanks
     M-706 Commando APC
     25-pounder guns
     120mm mortars
     106mm recoilless rifles

Reserves: about 10,000 men

NAVY

Personnel: 1,300

Major Units:
  4 fast missile patrol boats (PTFG) with short range SSM
  3 fast gunboats (PG)
  3 fast patrol craft (PTF)
  1 seaward defense craft (PCS)
  4 patrol vessels (YP)
  1 LST
  2 LCT
  6 small landing craft

AIR FORCE

Personnel: 1,000

Organization:
- 2 fighter squadrons (Hunter)
- 1 training squadron (Strikemaster)
  ((Note: this training squadron has a ground attack capability)
- 1 training squadron (SF-260)
- 1 communications and rescue squadron (Alouette III)
- 1 transportation and rescue squadron (Skyvan)
- 1 SAM squadron (Bloodhound)

Major Aircraft Types:
- 58 combat aircraft
  - 42 Hunter fighters
  - 16 Strikemaster armed trainers
- 27 other aircraft
  - 14 SF-260 trainers
  - 7 Alouette III helicopters
  - 6 Skyvan transports (3 have a SAR capability)

Equipment on Order: 40 A-4 Skyhawk fighter-bombers

Missiles: SAM Bloodhound

Major Air Bases: Tengah, Changi, Seletar

SRI LANKA
Republic of Sri Lanka
(Ceylon)

POWER POTENTIAL STATISTICS

Area: 25,332 square miles
Population: 13,500,000
Total Active Armed Forces: 8,600 (0.06% population)
Gross National Product: $2.2 billion ($163 per capita)
Annual Military Expenditures: $17 million (0.77% GNP)
Electric Power Output: 816 million kwh
Merchant Fleet: 28 ships; 13,107 gross tons
Civil Air Fleet: 2 jet, 1 turboprop, 2 piston transports

POLITICO-MILITARY POLICIES AND POSTURE

Since independence in 1948, this British Commonwealth nation has relied almost exclusively upon Great Britain for external security. The small armed forces are of little use other than for purposes of internal security and coastal sea and air

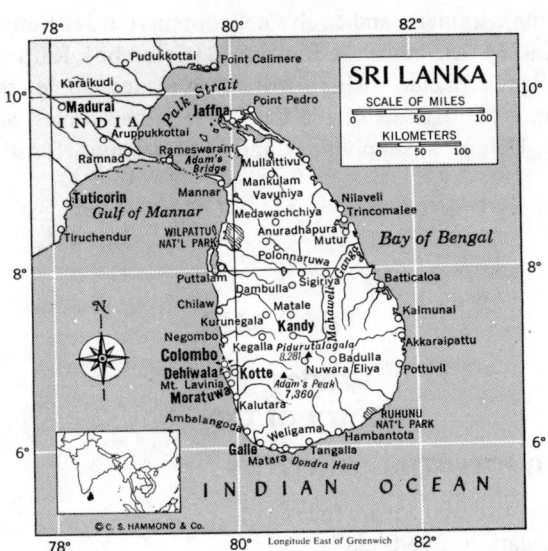

patrol. The regular forces are based entirely upon voluntary enlistment. There are also small Volunteer Army, Navy, and Air Force Militia establishments. Britain's withdrawal of forces from the Indian Ocean area in 1971 has not resulted in any significant military buildup.

The strategically placed British naval and air base complex of Trincomalee was turned over to Ceylon in 1957. It, with Colombo, is used by the Navy, but its facilities have largely remained idle and presumably are deteriorating, although the harbor is still useful.

There is some friction with India over ownership of tiny Kachchativu Island in the Palk Strait between the two countries, and over treatment of about 1,000,000 disenfranchised Indian Tamils residing in Ceylon. There is also internal friction between the native Tamils and the remaining Sinhalese population. A low rate of development, a stagnant economy, and population pressures, provide additional causes of internal unrest. Sri Lanka has been particularly hard hit by the changes in the world economic situation that began in late 1973 and continued in 1974.

In April 1971 an ultra-leftist rebellion led primarily by student groups attempted to overthrow the government. In its campaign to halt the rebellion, the government obtained aid (including small arms, fighter aircraft and helicopters, and armored cars) from all possible sources: Britain, East Germany, India, Pakistan, the Soviet Union, and the United States. The rebellion was quelled in May, after about 1,200 people, including 60 soldiers, had been killed.

The Regular Army totals about 5,000 men. The Navy based at Trincomalee has 2,000 men, one destroyer escort (DE), five patrol gunboats (PGM), ex-Chinese Shanghai class, 21 patrol craft (YP), a hydrofoil, and a tug. The Air Force has about 1,600 men, five MiG-17 fighters, eight Provost armed trainers, five Dove and four Heron coastal patrol and transport aircraft, three Pioneer CC2 liaison aircraft, one MiG-15 and nine

Chipmunk trainers, and twelve helicopters (ten Jet Ranger and two Ka-26). Air bases are Ratmalana (Colombo), Katunayaka, and eight smaller fields. Britain provides some training assistance for officers of the Ceylonese armed forces, and the Soviet Union is supplying some pilot training for the Air Force.

THAILAND
Prades Thai
Country of the Thai

POWER POTENTIAL STATISTICS

Area: 198,500 square miles
Population: 39,900,000
Total Active Armed Forces: 217,400 (including security forces; 0.54% population)
Gross National Product: $7.3 billion ($183 per capita)
Annual Military Expenditures: $301 million (4.12% GNP)
Refined Petroleum Products: 745,400 metric tons
Electric Power Output: 3.73 billion kwh
Merchant Fleet: 69 ships; 108,271 gross tons
Civil Air Fleet: 10 jet, 9 turboprop, 8 piston transports

DEFENSE STRUCTURE

The King of Thailand is a nominal commander in chief of the armed forces. Actual control is exercised by the Prime Minister who is Supreme Commander of the Armed Forces. In October 1973 Field Marshal Thanom Kittikachorn, the Premier and Commander of the Armed Forces, was overthrown in an uprising that involved heavy student activity and some bloodshed. He was replaced by Sanya Thammasak, a university dean and first civilian to hold this post since 1953.

POLITICO-MILITARY POLICY

Thailand's principal national objective is to preserve independence from foreign control.

Since 1950 Thailand has been committed firmly to the West in a determined but circumspect policy of opposing Communism in Southeast Asia. Thailand was an original signatory of the Southeast Asia Collective Defense Treaty in 1954, and the SEATO headquarters is located in Bangkok. The new government has been exploring its options and there have been renewed contacts with Peking.

In connection with the United States' military effort in South Vietnam, a number of operational US air bases were established on Thai territory. The numbers of men and aircraft present on Thai bases is slowly being reduced. In 1974 it was estimated that the United States had some 350 fighters and 50 B-52s in Thailand.

The armed forces are maintained by conscription. All men between the ages of 21 and 30 are subject to conscription to perform two years of military service; about 20 percent actually serve.

STRATEGIC PROBLEMS

Thailand has a number of serious strategic problems that pose severe challenges to the traditional Thai qualities of adroitness, compromise, and determination which kept Thailand independent during the colonial era in Southeast Asia.

Internal stability is uncertain; the nation has suffered a number of coups, counter coups, and attempted coups since World War II.

The ancient hostility between Burma and Thailand has not been in evidence since Burma regained its independence in 1948. The equally traditional and ancient enmity with Cambodia has also apparently abated since that country became actively involved in the Vietnam War (see Cambodia). Thai units, with intergovernmental approval, have apparently operated across the Cambodian border in reaction to communist activity.

While 85 percent of the people are ethnic Thais, three minority groups present serious defense problems. There are more than 3,000,000 Chinese in Thailand, about 10 percent of the population. The loyalty of these Chinese-Thais has not yet been really tested, but they are susceptible to pressures from China. Chinese have been prominent among the participants in exposed espionage groups, and apparently they play key roles in the subversive activities which have been going on for nearly ten years in northeastern and southern Thailand. How durable the new PRC pledges might be remains to be seen.

The communist-supported insurgency which exists in northeastern Thailand has been related to the Vietnam War, but it also represents an independent communist effort to penetrate the nations of Southeast Asia by exploiting ethnic minorities and economic underdevelopment. There are over 300,000 mountain tribal peoples in northern and northeastern Thailand who are not related to the Thais, and who feel little or no loyalty to Bangkok. This is relatively poor country, with few resources, and the central government has not, until recently, paid much attention to the area. As a result there are at least 1,000 active insurgent terrorists in the region, many of them mountain tribesmen, and they have considerable local sympathy and indirect support. Some 40,000 Vietnamese, many loyal to the Viet Minh, also inhabit this area.

In the southernmost provinces of Thailand, some 700,000 Malays make up a majority of the population. They, too, have little loyalty to the Bangkok government and thus are quite apathetic about communist terrorist activity. This activity has gone on along the rough, jungled Thai-Malaysia border since before 1960, when about 1,000 remnants of the Malayan insurgents retreated to this region after defeat by British and

Malay forces. Although a substantial number of these communist terrorists are Chinese, they also include Malays, who have been able to obtain some support from the local population just north of the border.

MILITARY ASSISTANCE

Before becoming involved in the Vietnamese War, Thailand had benefitted greatly from substantial US economic and military assistance. In recent years this military assistance has increased as both the United States and Thailand have seen mutual benefit in the strengthening of Thai military capabilities to make the nation a Free World bastion in Southeast Asia. Since 1950 this aid has totalled more than $610 million. In addition to the American combat and support forces in Thailand — totalling 32,000 troops — there is a US Military Advisory Group of over 600 assisting the Thai armed forces in the utilization of the American equipment which has been provided them. Many Thai military men receive training in the United States.

ALLIANCES

Thailand's two principal formal agreements are the collective security SEATO pact, and its bilateral military assistance agreement with the United States. In addition, Thailand is a member of the Association of Southeast Asian Nations, established in August 1967, with Indonesia, the Philippines, Malaysia, and Singapore.

ARMY

Personnel: 130,000

Organization:
- 4 infantry divisions
- 1 regimental combat team
- 11 artillery battalions
- 4 tank battalions
- 3 AAA battalions (1 with SAMs)
- 1 signal battalion
- 4 engineer battalions
- 1 transport battalion

Major Equipment Inventory:
- light tanks (M-24 and M-41)
- 144 light artillery pieces (105mm howitzers)
- 54 medium artillery pieces (155mm howitzers)
- 40 SAM launchers (Hawk; 1 battalion)
- armored half-tracks (M-2 and M-16)
- armored cars (M-8)
- scout cars (M3A1)
- 200 APCs (M-113)
- 60 light aircraft (Beech 99, O-1, L-18)
- 65 helicopters (FH-1100, Jet Ranger, UH-1, CH-47, H-23)

Reserves: Approximately 350,000 trained reservists

NAVY

Personnel: 26,400 (20,000 Navy, 6,400 Marines)

Organization:
- ASW squadron
- Mine squadron
- Patrol squadron
- Air squadron
- Service squadron
- Royal Thai Marine Brigade

Major Units:
- 2 destroyer escorts (DE)
- 6 patrol escorts (PF)
- 1 escort minesweeper (PF/MSF)
- 2 coastal minelayers (MMC)
- 4 coastal minesweepers (MSC)
- 21 escort/patrol vessels (PCE, PC, PCS, SC)
- 10 patrol gunboats (PGM)
- 8 patrol boats (YP)
- 6 river gunboats (PBR)
- 4 landing ships, tank (LST)
- 3 landing ships, medium (LSM)
- 1 survey/armed training ship
- 3 support gunboats (LSSL)
- 8 landing craft (2 LCI, 6 LCU)
- 5 coast guard patrol vessels (CGC)
- 15 auxiliaries and support craft maritime reconnaissance aircraft (S-2, and HU-16)

Under Construction: 1 general purpose frigate (PF); 2 corvettes (PCE)

Major Naval Bases: Paknam (mouth of Chao Praya River), Sattahip

Reserves: 30,000 trained naval reservists; 16,000 to 18,000 Marine reservists

AIR FORCE

Personnel: 25,000

Organization:
- 6 combat wings (1-3 squadrons each)
  - 3 fighter squadrons (F-5, F-86)
  - 6 COIN ground attack squadrons (T-28, T-6, OV-10)

2 transport squadrons (C-45, C-47, C-54, C-123, HS748, Caribou)
1 reconnaissance squadron (RT-33)
1 helicopter wing (UH-1, H-34, CH-47, H-43)
1 training and support wing (Chipmunk, CT-4, PL-2, SF-260, T-6, T-37, T-33)
4 battalions of airfield defense troops

Major Aircraft Types:
165 combat aircraft
   55 fighters (25 F-5, 30 F-86)
   105 COIN ground attack aircraft (30 OV-10, 45 T-28, 30 T-6)
   5 reconnaissance aircraft (RT-33)
356 other aircraft
   44 transports (5 C-45, 20 C-47, 2 C-54, 13 C-123, 2 HS748, 2 Caribou)
   77 helicopters (4 CH-47, 23 UH-1, 10 H-43, 40 H-34)
   235 trainer/support aircraft (see types listed above)

Major Air Bases: Bangkok, Udon Thani, Don Muang, Khorat, Takhli, Ubon, Nongkai, Prachuab, Kokekathion, Utapao, Nakhon Phanom

PARAMILITARY

The Provincial Police have a strength of 28,000. The Thai Border Patrol Police has a strength of 8,000 men, and is equipped with 46 aircraft, including 10 Bell 204B, 11 Bell 205, and 13 FH-1100 helicopters, and three Skyvan STOL transports. These, and all municipal highway and investigation police, are under Thai National Police Department, which is part of the Ministry of the Interior.

The Volunteer Defense Corps, with 10,000 men, is available for home guard type missions in times of emergency.

VIETNAM, NORTH
Viet-Nam Dan-Chu Cong-Hoa
Democratic Republic of Vietnam

POWER POTENTIAL STATISTICS

Area: 61,293 square miles
Population: 22,675,000
Total Active Armed Forces: 595,000 (includes 20,000 security police and border guards; 2.62% population)
Gross National Product: $2.2 billion ($97 per capita)
Annual Military Expenditures: $584 million (26.5% GNP)
Fuel Production: Coal: 3.3 million metric tons
Electric Power Output: 548 million kwh
Merchant Fleet: 5 ships; 713 gross tons

DEFENSE STRUCTURE

Formal command of the armed forces is constitutionally vested in the president of the Democratic Republic of Vietnam (DRV). Direct control of the military establishment has been since 1946 under the Minister of National Defense, General Vo Nguyen Giap, who is also Commander in Chief of the People's Army and a deputy Premier. The National Defense Council, a policy-making body (similar to the US National Security Council) includes the President, the Premier, the Defense Minister and other high civil and military officials. The Defense Minister exercises control largely through the General Staff, the Political Directorate, the Training Directorate, and the Logistics Directorate. Many of the top military officers and officials are also leading members of the all-powerful Communist Lao Dong Party, which controls the overall military policy.

The war in South Vietnam is directed from Hanoi by the Central Committee of the Lao Dong Party. A direct link runs from the Committee's politburo to the top echelon of the Lao Dong Party in the South—the Central Committee of the People's Revolutionary Party. This Committee has a select standing sub-committee known as the Central Office for South Vietnam (COSVN); both include several senior North Vietnamese generals. COSVN's Military Affairs Committee in turn directs the military effort through a Chief of the General Staff and a Political Department of the Army.

POLITICO-MILITARY POLICY

After the establishment of the DRV north of the 17th parallel, following the Geneva Agreement of July 1954, North Vietnam's communist regime had two major objectives: the survival and strengthening of the DRV as an independent nation; and the liberation of South Vietnam from its anti-communist government to permit Vietnam's unification under a centralized Marxist-Leninist system.

Growing US support of South Vietnam in the early 1960s in both economic development and pacification of the dissident Viet Cong (VC), and the start of American bombing of North Vietnam in 1965, gave an increased urgency to these twin objectives. The heavy bombing, dispersing but not destroying North Vietnam's limited industry, served to unite the people of the DRV in a strong resistance to the United States. Meanwhile, the DRV sent more units of its North Vietnamese Army (NVA) to help the communist-controlled VC guerrilla force in the South. The VC (or People's Liberation Army of South Vietnam), recruited initially from

328 ALMANAC OF WORLD MILITARY POWER

South Vietnamese, is the fighting arm of the National Liberation Front (NLF), the Southern resistance movement which is directed by Hanoi through COSVN.

The DRV strategy in the South concentrated on destroying America's will to win by maintaining an undefeated guerrilla force. While the US conducted a military war of attrition, the Hanoi-backed VC and its own NVA units needed only to survive and to maintain their ability to influence the population. The key to the war was: first, the US-South Vietnam inability to protect the villagers, who could be government-dominated by day but guerrilla-controlled by night; and second, a parallel inability to establish a mutually supportive relationship with the people. While the US forces—half a million strong by 1968—chased the North Vietnam regulars and VC main force units and won battlefield victories, the VC maintained a strong village organization throughout much of the heavily populated Mekong Delta and coastal plain regions.

The partially successful but costly North Vietnamese-VC Tet offensive of February-March 1968 shattered the American illusion that they were near victory. While the South Vietnam government did not topple nor its army revolt, as the VC and DRV had expected, the village security and rural development programs of South Vietnam were severely set back. However, NVA and VC follow-up offensives in May and August-September were largely futile and further costly in casualties. This punishment continued in successful limited objective operations by US and ARVN forces in the three subsequent years.

The overall DRV military policy had, however, succeeded in its primary objective of waring down the American desire to continue the war through successful resistance in South Vietnam and effective propaganda in the US and worldwide. In May, 1968, negotiations opened in Paris between North Vietnam and the United States, and were broadened in December to include South Vietnam and the NLF. In March, the United States cut back its air attacks to a small area above the DMZ, and on November 1 halted all bombing, thus giving the DRV the opportunity to rebuild its industrial and transportation system. Bombing of targets in the north was resumed briefly in 1972.

The 1973 agreements in Indochina were the product of a number of influences. The US had intensified bombing and undertaken serious harbor mining in an earlier effort to intimidate Hanoi. Although it cannot accurately be assessed, the Soviet Union and the People's Republic of China, concerned with the larger problems of detente and, in the Sino-Soviet case, preoccupied with one another, no doubt used their persuasive powers to lead Hanoi to agreement at the conference table. The Vietnam communists are not likely to forego their hopes for the future. In 1946 and again in 1964 they saw the South snatched from their grasp and they have fought too long and arduously to give up easily now. The current setting simply forces them to alter their style. A reunion of the two Vietnams under conditions that would satisfy both is difficult to conceive, and the only alternative is the maintenance of some level of combat.

In late 1968, a strategy debate among top DRV leaders reportedly centered on the question of continuing a big unit type of war or returning to the Maoist plan of protracted guerrilla warfare. The limited offensives during 1969 suggested a compromise strategy, as did a combination of medium-level unit and guerrilla attacks on Cambodia after the displacement of Prince Sihanouk in 1970. The initiation of a full-scale offensive by division-size units in early 1972 made it clear that big unit adherents were again determining strategy.

One payoff of this style was the establishment of control over sizable areas in hill country, effectively separating forces which might otherwise have cooperated against the North's troops. The ceasefire agreements in 1973 did not actually produce a halt in the fighting, although the larger engagements did decrease in number. The principal gain for Hanoi has been increased freedom of movement in the absence of US air elements. Each side maintains that the other is preparing a major strike. A major battle was fought in Chang Doc Province in December 1973.

STRATEGIC PROBLEMS

The NVA's basic weakness was its physical and military feebleness in comparison with the overwhelming wealth and power of its major enemy, the United States. However, the material aid from the USSR and Communist China, combined with US determination to avoid nuclear warfare and to avoid invasion of North Vietnam, enabled the DRV not only to survive, but to continue actively to fight for control of the southern half of Vietnam, which it regards as its own territory.

The DRV's dependence upon its two major communist allies has necessitated cautious and adroit diplomatic maneuvering between the feuding giants. It has shown remarkable skill in maintaining good relations with both Russia and China, and ensuring the continuance of their military, economic, and political support.

Recurrent food shortages—at times approaching famine—were alleviated by Soviet-funded rice imports, but lack of agricultural productivity remains a serious problem.

An acute shortage of new VC manpower has required the DRV to flesh out skeletonized VC guerrilla groups with its own soldiers. This is made difficult, however, by the Northerners' lack of familiarity with both the South and guerrilla fighting, and by the Southerners' traditional distrust of the Northerners. The South, on its part, is equally troubled by manpower problems.

MILITARY ASSISTANCE

The DRV has received heavy and continuing military support from the USSR and the PRC. Even before 1965, aid from the two Communist nations had totaled about $800 million, in conservative estimates, more than half coming from the Soviet Union. Since then Soviet aid has increased markedly and probably amounted to around $2.6 billion from 1966 through 1973. Aid agreements also exist with Czechoslovakia and East Germany. Besides weapons and military materials, technical aid has built or repaired many plants, and advisers have aided the DRV's power, engineering, mining and other industries. The number of Soviet military advisers is not available but surely exceeds 1,000. Until the Sino-Soviet feud intensified, much material traveled by rail across China, but in recent years, practically all has been delivered by ship to Haiphong. China has supplied some 30,000 engineer troops (with AA protection) for rail and road repair, and hospital and training facilities in China. Aid shipments, of weapons and some aircraft, amounted to an estimated $1.08 billion from 1966 through 1973.

ALLIANCES

The DRV is allied most closely with the Soviet Union and Communist China. There are agreements of friendship and mutual defense with other communist countries.

ARMY

Personnel: 500,000

Organization:
- 14 divisions (10,000-12,000 per division) plus support regiments
- 10 independent artillery regiments
- 3 independent armored regiments
- 20 independent infantry regiments
- 45-50 SAM battalions (SA-2 Guideline, 2 to 6 launchers per battalion)

Major Equipment Inventory:
- 175 medium tanks (65 T-34, 110 T-54)
- 300 light tanks (PT-76)
- 107mm, 122mm, and 140mm rocket launchers
- APCs (BTR-40, M-2, K-61)
- SU-76 and JSU-122 self-propelled guns
- various calibre guns and howitzers (75mm, 105mm, 122mm, 130mm and 152mm)
- 6,000 AAA pieces (100mm, 85mm, 57mm, 37mm—half are radar-directed; several thousand anti-aircraft machine guns; some are ZSU 57/2 self-propelled AA guns)
- SAMs (SA-2 Guideline, SA-3, SA-7)

Reserves: Unknown

NAVY

Personnel: 5,000

Major Units:
- 3 submarine chasers (SO-1 class, SC)
- 18 torpedo boats (12 P-4, 6 P-6, PT)
- 4 submarine chasers (Shanghai class, SC)
- 24 submarine chasers (Shanghai class, SC)
- 4 inshore minesweepers (MSI)
- 24 gunboats (PGM)
- 30 patrol boats (YP)
- 7 landing ships (LSM)
- 5 landing craft (LSSL)
- 100+ armed junks
- 10 auxiliaries

Major Naval Bases: Haiphong; Vinh

AIR FORCE

Personnel: 10,000

Organizationn:
- 1 light bomber squadron (Il-28)
- 6 interceptor squadrons (2 MiG-19, 4 MiG-21)
- 7 fighter/fighter-bomber squadrons (MiG-15/17, Su-7)

Major Aircraft Types:
- 185 combat aircraft
  - 100 MiG-15/17, Su-7 fighter-bombers (20 MiG-15, 70 MiG-17, 10 Su-7)
  - 40 MiG-21 interceptors (armed with Atoll AAMs)
  - 35 MiG-19 interceptors
  - 10 Il-28 light bombers
- 156 other aircraft
  - 89 transports (40 Il-14, 6 Il-12, 20 Li-2, 20 An-2, 3 An-24)
  - 25 trainer/support aircraft
  - 30 helicopters (Mi-1, Mi-4)
  - 12 heavy helicopters (Mi-6)

Major Air Bases: Gia Lam, Dien Bien Phu, Dong Hoi, Vinh, Hoa Lae

PARAMILITARY

The People's Armed Security Forces and the Frontier and Coastal Security Troops total an estimated 20,000.

An armed militia of some 425,000 for home defense is organized by regions.

VIETNAM, SOUTH
Vietnam Cong Hoa
Republic of Vietnam

POWER POTENTIAL STATISTICS

Area: 67,108 square miles
Population: 19,100,000
Total Active Armed Forces: 554,075 (includes regular forces only; 2.9% population)
Gross National Product: $4.2 billion ($220 per capita)
Annual Military Expenditures: $592 million (14.1% GNP)
Electric Power Output: 1.3 billion kwh
Merchant Fleet: 39 ships; 31,979 gross tons
Civil Air Fleet: 2 jet and 45 piston transports

DEFENSE STRUCTURE

Primary military authority rests with the President, who as head of state directly supervises the Minister of Defense and War Veterans, and is advised by a National Security Council. Administration of the armed forces is exercised by the Defense Minister. The Defense Ministry also directs the defense and pacification organizations and all military operations.

The Chairman of the Joint General Staff is subordinate to the Defense Minister. His chief of staff assists in directing the commanders of all Army units, as well as the staffs of the Air Force, Navy and Marine Corps. Deputy chiefs of staff supervise the general staff divisions and offices.

POLITICO-MILITARY POLICY

Since its formal proclamation on October 26, 1955, the basic goal of the Republic of Vietnam (RVN) has been to maintain its own territorial integrity and independence against the incessant efforts of southern Viet Cong (VC) insurgents, at the direction and with the aid of North Vietnam, to overthrow the Saigon government and unite the country under a communist regime.

Policy has concentrated on three aims: the unification and strengthening of a central government; the buildup of strong and self-sufficient armed forces; and the pacification of the predominantly rural countryside.

National military strategy long suffered from political dissension and turmoil directly and indirectly related to the ongoing conflict. The heavy increase in US economic and military aid and the growing Americanization of the war sustained governments during the first ten years of independence, despite numerous military coups. Since 1965, the government of General Thieu, now President, has maintained a relatively stable regime.

The various governments have recognized that an essential element of eventual success against the Viet Cong and the North Vietnamese must be to regain the support of the Vietnamese peasants and to guarantee their security against the guerrillas. The Rural Development (RD) program combines an emphasis on armed self-defense and government protection with a restoration of traditional village self-government (destroyed by the French during the colonial era).

The surprise Tet offensive of early 1968 shattered many of the village development programs and proved again that the national government could not provide security in many parts of the country. On the other hand, the offensive failed to achieve its announced aim to cause rebellion among the urban populations, defection of the Army of the Republic of Vietnam (ARVN), or the government's fall. Subsequent communist losses in May and September, and strong evidence of heavy VC casualties and dilution with impressed recruits, enabled the ARVN and self-defense forces to regain much lost ground and provide renewed hamlet and village security. US-North Vietnam peace negotiations began in May 1968, and were broadened to include South Vietnam and the VC in December.

By mid-1969 United States forces in Vietnam had grown to about 550,000 men. In June 1969 a US policy of gradual withdrawals, each reduction based on the strategic and tactical estimate of the then current situation, was started. It was January 1973 before the parties signed the Paris Agreement that embodied concrete actions to stop the fighting and begin movement toward the ultimate settlement of the dispute. The last US troops were withdrawn by the end of March, but fighting between North and South Vietnam continued, and in mid-1974 there is little evidence of willingness on either side to abandon armed force as the method of solution of their quarrel. In June 1973 a second ceasefire agreement was signed. The United States agreed to halt aerial reconnaissance over the North and to resume sweeping the mines laid earlier in northern waters. Bombing in the North had been halted in December 1972.

STRATEGIC PROBLEMS

The 1973 ceasefire in place produced a "leopard spot" phenomenon that ensured much local fighting. There have also been major attacks by both sides beyond the concept of the agreement. There seems little hope for any immediate reduction in activity; conversely, a final climactic military encounter does not seem likely. Both sides are gripped by the cost of maintaining forces far beyond their financial capabilities. South Vietnam has about half a million regular troops of all types, backed by an equal number of regional and popular forces and a large number of irregular type troops. They face, in the south, about 200,000 North Vietnam regulars and over 50,000 irregular troops. Both sides are well armed, but the balance in modern weapons favors the South.

The problem for the ARVN, as a result of American

withdrawal, has been far more than one of the expansion and accelerated training of combat forces. Logistical problems are formidable, resulting from the provision to ARVN of increased amounts of arms and equipment, much of it more sophisticated than the Vietnamese had been trained to operate or maintain. There is still a shortage of trained, experienced and resolute staff and leadership. There has been an overdependence on air support. The results of Vietnamization are still finally to be assessed in the ongoing operations.

At least until the beginning of the 1972 North Vietnamese offensive, the RD program has been making progress. However, the lack of a mutually supportive relationship between government and populace is still evident. Nevertheless, some progress toward a greater stability has been discernible, though slow.

Geographically, the country is open to direct attack not only from North Vietnam, but also from the western mountain and jungle vastnesses of Laos and Cambodia, which have been used as sanctuaries by both the Viet Cong and regular troops of the North Vietnam Army (NVA). South Vietnamese offensives, undertaken to reduce the usefulness of these sanctuaries, have been only partially successful.

MILITARY ASSISTANCE

Military assistance has come overwhelmingly from the United States, which by 1968 was spending some $2.5 billion a month on the entire war effort (or $30 billion a year). Between 1950 and 1972 total US military aid granted South Vietnam was announced as over $1.5 billion in addition to the expenses of the US's own commitment.

Thirty-seven other nations have contributed aid to South Vietnam, mainly nonmilitary assistance. Four nations, however, sent armed forces totalling some 70,000 men: South Korea – 50,000 in 2 infantry divisions and 1 marine brigade; Thailand – 12,000 in 1 infantry division and air units; Australia – 7,500 in 1 brigade group and air units; New Zealand – 600, including 1 artillery battery. Except for 38,000 in South Korean units, all were withdrawn by the end of 1971.

ALLIANCES

The extension of US military support to South Vietnam's government has been based upon the protocol of the SEATO treaty of September 1954 which designated the states of Cambodia and Laos and "the free territory under the jurisdiction of the State of Vietnam" to be protected by the Southeast Asia Treaty Organization. This was the basis whereby three other SEATO members – Australia, New Zealand, and Thailand – also had their military forces in South Vietnam.

South Vietnam is not a UN member, but has been admitted to all the specialized agencies. It is also a member of the Colombo Plan Council, the Afro-Asian Solidarity Conference, the Interparliamentary Union and a number of regional and world groups of an economic nature.

ARMY

Personnel: 450,000

Organization:
- 10 infantry divisions (approximately 12,000 per division)
- 1 airborne division (9 battalions)
- 3 independent infantry regiments
- 25 Ranger battalions
- 1 Special Forces Group
- 35 artillery battalions (105mm and 155mm howitzers)
- 6 independent armored cavalry regiments
    - 11 light tank squadrons (M-41, M-24, AMX-13)
    - 24 APC squadrons (M-59, M-113)
    - M-47 and M-48 medium tank battalions

Major Equipment Inventory:
- 500 medium tanks (M-47, M-48)
- 260 light tanks (M-41, M-24, AMX-13)
- 400 APCs (M-59, M-113)
- 275 armored cars (M-706 Commando and M-8 Greyhound)
- scout cars (M-3)
- 500 105mm and 155mm self-propelled howitzers and guns
- 1,000 light and medium artillery pieces (105mm, 155mm and 175mm howitzers)

NAVY

Personnel: 40,275 (not including Marines)

Major Units:
- 2 frigates (DER)
- 7 frigates (former US Coast Guard cutters)
- 1 submarine chaser (PC)
- 8 escorts (PCE)
- 22 gunboats (PGM)
- 8 landing ships, tank (LST)
- 7 landing ships, medium (LSM)
- 4 landing ships, support, large (LSSL)
- 5 landing ships, infantry, large (LSIL)
- 19 landing craft utility (LCU)
- 24 minesweeping launches (MLMS)
- 26 coast guard launches (CGC)
- 250+ landing craft, monitors, etc.

511 river patrol craft (PBR, PCF, YP)
500 auxiliary gunboats (junks)
6 oilers (AO)
165 auxiliaries

Naval Bases: Hue, Chu Lai, Qui Nhon, Cam Rahn Bay, Can Tho

MARINE CORPS

Personnel: 13,800

Organization:
8 battalions of infantry, plus support units, forming one division

AIR FORCE

Personnel: 50,000

Organization:
5 combat wings
- 8 fighter-bomber squadrons (F-5)
- 10 ground attack squadrons, jet, (A-37)
- 4 ground attack, piston squadrons (A-1)
- 3 gunship, ground attack squadrons (AC-47, AC-119)
- 8 transport squadrons (C-47, C-119, C-123, C-130)
- 8 light transport squadrons (Caribou, Beaver, U-17)
- 18 helicopter squadrons (CH-47, UH-1)
- 8 liaison squadrons (O-1)

Major Aircraft Types:
495 combat aircraft
- 126 F-5 fighter-bombers
- 224 A-37 jet ground attack aircraft
- 85 A-1 piston ground attack aircraft
- 60 gunships (20 AC-119, 40 AC-47)

1,110 other aircraft
- 172 transports, medium (45 C-47, 42 C-119, 53 C-123, 32 C-130)
- 180 transports, light (90 Caribou, 10 Beaver, 80 U-17)
- 678 helicopters (49 CH-47, 629 UH-1)
- 80 O-1 liaison aircraft

(Note: in addition to the above there are some 200 miscellaneous trainer and support aircraft)

Major Air Bases: Saigon (Tan Son Nhut), Nhatrang, Bien, Bienhoa, Binh Thuy, Dalat, Da Nang, Phan Rang, Pleiku, Cana

PARAMILITARY

Regional Forces: 285,000 (about 1,700 rifle companies controlled by provincial governors)
Popular Forces: 250,000 (7,500 platoons organized as light-armed militia)
National Police: about 20,000 (with light arms; some special units with helicopters and armored cars)
Civilian Irregular Defense Group: about 200,000 (engaged in counter-terror tactics and civic action in answer to Viet Cong infrastructure efforts and terror tactics)
People's Self Defense Forces: 1.5 million enlisted (500,000 trained, 300,000 armed). Goal is 2 million with 400,000 armed.

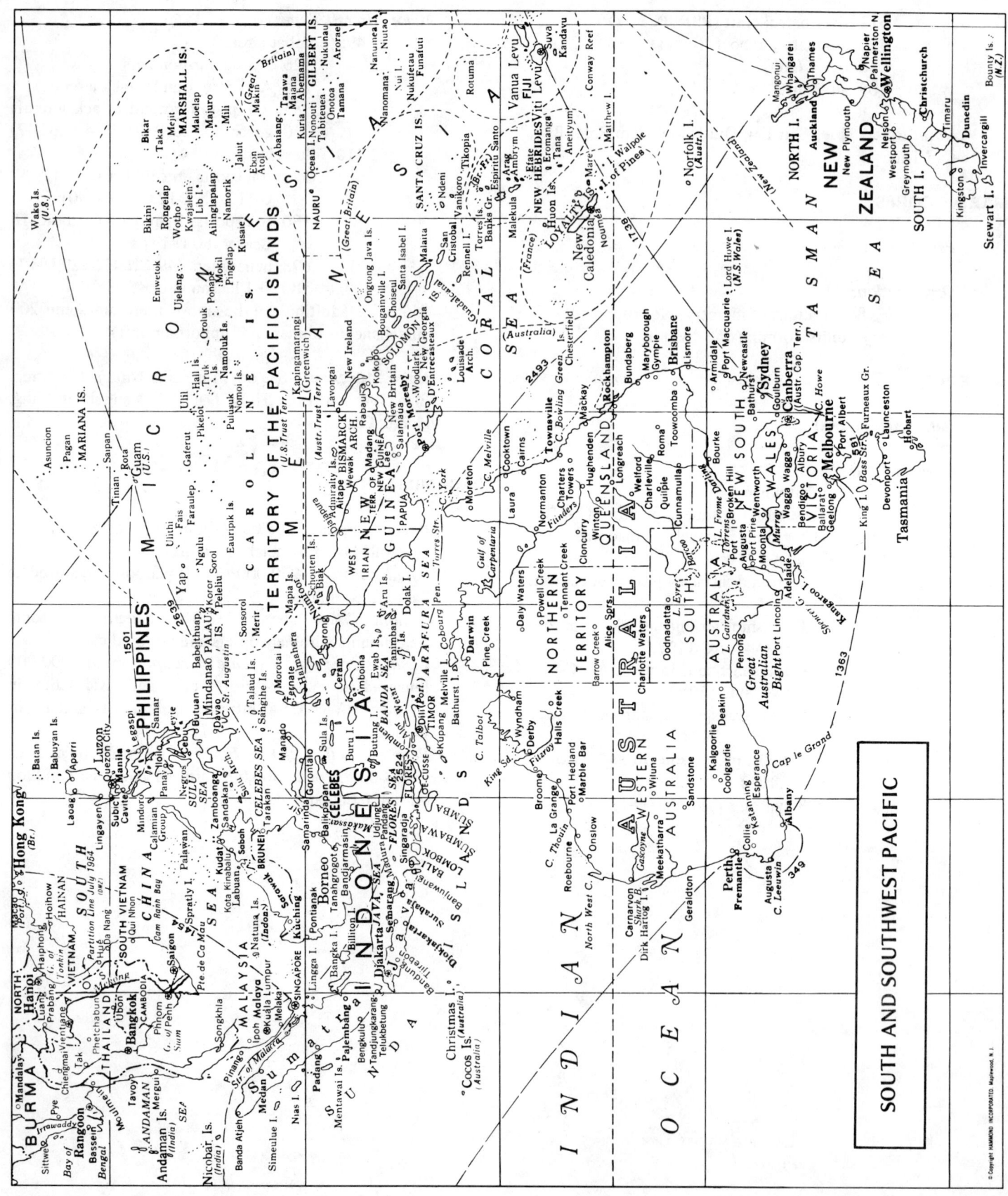

SOUTH AND SOUTHWEST PACIFIC

10

SOUTH AND SOUTHWEST PACIFIC

Regional Survey

MILITARY GEOGRAPHY

This region comprises the collections of archipelagos and great islands often known as Australasia. The principal nations of these archipelagos are the island continent of Australia, New Zealand, Indonesia, and the Philippines. To the north and east are a number of minor island groups with little military significance of their own, except as they provide bases from which larger powers can project military force across the reaches of the Pacific Ocean.

STRATEGIC SIGNIFICANCE

The Australasian archipelagos possess considerable natural wealth. Since these resources have been only partially developed, and since the populations are weak—either in numbers, or in technological development, or both—the region is vulnerable to penetration by more powerful nations. Efforts to accomplish such penetration have marked the history of the region for centuries; the most recent manifestations have been Japanese aggression in World War II, Soviet espionage and subversion in Australia, and Chinese Communist infiltration efforts in Indonesia since independence.

In the past, efforts to penetrate Australasia have been made only by powers with substantial maritime strength. The apparent ability of Communism to offset maritime weakness to some extent by means of ideological subversion suggests that Indonesia and the Philippines, at least, are more vulnerable to communist penetration than might have been expected in earlier, pre-nuclear eras when naked force could be exerted by nations possessing it without danger of precipitating conflicts elsewhere on the globe. Nevertheless, successful Indonesian resistance to Chinese Communist subversion in 1965, put down by a military coup, took place in a general climate of benevolent oversight by US Navy forces. Below the massive nuclear level, effective seapower is probably still the key to stability in the region.

ALLIANCES

There are two overlapping regional alliances which affect this region: The Southeast Asia Collective Defense Treaty (or Manila Pact, or SEATO) of September 1954 (see South and Southeast Asia Regional Survey) and the Australia, New Zealand, United States (ANZUS) Council Treaty, of August 1952, which had for its objective the preservation of peace in the Pacific.

The United States has a Mutual Defense Treaty with the Philippines, and in addition has bilateral mutual assistance agreements with the Philippines, Australia, and New Zealand.

RECENT INTRA-- AND EXTRA-REGIONAL CONFLICTS

The same kind of disorders and hostilities that have plagued South and Southeast Asia (q.v.) have also affected Indonesia and (to a lesser extent) the Philippines. A list of recent hostilities or crises involving the employment of armed forces is given below:

1963-1966	Sporadic Indonesian guerrilla attacks against Malaysia
1965	Military coup d'etat in Indonesia; massacre of Communists and sympathizers
1970	Moslem-Christian turbulence in Mindanao, Philippine Republic.

AUSTRALIA

The Commonwealth of Australia

POWER POTENTIAL STATISTICS
Area: 2,967,741 square miles
Population: 12,807,900
Total Active Armed Forces: 71,500 (0.56% population)
Gross National Product: $54.3 billion ($4,240 per capita)
Annual Military Expenditures: $1.96 billion (3.66% GNP)
Steel and Iron Production: 13.1 million metric tons
Fuel Production: Coal: 72.4 million metric tons
  Crude Oil: 15.4 million metric tons
  Refined Petroleum Products: 23.9 million metric tons
  Manufactured Gas: 1.5 billion cubic meters
Electric Power Output: 58 billion kwh
Merchant Fleet: 136 ships; 1,444,114 gross tons
Civil Air Fleet: 64 jet, 63 turboprop, 47 piston transports

336 ALMANAC OF WORLD MILITARY POWER

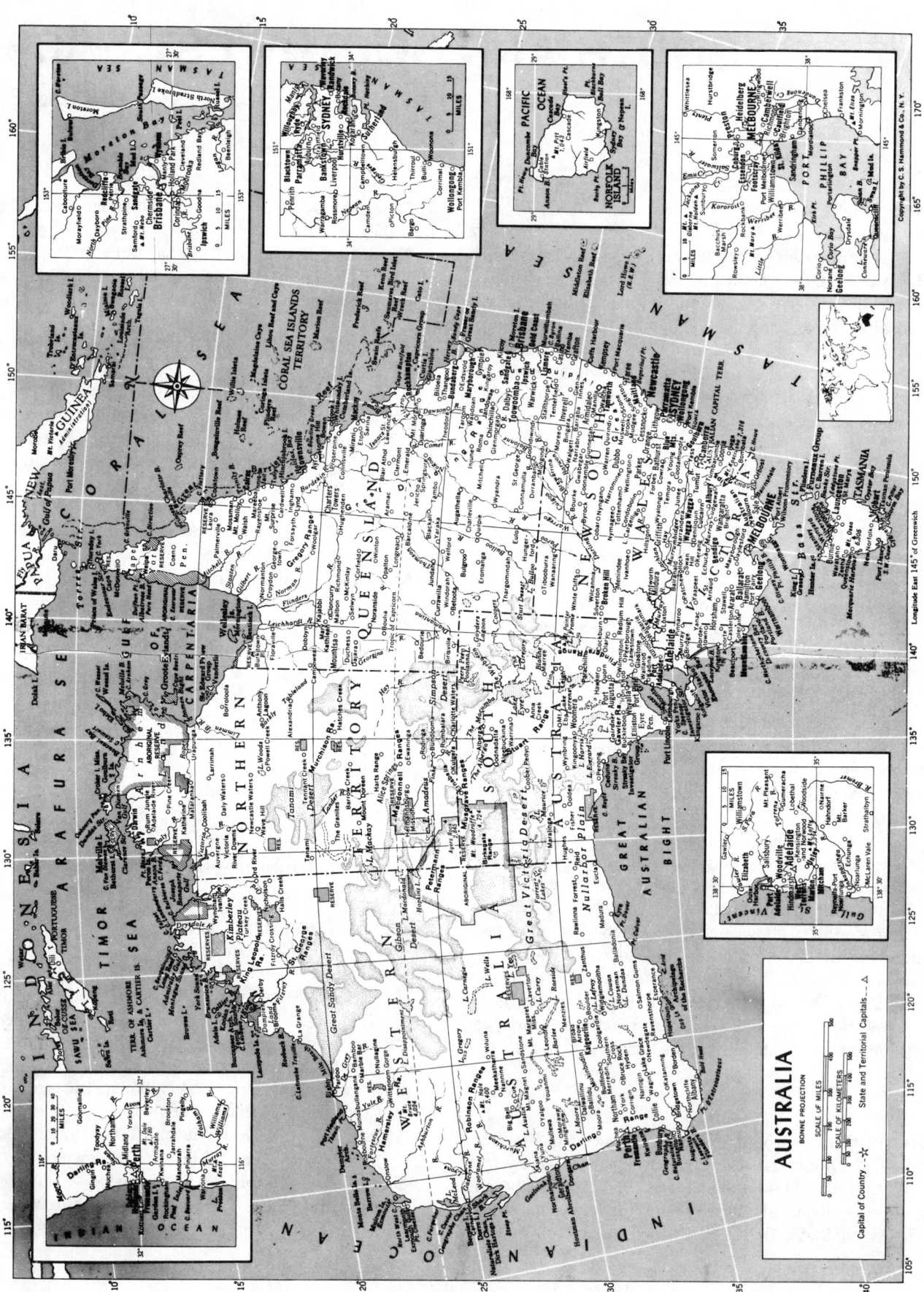

DEFENSE STRUCTURE

Nominally the Commander in Chief of the armed forces of the Commonwealth of Australia is the Governor General, representing the sovereign, who is also the sovereign of Great Britain. The Federal Government is parliamentary in form, with actual executive power—including that over the armed forces—vested in the Cabinet and the Prime Minister, who are responsible to Parliament. Principal responsibility within the Cabinet for the administration and control of the armed forces is exercised by the Minister of Defence. Each service is headed by a civilian Minister, but none of these is in the 12-member Cabinet. The Army, Navy and Air Force are administered, respectively, by the Military, Naval and Air Boards, each consisting of the Minister, the Chief of Staff, and four or five senior civilian officials and military officers. Joint operations are conducted by unified commands, and overall defense planning by a joint staff. Otherwise the three services remain separate.

POLITICO-MILITARY POLICY

In 1957 Australia made a fundamental decision to relate the organization and the equipping of its armed forces to United States patterns, which was a major shift from Australia's traditional military relationship with the United Kingdom. While this did not mean any loosening of Australia's Commonwealth ties, it did mean that Australia was realistically conforming to the changed pattern of power in the Pacific and Southeast Asia, where Britain was deliberately reducing its military commitments and responsibilities.

Australia supported the SEATO commitment to the defense of South Vietnam against Communist aggression. It sent troops to fight beside the Americans and South Vietnamese, while at the same time undertaking a civil program in South Vietnam coordinated with those of the Vietnamese and American governments. In 1971 the Australian troop contingent was withdrawn. A new Labor Party government stopped all participation in the Vietnam effort in 1972. This was one of several acts representing a new political orientation in Canberra.

The announced withdrawal of most United Kingdom forces from Southeast Asia by 1971 posed a difficult problem for Australia, with its limited population. However, the five-power pact of 1971 (see United Kingdom) has provided a solution that appears satisfactory to all concerned: Australia, Malaysia, New Zealand, Singapore, and the United Kingdom. Australia's contribution to the Australia-New Zealand-UK (ANZUK) Force consists of units of the three services, some on permanent station and some on rotation. With headquarters in Singapore, units serve also in Malaysia. In emergency, the bulk of the five power forces will come from Malaysia and Singapore. While insisting that the commitment to ANZUK remains firm, Australia's Labor Government has announced that it will withdraw its units from Singapore.

Several years after World War II Australia abandoned wartime conscription and returned to a policy of recruitment for the armed forces by voluntary enlistment. When this failed to provide adequate manpower, in 1965 Australia returned to a limited selective service system, in which selected young men over 20 serve for 18 months in the armed forces and three years in the reserve. Conscription was abolished again in 1972.

STRATEGIC PROBLEMS

In general, because of Australia's remoteness from the conflicts of Europe and Asia, combined with its insular geography, strategic problems have been relatively minor. However, the British decision to withdraw from Southeast Asia and the Indian Ocean, and the impact of modern weapons and transportation technologies, have caused Australia to become more directly concerned with affairs in Asia, and particularly Southeast Asia. Recently, for example, objection was registered to the US plan to improve the naval facility on Diego Garcia.

Australians are worried about the attraction that their large, rich, and sparsely-populated country has for the overpopulated nations of East and Southeast Asia. They are particularly concerned that Indonesia, having obtained West Irian (western New Guinea) from the Netherlands, may wish to extend further eastward to absorb the Australian dependencies in eastern New Guinea.

There are also possibly long-term strategic implications in the growing dependence of the Australian economy on trade with Japan.

The view is growing that any conflict involving Australia is less and less likely. This is accompanied by a new sense of separate identity and independence. ANZUS is increasingly seen as probably a necessary guarantee for the area, but one not likely to be invoked.

MILITARY ASSISTANCE

On a wholly cooperative basis, Australia exchanges students at military schools with the United Kingdom, New Zealand, Canada and the United States, and exchanges information with these nations within existing alliances. Otherwise, Australia is not the recipient of any formal military assistance.

Australia provided $40.6 million in military assistance to both Malaysia and Singapore between 1964 and 1969. This has been accomplished through training missions, by training in Australia, and by transfer of equipment.

ALLIANCES

Australia is a member of five major, overlapping, alliance systems. First, as a member of the Commonwealth, Australia maintains close military ties with the United Kingdom, New Zealand, and, to a lesser extent, with Canada and other

Commonwealth nations, and it is a member of the five-power pact (see above).

Second, Australia has had a bilateral mutual assistance treaty with the United States since 1951. Third, there have been formal and informal cooperative bilateral defense arrangements between Australia and New Zealand, aside from their Commonwealth relationship, since World War II. Fourth, these two bilateral relationships were linked together formally in the Australia-New Zealand-United States (ANZUS) Treaty of 1952. Finally, Australia is a member of the Southeast Asia Treaty Organization (SEATO), which was established in 1954.

ARMY

Personnel: 31,000 (includes about 2,500 Pacific Islands Regiment); proposed to be increased to 34,000

Organization:
- 6 infantry battalions
- 1 Pacific Islands Regiment (PIR; 2 battalions)
- 1 armoured regiment (tank)
- 1 cavalry regiment, plus 2 separate cavalry squadrons (mechanized)
- 1 Special Air Service regiment (air-mobile commandos)
- 3 field artillery regiments
- 1 medium artillery regiment
- 1 light AA regiment
- 1 aviation regiment
- 1 logistic support force

Deployment: logistic and administrative elements in ANZUK until 1975
- 1 battalion group in ANZUK
- 350 men, all ranks, detached to Papua, New Guinea, Defence Force

Major Equipment Inventory:
- 135 medium tanks (Centurion)
- 50 armored cars (Saladin)
- 265 scout cars (Ferret)
- 80 helicopters (Sioux, Kiowa)
- 25 light aircraft (Cessna 180, Pilatus Porter)
- 675 APCs (M-113)
- 235 105mm howitzers
- AAA pieces

Reserves: The Citizen Military Force, about 36,000 men, is available for rapid mobilization to form 25 additional battalions with supporting arms and services. There is also a 1,000 man Emergency Reserve Force. In addition, there are about 120,000 trained reservists.

NAVY

Personnel: 17,800

Major Units:
- 1 aircraft carrier (CVS; to ANZUK 3 months per year)
- 3 guided missile destroyers (with Tartar SAMs; DDG; several escort the carrier on rotation)
- 5 destroyers (DD; several escort the carrier on rotation)
- 9 destroyer escorts (6 with Seacat SAMS; DE)
- 1 destroyer tender (AD)
- 4 submarines (SS; 1 to ANZUK in rotation)
- 3 small patrol boats (SDB)
- 6 coastal minesweepers and minehunters (MSC)
- 20 patrol boats (PTF; 3 are unarmed)
- 13 auxiliaries and survey ships
- 12 landing ships, medium (LSM), assigned to Army
- 20 Skyhawk attack aircraft
- 14 S-2 Tracker ASW patrol aircraft
- 50 helicopters (including Wessex ASW helicopters and Wasp)
- 10 trainer/support aircraft (MB-236, Vampire, TA-4, A-4)

Equipment on Order: 10 Seaking helicopters

Major Naval Bases: Sydney, Nowra, Jervis, Freemantle

Reserves: There are 4,330 men in the Citizen Naval Forces and 1,075 in the Emergency Reserve. In addition, there are 65-70,000 trained reservists.

AIR FORCE

Personnel: 22,700

Organizationn:
- Operational Command (Headquarters, Sydney)
- Support Command (Headquarters, Melbourne)
  - 3 fighter squadrons (Mirage III)
  - 2 bomber squadrons (F-111)
  - 1 light bomber squadron (Canberra)
  - 2 maritime reconnaissance squadrons (P-2, P-3)
  - 5 transport squadrons (2 C-130, 2 Caribou, 1 special transport squadron, BAC-111)
  - 3 helicopter squadrons (UH-1, CH-47)
  - 1 SAM squadron (Bloodhound Mk 1)

Deployment:
- 2 fighter squadrons ANZUK Force (Mirage III)

Major Aircraft Types:
- 171 combat aircraft
  - 110 Mirage III fighters (Sidewinder AAM)
  - 24 F-111C bombers
  - 15 Canberra light bombers
  - 12 P-2 Neptune patrol bombers
  - 10 P-3 Orion maritime reconnaissance aircraft
- 289 other aircraft
  - 84 Aermacchi MB-326 trainers
  - 24 C-130 transports
  - 22 Caribou transports
  - 10 C-47 transports
  - 15 miscellaneous transports (2 BAC-111, 10 HS-748, 3 Mystere 20)
  - 47 helicopters UH-1
  - 87 trainer/support aircraft (CT-4, T-41, Winheel)
  - 12 CH-47 helicopters on order

Major Air Bases: Amberley, Point Cook, Canberra, Richmond, Tullarmarine, Woomera, Learmont, Laverton, Tindall, Darwin, East Sale, Williamtown, Fairbairn, Edinburgh, Townsville, Pearce

Reserves: There are 950 men in the Citizens Air Force available for prompt mobilization, plus about 580 in the Emergency Reserve. In addition, there are about 45,000 trained reservists.

INDONESIA
Republik Indonesia

POWER POTENTIAL STATISTICS

Area: 779,675 square miles
Population: 132,500,000
Total Active Armed Forces: 344,000 (includes 20,000 Police Mobile Brigade; 0.26% population)
Gross National Product: $11.9 billion ($90 per capita)
Annual Military Expenditures: $280 million (2.35% GNP)
Fuel Production: Coal: 173,000 metric tons
　Crude Oil: 53.8 million metric tons
　Refined Petroleum Products: 14.2 million metric tons
Electric Power Output: 1.87 billion kwh
Merchant Fleet: 513 ships; 618,589 gross tons
Civil Air Fleet: 15 jet, 32 turboprop, 4 piston transports

DEFENSE STRUCTURE

The President of the Republic of Indonesia is Minister of Defense and Security and the supreme commander of the armed forces. National defense policies are determined by the Cabinet Presidium in which the Minister of Defense and Security serves as chairman. The Chiefs of the Army, Navy, Air Force, and Police carry ministerial rank and advise and report to him.

POLITICO-MILITARY POLICY

In September and October 1965 leaders of the Army instituted a civic-action program throughout the country, partly to offset the disastrous effects of the economic and diplomatic policies of then-President Sukarno, and partly to insure Army influence at the village level to counter growing communist influence condoned or supported by Sukarno. The result was a confrontation between the President and the Army, which resulted in Sukarno's overthrow. This was followed by widespread massacres of known Communists and communist sympathizers. Since that time Indonesia's new rulers have established friendly relations with Malaysia, and they have stressed economic recovery and stability at home.

A selective service system and volunteers provide the manpower for the armed forces.

The Indonesian Army's relative lack of armor reflects both a doctrine that emphasizes guerrilla warfare and Indonesia's terrain, which is illsuited to heavy vehicles.

STRATEGIC PROBLEMS

The present military government still faces serious internal security problems in addition to massive economic troubles. Hard-core Communists remain in various parts of the republic, notably in east Java, and Army operations against communist guerrillas continue. An anti-Indonesian rebel movement on West Irian has emerged. Other dissident ethnic and religious factions continue to pose a potential threat. The student groups, which initially supported the military government and played a major role in the Army takeover are restless with the slow pace of progress. Since Indonesia is a major producer of petroleum, the energy crisis may produce a net advantage and reduce the economic ailments of the nation.

That there is still turbulence within Indonesia was demonstrated by a violent and unfriendly reception for the Prime Minister of Japan when he visited in January 1974. President Suharto was so concerned that he personally assumed command of the state security agency and dismissed four officials.

MILITARY ASSISTANCE

Between 1958 and 1965 Indonesia received some $1.2 billion in Sovet and East European military aid. The Navy and Air Force are still almost entirely equipped with Soviet craft, but much of this equipment has reached the end of its usefulness. An unknown, but substantial, number of Indonesian officers has been trained in the Soviet Union. Until 1965 a Soviet military technical mission of at least 400 experts was stationed in Indonesia. Since the October 1965 coup no new weapons aid has been provided, although Indonesia has been allowed to buy limited quantities of spare parts.

The United States in 1967 resumed a limited military aid program, which had been suspended in early 1965 over displeasure with former President Sukarno's "Crush Malaysia" policy. US military aid has totalled $98.4 million from 1950 through 1972.

ALLIANCES

Indonesia is a member of the UN and, except for military assistance agreements with the US and USSR, is a member of no military alliance or regional grouping.

ARMY

Personnel: 250,000
Organization:
    3 inter-regional commands (Sumatra, Kalimantan, East Indonesia)
    1 Strategic Reserve Command
    17 regional commands
        15 infantry brigades (organized into about 100 infantry battalions)
        4 mixed paratroop-infantry brigades (in Strategic Reserve Command)
        8 armored battalions
        1 paracommando regiment

Major Equipment Inventory:
    light tanks (PT-76 and AMX-13)
    armored cars (Saladin)
    scout car (Ferret)
    APCs (Saracen and BTR-152)
    light and medium artillery pieces
    AAA pieces (including Soviet radar-directed 57mm guns)
    helicopters (Alouette II)

NAVY

Personnel: 25,000 Navy; 14,000 Marine Corps (Korps Kommando—KKO)

Major Units: (A large number of these units are not operational)
- 2 Marine brigades
- 10 submarines (W class; SS)
- 3 destroyers (Skory class; DD)
- 10 frigates (DE)
- 18 submarine chasers (14 Kronstadt class; 4 ex-US PC)
- 6 fleet minesweepers (T-43 class; MSF)
- 20 coastal minesweepers (MSC)
- 21 torpedo boats (PT)
- 12 guided missile patrol boats (Komar class with Styx SSM; PTFG)
- 21 patrol gunboats (PGM)
- 34 patrol boats (YP/HDML)
- 8 landing ships, tank (LST)
- 1 landing craft, medium (LCM)
- 3 landing craft, infantry (LCI)
- 6 landing craft, utility (LCU)
- 3 submarine support ships (AS)
- 48 patrol craft (YP)
- 27 support ships and auxiliaries
- 6 Gannet AEW aircraft
- miscellaneous trainer/support aircraft

Major Naval Bases: Surabaja, Kemajaran (Djakarta), Gorontalo

AIR FORCE

Personnel: 35,000

Organization:
- 3 bomber squadrons (Tu-16, Il-28, B-26)
- 4 fighter squadrons (MiG-15/17, Sabre)
- 1 fighter-interceptor squadron (MiG-21)
- 1 fighter-bomber squadron (F-51)
- 1 ASW squadron (PBY, HU-16)
- 2 transport squadrons (An-12, C-130, C-47, Il-14)
- 3 helicopter squadrons (Mi-4, Mi-6, Alouette II, Iroquois)

Major Aircraft Types:*
- 117 combat aircraft
  - 37 bombers (22 Tu-16, 10 Il-28, 5 B-26)
  - 41 fighters (25 MiG-15/17, 16 Sabre)
  - 15 MiG-21 fighter-interceptors
  - 19 F-51 fighter-bombers
  - 5 ASW aircraft (PBY, HU-16)
- 293 other aircraft
  - 32 medium transports (6 An-12, 10 C-130, 6 C-47, 10 Il-14)
  - 31 helicopters (Mi-4, Mi-6, Alouette II, Iroquois)
  - 230 light transport, trainer, support aircraft (C-140, Otter, Skyvan, Twin Pioneer, T-33, T-34, U-17, Wilga)

Missiles: ASM: Kennel; AAM: Atoll; SAM: Guideline

Major Air Bases: Medan, Palembang, Djakarta, Husein (Bandung), Iswahjudi, Denpasar, Semerang, Lombok, Balikpapan, Amboina

PARAMILITARY

The Indonesian National Police of 110,000 is a separate service under the Minister of Defense. The 20,000-man Mobile Brigade supplements the Army's internal security mission and is trained in amphibious and airborne operations. The Sea Police, a paranaval force, assists the Navy in port and close inshore security missions. In time of martial law the police is under operational control of the Army. The police force is organized into 11 territorial units and the Djakarta metropolitan area. There is also a militia of about 100,000.

NEW ZEALAND

POWER POTENTIAL STATISTICS

Area: 103,736 square miles
Population: 2,960,000 (including island dependencies)
Total Active Armed Forces: 12,789 (0.43% population)
Gross National Product: $10.52 billion ($3,554 per capita)
Annual Military Expenditures: $190.8 million (1.81% GNP)
Fuel Production: Coal: 2.18 million metric tons
   Manufactured Gas: 59.7 million cubic meters
Electric Power Output: 17.3 billion kwh
Merchant Fleet: 54 ships; 182,124 gross tons
Civil Air Fleet: 11 jet, 23 turboprop, 65 piston transports

DEFENSE STRUCTURE

Nominally the Commander in Chief of the armed forces of New Zealand is the Governor General, who is the representative of the Queen in New Zealand. In New Zealand's parliamentary government, however, executive power—including authority over the armed forces—is vested in the Prime Minister and the Cabinet, who are responsible to Parliament. Principal responsibility for defense matters within the Cabinet rests with the Minister of Defence, who presides over the Ministry of Defence and who is chairman of the

---

*Many of these aircraft are in storage and many of the Soviet types are grounded due to lack of spare parts.

342 ALMANAC OF WORLD MILITARY POWER

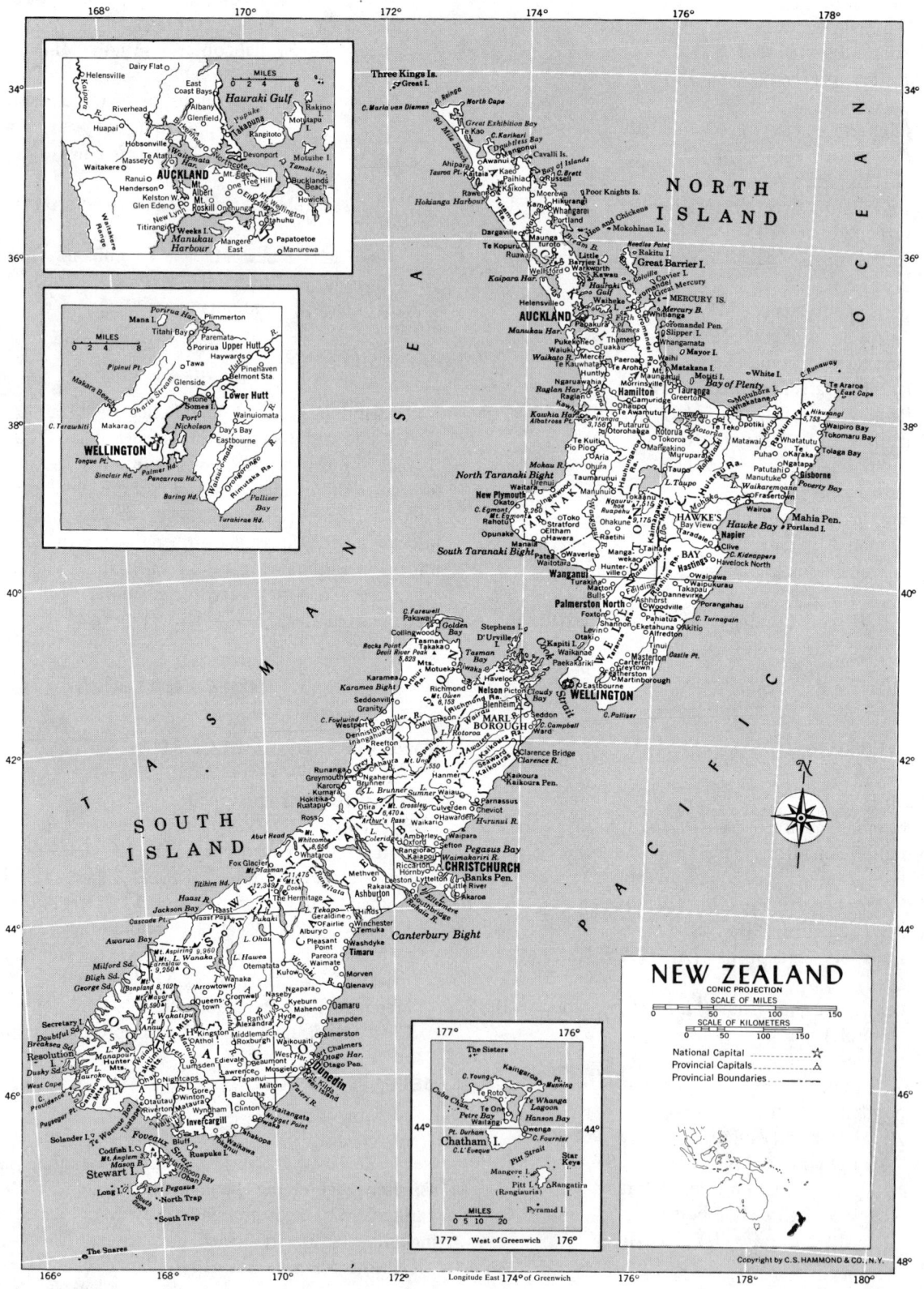

Defence Council, which directs the administration and command of the armed forces. The Defence Council also comprises the Chief of Defence Staff, who is the principal military adviser to the Minister, the Secretary of Defence, who is the permanent head of the Ministry of Defence and principal civilian adviser to the Minister, and the Chiefs of the General (Army), Navy and Air Staffs.

POLITICO-MILITARY POLICY

New Zealand seeks as far as possible to maintain independent means of self defense. The defense relationship with the United States, which finds formal expression in the ANZUS Treaty, is still a significant factor in New Zealand's defense policy, but less emphasis is placed on collective security than formerly. There are well developed defense ties with Australia which reflect shared strategic interests as well as a close identity of national character and outlook.

With the approval of the governments of Malaysia and Singapore, New Zealand, along with Britain, currently stations military forces in Singapore, under the Five Power Defence Arrangements. The purpose of this presence is to promote the stability and security of the South East Asian region. Mutually beneficial cooperation with regional neighbors in the field of defense training is being expanded as a means of strengthening friendly relations with the countries involved.

In the absence of any direct defense threat, New Zealand is placing increasing stress on the potential of its armed forces to carry out civilian aid activities, both within New Zealand and as part of aid programs to developing nations. However, such tasks are not performed at the expense of military capabilities.

New Zealand's defense forces are composed of regular servicemen, backed by an Army Territorial Force and smaller Air Force and Naval reserves. All military service is on a voluntary basis.

STRATEGIC PROBLEMS

New Zealand's strategic problems are related to its strategic advantages. New Zealand is a small country situated a considerable distance from any potential enemy. But on the other hand its remoteness, its lack of an industrial base, and its dependence on trade, create a heavy reliance on long maritime communication routes, which could be difficult to defend against persistent attack.

MILITARY ASSISTANCE

On a wholly cooperative basis, New Zealand exchanges students at military schools with the United Kingdom, Australia, and the United States, and exchanges information with these nations within existing alliances. Otherwise, New Zealand is not the recipient of any formal foreign military assistance.

ALLIANCES

New Zealand maintains military ties which do not form part of any formal military alliance with a number of Commonwealth nations. The two formal treaties of which New Zealand is a member are the Australian-New Zealand-United States (ANZUS) Treaty of 1952, and the South East Asia Treaty Organization (SEATO), established in 1954.

ARMY

Personnel: 5,600

Organization:
    1 brigade group (operational units plus cadre)
    1 reserve brigade group (mostly cadre)

Deployment:
    1 infantry battalion (light) in Singapore

Major Equipment Inventory:
    10 light tanks (M-41)
    9 scout cars (Ferret)
    59 APCs (M-113)
    28 howitzers (105mm)
    8 field guns (5.5 in.)
    12 field guns, 25-pounder

Reserves: The active Territorial Force numbers 4,247 and is available for rapid mobilization to fill out the Regular Army units

NAVY

Personnel: 2,900

Major Units:
    4 guided missile frigates (with Seacat SAMs, 2 Leander, 2 type 12 DEG)
    8 patrol craft (YP)
    2 training ships (ex-minesweeper MSF)
    1 survey ship (AGS)
    1 oceanographic survey ship (AGOR)
    2 auxiliaries
    3 helicopters (Wasp)
    5 trainer/support aircraft (including Vampire T-55)

Deployment:
    1 escort to Singapore under ANZUK

Major Naval Base: Auckland

Reserves: There are about 1,000 naval reservists operating five patrol craft.

AIR FORCE

Personnel: 4,222

Organization:
    Air Staff in Defence Headquarters
    1 Operations Group
    1 Training Group
    1 ground attack squadron (A-4)
    1 maritime patrol squadron (P-3)
    5 transport squadrons (C-130, Bristol Mk 31, C-47)

Major Aircraft Types:
    19 combat aircraft
        14 A-4 attack aircraft
        5 P-3 maritime reconnaissance aircraft
    89+ other aircraft
        20 transports (5 C-130, 9 Bristol Mk 31, 6 C-47)
        44 trainers (10 Strikemaster, 14 Devon, 16 Harvard, 4 Airtourer)
        25 helicopters (12 Sioux, 13 Iroquois)

Deployment: One transport squadron, No. 41 Squadron, is permanently based in Singapore as part of the RNZAF's contribution to the ANZUK Force. It is equipped with Bristol Freighter transport aircraft and Iroquois helicopters. No. 75 Squadron (A4K Skyhawks) based in New Zealand also forms part of this contribution and makes periodic deployments in the area.

Major Air Bases: Ohakea, Hobsonville, Wigram, Whenupai, Woodbourne

PHILIPPINES

Republika ng Pilipinas
Republic of the Philippines

POWER POTENTIAL STATISTICS

Area: 115,800 square miles
Population: 40,000,000
Total Active Armed Forces: 98,000 (including Constabulary; 0.25% population)
Gross National Product: $8.4 billion ($210 per capita)
Annual Military Expenditures: $97.5 million (1.16% GNP)
Iron Production: 2.1 million metric tons
Electric Power Output: 8.2 billion kwh
Merchant Fleet: 318 ships; 945,508 gross tons
Civil Air Fleet: 6 jet, 27 turboprop, and 13 piston transports

DEFENSE STRUCTURE

The Prime Minister of the Republic of the Philippines is the Commander in Chief of the Armed Forces of the Philippines (AFP) and as such has the sole power of employing them. He exercises this responsibility through the Secretary of National Defense. Within the Department, the senior military officer is the Chief of Staff of the Armed Forces, exercising military command functions over the major services.

POLITICO-MILITARY POLICIES

Since its independence in 1946 the Philippine Republic has relied almost exclusively upon the United States for external security, and has used its armed forces essentially for internal security purposes. Philippine officials have begun to discuss the establishment of formal relations with the Soviet Union and the PRC. This is part of a continuing search for the visible independence of Manila.

The strength of the armed forces is maintained by conscription, which is extremely selective, with only a small percent of the available manpower being drafted each year. Currently drafts are larger because of the situation in the south.

STRATEGIC PROBLEMS

Between 1946 and 1950 the communist-inspired Hukbalahap insurgency came close to destroying the republic. Then, between 1952 and 1954, under the leadership of Secretary of National Defense Ramon Magsaysay, the insurgency was almost eliminated by a combination of force and clemency. In recent years, however, the insurgency has revived. It is small, having no more than a few hundred armed militants. Of the three insurgent groups, the NPA of the Maoist Philippine Communist Party (CPP) overshadows both the Bagong Hukbong Mapagpalaya ng Bayan (BHMB) of the Traditional Communist Party and the original Hukbong Mapagpalaya ng Bayan (HMB) in the field of insurgency.

The imposition of martial law has dealt a severe blow to the local communist movement, but it continues to pose the main threat to Philippine national security.

Another troubled area is Mindanao, where Moslem secessionist rebels staged a series of well-planned and coordinated offensives in March 1973. The Moslem Revolutionary Forces (MRF), a rebel force composed of Moslem and Christian armed groups, attacked AFP troops in Lebak, Cotabato, on 1 March, precipitating attacks in the provinces of Lanao del Norte, Lanao del Sur, Sulu, Zamboanga del Norte, Zamboanga del Sur, and the island city of Basilan. Massive counteroffensive operations by the AFP seem to have calmed the area. At present there are 35,000 troops there.

Externally the Philippine Republic has a latent dispute with neighboring Malaysia over the ownership of the state of Sabah,

in northeastern Borneo. Malaysia now exercises sovereignty over Sabah, having inherited the 29,000 square mile region from Great Britain. The Philippines claims that Britain never legally owned Sabah, which was the territory of the Sultan of Sulu, whose island domain is now part of the Philippines. Neither side is likely to go to war over the dispute, and diplomatic relations, once severed, were resumed in December 1969 with agreement that the Sabah question be held in abeyance for the time being. The dispute could, nevertheless, be exploited by powers seeking to disrupt Southeast Asia and Australasia.

MILITARY ASSISTANCE

Since 1946 the United States has provided about $464.5 million in military assistance to its former dependency. In addition, the United States has given substantial economic aid and some $700 million in war rehabilitation grants and war damage claims. A US Military Advisory Group has provided extensive advice and assistance. This was particularly useful during the Hukbalahap insurgency. To bolster the defenses of the Philippines, three military agreements were entered into with the United States: (1) the Military Bases Agreement which gave the United States a 99-year lease over certain military, air, and naval bases in the Philippines; (2) Military Assistance Agreement wherein the US pledged to provide military assistance to the Philippines; and (3) the Mutual Defense Treaty in which the Republic of the Philippines and the United States pledged to assist each other in case of an armed attack against either or both of them by a foreign aggressor. By a memorandum signed 12 October 1959, however, the 99-year lease has been shortened to 25 years. Diplomatic negotiations are in process on the revision of the other military treaties.

Under the terms awarding Philippine independence, the United States retained a number of military bases in the archipelago, the most important being at Clark Field and Subic Bay and scattered facilities in the Southern Islands. With some modifications, these terms were confirmed by a Mutual Defense Treaty with the United States in 1952. However, the existence of these bases has aroused considerable resentment, despite the fact that sovereignty is recognized as joint, and continues to be a major political issue in the republic.

ALLIANCES

In addition to the alliance with the United States, the Philippines is an active member of the Southeast Asia Treaty Organization. Strongly opposed to the extension of communist influence in Southeast Asia and Australasia, the Philippines, as a member of SEATO, supported the American presence in South Vietnam and contributed a non-combat Philippine Civil Action Group of 2,000 men to assist in rehabilitation and community development.

ARMY

Personnel: 33,000

Organization:
- 2 infantry divisions
- 5 infantry brigades (separate)
- 1 artillery group
- 13 engineer construction battalions
- combat service support forces

Major Equipment Inventory:
- medium tanks (M-4)
- light tanks (M-24, M-41)
- half tracks (M-3)
- APCs (M-113)
- light and medium artillery pieces
- 20 light aircraft
- 1 SAM battalion (Hawk)

Reserves: There is an organized and trained reserve force of approximately one million. The existence of training division cadres greatly facilitates mobilization capability.

NAVY

Personnel: 16,000

Organization:
- 1 marine brigade
- 1 mine force
- 1 anti-submarine force
- 1 service force
- 2 naval construction battalions
- Coast Guard
- support forces

Major Units:
- 1 destroyer escort (DE)
- 2 escorts (converted fleet minesweepers; MSF)
- 10 patrol craft/escorts (PC; PCE)
- 2 coastal minesweepers (MSC)
- 3 command ships
- 9 patrol gunboats (PGM)
- 2 submarine chasers (PCS)
- 4 hydrofoil patrol craft (PCH)
- 6 landing ships (LST and LSM)
- 5 submarine chasers (SC)
- 6 patrol boats (PCF)
- 11 auxiliaries
- 3 helicopters

Major Naval Base: Sangley Point

AIR FORCE

Personnel: 15,000

Organization:
- 1 fighter wing
  - 2 day fighter squadrons (F-86)
  - 1 fighter-bomber squadron (F-5)
  - 1 fighter interceptor squadron, all weather (F-86)
- 2 airlift wings
  - 5 troop carrier squadrons
  - 1 liaison squadron
  - 1 COIN squadron
  - 1 air rescue squadron
  - 1 special mission squadron
  - 2 aviation engineer squadrons
  - support forces

Major Aircraft Types:
- 72 combat aircraft
  - 35 F-86 day fighters
  - 22 F-5 fighter-bombers
  - 15 F-86 all weather interceptors
- 211 other aircraft
  - 31 transports (4 C-130, 16 C-123, 11 C-47)
  - 8 other transports (F-27, HU-16, YS-11)
  - 142 training and utility (T-28, T-34, T-33, SF-260)
  - 30 helicopters (FH-1110, UH-1, H-34)

Major Air Bases: Clark AFB (US), Angeles, Pampanga; Basa AB, Florida Blanca, Fermando AB, Lipa, Batangas; Sangley Pt, Cavite; Mactan AB, Lapu City; Edwin Andrew AB, Zamboanga City; Nichols AB, Manila.

PARAMILITARY

The Philippine Constabulary, approximately 34,000 strong, is an efficient internal security organization. It is organized in 68 Provincial Commands and 8 Combat Battalions, with Combat and Service Support Units.

Other Paramilitary Forces include 57,000 Civilian Home Defense Forces, and 37,000 Armed Security Forces.

GLOSSARY

AAA. Anti-aircraft artillery (20mm to 130mm guns).

AAM. Air-to-air missile; guided or self-homing, rocket-propelled missile fired from one aircraft against another.

A-1, Skyraider (formerly AD). US, Douglas; single engine piston attack aircraft; first in service 1945; over 3,200 built; 10,000 pounds external armament; maximum speed 365 mph; maximum range 3,000 miles.

A-3, Skywarrior (formerly A3D), USAF designation B-66 (Destroyer). US, Douglas; carrier-based, twin engine jet, reconnaissance and light bomber; operational from 1956; 12,000 pounds of armament; maximum speed 610 mph; ceiling 41,000 feet; tactical radius 1,000 miles.

A-4, Skyhawk (formerly A4D). US, McDonnell-Douglas; originally designed as a carrier-based, single engine jet, single-seat, lightweight attack bomber; operational from 1956; still in production (over 2,500 built); maximum speed 676 mph; range with external tanks over 2,000 miles; 10,000 pounds of conventional or nuclear weapons carried on one center and four underwing attachment points; in service with US Navy and Marines, Argentina, Australia, Israel, and New Zealand.

A-5, Vigilante (formerly A3J). US, North American-Rockwell; carrier-based, twin engine jet, reconnaissance/attack bomber; maximum speed Mach 2.1; ceiling 70,000 feet; range 2,650 miles; can carry a combination of conventional and nuclear weapons on external attachment points; operational from 1960. RA-5C is multi-sensor reconnaissance version.

A-6, Intruder (formerly A2F). US, Grumman; carrier-based, twin engine jet, low-level attack bomber; all-weather capability; operational from 1963; maximum speed 685 mph; ceiling 41,000 feet; maximum range 2,800 miles; 18,000 pounds of conventional or nuclear weapons carried on five attachment points. EA-6B is an electronic intelligence and countermeasures version which retains some strike capability. KA-6 is a tanker version.

A-7, Corsair II. US, Ling-Temco-Vought; carrier-based, single engine jet, light attack bomber; operational from 1966; maximum speed 700 mph; combat radius 700 miles; 15,000 pounds of conventional or nuclear weapons can be carried on six attachment points. A-7A/B/E are Navy versions; A-7D is Air Force version.

A-32, Lansen. Sweden, Saab; single seat, single engine jet; attack version of Lansen (Lance) fighter-interceptor.

A-37. See T-37.

A-60 (Saab 105). Sweden, Saab; two-place, twin engine jet, trainer/utility aircraft; operational from 1965; can carry 1,500 pounds of armament; maximum speed 450 mph; ceiling 40,000 feet; range 850-1,000 miles.

A-106. Italy, Agusta; single-seat, single-engine helicopter designed for ASW operations; carries two torpedoes and equipment for contact identification; maximum speed, 110 mph; maximum range (with external tanks), 460 miles.

A-109, Hirundo. Italy, Agusta; twin engine, 8-seat high performance general purpose (turboshaft engine) helicopter; maximum speed 172 mph; service ceiling 17,400 feet; one engine 8,850 feet; maximum range, sea level 388 miles; 6,560 feet, 457 miles.

AB-47. Italy, Agusta-Bell; license-built version of Bell 47 (q.v.).

AB-204. Italy, Agusta-Bell; license-built version of UH-1 (q.v.).

AB-205. Italy, Agusta-Bell; license-built version of UH-1D/UH-1H; see UH-1.

AB-206. See Jet Ranger.

ABBOT (FV433). Britain, Vickers; operational from 1965; self-propelled 105mm gun, 1 howitzer, with full-traversing turret; also carries one 7.62mm machine gun; crew of four; weight 19 tons; maximum speed (road) 30 mph; range (road) 300 miles.

ABM. Anti-ballistic missile.

AC-47. Gunship version of C-47.

AC-119. US, Fairchild-Hiller; armed gunship conversion of C-119 (q.v.); equipped with Vulcan cannons and 7.2mm mini-guns and various lights, infra-red sensors, and light-intensifying equipment for night attacks; powered by two piston and two jet engines.

AC-130. US, Lockheed; armed gunship conversion of C-130 (q.v.); equipped approximately the same as AC-119 (above), but with larger overall number of guns.

AD. US designation for a destroyer tender.

AEC. Mk.3 armored cars.

ADC/NORAD. Air Defense Command/North American Air Defense (Command).

AERO COMMANDER (also designated L-26 or U-4). US; twin-engine piston, light transport; 230 mph cruising speed.

AGS. US designation for a survey ship.

AH-1, Huey Cobra. US, modification as gunship; pilot sits back of gunner in tandem; maximum speed 219 mph; various combinations of armament; 40mm grenade launcher; 7.62 mini-gun in nose; rocket and machine gun pods on stub wings.

AIM-9. See SIDEWINDER.

AIM-47A. US, Hughes; AAM; 12 feet long; range 40 nautical miles; speed Mach 5; 800 were ordered for F-12A which never entered series production; advanced infra-red and pulsed radar homing.

AIRTOURER. New Zealand, Aero Engine Services Limited; two-seat, single engine piston light trainer; maximum speed 164 mph; service ceiling 18,000 feet; range 670 miles.

AJ-37. See VIGGEN.

AJAX. See NIKE.

AKA. US designation for attack cargo ship.

AKL. US designation for a light naval cargo ship.

AL-60, Conestoga. Italy/Mexico, Lockheed Associates single engine, six-seat piston powered light utility transport; maximum speed 156 mph; 645 miles.

ALBATROSS (HU-16). US, Grumman; twin engine piston utility amphibian; operational from 1949; over 450 built; crew of five, 10 to 22 passengers; maximum speed 235 mph; ceiling 21,000 feet; range 2,800 miles.

ALIZE (Br 1050). France, Breguet; carrier-based, three-place, single engine turboprop ASW aircraft; operational from 1959; 87 built; 2,000 total pounds of armament carried internally and externally; maximum speed 285 mph; ceiling 26,000 feet; range 1,500 miles.

ALKALI (NATO codename). Soviet Union; AAM radar-guided, passive homing, solid fuel rocket motor, carried on MiG-17, MiG-19, and Su-9.

ALOUETTE. France, Aerospatiale; light helicopter; II model, nearly 1,300 sold from 1955; 4 passengers; 530-shp turbine; maximum speed 115 mph; ceiling 7,000 feet; maximum range 330 miles. III model; built from 1959 through present; 6 passengers; may be armed with combination of light and heavy machine guns and rockets; 870-shp turbine; maximum speed 131 mph; ceiling 19,650 feet; range (with 6 passengers) 190 miles; see also SA-315.

AM-3C. Italy, Aeritalia/Aermacchi; single engine, three-seat, piston-powered light armed trainer aircraft; maximum speed 173 mph; range 615 miles; armament two 7.62 machine gun pods.

AML-60. France; armored car for reconnaissance, convoy protection, and counterinsurgency operations; crew of 3; 5 tons; 55 mph; range 400 miles; 60mm mortar and 7.5mm machine guns.

AML-90. France; armored car; same as four-wheeled AML-60, but with 90mm gun.

AMX-13. France; light tank; 14.8 tons; 75mm gun; crew of 3; latest models also carry four SS-11 antitank guided missiles; operational since 1952.

AMX-30. France; medium tank; 32.5 tons; 105mm gun; deep fording capability; 800 hp; 250-mile range; co-axial 7.62mm machine gun; 12.7mm AA machine gun; 40 mph.

AMX-105. France; self-propelled 105mm howitzer; two versions—one with howitzer mounted in fully traversing turret; both versions mounted on AMX-13 chassis; 16 to 16.5 tons; howitzer range 15,000 to 16,000 yards.

AMX-155. France; self-propelled 155mm howitzer mounted on modified AMX-13 chassis; howitzer range over 20,000 meters.

AMX-VTT. France; armored personnel carrier; 12 troops and crew of 2; 14 tons; AMX-13 chassis.

AN. US designation for an ASW net-laying ship.

AN-2 (NATO codename Colt). Soviet Union, Antonov; single engine piston utility bi-plane; operational from 1947; over 5,000 built; maximum speed 160 mph; ceiling 16,000 feet; range 560 miles; 10-14 passengers.

An-12 (NATO codename Cub). Soviet Union, Antonov; heavy cargo plane; four engine 4,000-hp turboprops; 44,000-pound payload; maximum cruising speed 370 mph; range with half payload 2,000 miles; 100 passengers; operational from 1959.

An-14 (NATO codename Clod). Soviet Union; twin engine, six-seat, piston powered light transport; maximum cruising speed 118 mph; range 290 miles. A later fifteen passenger turboprop model AN-14M appeared in 1972.

An-22 (NATO codename Cock). Soviet Union, Antonov; ultra-heavy cargo plane; four engine 15,000-hp turboprops; maximum payload 221,443 pounds; maximum speed 460 mph; maximum range 6,800 miles; 300-350 passengers; operational from mid-1967.

An-24/An-26 (NATO codename Coke). Soviet Union, Antonov; twin engine turboprop transport; 44-50 passengers; 300 mph speed; ceiling 27,000 feet; range (depending on load) 325-1,500 miles; operational from 1962.

ANAB (NATO codename). Soviet Union; AAM with infra-red and semi-active homing versions; carried by Yak-28P (Firebar), Su-9 (Fishpot), and Su-11 (Flagon-A).

ANDOVER (HS-748). Britain, Hawker-Siddeley; twin engine turboprop, rear-loading transport; 58 troops or 40 paratroops; 15,000-pound payload; civilian version carries up to 62 passengers; operational from 1961; maximum cruising speed 290 mph; ceiling 25,000 feet; range with maximum payload 700 miles.

AO. US designation for fleet oiler.

AOE. US designation for fast combat support ship; provides the fleet with both fuel and ammunition through underway replenishment.

AOR. US designation for a replenishment oiler; provides both fuel and supplies to fleet through underway replenishment.

APA. US designation for an attack transport; usually carries a reinforced infantry battalion and the landing craft with which to land it.

APD. US designation for a high speed transport; usually converted from a destroyer or destroyer escort.

AR. US designation for a repair ship.

ARGOSY. Britain, Hawker-Siddeley; four engine turboprop, medium-range transport; operational from 1962; 69 troops or 54 paratroops; maximum payload 29,000 pounds; cruising speed 270 mph; ceiling 21,000 feet; maximum range 2,500 miles.

ARGUS. See CL-28.

AS. US designation for a submarine tender.

AS-11. See SS-11 (France, Nord).

AS-12. France, Nord; SS-12 wire-guided antitank missile converted to use automatic telecommand guidance from an aircraft; weight 167 pounds; range approximately 4 miles; 63-pound warhead.

AS-20. France, Nord; radio-controlled, air-to-surface missile; 315 pounds; 3 3/4 nautical mile range; 9 1/2 feet long.

AS-30. Improved version of AS-20; range up to 6 1/2 nautical miles; weight 1,150 pounds; 507-pound warhead.

AS-33. Similar to AS-30, but with inertial guidance; operational from 1966; 6.2-nautical mile range; weight 1,150 pounds.

ASH (NATO codename). Soviet Union; AAM with infra-red and radar-homing versions; carried by Tu-28 (Fiddler).

ASM. Air-to-surface missile; guided or self-homing, rocket-propelled or free-fall projectile launched from an aircraft against ground or sea target.

ASROC (RUR-5A; Anti-Submarine Rocket). US, Honeywell; rocket-assisted antisubmarine ballistic weapon; operational from 1961; equips destroyers, escort vessels, and cruisers in US Navy and others (e.g., Japan); weapon has its own eight-missile launcher, but can also be fired from Terrier launchers (q.v.); is essentially a ballistic rocket carrying acoustic homing torpedos or a nuclear depth charge; range 1 to 6 miles; firing weight 1,000 pounds.

ASU-57. Soviet Union, self-propelled 57mm gun on tracked chassis; designed for airborne operations; crew of two; weight 3.5 tons.

ASW. Anti-submarine warfare.

AT. Antitank.

AT-26, Xavante. See MB326B.

ATLANTIQUE (BR-1150). France, Breguet; maritime patrol aircraft, twin engine, turboprop two 6105 shp RR

Tyne engines; maximum speed 409 mph; service ceiling 32,800 feet; cruise speed 345 mph; maximum range 5,590 miles; standard bombs; HVAR (high velocity air rocket), depth charges, homing torpedoes, ASM nuclear warheads, MAD, sonobuoys.

ATOLL (NATO codename). Soviet Union; AAM with infra-red, heat-seeking guidance; similar to US Sidewinder.

AU-23A. See PC-6.

AUSTER (BEAGLE) AOP 6. Britain, Auster/Beagle; single engine piston, light liaison aircraft; operational from 1945; maximum speed 125 mph; ceiling 14,000 feet; range 315 miles.

AVP. US designation for a small seaplane tender.

AWL (NATO codename). Soviet Union; AAM little known radar or infrared guidance carried by interceptors. (Similar in configuration to US AAM Sparrow).

B-1. US, North American Rockwell; four engine jet; proposed new supersonic strategic bomber for USAF.

B-25, Mitchell. US, North American; World War II twin-engine, piston light bomber; over 4,300 built; 4,000 pounds of armament; maximum speed 275 mph; ceiling 24,000 feet; range 1,350 miles.

B-26, Counter Invader. US, twin-engine piston; modification and modernization of Douglas B-26 Invader for counter-insurgency operations; armed with eight .50 caliber machine guns in nose and up to 11,000 pounds of bombs; maximum 395 mph; ceiling 30,000 feet, range 1,500 miles; over 40 converted from 1963.

B-47, Stratojet. US, Boeing; six engine jet, medium bomber; operational from 1949; 1,500 built; 20,000-pound payload; maximum speed 650 mph; ceiling 42,000; range 3,500 miles.

B-52, Stratofortress. US, Boeing; eight engine jet, long-range, heavy bomber; operational from 1955; 744 built; 35-ton payload; maximum speed over 650 mph; ceiling over 50,000 feet; maximum range 12,500 miles.

B-57. US, Martin; license-built version of British Canberra (q.v.) twin engine jet, light bomber.

B-58, Hustler. US, Convair; four engine jet, delta-wing, supersonic, medium bomber; operational from 1960; maximum speed Mach 2; ceiling over 60,000 feet.

BA-64. Albania; APC.

BAC 167, Strikemaster. Britain, BAC; light single engine jet ground attack aircraft based on Jet Provost BAC-145 trainer.

BANTAM. Sweden; antitank guided missile; range 2,000 meters; speed 190 mph; weight 13 pounds; wire-guided, optically-tracked.

BARAK. Israeli version of Mirage (q.v.).

BATTALION. Usually a unit of 500 to 1,000 men of one arm which combined with one or more like units becomes a brigade or regiment (q.v.). Battalion-sized units of artillery and armor in British, Commonwealth, and some other armies are known as regiments. Battalion-sized units of US cavalry are known as squadrons. Soviet SAM battalions consist of only 80 to 150 men.

BATTERY. The basic firing unit of artillery, usually four to eight guns, depending upon the army. Three batteries usually comprise an artillery battalion (US practice) or regiment (British practice).

Be-12 (NATO codename Mail). Soviet Union, Beriev; twinturboprop maritime-reconnaissance amphibian; operational from 1965.

BEAGLE 206, Basset. Britain, Beagle; twin engine piston, light transport carrying 5-8 people; maximum speed 220 mph; maximum range 1,645 miles.

BEAGLE PUP. Britain, Beagle; two-seat, single engine piston light aircraft; used as primary trainer; maximum speed (estimated) 125 mph; range (estimated) 300 miles.

BEAVER (U-6A, US; DHC-2, Canada). Canada, De Havilland; single engine piston, STOL utility transport; maximum speed over 160 mph; ceiling 18,000 feet; range with maximum payload 480 miles; 7 passengers; over 1,600 built since 1948.

BEECH F33C, Bonanza. US, Beech; four-or five-seat single engine piston trainer; advanced version of commercial Beech Bonanza to be used in training and liaison; maximum speed 204 mph; service ceiling 18,300 feet; range 890 miles.

BEECH 99. US, Beechcraft; twin engine, turboprop, seventeen-seat aircraft; operational from mid-1968; maximum cruising speed (depending on version) 254 to 284 mph; range (with maximum fuel and 1,800 pounds payload) 1,100 miles; ceiling (depending on version), 24,000 to 26,000 feet.

BEECH QUEEN AIR (U-8F), Seminole. US, Beechcraft; light, twin engine piston transport; maximum speed 214 mph; ceiling 31,000 feet; range 1,600 miles; over 400 built since 1959.

BELFAST. Britain, Short Brothers; 4 engine turboprop military transport; 200 men or 78,000 pounds of cargo; maximum speed 310 mph; ceiling 30,000 feet; range with maximum payload 1,000 miles; operational from 1964; only 10 built.

BELL 47 (OH-13), Sioux. US, Bell; three-place, utility helicopter; maximum speed 105 mph; ceiling 18,500 feet; maximum range 250 miles; operational from 1960.

BELL 204. See UH-1.

BELL 206. See Jet Ranger.

BEN GURION. Israel; an Israeli modification of early-model Centurion medium tanks made by conversion to 105mm gun and other improvements.

BLOODHOUND. Britain, BAC; surface-to-air missile; semiactive homing guidance; effective against aircraft under 1,000-feet altitude and up to over 50,000-feet altitude; maximum range 50 miles or more; operational since 1958.

BLUE STEEL. Britain, Hawker-Siddeley; air-to-surface missile; a liquid-rocket stand-off bomb for "V-bomber" force; 200-miles range; thermo-nuclear warhead.

BMP-76PB. Soviet Union; see BTRM-1967.

BN2A, Islander, Defender. Britain, Britten-Norman; land based twin engine, piston-powered, multi-seat light transport (also light attack, search and rescue (SAR), reconnaissance) aircraft; cruising speed 160 mph; maximum range with tip tanks 1,040 miles; proposed armament, fixed guns, gun or rocket pods.

BO-5. Germany, Messerschmidt-Bolkow-Blohm; five-seat turbo-shaft high speed helicopter; gross weight 5,600 pounds, maximum speed 231 mph.

BOEING MODEL 707, 720 (USAF designation VC-137). US, Boeing; four-engine jet, long range transport; initial flight July 1954; many stages of development since then; four jet engines (turbo-jet or turbo-fan) each 17,500 pounds thrust; maximum speed Mach .95; service ceiling 42,000 feet; range 7,600 miles; can carry as many as 215 passengers; tanker model built for USAF KC-135 (Stratotanker).

BOMARC (MIM-10). US, Boeing; long-range surface-to-air missile; built with various modifications from 1952; speed Mach 2.8; range 440 miles; intercept capability from low-level to 100,000 feet; nuclear warhead.

BRDM. Soviet Union, 1959; four-wheeled amphibious armored reconnaissance vehicle; crew of 3; later models equipped with antitank missiles.

BREGUET 765. See SAHARA.

BREGUET 1150. See ATLANTIQUE.

BRIGADE. A formation of from 3,000 to 6,000 men, usually of several battalions of the same arm. In the US Army a brigade is essentially the equivalent of the former three-battalion regiment.

BRIGADE GROUP. Britain; an infantry brigade reinforced by artillery, tanks, and other supporting units.

BRITANNIA. Britain, Bristol; four-engine turboprop, medium transport; operational from 1957; 82 built; up to 133 passengers; maximum cruising speed 402 mph; range 4,160 miles.

BRONCO. See OV-10.

BROUSSARD. France, Max Holste; utility aircraft; six passengers; operational from 1953; 335 built; maximum speed 160 mph; ceiling 17,000 feet; range 745 miles.

BT-13. US, Vultee; World War II; single engine, piston, two-place basic trainer; maximum speed 164 mph; range 560 miles; ceiling 21,000 feet.

BTR-40. Soviet Union, 1950s; four-wheeled armored personnel carrier and scout car; 5.3 tons; 50 mph; range 175 miles; driver plus 9 troops.

BTR-50P. Soviet Union; tracked amphibious armored personnel carrier; suspension and power train similar to PT-76 light tank; 16 tons; 27 mph; driver plus 14 troops.

BTR-60P. Soviet Union; eight-wheeled amphibious armored personnel carrier; 12.7mm machine gun.

BTR-152. Soviet Union, 1950s; six-wheeled armored personnel carrier; 9.2 tons; 34 mph; crew of 3 plus 12 troops.

BTRM-1967, BMP-76. Soviet Union, fully-tracked armored infantry combat vehicle (AICV); carries 8-10 troops; armed with 76.2mm gun and wire-guided antitank missile; has amphibious capabilities; operational from 1967.

BUCCANEER. Britain, Hawker-Siddeley; twin-engine jet two-seat strike aircraft; operational from 1962; speed Mach 0.9.

BUFFALO (CV-7A or C-8A US; DHC-5 or CC-115, Canada). Canada, De Havilland; twin engine turboprop, STOL tactical transport; Canadian Forces version (CC-115) has more powerful engines; operational from 1965; crew of three, 41 troops, 35 paratroops, or 24 stretchers and six seats; maximum payload 13,843 pounds; maximum speed 271 mph; ceiling, 30,000 feet; range with maximum payload 507 miles; aircraft is basically a developed version of the Caribou (q.v.) with an enlarged fuselage and two turbo-prop engines.

BULLDOG. Britain, Scottish Aviation; single engine, two seat, piston-powered primary trainer; maximum speed 150 mph; range 621 miles.

BULLPUP (AGM-12). US, Maxson Corp.; air-to-surface missile; radio command guidance. AGM-12B, Bullpup A; 10 1/2 feet long; range 6 nautical miles; 250-pound HE warhead; overall weight 571 pounds; used by Navy and Air Force. AGM-12C, Bullpup B; 12 3/4 feet long; range 8.5 nautical miles; 1,000-pound HE warhead; overall weight 1,785 pounds; Navy only. AGM-12D; nuclear warhead. AGM-12E; high fragmentation warhead.

BV-202. Norway, armored personnel carrier (APC) in the Norwegian Army.

C-5, Galaxy. US, Lockheed; four-engine jet, long-range heavy transport; maximum payload 265,000 pounds; maximum speed 571 mph; maximum range 6,500 miles; operational from late 1969; ceiling 34,000 feet.

C-9, Nightingale. US, McDonnell-Douglas; twin engine jet military version of DC-9 commercial jet liner; used exclusively for medical evacuation purposes by Military Airlift Command.

C-42, Regente. Brazil, Neiva; four-seat utility, liaison and observation, single engine piston aircraft; maximum speed 137 mph; service ceiling 11,800 feet; maximum range 576 miles.

C-45, US, Beechcraft; twin-engine piston, light transport; 4 passengers; T-7 navigational training version; T-11 bombing training version.

C-46, Commando. US, Curtiss-Wright; World War II twin-engine piston transport; 36 passengers; 3,180 built.

C-47, Dakota or Skytrain (DC-3). US, Douglas; twin-engine transport; 21 passengers; over 10,000 built.

C-54, Skymaster (DC-4). US, Douglas; World War II four-engine piston transport; 44 passengers; over 1,000 built.

C-82, Packet. See C-119.

C-95, Bandeirante. Brazil, Embraer; twelve passenger, twin turboprop, light transport/utility aircraft; two 550 shaft hp engines; maximum cruising speed 267 mph; service ceiling 25,000 feet; maximum range 1,240 miles.

C-118, Liftmaster (DC-6). US, Douglas; four-engine piston transport; 64-92 passengers; 27,000 pounds of cargo; maximum speed 360 mph; range 4,900 miles.

C-119, Flying Boxcar. US, Fairchild-Hiller; twin engine piston transport; 62 paratroops; 30,000 pounds cargo; maximum speed 295 mph; range 3,480 miles; developed from C-82 Packet. Latest version, AC-119K Shadow, is an attack gunship carrying 20mm Vulcan cannon and 7.62mm Minigun machine guns (each firing 6,000 rounds per minute) plus advanced detection equipment.

C-121, Constellation and Super Constellation. US, Lockheed; four-engine piston transport; operational from 1951; 63-99 passengers; 40,000 pounds cargo; maximum speed 375 mph; range 2,100 miles.

C-123, Provider. US, Fairchild-Hiller; twin-engine piston tactical transport; maximum speed 253 mph; payload 19,000 pounds; range with maximum payload 1,340 miles; first built in 1954; C-123K was converted from C-123B in 1966-67 with addition of two 2,850 pound thrust turbojets to improve performance.

C-124, Globemaster. US, Douglas; four-engine piston transport; 200 troops; 74,000 pounds of cargo; maximum speed 300 mph; maximum range 6,820 miles.

C-130, Hercules. US, Lockheed; four-engine, turboprop transport; over 1,000 built since 1956 in various versions; payload 35,000 to 45,000 pounds; maximum speed 380 mph; ceiling 40,000 feet; range 1,800 to 4,700 miles depending on model.

C-131, Samaritan. US, Convair; twin engine piston transport; 48 passengers; maximum speed 313 mph; range 1,600 miles; military version of Convair 240/440-series commercial airliners.

C-133, Cargomaster. US, Douglas; four-engine turboprop, heavy transport; operational from 1957; over 200 troops; 80,000- to 100,000-pound payload; maximum speed 359 mph; ceiling 24,000 feet; range 2,200 to 4,300 miles.

C-135, Stratofreighter. US, Boeing; long-range four-engine jet transport; operational from 1961; 126 troops; maximum payload 50,000 pounds; maximum speed 640 mph; range 4,500 miles; military version of Boeing 707-series commercial jet liner. See KC-135 and Boeing Model 707, 720.

C-140, Jet Star. US, Lockheed; four-engine jet light transport; used for VIP transport, liaison duties, etc.

C-141, Starlifter. US, Lockheed; four-engine turbofan, long-range cargo and troop transport; operational from 1965; 154 troops or 123 paratroops; maximum payload 71,000 pounds; maximum speed 570 mph; ceiling 41,000 feet; range with maximum payload 4,000 miles.

C-160. See TRANSALL.

C-212, AVIOCAR. Spain, CASA; 15 seat, twin engine, turboprop paratroop or aeromedical transport aircraft; maximum speed 249 mph at 12,000 feet; service ceiling 24,606 feet; range with maximum fuel 1,198 miles.

C-class, (Charlie). Soviet Union; NATO designation for a class of nuclear-powered submarines; eight tubes for launching SS-N-7 missiles; these missiles have a range of approximately 25 miles and can be launched from underwater against both surface ships and submarines.

CA. US designation for a heavy cruiser, armed with 8-inch guns.

CA-27. See CF-86.

CACTUS. France, surface-to-air missile; Mach 1.2.

CANBERRA. Britain, BAC; twin-jet, light bomber; operational from 1951; 1,329 built, including 403 in US as B-57; 6,000 pounds of armament; maximum speed 600 mph; ceiling 48,000 feet; maximum range over 2,300 miles.

CARIBOU (C-7A or CV-2A, US; DHC-4, Canada). Canada, DeHavilland; twin-engine, piston STOL transport; 159 built for US from 1959; total 248 built; 32 passengers or 26 paratroops; maximum payload 8,700 pounds; maximum speed 215 mph; ceiling 27,000 feet; range with maximum payload 240 miles.

CARL GUSTAV. Sweden; a recoilless 84mm antitank weapon.

CASA 3524. Spain, CASA; light twin-engine turboprop transport.

CC-106, Yukon. Canada, Canadair; license-built piston-engine version of Britannia (q.v.).

CC-109. See COSMOPOLITAN.

CC-115. See BUFFALO.

CC-138. See TWIN OTTER.

CENTURION. Britain; medium tank in production from post-World War II to 1960s; Mk. III to VIII armed with 20-pounder (83.4mm) gun; IX and X with 105mm gun; 51 tons; 21.5 mph; road range 115 miles; cross-country range 75 miles; crew of 4.

CESSNA 180. US, Cessna; single-engine piston, utility aircraft; 6 passengers; maximum speed 170 mph; ceiling 19,000 feet; range 900 miles; over 5,000 built.

CESSNA 185 (Skywagon). See U-17A.

CESSNA 310 (U-3). US, Cessna; twin-engine, 6-passenger aircraft; over 2,700 built from 1953; maximum speed 242 mph; ceiling 21,300 feet; range 1,340 miles.

CESSNA FR-172. France, Reims Aviation; four-seat, single engine piston, light aircraft; license-built Cessna 172; equipped to carry Matra rocket launchers in counterinsurgency (COIN) role; maximum speed 153 mph; service ceiling 17,000 feet; range 740 miles.

CF-5. Canadian-built version of F-5 jet fighter.

CF-86 (CA-27), Sabre. Canadian Forces version of F-86 jet fighter; built in Australia.

CF-100, Canuck. Canada, Avro; twin-engine jet two-seat interceptor in service from 1951; maximum speed 650 mph; range 2,000 miles; carries fifty-two 2-3/4 inch air-to-air rockets in each of two wing-tip pods or eight .50 cal. machine guns in a belly-pack; over 500 built; one version served with Belgian Air Force.

CF-101, Voodoo. Canadian-built version of F-101 jet interceptor.

CF-104, Starfighter. Canadian-built version of F-104.

CH-46, Sea Knight. US, Boeing-Vertol; twin-rotor, medium helicopter; operational from 1962; over 500 built; 17-25 troops; maximum speed 166 mph; ceiling 14,000 feet; range with maximum fuel 750 miles.

CH-47, Chinook. US, Boeing-Vertol; twin-rotor, medium helicopter; operational from 1962; 33-44 troops or 23,450 pound maximum payload; maximum speed 190 mph; 9,500 foot ceiling; combat radius 115 miles.

CH-53 (S-65), Sea Stallion. US, Sikorsky; heavy assault helicopter; operational from 1966; over 100 built; 38 troops or 28,000-pound payload; maximum speed 195 mph; ceiling 21,000 feet; range 255 miles (up to 540 with external tanks).

CH-54 (S-64), Sky Crane. US, Sikorsky; crane helicopter for lifting external loads or pods of up to 22,890 pounds;

maximum speed 127 mph; ceiling 13,000 feet; range with maximum fuel 253 miles.

CH-113, Labrador. Canada; version of US Boeing-Vertol CH-46 built in US for Canadian Armed Forces.

CHAPARRAL/VULCAN. US; a low-altitude air defense system comprising Sidewinder AAMs (q.v.) modified for use as SAMs and mounted on a tracked vehicle, combined with a radar-directed Vulcan 20mm cannon mounted on a modified M-113 APC.

CHARIOTEER. Britain; World War II medium tank; a Cromwell tank rearmed with a 20-pounder (83.4mm) gun; 28.5 tons; crew of 3-4.

CHIEFTAIN. Britain; main battle tank; 120mm gun; 50 tons; maximum speed 25 mph; range 250 miles; crew of 4.

CHIPMUNK. Britain, Hawker-Siddeley; single engine piston primary trainer; maximum speed 138 mph; range 280 miles.

CIVIC ACTION. Employment of military units in building up the economic infrastructure of a developing nation or in providing various social services to civilians in remote areas.

CL. US designation for a light cruiser, armed with 6-inch guns.

CL-13, Sabre. Canada, Canadair; license-built version of F-86 Sabre.

CL-28, Argus. Canada, Canadair; long-range maritime reconnaissance version of Britannia (q.v.); 8,000 pounds internal and 7,600 pounds external armament; ASW equipment; maximum speed 288 mph; range 4,000 miles.

CL-41, Tutor. Canada, Canadair; two-seat, single engine jet trainer; 200 produced from 1961; G model can be armed with 4,000 pounds of gun pods, bombs, or rockets; maximum speed 480 mph; ceiling 44,500 feet.

CLAA. US designation for an anti-aircraft cruiser armed predominantly with anti-aircraft guns.

CLG. US designation for a guided missile light cruiser; armament includes surface-to-air missiles.

COBRA. Germany, Bolkow; wire-guided antitank missile; 30.7 inches long; 20.2 pounds; 190 mph; range 400-1,600 meters. Not to be confused with AH-1G Huey Cobra helicopter gunship (see UH-1).

COH-58. Canada; version of US Bell OH-58 (q.v.).

COIN. US acronym for counter-insurgency.

COMET. Britain; medium tank from late World War II period; 17-pounder (77mm) gun; 33.5 tons; crew of 5.

COMET. Britain, De Havilland; four-engine jet transport; operational from 1958; range 2,590 miles; service ceiling 39,000 feet; cruising speed 542 mph.

COMMANDO (XM706). US, Cadillac-Gage; 4-wheeled amphibious armored car/armored personnel carrier; 65 mph; range 300 miles; some carry turret-mounted 20mm cannon; crew of 4 (plus 7 troops in APC version); used by South Vietnam and other countries.

CONDOR (AGM-53A). US, North American-Rockwell; air-to-surface missile; TV guidance; 40 nautical mile range; for use from A-6A and A-7 aircraft.

CONVAIR 440. See C-131.

CORPS. A type of unit common throughout an army, as Ordnance Corps; more commonly a large formation of two or more divisions plus supporting combat and logistical units.

CORVETTE. Designation, principally British, of a class of ASW convoy escort ships, about 180-foot, with 3 inch gun and ASW weapons; often converted from another type such as minesweeper; US designation is PCE (q.v.).

COSMOPOLITAN CC-109. US, General Dynamics (Convair); twin engine turboprop Canadian-built version of C-131 (q.v.); powered by Allison 501D-13 turboprops; maximum speed 309 mph; service ceiling 24,000 feet; range 1,230 miles; used by Canadian Armed Forces as medium range transport.

CROTALE. France, Thomson-CSF; land-mobile, automatic, all weather surface-to-air guided missile; propulsion single stage solid propellant, infrared and radar guidance.

CUH-1N. Canada; Iroquois (q.v.) helicopter for Canadian Armed Forces.

CVA. US designation for an attack aircraft carrier; fleet carrier of the largest type, carrying up to 100 aircraft.

CVAN. Nuclear-powered CVA.

CVL. US designation for a light aircraft carrier; smaller than CVA and carrying fewer planes; many converted from other hulls.

CVS. US designation for a support aircraft carrier; usually carry ASW aircraft.

D-18. See C-45.

DAF-YP-408. Netherlands; 8-wheeled armored personnel carrier; 12 tons; 50 mph; range 310 miles; crew of 2 plus 10 troops.

DAPHNE. France; class of diesel attack submarines; 850 tons; 190 feet; twelve 21-inch torpedo tubes; speed 16 knots surfaced or submerged.

DC-3. See C-47.

DC-4. See C-54.

DC-6. See C-118.

DD. US designation for a fleet destroyer; armed with two to six 3- or 5- inch guns; ASW weapons; top speed 35 knots.

DDG. US designation for a guided missile destroyer; partially armed with surface-to-air missiles.

DDR. US designation for radar picket destroyer.

DE. US designation for a destroyer escort; a convoy escort of slower speed and less armament than a destroyer.

DEG. US designation for a guided missile destroyer escort; partially armed with surface-to-air missiles.

DELFIN (L-29). Czechoslovakia, Aero; single engine jet trainer; NATO codename Maya, may be armed with 2 machine guns or 8 rockets; maximum speed 407mph; ceiling 36,100 feet; maximum range (with external tanks) 555 miles.

DEVON. Military version of Dove (q.v.).

DHC-2. See BEAVER.

DHC-3. See OTTER.

DHC-4. See CARIBOU.

DHC-5. See BUFFALO.

DHC-6. See TWIN OTTER.

DIVISION. A formation of combined arms, that is infantry, armor, artillery, etc.; usually from about 10,000 to 15,000 men; infantry may be mechanized or motorized (infantry in armored personnel carriers and strong in tanks), airborne (parachute-landed), air mobile (helicopter-borne) or Marine (specially structured and equipped for landing across a defended beach). In the U.S. Air Force, a division consists of two or more wings.

DJINN (SA-1221). France, Sud-Aviation; two-seat, light helicopter; 178 made from 1956; maximum speed 81 mph; maximum range 200 miles; ceiling 5,900 feet.

DL. US designation for frigate (originally destroyer leader); roughly comparable in size to a light cruiser; 5,000 to 10,000 tons displacement.

DLG. US designation for a guided missile destroyer leader; also classified as a frigate; large destroyer equipped as a flagship and partially armed with guided missiles.

DLGN. US designation for nuclear-powered guided missile frigate.

Do-27, Skyservant. West German, Dornier; single engine piston utility aircraft carrying up to 6 passengers; 680 built from 1956; maximum speed 174 mph; ceiling 10,000 feet; range 492 miles.

Do-28, Skyservant. West Germany, Dornier; twin engine piston version of DO-27; maximum speed 184 mph; ceiling 20,500 feet; range 745 miles.

DOVE. Britain, Hawker-Siddeley; twin-engine piston, light transport seating up to 11 passengers; 540 built; maximum speed 230 mph; ceiling 21,000 feet; range 880 miles.

DRAGONFLY. See T-37.

DRAKEN (Dragon, J-35, S-35). Sweden, Saab; single-seat, double-delta-wing, supersonic, single engine jet fighter; entered service in 1960; still in production; maximum speed Mach 2.2; ceiling 65,000 feet; armed with two 30mm cannon, air-to-air missiles, bombs or rockets; "J" is fighter version, "S" and "RF" reconnaissance version, "F" fighter- bomber version.

E-class (Echo). Soviet Union; NATO designation for a class of nuclear-power missile submarines; E-1 class carry 6 Shaddock missile tubes; E-2 class carry 8 Shaddock launching tubes which elevate from the flush deck; E-2 is basically a lengthened E-1.

EA-6B, Intruder. US, Grumman; enlarged-fuselage version of A-6 (q.v.) with crew of four; the two additional crewmen operate electronic devices to suppress enemy electronic activity and obtain tactical electronic intelligence data.

EBR-75. France, Panhard; 8-wheeled armored car with 75mm gun; there are two versions differing only in turret design and weighing 13.5 to 15.2 tons; crew of 4. Another version of the basic design mounts a 90mm gun.

EBR-ETT. France, Panhard; 8-wheeled armored personnel carrier based on EBR armored car chassis; 13.5 tons; 65 mph; driver plus 14 troops.

EMB326G Xavante. See MB326G.

ENTAC (US, MGM-32A). France, Nord; wire-guided antitank missile; in service from 1957; weight 27 pounds; speed 190 mph; range 2,000 meters.

ETENDARD IV. France, Dassault; single engine jet carrier-based, transonic, attack aircraft; operational from 1962; two 30mm cannon and 3,000 pounds of external armament; maximum speed Mach 1.08; ceiling 49,000 feet; combat radius 460 miles (1,000 miles with external fuel).

EXOCET. France, Aerospatiale (Nord); SSM designed for use by warships against other surface ships; length 16 feet, 9-1/2 inches; range about 20 miles; launching weight 1,587 pounds; designed to fly 6 to 10 feet above the water and operate efficiently in an ECM environment; terminal guidance is by active homing head.

F-class (Foxtrot). Soviet Union; NATO designation for a class of diesel-powered attack submarines; 2,000 tons; 300 feet long; eight 21- inch torpedo tubes; 20 knots on surface, 15 knots submerged.

F-4 (formerly Navy F4H, Air Force F-110), Phantom II. US, McDonnell-Douglas; twin engine jet, two-seat, long-range attack fighter; operational from 1959; various models for US services and foreign countries; carries 16,000 pounds of armament; maximum speed Mach 2.4; ceiling 71,000 feet; combat radius 1,000 miles.

F4U, Corsair. US, Chance-Vought; World War II single engine piston fighter; featured unusual inverted-gull wing; last model built in 1953; served with US Navy and Marine Corps, French Navy, and other air forces; four 20 mm cannon; maximum speed 470 mph; range 1,120 miles; ceiling 40,000 feet; over 12,000 built.

F-5, Tiger II, formerly Freedom Fighter. US, Northrup; light, twin-jet, tactical fighter; maximum speed Mach 1.38; operational from 1963; ceiling over 50,000 feet; range with maximum fuel 1,750 miles, with maximum payload 380 miles; carries up to 6,200 pounds of armament including two 20mm cannon plus rockets, bombs, and Sidewinder AAMs.

F6F, Hellcat. US, Grumman; World War II single-engine piston, single-seat fighter.

F-8, Crusader. US, Ling-Temco-Vought, single engine jet carrier-based fighter; operational from 1956; maximum speed Mach 1.97; four 20mm cannon and 2 to 4 Sidewinder AAMs.

F-9. People's Republic of China, Shen Yang Aircraft Production Complex; single engine jet; single-seat strike fighter; maximum speed Mach 2.0; combat radius 300 to 500 miles; loaded weight 22,000 pounds; possibly a Chinese copy of MIG-21; production rate of about 10 per month. 10 per month.

F9F-2, Panther. US, Grumman; single engine, single-seat jet naval fighter; operational from 1948; four 20mm cannon; maximum speed 640 mph; range 1,500 miles; ceiling 50,000 feet; swept wing development became F9F-6, Cougar (q.v.).

F9F-6, Cougar, US, Grumman; carrier-based transonic fighter; operational from 1950s.

F-27, Friendship. Netherlands, Fokker (US, Fairchild-Hiller, FH-227); twin engine turboprop transport; operational from 1958; 40-52 passengers; cruising speed at 20,000 feet 265 to 290 mph, depending on model; ceiling 28,000 feet; range with maximum fuel 1,200 miles (430-670 miles with maximum payload).

F-27M, Troopship. Netherlands, Fokker; military version of F-27;45 troops or 13,800 pounds of cargo; large cargo and parachute-drop doors on each side of fuselage.

F-28, Fellowship. Netherlands, Fokker MK 1000; 79 passenger, twin engine jet transport; gross weight 65,000 pounds; maximum cruising speed 528 mph; maximum crusing altitude 30,000 feet; range 1,266 miles.

F-47, Thunderbolt. US, Republic; World War II single engine piston fighter; WWII designation P-47; eight .50 cal. machine guns; a total of 15,329 built; maximum speed 426 mph; range with wing tanks 2,700 miles; ceiling 43,000 feet.

F-51, Mustang. US, North American; World War II single engine piston fighter; maximum speed 437 mph; ceiling 40,000 feet; six .50 caliber machine guns; over 15,000 built.

F-80, Shooting Star. US, Lockheed; single engine jet fighter-bomber; operational from late 1945; over 1,600 built; six .50 caliber machine guns in nose; two 1000-pound bombs; maximum speed 590 mph; range 1,300 miles.

F-84, Thunderjet. US, Republic; single engine jet fighter-bomber; operational from 1946; 4,457 built; six .50 caliber guns (four in nose, two in wing roots) and 4,000 pounds of bombs; maximum speed 620 mph; ceiling 40,000 feet; range with maximum fuel 2,000 miles; F84F, Thunderstreak, is the swept-wing version of the straight-wing F-84G; six .50 caliber guns and 6,000 pounds of bombs; maximum speed 695 mph; 2,711 built; maximum range 1,600 miles.

F-86, Sabre. US, North American; single engine jet fighter; operational from 1948; 4,500 built; maximum speed 707 mph; ceiling 50,000 feet; range 900 miles; F86D and K are all-weather versions.

F-100, Super Sabre. US, North American; single engine jet; operational from 1954; 2,300 built; four 20mm cannon and 7,500 pounds of bombs and rockets; maximum speed Mach 1.3; range 1,500 miles.

F-101, Voodoo. US, McDonnell; supersonic, twin-engine jet, fighter-interceptor; operational from 1957; over 800 built; four 20mm cannon, three Falcon AAMs, or 2 Genie nuclear-armed rockets; maximum speed Mach 1.85; ceiling 52,000 feet; maximum range with external tanks 2,980 miles.

F-102, Delta Dagger. US, Convair; single engine jet all-weather interceptor; operational from 1956; 875 built; six Falcon AAMs and 24 2 3/4 inch rockets; maximum speed Mach 1.25; ceiling 54,000 feet; combat radius 550 miles.

F-104, Starfighter. US, Lockheed (also built in Canada, Belgium, Japan, Germany, Netherlands, and Italy); single engine jet multimission fighter; operational from 1958; maximum speed Mach 2.2; ceiling 58,000 feet; combat radius 750 miles; 4,800 pounds of armament (one 20mm Vulcan cannon plus various combinations of rockets, bombs, and Sidewinder AAMs).

F-105, Thunderchief. US, Republic; single engine jet all-weather fighter-bomber; operational from 1958; maximum speed Mach 2.15; ceiling 60,000 feet; range with maximum fuel 2,000 miles; 12,000 pounds of armament (20mm Vulcan cannon, three 3,000-pound bombs, 16 750-pound bombs, rocket pods, etc.).

F-106, Delta Dart. US, Convair; single engine jet all-weather interceptor; operational from 1959; 320 built; two Genie nuclear-armed rockets plus six Falcon AAMS; maximum speed Mach 2.31; ceiling 57,000 feet; range 1,500 miles.

F-111. US, Convair; two-seat, twin engine jet, tactical fighter-bomber with variable-geometry wings; operational from 1967; maximum speed Mach 2.5; ceiling over 60,000 feet; range with maximum fuel over 3,800 miles.

FALCON (Mystere 20). France, Dassault; light, twin-engine jet, executive transport; operational from 1963; 14 passengers; maximum speed Mach 0.85; ceiling 42,000 feet; maximum range 1,900 miles.

FALCON (AIM-4A/C/D; Super Falcon AIM-4E/G; Nuclear Falcon AIM-26A). US, Hughes; air-to-air missile; 6.5 feet long; 120 pounds; speed Mach 2 plus; range 5 nautical miles. Super Falcon is 8 1/4 feet long; range of 5 nautical miles; speed Mach 2.5. Nuclear Falcon is 6 3/4 feet long with a nuclear warhead; 5-nautical mile range; speed Mach 2.

FB-111. US, General Dynamics; strategic bomber version of F-111; slightly longer wingspan; improved range.

FERRET. Britain, Daimler; 4-wheeled armored scout car; 4 to 5 tons; 58 mph; range 190 miles; crew of 2.

FH-1100. US, Fairchild-Hiller; light observation helicopter.

FIRESTREAK. Britain, Hawker-Siddeley; air-to-air missile; length 10 1/2 feet; 300 pounds; speed Mach 2 plus; range 4.3 nautical miles; infra-red guidance.

FLAMANT (M.D.315). France, Dassault; light, twin-engine, prop transport; operational from 1949; 10 passengers; maximum speed 236 mph; ceiling 26,240 feet; range 755 miles.

FN4RM/62FAB. Belgium; lightweight four-wheeled armored reconnaissance vehicle; 8-9 tons; 130 hp; 65 mph; range 350 miles. One version armed with 90mm cannon, the other with a 60mm mortar and two machine guns; both carry crew of 3.

FOKKER S-11 Instructor. Netherlands, manufactured in Brazil; land based single engine 2 seat piston powered primary trainer; maximum speed 400 mph; range 400 miles.

4K4F. Austria; armored personnel carrier; capacity 10 fully equipped men; 12.5 tons; 220-hp engine; carries 12.7mm machine guns or 20mm cannon. A variant, the JPz-4K, has the APC's hull, tracks and suspension, but is armed with a 105mm gun in a French AMX-13 turret; crew of 3; 16.8 tons; 300-hp engine; maximum speed 40 mph.

FRIGATE. UK, France and others; roughly comparable to US DEs, but not to DLs; displacements from less than 2,000 to over 5,500 tons.

FROG (Free Rocket Over Ground). Soviet Union; NATO designation for unguided tactical surface-to-surface rockets with conventional, chemical, or nuclear warheads. FROG-1 mounted on a JS-3 tank chassis; operational from 1957; estimated range of 15 miles. FROGs 2-5 in slightly different forms; mounted on modified PT-76 tank chassis; estimated ranges up to 30 miles. FROG-7 first seen in 1967 is mounted on large 8-wheeled vehicles.

FUG-1966, FUG-A. Hungary; license-built versions of Soviet BRDM/BTR-40 type armored vehicles.

FV-432, Trojan. Britain; tracked armored personnel carrier; 14 tons; 32 mph; range 400 to 500 miles; crew of 2 plus 10 troops; similar to US M-113.

FV-1609. Armored personnel carrier.

G-91. Italy, Fiat; single engine jet light fighter-bomber; later version is twin-engine jet; operational from 1959; 1,500 pounds of armament on four attachment points and four .50 caliber machine guns; maximum speed 675 mph; ceiling 40,000 feet.

G-class (Golf). Soviet Union; NATO designation for a class of diesel-powered missile submarines with 3 vertical launch tubes for Serb/Sark-type ballistic missiles in conning tower.

GAINFUL. Soviet Union; NATO codename for SA-6 (US designation); first seen in 1967; mobile surface-to-air missile; probably now operational with Soviet ground forces; three missiles (exact propulsion system unknown) mounted on fully-tracked chassis similar to that of ZSU-23/4 (q.v.); apparently designed as a low-altitude complement to the SA-4 Ganef (q.v.).

GALEB (Soko G2-A, Seagull). Yugoslavia, Soko; two-seat, single engine jet, basic trainer; maximum speed 500 mph; maximum range 770 miles; can be armed with two .50 caliber machine guns, bombs, and rockets.

GANEF. Soviet Union; NATO codename for SA-4 (US designation); mobile surface-to-air missile; deployed for use of Soviet ground forces (including some believed deployed with Soviet forces in Egypt); two ramjet powered missiles (each with 4 strap-on, solid-fuel boosters) mounted on a fully-tracked chassis; range comparable to SA-2; altitude capability thought to be lower than SA-2 (because of less high-altitude threat in tactical situations).

GANNET. Britain, Westland; 3-seat, single engine, double turboprop, powered airborne early warning aircraft; maximum speed 250 mph; range 800 miles; carries 2 radar operators in the midships cabin.

GENIE (AIR-2A). US, Douglas; unguided air-to-air rocket with nuclear warhead; length 9 1/2 feet; weight 820 pounds; speed Mach 3; range 6 miles; carried by F-101 and F-106.

GILOIS. France; tank-mounted scissors bridge for spanning canals, antitank ditches, and small watercourses impeding an armored advance. The smaller model, mounted on an AMX-13 tank chassis, spans 38 feet with a 35-ton capacity; the larger model, on an AMX-30 tank chassis, has a greater capacity.

GNAT. Britain, Folland (also built in India by Hindustani); single-seat, single engine jet lightweight fighter; maximum speed Mach 0.98; ceiling 40,000 feet; combat radius 250 miles; two 30mm cannon and 2,000 pounds of external armament.

GOA. Soviet Union; NATO codename for SA-3 (US designation); surface-to-air missile about 20 feet long; range 13 miles to an altitude of 45,000 feet; intended for low-altitude air defense; GOA's fire-control radar is codenamed Low Blow; acquisition radar is codenamed Flat Face; naval version is SA-N-1 with Peel Group guidance radar.

GOMHOURIA. Egypt; single engine piston primary trainer; 130 mph; ceiling 15,000 feet; range 600 miles.

GORDY. Soviet Union; NATO designation for a class of DD built in 1936 and now obsolete; remaining units transferred to Communist China; 1,650 tons; 358 feet long; 36 knots; four 5.1-inch guns; eight 37mm guns; 8 depth-charge projectors; six 21-inch torpedo tubes.

GRAIL. Soviet Union. NATO code name for SA-7; small warhead optically sighted infrared heat-seeking shoulder-fired surface to air missile; can also be mounted in batteries of four or eight on scout cars or trucks.

GRIFFON. Soviet Union; NATO codename that has been applied to SA-5 surface-to-air ABM type, long range air defense missile; radar homing, 2-3 stage solid propellant; length 54 feet; diameter-booster 3¼ feet, second stage 2 2/3 feet; launch weight 22,000 pounds; range 155 miles.

GROUP. A unit consisting of two or more aircraft squadrons, although in some air forces squadron-sized units are referred to as groups. In Britain's RAF and other air forces patterned on it, a group consists of two or more wings (each of two or more squadrons). In armies usually applied to a temporary composite formation of like or different combat units.

GUARANI II. See IA-50.

GUIDELINE. Soviet Union; NATO codename for SA-2 (US designation); surface-to-air missile; Soviet designator is VK750 or V750VK; operational from 1957; solid-fuel booster, liquid-fuel sustainer; length with booster 35 feet; weight with booster is 4,875 pounds; naval version is SA-N-2; 288-pound HE warhead; command guidance; speed Mach 3.6; ceiling over 80,000 feet; fire-control radar is codenamed Fan Song and acquisition radar is Spoon Rest.

GY-80. Horizon. France, SOCATA; four-seat single engine piston light monoplane; estimated maximum speed 150 mph; estimated range, 800 miles.

H-6. See OH-6.

H-13. See OH-13.

H-19, Chickasaw (also referred to as UH-19). US, Sikorsky; transport helicopter; operational from 1950; over 1,200 built; up to 10 passengers; maximum speed 115 mph; range 400 miles; non-military version is Sikorsky S-55.

H-23, Raven. US, Hiller; three-place, utility helicopter; operational with US Army from 1957; over 1,200 built; maximum speed 100 mph; ceiling 15,000 feet; range 500 miles.

H-34, Choctaw. US, Sikorsky; piston-engine utility helicopter used for troop transport (CH-34) and ASW (SH-34 Seabat); up to 16 passengers; maximum speed 134 mph; ceiling 9,500 feet; range with maximum fuel 250 miles; over 1,000 built; later models are turbine-powered; non-military version is Sikorsky S-58.

H-37, Mojave. US, Sikorsky; twin-engine, heavy helicopter; operational from 1956; 26 troops; maximum speed 130 mph; range 220 miles; ceiling 8,700 feet; also referred to as CH-37 and Sikorsky S-56.

H-43, Huskie. US, Kaman; turbine-powered, twin-rotor, utility helicopter; rescue version is HH-43; maximum payload 3,800 pounds; maximum speed 120 mph; ceiling 25,000 feet; range 275 to 500 miles.

H-53. See CH-53.

H-class (Hotel). Soviet Union; NATO designation for a class of nuclear-powered missile submarines with 3 vertical missile tubes in sail or conning tower for Serb missiles.

HA-200. See SAETA.

HA-220. Spain, Hispano; single-seat, ground attack version of HA-200 (above).

HAI. East Germany; class of PC; 300 tons; 175 feet; 25 knots; diesel and gas turbine drive; 2 twin-37mm guns.

HARRIER. Britain, Hawker-Siddeley; the western world's only operational fixed-wing V/STOL fighter; operational from 1968; in service with Royal Air Force and US Marine Corps; maximum speed 737 mph; ceiling over 50,000 feet; range (ferry) 2,300 miles; armed with various combinations of rockets, bombs, missiles and guns — all carried externally; powered by single vectored thrust turbo-fan jet engine.

HARVARD. See T-6.

HAWK (MIM-23A). US, Raytheon/Northrup (also built by a 5-nation NATO consortium); small transportable surface-to-air missile; acronym stands for Homing All-Way Killer; homes on radar reflections from ground-based radar (semi-active); effective from low-level to normal tactical aircraft altitudes; 16 1/2 feet long; 1,295 pounds; speed Mach 2.5; slant range 22 miles; three missiles on each launcher.

HC-54. US, Douglas; a variant of C-54 (q.v.) equipped for search/rescue missions.

HE-111. Germany, Heinkel; twin engine piston World War II bomber; now obsolete but still in service with Spanish Air Force.

HERALD. Britain, Handley-Page; twin turboprop, medium transport; operational from 1959; 50 passengers or maximum payload of 11,700 pounds; maximum speed 350 mph; ceiling 28,000 feet; range with maximum fuel 1,750 miles.

HERCULES. See C-130.

HERON. Britain, Hawker-Siddeley; four-engine piston, light transport; up to 17 passengers; cruise speed 180 mph; range 1,500 miles.

HH-52. US, Sikorsky; twelve passenger helicopter; turbo-shaft engine; single rotor and tail rotor; maximum speed 109 mph; maximum range 474 miles.

HH-53. See CH-53 SEA STALLION.

HJT-16, Kiran. India, HAL; two-seat single engine jet basic trainer; maximum speed 432 mph; endurance one hour forty-five minutes on internal fuel.

HONEST JOHN (MGR-1A/B). US, McDonnell-Douglas/ Emerson; unguided tactical surface-to-surface rocket in service in 1950s and 1960s; still in service with some armies; conventional, chemical, and nuclear warheads; 26 feet long; 4,700 pounds; speed Mach 1.5; range 12 miles; launched from a rail mounted on a 5-ton truck.

HORNET. See SUPER FRELON.

HOT (High-subsonic, Optically-guided, Tube-launched). France, Nord, and West Germany, Bolkow; wire-controlled antitank missile; operational from 1968; length 4 1/4 feet; weight (missile and launcher container) 55 pounds; maximum speed 625 mph; range 75 to 4,000 meters.

HOUND DOG (AGM-28B). US, North American-Rockwell;

air-to-surface stand-off missile; thermo-nuclear warhead; two carried by B-52G/H bombers; speed Mach 2; range over 600 miles; operational from 1960; 400 in service.

HS-30. West Germany; armored personnel carrier; 14 tons; 40 mph; range 180 miles; driver plus 7 troops; one of a family of armored vehicles including a reconnaissance vehicle with 20mm gun, a mortar carrier, a command vehicle, and an antitank missile carrier.

HS-125, Dominie. Britain, Hawker-Siddeley; originally the de Havilland 125; twin-engine, light jet transport; both civilian and military versions; maximum cruising speed 510 mph at 31,000 feet; ceiling 41,000 feet; range (maximum fuel and payload) 1,940 miles; over 200 built since 1964.

HS-748. See ANDOVER.

HSS-1, Seabat. US, Sikorsky; old designation for SH-34; see H-34.

HT-2. India, HAL; 2-seat, single engine piston trainer; operational from 1953; maximum speed 130 mph; ceiling 16,500 feet; range 350 miles.

HU-16. See ALBATROSS.

HU CHWAN. Peoples Republic of China; US designation for a class of hydrofoil patrol boat; two 21-inch torpedo tubes, two twin 14.5mm machine guns; name means Little Tiger.

HUEY COBRA. See AH-1.

HUGHES-269. Brazil (US designation H-55 Osage); 2-3 seat light helicopter trainer; piston powered; maximum speed 86 mph; range 204 miles.

HUGHES 500. See OH-6 Cayuse.

HUMBER MK. IV. Britain, Humber; armored car; World War II; crew of three; one 37mm gun, one 7.92mm machine gun; maximum speed 45 mph; range 250 miles; weight 7.1 tons.

HUNTER. Britain, Hawker; single engine jet fighter-bomber; operational from 1954; 1,985 built; four 30mm cannon in nose plus 7,000 pounds of external armament; maximum speed 715 mph; ceiling 50,000 feet; maximum range 1,800 miles.

HUSKIE. See H-43.

IA-35, Huanquero. Argentina, FMA; multi-role eight-seat twin engine (750 hp. each) piston aircraft; used for advanced training, instrument and weapon training; also as ambulance aircraft; maximum speed 225 mph; service ceiling estimated at 20,000 feet; range 975 miles; weapon trainer version can carry two .50 cal machine guns plus underwing bombs or rockets; weight 440 pounds.

IA-50, Guarani II. Argentina, FMA; twin engine turboprop, light transport; operational from 1967; up to 15 passengers or maximum payload of 3,300 pounds; maximum speed 310 mph; ceiling 41,000 feet; range with maximum fuel 1,600 miles (with maximum payload 1,250 miles).

IA-58, Pucara (A-X2). Argentina, FMA; twin engine turboprop COIN combat aircraft; maximum speed 308 mph; ceiling 29,000 feet; range with maximum fuel 2,235 miles; armament two 20mm Hispano cannon; four 7.62FN machine guns.

IAI-201, Arava. Israel Aircraft Industries; twin engine turbo-prop STOL light transport; maximum speed 217 mph; service ceiling 28,550 feet, one engine 11,150 feet; range, maximum fuel, 867 miles, maximum payload 301 miles.

ICBM. Intercontinental ballistic missile; 4,000- to 8,000-mile range; thermo-nuclear warhead.

IKV-91. Sweden, Hagglund and Soner; tank destroyer with 90mm gun in fully traversing turret; two machine guns; maximum speed (road) 42 mph; (water) 5 mph; weight 16.5 tons; range 375 miles.

Il-12 (NATO codename Coach). Soviet Union, Ilyushin; twin engine piston transport; operational from 1946; over 3,000 built; carries 27-32 passengers; maximum speed 252 mph; range 1,240 miles.

Il-14 (NATO codename Crate). Soviet Union, Ilyushin; twin engine, piston transport; operational from 1953; 32 passengers; maximum speed 258 mph; ceiling 22,000 feet; range over 900 miles.

Il-18, Moskva (NATO codename Coot). Soviet Union, Ilyushin; 4-engine turboprop, medium transport; operational from 1957; up to 110 passengers or maximum payload of 30,000 pounds; maximum cruising speed 400 mph; range with maximum fuel 4,000 miles (with maximum payload 2,300 miles); resembles Lockheed Electra.

Il-28 (NATO codename Beagle). Soviet Union, Ilyushin; twin-engine jet, light bomber; operational from 1950; 4,500 pounds of internal armament; maximum speed 580 mph; ceiling 41,000 feet; range 1,500 miles.

Il-38 (NATO codename May). Soviet Union, Ilyushin; a modification of Il-18 Coot for ASW; changes include

MAD (magnetic anomaly detection) boom in tail and an internal weapons bay in center-fuselage; conversion is similar to that of Lockheed Electra into P-3 Orion ASW aircraft.

IMPALA. South Africa, Atlas (Aermacchi MB-326 being built under license); light single engine jet trainer/counter-insurgency aircraft; operational since 1966; maximum speed 525 mph; ceiling 39,000 feet; combat radius 75 miles; 3,000 pounds of armament.

IRBM. Intermediate range ballistic missile; range 500 to 3,000 miles; thermo-nuclear warhead.

IROQUOIS. See UH-1.

ISKRA. See TS-11.

ISKU. Finland; a class of guided missile patrol boat (PTG); first built in 1970; first non-Soviet design to fire Styx SSM; length 86-1/2 feet; displacement 115 tons; maximum speed 25 knots; four Styx, one twin 30mm gun.

J-32, Lansen (Lance). Sweden, Saab; a single engine jet all-weather interceptor; operational since 1950s.

J-35. See DRAKEN.

J-37. See VIGGEN.

J-class (Juliet). Soviet Union; NATO designation for a class of diesel-powered missile submarines with 4 elevating launch tubes for Shaddock cruise missiles mounted flush with the deck.

JASTREB (Hawk). Yugoslavia, Soko; light ground attack version of Galeb jet trainer; operational from 1967; maximum speed 500 mph; three .50 caliber machine guns plus bombs and rockets.

JAVELIN. Britain, Gloster; delta-wing, all-weather single engine jet fighter; operational from 1956; four 30mm cannon or 2 cannon and 4 Firestreak AAMs; maximum speed 695 mph.

JET PROVOST (BAC 145). UK; single engine jet two-seat primary and basic trainer; maximum speed 440 mph; service ceiling 36,750 feet; maximum range 900 miles; can carry two 7.62mm machine guns and up to 3,000 pounds of bombs; later modification is BAC 167 Strikemaster (q.v.).

JET RANGER. (TH-57A SeaRanger, US Navy; OH-58A, Kiowa, US Army; also Bell 206A). US, Bell; five-seat turbine powered helicopter; see also OH-58.

JPz4-5. West Germany; tank destroyer with hull-mounted 90mm gun; 49 mph; range 240 miles; 23 tons; one of a family of tracked armored vehicles designed to operate with Leopard medium tank as a team; also includes APC, 120mm mortar carrier, and SS-11 antitank missile carrier.

JS-2. Soviet Union; World War II heavy tank; 122mm gun; 45 tons; maximum speed 23 mph; crew of 4.

JS-3. Soviet Union; post-World War II heavy tank; 122mm gun; 46 tons; maximum speed 23 mph; crew of 4.

JSU-122. See SU-122.

JSU-152. See SU-152/JSU-152.

JU-52. Germany, Junkers; pre-World War II three engine piston transport; produced in civil and military versions; total of 3,234 built; maximum speed 165 mph; range 800 miles.

K-61. Soviet Union; amphibious assault vehicle.

Ka-25 (NATO codename Hormone). Soviet Union, Kamov; armed ASW helicopter assigned to Moskya and Leningrad ASW helicopter cruisers.

KANGAROO (NATO codename). Soviet Union; air-to-surface missile carried by Tu-20 Bear heavy bomber; turbojet powered; 50 feet long; 30-foot span; range 300 miles plus.

KASHIN. Soviet Union; NATO designation for a class of DLG; 5,200 tons; 476 feet long; 35 knots; four 3-inch guns; five torpedo tubes; two twin Goa (SA-N-1) SAM launchers; two 12- and two 6-barrel ASW rocket launchers.

KC-130. Hercules. US, Lockheed; tanker version of C-130 (q.v.).

KC-135. Stratotanker. US, Boeing; jet tanker. See C-135. 820 C-135/KC-135 delivered.

KELT (NATO codename). Soviet Union; air-to-surface missile carried by Tu-16 Badger medium bomber; 31 feet long; 15-foot span; range over 100 miles.

KENNEL (NATO codename). Soviet Union; air-to-surface antishipping missile carried under the wings of Tu-16 medium bombers. These missiles are swept-wing and resemble a small jet fighter; turbojet-powered; 26 feet long; 14-foot span; range 50 miles plus. As a surface-to-surface missile launched by rocket booster it is used for coast defense by Poland and Cuba and bears the NATO codename Samlet.

KH-4. Japan, Kawasaki; four-seat, piston powered light general purpose helicopter developed by Kawasaki from the Bell 47 (q.v.); see also OH-13.

KILDIN. Soviet Union; NATO designation for a class of DD; 3,000 tons; 427 feet; one SS-N-1 launcher (SSM); two rocket launchers; four quadruple 45mm guns; 35 knots.

KIOWA. See OH-58.

KIPPER. (NATO codename). Soviet Union; air-to-surface missile carried by Tu-16; 31 feet long; 16-foot span; range over 120 miles.

KITCHEN. (NATO codename). Soviet Union; air-to-surface missile carried by Tu-22 Blinder supersonic, medium bombers; 36 feet long; 8-foot span; range over 200 miles.

KM, KM-2. See LM-1, LM-2.

KOMAR. Soviet Union; NATO designation for a class of guided missile patrol craft (PTG); converted from P-6 class torpedo boats; 85 feet long; 40 knots; two Styx SSMs and twin 25mm AA gun; operational from 1960; in service in USSR, Algeria, Cuba, Indonesia, Syria, Egypt, and China; name means mosquito.

KOTLIN. Soviet Union; NATO designation for a class of DDG/DD; 2,850 tons; 425 feet long; one twin Goa (SA-N-1) SAM launcher; two 3.9-inch guns, one quadruple 57mm gun, and 6 depthcharge projectors; or four 5.1-inch guns, four quadruple 45mm guns, six depthcharge projectors, and ten 21-inch torpedo tubes; 36 knots.

KRAGUJ. Yugoslavia; single-seat, light, piston-engine counterinsurgency aircraft; operational from 1967; two 7.9mm machine guns, light bombs, two 12-round rocket pods.

KRESTA. Soviet Union; NATO designation for a class of DLG; 7,000 tons; 509 feet long; two twin Shaddock SSM launchers; two twin Goa SAM launchers; ASW depth charges and torpedoes; two twin 57mm guns; 34 knots.

KRISHAK. (HAOP-27). India, HAL; liaison and utility single engine piston aircraft; operational from 1964; maximum speed 130 mph; ceiling 19,000 feet; range 290 miles.

KRONSTADT. Soviet Union; NATO designation for a class of submarine chasers (PC); operational from 1948; 167 feet long; 23 knots; one 3.9-inch gun; two 37mm AA guns; three 20mm AA guns; depthcharge projectors.

KRUPNY. Soviet Union; NATO designation for a class of DD; 3,650 tons; 450 feet long; two SS-N-1 SSM launchers; four quadruple 57mm guns; six ASW torpedo tubes; 34 knots.

KURIR. Yugoslavia; three-place, single engine piston liaison/utility aircraft; maximum speed 115 mph; ceiling 10,000 feet; range 470 miles.

KV-107. Japan, Kawasaki; Boeing Vertol CH-46, Sea Knight (q.v.), built in Japan.

KWH. Kilowatt hour; measurement of work performed by 1,000 watts of electricity during one hour, one watt for 1,000 hours, 250 watts for four hours, etc.

KYNDA. Soviet Union; NATO designation for a class of DLG; 6,000 tons; 492 feet; two quadruple Shaddock SSM launchers; one twin Goa SAM launcher; two twin 3.3-inch guns; six 21-inch torpedo tubes; depthcharge projectors; 35 knots.

L-4. US, Piper; two-seat, single engine piston light aircraft; utility version of the Piper Cub.

L-19. See O-1.

L-21. US, Piper; a version of the Piper Cub (see L-4) with a more powerful engine.

L-29, Delfin (NATO code name Maya). Czechoslovakia, Aero Vod; one or two-seat, single engine jet; basic and advanced trainer; counterinsurgency version; nose camera and underwing stores two 1,100 pound bombs; eight AG rockets; two 7.62mm machine guns; maximum speed, 16,400 feet, 407 mph; service ceiling 36,000 feet; maximum range 397 miles, external tanks, 555 miles.

L-39. Czechoslovakia, Aero Vod; single engine jet; two-seat advanced trainer; maximum speed 454 mph, Mach.83; average ceiling 37,225 feet; maximum range tip tanks empty, 680 miles; tip tanks full, 930 miles.

L-42. Regente. Brazil, Neiva; four seat, liaison and observation single engine piston aircraft (a later development of the C-42); maximum speed 149 mph; service ceiling 12,000 feet; maximum range 590 miles.

L-188. Electra. US, Lockheed; four-engine turboprop transport.

LABRADOR. See CH-113.

LACROSSE (MGM-18A). US; field artillery surface-to-surface missile; operational from 1958; radar-command terminal guidance; 19 feet long; 2,360 pounds; range 20 miles; nuclear or conventional warheads.

LAMA. See SA-315.

LANCE. (MGM-52A). US, Ling-Temco-Vought; tactical

surface-to-surface missile; replacement for Little John (q.v.) and Honest John (q.v.); 20 feet long; 3,200 pounds; launched from tracked transporter or a lightweight, wheeled launcher; ranges from 30 to 75 miles; operational from 1969; nuclear or conventional warhead.

LANSEN. See J-32.

LCG. Britain; landing craft, gun; a landing craft like an LCU, armored and armed with a 3-inch or larger gun and rockets for close-in support of a landing. US designation, LSSL (landing ship, support, large)

LCI. US and Britain; World War II landing craft, infantry; 158 feet long; 15 knots; capable of beaching and debarking 60-100 troops over ramps.

LCM. US; landing craft, mechanized; 50 to 75 feet long; 10 knots; carries one tank or its equivalent weight (30 to 60 tons) in other mechanized equipment which is landed over a bow ramp when beached; transported deck-loaded on APA and AKA, well-loaded in LSD and LPD.

LCU. US; landing craft, utility; 105 to 135 feet long; 10 knots; carries 3 to 5 tanks or their equivalent (175 tons) in other mechanized equipment which are landed over bow ramp when craft is beached.

LCVP. US; landing craft, vehicle-personnel; 36 feet long; 10 knots; carries 30 troops or a small vehicle which are landed over a bow ramp when beached; transported deck- or davit-loaded on APA and AKA.

LEANDER Class. Britain; class of general purpose frigates in service with Royal Navy and others; operational from 1964; displacement 2,450 tons (standard); 2,860 tons (full load); one Wasp (q.v.) ASW helicopter, quadruple Seacat (q.v.) SAM launcher, two sextuple 3 inch mk. 4 launchers, two twin 4.5 inch dual purpose guns, two single 40mm guns (or two single 20mm guns on Seacat equipped versions), depth charges; overall length 372 feet; speed 30 knots.

LEAR 23. US, Lear; twin-engine jet, light transport; operational from 1964; up to six passengers or 2,300 pounds; maximum speed 560; ceiling 45,000 feet; maximum range 1,000 to 1,800 miles depending on load.

LEOPARD. West Germany, Krauss-Maffei; medium tank; 105mm gun; 39 tons; 43 mph; range 350 miles; crew of 4.

Li-2. (NATO codename Cab). Soviet Union, Lisunov; World War II (and after) license-built version of US C-47 twin engine piston transport.

LIGHTNING. Britain, BAC; supersonic, twin-engine jet, all-weather interceptor, or multi-role, ground attack fighter; operational from 1958; maximum speed Mach 2.1; ceiling 60,000 feet.

LITTLE JOHN (MGR-3). US, Emerson; lightweight, transportable surface-to-surface tactical rocket; rocket and launcher together weigh less than 3,000 pounds (rocket alone weighs 780 pounds); nuclear or conventional warheads; range over 10 miles.

LM-1, LM-2, Nikko. Japan, Fuji Heavy Industries; four-seat single engine piston trainer; modification of the T-34 (q.v.).

LPD. US designation for landing platform, dock; an amphibious ship developed from the LSD; has a floodable well deck which carries LCU, LCM, or LVT; well is covered by a flight deck for six transport helicopters; 500 to 570 feet long; 20 knots; eight 3-inch automatic AA guns; 840 to 930 troops.

LPH. US designation for landing platform, helicopter; an amphibious ship with the appearance of an aircraft carrier (may be converted from a CVS or CVL); 600 feet long; 20 knots; carries 30 transport helicopters and 2,000 troops.

LSD. US designation for landing ship, dock; World War II and later; amphibious ship with floodable well deck for carrying LCU, LCM, and LVT; 450-550 feet long; 15 to 24 knots; 400 to 600 troops; other decks carry vehicles; some are fitted with helicopter platforms.

LSIL. US designation for landing ship, infantry, large; World War II; 160 feet long; 14 knots; capable of beaching and debarking 60 to 100 troops over a bow ramp.

LSM. US designation for landing ship, medium; World War II; 200 feet long; 12.5 knots; ocean-going; carries 3 to 5 tanks or equivalent mechanized equipment which it lands over a bow ramp when beached.

LSSL. US designation for landing ship, support, large; World War II; an LSM converted with one 5-inch gun and multiple barrage-rocket launchers for close support of landings.

LST. US designation for landing ship, tank; World War II and later amphibious ship for landing tanks and mechanized equipment which it lands over a bow ramp when beached; 300-525 feet long; 10 to 20 knots; 150-430 troops; 15,000 to 20,000 square feet of space for vehicles; up to 2,000 tons cargo.

LVTP5. US; landing vehicle, tracked, personnel; used by Marine Corps in 1950s-60s; 40 tons; crew of 3 plus up to 34 troops; land speed 30 mph, water 6-8 mph, land range 190 miles, water 57 miles.

M-2/M-3. US, White; half-tracked armored personnel carrier or scout car; World War II; over 41,000 built; still in extensive use by Israel.

M3A1/M5, Stuart I-IV. US; World War II light tank; 37mm gun; 13 1/2-16 1/2 tons; 35-40 mph; crew of 3 or 4.

M-4, Sherman. US; World War II medium tank; the few still in use are probably the later M4A3E8 with high-velocity 76mm gun; either US or Canadian-made; 36 tons; 30 mph; crew of 5; 50,000 produced.

M-6. US; armored car.

M-8, Greyhound. US; World War II 6-wheeled armored car; 7.4 tons; 37mm gun; 56 mph; over 8,500 built; unarmed version is M-20.

M-16. US; APC based on M-3 half-track (see M2/M3).

M-18 Hellcat. US; 76mm gun on tracked chassis in a full-traversing turret; operational from World War II; crew of five; weight 18.5 tons; also carries one 0.50 cal. machine gun; maximum speed (road) 55 mph; range over 200 miles.

M-20. See M-8.

M-24, Chaffee. US; World War II and later; light tank; 75mm gun; crew of 5; 34 mph; 19 tons.

M-36, Slugger. US; World War II; tank destroyer; 90mm turret-mounted on M-4 tank chassis; 30 tons; crew of 5; 28 mph.

M-41, Walker Bulldog. US; 1950s; light tank; 76mm gun; 23 tons; 41 mph; crew of 4.

M-42, Duster. US; twin 40mm AA gun mounted on M-41 tank chassis.

M-44. US; self-propelled 155mm howitzer; operational from 1956; weight 28.4 tons; crew of five; maximum speed (road) 35 mph.

M-47, Patton. US; 1950s; medium tank; 90mm gun; 48 tons; 37 mph; crew of 5.

M-48, Patton. US; 1950s/60s; medium tank; 90mm gun; 49.5 tons; 32 mph; crew of four; range 160 miles (except diesel M48 A3, 300 miles).

M-59. US; APC on tracked chassis; crew of two and ten troops; weight 18 tons; operational from 1953; maximum speed (road) 33 mph.

M-60, Patton. US; 1960s; main battle tank; 105mm gun; 51 tons; range 310 miles; 30 mph; crew of four.

M-60A1E2. US; main battle tank; 152mm gun launcher; weight 57 tons; range about 280 miles.

M-103. US; 1950s/60s; heavy tank; 120mm gun; 54.4 tons; 21 mph; range 100 miles; crew of five.

M-106. US; APC.

M-107. US; self-propelled 175mm gun on a tracked chassis; gun's range is 18.8 miles; crew of six; weight 25 tons; maximum speed 34 mph; cruising range 450 miles.

M-109. US, self-propelled 155mm howitzer on a tracked chassis; gun's range 18,000 yards; weight 26 tons; range 440 miles.

M-110. US; self-propelled 8 inch howitzer on a tracked chassis; gun's range 10.2 miles; rest of characteristics same as M-107 (q.v.).

M-113. US; 1960s; amphibious armored personnel carrier; 11.5 tons; 42 mph; crew of two plus 11 infantry men.

M-114. US, tracked APC; improved version of M-113 (q.v.).

M-577. US; APC on tracked chassis; crew of two plus 12 troops.

M-706. US; armored car.

MAC-1. US, Chrysler; 4-wheeled armored car used by Mexico; 6.7 tons; 65 mph; range 300 miles; 20mm gun; crew of four.

MAGISTER (CM170). France, Fouga; light, twin-engine jet, trainer; operational from 1956; about 900 built in France and abroad under license; maximum speed 443 mph; ceiling 40,000 feet; range 575 miles; two .50 caliber machine guns plus two rocket pods, two 110-pound bombs, or two AS-11 missiles.

MALAFON. France, Latecoere; surface-to-surface or surface-to-under-water winged naval missile; solid-fuel rocket boosters; 21-inch, acoustic-homing torpedo weighing 1,150 pounds; launch weight 2,865 pounds; range 11 miles; operational from 1965.

MANDRAKE. Soviet Union, Yakovlev; NATO codename for a long range, twin-engine jet, very high altitude, strategic reconnaissance aircraft; single seat; operational since 1963; exact YAK designation unknown but it is thought to be a development of the YAK-25 with a new straight wing extended span, much like the US U-2 and RB-57F Canberra.

MARDER. West Germany; full-tracked APC; carries 10 (including crew); maximum speed 45 mph; one 20mm cannon.

MARTEL, AS-37 (Missile, Anti-Radar and Television). France and Britain, Matra and Hawker-Siddeley; television-guided or radar-homing air-to-surface missile; operational from 1967; range "tens of miles"; length 12 feet.

MARUT, HF-24. India, HAL; supersonic, single-seat, twin-engine jet fighter; operational from 1964; maximum speed Mach 1.02; range 400 miles; four 30mm cannon; retractable pack of 48 air-to-air rockets or four 1,000-pound bombs.

MASURCA, Mk.2. France; naval surface-to-air missile; length 28 feet; launch weight 4,387 pounds; range over 25 miles.

MATRA R-511. France, Matra; air-to-air guided missile; operational from about 1960; length 10 feet; weight 400 pounds; maximum speed Mach 1.8; range four nautical miles; semi-active homing.

MATRA R-530. France, Matra; air-to-air guided missile; operational from 1967; interchangeable semi-active radar and infra-red homing heads; 60-pound, proximity-fuse HE warhead; weight 430 pounds; speed Mach 2.7; range 11 miles.

MB-326B. Italy, Aermacchi; light single engine jet trainer/ground attack aircraft; operational from 1961; maximum speed 509 mph; ceiling 41,000 feet; range 690 miles; two .50 caliber machine gun pods; four air-to-air rocket pods or six 260-pound bombs; South African version, Impala; Brazilian version, Xavante.

MB-326G. Higher powered version of MB-326B; up to 4,000 pounds of armament on six underwing attachment points; maximum speed 539 mph; ceiling 47,000 feet; combat radius, armed, 800 miles.

MENTOR. See T-34.

METEOR. Britain, Gloster; twin-engine jet fighter; operational from 1946; maximum speed 592 mph; range 710 miles; ceiling 44,000 feet; carries four 20mm cannon, 2,000 pounds of bombs and rockets.

Mi-1 (NATO codename Hare). Soviet Union, Mil; utility helicopter; up to 3 passengers; maximum speed 125 mph; range 200 miles.

Mi-2. Soviet Union, Mil; a variant of the Mi-1 (q.v.) equipped with two turboshaft engines in place of the Mi-1's single piston engine; now produced solely in Poland; carries six to eight passengers; maximum speed 130 mph; maximum payload 1,765 pounds; ceiling 13,755 feet; range (with maximum fuel) 360 miles.

Mi-4 (NATO codename Hound). Soviet Union, Mil; utility helicopter; 8-11 passengers, or up to 14 troops; operational from 1952; maximum payload 3,800 pounds; maximum speed 130 mph; ceiling 18,000 feet; range 150-250 miles; several thousand built; one 1,700-hp piston engine.

Mi-6 (NATO codename Hook). Soviet Union, Mil; heavy utility helicopter; operational from 1957; two 5,500-shp turbines; 65 passengers; maximum payload 26,000 pounds; maximum speed 185 mph; ceiling 14,750 feet; range with 17,000-pound payload, 385 miles.

Mi-8 (NATO codename Hip). Soviet Union, Mil; general purpose two turboshaft-powered transport helicopter; crew of two or three and 28 passengers; can carry 12 stretchers; internal freight 8,820 pounds; externally carried freight, 6,614 pounds; maximum speed 155 mph; range 233 miles.

Mi-10 (NATO codename Harke). Soviet Union, Mil; a flying crane development of Mi-6 using same engines; first seen in 1961; maximum payload 33,070 pounds.

Mi-12 (NATO codename Homer). Soviet Union, Mil; world's largest and heaviest helicopter; maximum payload 88,636 pounds; crew of 6; four 6,500-shp turbines; fuselage is 121 feet long; span over rotor tips is 220 feet.

MiG-15 (NATO codename Fagot). Soviet Union, Mikoyan-Gurevich; swept-wing single engine jet fighter; operational from 1948; two 23mm and one 37mm cannon; two 550-pound bombs; maximum speed 668 mph; ceiling 48,000; range 560 miles; two-seat trainer version is MiG-15 UTI (NATO codename Midget).

MiG-17 (NATO codename Fresco). Soviet Union, Mikoyan-Gurevich; swept-wing single engine jet fighter; operational from 1953; three 23mm cannon; ceiling 55,000 feet; range 600 miles; "D" and "E" models have limited all-weather capability and are armed with both cannon and AAMs.

MiG-19 (NATO codename Farmer). Soviet Union, Mikoyan-Gurevich; swept-wing twin-engine, jet fighter; "A" model is day fighter; "B" model limited all-weather interceptor; operational from 1955; three 30mm cannon and AAMs; maximum speed 900 mph; ceiling 58,000 feet; range with external tanks 1,370 miles.

MiG-21 (NATO codename Fishbed). Soviet Union, Mikoyan-Gurevich; short range, delta wing, single engine jet, supersonic fighter; operational since 1956; maximum speed Mach 2.1 above 36,000 feet; Mach 1.06 at low level; combat radius varies with altitude, external stores and mission but averages approximately 350 miles; in the fighter role it carries ATOLL AAM or two pods, each containing 16 55mm rockets, or a gun pod with a twin barrel 23mm cannon; in the fighter-bomber role, four 240mm ASM, two 1,100-pound and two 550-pound bombs; in the reconnaissance role, a camera pod or infrared or other sensors. Later models have a limited all weather capability with airborne intercept radar, the two-seat trainer version has the NATO codename Mongol.

MiG-25 (NATO codename Foxbat). Soviet Union, Mikoyan-Gurevich; high-altitude, twin engine jet all-weather interceptor; operational from 1969; maximum speed Mach 3; ceiling over 70,000 feet; reported based in Egypt, and possibly Algeria, with Soviet forces; also equips Soviet units in USSR and East Europe.

MILAN. France-West Germany. Nord-Bolkow; wire-guided antitank missile; 2 1/2 feet long; 24 pounds; 400 mph; range 25-2,000 meters.

MINUTEMAN I/II/III (LGM-30A/B/F/G). US, Boeing; three-stage, solid-fuel ICBM; one-megaton thermonuclear warhead; 800 Minuteman I were operational by 1965; 200 Minuteman II became operational in 1966-67; Minuteman III is now replacing some of the earlier models and is equipped with a MIRV (multiple independently targetable re-entry vehicle) containing three warheads; launch weight 65,000-70,000 pounds; speed Mach 22; range 6,000 to 7,000 miles.

MIRAGE III. France, Dassault; single engine jet supersonic, all-weather, delta-wing, interceptor and ground support aircraft; operational from 1960; about 1,000 built; maximum speed Mach 2.17; ceiling 54,000 feet; ground attack combat radius 560 miles; high-altitude subsonic combat radius 745 miles; III B is a two-seat trainer retaining full combat capability; III C is all-weather interceptor and day ground attack fighter; III D is two-seat version of III O, the Australian license-built version of the III E; III E is the long-range, fighter-bomber/intruder version; III R is a reconnaissance version of III E; III S is the Swiss-built version of III E with improved radar and Falcon AAMs.

MIRAGE IV. France, Dassault; two-seat, twin-engine jet, supersonic, delta-wing atomic bomber operational from 1964; 62 built; operational radius of over 1,000 miles at Mach 1.7 at high altitude; maximum speed Mach 2.2; ceiling 65,000 feet.

MIRAGE 5. France, Dassault: single engine jet fighter-bomber; operational late 1971; essentially a simplified version of III E; in service with Peruvian and Belgian air forces.

MIRV. Multiple independently-targetable re-entry vehicle warhead for ICBMs.

MMC. US designation for coastal minelayer; usually a small, short-range ship carrying a limited number of moored contact or controlled mines to be laid off friendly coasts.

MMF. US designation for fleet minelayer; an ocean-going ship which can operate with the high-seas fleet, defend itself from air and surface attack, and lay mines offensively. US MMFs carry up to 1,000 mines.

MO-VI. Soviet Union, small submarine chaser; in production from 1956 to 1960; adaptation of P-6 motor torpedoboat; maximum speed 38.5 knots; displacement 79.5 tons; two depth charge mortars and two depth charge racks with total of 24 charges, in place of torpedo tubes; two twin 25mm guns; about 80 constructed or converted from P-6s.

MODEL 61. Japan; operational 1962; medium tank; 90mm gun; 35 tons; crew of four.

MOSKVA (Moscow). Soviet Union; NATO designation for a class of ASW cruiser and helicopter carrier; 15,000 tons; 30 knots; carries 20 or more Ka-25 Hormone armed ASW helicopters; variable-depth sonar; two twin 57mm guns; two twin SAM launchers (SA-N-3); two 12-barrel ASW rocket launchers; one twin launcher for ASROC/SUBROC-type weapon; torpedo tubes mounted amidships, below decks.

MOSS (NATO codename). Soviet Union, Tupolev; four-engine turboprop AWACS (Airborne Warning and Control System) aircraft version of Tu-114 transport (q.v.).

MRBM. Medium-range ballistic missile; range up to 1,000 or 1,500 miles; thermo-nuclear warhead.

MRV. Multiple re-entry vehicle; multiple warhead for ICBMs; not independently targeted.

MS-760 (Paris III). France, Potez; twin-engine jet, light transport; five passengers; maximum speed 415 mph; ceiling 39,000 feet; range 970 miles.

MSBS M-1. France; SLBM with range of 1,380 miles; carries a 500 kiloton warhead; from 1976 forward M-1 is to be replaced by M-2 with a thermonuclear warhead of one megaton yield and a range of 1,864 miles.

MSC. US designation for coastal minesweeper; small, under 140 feet long; non-magnetic; capable of mechanized and influence sweeps in shallow coastal waters.

MSF. US designation for fleet minesweeper; large ocean-going mechanical sweeper to accompany fleet.

MSI. US designation for inshore minesweeper; non-magnetic; small, about 110 feet, and shallow draft for mechanical and influence sweeps in inshore waters in advance of landings or in harbor approaches.

MSO. US designation for ocean minesweeper; large, ocean-going, non-magnetic ship capable of mechanical and influence sweeping with the fleet; a more modern type than the MSF.

MUSKETEER. US, Beech; two-seat, single engine piston light trainer; in production since 1962; maximum speed 140 mph; range 880 miles.

Mya-4 (NATO codename Bison). Soviet, Myasishchev; four engine jet heavy bomber; now used primarily in tanker and maritime-reconnaissance roles; operational from 1958.

MYSTERE IV. France, Dassault; swept-wing, single engine jet fighter; operational from 1954; over 400 built; two 30mm cannon; maximum speed Mach 0.94; ceiling 45,000 feet; range 575 miles.

N-class (November). Soviet Union; NATO designation for a class of nuclear-powered attack submarines with six bow-mounted torpedo tubes; 25-30 knots submerged.

NANUCHKA. Soviet Union; NATO designation for a class of fast guided missile gunboat (PG); length 198 feet; displacement 650 tons; maximum speed 32 knots; two triple SSM launchers, one twin 57mm dual-purpose gun, possible SAM; 6 in service with Soviet Navy.

NEPTUNE. See P-2.

NF-5. Canada, Canadair; version of F-5 aircraft (q.v.) built for the Netherlands.

NIKE-AJAX (MIM-3A). US, Douglas; surface-to-air missile; operational from 1953; 15,000 built; length 34 feet; 2,455 pounds; speed Mach 2.25; range 25 miles; ceiling 63,000 feet.

NIKE-HERCULES (MIM-14A). US, Douglas; surface-to-air missile; operational from 1958; 15,000 built; nuclear or HE warhead; length 41 1/2 feet; 10,400 pounds; speed Mach 3.65, range 80 miles; ceiling 153,000 feet.

NIMROD. Britain, Hawker-Siddeley; highly modified version of Comet four-engine jet transport; used for maritime reconnaissance and ASW; 41 in service.

NORATLAS. France, Norad; twin-engine piston transport; operational from 1952; up to 45 passengers; maximum speed 270 mph; ceiling 24,000 feet.

NUOLI. Finland; class of fast patrol boat (PTF); production started 1961; length 72 feet; displacement 46.5 tons; maximum speed over 40 knots; one 40mm and one 20mm gun; mines and depth charges.

O-1, Bird Dog (L-19). US, Cessna; two-place, single engine piston liaison aircraft; operational from 1950; about 5,500 built; maximum speed 115 mph; ceiling 8,000 feet; range 530 miles.

O-2. US, Cessna; military version of 337 Super Skymaster; twin engine, piston liason/utility aircraft; four passengers or equivalent cargo or armament; four armament attachment points under wings; maximum speed 200 mph; ceiling 20,000 feet; range 750 miles; operational in 1968; 200 built.

OBERON-class. Britain; class of diesel submarines in service with Royal Navy and other navies; overall length, 295 feet; displacement, 1,610 tons (standard), 2,030 (surface), 2,410 (submerged); eight 21-inch torpedo tubes; speed, 12 knots (surface), 17 knots (submerged); operational from mid-1960s.

OH-6, Cayuse. US, Hughes; light observation helicopter; operational from 1966 when deliveries began on order of over 700; 317-shp turbine; four troops or various machine gun and rocket pod combinations; maximum speed 140 mph; ceiling 15,000 feet; range 410 miles.

OH-13, Sioux (Model 47). US, Bell (built under license in Italy, Japan, and Britain); three passengers or 1,000 pounds of cargo; 280-hp engine; maximum speed 105 mph; ceiling 20,000 feet; range 300 miles.

OH-23. Raven. See H-23.

OH-58, Kiowa. US, Bell; four-seat, turbine-powered helicopter; civil version is called Jet Ranger.

OSA (Bee). Soviet Union; NATO designation for a class of guided missile patrol craft (PTFG); length 130 feet; displacement 200 tons; maximum speed 36 knots; range at 25-knot cruising speed 600 to 800mm; four Styx SSMs and two twin 30-mm guns; Drum Tilt fire-control radar for guns; Osa I has original version of Styx; Osa II probably has folding-wing variant of Styx; in service in USSR, Algeria, China, Cuba, East Germany, Egypt, India, Poland, Romania, and Yugoslavia.

OT-62, OT-64, OT-65, OT-66. Czechoslovakia; license-built versions of Soviet BTR-50 and -60 series APCs.

OTTER (US designation, U-1A; Canadian, DHC-3). Canada, De Havilland; single-engine, piston STOL utility aircraft; operational from 1953; over 500 built; 9-10 passengers; maximum speed 160 mph; ceiling 18,000 feet; range 960 miles; can also operate on skis or floats.

OURAGAN (Hurricane). France, Dassault; single engine jet fighter.

OV-10, Bronco. US, North American Rockwell; two-seat twin-turboprop COIN aircraft; operational from 1967; used by US Air Force, Marines, and Navy as forward air control aircraft, helicopter escort, light attack aircraft, etc.; also in service with Thai Air Force and West German Luftwaffe; can carry various combinations of guns, bombs, and missiles up to a maximum payload of 3,600 pounds; maximum speed 288 mph; maximum range 1,428 miles; combat radius 228 miles.

P-2, Neptune (formerly P2V). US, Lockheed; twin engine piston maritime reconnaissance and ASW aircraft; operational from 1945; over 1,000 built; two turbojets added later to improve performance; 8,000 pounds of armament; ASW detection gear; maximum speed over 300 mph; ceiling 22,000 feet; range 3,850 miles.

P-2J. Japan, Kawasaki; Lockheed SP-2H Neptune with stretched fuselage, added electronics, and piston engines replaced by two 2,850-shp turboprops, two 3,085-pound thrust turbojets; normal cruising speed 253 mph; long-range cruising speed 196 mph; ceiling 30,000 feet; maximum speed 390 mph; cruising range 2,765 miles; total of 46 on order; began entering service in 1970.

P-3, Orion (formerly P3V). US, Lockheed; maritime patrol and ASW aircraft; operational from 1961; based on Electra, four-engine, turboprop airliner; maximum speed 475 mph; ceiling 28,000 feet; maximum radius 2,500 miles; maximum radius with three hours on station 1,900 miles; 20,000 pounds of mines, depth charges, torpedoes, sonobuoys, flares, and markers can be carried internally and on six underwing points.

P-4 (NATO class designator, Komsomolets). Soviet Union; motor torpedo boat; entered service in 1951; aluminum hull; maximum speed over 50 knots; length 63 feet; displacement 21 tons; two 18-inch torpedo tubes; one twin 14.5mm machine gun mount; depth charges; in addition to USSR is in service in Albania, Bulgaria, China, Cuba, Cyprus, North Korea, Romania, North Vietnam, and Yemen (Aden).

P-5M, Marlin (also P-5B). US, Martin; maritime reconnaissance flying boat; 12,000 pounds of armament; ASW detection gear; two piston engines supplemented by tailmounted jet engine; maximum speed 250 mph; range 2,000 miles.

P-6. Soviet Union; motor torpedoboat; entered production in 1954; wooden hull; length 85 feet; displacement 65 tons; maximum speed about 45 knots; range at 30-knot cruising speed about 450nm; two 21-inch torpedo tubes, two twin 25mm power-operated cannon, depth charges (two sizes) and mines; Pot Head radar; in service in USSR, Cuba, Algeria, Egypt, East Germany, Indonesia, Iraq, Poland, North Vietnam, Guinea; China has constructed about 80 duplicates, some of which may have been given to N. Korea; total of about 600 built if Komar and MO-VI (q.v.) variants are included.

P-149. Italy, Piaggio; single engine piston trainer developed from the similar P-148; up to 5 seats; 190 mph; ceiling 19,000 feet; range 680 miles.

P-166M (Albatross). Italy, Piaggio; twin engine, two-seat piston powered coastal patrol aircraft; maximum speed 222 mph; range 1,200 miles.

PA-28-140, Cherokee. US, Piper; single engine, two/four-seat piston light trainer/utility aircraft; maximum speed 142 mph.; maximum range 839 miles.

PBM, Mariner. US, Martin; twin engine piston flying boat, patrol bomber; operational from late World War II.

PBR. US designation for river patrol boat; 30 to 50 feet long; shallow draft, fast; often hydrojet-propelled; armored and armed with a combination of machine guns, mortars, and recoilless weapons.

Pbv 301. Sweden, Hagglund; APC on tracked chassis; driver plus nine troops; weight 11.7 tons; maximum speed 28 mph; one 20mm cannon; operational from 1962.

Pbv 302. Sweden; tracked amphibious armored personnel carrier; 13 tons; 40 mph; range 190 miles; 20mm gun; crew of 2 plus 10 troops.

PBY, Catalina. US, Consolidated-Vultee; World War II; twin engine piston maritime reconnaissance/patrol bomber flying boat; over 2,000 built; maximum speed 195 mph; range 2,500 miles.

PC. US designation for a class of submarine chaser; 170 feet long; one 3-inch gun and ASW weapons; any ASW-capable ship of about this size.

PC-6, Porter. Switzerland, Pilatus, and US, Fairchild (AU-23A); land-based, eight or ten-seat single engine piston-powered STOL light transport; maximum speed 161 mph; maximum range 1,006 miles; later version PC-6A, (q.v.) turboprop-powered.

PC-6A, Turbo-Porter. US/Switzerland, Fairchild/Pilatus; single engine, eight-ten seat turboprop-powered light transport; maximum cruising speed 161 mph; maximum range 1,006 miles; armament 20mm cannon and guns or rocket pods.

PCE. US designation for a class of escort ships; 180 feet long; one 3-inch gun and ASW weapons; any ASW-capable ship of about this size.

PCF. US designation for a class of fast patrol craft for inshore interdiction and control of fishing and coastal craft; 50 feet long; 25 knots; one 81mm mortar and three .50 caliber machine guns.

PCH. US designation for a class of submarine chasers equipped with hydrofoils.

PCS. US designation for a class of submarine chaser; 136 feet long; armed with 40mm guns and ASW weapons; equivalent of British seaward defense craft.

PD-808. Italy, Piaggio; six-nine seat, twin engine jet, VIP transport, ECM, or navigation trainer aircraft; maximum speed 529 mph; range 1,322 miles.

PEMBROKE. Britain, Hunting; twin-engine piston transport; operational from 1952; 10 passengers; maximum speed 224 mph; ceiling 22,000 feet; range 1,100 miles.

PENGUIN. Norway; Norwegian-designed and built SSM; entered service in 1970; length 9 feet, 7 inches; weight 740 pounds (including 264-pound warhead); inertial guidance and passive infrared homing; range of 10 to 15 miles.

PERSHING (MGM-31A). US, Martin; two-stage, selective-range, surface-to-surface missile; highly mobile; nuclear warhead; simplified support equipment; air transportable in CH-47, C-123, or C-130; operational from 1962; originally designed with launcher and support equipment in wheeled or tracked versions; four vehicles—erector-launcher with missile (less warhead), test and power vehicle, communications vehicle, and warhead transporter; launch weight 10,000 pounds; range 115-460 miles.

PETYA. Soviet Union; NATO designation for a class of DE; 250 feet long; 30 knots; two twin 3-inch guns; ASW rocket launchers and torpedoes; diesel and gas-turbine propulsion.

PF. US designation for a class of patrol escort; over 200 feet long; guns and ASW weapons same as British frigate.

PG. US designation for a class of fast gunboat; 165 feet long; over 40 knots; one 3-inch automatic gun; one 40mm gun; combination diesel and gas-turbine (CODAG) propulsion.

PGM. US designation for a class of motor gunboat; 95 feet long; 15 knots; one 40mm gun; .50 caliber machine guns; any craft of from 100 to 150 feet without an ASW capability; standard patrol craft supplied through US Military Assistance Program.

PHOENIX (AIM-5A). US, Hughes; air-to-air missile; 1,400 pounds; 13 feet long; range 40 nautical miles; for fleet defense by F-14 Tomcat (originally designed for use with F-111B); radar homing by prime source.

PL-1, PL-2, Chienshou. Republic of China (Taiwan); two seat single engine piston-powered primary trainer built in Taiwan at the Aeronautical Research Laboratory, Taichung; also being built in Vietnam, Thailand, and S. Korea; maximum speed 150 mph; maximum range 405 miles.

PLEJAD. Sweden; a class of fast patrol boat (PTF) constructed in West Germany between 1955 and 1960; length 157 1/2 feet; displacement 170 tons; maximum speed 37.5 knots; range at 30-knot cruising speed 600nm; six 21-inch torpedo tubes, two 40mm guns, mines.

PO-2 (NATO codename Mule). Soviet Union, Polikarpov; operational from 1928; a two-seat single engine piston biplane trainer; maximum speed 97 mph; ceiling 13,000 feet.

PO-2. Soviet Union; class of minesweeping launch; employed for use in harbor, coastal, inshore and estuarial areas and for general purpose duties.

POLARIS/POSEIDON. US, Lockheed; ballistic missiles designed to be launched from submerged submarines; Polaris versions have ranges of from 1,500 to 2,500 miles. Poseidon has range of almost 3,000 miles and can carry MIRV warhead.

POLNOCNY. Soviet Union; NATO designation for a class of landing ship.

POLUCHAT. Soviet Union; designation for a class of PGM; length about 100 feet; 18 knots; armed with 37mm, 25mm, or 14.5mm automatic guns.

POTI. Soviet Union; NATO designation for a class of submarine chaser; in service from 1960; length 197 feet; displacement 500 tons; two automatically-reloading, 12-tube ASW rocket launchers, four 16-inch ASW torpedo tubes, twin 57mm dual-purpose guns; in service in USSR and Romania.

PROVOST. Britain, Hunting; single engine, two-seat piston-powered; armed trainer/reconnaissance aircraft; maximum speed 200 mph; armament, two .30 cal machine guns; 500 pounds bombs; or 60 pounds rockets.

PT. US designation for motor torpedo boats; 60 to 120 feet long; over 40 knots; 2 to 4 torpedoes.

PT-13,17. US, Stearman design, Boeing; (Kaydet); World War II (and earlier); two-seat, single-engine piston biplane, primary trainer; over 10,000 built when production ceased in 1945; maximum speed 105 mph; range 385 miles; ceiling 13,000 feet.

PT-19. US, Fairchild; World War II; single-engine piston monoplane, two-seat primary trainer; maximum speed 125 mph; range 430 miles; ceiling 13,000 feet.

PT-76. Soviet Union; amphibious light tank; 1950/60s; 76mm gun; 15 1/2 tons; 31 mph on land, 7 mph on water.

PTF. US designation for fast patrol craft employed for various special missions; essentially PT boats without torpedoes but mounting light guns (e.g., 40mm). **PTFG.** US designation for patrol torpedo fast guided missile boat.

PUMA. France/Britain, Aerospatiale/Westland; twin-turbine, single-rotor medium transport helicopter; operational from 1970; maximum speed 174 mph; maximum range 390 miles (with extra tanks, 865 miles); ceiling 15,750 feet; crew of 2 plus 20 troops (or over 2.5 tons of cargo).

PV-2, Harpoon. US, Lockheed; World War II maritime reconnaissance bomber; two piston engines; carries 4,000 pounds of bombs internally and an additional 2,000 pounds externally, also carries 0.50-inch machine guns; maximum speed 265 mph; maximum range about 2,000 miles; over 500 built.

PX-S. Japan, Shin-Meiwa; STOL maritime reconnaissance flying boat; four 2,850-shp turboprop engines; maximum speed 340 mph; range 3,000 miles; ceiling 29,000 feet.

Pz-61. Switzerland; medium tank; 105mm gun; 35 tons; 30 mph; range 190 miles.

Pz-68. Switzerland; improved version of Pz-61 tank.

PZL-104. See WILGA.

Q-class (Quebec). Soviet Union; NATO designation for a class of short-range, diesel-powered submarines; probably used now for coastal defense patrols.

QUAIL (AIM-20). US, McDonnell-Douglas; decoy missile carried internally by B-52s; launched to confuse enemy radars because its radar profile is very similar to a B-52.

R-class (Romeo). Soviet Union; NATO designation for a class of modified W-class submarines with modernized super-structure, conning tower, and sonar installation.

RAPIER. Britain, BAC; surface-to-air missile; operational in 1970; for low-altitude defense.

Rb08. Sweden, Saab; SSM for ship-to-ship or surface-to-surface use; evolved from a French-designed target drone; operational from 1970; also called Aerospatiale M.20; operated from coastal defense batteries and two destroyers; terminal homing; launch weight 1,985 pounds.

REDEYE. US, General Dynamics; portable, tube-launched SAM; carried and fired by one man; uses infra-red homing; version proposed for air-launch from helicopters, called MRAM (Multi-Mission Redeye Air-Launched Missile); two each in pods on each side of helicopter; for air-to-ground use against such targets as tanks; Redeye is operational with US Army and Marine Corps.

RED TOP. Britain, Hawker-Siddeley; air-to-air missile; 11 1/2 feet long; speed Mach 3; range 6 nautical miles; infra-red homing; carried as standard armament on later marks of the Lightning and Sea Vixen.

REGIMENT. US Marine Corps: an infantry regiment consists of three infantry battalions, and an artillery regiment consists of three light and one medium artillery battalions. Britain: an infantry regiment is a traditional and administrative unit parent to a number of separate infantry battalions which may be deployed with different infantry brigades; artillery and armored regiments of 24 guns or 35 to 50 armored vehicles, respectively, are the equivalent of US artillery or armored battalions. The artillery regiments comprise two batteries of two troops each; the armored regiments are composed of squadrons (US equivalents being company or troop) which consist of troops (US equivalent being platoons). U.S. Army: The British infantry regiment example has been followed for all of the combat arms.

REGIMENTAL LANDING TEAM. US; a Marine infantry regiment reinforced with the necessary supporting arms and services to enable it to conduct an amphibious operation.

RF-4, RF-5, RF-80, RF-84, RF-86, RF-101, RF-104, RT-33, etc. US; reconnaissance versions of the basic aircraft; usually stripped of guns and armor for greater speed and mounting a variety of cameras and other sensors.

RIGA. Soviet Union; NATO designation for a class of DE; 1,200 tons; 279 feet long; three 3.9-inch guns; three 37mm guns; 28 knots; depth-charge projectors and ASW torpedoes.

ROLAND. France-West Germany, Nord-Bolkow; light surface-to-air missile for use against low-flying aircraft; launched from a light armored vehicle; eight feet long; launch weight 140 pounds; speed Mach 2; range 1,600 to 19,700 feet.

RUISSALO. Finland; a class of motor gunboat (PGM); convertible to minesweeper; built from 1959; length 114 feet; displacement 130 tons; maximum speed 20 knots; one 40mm and one 20mm gun, one Squid ASW mortar, mines and sweep gear; versions sold to Colombia are used as customs launches and carry only a single 20mm gun.

S-2 (S-2D, S-2F), Tracker. US, Grumman; twin-engine, piston carrier-based, anti-submarine search and attack aircraft; operational from 1954; over 1,000 built; maximum speed 265 mph; ceiling 21,000 feet; range 970 miles or patrol endurance of nine hours; ASW detection gear; homing torpedoes; depth charges, bombs, rockets, and sonobuoys. The C-1A Trader is a utility transport version for carrier-onboard-delivery (COD) of passengers and high-priority cargo. The E-1B Trader is an airborne early-warning and fighter direction version.

S-32. Sweden, Saab; reconnaissance version of A-32 (q.v.).

S-35. Sweden, Saab; reconnaissance version of Draken (q.v.).

S-37. Sweden, Saab; reconnaissance version of Viggen (q.v.).

S-51. US, Sikorsky; four-seat single-rotor helicopter; operational from 1947; over 300 built in both civil and military versions; maximum speed 95 mph; ceiling, 13,200 feet; maximum range 300 miles.

S-55. See H-19.

S-58. See H-34.

S-65-OE. US, Sikorsky; a variant of the CH-53 (q.v.).

SA-2. See GUIDELINE.

SA-3. See GOA.

SA-4. See GANEF.

SA-5. See GRIFFON.

SA-6. See GAINFUL.

SA-7. See GRAIL.

SA-315, Lama. France, Aerospatiale; helicopter; Alouette III engine on Alouette II airframe; Indian version built by HAL called Cheetah.

SA-330. See PUMA.

SA-341, Gazelle. Brazil, Aerospatiale (France origin), built under license by Embraer in Brazil; 5-seat light observation helicopter; single engine turboshaft powered, maximum speed 165 mph, hovering ceiling 10,170 feet, maximum range 403 miles.

Saab 105; See A-60.

Saab MFI-15. Sweden; single engine two/three-seat piston-powered light trainers; maximum speed 160 mph; endurance 4 hours 45 minutes.

SABRA. Israel; main battle tank; built by Israel Army Ordnance; 40 tons; mounts 105mm gun (British); 1,000 hp diesel engine (American); entered service 1972.

SABRE 27. Australian license-built version of the F-86 (q.v.).

SABRE 32. Later version of SABRE 27.

SAETA (E-14). Spain, Hispano; also referred to as HA-200; twin-engine jet, armed trainer; operational from 1960; over 100 built in Spain; 90 built in Egypt under license as Al-Kahira; maximum speed 435 mph; ceiling 40,000 feet; range 1,050 miles; two underwing attachment points for armament.

SAFIR (Saab 91-D). Sweden, Saab; single engine piston four-seat, training and utility aircraft; over 300 built; maximum speed 165 mph; ceiling 16,000; range 650 miles; can be armed with two light machine guns.

SAGE. Semi-automatic ground environment; air defense system built about an electronic digital computer that reports and acts on a developing situation; operational in U.S. Aerospace Defense Command.

SAHARA. France, Breguet; four-engine piston, heavy transport; operational from 1958; 145 troops or 34,000 pounds of cargo; maximum speed 230 mph; range 2,900 miles.

SALADIN. Britain, Alvis; post-World War II; 6-wheeled armored car; 11 tons; speed 45 mph; 76mm gun; range 250 miles; crew of 3.

SALISH. Soviet Union; NATO codename; SSM similar to Samlet.

SAM. Surface-to-air missile.

SAMLET. See KENNEL.

SARACEN. Britain, Alvis; 6-wheeled armored personnel carrier; 10 tons; 43 mph; range 240 miles; crew of 2 plus 10 troops.

SC. US designation for a class of submarine chaser; 110 feet long; small gun and ASW weapons; equivalent of British seaward defense craft.

SCORPION (M-56). US; self-propelled antitank gun (SPAT); 90mm; 7.5 tons; crew of 4; 27 mph; air droppable.

SCORPION. Britain, Alvis; tracked light reconnaissance vehicle; weight 7.5 tons; range 400 miles; maximum speed (road) 45mph; lightweight 76mm gun; aluminum; zinc-magnesium alloy armor.

SCOUT. See WASP.

SCUD. Soviet Union; NATO designation for mobile tactical surface-to-surface missile; various versions are mounted on tracked or wheeled launchers; ranges of 50 to 100 miles; nuclear capability.

SEACAT. Britain, Short Brothers and Harland; short-range naval surface-to-air missile.

SEA HAWK. Britain, Armstrong-Whitworth; carrier-based, twin-engine jet, fighter-bomber; four 20mm cannon; 1,000 pounds of external armament; maximum speed 600 mph; combat radius 230 miles.

SEAKILLER. Britain; short range, surface-to-surface missile.

SEA KING. US, Sikorsky; twin turbine, single rotor helicopter; used as transport (26 troops), for ASW duties, air/sea rescue, astronaut recovery, etc.; used by US, Danish, Canadian, Malaysian, Brazilian, Japanese, Italian, British, and German armed forces; license-built in Canada, Britain, Japan, and Italy.

SEA VENOM. Britain, DeHavilland; carrier-based single engine jet, two-seat fighter; four 20mm cannons; 500 pounds of external armament; maximum speed 560 mph; ceiling 37,000 feet; operational from early 1950s.

SEA VIXEN. Britain, DeHavilland; carrier-based single engine jet, two-seat, all-weather fighter; operational from 1959; 2,000 pounds of external armament.

SEKSTAN. Soviet Union; NATO designation for a class of trawler-type craft; probably used for collecting intelligence; 134 feet long.

SERGEANT (MGM-29A). US, Sperry; medium-range tactical surface-to-surface missile; operational from 1962; launch weight 10,000 pounds; range 28 to 85 miles.

SF-5. Spain, CASA; a version of the F-5 (q.v.) being produced in Spain with co-operation of Construcciones Aeronauticas SA (CASA).

SF-260 MX. Italy, SIAI Marchetti; light three-seat single engine piston armed trainer; maximum speed 211 mph; service ceiling 21,370 feet; maximum range 894 miles; can be armed with wing pylons carrying bombs and rockets.

SH-3. See SEA KING.

SH-34. See H-34.

SHACKLETON (MR Mk.3). Britain, Hawker-Siddeley; maritime reconnaissance aircraft; operational from 1960; four turboprops plus two auxiliary turbojets.

SHADDOCK (NATO codename). Soviet Union, a surface-to-surface cruise missile; comes in shipborne or vehicle-launched versions; about 40 feet long; range somewhere between 200 and 400 miles.

SHAFRIR. Israel; air-to-air missile; very much like the US Sidewinder heat-seeking missile carried on Mirage and Israeli version of Mirage, the Barak.

SHANGHAI. People's Republic of China; US designation for a class of PGM/PT; 144 feet long; 30 knots; two twin-37mm guns; two twin-25mm guns; later versions have two torpedo tubes; over 60 built from 1959.

SHERIDAN, (M-551). US; lightweight assault vehicle; air-droppable; aluminum hull; mounts 152mm gun/launcher in fully-traversing turret.

SHERMAN. See M-4.

SHERSHEN. Soviet Union; NATO designation for a class of motor torpedo boat (PT); length 110 feet; displacement 150 tons; maximum speed 45 knots; four 21-inch torpedo tubes, two twin 30-mm guns, 12 depth charges; Drum Tilt and Pot Head radars; also has minelaying capability; in service in USSR, East Germany, and Yugoslavia.

SHRIKE (AGM-45). US, Texas Instrument; air-to-surface antiradar missile; 10 feet long; 390 pounds; range 8 1/2 nautical miles; S-band, passive homing.

SIDEWINDER (AIM-9B/C/D). US, Philco, Raytheon, and Motorola; air-to-air missile; operational from 1954; "C" version uses semi-active radar homing; "B" and "D" versions use infra-red homing; launch weight 185 pounds; warhead weight 25 pounds; range from 2-11 miles depending on version; modified missiles serve as basis for Chaparral SAM system (q.v.); Sidewinder also produced in Europe for NATO.

SK-37. See VIGGEN.

SK-60. Sweden, Saab; light attack version of A-60 (q.v.).

SKORY. Soviet Union; NATO designation for a class of DD; 394 feet long; 36 knots; four 5.1-inch guns; two 3-inch guns; four twin-37mm AA guns; depthcharge throwers; 10 torpedo tubes; can also carry 80 mines; operational from about 1953; 75 built of which at least 20 have been transferred to foreign navies.

SKYVAN. Britain, Short; operational from 1963; light twin-turboprop transport; maximum payload 4,600 to 5,000 pounds; maximum cruising speed 201 mph; maximum range 660 miles; ceiling 22,500 feet.

SLBM. Submarine-launched ballistic missile.

SM-1. Poland; license built version of Mi-1 (q.v.).

SM-2. Poland; a development of the SM-1.

SM-4. Poland; a three-seat light helicopter powered by a single piston engine; cruising speed 72 mph; ceiling 10,800 feet; range (with maximum fuel) 185 miles.

SM-1019. Italy, SIAI-Marchetti; two-seat, single engine turboprop version of the O-1 produced in Italy; powered by a 317 shp Allison 250-B15G turboprop; maximum cruising speed 155 mph; can carry up to 500 pounds of rockets, bombs, or camera packs on two underwing racks.

SNAPPER, SWATTER, SAGGER (NATO codenames). Soviet Union; wire-guided antitank missiles. Snapper weighs 50 pounds; 3.7 feet long; speed 200 mph; range of 500 to 2,300 meters; can penetrate over 12 minches of armor. Swatter and Sagger are improved versions; usually carried in multiple launchers on BRDM armored car.

SO-1. Soviet Union; class of PCS; 138 feet long; 28 knots, two twin-25mm guns; four multiple ASW rocket launchers; operational since 1957; over 100 built.

SP-2. See P-2.

SPARROW IIIB (AIM-7E). US, McDonnell-Douglas; air-to-air missile; launch weight 400 pounds; warhead weight 60 pounds; speed Mach 2.5; range 12 nautical miles; semi-active homing.

SPICA. Sweden; a class of fast patrol boats (PTF) built in Sweden between 1966 and 1968; length, 141 feet; displacement 200 tons; maximum speed over 40 knots; six 21-inch torpedo tubes, one 57mm gun, mines; Spica II on order for Sweden and Denmark is two feet longer and eight tons heavier.

SQUADRON. A unit of from 9 to 25 aircraft depending on the air force and the size of the aircraft; a battalion-sized unit of US cavalry; a unit of British, Commonwealth, or other armies' cavalry or armor of 100 to 200 men or 10 to 15 tanks.

SR-71, Blackbird. US, Lockheed; two-seat twin-jet strategic reconnaissance aircraft; maximum speed more than Mach 3; range 2,982 miles at Mach 3 at 78,750 feet.

SRAM (AGM-69). US, Boeing; acronym for "short-range attack missile", air-to-surface missile; 14 feet long; 2,200 pounds; inertial guidance; range 120 nautical miles; for B-52G/H, FB-111A, and B-1A.

SRN-6. Britain, British Hovercraft Corporation; a class of hovercraft.

SS. US designation for diesel-powered submarine; SSN denotes nuclear-powered submarine; SSBN stands for nuclear-powered ballistic missile submarine; SSC is a small coastal submarine; SSB denotes a diesel-powered missile submarine.

SS-4. (NATO codename Sandal). Soviet Union; single-stage, liquid-fuel MRBM; range 900 to 1,100 miles; type based in Cuba in 1962.

SS-5. (NATO codename Skean). Soviet Union; single-stage, storable liquid-fuel IRBM; range about 2,000 miles.

SS-6 (NATO codename Sapwood). Soviet Union; liquid-fuel ICBM; first Soviet ICBM; basic missile plus various upper stages is launch vehicle for Vostok and Soyuz manned spacecraft.

SS-7 (NATO codename Saddler). Soviet Union; storable liquid-fuel ICBM.

SS-8 (NATO codename Sasin). Soviet Union; two-stage, storable liquid-fuel ICBM; range about 6,200 miles.

SS-9 (NATO codename Scarp). Soviet Union; ICBM; range over 9,000 miles; can carry one 25-megaton, three 4-to 5-megaton, six 1- to 2-megaton or eighteen 200-kiloton warheads (MRVs); FOBS (Fractional Orbit Bombardment System) launcher; has depressed trajectory capabilities for sending warheads in below early-warning radar coverage.

SS-10. (NATO codename Scrag); Soviet Union; three stage storable, liquid fuel ICBM; length 121 feet; diameter of first stage base approximately nine feet; range estimated at 4,950 miles.

SS-11 (US, AGM-22A). France, Nord; wire-guided antitank missile; operational from 1962; over 120,000 built; 4 feet long; launch weight 66 pounds; speed 360 mph; range 500 to 3,000 meters; air-launched version called AS-11.

SS-11. Soviet Union; storable liquid-fuel ICBM; performance is comparable to US Minuteman (a solid-fuel ICBM).

SS-12. France, Nord; more powerful development of SS-11; launch weight 167 pounds; range 6,000 meters; air-launched version called AS-12.

SS-13 (NATO codename Savage). Soviet Union; three-stage, solid-fuel ICBM; similar to US Minuteman; range 5,000 to 6,000 miles.

SS-14 (NATO codename Scapegoat). Soviet Union; two-stage, solid-fuel IRBM; range 2,500 miles.

SSBS. S-2. France; IRBM with range of 1,864 miles; carries 150-kiloton warhead; fired from underground silos.

SSM. Surface-to-surface missile.

STAGHOUND (T-17E1). US-built, used by British; World War II, 4-wheeled armored car; 12 tons; 37mm turret-mounted gun.

STANDARD ARM (AGM-78A). US, General Dynamics; air-to-surface anti-radar missile; 14 feet long; 1,300 pounds; HE warhead; passive radar homing; carried by A-6A and F-105D.

STENKA. Soviet Union; NATO designation for antisubmarine version of Osa PTFG two twin 30mm guns; four fixed 16-inch ASW torpedo tubes and two depth charge racks in place of SSMs; operated in peacetime by KGB Border Guards; about 30 built, none exported.

STOL. Short Take-Off and Landing; applied to aircraft with capability of operating from fields of less than 1,000 feet in length through use of special flaps, slots, and wing designs (cf. V/STOL and VTOL).

STORM. Norway; a class of motor gunboat (PGM) built from 1965; length 118 feet; displacement 125 tons; maximum speed 35 knots; one 76mm dual purpose gun (Swedish boats have a 57-mm gun), one 40-mm gun, six Penguin SSMs; in service in Norway, Sweden, and Venezuela.

STRIKEMASTER. See BAC 167.

Strv-74. Sweden; operational from 1958; light tank with 75mm gun and one or two machine guns; weight 26 tons; two 170 hp engines.

Strv-S. Sweden, Bofors; medium tank; 105mm gun and two machine guns mounted rigidly in hull and aimed by steering tank or lowering and elevating suspension; a third machine gun is mounted on top of the hull for AA defense; 37 tons; crew of 3.

STYX (NATO codename). Soviet Union; naval surface-to-surface missile; solid-fuel rocket booster; rocket sustainer; radar homing guidance; 20 feet long; 9-foot wingspan; range over 15 miles; carried by Komar and Osa class PTFG.

Su-7 (NATO codename Fitter). Soviet Union, Sukhoi; single-seat, single engine jet ground attack fighter; operational from 1960; maximum speed about Mach 1.6; two 30mm cannon plus two wing and two fuselage attachment points for bombs or other stores.

Su-9 (NATO codename Fishpot). Soviet Union, Sukhoi; single-seat single engine jet all-weather fighter; probably operational 1958-1959; can carry four Alkali or two Anab AAMs (in latter configuration, one is radar homing head version, the other Anab is equipped with an IR homing head); maximum speed Mach 1.8; only about 200 produced for service with Air Defense Command.

Su-11 (NATO codename Flagon-A). Soviet Union, Sukhoi; single-seat, twin-engine jet delta-wing fighter; probably operational from 1969; normally carries two Anab AAMs (one radar homing version, one with IR homing head); maximum speed Mach 2.5; aircraft of this type are reported to be serving with Soviet forces in Egypt.

SU-76. Soviet Union; World War II assault gun; 76mm gun mounted on a lengthened T-70 light tank chassis; 12 1/2 tons; 25 mph; crew of four; also used in Korean War.

SU-85. Soviet Union; World War II assault gun; 85mm gun hull-mounted on T-34 medium tank chassis; 29 tons; 24 mph; crew of 5.

SU-100. Soviet Union; World War II and after assault gun; 100mm gun hull-mounted on T-34 chassis; 32 tons; 32 mph; crew of four.

SU-122. Soviet Union; World War II and after; assault gun; 122mm gun/howitzer hull-mounted; 32 tons; 34 mph; crew of 4. JSU-122 featured same gun hull-mounted on heavy tank chassis; 46 tons; crew of five.

SU-152/JSU-152. Soviet Union; 152mm gun/howitzer on heavy tank chassis.

SUBROC (UUM-44A; SUBmarine ROCket). US, Goodyear; advanced tactical missile for use by submarines against other submarines; operational in late 1965; carries a nuclear depth charge; launching weight 4,000 pounds; range 22-26 miles; fired from the submarine's torpedo tubes.

SUPERCONSTELLATION. See C-121.

SUBROTO. India; license-built version of Andover transport aircraft (q.v.).

SUPER FRELON. France, Sud; heavy transport and antisubmarine helicopter; three 1,500-shp turbines; operational from 1966; 30 troops; maximum speed 149 mph; ceiling 10,000 feet; range 585 miles.

SUPER MYSTERE. France, Dassault; supersonic single engine jet interceptor and fighter-bomber; two 30mm cannon; 2,200 pounds external armament; maximum speed Mach 1.125; ceiling 55,000 feet.

SUPER SHERMAN or ISHERMAN. Israel; a US World War II M4 Sherman medium tank modernized with a diesel engine, wider tracks for desert use, and a French 105mm gun.

SVERDLOV. Soviet Union; NATO designation for a class of CL; 14 built from 1951; 689 feet long; 15,450 tons; 34 knots; twelve 5.9-inch guns; twelve 3.9-inch guns; 16 twin-37mm AA guns; 10 torpedo tubes.

SWATOW. People's Republic of China; US designation for a class of PTF/SC; 84 feet long; 40 knots; two twin-37mm guns; two 12.7mm guns; depth charges; over 45 built from 1958.

SWINGFIRE. Britain, BAC; ground- or air-launched wire-guided antitank missile; 3 1/2 feet long; range 150 to 3,000 meters; operational from 1967.

SYCAMORE. Britain, Bristol; operational from 1949; four-seat single-rotor helicopter; maximum speed 127 mph; ceiling 15,500 feet; maximum range 324 miles.

T-2. Buckeye; North American Rockwell land-or carrier-based two-seat general purpose trainer; maximum speed 540 mph; service ceiling 42,000 feet; range 1,047 miles; armament can be installed (guns, practice bombs, rockets); early version single engine jet, later twin.

T-6, Harvard or Texan (formerly AT-6, SNJ). US, North American; single engine piston, two-seat training aircraft operational from 1938; over 10,000 built; T-6G is armed version; maximum speed 210 mph; ceiling 24,000 feet; range 870 miles.

T-7. See C-45.

T-10. Soviet Union; 1957; heavy tank; 122mm gun; 50 1/2 tons; 26 mph; range 160 miles; crew of 4.

T-11. See C-45.

T-23, Uirapuru. Brazil, Aerotec; two-seat single engine piston, primary trainer, side-by-side seating; maximum speed 140 mph; maximum range 495 miles; service ceiling 14,760 feet.

T-25, Universal. Brazil, Neiva; two-seat, single engine piston basic trainer with side-by-side seating; maximum speed 201 mph; maximum range 620 miles, service ceiling 26,250 feet.

T-28, Trojan. US, North American; single engine piston, two seat trainer; operational from 1950; almost 2,000 built; T-28D armed COIN version; maximum speed 346 mph; ceiling 37,000 feet.

T-29. See C-131.

T-33, Shooting Star (also formerly, Navy, TV-2). US, Lockheed; single engine jet, two-seat trainer version of F-80 jet fighter; operational from 1949; over 5,700 built; armed and reconnaissance versions in service; maximum speed 600 mph; ceiling 47,000 feet; range 1,345 miles. Armed version carries machine guns, bombs, rockets; reconnaissance version carries cameras.

T-34. Soviet Union; World War II and after; medium tank; 85mm gun; 32 tons; 32 mph; crew of 5.

T-34, Mentor. US, Beechcraft; single engine piston, two-seat trainer; operational from 1950; 1,000 built; maximum speed 185 mph; ceiling 18,000; range 735 miles.

T-37, Dragonfly. US, Cessna; twin engine jet trainer; operational from 1954; over 1,000 built; "B" and "C" models have provision for light armament; maximum speed 425 mph; ceiling 38,000 feet; range 930 miles. AT-37D or A-37B is more powerful and heavily armed COIN version; internally mounted 7.62mm GE Minigun (six barrels; 6,000 rounds per minute) and 4,700 pounds of external armament; maximum speed 507 mph; ceiling 41,765 feet; range 1,012 miles.

T-38, Talon. Two seat trainer version of F-5 (q.v.)

T-39, Sabreliner. US, North American; twin engine jet, combat readiness trainer and utility transport; maximum speed 595 mph; Mach .8; service ceiling 45,000 feet; range 1,950 miles.

T-41, Mescalero (Cessna 172). US, Cessna; four-place single engine piston, training/utility aircraft; operational from 1966; used by US Air Force and Army and many foreign countries; over 400 built (over 11,000 commercial versions previously built); maximum speed 150 mph; ceiling 17,000 feet; range 800 miles.

T-42, Cochise. US, Beech; four- or six-seat, light transport twin-engine piston-powered; maximum speed 236 mph; range 1,225 miles.

T-43. US, Boeing; military version of the civil air liner, Boeing Model 737-200 twin-engine jet; navigational trainer and transport; crew of two, 12 navigator trainees, four navigation proficiency positions and three navigation instructors; maximum speed 586 mph, service ceiling 42,000 feet (estimated); range 3200 miles (estimated).

T-43. Soviet Union; class of MSF; 500 tons; 200 feet long; four 37mm guns; eight 13mm AA guns; 17 knots.

T-54. Soviet Union. 1953; medium tank; 100mm gun; 36 tons; 32 mph; crew of 4.

T-55. Soviet Union, early 1960s; medium tank; 100mm gun; 36 tons; 32 mph; crew of 4.

T-59. Communist China; medium tank; a Chinese-built version of T-54B which includes a smoke discharger, but no infra-red equipment.

T-62. Soviet Union; late 1960s; medium tank; 115mm smooth-bore gun; 37 tons; crew of 3; replacing T-54 and T-55 in Soviet and Warsaw Pact armies.

T-62. Chinese light tank.

T-64. Soviet Union; medium tank; weight 45 tons; 120mm gun/launcher; crew of four; speed 25 mph.

T-301. Soviet Union; class of MSC; 100 feet long; 10 knots; one twin-37mm gun; one twin-25mm gun; over 70 built from 1946 to 1956.

TALOS (RIM-8). US, Bendix; long-range naval surface-to-air missile; solid-fuel booster, ramjet sustainer; range over 65 miles.

TARTAR(RIM-24). US, General Dynamics; naval surface-to-air missile for use against both low- and medium-altitude targets; operational from 1961; launch weight 1,200 pounds; speed Mach 2.5; range over 10 miles; effective from 1,000 to 40,000 feet.

TEBUAN (Wasp); see CL-41 Tutor; Malaysian Air Force designation for the CL-41 ground attack/trainer aircraft.

TERRIER. US, General Dynamics; two-stage naval SAM; one variant designed for land use by US Marine Corps; length 27 feet; launch weight 3,300 pounds; range over ten miles.

TF-26, Xavante. See MB326-G.

TH-55. See Hughes 300, Hughes 269.

THUNDERBIRD. Britain, BAC; mobile surface-to-air missile; operational from 1958; solid-fuel rocket boosters and sustainer; semi-active radar homing; 21 feet long; range 15 miles.

TI-67. Israel; Israeli designator for captured T-54/55 tanks fitted with a 105mm gun and otherwise modified.

TIGERCAT. Britain, Short Brothers and Harland; mobile, land based version of Seacat surface-to-air missile.

TITAN II. US, Martin; two-stage, storable liquid-fuel ICBM; operational from 1961; launch weight 329,000 pounds; range over 9,000 miles; 54 in service; carries over a 5-megaton warhead.

TOW (MGM-71A; Tube-launched, Optically-tracked, Wire-guided). US, Hughes; high-performance antitank missile; fired from tripod, vehicles, or helicopters; range over one mile; to replace 106mm recoilless rifle and the Entac and SS-11 missiles with US forces; also ordered by other countries.

TRACKER. See S-2.

TRANSALL (C-160). French-West German consortium; twin-turboprop, military transport; operational from 1968; 93 troops or 60 to 80 paratroops; maximum payload 35,000 pounds; maximum speed 330 mph; ceiling 28,000 feet; range with maximum payload 730 miles.

TROJAN. See FV-432; T-28.

TROOP. In the British, Commonwealth, and some other armies a small unit of cavalry or armor equivalent to the platoon in US practice, or one-half (four guns) a battery of artillery. In US cavalry or armor a company-sized unit, 100 to 200 men or 15-17 armored vehicles.

TROOPSHIP. See F-27M.

TS-11; Iskra (Spark). Poland; single-engine jet, two-seat advanced trainer; maximum speed 447 mph; gross weight 8,377 pounds; range 907 miles; armament 23mm gun and four racks for bombs or rockets.

TU-4. Soviet Union, Tupolev, Soviet built version of the Boeing B-29 Superfortress piston four engine bomber;

classed as very long range bomber in WWII, later reclassified as medium bomber; maximum speed 261 mph, (sea level); maximum speed 354 mph, (at 32,808 feet); range at 9,845 feet 3,107 miles; 11,000 pound bombload.

Tu-16 (NATO codename Badger). Soviet Union, Tupolev; twin-engine jet, medium bomber; operational from 1954; about 2,000 built; maximum speed 620 mph; range 4,250 miles; carries conventional or nuclear bombs internally, anti-shipping missiles or stand-off ASMs externally; three twin-23mm cannon for defense; a Chinese-built version is being assembled at the rate of six per month.

Tu-20 (NATO codename Bear). Soviet Union, Tupolev; four-engine turboprop, long-range, heavy bomber and reconnaissance aircraft; carries Kangaroo ASM in addition to 23mm cannon in turrets; also known as Tu-95.

Tu-22 (NATO codename Blinder). Soviet Union, Tupolev; twin engine jet medium-range bomber; maximum speed Mach 1.5; ceiling 60,000 feet; range 1,250 miles; some carry Kitchen ASM; also in service with Soviet Navy.

Tu-28 (NATO codename Fiddler). Soviet Union, Tupolev; twin-engine jet long-range interceptor; maximum speed Mach 1.75.

Tu-104 (NATO codename Camel). Soviet Union, Tupolev; twin-engine jet, medium-range transport; up to 100 passengers; maximum payload 19,000 to 26,000 pounds; maximum speed 614 mph; ceiling 37,000 feet; range 1,860 miles; operational from 1956.

Tu-114 (NATO codename Cleat). Soviet Union, Tupolev; four-engine turboprop, long-range transport based on Tu-20 Bear; a modified Tu-114 serves as the basis for the Moss AWACS aircraft.

Tu-124. (NATO codename Cookpot). Soviet Union, Tupolev; twin-engine jet transport; 22 to 56 passengers; maximum payload 13,228 pounds; maximum speed 603 mph; ceiling over 33,000 feet; maximum range 1,305 miles; operational from 1961.

TUTOR. See CL-41.

TWIN OTTER (DHC-6). Canada, DeHavilland; twin-engine turboprop, STOL light transport; operational from 1967; 13-20 passengers or maximum payload of 5,100 pounds; maximum cruising speed 210 mph; ceiling 26,700 feet; range with maximum payload 100 miles, with maximum fuel 945 miles.

U-2. US, Lockheed; single engine, single seat, high altitude long range reconnaissance aircraft; maximum speed 520 mph above 36,000 feet; ceiling over 60,000 feet.

U-4. See AERO COMMANDER.

U-6. See BEAVER.

U-8, Seminole. US, Beech; military version of commercial Queen Air 65; four- to six-seat twin engine piston-powered light transport; maximum speed 239 mph.; range 1,220 miles.

U-10, Helio H-295 Super Courier. US, Helio; single engine piston; six-seat STOL utility monoplane; maximum speed 165 mph; service ceiling 20,500 feet; range 660 miles.

U-17 (Cessna 185E Skywagon). US, Cessna; six-place single engine piston utility aircraft; operational from 1965 (over 1,200 commercial versions built from 1961); maximum speed 175 mph; ceiling 17,000 feet; range 885 miles.

U-22, Bonanza. US, Beech; two-seat single engine piston trainer; maximum speed 204 mph; range 880 miles.

UH 1, Iroquois (Bell 204B). US, Bell; turbine-powered military helicopter; operational from 1960; over 6,000 built; "B" models converted to "gunships" with combination of machine guns, rocket pods, and 40mm grenade launchers; "E" model is a 10-place troop transport; maximum speed 140 mph; ceiling 12,000 feet; range 350 miles; nickname Huey.

UH-1N (212 Bell). US, Bell; a twin engine version of the UH-1 which has a Twin Pac Pratt and Whitney PT6T turboshaft; maximum speed, 121 mph; service ceiling, 11,500 feet; maximum range, 296 miles; can carry 14 passengers; has 220 cubic feet internal cargo space or 4,000 pounds externally.

UH-12. US, Hiller; a variant of the H-23 (q.v.).

UH-19. See H-19.

UH-23. See H-23.

V750VK (or VK750). Soviet designation for SA-2 Guideline (q.v.).

VAMPIRE. Britain, DeHavilland; single engine jet fighter-bomber; operational from 1946; four 20mm cannon; 2,000 pounds external armament; maximum speed 570 mph.

VAUTOUR. France, Sud; twin-engine jet, attack bomber and interceptor; operational from 1956; 30 built; four 30mm cannon; 3,000 pounds internal and 2,000 pounds external armament; maximum speed Mach 0.9; range 2,400 miles.

VC-10. Britain, BAC; four-engine jet, long-range transport; operational from 1964; up to 174 passengers; maximum speed Mach 0.86; ceiling 42,000 feet; range with maximum payload 5,000 miles.

VENOM. Britain; De Havilland; a development of the Vampire (q.v.); single engine jet fighter operational from 1950; maximum speed 585 mph; ceiling over 40,000 feet; range over 800 miles; carries four 20mm cannons and up to 2,000 pounds of bombs and rockets.

VICTOR. Britain, Handley-Page; four-engine jet, medium bomber; operational from 1958; cruising speed Mach 0.92; cruise ceiling 55,000 feet; combat radius high-low 1,700 miles, high 2,300 miles; carries nuclear weapons, stand-off ASMs, or 35 1,000-pound bombs.

VIGGEN (Thunderbolt; AJ-37, JA-37, S-37, SK-37). Sweden, an advanced multi-mission combat aircraft; AJ-37 is single-seat single engine jet, delta canard configuration, all-weather attack fighter, with secondary interceptor capability, designed to replace A-32 (q.v.); JA-37 is single-seat interceptor version, with secondary attack capability, designed to replace J-35 Draken (q.v.); S-37 is single-seat reconnaissance version to replace S-32 (q.v.); SK-37 is two-seat trainer version to enter service simultaneously with AJ-37; maximum speed Mach 2.0; maximum range (with external armament) over 1,000 miles; carries various combinations of guns, bombs, rockets, missiles, and mines.

VIGILANT (Visually Guided Infantry Light Anti Tank). Britain, BAC; wire-guided antitank missile; operational from 1963; launch weight 31 pounds; warhead 13 pounds; speed 350 mph; range 230 to 1,600 meters.

VIGILANTE. See A-5.

VIJAYANTA. India, Avadi; 105mm gun; 37 tons; crew of four resembles British Chieftain tank with Centurion turret; initially made with British help and components; now totally Indian-built.

VISCOUNT. Britain, Vickers; four-engine turboprop, medium transport; operational from 1953; 444 built; up to 72 passengers; maximum payload 14,500 pounds; maximum cruising speed 355 mph; ceiling 28,500 feet; range 1,700 miles.

VTOL. Vertical Take-Off and Landing; applies to aircraft which, by means of tiltable propellers, directed fans, jets, or a combination of these means, can rise vertically and change from vertical to horizontal flight. V/STOL applies to aircraft combining features of both STOL and VTOL, but using a vertical approach only when necessary.

VULCAN. Britain, Hawker-Siddeley; four-engine jet, medium bomber; operational from 1956; maximum speed Mach 0.94; cruising ceiling 55,000 feet; combat radius high-low 1,700 miles, high 2,300 miles; carries nuclear weapons, stand-off ASMs or 21 1,000 pound bombs.

VULCAN. US, GE; a six-barrel 20mm cannon; maximum rate of fire is 6,000 rounds per minute; used in both aircraft role (e.g., F-4E, F-104, F-105, AC-119, AC-130, etc.) and as land-based weapon as part of the Chaparral/Vulcan system (q.v.)

W-Class (Whiskey). Soviet Union; NATO designation for a class of diesel submarine. Three missile-launching versions exist—the Long Bin version has four inclined Shaddock launch tubes built into the forward portion of an enlarged conning tower; the single- and twin-cylinder types have Shaddock launching tubes aft of the conning tower and firing toward the stern. The standard W-class is a diesel-powered attack submarine operational from 1950; over 170 built; 240 feet long; 1,030 tons; 17 knots surfaced, 15 knots submerged; six 21-inch torpedo tubes; radius 13,000 to 16,000 miles.

WALLEYE. US, Martin/Hughes; a television-guided glide bomb; 1,100 pounds; 11 feet long.

WASP/SCOUT. Britain, Westland; naval ASW helicopter is named Wasp; army version is named Scout; four passengers or two ASW homing torpedoes; maximum speed 120-130 mph; ceiling 12,000 feet; range 270-315 miles.

WELLINGTON. Britain, British Hovercraft Corporation; a class of hovercraft.

WESSEX. Britain, Westland; turbine-powered version of the Sikorsky S-58/H-34 utility helicopter (q.v.); operational from 1961; up to 16 passengers; maximum speed 130 mph; ceiling 14,000 feet; range 300 to 600 miles depending on amount of fuel.

WHIRLWIND. Britain, Westland; Series 3, Mk. 9/10 military helicopter is a turbine-powered conversion of earlier piston version which, in turn, was a British model of the US Sikorsky S-55/H-19; operational from 1962; 10 passengers; maximum speed 105 mph; ceiling 16,000 feet; range 300 miles.

WILGA/GELATIK (PZL-104). Poland/Indonesia; four-seat piston engine powered light training/utility/liaison monoplane; built in Poland as the Wilga (Thrush) and in Indonesia as the Gelatik (Rice Bird); maximum speed 127 mph; range 435 miles.

WING. In US Air Force practice, a combat group plus the logistical and control units which render it self-supporting. In US Marine practice, a large unit of several combat groups and specialized squadrons plus logistical and control organizations to render it self-sufficient. In RAF practice, two or more squadrons.

WINJEEL, CA-25. Australia, two-seat piston powered Australian built primary trainer.

WPB. US; designation for US Coast Guard patrol boats; lengths vary from 82 to 95 feet; displacement varies from 65 to 106 tons; speed about 20 knots; lightly armed with 20mm or 40mm cannon, 81mm mortar, etc.

XAVANTE. See MB326-G.

Y-Class (Yankee). Soviet Union, NATO designation for a class of nuclear-powered fleet ballistic missile submarines similar to US Polaris submarines; 16 missile tubes for underwater launching.

Yak-11 (NATO codename Moose). Soviet Union, Yakovlev; two-seat single engine piston trainer; operational from 1946; maximum speed 286 mph; ceiling 23,000 feet; range 800 miles.

YAK-12. USSR, Yakovlev; single engine two-seat light piston primary trainer.

Yak-18 (NATO codename Max). Soviet Union, Yakovlev; two-seat single engine piston trainer; operational from 1946; maximum speed 185 mph; range 400 miles; there is a four-passenger version.

YAK-25 (NATO codename Flashlight). Soviet Union, Yakovlev; two-seat, twin jet, all weather, interceptor fighter; operational since 1955; swept wing (45°); maximum speed Mach 0.95 at 36,000 feet; armament, one 30mm cannon plus bombs.

YAK-26 (NATO codename Mangrove). Soviet Union, Yakovlev; two-seat, twin jet, tactical reconnaissance aircraft, a development of the Yak-25 Flashlight fighter; this aircraft has extended wing tips and reduced armament (one 30mm cannon), and a transparent nose section for an observer.

YAK-28 (NATO codename Brewer); Soviet Union, Yakovlev; two-seat multi purpose tactical bomber version of the Yak-28P Firebar; performance that of Yak-28P but armament includes internal weapon bay and two 30mm cannon in fuselage.

YAK-28P (NATO codename Firebar). Soviet Union, Yakovlev; two-seat, twin jet all weather, interceptor fighter; first seen in 1961; a development of the Yak-25; swept wing (45°); maximum speed Mach 1.1 at 36,000 feet; range 1200-1600 miles at 570 mph; armed with 2 Anab AAM; a light bomber version is called Brewer.

YDT. A US Navy designation for a diving tender.

YNG. A US Navy designation for a gate vessel; i.e., a ship that tends antisubmarine nets.

YP. US designation for a local patrol craft; under 100 feet long; armed with machine guns; short endurance and low sea-keeping ability.

YS-11. Japan, NAMC; twin-engine turboprop, medium-range transport; operational from 1964; over 180 built; up to 60 passengers; maximum payload 12,000 to 16,000 pounds; maximum cruising speed 300 mph; range 700 to 1,300 miles depending on payload and fuel.

Z-Class (Zulu). Soviet Union; NATO designation for a class of diesel submarine; original Z-Class was a diesel-powered attack submarine with 8 torpedo tubes (6 bow, 2 stern); some were later converted to missile submarines by addition of larger conning tower with 2 vertical launch tubes for Sark-type missiles.

ZLIN 326. Czechoslovakia, Moravan; two-seat, single engine piston trainer; maximum speed 143 mph; service ceiling 18,050; range 403 miles.

ZSU-23/4. Soviet Union; 1967; self-propelled anti-aircraft gun; quadruple 23mm cannon mounted in turret with integral gun-laying radar (NATO codename Gun Dish); 800-1,000 rounds per minute per gun; tracked chassis apparently same as that used for SA-6 Gainful (q.v.).

ZSU-57/2. Soviet Union; 1957; self-propelled twin 57mm AA guns mounted in open turret on a T-54 tank chassis.

SOURCES

Sources used in the preparation of this book include the following:

Books.

Munson, Kenneth. *Civil Airliners Since 1946*. New York: The Macmillan Co. 1967.
Taylor, John W.R., and Swanborough, Gordon. *Military Aircraft of the World*. New York: Charles Scribner's Sons, 1973.

Public Documents.

Britain 1973, An Official Handbook. London: Her Majesty's Stationery Office: 1973.
Department of National Defence, Ottawa, Canada. *Defense 1973*. Ottawa: Information Canada, 1974.
Minister of National Defence. *White Paper on Defence*. Ottawa: Information Canada, 1971.
Statement on the Defence Estimates, 1973. Presented to Parliament by the Secretary of State for Defence February 1973. London: Her Majesty's Stationery Office.
U.S. Agency For International Development. Bureau For Program and Management Services. *Gross National Product, Growth Rates and Trend Data, By Region and Country*. Washington, D. C.: AID, 1973.
U. S. Arms Control and Disarmament Agency. Bureau of Economic Affairs. *World Military Expenditures, 1971*. Washington, D.C.: USACDA, 1972.
U. S. Congress. House of Representatives. Defense Appropriations Subcommittee of the House Committee on Appropriations. Statement by Admiral Thomas H. Moorer, USN, Chairman, Joint Chiefs of Staff, on *United States Military Posture for FY 1974*. 3 April 1973.
U. S. Department of Defense. Security Assistance Agency. *Military Assistance and Foreign Military Sales Facts, May 1973*. Washington, D.C.: DOD, 1973.
U. S. Department of the Interior. Bureau of Mines. *International Petroleum Annual, 1972*. Pittsburgh Pa.: Bureau of Mines, 1974.
U.S. Department of State. *Background Notes, 1972, 1973*. Washington D. C.: GPO.
U. S. Department of State. *Geographic Bulletin. Status of the World Nations*. Washington D. C.: GPO, 1973.
World Bank Atlas, Population, Per Capita Product and Growth Rates. Washington, D. C.: International Bank for Reconstruction and Development, 1972.

Periodic Publications

Air Enthusiast.
Air Force Magazine.
Air Progress.
The Americana Annual 1973.
Army.
Asia Yearbook, 1973. Hongkong: Far Eastern Economic Review, 1973.
Aviation Week and Space Technology
Britannica, Book of the Year, 1973.
Facts on File.
International Defense Review.
Jane's All the World's Aircraft, 1973-74. London: Janes, 1973.
Jane's Fighting Ships, 1973-74. London: Janes, 1973.
Jane's Weapon Systems, 1973-74. London: Janes, 1973.
Keesing's Contemporary Archives.
Marine Corps Gazette.
Military Balance 1973-1974. London: The International Institute for Strategic Studies, 1973.
Military Review.
National Defense.
NATO's Fifteen Nations.
Naval War College Review.
New York Times.
Newsweek.
Proceedings. United States Naval Institute.
Statesman's Year-book, 1971-72. London: Macmillan London Ltd., 1971.
Strategic Review. Washington, D. C.: United States Strategic Institute, 1973, 1974.
Strategic Survey 1973. London: The International Institute for Strategic Studies, 1974.
Survival 1972, 1973, 1974. London: The International Institute for Strategic Studies.
Time.
Times of the Americas.
U. S. Air Force. *Air Force Policy Letter for Commanders, 1973-74*. Washington, D. C. 1973-74.
U. S. Air Force. *Air University Review, The Professional Journal of the United States Air Force*. Washington D. C.: GPO, 1972-74.

U. S. News and World Report.
Wall Street Journal.
Washington Post.
Weyer's Warships of the World, 1973. Annapolis Maryland.: Naval Institute Press, 1973.
World Aviation Directory, Summer 1973. Washington, D. C.: Ziff-Davis Publishing Co., 1973.

INDEX OF COUNTRIES, REGIONS AND INTERNATIONAL ORGANIZATIONS

Abu Dhabi	171
Afars and Issas	
(see French Territory of the Afars and Issas)	—
Afghanistan	300
Africa	203
African-Malagasy Common Organization (OCAM)	205
Ajman	171
Albania	135
Algeria	207
Angola	243
Anguilla	24
Antigua	24
ANZUK (see Five Power Pact)	—
ANZUS Pact	335
Arab Gulf States	171
Arab League	170, 204
Argentina	42
Aruba	35
Australia	335
Austria	74
Baghdad Pact	
(see Central Treaty Organization)	—
Bahamas	24
Bahrain	171
Bangladesh	302
Barbados	23
Belgium	76
Belize	25
Bermuda	24
Bhutan	303
Bolivia	44
Botswana	209
Brazil	47
British Honduras (see Belize)	
British Virgin Islands	25
British West Indies	24
Brunei	304
Bulgaria	137
Burma	304
Burundi	210
Cambodia	307
Cameroon	211
Canada	2
Caribbean Community	23
Caribbean Free Trade Association (CARIFTA)	23
Cayman Islands	25
CENTO (see Central Treaty Organization)	—
Central African Republic	212
Central America	21
Central American Common Market (CACM)	23
Central American Defense Council (CONDECA)	23
Central Treaty Organization (CENTO)	170
Ceylon (see Sri Lanka)	
Chad	213
Chile	50
China (PRC)	276
China (Taiwan)	283
Colombia	53
COMECON (see Council for Mutual Economic Assistance)	—
Common Organization of Africa and Mauritius (OCAM)	205
Congo	214
Congo (Kinshasa) (see Zaire)	—
Conséil de l'Entente	205
Costa Rica	25
Council for Mutual Economic Assistance	134
Cuba	26
Curacao	35
Cyprus	78
Czechoslovakia	139
Dahomey	215
Denmark	80
Dominica	24
Dominican Republic	28
Dubai	171
Dutch Guiana (see Surinam)	—
East African Community	205
Eastern Europe	133
Ecuador	55

385

Egypt	173
Eire	98
El Salvador	30
Equatorial Guinea	215
Ethiopia	216
European Economic Community	73
Falkland Islands	25
Finland	83
Five Power Pact	300
France	85
French Guiana	31
French Territory of the Afars and the Issas	220
Fujairah	171
Gabon	221
The Gambia	222
Germany (East)	142
Germany (West)	90
Ghana	222
Greece	94
Grenada	32
Guadeloupe	31
Guatemala	32
Guyana	57
Guinea	224
Guinea-Bissau	246
Haiti	33
Honduras	33
Hungary	146
Iceland	97
India	309
Indonesia	339
Inter-American Defense Board (IADB)	21
Iran	176
Iraq	179
Ireland	98
Israel	182
Italy	100
Ivory Coast	225
Jamaica	34
Japan	286
Jordan	186
Kenya	226
Korea (North)	290
Korea (South)	293
Kuwait	189
Latin American Free Trade Association (LAFTA)	41
Laos	313
Lebanon	190
Lesotho	227

Liberia	228
Libya	229
Luxembourg	103
Maghreb	204
Malagasy Republic	232
Malawi	233
Malaysia	315
Mali	234
Malta	104
Martinique	31
Mauritania	235
Mexico	6
Middle East	169
Mongolia	295
Montserrat	25
Morocco	236
Mozambique	244
Nepal	317
Netherlands	104
Netherlands Antilles	35
New Zealand	341
Nicaragua	36
Niger	239
Nigeria	240
North America	1
North Atlantic Treaty Organization (NATO)	71
Norway	107
Oman	191
Organization of African Unity (OAU)	204
Organization of American States (OAS)	21
Organization of Central American States (ODECA)	23
Organization of Latin American Solidarity (OLAS)	23
Organization of Petroleum Exporting Countries	171, 205
Pakistan	318
Panama	37
Paraguay	58
Peru	61
Philippines	344
Poland	148
Portugal	110
Portuguese Africa	242
Portuguese Guinea	246
Qatar	171
Ras al Khaimah	171
Rhodesia	247
Romania	152
Rwanda	249
Sahara Group	205

St. Christopher-Nevis	24	Tunisia	265
St. Lucia	24	Turkey	122
St. Vincent	24	Turks and Caicos Islands	25
Saudi Arabia	193		
Senegal	250	Uganda	267
Sharjah	171	Umm al Qaiwain	171
Sierra Leone	251	Union of Soviet Socialist Republics	154
Sikkim	321	UNITAS	23
Singapore	321	United Arab Emirates	170
Somalia	252	United Kingdom	125
South Africa	254	United States	9
South America	41	Upper Volta	268
South Asia	299	Uruguay	63
South East Asia Treaty Organization	299		
Southern Yemen	199	Venezuela	67
South Pacific	335	Vietnam (North)	327
South West Africa	254	Vietnam (South)	331
Southwest Pacific	335		
Spain	112	Warsaw Pact	133
Sri Lanka	323	West African Economic Community (CEAO)	205
Sudan	259	Western Europe	71
Surinam	36	Western European Union	72
Swaziland	261	West Indies	21
Sweden	117		
Switzerland	119	Yemen (Aden)	199
Syria	196	Yemen (San'a)	200
		Yugoslavia	165
Tanzania	262		
Thailand	324	Zaire	269
Tibet (see China, PRC)	—	Zambia	271
Togo	264		
Trinidad and Tobago	38		

Ref
UA
15
D9
1974

MAR 19 1975